Library of
Davidson College

Prehistoric Greece and Cyprus

Prehistoric Greece and Cyprus

An Archaeological Handbook

by Hans-Günter Buchholz
and Vassos Karageorghis

Translated from the German by Francisca Garvie

Phaidon

Phaidon Press Limited, 5 Cromwell Place, London SW7

Published in the United States of America by Phaidon Publishers, Inc.
and distributed by Praeger Publishers, Inc.
111 Fourth Avenue, New York, N.Y. 10003

First published 1973
Originally published as ALTÄGÄIS UND ALTKYPROS
© 1971 by Verlag Ernst Wasmuth, Tübingen
Translation © 1973 by Phaidon Press Limited

ISBN 0 7148 1501 2
Library of Congress Catalog Card Number: 72 - 88536
All rights reserved

No part of this publication may be reproduced, stored in a
retrieval system or transmitted in any form or by any means,
electronic, mechanical, photocopying, recording or otherwise,
without the prior permission of the Copyright owner

Printed in Germany

To FRIEDRICH MATZ

on his 80th birthday, 15 August 1970

CONTENTS

	page	cat. no.
FOREWORD	9	
PREHISTORIC GREECE	11	
INTRODUCTION	11	
Palaeolithic period	11	
Neolithic period	13	
Early Bronze Age	17	
Middle Bronze Age	19	
Late Bronze Age	20	
Conclusion and Transition	23	
THE AEGEAN – BRONZE AGE IRON FINDS	27	
ANCIENT AEGEAN CHRONOLOGY	29	
Chronological table	30	
CATALOGUE	31	
Excavated sites. Architecture	31–39	*1–130*
Cave dwellings and sacred caves – Thessalian magoulas – Early and Middle Bronze Age domestic and defensive architecture – urban buildings of Hagia Irini, Keos	31	*1–40*
Cretan palaces, cities, and private houses	33	*41–75*
Mycenaean fortresses, settlements, bridges, and streets	35	*76–130*
Tombs. Tomb architecture	39–44	*131–91*
Early Bronze Age graves	40	*131–40*
Middle Bronze Age and Late Helladic I tombs	40	*141–57*
Mycenaean tholos tombs	42	*158–81*
Cist graves and chamber tombs – pithos and urn burials	44	*182–91*
Small finds. Implement and weapons	44–60	*192–752*
Stone – clay	46	*192–456*
Moulds and matrices	49	*457–64*
Bone – horn – ivory	50	*465–516*
Metal	51	*517–738*
Ingots	59	*739–52*
Pottery	60–78	*753–1042*
Neolithic period. Thrace – Thessaly – Boeotia – Attica – Aegina – Arcadia – Leukas	62	*753–90*
Early and Middle Bronze Ages. Troy – Lemnos – Kos – Aegina – Attica – the Argolid – Boeotia – Leukas	64	*791–832*
Early Minoan Period – Crete	66	*833–40*
Early and Middle Bronze Ages – The Cyclades	66	*841–63*
Middle Helladic period. Attica – Aegina – the Argolid – Boeotia	68	*864–84*
Middle Minoan Period. Crete – eastern Mediterranean	69	*885–97*
Late Bronze Age, Phase I. Crete – Attica – Egypt	70	*898–903*
Unpainted relief pithoi. Crete and Mycenae	70	*904–7*
Late Bronze Age, Phases I–III. Greece – northern and eastern Aegean – Cyclades – Crete – Syria – Egypt – Italy	70	*908–1024*
Late Bronze Age. The Argolid – Attica – Keos – Crete – eastern Aegean	76	*1025–42*
Wall-painting	78–81	*1043–60*
Painted sarcophagi and stelai	82–84	*1061–71*
Metal vessels	84–88	*1072–1117*
Gold – silver – lead – copper (Early and Middle Bronze Ages)	85	*1072–84*
Gold – silver – copper – bronze (Late Bronze Age)	86	*1085–1117*
Stone vessels and reliefs	88–94	*1118–71*
Vases	90	*1118–67*
Reliefs	94	*1168–71*
Sculpture in the round	95–105	*1172–1271*
Neolithic and Early Bronze Age female statuettes and animal figures	98	*1172–93*
Early Cycladic stone sculpture and related work	99	*1194–1212*
Minoan terracottas (MM/LM)	101	*1213–23*
Cretan bronze and faience sculpture (MM/LM)	101	*1224–33*
Late Bronze Age animal sculpture, especially animalhead rhytons	102	*1234–42*
Mycenaean gold masks – clay and stucco sculpture – animal figures	103	*1243–65*
Late Bronze Age terracotta sculpture. Crete and Rhodes	104	*1266–71*
Ivories	105–7	*1272–90*
Jewellery	108–12	*1291–1358*
Early Bronze Age – Middle Bronze Age – Shaft Grave period – semi-precious stones and gold	108	*1291–1305*
LH II and LH III – gold – bronze – iron – semi-precious stones – faience – glass	109	*1306–58*

	page	cat. no.
Seals and signet rings	112–7	*1359–1408*
Neolithic period – Early Bronze Age – Middle Bronze Age	112	*1359–74*
Late Bronze Age	114	*1375–1408*
Written remains	118–22	*1409–22*

ANCIENT CYPRUS 123

Introduction 123

	page	
The Stone Age	123	
The Chalcolithic period	124	
Early Bronze Age	132	
Middle Bronze Age	133	
Late Bronze Age	134	

Cypriot Chronology 138

Catalogue 139

	page	cat. no.
Excavated sites. Architecture	139–40	*1423–62*
Neolithic and Chalcolithic settlements and buildings	139	*1423–50*
Early and Late Bronze Age buildings and fortifications	140	*1451–62*
Tombs	140–43	*1463–84*
Neolithic burials	140	*1463–78*
Early and Middle Bronze Age tombs	142	*1479–84*
Pottery	144–54	*1485–1656*
Neolithic and Chalcolithic periods	144	*1485–93*
Early Bronze Age	145	*1494–1527*
Middle and Late Bronze Ages	148	*1528–1656*
Stone vessels and conical stones	155–6	*1657–70*
Neolithic period	155	*1657–64*
Late Bronze Age	156	*1665–70*
Faience and glass	157	*1671–81*

	page	cat. no.
Metal vessels and implements	158	*1682–8*
Sculpture in the round	159–63	*1689–1741*
Neolithic and Chalcolithic periods: stone and clay	160	*1689–1703*
Early Bronze Age: terracotta	161	*1704–16*
Middle and Late Bronze Ages: terracotta	161	*1717–31*
Late Bronze Age: metal	162	*1732–41*
Ivories	163	*1742–9*
Seals	164	*1750–60*
Ornaments and toilet articles	165–68	*1761–1827*
Stone, shell, and glass paste	166	*1761–72*
Gold	166	*1773–1803*
Bronze and bone dress pins and fibulae	168	*1804–20*
Bronze toilet articles	168	*1821–4*
Gold, silver, and bronze hair-grips	168	*1825–7*
Tools – lamps – weapons – ingots	169–72	*1828–99*
Stone and bone	169	*1828–39*
Terracotta, ivory, steatite	169	*1840–56*
Copper and bronze	170	*1857–99*
Texts in syllabic script and writing implements	172	*1900–11*
Syllabic script documents and writing implements	173	*1900–11*

List of figures in the text and sources of plates 174

Bibliographical notes 176

List of abbreviations 184

Plates 189

Index of sites 509

782 Arapi Magoula near Larissa, Thessaly. Neolithic vessel

890 Phaistos, Crete. Cup of Kamares type

Colour plate 1

FOREWORD

The series published by Ernst Wasmuth with the title *Die ältesten Kulturen des Mittelmeerkreises* commenced in 1923 with *Altkreta*, by HELMUTH T. BOSSERT; but it still awaits completion. Since the succeeding volumes, *Altanatolien*, 1942, and *Altsyrien*, 1951, by BOSSERT in collaboration with RUDOLF NAUMANN, have been out of print for some years, it was clearly opportune to revive the old project. Thus the present volume makes its appearance. Its scope is wider than that of *Altkreta,* in that it includes documents of the prehistoric Cypriot civilization. It is so closely bound up with the life work and enquiring mind of Friedrich Matz, the Nestor of ancient Aegean research in Germany, that the authors have dedicated their work to him.

Illustrated works of this kind no longer require any justification. Even the pictorial volume that appeared in 1900, *Kunstgeschichte in Bildern* by FRANZ WINTER and GEORG DEHIO, aroused worldwide interest in its time, and served the young archaeologists and art historians of the beginning of the century as a standard introduction to their subjects, transmitting as it did the lifetime's experience of two scholars.

With respect to the Minoan civilization, one could of course say that such standard works as *L'Art de la Crète* by CHRISTIAN ZERVOS, *Kreta und das mykenische Hellas*[1] by SPYRIDON MARINATOS (with photographs by MAX HIRMER), *Kreta und Frühes Griechenland*[2] by FRIEDRICH MATZ, *Die minoische Kultur des alten Kreta* by FRITZ SCHACHERMEYR, *Greece in the Bronze Age* by EMILY VERMEULE, and *Das antike Kreta* by LEONHARD VON MATT have already covered all possible aspects, and that there is no room for a new work on the same subject or of a related one. Our book has to prove itself beside these works as a cheap and yet comprehensive archaeological documentation.

From the outset we decided to enter into only a moderate amount of detail, and to combine graphically compendious archaeological information with some two thousand illustrations, within as small a space as possible, both of familiar objects, often photographed from unfamiliar angles, and of new finds. Naturally, we have paid necessary attention to important excavations in recent years; but the craze to be up to date has played no part either in our choice of subjects or in our interpretation of archaeological discoveries. An important find by SCHLIEMANN seemed essential for our purpose, and certainly not to be supplanted by some second-rate new find! The editors also consider *Kretischmykenische Kultur* by DIETRICH FIMMEN, 2nd ed., 1924, such an outstanding compilation of the known facts and opinions of the time that in many respects it still deserves attention today.

This book familiarizes the reader with all the aspects of prehistory and early history in the Aegean and Cyprus. It tells of shrines, domestic and defensive architecture, citadels, palaces, and private houses, of burial customs and of tombs; it includes implements and weapons of stone, clay, bone, horn, and metal. With its considerable variants, its pictures and its ornaments (classified by periods and regions), pottery occupies a major place. Selected examples of painted sarcophagi and of the great wall-paintings in the palaces lead the observer deeper into the world of art, as do the group of gold and silver vessels chiselled in rich relief, the different types of colourful painted faiences, and the equally precious stone vases, with and without relief decoration. Besides sculptured works in clay, stone and metal—figures of gods, men, and animals—we have given due place to ivories, seal-stones and rings, and also to jewellery of coloured glass or precious metal. Inscribed remains and writing implements round off the picture; they remind us that the Bronze Age civilizations of Greece and Cyprus were familiar with writing. The Mediterranean basin was and is a geographical focus for historical and cultural currents leading to fruitful intercourse; we wished to stress this point especially with regard to the early period.

1 English edition: *Crete and Mycenae*, 1960.
2 English edition: *Crete and Early Greece*, 1962.

It would have been impossible to procure all the photographs, drawings, plans, and information without the assistance of numerous colleagues, both at home and abroad; and we offer our thanks to the individuals and institutions listed on pp. 175 f. We owe thanks also to our friends K. Grundmann and W. Kühne, both formerly of Berlin, who contributed to the success of this work—the one with his drawings, the other with his photographs—although they were unable to see its completion. Mrs. M. Heiber and Mr. G. Jöhrens, both of the Deutsches Archäologisches Institut in Berlin, have worked tirelessly in their free time, translating, checking corrections, and compiling entries. The technical staff of the Department of Antiquities in Nicosia provided the text illustrations and plates relating to Cyprus, and Dr. Angeliki Pieridou, Nicosia, assisted in arranging them. All the plates published in the Ancient Cyprus section were made available by the Cyprus museum in Nicosia, except for the following: nos. *1682, 1683, 1686, 1747, 1789, 1794a, b, 1880, 1899* (by courtesy of the Trustees of the British Museum, London); *1685a, b* (from the Staatliche Museen, East Berlin); *1735a, b* (from Medelhavsmuseet, Stockholm); and *1718* (from the Département des Antiquités Orientales, Musée du Louvre, Paris). The publishers and authors are especially indebted to these institutions. We must mention also the support and indefatigable interest of Mrs. V. Hankey (Westerham, Kent), Professor P. Åström (Göteborg), Professor S. Iakovidis (Athens), and Professor K. Parlasca (Frankfurt, now at Erlangen). We would also like to express personal thanks to the advisers to the photographic archives of the departments of the Deutsches Archäologisches Institut in Athens and Rome, Drs. R. Tölle, H. Sichtermann, and D. Willers, and to their assistants; to Professors A. Greifenhagen and A. von Müller, and Drs. U. Gehrig, W. Nagel, and E. Rohde at the Staatliche Museen, Berlin; and to Drs. R. D. Barnett and R. Higgins, and Mr. D. E. L. Haynes, of the British Museum, London. Finally we must also make grateful mention of Drs. T. Haevernick (Mainz), G. Daltrop (formerly of Hamburg, now of Rome), and O. Höckmann (Mainz), and Professor V. Milojcic (Heidelberg).

For reasons of space we have not always noted the precise scales of the objects; the catalogue entries give the measurements. We hope that the concise form of the text has not affected its intelligibility. The bibliography should assist the reader to explore the subject further; we have noticed recent literature as far as possible. Perhaps we should make special mention of the monumental work by the late Dr. P. Dikaios with the title *Enkomi*. This was not completed when this text went to press, and therefore could be cited only at a few points. The new three-volume modern Greek work *Perati* by S. Iakovidis also reached us too late for adequate notice here.

Giessen and Nicosia

Hans-Günter Buchholz
Vassos Karageorghis

PREHISTORIC GREECE

Introduction

The Stone and Bronze Age civilization surveyed here forms a geographical unity. It embraced the Greek mainland, the coastal areas of Thrace and Anatolia, and the islands, with Crete as the southern boundary (maps: Figs. 1, 2). The interpenetration of land and sea and the variety of the landscape are characteristic features. Mountain chains and sea lie close together; valleys, large and small plains of greater or less fertility open out into the sea, and are protected against each other and against the hinterland by mountain ranges. Even the great plains of central and northern Greece lie close to the sea.

This characteristic of the land already exerted a very definite influence on Stone Age man. The relative seclusion of smaller and larger areas of settlement produced a canton-like cultural development from the very beginning; but at the same time this isolation never proved so inhibiting as to prevent a constant, active exchange of ideas and materials, thanks largely to the intercommunicating sea.[1]

But the unity of the geographical area as a whole did not involve complete absence of relations with the outside world. It can be shown that from the earliest times the valleys of the rivers flowing to the Aegean Sea formed the lines of communication between Greece, the Balkans and Danube countries. Although the Bosphorus, the Sea of Marmara, and the Dardanelles separate the continents, they do not represent an insuperable barrier; the peninsula of Anatolia extends to the islands, including Crete. The cultural bridging function of the Aegean derives from these geographic conditions. On the whole the Aegean can be regarded as open towards the east and south, and more secluded from the north and west. The phrase coined by Schachermeyr for the Stone Age, the 'Near Eastern cultural drift,'[2] takes account of these natural conditions, as does Matz's discovery of 'the true role of early art and civilization in the Aegean: to assert itself in this field of tension.'[3]

PALAEOLITHIC PERIOD

A well-preserved mammoth's skull, 1.25 m. long, was recently discovered on the island of Chios. No doubt a number of the many caves in the area could throw light on the earliest appearance of man. A list compiled by the Greek Society for Speleology in 1968 includes 3,982 caves. The earliest evidence of human presence in Hellas are hearths, single teeth, and a Neanderthal skull (cf. Kokkoros-Kanellis, *L'Anthropologie* 64 [1960], 438 ff.; *Hellenika*, 1968, 97), and, above all, Palaeolithic flints, hand axes and other stone implements from southern Macedonia, Thessaly, Epiros, central Greece, and recently Argolid and Elis (cf. *192 a—c, 193, 194, 199, 202—214*).[4] Late Palaeolithic implements from the Seidi cave in Boeotia, and from Skyros, Cephallenia, and Zakynthos, were also described as 'Epipalaeolithic'

---

1 Lesky, *Thalatta, der Weg der Griechen zum Meer* (1947).
2 Schachermeyr, *Die ältesten Kulturen Griechenl.* (1955), 49 ff.
3 Matz, *Kreta und frühes Griechenland* (1962), 10.
4 Müller-Karpe, *Handbuch der Vorgeschichte* I (1966), 81 f. and 329 f., No. 308 ff.; for details see Milojcic, *Germania* 36 (1958), 319; Theocharis–Milojcic, *Delt.* 16 (1960), Chron. 182 f., 186 f.; Hood, *JHS.* 81 (1961), Arch. Rep. 3; Servais, *BCH.* 85 (1961), 1 ff.; Bialor–Jameson, *AJA.* 66 (1962), 181 f.; Schachermeyr, *AA.* 1962, 175, 179, 186;

Higgs, *Man* 63 (1963), 2 f.; Dakaris–Higgs, *Delt.* 18 (1963), Chron. 154 ff., Fig. 5, Pls. 188 a, 191; Daux, *BCH.* 87 (1963), 767 ff., Pl. 15; Dakaris–Higgs–Hey, *PPS.* 30 (1964), 199 ff.; Leroi-Gourhan, *BCH.* 88 (1964), 1 ff.; Milojcic, *Paläolithikum um Larissa in Thessalien* (1965); Higgs, *PPS.* 33 (1967), 1 ff.; Chavaillon, *BCH.* 91 (1967), 151 ff. and 93 (1969), 97 ff.; Megaw, *JHS.* 88 (1968), Arch. Rep. 11. – Compare the report also on new Palaeolithic finds in Anatolia by Müller and Beck, *PZ.* 38 (1960), 111 ff.

1 Kastritsa, Dodona
2 Kokkinopilos
3 Nidri
4 Chiorospilia
5 Palaiokastro
6 Kokkinospilia, Hag. Elias
7 Kallithea
8 Teichos Dymeion
9 Olympia, Babes Makrysia
10 Peristeria
11 Kakovatos
12 Pylos
13 Malthi
14 Sparta, Amyclae, Vaphio
15 Asea
16 Argos, Asine, Berbati, Dendra, Kasarmi, Lerna, Midea, Mycenae, Prosymna, Tiryns
17 Iria
18 Zougitza Cave, Zygouries, Korakou, Corinth
19 Galaxidi, Delphi
20 Eutresis, Thebes, Gla, Orchomenos, Chaironeia, Hyria Drachmani, Dramesi
21 Tanagra, Anthedon
22 Eleusis, Sparta, Athens, Hag. Kosmas, Vari
23 Thorikos
24 Perati, Marathon, Pyrgos
25 Oxylithos Paralia
26 Leukandi
27 Chalcis
28 Kyme
29 Lianokladi
30 Zerelia, Pthiotic Thebes
31 Sesklo, Dimini, Tsangli
32 Iolkos, Volos
33 Tsani Magoula
34 Larissa, Argissa, Arapi Otsaki, Souphli Magoula
35 Marmariane, Rhachmani
36 Palaikastro, near Kozani
37 Hag. Mamas, near Olynthos
38 Dikeli Tash
39 Komotini
40 Poliochni
41 Troy
42 Antissa
43 Thermi
44 Smyrna
45 Samos Heraion, Tigani
46 Miletus
47 Kos Seraglio,
— Eleona
— Askloupis
48 Aspripetra
49 Iasos
50 Ialysos
51 Lindos
52 Camirus
53 Phylakopi
54 Chalandriani

Fig. 1   Aegean, survey of sites mentioned in the text

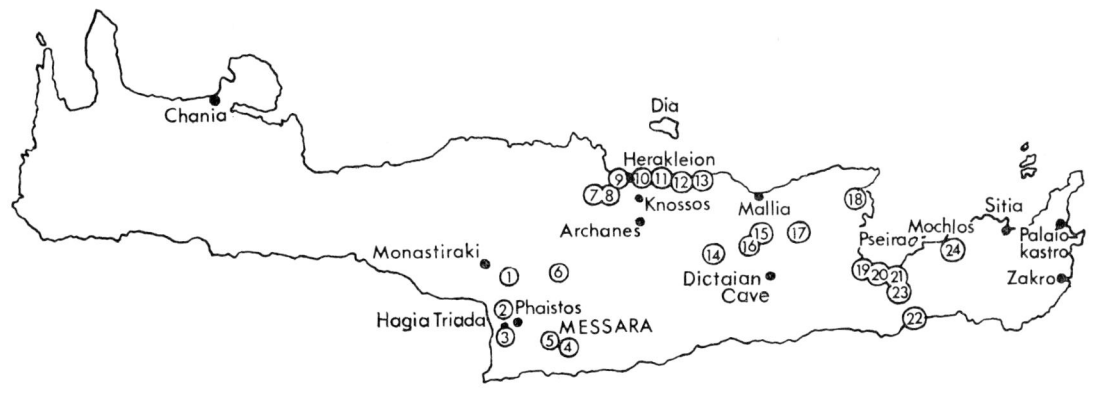

1 Kamares Cave	9 Gazi	17 Cave of Trapeza
2 Hag. Onouphrios	10 Zapher Papoura	18 Olous
3 Kamilari	11 Katsamba	19 Vrokastro
4 Koumasa	12 Amnisos	20 Gournia
5 Platanos	13 Nirou Chani	21 Pachyammos
6 Vorou	14 Arkalochori	22 Hagia Photia
7 Tylissos	15 Karphi	23 Vasiliki
8 Isopata	16 Cave of Psychro	24 Mouliana

Fig. 2 Crete, survey of sites mentioned in the text

For further archaeological maps cf.:
p. 25, Fig. 8, *107* (the Argolid); p. 28, Fig. 9, *129* (West Anatolia) and *130* (Rhodes); p. 36, Fig. 13 (region of Mallia, Crete); p. 51, Fig. 21 (overall Aegean); p. 60, Fig. 26 (Cyprus – Aegean – Sicily – Sardinia); p. 123, Fig. 44 (Cyprus); p. 124, Fig. 45 (Eastern Mediterranean)

in order to indicate that these are very ancient forms, although possibly of a somewhat later date.[5] Quite unmistakable microliths which point typologically to the existence of a Mesolithic Age were discovered recently in Thessaly. We must regard the reports of Early Stone Age works of art (cave drawings, red-ochre drawings on pebbles, and slate tablets), also noted there, with some hesitation for the time being. Recently, uninterrupted sequences of Palaeolithic, Mesolithic and Neolithic deposits were found in the Franchthi cave near Koilada in the Argolid.[6] Blegen's finds in the Zougitza cave near Nemea, unfortunately not yet published, are also very informative; these are now in the Archaeological Museum, Corinth.

NEOLITHIC PERIOD

The age of food-gatherers and hunters living in caves was followed in the sixth millennium B.C., even before the invention of pottery, by the definite transition to farming and the settled life this entailed. This was the Neolithic period. It has been demonstrated that in Thessaly emmer wheat, together with einkorn wheat, barley, peas, and lentils, were the main crops, to be joined in the late Neolithic period by wheat, beans, figs, and almonds. Wild olives were also grown. Animal husbandry began with sheep and goats. Fishhooks show that fishing also was practised.

---

5 Zapfe, *Wiener PZ.* 24 (1937), 158 ff.; Stampfuss, *Mannus* 34 (1942), 132 ff.; Schachermeyr, *Die ältesten Kulturen*, 49 f., Fig. 2; Marinatos, *Delt.* 16 (1960), Chron. 41 ff.; also Müller-Karpe, op. cit., 330, No. 311, and Weinberg in Ehrich, *Chronologies in Old World Archaeology* (1965), 85.

6 Fraser, *Archaeological Report for 1968/69*, 14 f.

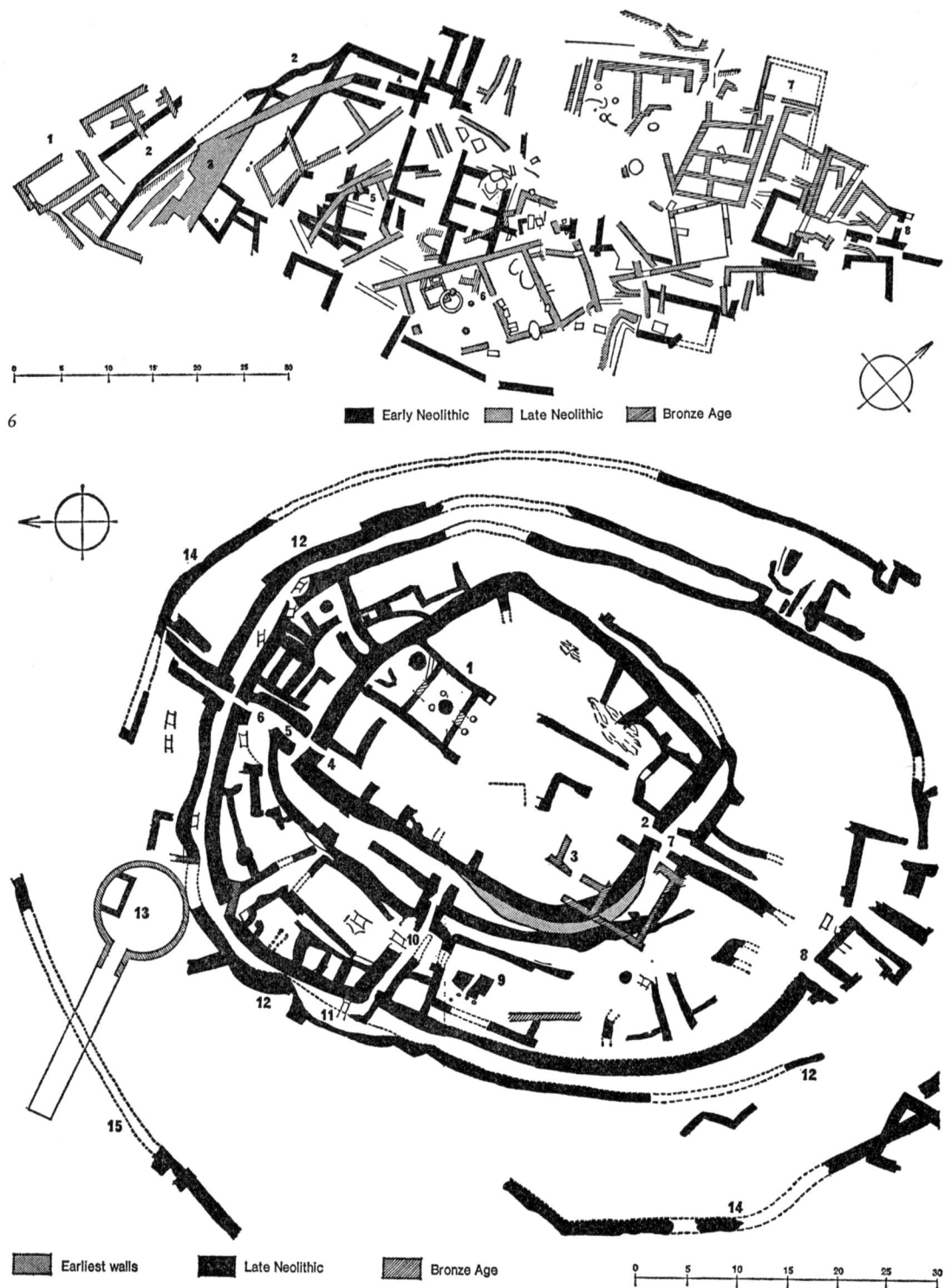

Fig. 3 6 Sesklo, 1 Bronze Age buildings 2 Early Neolithic retaining wall 3 Late Neolithic retaining wall 4 Gateway 5 Depot, sling shots 6, 7 Late Neolithic megara 8 Early Neolithic megaron; 7 Dimini, 1 Megaron A 2 South gate, Wall I 3 Bronze Age buildings 4 North gate, Wall I 5 North gate, Wall II 6 North gate, Wall III 7 South gate, Wall II 8 South gate, Wall III 9 Megaron B 10 West entrance 11 Tomb 12 Wall IV 13 Bronze Age tholos 14 Wall 15 Wall VI

In Greece, polished axes of hard rock are found throughout the mainland and the islands *(217—223)*. Neolithic stone clubs were designed for hand-to-hand fighting *(233)*, and the evidence of numerous finds of slingstones of clay and limestone *(235—237)* show that the sling was the major long-distance weapon, although bows and arrows also were used *(410)*. Implements made of flint and obsidian (vitreous lava) are extremely numerous *(200, 201, 215, 216, 245—289, 348—351)*; knives, scrapers, borers, and sickle blades all occur. Since obsidian only occurs in a few volcanic sites, we must assume that the distribution of implements made of this material beyond the borders of their natural occurrence indicates the existence of wide-ranging trade relations from the pre-ceramic Neolithic period onwards.

Clay spindle-whorls and conical weights *(413—415, 428, 429)* show that the use of wool and weaving were known.

The carefully worked Neolithic pottery, made without the wheel *(753—791)*, assumes a wealth of forms, highly differentiated according to regions and stylistic periods, and evinces a remarkable joy in incised, polished, and in particular painted ornaments (Col. Pl. 1, *782*). They give us an idea of the nature of their makers and, at times, of connections with non-Aegean work.

Cave-dwelling continued until far into the Neolithic period *(1—3)*; later the caves occasionally served cultic purposes *(2, 3)*. But in the fertile plains of central and northern Greece, even before the introduction of pottery, hill settlements (magoulas) appeared, where the rubble reached considerable heights over thousands of years of human occupation. In the area between Larissa and Volos alone there are 150 such magoulas *(4, 5)*. For the finds from the Alepotrypa cave in Southern Peloponnesos see most recently: Lambert, *AAA.* 5 (1972), 199 ff.

The first permanent dwellings—huts made of posts and wattling—were followed in the Sesklo culture by almost square houses of sun-dried brick *(8, 9)* and then by large megaron buildings *(6;* cf. *12* [Dimini, late Neolithic period]), whose origins can be traced to the Near East, but which exhibited their ancient Aegean influence in the small porch supported by two posts at the narrow end. Even in the Stone Age the settlements became more compact than the farming and village colonies.

More sophisticated needs are expressed in the abundance of Neolithic idol sculpture *(1172—1183, 1191)*; it reflects the belief, extending beyond Hellas, in the maternal aspect of the divine being; for it was mainly the female element that was represented, or at times a mother and child *(1180)*. The coloured ornamentation of these figures suggests body pigmentation and tattooing. The famous menhir statue from the Souphli magoula in Thessaly (Biesantz, *AA.* 1959, 57 f., Figs. 1, 2) is not discussed here because its Stone Age dating is not yet certain. The dead were buried with care; for instance, an Early Neolithic joint burial of mother and child was found in Nea Nikomedia.[7]

Naturally we know nothing of the language and racial characteristics of the Stone Age inhabitants of Greece. But the examination of skeletons and skulls has produced a surprisingly variegated picture,[8] indicating that the most heterogeneous ethnic elements flowed into the Aegean and confirming that the area served as a cultural as well as geographical bridge.

---

[7] Vermeule, *Greece in the Bronze Age* (1964), Pl. 1; list of Neolithic burials in Matz, *Hdb. d. Arch.* II (1954), 185, note 6; Weinberg, 'The Stone Age in the Aegean', *CAH.²*, I.i (1970), 551–618.

[8] Fürst, *Zur Anthropologie der prähistorischen Griechen in der Argolis* (1930); Angel, *Amer. Journ. of Physical Anthropology* 1 (1943), 229 ff., and 4 (1946), 69 ff.; and *AJA.* 49 (1945), 252 ff. and 62 (1958), 221 ff.; also Vermeule, 332, note 6; Charles, 'Anthropologie Archéologique de la Crète', in *Et. Crét.* XIV (1965).

Early Bronze Age

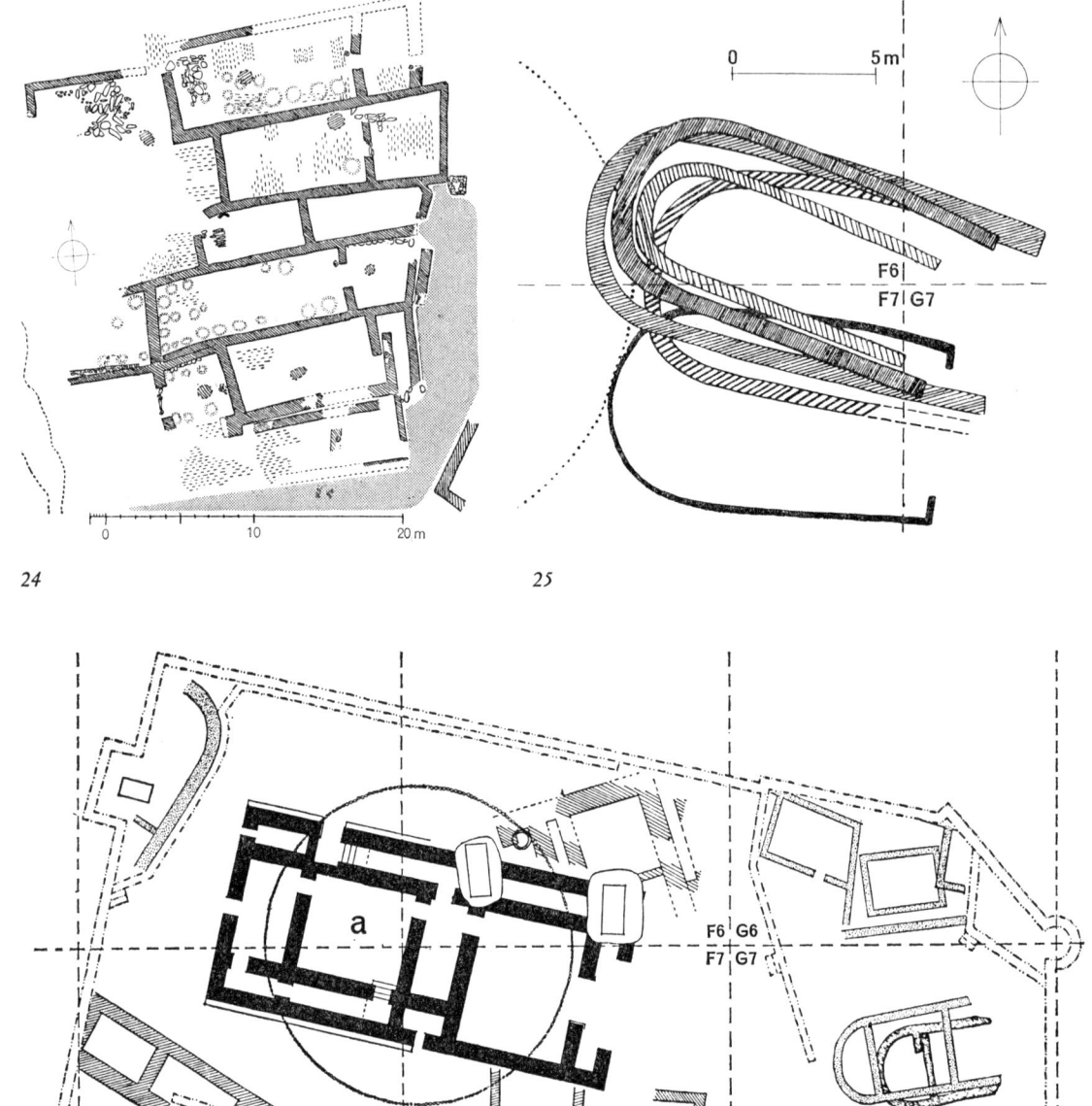

Fig. 4 *24* Thermi, Lesbos, Phase 1   *25* and *26* Lerna, the Argolid (a: House of Tiles, b: Early Helladic fortifications; F6 / F7 / G6 / G7 in *25* and *26* to be superimposed)   *27* Orchomenos, Boeotia   *28* Poliochni, Lemnos

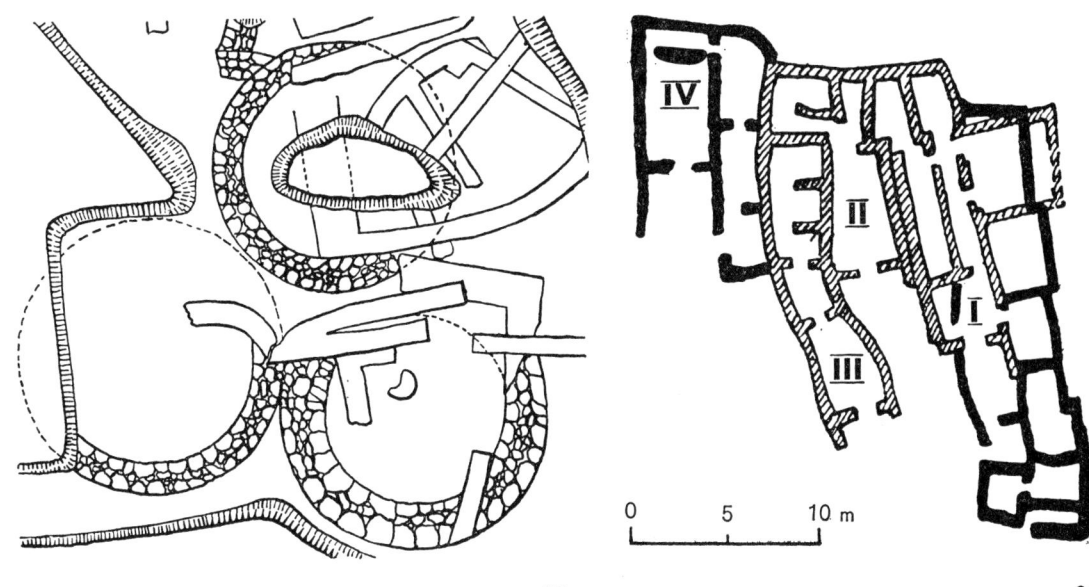

27 28

EARLY BRONZE AGE

The third millennium B.C. was of great historical importance in Greece: trades and crafts were given great impetus thanks to the development of metallurgy (cf. implements p. 53, Fig. 22). The islands of the central Aegean had a major share in this (cf. map, p. 51, Fig. 21). And it was here that a curious form of marble sculpture evolved (see below, p. 96, and Preziosi-Weinberg, 'Evidence for Painted Details in Early Cycladic Sculpture,' *AntK.* 13 [1970], 4 ff.). The general cultural character underwent a change; yet the indigenous Aegean-Anatolian urbanization consolidated itself during the exposure to external influences. Further areas of contact now came into being. J. L. Caskey's excavations in Lerna made it even clearer that there were communications between the Argolid, the Cyclades, and Crete (*AJA.* 64 [1960], 183; 72 [1968], 313 ff.). Discoveries on Kythera brought to light both Early Minoan and local finds. Gold and silver vases from Euboea tell of the central Anatolian influence *(1079— 1081)*; contacts between north-west Asia Minor and the Cyclades are shown by the existence of Troy II beakers in Kastri on Syros (Caskey, in *Essays in Memory of K. Lehmann* [1964], 63 ff., Fig. 8; Megaw, *JHS.* 88 [1968], Arch. Rep. 19; cf. *799* [Troy], *796* [Poliochni], *797* [Orchomenos], also Tiryns, Keos and Samos).

Finally, 'Ishtar at Troy,' a study by Henri Frankfort (*JNES.* 8 [1949], 194 ff.) shows that there were perhaps contacts reaching far beyond the Aegean; for instance, similarly decorated bone implements *(500—505)* occurred both in the Cyclades and in Syria about the middle of the millennium (Hennessy, *The Foreign Relations of Palestine during the Early Bronze Age* [1967], Pl. 77). Minoan weapons and vases from the end of this period found in Cyprus tell of similar contacts between Cyprus and Crete *(1572, 1876, 1877)*. Mention must also be made of an Oriental cylinder seal from Amorgos *(1362 a—c)* and of the study of cylinder seals found in the Aegean cultural area (Buchholz, *TrAPhSoc.* 57, Part 8 [1957], 148 ff.).

The cultural turning-point appears to have been related to new forms of economy and organization, including the sealing of vessels, as can be seen from seal impressions from Crete and the Argolid (Persson, *Asine*, 217 f., No. 15, Fig. 160: 2 [repeated 25 times], 235 ff., Fig. 172: 5—7; Vermeule, *Greece in the Bronze Age*, Pl. 5 [Lerna]). A scarab impression on an EM III vase handle from east Crete *(1371)* and a Cycladic vase with four identical impressions of an Egyptian stamp seal *(851)* show that there were wide-ranging relations in the use of seals. The Early Bronze Age proved to be

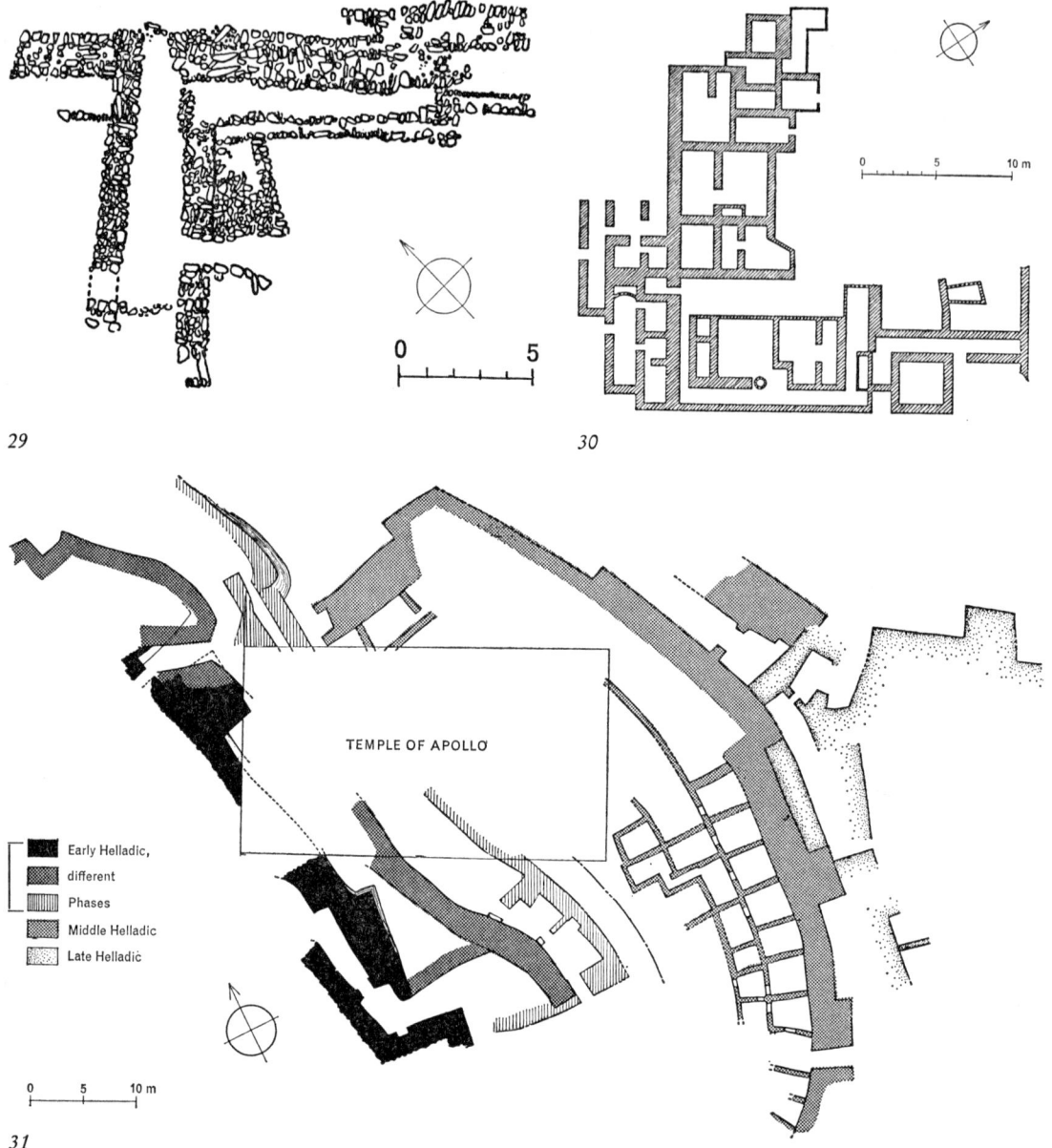

Fig. 5 *29* Thermi, Lesbos *30* Vasiliki, East Crete *31* Aegina

the first flowering of glyptic, and the early seals of Crete are of great importance to art history *(1363—1370;* Matz, *Die Frühkretischen Siegel* [1928]).

In architecture this period saw the breakthrough to representative forms. Even tomb architecture made progress *(131, 134—140,* Fig. 16), reaching as far as the great circular tombs of south Crete *(132, 133).* Buildings were executed in traditional indigenous ashlar with the Oriental sun-dried brick technique *(18—20;* Fig. 11, *21).* Earlier forms of house—round, oval and apsidal buildings—continued also; cf. Tiryns, Orchomenos, Eutresis (Fig. 4, *26, 27)* and an early Cycladic model *(1122 a, b),* also Caskey, *Hesperia* 29 (1960), 139, Fig. 6 and p. 162 f.; and 26 (1957), Pl. 42. At the beginning of the following millennium (MM I), there were still oval houses beside the palaces, for instance in Chamaizi, east Crete (Xanthoudides, *Ephem.* 1906, 119, Fig. 1; Bulle, *Orchomenos* I [1907], 125 f., Fig. 37; Noack, *Ovalhaus und Palast in Kreta* [1908], 55 ff., Figs. 6, 7; Glotz, *La Civilisation Egéenne*[2] [1937], 155, Fig. 23; Davaros, *AAA.* 1972, 283 ff.).

We possess beautiful examples of well-planned urban settlements with gates, roads and drainage from as early as the third millennium (Overbeck, 'Greek Towns in the Early Bronze Age,' *Class. Journ.* 65 [1969], 1 ff.). The northern Aegean also had a part in this development: Thermi (Fig. 4, *24*; 5, *29*), Poliochni (Fig. 4, *28*). Palace-like buildings, for instance in Lerna (Fig. 4, *25*), and in Vasiliki, east Crete (Fig. 5, *30*, cf. Sinos, *AA.* 1970, 1 ff.) as well as mighty fortification walls, for example in Lerna (Fig. 4, *25*), Aegina (Fig. 5, *31*), Poliochni *(22)* and Troy *(23)*, and characteristic cult equipment, such as a ceremonial hearth in Lerna (*Hesperia* 28 [1959], Pl. 42a; Vermeule, *Greece in the Bronze Age* [1964], Pl. 4c)—presuppose differentiations in social structure and powerful leaders.

We would like to have more anthropological knowledge about the third millennium. There are skeleton remains from Leukas (Velde, *ZfE.* 1912, 845 ff.), Attica (Angel in Mylonas, *Aghios Kosmas* [1959], 167 ff.) and Troy (Angel, *Troy-Suppl.* I ([1951])). 'The People of Lerna' have also been described by Angel (*AJA.* 62 [1958], 221); while Gejvall made a scientific study of animal remains from various deposits some time ago (*Årsberättelse Lund*, 1937/38 and 1938/39).

For parallel phenomena and diverging features in contemporary culture on the island of Cyprus, see p. 132. *Die mittelmeerischen Grundlagen der antiken Kunst* [The Mediterranean foundations of ancient art], by Kaschnitz-Weinberg, 1944, were not only visible in the Early Bronze Age, even if they were most striking there. Probably we are usually too little aware of the level of civilization in the East at that time: the forms of culture during the Early Minoan and Helladic period in Greece were contemporaneous with important imperial structures in the Orient and with the pyramids of Egypt!

Further literature: S. Weinberg, 'Aegean Chronology: Neolithic Period and Early Bronze Age' (*AJA.* 51 [1947], 165 ff.); F. Schachermeyr, *Die ältesten Kulturen Griechenlands* (1955), 151 ff.; T. L. Caskey, 'Greece, Crete and the Aegean Islands in the Early Bronze Age' (*CAH.*²); id., 'The Early Helladic Period in the Argolid' (*Hesperia* 29 [1960], 285 ff.).

MIDDLE BRONZE AGE

Selected bibliography: T. L. Caskey, 'Greece and the Aegean Islands in the Middle Bronze Age' (*CAH.*² [1966], No. 45); Buck, 'The MH-Period' (*Phoenix* 20 [1966], 193 ff.); Howell, 'The Regional Variations in Middle Helladic Pottery' (*BICS.* 13 [1966], 116); S. Hood, 'The Early and Middle Minoan Periods at Knossos' (loc. cit., 110 f.). Note also the general summary of Cyprus during the Middle Bronze Age below (p. 000).

The 'Earlier Palace Period' was of greater importance in world history than the period just described. Crete became the undisputed centre of power in the Aegean, and the Middle Minoan fleet ruled the sea, largely without resistance. Compared to the third millennium, this represented a consolidation of the Aegean area as a whole, together with a decline in the importance of the Cyclades. In any case the Middle Helladic culture taking shape on the mainland was initially more exposed to Anatolian than to Minoan influences. The cultural power of the Minoans is, however, demonstrated at Lerna in the Argolid by Cretan Barbotine and Kamares ware (Caskey, *Hesperia* 26 [1957], Pl. 43c; and *AJA.* 64 [1960], 183), and also by Cretan vessels or local imitations in Aegina *(864 a, b)* and in Athens *(875)*. Kamares ware even reached Cyprus *(1573 a, b)* and north Syria *(897*, Ras Shamra); conversely, stone vases from Egypt reached Crete: the lid found in Knossos inscribed with the name of Pharaoh Khyan has become famous (c. 1680 B.C., *1144*). Tel-el-Yahudiyeh juglets in the Thera Museum are documents for Middle Bronze Age contacts, as well (Åström, *Acta of the 1st. Int. Scient. Congress on the Volcano of Thera 1969* [1970], 415 ff.).

In technical and cultural terms, and in respect of religion and art history, the astonishingly dynamic culture of the island of Minos at that time was of such high quality and at the same time so individual that it can be defined as a 'high culture.' Schachermeyr, whom we follow here, defined the characteristics of culture in the Middle Minoan period as having produced such elements as: 'the presence of development, its independence, the completeness of the cultural structure, and the attainment of correspondingly high and serious cultural achievements' (*Die minoische Kultur des alten Kreta* [1964],

268 ff.). Equally noteworthy are the largely independent development of writing (p. 118) and the creation of a carefully balanced structure of society and power, which was fully reflected in the palace architecture—in fact, in the least product of craftsmanship.

The culmination of Minoan culture as a whole in MM II noted by Schachermeyr and others makes it impossible, strictly speaking, to regard the second culmination—during the flowering of the later palaces—as equally outstanding. In analogy, there is now a new and deeper appreciation of the Middle Kingdom in Egypt: 'from our point of view the concepts of balance, vigour and a conscious life form between the two extremes may well justify the application of the term Classical to Egypt in the Middle Kingdom' (Otto, *Ägypten — der Weg des Pharaonenreiches* [1953], 132). In this sense we may also call the Middle Minoan period, the age of the earlier palaces, 'classical'.

LATE BRONZE AGE

The period from the mid-millennium until 1200 B.C. was a crucial moment of development and one of great importance to the history of civilization. In Crete this was called the 'Later Palace Period' (Chronological Table: pp. 29 f.; for Knossos, Phaistos, Hagia Triada, Mallia, and Kato Zakro, see Fig. 6, *41, 42*; Fig. 12, *53*; Fig. 14, *70, 75*, also *43 ff.* [Knossos] and *54 ff.* [Phaistos]); its sophisticated courtly life led Matz aptly to define the essence of the period in the title of his work 'Minoan Civilization: Maturity and Zenith' (*CAH.*² II, Ch. iv and xii [1962]). Prosperity, luxury, and a fastidious taste are evident from the surviving wall paintings (79, Fig. 29; *1043, 1045—1054*); the examples from the palaces of the Cyclades are remarkable examples of the art of this period (Phylakopi, Melos: *1044*; recently also Thera: *AAA.* 4 [1971], 66 ff., Figs. 13—15, Col. Pl. A 1).

Since 1962 excavations in the palace of Kato Zakro, destroyed by a natural disaster but never plundered, have produced thousands of finds in more than seventy rooms (Fig. 14, *75*). The total number of rooms must have been between 250 and 300. There can be no doubt that centres of this kind were the real seats of authority, culture, and economy. Everywhere one can see the beginnings of a truly urban life style.

Instead of the desire for massiveness and artistic representation, we find in Crete a predilection for small forms and correspondingly intimate and dainty objects: gold and silver work, bronze statuettes (*1224 ff.*), and outstanding gem carvings (see bibliography on seals below, p. 182). We are faced here almost with a picture of a surfeit of cultural maturity. At the same time, this is the period when the administrative system was rationalized; (there is increased evidence of writing: *1410 ff.*; p. 120, Fig. 41 and p. 122, Fig. 43; see documents of Cypro-Minoan script: *1892, 1893, 1901 ff.*). And all this bore the imprint of the priest-kings' households. In Greek tradition the name 'Minos' probably derived from an ancient Cretan royal title. So-called 'portrait gems' give us an idea of the form of the ruling class of the time; the Prince Cup *(1166)* and wall frescoes *(1052, 1053)* give an impression of the different degrees of nobility, dignity, and rank.

Government and administration, activities of social life such as dancing and bull-jumping *(1054, 1214, 1384, 1620)*, all the artistic media—in fact, life in its totality as well as death—were deeply entrenched in an all-pervasive, ubiquitous religion (Guthrie, 'The Religion and Mythology of the Greeks,' *CAH.*², Ch. xl [1961]). The 'Temple Tomb' of Knossos (Fig. 16, *141, 142*, and *143 ff.*) is evidence of this; however, note also a number of the individual details in the palace complexes! The cultic function of the open stairway *(54)* becomes quite clear from the pictures on the small frescoes from Knossos. Note in particular the religious implications of the frescoes in the Throne Room at Knossos (48; cf. Reusch in *Minoica: Festschrift zum 80. Geburtstag v. Sundwall* [1958], 334 ff.).

Indeed, the often-mentioned alleged naturalism of Minoan art was simply a materialistic rendering of a primitive conception of the world, misunderstood in our day; for the rendering of nature in Ancient Cretan art, see Banti, in *Geras Keramopoullou* (1953), 119 ff.; for the composition cf. Schachermeyr, *Kret. Chron.* 15/16 (1961/1962), Part I, 177 ff. Even such an unholy coquette as the Petite Parisienne is characterized as a priestess by the cult knot attached at the neck of her dress *(1048)*. Women also dominate on the Hagia Triada sarcophagus in the role of priestesses *(1065)*. Their pre-

41

42

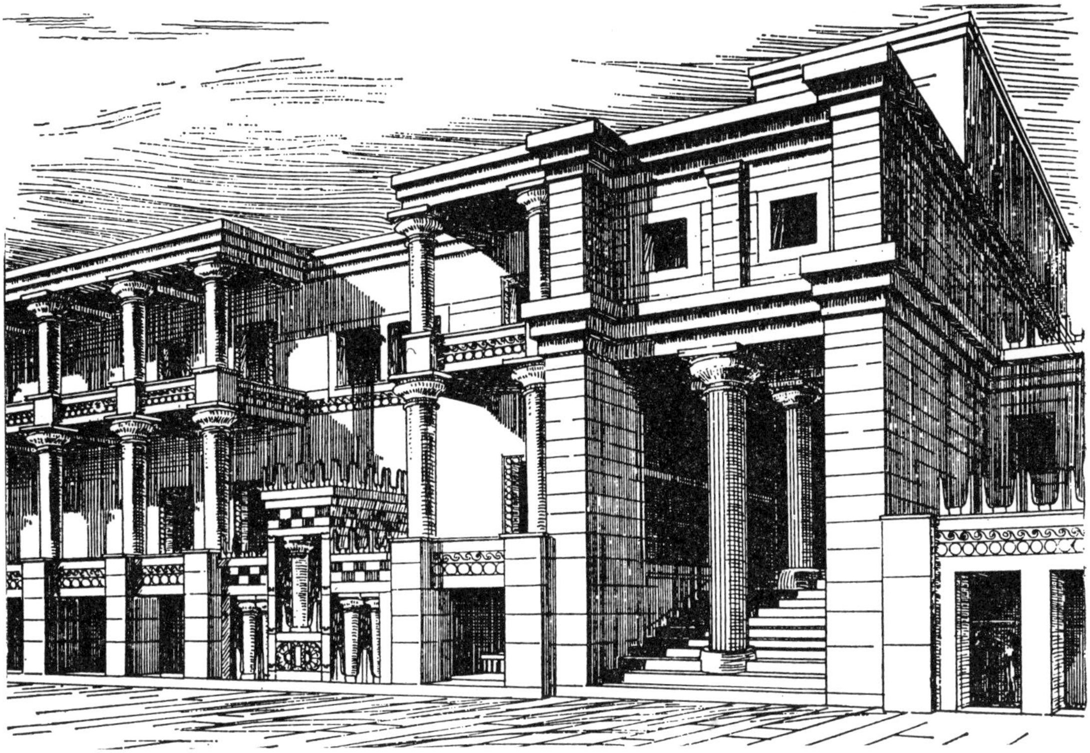

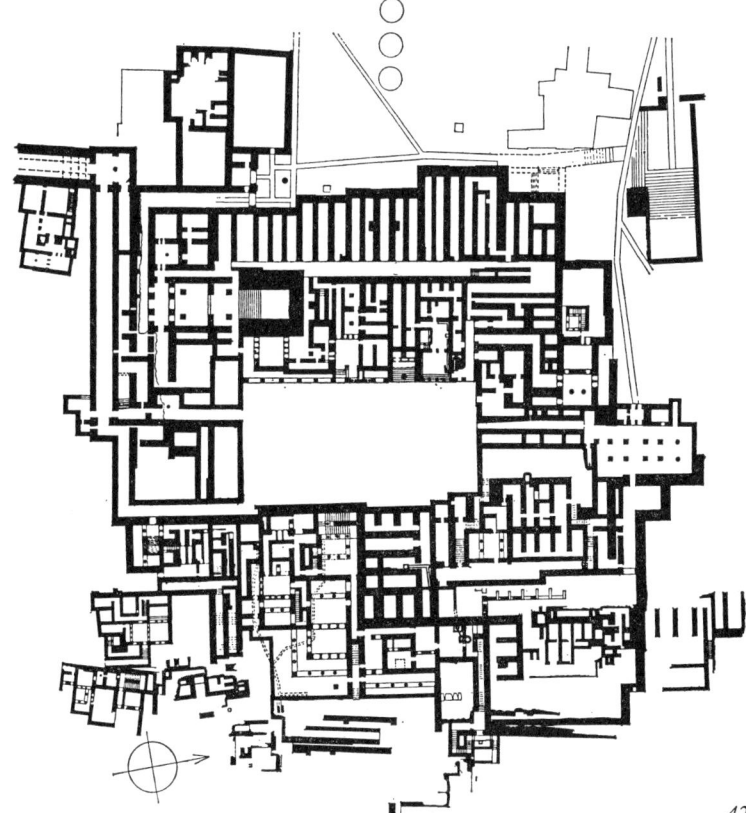

Fig. 6 *41* and *42* Knossos, diagrammatic reconstruction of the east front of the west wing and plan of the palace at the level of the central court

eminence in every sphere of life was reflected in the preference for the female principle in the Pantheon (see the bibliography p. 183; and that in G. Thomson, *Aeschylus and Athens* [2nd ed. 1946]);[9] *1233* (faience goddess, Knossos), *1290* and *1400* (Potnia Theron on ivory lid, Ras Shamra, and on seal, Crete), *1280* (ivory group, Mycenae), *1381, 1384, 1385*, and *1397* (cult scenes on rings and seals). The bee was seen as a giver of life and symbol of the eternal feminine *(1356,* cf. *1296).* The high esteem of the female is also discernible in the religion of the more masculine Mycenaean civilization, from the evidence of countless idols *(1258 ff.)*: see *1069* (female mourners on sarcophagus), *966* (female winged being, vase painting). There were also mother goddesses in Cyprus: *1722, 1723* (clay idol), *1734* (bronze statuette), and *1759* (enthroned goddess on seal). Her symbols of fertility included pomegranates *(1678)*. Alexiou has interpreted the female figures with upraised arms as goddesses in a gesture of revelation (e.g. *464, 1267—1269*; cf. especially Matz, *Göttererscheinung u. Kultbild im minoischen Kreta* [1958]).

The group of sculpture from Kamilari, south Crete *(1223)*, is a cultic document of a particular kind. The Harvester Vase from Hagia Triada *(1165)* makes it clear that rural festivals existed side by side with the more sophisticated rites of court society and were also considered worthy of representation. Because of the *sistrum* (sacred rattle) depicted there, Egyptian influence has been suggested; but frame rattles of the *sistrum* type as seen on the Harvester Vase have also been found from the central Anatolian Bronze Age (Horoz Tepe).

The male element was by no means suppressed in ancient Cretan culture. In the religious sphere we need only recall the youths serving as officers of the temple *(1053, 1065 b;* Fig. 35, *1167)* and the many praying youths with right hand laid reverently on their brows *(1225, 1226, 1231, 1232)*. The Mycenaean world, it is true, had an even greater reverence for the gods; noteworthy here are the figure of Potnios Theron from Aegina *(1305)* and the Orpheus of Pylos, enthroned on a high cliff *(1059)*, as well as the so-called 'Zeus with the scales of fate' on a Cypro-Helladic vase *(1621)* and two bronze horned gods *(1740, 1741)*, all from Enkomi. There is a virile, heroic, Asiatic effect in the cycles of myths about liberators attacking evil spirits and huge beasts ('Arimasp' motif, lion tamer: *1747* and *1748*).

Bronze Age civilization on the mainland is distinguished from that in Crete by a preference for war and the hunt *(1383,* and Fig. 39, *1388)*: finds of weapons for hand-to-hand fighting and engagements at a distance (e.g. arrowheads: Fig. 20, *410* and *600 ff.)*, armour, and helmets *(710, 712)* show this very clearly indeed. The chariot was the formal accontrement of a knightly prince, as we can still see in Homer *(999—1001, 1170, 1171;* Fig. 39, *1395;* cf. also the snaffle bit in Fig. 24, *709)*. The Cyclopean defensive walls of the forts tell of the careful security measures (Col. Pl. 2, *78,* Mycenae; see also pp. 35 ff.), while at the same time reflecting a desire for massiveness. Settlements in Keos *(37,* Hagia Irini) and Cyprus *(1456 ff.,* Palaiokastro Maa, Enkomi, Kition) were just as strongly defended. The mighty Late Helladic tombs—like the two grave circles of Mycenae *(156, 157;* Figs. 7, *95* and 17, *153)* and the tholoi found wherever there were Late Bronze Age ruling dynasties in Greece *(159 ff.;* Fig. 17, *180,* Col. Pl. 2, *177)*—were also the expression of a vivid sense of the massiveness inherent in such buildings.

The architectural rendering of the concept of domination in this civilization is found chiefly in the megara and their throne rooms (Pylos, *122, 123)*. Other insignia of warrior kingship were the lance and sceptre, like Agamemnon's ruler's staff in the *Iliad* (Col. Pl. 4, *1788:* gold sceptre with pair of falcons; cf. Alföldi, 'Hasta-Summa Imperii,' *AJA*. 63 [1959], 1 ff.). Insignia of rank appear to have been represented through the distinctions between victors and vanquished, conquerors and prisoners of war (Lencman, *Die Sklaverei im mykenischen u. homerischen Griechenland* [1966]).

We can establish more than just superficial differences between the Minoan island civilization and the Late Helladic mainland civilization; Biesantz has attempted to differentiate between the two 'structures' in so far as they are visible in art (*Ullstein Kunstgeschichte* IV [1963]) and Schachermeyr has stressed both the barbaric element in the mainland culture and its internal dependence on the Minoan flowering, in the sense of its being a 'satellite culture' *(Die min. Kultur des alten Kreta* [1964], 268 ff.). But following the routes mapped out by the Minoan seafarers (maps: Fig. 9, *129, 130*; Figs. 45 and 60)—and even beyond this—the Mycenaeans asserted themselves as traders and colonizers as far

---

[9] The German edition of the present work gives a reference to p. 30, note 11, of the German edition, *Aischylos und Athen* (1957).

as Egypt (Fig. 34; *900, 912*; Egyptian counter-current: *1140, 1141, 1305*), Syria and Palestine (*873*; oriental counter-current: ivory, *956 b* [Canaanite jug, Athens], *1350—1352* [oriental amulets, Perati], *1374 ff.* [cylinder seals]), Cyprus (*1616 ff.*; Cypriot counter-influence: *1160* and White Slip ware), Malta—southern Italy—Sicily—Lipari—Sardinia—Etruria (p. 76, Fig. 28 [pottery, Tarentum], p. 60, Fig. 26 [copper ingots]) and south-west England *(699)*. 'Pottery as Evidence of Trade and Colonisation' by Wace and Blegen (*Klio* 32, 1939, 131 ff.) has become a standard article.

CONCLUSION AND TRANSITION

'The Fall of the Mycenaean Empire' (Vermeule, *Archaeology* 13 [1960], 66 ff.), 'Das Ende der mykenischen Fundstätten auf dem griechischen Festland' (Ålin, 1962)—these are the archaeological themes corresponding to the historic events of the Dorian migration and the wave of Aeolian settlement towards north-west Anatolia, together with the momentous Central European 'urnfield peoples' migration and the movement of the 'Sea Peoples' in the eastern Mediterranean (Philistine seal from Enkomi: *1760*). The same awareness of a causal connection is reflected in the title 'Seevölkerbewegung und Urnenfelderkultur' (Kimmig, in *Studien aus Alteuropa* I [1964], 220 ff.).

In literature, this period includes the background to the legend of the Trojan war; in archaeology, the chronology of the destructions from the thirteenth to eleventh century in Greece. Following *Lakonien u. Sparta: Untersuchungen zur ethnischen Struktur u. zur politischen Entwicklung Lakoniens u. Spartas...* (1963), I gave an affirmative answer (*Histor. Zeitschr.* 200 [1965], 360 ff., esp. 364 f.) to Matz's question whether the great destruction of the later thirteenth century was caused by the invasion of the Dorians (*Atti 7. Congr. Internaz. di Arch. Class.* I [1961], 197 ff.): Even if there were several Dorian invasions, I have no doubt that was the decisive one. Several waves of north-west Greek immigration have also become evident from the investigation 'Die Dorische Wanderung im Lichte der vorgeschichtlichen Funde' (Milojcic, *AA*. 1948/49, 12 ff.). This is why it is not surprising to find 'Balkan elements in Late Mycenaean and Geometric Greece' ('Balkanische Elemente im spätmykenischen u. geometrischen Griechenland,' Bouzek, *Acta Antiqua Acad. Scient. Hungaricae* 15 [1967], 261 ff.; and *Op. Athen*. IX [1969], 41 ff.). From the point of view of linguistics, Krahe's works are still worth note: *Die Indogermanisierung Griechenlands u. Italiens* (1949) and 'Die Vorgeschichte des Griechentums nach den Zeugnissen der Sprache' (*Antike* 15 [1939], 175 ff.).

With regard to the question of the Greek nationality of the carriers of Mycenaean culture, the issue of the continuity or discontinuity between the Helladic Bronze and Iron Ages should be decisive: Carpenter, *Discontinuity in Greek Civilization* (1966), cf. East, *JHS*. 87 (1967), 176 f.; and Pugliese Carratelli, 'Dal Regno Miceneo alla Polis' (*Problemi Attuali di Scienza e di Culture* 54 [1962], 175 ff.). In my opinion there are so many archaeological links between the two periods as to make the existence of Greek-speaking elements in the population before the Dorian migrations beyond question. For the latter, cf. Cook, 'The Dorian Invasion,' *Proceedings of the Cambridge Society*, N.S. 8 (1962), 16 ff.; cf. also Nixon, *The Rise of the Dorians* (1968), and Burn, *Antiquity* 43 (1969), 232 f.; Lang, *Class. World* 62 (1969), No. 9; Bennett, *American Historical Review* 75 (1970), 1084; MacKendrick, *Classical Journal* 66 (1970), 80 f. Grumach maintains that pre-Dorian Hellenes first appeared in Greece c. 1200 B.C. ('The Coming of the Greeks,' *Bulletin of the J. Rylands Library* 51 [1968/69], Nos. 1, 2). For the history of the Sea People, note finally Wainwright, 'A Teucrian at Salamis' (*JHS*. 83 [1963], 146 ff.) and, more recently, Pritchard's study, 'New Evidence on the Role of the Sea Peoples in Canaan at the Beginning of the Iron Age' (*The Role of the Phoenicians* [1969], 99 ff.). Cyprus played a lively part in determining the fate of the eastern Mediterranean coasts inflicted by these peoples (see the Philistine seal: *1760*, and the bronze figure of a god from Enkomi: *1441*).

Most of our archaeological knowledge of the transitional period and the period of unrest stems from the finds in the cemetery of Kerameikos in Athens, in the large chamber-tomb necropolis of Perati in east Attica *(191)*, and in the cemetery of the island of Salamis. This is where Styrenius embarked on his *Submycenaean Studies* (1967); they have enriched our picture of this transitional phase, defining

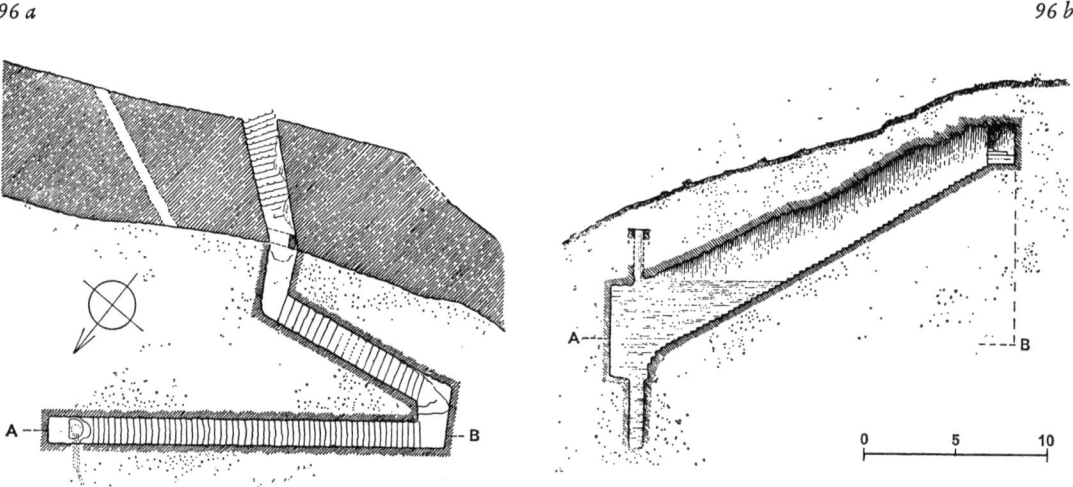

Fig. 7 *94–96 b* Mycenae, plan of the citadel (*94:* 1 Lion Gate, 2 Grave Circle A [cf. *95*], 3 Palace, megaron, 4 North terrace wall, 5 North sally-port, 6 Perseia [cf. *96 a,b*], 7 House of Columns 8 Tower on the descent to the Chaos ravine; Grave Circle A with Shaft Graves I–IV (*95:* 1 Lion Gate, 2 Ramp); Perseia (*96 a:* ground-plan, *96 b:* section)

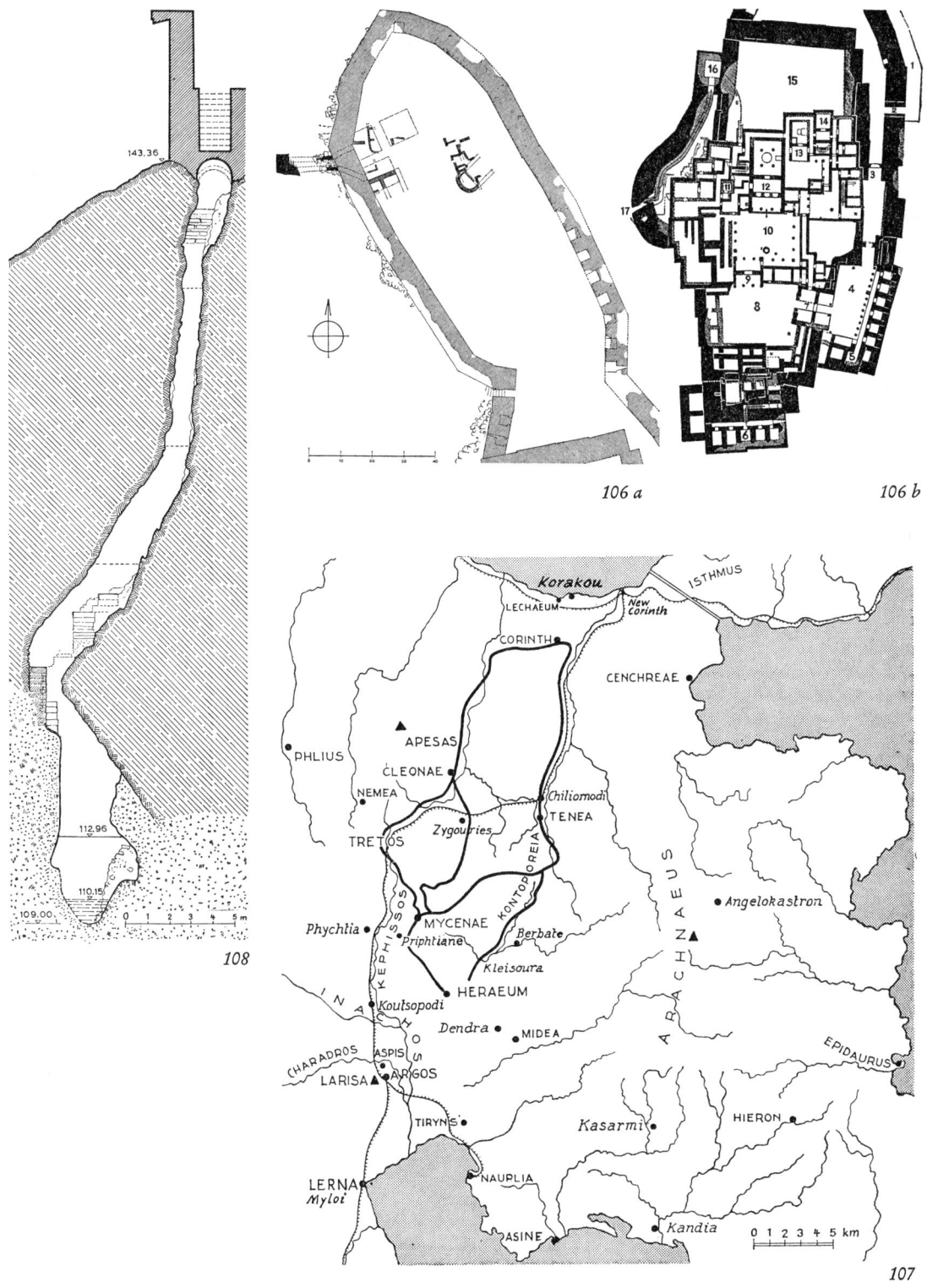

Fig. 8 *106–108:* Tiryns, lower citadel (*106 a*) and upper citadel (*106 b:* 1 Ramp, 2 Outer gate, 3 Inner gate, 4 Forecourt, 5,6 Casemates, 7 Outer propylon, 8 Outer palace court, 11 Bathroom, 12 Megaron with Throne Room, 13,14 Small megara, 15 central citadel, 16 Tower, 17 West Gate); the Argolid, Mycenaean system of routes, citadels and settlements (*107*); Athens, Acropolis, Mycenaean well-shaft (*108*)

it more precisely, and have taken into consideration the area outside Attica (e.g. Leukandi in Euboea: *126—128*; cf. also Warren's summary in *Erasmus* 19, 1967, 493 ff.; Boardman, *Classical Review* 18 [1968], 244 ff.; Bennett, in *Classical World* 61 [1968], 421, and Bouzek, in *Eirene* VII [1968], 150). Desborough has prepared the ground even more thoroughly for a historical understanding of these processes in *The Last Mycenaeans and their Successors* (1964; review by Ålin, *Gnomon* 37 [1965], 723 ff.).

The latest Mycenaean finds (LH III c and sub-Mycenaean, cf. chronological table p. 30), different from earlier ones, come not only from the Greek mainland, and at times from new areas of concentrated settlement, but also from Rhodes (see map Fig. 9, *130*), from the west coast of Anatolia (see map Fig. 9, *129*), Cyprus *(1646 ff.)*, and even Palestine (Beth Shan), as well as the west (Tarentum, cf. Fig. 28, *1012, 1019, 1021, 1022*). In Crete, the Ancient Minoan spirit continued to manifest itself even in the final works of the transitional and degenerate period, for instance in the figures of goddesses with raised arms *(1267—1269)*. During the period of unrest, Cyprus was finally won over to the Greek language and civilization by admitting refugees (cf. p. 135).

Finally, we must also mention that with the end of the Bronze Age there came a marked change in burial customs; instead of interring the corpse *(134, 135, 151, 152, 188, 1463 ff.)*, the body was more often cremated and placed in urns (Perati: *190*), as we know from Homer (Andronikos, 'Totenkult', in Matz-Buchholz, *Arch. Hom.* [1968], and below, p. 39). So the characteristic new elements found at the end of the Bronze Age include: Balkan elements among the finds (e.g. bird's head knife: *665*), new features in armour (laced greaves: *711, 1880, 1881*), destruction in large parts of Greece, LH III c- and sub-Mycenaean pottery *(1025 ff.)*, together with the gradual emergence of iron. In his *Allegories to Homer*, Heraclitus rightly considers, with reference to the *Iliad* (XIII, 340 ff.), that 'in fact at that time iron was still rare' (31; first century A.D.). So one of the questions of modern historians, relating to the decline of Bronze Age civilization and the rise of the early Greek culture, also hinges on the historical significance of the new metal. In his poem *Works and Days*, which discusses the periods named after metals, Hesiod concludes the line of metallic decadence with the 'Iron Age,' thus giving iron a negative symbolic value after the turn of the Heroic period (perversion of power, corruption of the law into a means of piracy; cf. Walcot, *Hesiod and the Near East* [1966]). But the new metal did not come from the North with the Dorians at all, so one cannot hold that the latest of the Greek waves of immigration was the channel through which the Aegean culture became familiar with iron. It was already known in central Anatolia in the third and second millennia B.C. (Alaça Hüyük; Hittite correspondence). It has also been traced in the period between the nineteenth and the fourteenth centuries B.C. in Alalakh, Ras Shamra (Ugarit), Qatna, and Byblos, at the beginning of the second millennium from tombs in Cyprus (as shapeless lumps, Lapithos; cf. Stewart, *SCE.* IV 1 A [1962], 256), and in *c.* 1200 B.C. in Enkomi, Kourion, and Old Paphos (cf. Iakovidis, *Perati* II [1970], 378).

Developments in the Aegean ran parallel to those in the ancient Near East. Even in the early second millennium meteoric iron and magnetite were known as precious magic stones (see list below); from around the mid-millennium forged mineral iron occurs for ornamental purposes (e.g. a Mycenaean iron ring, still fixed to the finger bone: *1357*). We note a striking increase in such finds from the fourteenth and thirteenth centuries. Finally, in the twelfth century, the first iron knives and daggers with bronze rivets appear *(638, 675)*; towards 1000 B.C. came the mass production of fairly large agricultural tools (cf. sickle point from Tiryns, No. 28 in the list below). We know of Late Bronze Age iron production from a trading outpost in the valley of Axios (Iakovidis, *AAA.* 3 [1970], 296).

The following list of Bronze Age iron finds from the Aegean does not include haematite and meteorite seals.

For literature on iron in Mycenaean times, see the bibliography for 'Metallurgy' below (p. 182) and Richardson, 'Iron, Prehistoric and Ancient,' *AJA.* 38 (1934), 555 ff.—Müller-Karpe, 'Die Metallbeigaben der früheisenzeitlichen Kerameikos-Gräber,' *JdI.* 77 (1962), 59 ff.—Forbes, 'Bergbau,' in Matz-Buchholz, *Arch. Hom.* (1967), 29 f.—Bielefeld, 'Schmuck,' vol. cit. (1968), 34 f.—Bouzek, *Homerisches Griechenland* (1969), 43 f., Fig. 10 and p. 115 ff.—R. Pleiner, *Iron Working in Ancient Greece* (1969). —Tholander, Evidence of the Use of Carburized Steel and Quench Hardening in Late Bronze Age Cyprus, *Op. Ath.* 10 (1971), 15 ff.—Desborough, *The Greek Dark Ages* (1972), passim.

THE AEGEAN – BRONZE AGE IRON FINDS

A. BEFORE 1500 B. C.

1. PLATANOS, Messara, south Crete, large tholos tomb. Iron slag, 'earliest evidence of iron produced by man in Crete', EM III. Foltiny, *AJA.* 65 (1961), 290 f.; Marinatos, *Pragmat. Akad. Athens* 24 (1963), No. 4, p. 44.
2. MAVRO SPILIO near Knossos, Crete; chamber tomb. Small corroded cube, probably meteoric iron; MM II (eighteenth century B. C.), Arch. Mus., Herakleion. – *BSA.* 28 (1926/27), 279 and 296; Pendlebury, *Arch. of Crete,* 140; Lorimer, *HM.* (1950), 111, No. 1; Foltiny; Marinatos; Iakovidis, 295.
3. HAGIA TRIADA, palace, south Crete. Unworked piece of meteoric iron with traces of notching and sawing; length 29 cm., weight 20 pounds, LM I, Arch. Mus., Herakleion. – Marinatos, 43 f. and plate 1; Iakovidis, 288, Fig. 1.

B. FIFTEENTH CENTURY B. C.

4. KNOSSOS: Iron nail with gilt head, precise date not known, LM I/II. – *BSA.* 6 (1899/1900), 66; Lorimer, *HM.* 111, No. 4; Iakovidis, 295.
5. KAKOVATOS, west Peloponnese, tholos tomb. Iron ring bezel set in gold. Nat. Mus., Athens. – K. Müller, *AM.* 34 (1909), 275, Plate 13:35; Montelius, *La Grèce préclass.,* p. 197, fig. 687; Lorimer, No. 3; Karo, *RE.* Suppl. VI, 591, cf. also *Myk. Kultur*; Iakovidis, 295.
6. VAPHEIO, Laconia, tholos tomb. Iron ring set in gold. Nat. Mus., Athens. – Tsountas, *Ephem.* 1888, 199 and 1889, 147; Lorimer, No. 2; Bielefeld, 'Schmuck', in Matz–Buchholz, *Arch. Hom.* (1968), 35; Iakovidis, 295. No entry in *CMS.* I!
7. VOLOS, Thessaly, tholos tomb. Small square plaque of sheet-iron, LH II b. Arch. Mus., Volos. – Kourouniotis, *Ephem.* 1906, 236 f.; Iakovidis, 295.

C. FOURTEENTH AND THIRTEENTH CENTURIES B. C.

8. PHAISTOS, south Crete, tomb find. Fragment of finger-ring bezel with bronze core plated with gold and iron; Arch. Mus., Herakleion. – *Mon. Ant.* 14 (1904), 593, No. 5, Fig. 55; Lorimer, No. 5; Foltiny, *AJA.* 65 (1961), 290 f.; Iakovidis, 295.
9. IALYSOS, Rhodes, Tomb LXIX. Several small amorphous fragments of iron. Arch. Mus., Rhodes. – Jacopi, *ASAtene* 13/14 (1930/31), 248; Iakovidis, 295.
10. MELATHRIA, Laconia on the far bank of the Eurotas, opposite Vapheio, near Skoura. Iron finger-ring from chamber tomb. Arch. Mus., Sparta. – Dimakopoulou, *AAA.* 1 (1968), 41; id., *Delt.* 22 (1967), Chron. 198; Megaw, *Arch. Rep.* 1967/68, 10; Iakovidis, 295.
11.–14. MYCENAE, chamber tombs in the lower town. Two simple iron rings and two finger-rings with gold-plated bezels and hoop over iron core. Nat. Mus., Athens, Inv. No. 2856. – Tsountas, *Ephem.* 1888, 135 and 147; Schachermeyr, *AM.* 41 (1916), 411 f.; Evans, *PM.* I, 687, Fig. 505 and IV, 565, Fig. 538; Lorimer, *HM.* 112, No. 10; Coghlan, *Notes on Prehistoric and Early Iron in the Old World,* 64; Biesantz, *Kret.-myk. Siegelbilder* (1954), 2; *CMS.* I, No. 91; Iakovidis, 295.
15. ASINE, the Argolid, Chamber Tomb 1. Fragments of an iron ring. LH II/III. Arch. Mus., Nauplia. – Persson, *Asine,* 373; Lorimer, 112, No. 9; Iakovidis, 295.
16. DENDRA, the Argolid, Chamber Tomb 2. Cylindrical iron ornamental stud, set in gold at both ends, thirteenth century B. C. Nat. Mus., Athens. – Persson, *Dendra* I, 79, and 102 f., No. 14, Plate 33:6; Lorimer, Nos. 7–8; Iakovidis, 289, Fig. 3.
17.–19. DENDRA, tholos tomb. Three finger-rings, with oval ring bezels of layers of silver, lead, copper, and iron hammered on one another; first half of fourteenth century B. C. Nat. Mus., Athens. – Persson, 33 and 56 f., Fig. 35; Lorimer, No. 6; Foltiny, *AJA.* 65 (1961), 290 f.; Bielefeld, 'Schmuck' in Matz–Buchholz, *Arch. Hom.* (1968), 35; Iakovidis, 289, Fig. 2.
20. THEBES, Boeotia, chamber tomb. Corroded iron ring with finger bone, LH III a/b. Arch. Mus., Thebes. – Unpublished: *1357.*
21. GLA, Boeotia, palace. Remains of iron on a lead clamp from a door hinge, LH III. – De Ridder, *BCH.* 18 (1894), 293; Tsountas-Manatt, *Myc. Age,* 381; Lorimer, No. 11; Iakovidis, 295.
22. KNOSSOS GYPSADES, Crete, Chamber Tomb VII. Single-edged iron knife with bronze rivets, LM III b 2. Arch. Mus., Herakleion. – Hood, *BSA.* 53/54 (1958/59), 248, No. VII, 12, Fig. 32 and Plate 60 a; Sandars, *AJA.* 67 (1963), 135; Iakovidis, 295.

D. TWELFTH CENTURY B. C. AND LATER

23. TYLISSOS, north Crete, cremation tomb. Fragments of iron knife with bronze rivets, LH III b/c. Arch. Mus., Herakleion. – Marinatos, *AM.* 56 (1931), 114, Figs. 2 and 3:6; Furumark, *Op. Arch.* III (1944), 227 ff.; Desborough, *Protogeometric Pottery* (1952), 255; Iakovidis, 295.
24. VROKASTRO, east Crete, Chamber Tomb V. Iron knife with bronze rivets, sub-Minoan. Arch. Mus., Herakleion. – Hall, *Excavations in Eastern Crete:* 'Vrokastro' 151, Plate 21 a, Bouzek, *Homerisches Griechenland* (1969), 71; Iakovidis, 295.
25. IALYSOS, Rhodes, chamber tomb. Iron bracelet, 1200 to 1050 B. C. Arch. Mus., Rhodes. – Maiuri, *ASAtene* 6/7 (1923/24), 127; Iakovidis, *AAA.* 3 (1970), 295; id., *Perati* II (1970), 377.
26. NAXOS, Tomb Gamma. Amorphous pieces of iron, 1200

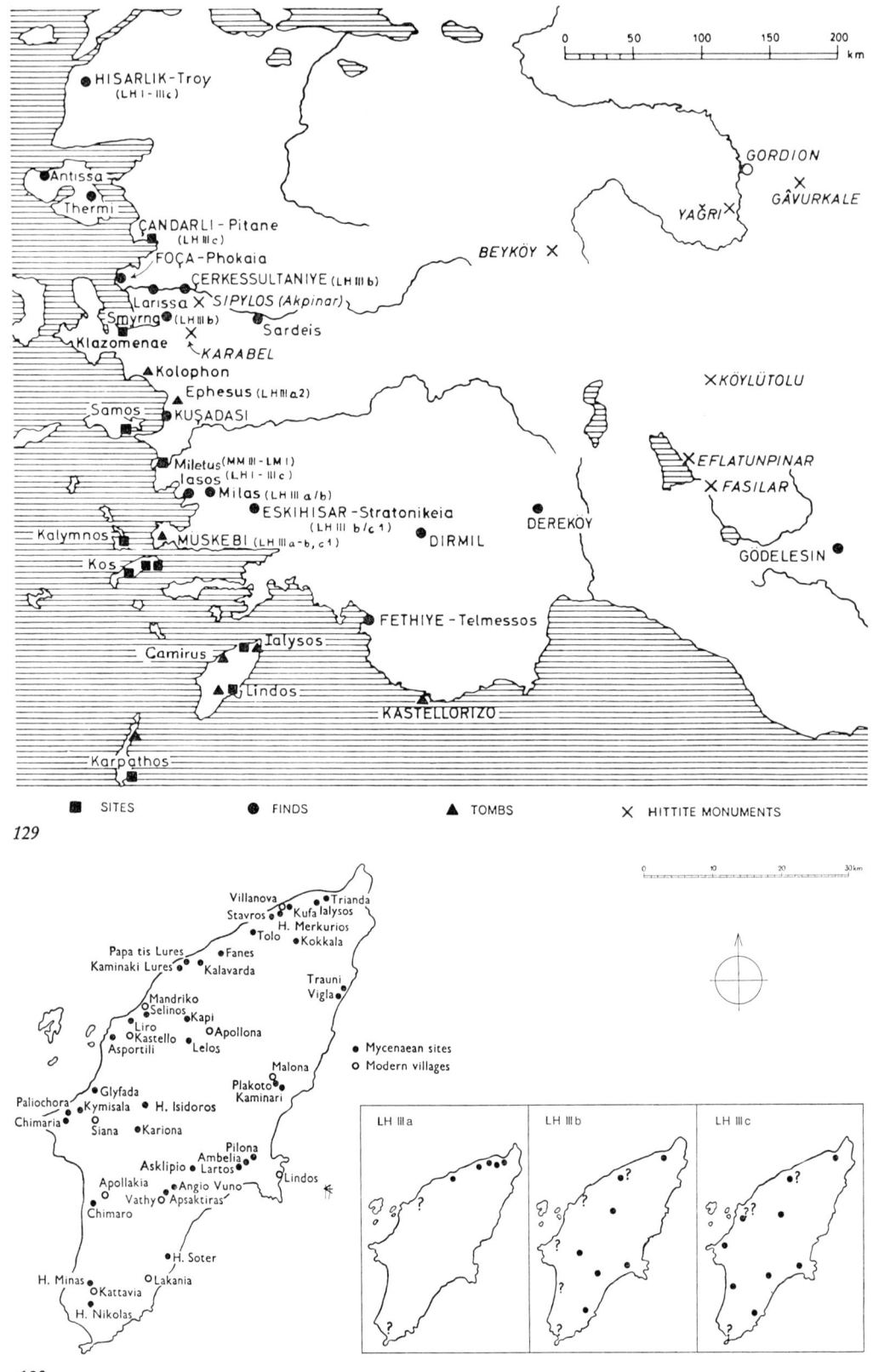

Fig. 9 129 and 130: Mycenaean sites in the eastern Aegean (129) and in Rhodes (130)

to 1050 B. C. – *Ergon* 1969, 144; Iakovidis, *AAA.* 3 (1970), 295.

27. Kamini, Naxos, tomb find. Iron dagger or knife with bronze rivets, LH III c. – Zapheiropoulos, *Prakt.* 1960, 332 and *Delt.* 15 (1960), Chron. 250; Bouzek, 44 and 55; Iakovidis, *AAA.* 3 (1970), 295.
28. Tiryns, hoard find. Point of an iron sickle, LH III c. Nat. Mus., Athens. – Karo, *AM.* 55 (1930), 135 f., Fig. 6; Foltiny, *AJA.* 65 (1961), 291; Iakovidis, 293, Fig. 4.
29. Perati, Attica, Chamber Tomb 28, Find No. M 75. Triangular dagger or knife blade of iron, with bronze rivet, length 10.5 cm., LH III c. Nat. Mus., Athens. – Iakovidis, *Prakt.* 1954, 98, Fig. 20; id., *AAA.* 3 (1970), 295, Fig. 6; id., *Perati* I (1970), 17 f. and II, 341 f., Fig. 147 a, pp. 348, 376, and 463, Plate 3 a; Bouzek, 28, Fig. 6:14 and Fig. 10:2 (map); *675* below.
30. Perati, Chamber Tomb 38, Find No. M 85. Iron knife with bronze rivets, length 14 cm., LH III c. Nat. Mus., Athens. – Schachermeyr, *AA.* 1962, 232; Iakovidis, *Delt.* 19 (1964), Chron. 94, Plate 90 e; id., *AAA.* 3 (1970), 295; id., *Perati* I (1970), 283 f. and II, 341, 344 f., Fig. 149 b, p. 415, Plate 82 c; *638* below.
31. Perati, Chamber Tomb 108, Find. No. D 142. Iron fragment of pin with pale glass head, 1200–1050 B. C. Nat. Mus., Athens. – Iakovidis, *AAA.* 3 (1970), 295; id., *Perati* I (1970), 391 and 394 and II, 288 ff. and 402.
32. Perati, Chamber Tomb S 2. Amorphous pieces of iron, 1200–1050 B. C. Nat. Mus., Athens. – Iakovidis, *AAA.* 3 (1970), 295; id., *Perati* II (1970), 463.
33. Leukandi, Euboea, Settlement Layer II. Iron knife, LH III c. – Popham–Sackett, *Excav. at Lefkandi* (1968), 14, Fig. 22; Iakovidis, *AAA.* 3 (1970), 295.

We have mentioned a few salient points—of which the appearance of iron is only one—in order to make it clear that there was a turning-point in the twelfth century B.C. 'which has no parallel until the turning-point between Antiquity and the Middle Ages' (Matz, *Geschichte der griechischen Kunst* I [1950] 37).

Ancient Aegean Chronology

Research on the earlier periods is summarized in Milojcic, *Chronologie der jüngeren Steinzeit Mittel- und Südosteuropas* (1949), Schachermeyr, (*AA.* 1962, 179 ff.: classification of the Thessalian Stone Age) and Weinberg, in Ehrich, *Chronologies in Old World Archaeology* (1965), 285—320, which also includes a list of published radio-carbon dates (310 ff.).

The dates are not yet definitive, so we must continue to regard them as estimates at present (Palaeolithic, 'Epipalaeolithic,' Neolithic). With the beginning of metallurgy (Early Bronze Age), the dating becomes a little more trustworthy, since the finds show increasing connections with the more highly developed art and material culture of the kingdoms of Egypt and the Near East, who possessed written records. In our chronological table, the dating of the Egyptian dynasties follows the figures given in the second edition of the *Cambridge Ancient History* (cf. also Matz, *Kreta und frühes Griechenland* [1962], 242 f.).

The classification into Early, Middle, and Late Minoan, or Early, Middle, and Late Helladic, with further subdivisions, is based on observations in the development of pottery (EM, MM, LM; EH, MH, LH). The two works by Furumark, *The Chronology of Mycenaean Pottery* (1941) and *The Mycenaean Pottery—Analysis and Classification* (1941) are fundamental for the classification of the LH phases although some points have been revised by others.

Since the development of some groups of monuments—above all architecture—does not coincide exactly with the chronology of pottery, we have also introduced the terms 'pre-palatial Period,' 'Earlier Palace Period,' 'Later Palace Period,' and 'post-palatial Period' into the terminology of ancient Cretan chronology.

The concepts 'sub-Minoan and sub-Mycenaean' again derive from the pottery; cf. Desborough, *The Last Mycenaeans and their Successors* (1964), and 'History and Archaeology in the Last Century of Mycenaean Age' (in *Atti e Memorie del I. Congresso Internaz. di Micenologia*, Rome 1967).

The following table is based on stratigraphic evidence and commences at the fort. To round off the picture of the chronological relationship, see also the chronological table for the Cypriot Stone and Bronze Age (p. 138).

B.C.	Egypt	Troy	Crete	Cyclades	Greek Mainland	B.C.
1000			Proto-geometric period and sub-Minoan period	Protogeometric Period and sub-Mycenaean Period		1000
1100	20th Dynasty (1200–1085)	Late Bronze Age town VII a, b				1100
1200	19th Dynasty (1320–1200)		LM III a–c (post-palatial period)	LH III a–c	LH III c	1200
1300		Late Bronze Age town VI c			LH III b	1300
1400	18th Dynasty (1567–1320)				LH III a	1400
1500		Middle Bronze Age town VI b	LM II Palace style (Age of later Palaces) / LM I a, b	Hagia Irini, Keos	LH II (Middle Mycenaean)	1500
1600	2nd transitional period: Hyksos (1786–1567)		MM III a, b	Middle Cycladic Period		1600
1700		Middle Bronze Age town VI a	MM II Kamares style (Age of Earlier Palaces)		LH I a and b (Early Mycenaean/Shaft Grave period)	1700
1800	11th and 12th Dynasty (Middle Kingdom 2133–1786)					1800
1900		Early Bronze Age town III–V	MM I b		EH III	1900
2000			(MM I a)	Early Bronze Age: Syros group		2000
2100	1st transitional period		EM II and III		EH II	2100
2200		Early Bronze Age town II	(Pre-palatial Period)			2200
2300	4th–6th Dynasty (2613–2181)				EH I	2300
2400			EM I	Early Bronze Age: Pelos group		2400
2500		Early Bronze Age town I				2500
2600					Neolithic period: Arapi and Dimini phases	2600
	1st–3rd Dynasty (3100–2613) and predynastic period (pre-3100)	sub-Neolithic and Neolithic period	Late Neolithic period Middle Stone Age, and Early Stone Age	Neolithic period: Saliagos and Kephala/Keos ↓ ?	Neolithic period: Sesklo stages I–III	
					Pre-ceramic and Early Ceramic Neolithic period; proto-Sesklo: Thessaly	
6th Mill.			↓ ?		Mesolithic not yet certain. Microlithic finds in Thessaly	6th Mill.
c. 10 000					'Epipalaeolithic' and late Palaeolithic: Epiros, Zakynthos, Boeotia	c. 10 000
c. 50 000					Early Palaeolithic: Epiros, Macedonia, Thessaly, Elis	c. 50 000

CATALOGUE

Excavated sites—architecture

For the history of archaeological discoveries, see Schachermeyr, *Die ältesten Kulturen Griechenlands* (1955), 21 ff., Matz, *Kreta und frühes Griechenland* (1962), 11 ff. and the works listed in our bibliography (p. 176 ff., maps pp. 12 and 13, Figs. 1, 2). For details on the development of architecture from the Neolithic period to the Late Bronze Age, see the remarks in the Introduction. See also the model house *1122 a, b*. Noack, *Ovalhaus und Palast in Kreta — ein Beitrag zur Frühgeschichte des Hauses* (1908), can be supplemented by the reports of more recent excavations. In 1903 the same author compared the descriptions in early Greek epics with the remains of Bronze Age architecture in *Homerische Paläste — eine Studie zu den Denkmälern und zum Epos* (cf. also Dörpfeld, *AM* 30 [1905], 257 ff., and Wace, *JHS* 71 [1951], 203 ff.), while Drerup compares them with the architecture of the Geometric Period in *Archaeologia Homerica* (1969).

There are general studies of pre-Greek architecture, from its beginnings until the end of the Mycenaean Age, in Robinson, *RE*. Suppl. VII (1940), 224 ff. s. v. *Haus — Prähistorische und griechische Häuser*, and in Lawrence, *Greek Architecture* (1957), 1—82. For comparison it is worth referring to Naumann, *Architektur Kleinasiens von ihren Anfängen bis zum Ende der hethitischen Zeit* (1955, second edition 1971). There is a detailed study of the monumental architecture of ancient Crete in Graham, *The Palaces of Crete* (1962). The latest study is: Sinos, *Die vorklassischen Hausformen in der Ägäis (1971)*.

Urban building in the Minoan culture is discussed in Hutchinson, 'Prehistoric Town Planning in Crete,' (*Town Planning Review* 21 [1950], 199 ff.) and, in a broader context, by Kriesis,' Ancient Greek Town Building' (*Acta Congressus Madvigiani* IV, Copenhagen 1954 [1958], 27 ff.). Finally, a recent addition is Weissengruber, 'Eine Entwicklungsstufe im griechischen Städtebau' (*ÖJh.* 48 [1966/67], 76 ff.). Heinrich has noticed far-reaching similarities in 'Inselarchitektur des Mittelmeergebiets,' *AA*. (1958), 89 ff.

For the question of the roofing of Early and Middle Helladic houses, see Caskey, *Hesperia* 23 (1954), Pl. 5 c and e, also Lawrence, 5, Fig. 2; for Mycenaean building see the clay roof tiles from Berbati *(451—453)*. Stone Horns of Consecration *(449, 450)* are important both as documents of religious history and as a form of decoration in Aegean religious architecture (cf. *144, 1303*). Moreover, there were formal and technical interrelations between domestic and religious architecture on the one hand, and tomb architecture on the other; for examples of this latter, see *131—191*; for the development of Cypriot architecture from its beginnings to the end of the Bronze Age, see *1425—1462*.

1–40: CAVE DWELLINGS AND SACRED CAVES – THESSALIAN MAGOULAS – EARLY AND MIDDLE BRONZE AGE DOMESTIC AND DEFENSIVE ARCHITECTURE – URBAN BUILDINGS OF HAGIA IRINI, KEOS

1 Kokkinospilia, near Hagios Elias, Aetolia. Cave inhabited at least from the Neolithic period. Huge deposits in front of cave entrance. Surface finds: Neolithic and EH sherds, stone hand-axes, flint and obsidian blades. – Mastrokostas, *Prakt.* 1963, Pls. 185 b, 186 b, c.

2 Cave of Psychro, Lasithi Mountains, Crete. Inhabited in Neolithic period, later a place of worship. This change of function is frequent in the Aegean; the Cave of Pan, near Marathon, was similarly used. – Nilsson, *MMR.*[2], 61 ff.; Faure, *Fonctions des Cavernes Crétoises* (1964), 151 ff., Pl. 2; Zervos, *Crète*, Pls. 53, 54. Boardman, *The Cretan Collection in Oxford* (1961): detailed study of the finds (cf. *723–34*) from the Bronze Age and the Early Iron Age.

3 Cave of Eileithyia, near Amnisos, 6 km. east of Herakleion. Inhabited in Neolithic period, later a place of worship. – Faure, *op. cit.*, 55 f., Pl. 7; Nilsson, *MMR.*[2], 58; Marinatos–Hirmer, 66, Figs. 1, 2, Pl. 1; Jameson, *Archaeology* 13 (1960), 36, Fig. 4; *Od.* XIX 188.

4 Dimini, Thessaly. Overall view of the late Neolithic hill settlement (cf. *7*).

5 Tzalma Magoula, Thessaly. Neolithic hill settlement, not yet fully studied by archaeologists. – Zervos, *Naissance* I, Pl. IX lower.

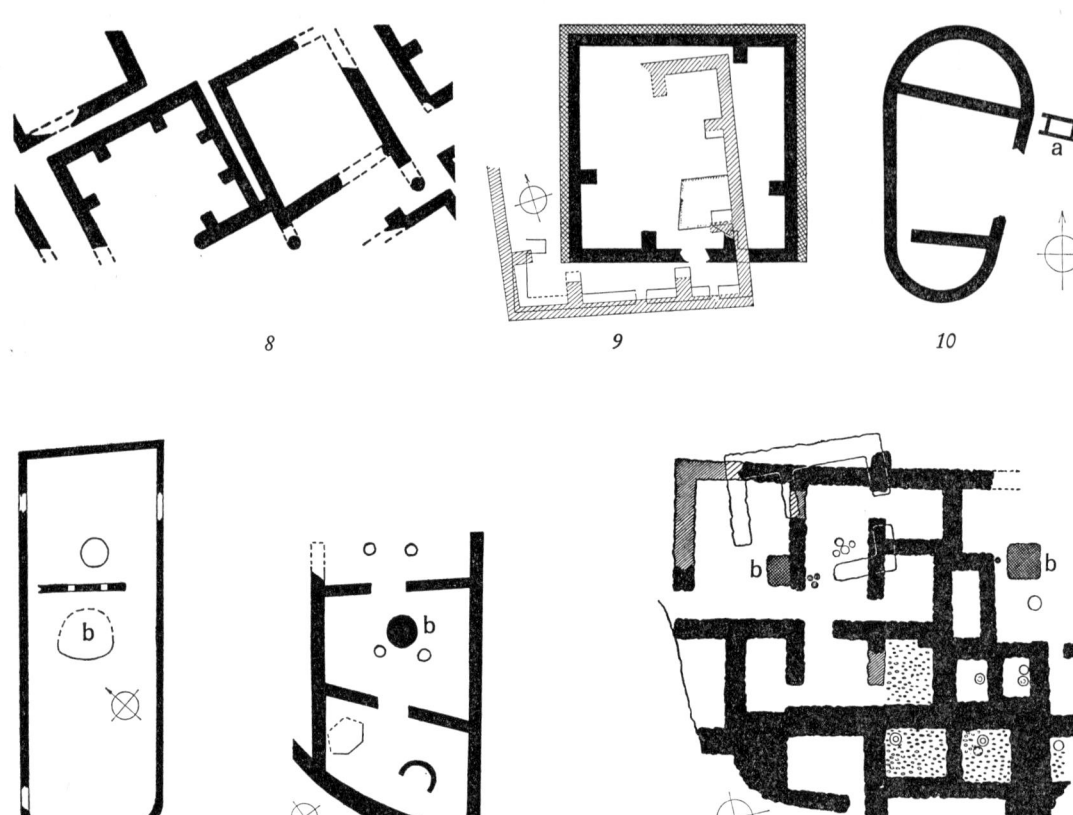

Fig. 10 8–13 Neolithic buildings (a: grave, b: hearth)

6 p. 14, Fig. 3: Sesklo, Thessaly. Plan of early Neolithic settlement (cf. building, 14). – Tsountas, DS., Pl. 3; Zervos, Naissance I, 76 f.; Müller-Karpe, Hdb. d. Vorgesch. II (1968), Pl. 132 a.

7 p. 14, Fig. 3: Dimini. Plan of Late Neolithic settlement (cf. 4, individual buildings: 12, 15, 16). – Tsountas, DS., Pl. 1; Zervos, Naissance I, 84 f.; Müller-Karpe, Pl. 132 b.

8 Fig. 10: Otzaki Magula, Thessaly. Middle Neolithic group of buildings, consisting of square houses. – Milojcic, Neue deutsche Ausgrabungen, 225 ff.; Schachermeyr, AA. (1962), 180 ff., Fig. 21; Zervos, Naissance I, 87 upper; Müller-Karpe, Pl. 127:33.

9 Fig. 10. Tsangli, central Thessaly. Order of early Neolithic square houses P, Q and R. – Wace–Thompson, Prehist. Thess. 116 f., Figs. 65, 66; Lawrence, Greek Architecture (1957), 14, Fig. 9; Zervos, Naissance I, 89 upper; Müller-Karpe, Pl. 130:43.

10 Fig. 10: Rhini, central Thessaly. Late Neolithic oval house. – Wace–Thompson, Prehist. Thess., 132 f., Figs. 80, 81; Zervos, Naissance I, 89 lower.

11 Fig. 10: Rhachmani, northern Thessaly. Late Neolithic apsidial house P with large hearth; only the stone base survives; probably originally surmounted by sun-dried brick walls. – Wace–Thompson, Prehist. Thess., 38, Fig. 17; Zervos, Naissance, I, 87 lower.

12 Fig. 10: Dimini. Late Neolithic megaron, backing on to a curved wall (cf. 7, 15). – Tsountas, DS., 50, Fig. 9; Lawrence, op. cit., 15, Fig. 10; Zervos, Naissance I, 89 lower.

13 Fig. 10: Knossos, Crete. Late Neolithic, small-roomed houses (cf. Knossos, other Neolithic rooms, 17). – Evans, PM. II, 19, Fig. 8 a; Pendlebury, Arch. of Crete, 40, Fig. 3; Schachermeyr, Die ältesten Kulturen, 83, Fig. 13; Müller-Karpe, Hdb. d. Vorgesch. II (1968), Pl. 139:19.

14 Sesklo. Early Neolithic megaron (cf. plan p. 14, Fig. 3, 6). Tsountas, DS., 89, Fig. 18; Zervos, Naissance I, Pl. XI.

15 Dimini. Late Neolithic megaron and other building
16 (cf. plan p. 14, Figs. 3, 7; 10, 12).

17 Knossos. Neolithic House C from the west (stratum III, excavated 1960). – Evans, BSA., 59 (1964), Pl. 32:2.

18 Lerna, the Argolid. Early Helladic wall of sun-dried
19 bricks on herringbone masonry foundations (cf. plan p. 14, Fig. 4, 25). – Hesperia 27 (1958), Pl. 33 b; see also references to 25, 26.

20 Troy I. Early Bronze Age herringbone masonry. Schliemann's large section, Square D 4–5 in the American excavations. – Dörpfeld, Troja und Ilion I (1902), 47, Fig. 9; Blegen, Troy I, 2 (1950), Pl.-Fig. 56.

21 Fig. 11: Thermi I (E 2), Lesbos. Early Bronze Age herringbone masonry. – Lamb, Excavations at Thermi in Lesbos (1936), Pl. 2:6; Naumann, Architektur 59, Fig. 35.

22 Poliochni, Lemnos. South corner of Early Bronze Age fortification wall, with window aperture and gate subsequently walled-in (megara, Poliochni: 28). – Bernabò-Brea, *Poliochni* I, 1 (1964), 123, Fig. 68; Riemann, *AA*. (1937), 161 f., Fig. 18.

23 Troy, South-west ramp and fortification wall of Troy II. – cf. Matz, *Kreta–Mykene–Troja*, Pl. 9 lower; Mellaart, 'Notes on the Architectural Remains of Troy I and II' in *Anat. Stud.* 9 (1959), 131 ff.

24 p. 16, Fig. 4; Thermi I, section. Early Bronze Age arrangement of buildings (for Thermi, cf. also 21 and 29). – Lamb, Plan 1; Naumann, *Architektur*, 312, Fig. 389.

Fig. 11 21 Thermi, Lesbos

25 p. 16, Fig. 4: Lerna. Overall plan and sequence of
26 buildings of Early Helladic houses with apse. – Caskey, *Charist. eis A. K. Orlandon* III (1966), 150, Fig. 5; Schachermeyr, *AA*. (1962), 193 f., Fig. 24; Caskey, *Hesperia* 23 (1954), 13, Fig. 2; 24 (1955), 30, Fig. 2; 26 (1957), 149, Fig. 4 (apsidial house, MH). Further descriptions in: *Hesperia* 27 (1958), 126 ff.; 28 (1959), 202 ff., Fig. 1 (overall plan); 29 (1960), 285 ff.

27 p. 17, Fig. 4: Orchomenos, Boeotia. Round buildings (EH). – Bulle, *Orchomenos* I (1907), 36 ff., Pls. 4–6; Schachermeyr, *Die ältesten Kulturen*, 188, Fig. 58.

28 p. 17, Fig. 4: Poliochni (cf. 22). Early Bronze Age megara (I–IV in plan). – Doro Levi, *Bd'A*. 37 (1952), 345, Fig. 42; Schachermeyr, *AA*. (1962), 205 f., Fig. 26 (overall plan).

29 p. 18, Fig. 5: Thermi (cf. 21, 24). Early Bronze Age town gate, Phase V. – Lamb, *Excavations at Thermi in Lesbos*, Plan 5; Naumann, 251, Fig. 296.

30 p. 18, Fig. 5: Vasiliki, east Crete. Small palace (EM II). – Pendlebury, *Arch. of Crete*, 62, Fig. 5; Lawrence, *Greek Architecture*, 19, Fig. 15; Gruben, *Die Tempel der Griechen* (1966), 14, Fig. 2; Sinos, *AA*. (1970), 1 ff.

31 p. 18, Fig. 5: Aigina, hill of Kolonna. Early Helladic town fortification. – Harland, *Prehistoric Aigina* (1925); Wolters, *Gnomon* 1 (1925), 46 ff.; id., *AA*. (1925), 1 ff.; Welter, *AA*. (1925), 318 ff.; Buschor, *Gnomon* 2 (1926), 120 ff.; Welter, *Gnomon* 5 (1929), 185 ff. and 269; id., *Aigina* (1938), 11, Fig. 9; Schachermeyr, *Die ältesten Kulturen*, 186, Fig. 57.

32 Olympia, Elis. House 3, ending in apse; part of a
a, b village settlement in the Altis region (MH; cf. corresponding EH ground plans: 26). – Dörpfeld, *Alt-Olympia* I (1935), 82, Fig. 7, II, Suppl. 3 a, Pl. 17 (plan); Herrmann, 'Zur ältesten Geschichte von Olympia' in *AM*. 77 (1962), 3 ff., 16, Fig. 2 (plan).

33 Peristeria, near Kyparissia, west Peloponnese. House of rubble masonry, with dry stone walling (MH, excavated by Marinatos; state in 1967).

34 Heraion, Samos. Prehistoric buildings and walls. In
a, b the background, foundations of the Temple of Hera (34 a). – cf. Milojcic, *Die prähistorische Siedlung unter dem Heraion, Samos* I (1961); Buschor, *Neue deutsche Ausgrabungen*, 197 ff.

35 Troy VI. Middle/Late Bronze Age east wall of regu-
a, b larly laid ashlar, view from the south-east. Wall sections separated by careful vertical profiles ('saw cut', detail: 35 b). – Blegen, *Troy III*, 2 (1953), Pl.-Fig. 12; Akurgal, *Die Kunst Anatoliens* (1961), Col. Pl. 1 a; Alkim, *Anatolien* I (1968), Fig. 77.

36 Troy VI. Wall corner at South Gate VI S; statically stable and earthquake-proof ashlar bond – Blegen, op. cit., Pl.-Fig. 34.

37 Hagia Irini, Keos (excavated by Caskey). 37: Town
to wall of the sixteenth century B. C. (*Late Bronze Age* I),
40 fortification sections running from beach to beach. 38: Town gate from the inside, with huge threshold and stone ledge on the edge of the road. 39: Detail of the town wall and corner of a covered well in front of it. 40: Cellar steps in palace-like House A. – For preliminary plans of the courses of the city wall, of House A and of the subterranean well, cf. Caskey, *Epeteris Hetaireias Kykl. Meleton* 5 (1965), 708 ff., Figs. 2–7; further preliminary accounts by Caskey, *Hesperia* 31 (1962), 263 ff.; *Archaeology* 16 (1963), 284 ff.; *Hesperia* 33 (1964), 314 ff.; 35 (1966), 361 ff.; *Delt*. 17 (1961/62), Chron. 275 ff.; 19 (1964), Chron. 413 ff. and Plan. 1; 20 (1965), Chron. 527 ff., Pls. 661–666; Megaw, *JHS*. 16 (1964), Arch. Rep. 17; Daux, *BCH*. 88 (1964), 822 ff., Ervin, *AJA*. 72 (1968), 275, Pl. 95:45: Vermeule, *Greece in the Bronze Age* (1964), Pl. 15 b (overall view).

41–75:   CRETAN PALACES, CITIES AND PRIVATE HOUSES

41 p. 21, Fig. 6: Knossos. Minoan palace, spiritual and
42 political centre of the island (MM III–LM II); English excavations. 41: Diagrammatic reconstruction of the east front of the west wing facing the Central Court; on the far right, part of the Throne Room (cf. 48); adjacent to this are the steps to the main floor, leading to the Shrine and verandas. – Matz, *Kreta–Mykene–Troja*, Pl. 28; Gruben, *Die Tempel der Griechen* (1966), 16, Fig. 5. 42: Plan of the palace on the Central Court level. – cf. Evans, *PM*. I–IV; Pendlebury, *Arch. of Crete*, 128, Fig. 20; Matz, Pl. 24; Gruben, 15, Fig. 3.

43 Knossos. Palace, extensively reconstructed (MM III–
to LM II). 43: North entrance, Hall of Columns on the
52 left; on the right, colonnades with reliefs of bulls. 44: East wing, ante-room leading to the Hall of the Double Axes (cf. Marinatos–Hirmer, Pl. 39). 45: Balustrade with reconstructed shield-fresco (cf. Evans, *PM*. III, 303, Fig. 196). 46, 47: East wing, grand

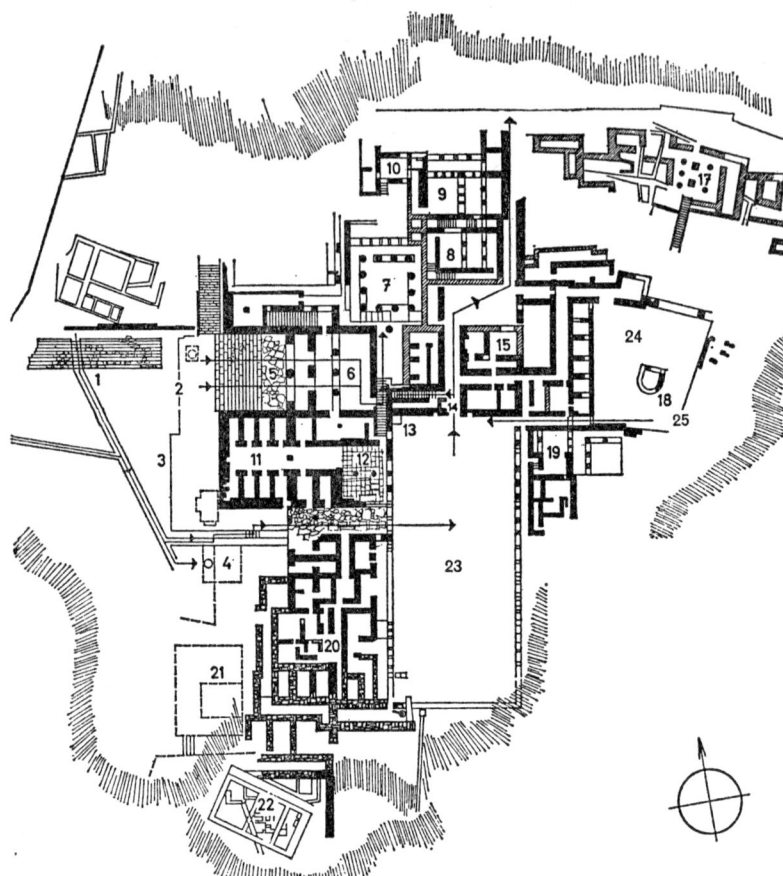

Fig. 12 53 Phaistos

1 Grand Staircase
2 Old Palace
3 West Court
4 Entrance to Old Palace
5 Propylon of New Palace
6 Court
7 Court of Peristyles
8 Double room
9 Double hall
10 Cleansing basin
11 Magazine
12 Hall
13 Altar
14 Central corridor
15 Womens' apartments
16 Outhouses
17 Domestic buildings
18 Furnace
19 Living wing
20 Servants' wing
21 New excavations
22 Greek temple
23 Main court
24 East court
25 East entrance

staircase with Hall of Columns. *48:* Throne Room in the west wing (cf. *41*): on either side of the throne griffin frescoes and stone wall benches (Reusch, 'Zum Wandschmuck des Thronsaales in Knossos' in *Minoica, Festschr. zum 80. Geburtstag von Sundwall* [1958], 334 ff.). *49:* Street of the Procession and steps to the north corner of the palace. *50:* Bath for washing the feet in the 'Caravanserai' south of the palace (Pendlebury, *Handbook of the Palace of Minos* [1933/ 1954], Pl. 14, 1). *51:* Part of the West Magazine with pithoi *in situ* (cf. Pendlebury, op. cit., Pl. 2:2; Marinatos–Hirmer, Pl. 41). *52:* Foundations of the viaduct south of the palace on the Vlychia Ravine (plan: Pendlebury, op. cit., 58, Fig. 4). – A wealth of pictorial material from Knossos is to be found in Marinatos–Hirmer, Pls. 26–45.

53 Fig. 12: Phaistos, south Crete; Italian excavations. Plan of the Minoan palace (MM–LM), and of remains of the earlier palace, especially on the west edge and in the north east. – Pernier-Banti, *Il Palazzo Minoico di Festòs* II (1951): Marinatos–Hirmer, 83, Fig. 12, Pls. 48–51. – D. Levi, 'The Recent Excavations at Phaistos' in *Studies in Mediterranean Archaeology* XI (1964).

54 Phaistos. *54, 55, 57:* West court, great stairway and
to open steps to the main portal; Foundations of the west
59 wall of the earlier palace (MM). – cf. Levi, *Bd'A.* 37 (1952), 323, Fig. 6 (plan); Matz, *Kreta–Mykene–Troja*, Pl. 42 upper. *56:* West court and west area of the earlier palace, behind it, the central court (white area). *58 a, b, 59:* Northern part of the Central Court, south front of the northern tract, with an entrance flanked by two half-columns; stepped altar in the north-west corner of the court (cf. Matz, Pl. 41 upper).

60 Hagia Triada, south Crete. Small palace (LH I/II);
a, b Italian excavations. Propylaeum (Room 4, counting from west to east) with stone benches, wall incrustation and pillar bases in the front – Marinatos–Hirmer, 86, Fig. 13, Pls. 52–55 and Col. Pl. 19.

61 Also Figs. 13 and 14: Mallia, north Crete; French
to excavations. Palace and area of the Minoan town
70 *61 a, b:* Circular stone libation table with central hollow and little 'bowls' around the rim, diam. 90 cm., Room XVI 1, south-west corner of the Central Court. Its identification as a gaming table is unlikely; note the votive use of a similar stone in the tombs of Chrysolakkos. – *BCH.* 50 (1926), 575 f., Fig. 15; Chapouthier, *BCH.* 52 (1928), 292 ff.; Chapouthier–Joly, *Et. Crét.* IV (1936), frontispiece (diagrammatic reconstruction); Evans, *PM.* III, 392 ff.; Yavis, *Greek Altars* (1949), 14 f., Fig. 7: Nilsson, $MMR.^2$, 129 f., Fig. 39 and p. 450 ff.; Pernier-Banti, *Festòs* II, 206, Fig. 128; Zervos, *Crète*, Pl.-Fig. 17: Marinatos–Hirmer, Pl. 56 lower; Graham, *The Palaces of Crete*, Fig. 61; Demargne, *Naissance de l'art grec* (1964), 92, Fig. 119; Schachermeyr, *Die minoische Kultur des alten Kreta* (1964), 161, 336, Note 67, and Pl. 33. *62, 64:* Paved north entrance with pithoi (MM, cf. *905*). *63:* Silos in

the south west tract of the palace (round 'silos' also in Knossos: Evans, *PM.* IV, 62, Fig. 36). *65:* Façade on the west side of the Central Court with large open stairway. *66:* Stairway XXII 3 from the west; at front right is a balustrade post with groove for inserting slabs, as in the later palace at Phaistos (Pernier–Banti, *Festòs* II, 148 f., Figs. 88, 89; Mallia: Graham, *The Palaces of Crete* [1962], Fig. 60). *67–70:* (Figs. 13, 14): Plan of the surroundings of the palace, ground-plans of Houses Zeta b and Delta a, plan of the palace. – Tiré-van Effenterre, *Guide des fouilles françaises en Crète* (1966); cf. Marinatos–Hirmer, 88, Fig. 14; Demargne–Gallet de Santerre, *Et.Crét.* IX (1953), Pl. 1 (overall plan), Pls. 17–20 and 63–67 (House Delta a); Graham, *The Palaces of Crete* (1962), Figs. 21, 22 (House Delta a); 27 (House Zeta b) *BCH.* 90 (1966), 552 ff. (domestic architecture).

71 Vathypetro, central Crete; on the road from Archanes to Ligourtino, Messara. Minoan private house (LM I). Other Minoan private houses, not illustrated here: Achladia, Amnisos, Nirou-Chani, Sklavokampos, Tylissos.

– Marinatos–Hirmer, Pls. 60–62 and Col. Pl. 21 (Vathypetro). Pls. 63–65 (Amnisos, Tylissos, Nirou-Chani).

72 Gournia, on the Gulf of Mirabello; American excavation. Minoan town (LM I), with houses, and paved
74 paths occasionally stepped, *(72, 74),* and small palace *(73,* hill town from the south). – Hawes, *Gournia* (1908); cf. Matz, *Kreta–Mykene–Troja,* Pl. 44; id. *Kreta u. frühes Griechenland,* 104 ff. (with plan); Marinatos–Hirmer, Pls. 66, 67. Col. Pl. 23.

75 Fig. 14: Kato Zakro, east Crete. Plan of the important Minoan palace (LM I/II, excavations in progress under the direction of Platon). Finds: *722, 739–744, 1154, 1156.* – Preliminary reports and plans: Platon, *Prakt.* 1963 (1966), 160 ff., Fig. 3; 1964 (1966). Pl. 1 to p. 160 f.; 1965 (1967), Pl. 1 to p. 216 f.; 1966 (1968), Pl. 1 to p. 144 f.; *Ergon* 1964, Pl. 1 to p. 164 f.; 1965, Pl. 1 to p. 136 f.; 1966, 120, Fig. 142; Daux, *BCH.* 90 (1966), 920, Fig. 1; Platon in: von Matt, *Das antike Kreta* (1967), 163 ff.; *Ergon,* 1968, 118 ff., Fig. 138 (plan of palace, as excavated in 1968).

76–130: MYCENAEAN FORTRESSES, SETTLEMENTS, BRIDGES AND STREETS

76 Gla, Boeotia (cf. plan: p. 38, Figs. 15, *120*) and Myce-
77 nae, the Argolid (cf. plan: p. 24, Fig. 7, *94*); aerial photographs of Mycenaean fortresses. In both cases the natural defences of the area are visible. Gla was originally an island in the former Lake Copais, now drained; the remains of the surrounding Cyclopean walls are visible as a distinct line (cf. *111–119*). Mycenae: Lion Gate and Grave Circle A at the lower edge of the picture (cf. *83, 84, 154–157*). Palace complex in the centre in lighter tone (cf. *87*). – *Ephem.* 1962, Pl. 1: Mylonas, *Myc. and the Myc. Age,* Pl.-Figs. 8, 48; Vermeule, *Greece,* Pl. 24 a.

78 Also p. 24, Fig. 7 and Col. Pl. 2 after p. 40: Mycenae.
to 78, 79: Overall view of the citadel from the south-
96 west and from the surmounting eastern slope of Hagios Elias (cf. Lord William Taylour, *The Mycenaeans,* Pl. 35). *80:* Gateway in the northern extension of the Cyclopean wall from the outside, before its restoration (for its present state: Mylonas, *Myc. and the Myc. Age,* Pl.-Fig. 17 and in *Charisterion Orlandos* I [1965] 213 ff.). *81, 82:* Sally port of the eastern extension with pointed arch. – cf. Wace, *Mycenae* (1949), Fig. 109 b; interior and exterior (details: *91 a, b;* and *155* foreground). *83, 84:* Lion Gate; Mylonas, Pl.-Fig. 39. *85, 88:* Cyclopean fortification wall, north-west and south-west reach. *86:* Perseia, descent to the subterranean spring, near the north-east corner of the citadel (cf. *93, 96 a, b:* Mylonas, 19, 20). *87:* Megaron, palace region of the citadel. *89:* Ramp to the palace near Grave Circle A. *90:* House of the Warrior Vase directly south of Grave Circle A (cf. Wace, op. cit., Fig. 81 a, b; Warrior Vase: *1025*). *91 a–c:* Structural details of the Lion Gate *(83, 84),* threshold with marks of chariot wheels (cf. Daux, *BCH.* 83 [1959], 609, Fig. 12; Mylonas, Pl.-Figs. 15, 25). *92:* Corridor with steps adjacent to the Cyclopean north wall (excavated in 1962: Mylonas, op. cit., Pl.-Fig. 37). *93, 96 a, b* (Fig. 7 cf. *86*); Perseia, subterranean stepped tunnel, section and ground plan (Karo, *AJA.* 38 [1934], 123 ff., Pls. 12, 13; Wace, op. cit., Fig. 35). *94:* (Fig. 7): Overall plan of the citadel (cf. Wace, op. cit., Fig. 19; Mylonas, op. cit., 31, Fig. 7: Megaw, *JHS.* (87 [1967], Arch. Rep. 8, Fig. 11). *95* (Fig. 7): Plan of Grave Circle A (LM I, cf. *154–157; BSA.* 25 [1921/23], Pl. 1; Mylonas, 74, Fig. 19).

97 Kasarmi, between Nauplia and Epidauros. Bed of a stream with Mycenaean culvert, crossed by an LH III road; built with the technique of the 'false arch', similar to the tunnel *(93),* gates *(98)* and casemates *(99).* – Tsountas–Manatt, *Myc. Age,* 37, Fig. 9; Lord, *AJA.* 43 (1939), 81, Pl. 4 c; Wace, *Mycenae,* 27; McDonald, in Bennett, *Mycenaean Studies* (1964), Fig. 10 after p. 222.

98 Also p. 25, Fig. 8: Tiryns, the Argolid; Mycenaean
to fortress, German excavations. *98:* Gate of the stairway
106 added to the upper fortress in the west, seen from the outside (cf. *101* and plan: Fig. 8, *106 b*). *99:* Pointed-arched vault of the defensive passage in the south-west part of the fortress wall. *100, 102:* Intermediate gates in the eastern ascent to the upper fortress. *101:* Stairway of the west front (cf. *98* and Sulze's model in *Tiryns* III, 49, Fig. 33). *103 a, b:* Interior of the eastern wall of the lower fortress, with chamber interior (cf. Grossmann, *AA.* 1967, 99, Fig. 4). *104:* Cyclopean wall, south-east corner from the outside, resting on a ridged base of rock. *105:* Remains of the megaron; foreground: palace court, two flat steps to the vestibule and column bases. *106 a, b:* Plans of the lower and upper fortress (p. 25, Fig. 8 shows the newly discovered tunnels in the north-west of the lower fortress). – Frickenhaus–Rodenwaldt–Müller, *Tiryns* I–IV (1912–1944); Karo, *Führer durch Tiryns*[2] (1934); preliminary reports of more recent examinations since 1967 are given in *AA.*

107 p. 25. Fig. 8: Map of the Argolid in Mycenaean times. Fortresses, settlements and network of roads. – Wace, *Mycenae,* Fig. 7 (after Steffen-Lolling, *Karten von Mykenai* [1884]; cf. Taylour, *Mycenaeans* (1964), 137, Fig. 51.

108 Also p. 25, Fig. 8: Athens, Acropolis. Architectural
to remains of the thirteenth and twelfth centuries B. C.
110 *108* (Fig. 8): Well shaft, LH III. – Broneer, *Hesperia* 8 (1939), 317 ff.; Iakovidis, *Mykenaiki Akropolis ton*

Fig. 13

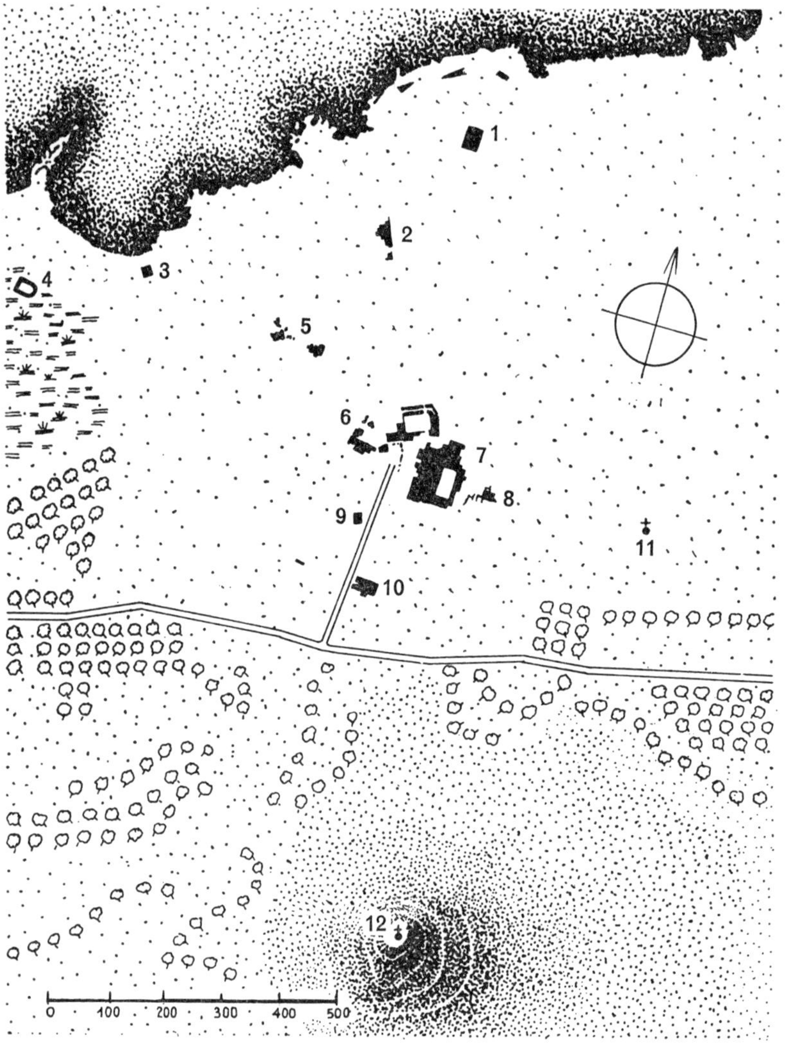

67 Mallia and surroundings

1 Chrysolakkos
2 Area Alpha
3 House Theta
4 Basilica
5 Area Gamma
6 Area Delta
7 Palace
8 Area Zeta
9 Area Beta
10 House Epsilon
11 Hagios Nikolaos
12 Hagios Elias

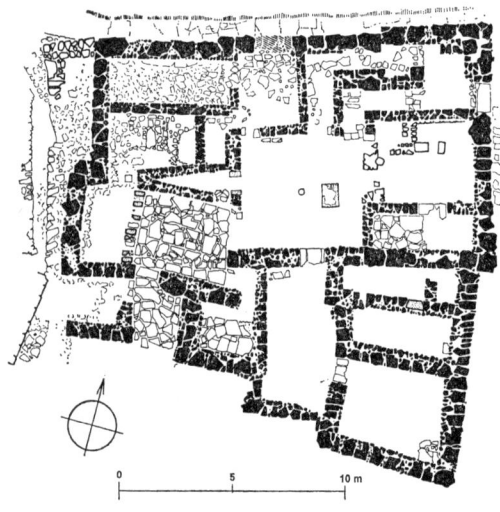

68 Mallia, House Zeta b

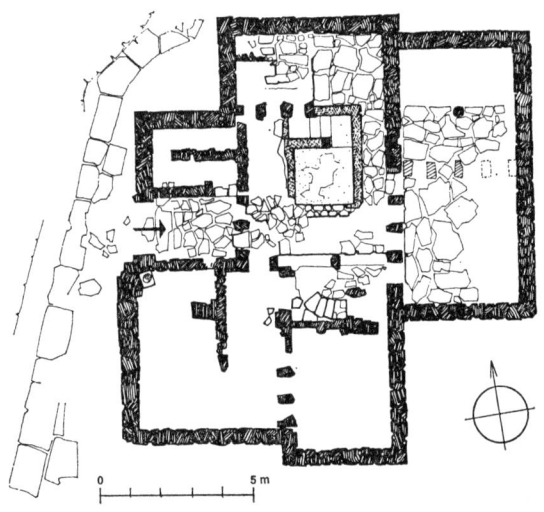

69 Mallia, House Delta a

Fig. 14

70 Mallia, Palace

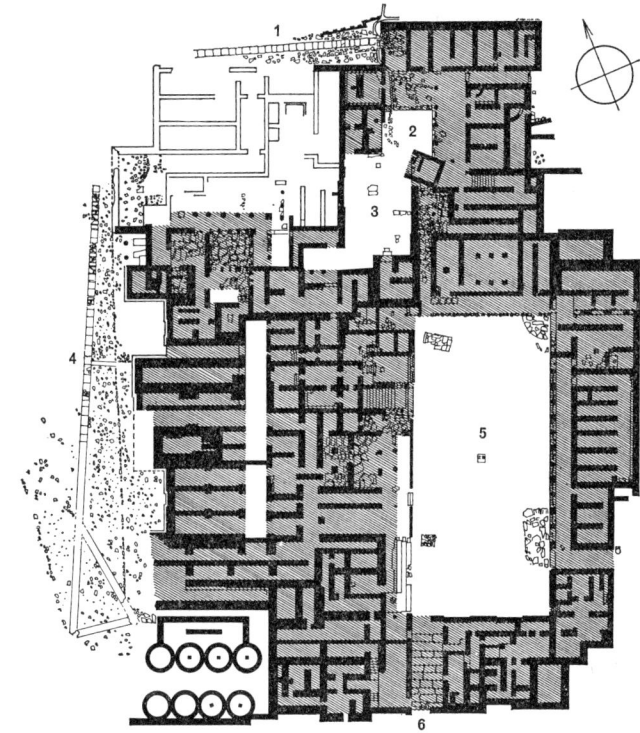

1 North Gate
2 Northern Forecourt
3 Guards' Court
4 West Esplanade
5 Central Court
6 South Gate

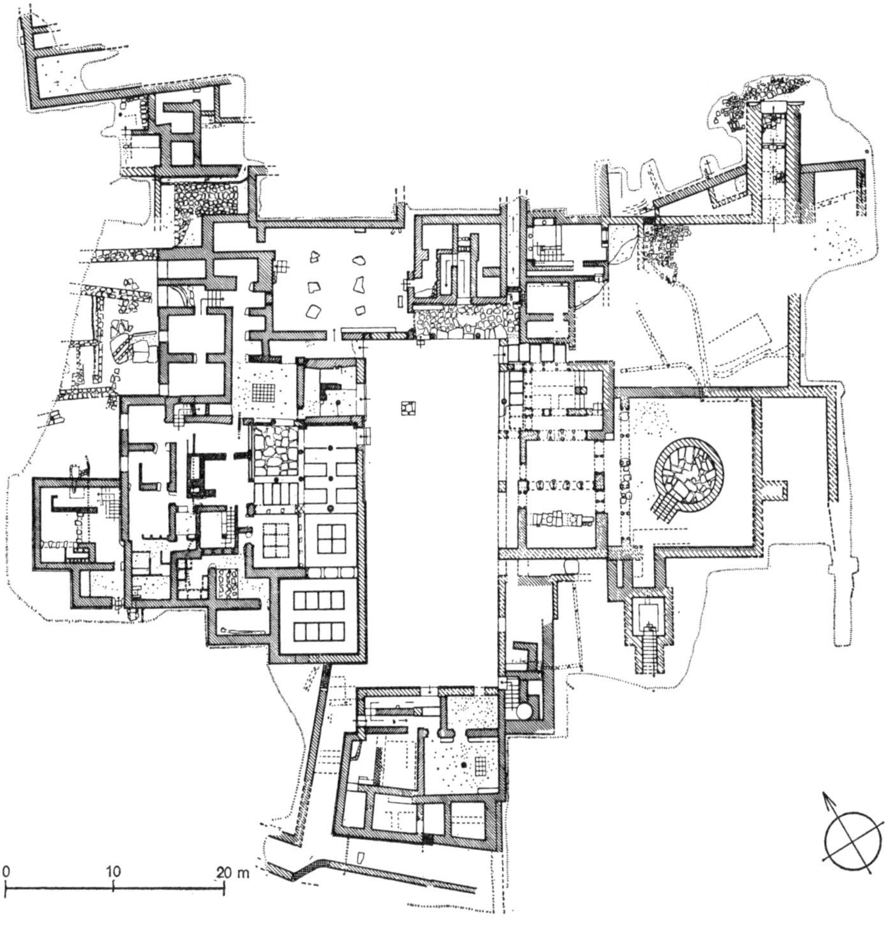

75 Kato Zakro, Palace (state of excavation: 1967)

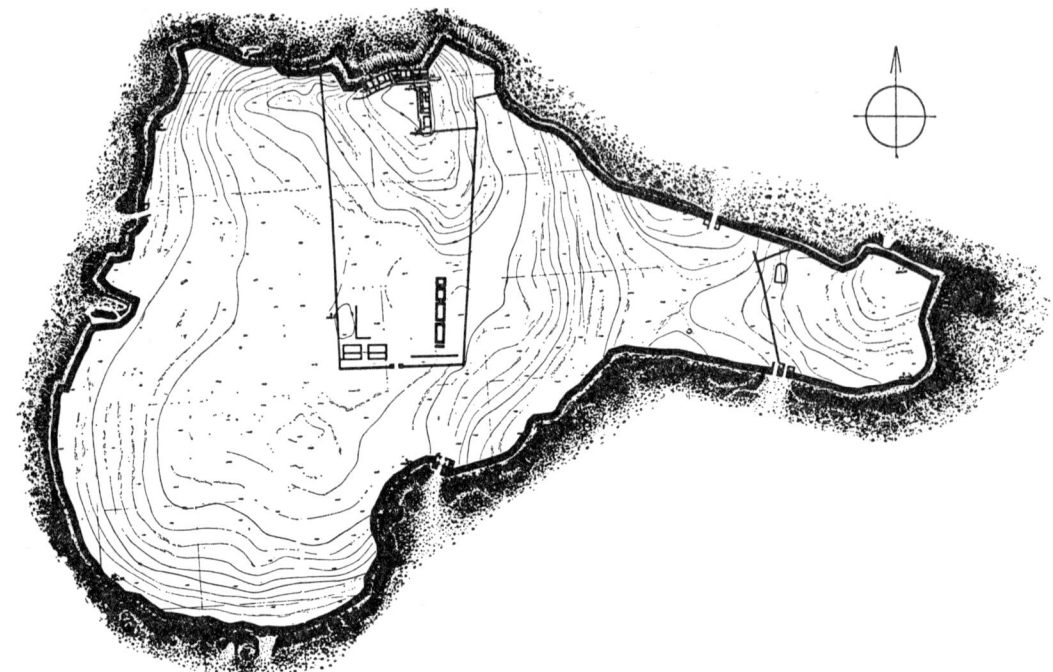

120 Gla, Boeotia

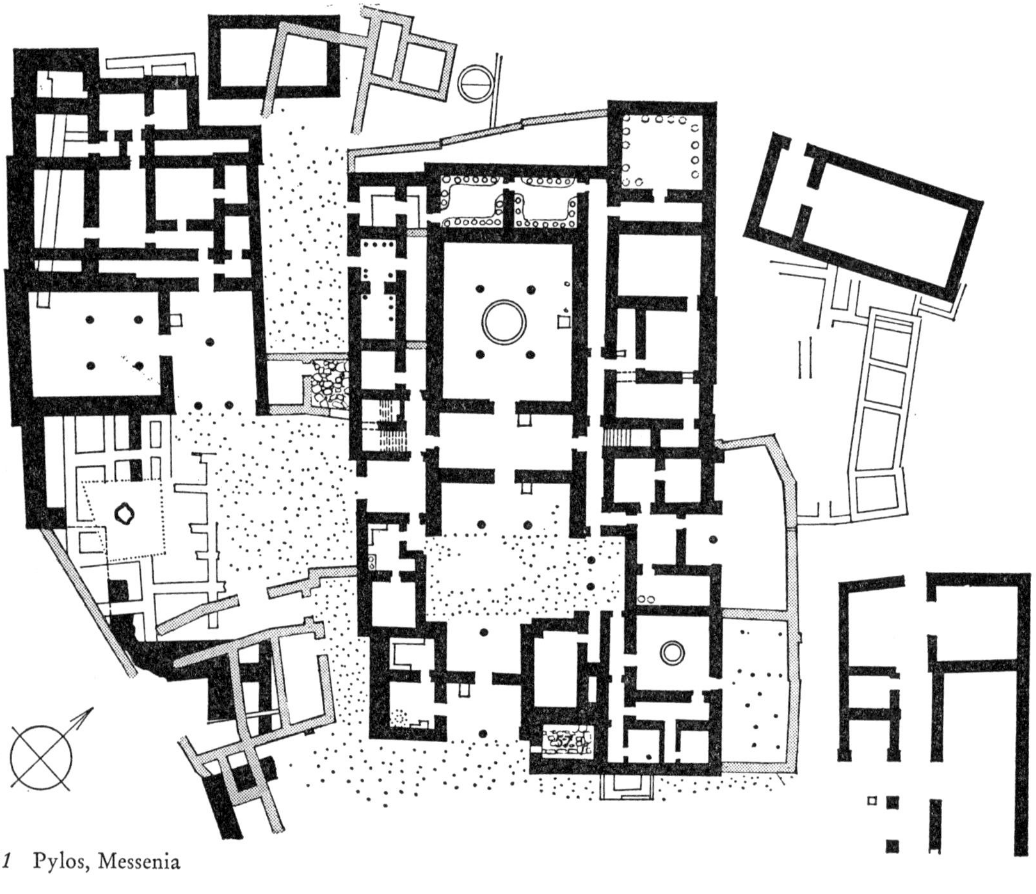

121 Pylos, Messenia

Fig. 15

Athenon (1960, mod. Gk.), 128 ff.; Mylonas, *Myc. and the Myc. Age*, 42, Fig. 10. *109*: Steps on west hewn out of the rock. *110*: Cyclopean wall. – Iakovidis, op. cit., 147, Fig. 24. Vermeule, *Greece in the Bronze Age*, Pl. 23 a (simplified plan).

111 Also Fig. 15: Gla, Boeotia. Huge Mycenaean fortress
to on an island in the dried-up Lake Copais (cf. aerial
120 view: 76). *111*: Southern main gate from within. *112, 113*: Steep slope in the north-west with fortification wall (*113* left: retaining wall of the palace, as it was in 1964). *114, 116*: North wing of the palace from the west and east. – cf. Mylonas, *Myc. and the Myc. Age*, Pl.-Fig. 77. *115*: Surrounding wall, southern section. – Fimmen, *Kret.-myk. Kultur*, 37, Fig. 26: Mylonas, op. cit., Pl.-Fig. 49. *117*: Right corner tower of the North Gate from within. – Taylour, *Mycenaeans* (1964), Pl. 43. *118, 119*: Southern main gate from outside and left side from within with 'guard-room' (cf. *111*). *120* (Fig. 15): Plan of the fortress in the thirteenth century B.C. – Literature on Gla and Lake Copais: Kambanis, *BCH*. 16 (1892), 121 ff. and 17 (1893), 322 ff.; de Ridder, *BCH*. 18 (1894), 271 ff., 446; Noack, *AM*. 19 (1894), 405 ff.; id., *Homerische Paläste* (1903), 19 f.; Kenney, *Liv. Ann.* 22 (1935), 189 ff.; Kahrstedt, 'Der Kopaissee im Altertum u. die "minyschen" Kanäle' in *AA*. 1937, 1 ff.; Marinatos–Hirmer, Pls. 158, 159; Vermeule, *Greece in the Bronze Age*, Pl. 22 b; Mylonas, op. cit., Pl.-Figs. 47, 74–77. New excavations are reported by Threpsiadis, *Prakt*. 1955, 121 ff.; 1956, 90 ff.; 1957, 48 ff.; 1961, 28 ff.; *BCH*. 82 (1968), 745 ff.; Schachermeyr, *AA*. 1962, 289 ff., Figs. 57, 58.

121 Also Fig. 15: Pylos, Messenia, Palace of Nestor, near
to Ano Englianos (LH III, American excavation). *121*
125 (Fig. 15): Plan of the palace. *122–124*: Megaron with Throne Room, and round, central hearth (*123 a, b*: flame-pattern painting on the stucco rim; a similar round hearth is in the megaron of Mycenae: Wace, *Mycenae*, Figs. 96, 97 a); background: anteroom and portal (*124*: corner of the passage to the Throne Room, seen from the vestibule); foreground: rooms with inset storage pithoi (cf. *123 b*). *125*: Probably sacred bathroom, with built in, richly painted bath tub (Graham, *Archaeology* 13 [1960], 53, Fig. 14; Taylour, *Mycenaeans*, Pl. 39; for its interpretation, cf. Platon in *Europa – Festschr. f. Grumach* [1967], 236 ff.; similar baths: *1066, 1068*. – Blegen–Rawson, *The Palace of Nestor at Pylos I* (1966).

126 Leukandi, Euboea. Mycenaean settlement. LH III;
to English excavation in progress. *126*: Sequence of strati-
128 fication, LH III – Protogeometric. *127, 128*: House walls of rubble (LH III c; state: autumn 1967). – Popham–Sackett, *Excavations at Lefkandi, Euboea, 1964–1966, Preliminary Report* (1968).

129 p. 28, Fig. 9 (map): Mycenaean sites on the west coast of Anatolia. – Hope Simpson, *A Gazetteer and Atlas of Mycenaean Sites* (1965): also Bittel, *MDOG*. 98 (1967), 18, Fig. 17.

130 p. 28, Fig. 9 (maps): Mycenaean sites in Rhodes, LH III a–c. – Stubbings, *Mycenaean Pottery from the Levant* (1951), 6, Fig. 1; cf. also Blinkenberg, *Lindos* I (1931), Pl. 3:20–37 and 40 c, and Maiuri, *AS Atene* 6/7 (1923/24), 251 ff. (list of Mycenaean cemeteries in Rhodes).

Tombs—tomb architecture

Even in the earliest Greek cultures reverent attention was given to the repose of the dead (p. 15 and note 7), as was customary in all civilized communities. Until the end of the Bronze Age the corpse was almost always buried (sometimes the skeleton lies on its back *[152]*, sometimes on its side [cist graves, *151, 188*]). Small children were often interred in large storage urns *(187)*. Individual and family burials alternated throughout the period.

The use of cremation was not widespread in the Neolithic period (Blegen, *Prosymna*, 27 ff.; Biesantz, *AA*. 1959, 70 ff.), in EH (Dörpfeld, *Alt-Ithaka* [1927], 220 f.), in MH (Argos: Ervin, *AJA*. 72 [1968], 270, Pls. 92, 93) and MM (Ailia near Knossos: *JHS*. 76 [1956], Arch. Rep. 32) and c. 1400 B.C. (Tragana near Pylos: Marinatos, *Ergon* 1955, 89 ff.); but the custom spread so rapidly after LH III c that it was the sole form of burial in the age of Homer. Eighteen cremations have been counted (*190*; Iakovidis, *Ergon* 1963, 21) in the late Mycenaean necropolis at Perati alone (*191*, LH III c).

Grave goods—death masks *(1243, 1244)*, ornaments, weapons, vessels containing foodstuffs *(151, 152, 182, 188)*—have made it possible to date finds and make conjectures about the social status of the dead. For instance, a fifteenth-century noble was accompanied to his grave by his sacrificed chariot horses *(181)*. Furthermore, archaeological finds can tell us about the cult of the dead and the belief in the soul and in after-life; this has been studied in detail by Wiesner, *Grab und Jenseits* (1938) and Andronikos, 'Totenkult,' in *Arch. Hom. Lieferung W* (1968).

The tombs were originally simple pits dug in the earth in natural caves or in the open, but already they had reached a considerable size in the Early Bronze Age tholoi of Crete *(132, 133)*. There were contemporary small, modest graves in other parts of Greece (Attica: *134—140*). The ancient Mediterranean idea of the cave tomb found its most impressive form in the palatial architecture of the 'temple-tomb' of Knossos *(141—149)*, which served as place of rest for members of the Minoan royal family. There is a detailed study of developments in Crete in Pini, *Beiträge zur Minoischen Gräberkunde* (1968), which also lists recent literature on the subject.

On the Greek mainland we find chamber tombs with long corridors (dromos, *183—186, 189, 956 b*), developed from the artificial cave tombs; they were in use until the end of the Bronze Age. The princely tombs of Mycenae in LH I—deep shaft graves—became architecturally more elaborate by being assembled into a complex by encircling them with a double ring of slabs (Grave Circle A: *154—157*). The desire for a monument to the dead was expressed by means of tomb stones (stelae: *1071, 1170, 1171*), which we find from MH onwards (Lerna: *150*).

The clearest manifestation of the spirit of Mycenaean fortified architecture is in the imposing architecture and design of the princely tholos tombs (see the schematic sectional drawing in Fig. 17, *180* and note the façade and ceiling decoration: *163, 167, 168*). There are considerably more tholoi than we have been able to show here *(158—179)*, amongst others, those in Thessaly (e.g. in Dimini, cf. p. 14, Fig. 3, 7 left; Lolling-Wolters, *AM.* 11 [1886], 435, and 12 [1887], 136). Hood has compiled a map of distribution of similar tombs in the Aegean (*Antiquity* 34 [1960], 166 ff., Fig. 1) and has demonstrated the formal and technical dependence of Late Bronze Age tholoi on the Early Bronze Age Messara tombs of Crete. The vaulted circular tomb persisted in small, debased forms until the Protogeometric and later periods (e.g. at Messenia: Choremis, *AAA.* 1 [1968], 205 ff.; and at Maltepe, south Bulgaria: Welkow, *AA.* 1931, 418 ff.).

Burial of corpses in painted sarcophagi of various materials, in the form of painted chests or baths, first became customary in Crete *(1061—1068)*; it reached the mainland in the thirteenth century B.C. *(1069, 1070)*.

For tombs in Cyprus, see *1463—1484*; for the area east of the Aegean, see Özgüç, *Die Bestattungsbräuche im vorgeschichtlichen Anatolien* (1948), and Orthmann, *Das Gräberfeld bei Ilica* (1967). Besides accounts of burials and the literature on Aegean burial customs and tomb architecture mentioned in the text and in the catalogue, reference may be made to Evans, 'The Prehistoric Tombs of Knossos' *Archaeologia* 59 (1905), 391 ff.; Zehetmaier, *Leichenverbrennung und Leichenbestattung im alten Hellas* (1907); Mylonas, 'The Cult of the Dead in Helladic Times' *(Studies presented to David Moore Robinson on his Seventieth Birthday* I [1951], 64—105); further references are given by Andronikos, in *Arch. Hom. Lieferung* W (1968), 136 ff.

131–140: EARLY BRONZE AGE GRAVES

131 Hagia Irini, Keos. Early Bronze Age 'Hero's Tomb' in front of the main gate of the town; evidently preserved until LH and not built over (excavation: Caskey, unpublished; state in 1967).

132 Hagia Triada, south Crete. Remains of a large circular tomb on the ascent of the slope; family tomb (EM). – Pendlebury, *Arch. of Crete*, 77 (bibliography); Marinatos–Hirmer, Pl. 3 upper.

133 Kamilari, district of Gligori Korphi, south Crete. Circular tomb from the west, entrance on the eastern side. Wallfacing of dressed-stone blocks filled in with small stones; inner diam. 7.65 m. Use: MM II/III and LM III a. – Levi, *ASAtene* 39/40 (1961/62), 7 ff., and *The Recent Excavations at Phaistos* (1964), 9 f., Figs. 1–5; Pini, *Beiträge zur Minoischen Gräberkunde* (1968), 5, 81, No. 108, Figs. 1–5.

134 Hagios Kosmas, Attica. Small EH Tombs Nos. 28 (also

135 Fig. 16, *139*) and 32 (also Fig. 16, *140*). Type of tomb influenced by the Cyclades. The false doors are too small for practical use, and interment was from above – Mylonas, *Aghios Kosmas* (1959), Figs. 106, 115; Schachermeyr, *Die ältesten Kulturen*, 189 f.

136 Fig. 16: Hagios Kosmas. EH Tombs Nos. 3 (section: to *136*), 15 (section: *137*), 20 (section: *138*), 28 (plan: *139*, *140* cf. *134*) and 32 (plan: *140*, cf. *135*). – Mylonas, Figs. 13:3; 19:15; 19:20; 43:47.

141–157: MIDDLE BRONZE AGE AND LATE HELLADIC I TOMBS

141 Also Fig. 16: Knossos. Temple-tomb, covering a large
to area with several rooms and a rock-cut chamber for
149 interments. Use: MM III b–LM II and LM III a 2. – Pendlebury, *Handbook to the Palace of Minos, Knossos* (1933/1954), Pl. 10:2. Evans, *PM*, IV, 962 ff.; Matz, *Kreta-Mykene-Troja*, 61; Marinatos–Hirmer, 34, 81, text Figs. 10, 11, p. 127, note 19, Pl.-Figs. 46, 47: Pini, *Beiträge zur minoischen Gräberkunde* (1968), 84, Fig. 36.

78   Mycenae, view of the citadel from the south-west

177   Mycenae, Tomb of Clytemnestra

Colour plate 2

136–138 Hagios Kosmas, Attica

139, 140 Hagios Kosmas, Attica

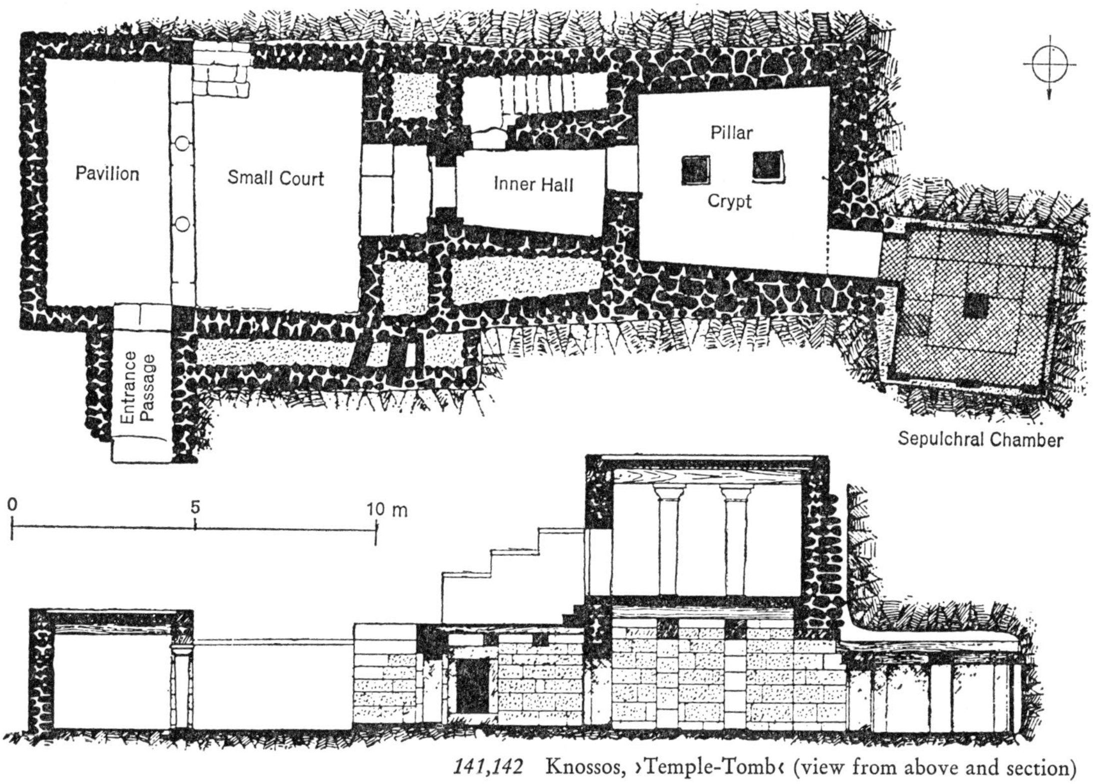

141, 142 Knossos, ›Temple-Tomb‹ (view from above and section)

150 Lerna, the Argolid. Tomb A 7 (MH, late phase), with grave stele *in situ*. Caskey, *Hesperia* 23 (1954), 14, Pl. 3 c; Adronikos, 'Totenkult' in *Arch. Hom. Lieferung W* (1968), Pl. 7 a.

151 Also Fig. 17: Mycenae, Grave Circle B (MH/LH I a).
to *151:* Tomb Eta, skeleton doubled up on its side in the
153 grave shaft with grave goods. *152:* Tomb Epsilon, skeleton at full length on its back, with numerous funerary vessels. *153:* Plan of Grave Circle B (Fig. 17, cf. Grave Circle A: *95*). — Marinatos, in *Geras Keramopoullou* (1953), 54 ff.; Mylonas, *Anc. Myc.*, Figs. 55, 82, 87; id., *Myc. and the Myc. Age*, Pl.-Fig. 88.

154 Mycenae, Grave Circle A (LH I). Details of the ring
to of slabs, of the grave shafts and their position within
157 the Cyclopean wall; cf. plan: *95*. — Karo, *SchGr.*; Wace, *Mycenae* (1949), Figs. 20 b–22, 77 a, b.

158–181: MYCENAEAN THOLOS TOMBS

158 Kakovatos, west Peloponnese. North of the prehistoric acropolis are three large tholos tombs rich in pottery, ornaments, and amber. Remains of Tholos A, LH II (Excavation: Dörpfeld; state: 1967). — Dörpfeld, *AM.* 33 (1908), 295 ff.; Müller, *AM.* 34 (1909), 269 ff., Pls. 12–24; Dörpfeld, *AM.* 38 (1913), 97 ff., Pl. 5 (plan of site); Fimmen, *Kret.-myk. Kultur*, 10, 55, Fig. 45.

159 Thorikos, Attica. Tholos with oval ground-plan (LH II), during excavation. — Stais, *Prakt.* 1893, 12 ff. and *Ephem.* 1895, 221 ff.; Frazer, *Pausanias* V, 523; Fimmen, 7 f., Fig. 2 (plan of site).

160 Tiryns. Tholos, 800 m. east of the fortress on the west
161 slope of Hagios Elias. Diam. of vault 8.5 m., length of dromos 13.7 m. *160:* View of the vault. *161:* Entrance and dromos from within. — Dragendorff, *AM.* 38 (1913), 347 ff.; Karo, *AA.* 1914, 136, Figs. 2, 3; id., *Führer durch Tiryns* (1934), 35 f., Fig. 11 (groundplan).

162 Vapheio, Laconia. Tholos after partial reconstruction (cf. Chrestou, *Delt.* 18 [1963], Chron. Pl. 102 a, b); among the important finds from this tomb are two gold cups: *(1105 a, b, 1106)*. — *Ephem.* 1888, 197 ff.; 1889, 129 ff.; Fimmen, 10, 68.

163 Orchomenos, Boeotia. Fourteenth-century tholos (diam.
to 14 m.). *163:* Ceiling relief of the side-chamber of green
165 schist, with spiral and rosette decoration (originally 3.74×2.75 m., described by Pausanias, ix, 38). *164:* Entrance to the tholos, from the inside. *165:* Door to the side-chamber. — Perrot–Chipiez VI (1894), 434 ff., Figs. 160–165, 220, 221; Bulle, *Orchomenos* I (1907), Pl. 27:1, 2 (old state); Fimmen, 5, 62, Fig. 53; Matz, *Kreta–Mykene–Troja*, Pl. 82 upper: Marinatos-Hirmer, Pls. 160, 161.

166 Dendra, the Argolid. Tholos; door blocked, vault caved in. — Persson, *Dendra* I (1931), 13, Fig. 9.

167 Mycenae. The Treasury of Atreus. Fragments of the
168 façade decoration. Reconstructions of the façade may be found in: Wace, *Mycenae*, Fig. 51; Graham, *Archaeology* 13 (1960), 51, Fig. 10. *167:* Fragment of the capital; Badisches Landesmuseum, Karlsruhe. — Perrot–Chipiez VI, 630, Fig. 280; Michaelis, *AM.* 21 (1896), 121 ff.; Lawrence, *Greek Architecture* (1957), Pl. 12 b (wrongly described as in British Museum); Meurer, 'Form und Herkunft der mykenischen Säule', in *JdI.* 29 (1914), 1 ff. Columns tapering towards the base: Naumann, *Jahrb. f. kleinasiat. Forsch.* 2 (1953), 246 ff. *168:* Fragment of panel from the relieving triangle, with spiral decoration; British Museum, London. — Wace, *Mycenae*, Fig. 49 a; Marinatos-Hirmer, Pl.-Fig. 149.

169 Mycenae. The Treasury of Atreus, fourteenth-century
to B. C. tholos; well-preserved vaulting, main entrance,
171 relieving triangle and door to side-chamber *(169)*; entrance and dromos from within *(170)*; dromos and façade from without *(171)*. — For references, see *167*, *168*; also: Thiersch, *AM.* 4 (1879), 177 ff., Pls. 11–13 (technical comments); Robertson, *JHS.* 51 (1941), 14 ff.; Wace, *JHS.* 46 (1926), 110 ff.; id., in Persson, *Dendra* I (1931), 40 ff.; id., in *Antiquity* 14 (1940), 233 ff.; in *Geras Keramopoullou* (1953), 310 ff.; and *Mycenae* (1949), Figs. 5 (plan), 8–10 (subsequent excavation in 1939), 74 b (façade).

172 Mycenae. Lion Tomb, vault collapsed; the lintel, form-
173 ed of huge blocks, has a profile carefully adapted to the curve of the tholos *(172)*; the entrance consists of large, carefully hewn ashlar; the ascending walls are of small ashlar masonry *(173)*). — Wace, *Mycenae*, Figs. 13 (section and ground-plan). 17 a (plan of site), 62 a, b (details).

174 Also Col. Pl. 2: Mycenae. The Tomb of Clytemnestra,
to with long dromos (37.40 m., width 6 m.), high door
177 and high relieving triangle. Diam. of tholos: 13.80 m. Good ashlar construction *(175–177)*, half-column on right beside entrance *(174)*. — Perrot–Chipiez VI, 644, Fig. 288; Wace, *Mycenae*, Figs. 6 (section and ground-plan), 53, 54 (details).

178 Hagios Elias, Aetolia. Four small tholoi in the im-
179 mediate neighbourhood of Kokkinospilia (cf. *1 a, b*): in part carefully constructed of ashlar, in part of rubble (LH III a–c). Among the finds: Skarabaeus Amenophis III). All vaulting collapsed. — Mastrokostas, *Prakt.* 1963, 203 ff.; *Ergon* 1963, 126 ff.; *Delt.* 19 (1964), Chron. 295 ff., Pl. 323 ff.; Daux, *BCH.* 88 (1964), 762 ff.

180 Fig. 17: Mycenaean tholos, schematic diagram. — cf. Wace–Stubbings, *A Companion to Homer* (1962), 483, Fig. 49; Andronikos, *Arch. Hom. Lieferung W* (1968), 79, Fig. 6 b; clear isometric drawing: Taylour, *Mycenaeans* (1964), 83, Fig. 29.

181 Marathon, Attica. Burial of two horses in the dromos of a tholos (LH II; excavated by Papadimitriou). — *Ergon*, 1958, 25, Fig. 23; Daux, *BCH.* 83 (1959), 583 ff., Fig. 7; Jameson, *Archaeology* 13 (1960), 34, Fig. 2; Schachermeyr, *AA.* 1962, 224 ff., Fig. 30; Mylonas, *Myc. and the Myc. Age*, Pl.-Fig. 111; Andronikos, 85, Pl. 4 b.

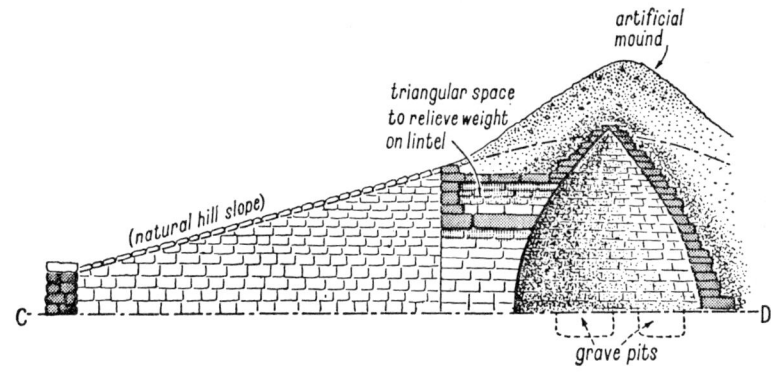

180 Tholos, schematic view

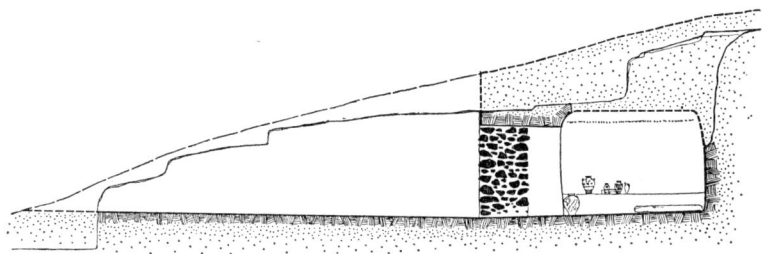

183 Athens, Areopagus, chamber tomb (cf. *956 a,b*)

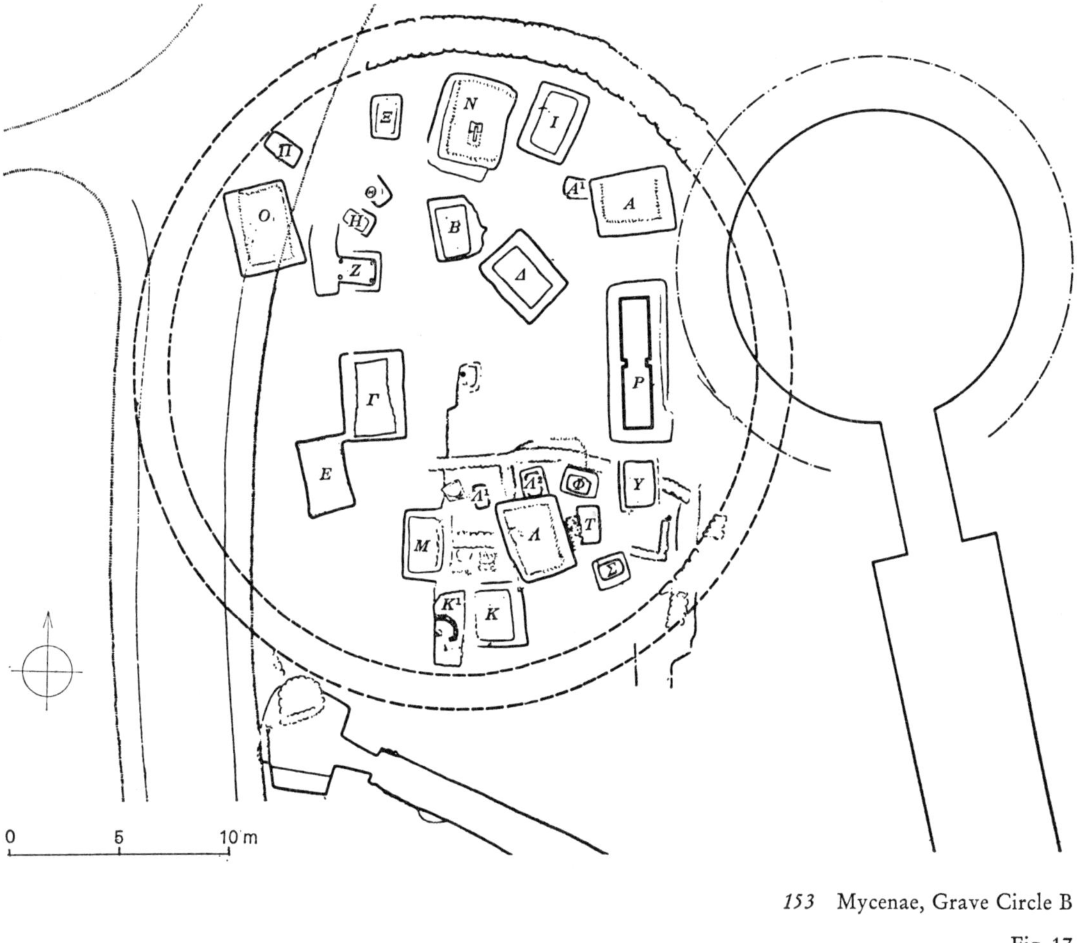

153 Mycenae, Grave Circle B

Fig. 17

182 Olous, east Crete; large necropolis. Sub-Minoan tombs 10–12, *in situ.* – Van Effenterre, 'Nécropoles du Mirabello' in *Et. Crét.* VIII (1948), Pl. 35; Andronikos, 99, Fig. 7.

183 Fig. 17: Areopagus, Athens. Sectional drawing of a Mycenaean chamber tomb. – cf. *956 a, b*.

184 Olympia. Mycenaean chamber tomb necropolis on the
185 slope behind the New Museum. Dromoi (6×1.50 m.), and entrances to two tombs blocked with boulders (LH III a, b). Excavated by Yalouris and Themelis. – *BCH.* 84 (1960), 720; *Delt.* 17 (1961/62), *Chron.* 105 f.; *Delt.* 20 (1965), *Chron.* 209.

186 Tiryns. Chamber Tomb XVI, at the foot of Hagios Elias, at the time of the discovery of the dromos.

187 Mycenae, Cyclopean terrace building. Burial of a child in a pithos, lying on its side (= *907*; height 1.70 m.; LH III c). Closed by a small handled vessel of red clay; the grave goods are small pots and stirrup jar. Arch. Mus., Nauplia. – Wace, *Mycenae*, 46, Fig. 68 a, b; id., *BSA.* 25 (1921–23), Pl. 62, 2.

188 Perati, Attica. Large chamber tomb necropolis (LH
to III c). *188:* Tomb 84, burial pit, skeleton on right side,
191 with knees drawn up, and grave goods behind head and shoulders. *189:* Tomb S 15, dromos. *190:* Tomb 1. Urn with cremated corpse *in situ. 191:* Part of the necropolis from the south; state 1963. – Jakovidis. *Prakt.* 1963, pl. 24 a; other preliminary reports: *Ergon* (1961), 13 ff.; 1962, 21 ff.; *Prakt.* 1961, 19 ff.;1962, 16 ff.; 1963, 32 ff.; *Delt.* 19 (1964), *Chron.* 87 ff.; *AJA.* 70 (1966), 43 ff.; Schachermeyr, *AA.* 1962, 228 ff. (bibliography of older reports).

Small finds—implements—weapons

'Small finds' include utilitarian implements, which generally provided their makers with little opportunity for artistic embellishment, although one finds stone implements of marked formal beauty *(226, 232)*. Such objects are of value to archaeologists because they provide a typological inventory of early times, help to establish a chronology, and give information on the state of technical knowledge at the time (e.g. polished stone axes: *217—223*; moulds: *457—464*), on the various types of craft (e.g. spindle-whorls, loom-weights, spindles: *413—429, 431—438, 508*; basketwork: *454, 455*). We learn also about trade intercourse from rare raw materials (obsidian, semi-precious stones), and in particular from ivory, which was always imported into the Aegean *(506—508, 511, 512, 514—516; also 1272—1290)*. The question of whether ivory carving was produced exclusively in Crete in the Helladic epoch has been answered by the discovery of a workshop in Mycenae *(509)*.

Arms can provide us with general information on the methods of warfare: long-range weapons played an important role in the Stone Age and Early Bronze Age: slings (missiles *235—237*) and bows and arrows (with heads of flint and obsidian, *294, 295, 353—376*), besides the weapons for hand-to-hand combat, such as the battle-axe *(226—231)* and the stone club *(233)*. In the Middle Bronze Age the traditional sling became rarer, but arrow-heads are evidence of the continued importance of long-range weapons *(377—391)*; even the courtly Late Helladic culture could not do without this Stone Age invention *(392—409;* also arrow polishers: *411, 412*, and Fig. 20, *410)*. In the fully developed Bronze Age, the boar's tusk helmet—a leather or felt cap covered with little plates of tusk—still remained as a very ancient piece of armour *(510*; and note pictures of 'zone' and boar's tusk helmets: *717, 938, 1286—1289)*. For further details, of metal arms in particular, see pp. 169 ff.

A number of Early Bronze Age metal objects are made of relatively pure copper (e.g. *518—520, 523—525, 528, 529, 531, 536, 538)*. Arsenical bronze was also used (e.g. *526, 527, 530, 532, 539, 540)* and also leaden bronze (e.g. *533, 563*) and tinned bronze.

For the typological distribution of Aegean metal objects in the third millennium, see Fig. 21, *517*. There are analyses of the metals in Buchholz, *BJbV.* 7 (1967), 189 ff. For a detailed study of bronze implements in the second half of the second millennium, see H. W. Catling, *Cypriot Bronzework in the Mycenaean World* (1964). For the Late Bronze Age copper trade, see the copper ingots *(739—752, 1898, 1899* and Fig. 26). The first appearance of iron weapons at the end of the Mycenaean Age deserves special mention *(638, 675)*.

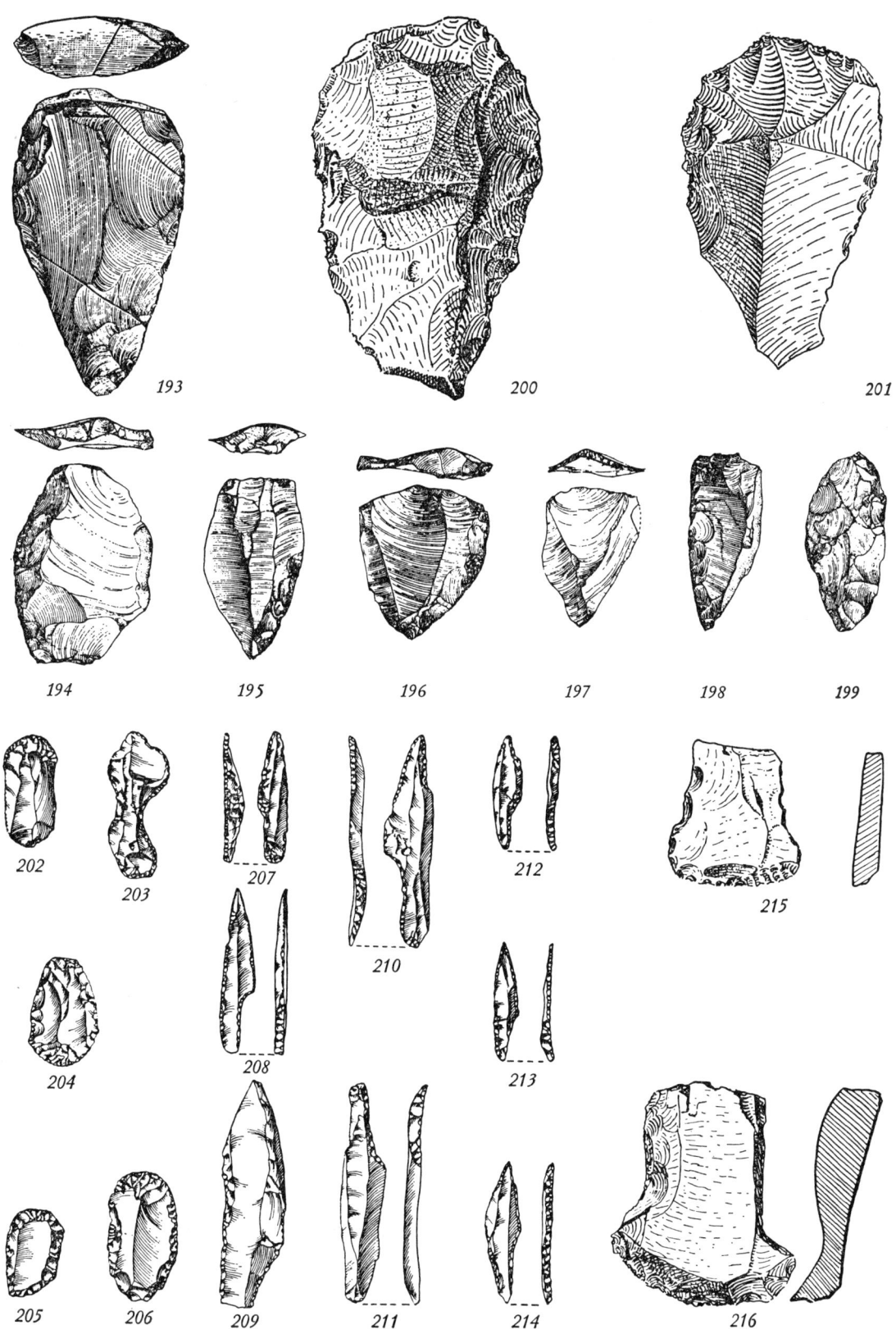

193–216 Palaeolithic and later stone implements, Macedonia, Epiros, and Samos
Fig. 18

192 Also Fig. 18: Palaiokastro, near Kozani, Macedonia.
a–c Hand-axe of Acheulian type, length 15.3 cm., width
193 10 cm., diam. 3.6 cm.; surface find (other hand-axes from the same area: Petsas, *Delt.* 20 [1965], Chron. Pl. 502 a-d; *Makedonika* 1966-7, Pl. 56 g; Veria, Arch. Mus.); Museum of Archeology and Ethnology, Cambridge. – Higgs, *Antiquity* 38 (1964), 54 f., Pl. 12; Müller-Karpe, *Hdb. d. Vorgesch.* I (1966), 329, No. 309, Pl. 239 b.

194 Fig. 18: Kokkinopilos, near Hagios Georgios, Preveza/
to Epiros. Middle Palaeolithic flints – points, flake points,
199 scrapers, scratchers, blade-like instruments, and Levalloisien fragments – found under a 1.50 m. thick deposit of clay. – Dakaris–Higgs, *Delt.* 18 (1963), Chron. 154 ff., Fig. 5, Pls. 188 a, 191; Higgs, *Man* 1963, 2 f.; id., *PPS.* 30 (1964), 213 ff.; Müller-Karpe, 329, No. 308, Pl. 239 c.

200 Fig. 18: Tigani, Samos. Flint points, probably 'Epi-
201 paleolithic' or later. – Buttler, *AM.* 60/61 (1935/36), 197, Fig. 7:1, 2.

202 Fig. 18: Kastritsa, near Joannina, Epirus. Late Paleo-
to lithic flint implements, c. 20,000 B. C. – Megaw,
214 *JHS.* 87 (1967), Arch. Rep. 13 f., Fig. 20; id., *JHS.* 88 (1968), Arch. Rep. 13; Higgs, *Antiquity* 42 (1968), 235. On other Paleolithic sites in Epirus, see *194–199*, and Higgs, *Delt.* 20 (1965); Chron. 361 ff.

215 Fig. 18: Tigani, Samos. Flint scraper, probably Early
216 Neolithic. – Buttler, *AM.* 60/61 (1935/6), 199, Fig. 9.

217 Also Fig. 19: Early Neolithic to Early Bronze Age
to (mainly Late Neolithic) polished stone axes, cutting
223 edges usually whetted on one side, necks pointed or round. *217, 218:* Kouphovouno, Laconia. Finds 1957; hard, grey-green stone, length 7.5 cm. (Neolithic or EH) and hard black stone with lighter patches, length 4 cm., width 3.4 cm (probably EH). – Waterhouse-Simpson, *BSA.* 55 (1960), 74, 80, Fig. 6:1, 2, Pl. 23 c:4, 5: cf. Blegen, *Zygouries*, Pl. 22:2. *219:* Argos, found between Larissa and Aspis. Diorite. – Vollgraff, *BCH.* 30 (1906), 6, Fig. 1. *220:* Knossos, Stratum IV (Early Neolithic II). – Evans, *BSA.* 59 (1964), 209, Fig. 49:8. *221:* Poliochni, Lemnos; Early Bronze Age. – Bernabò-Brea, *Poliochni* I, 2 (1964), Pl. 101:3. *222:* Nea Stryme, Thrace; dark grey granite, length 22 cm., Late Neolithic. Arch. Mus., Komotini, probably from the cave dwellings mentioned by Schachermeyr (*AA.* 1962, 187). – Daux, *BCH.* 90 (1966), 88 f., Fig. 4. *223:* Lerna, the Argolid. Arch. Mus., Argos. – Zervos, *Naissance* II (1963), 339, Fig. 460. Similar forms frequent throughout Greece, e. g. Thessaly (Wace–Thompson, *Prehist. Thess.* 23 f.), Epirus (Hammond, *BSA.* 32 [1931/32], 136, Fig. 5), central Greece (Soteriades, *REG.* 25 [1912], 254, Fig. 1; Marinatos, *AAA.* 1 [1968], 11, Fig. 16), Imbros (Fredrich, *AM.* 33 [1908], 102, Figs. 7–9), Peloponnese (Tsountas, *Ephem.* 1901, 84 ff., Pl. 5).

224 Hagios Elias, Aetolia. Acropolis. Late Neolithic pick with grooved shaft, length 11.6 cm., width 6 cm.; Arch. Mus., Agrinion, Inv. L 16. Compare the stone shaft-groove implements from Olympia and Malthi: Valmin, *Das adriatische Gebiet in Vor- und Frühbronzezeit* (1939), 208, Fig. 47: 9–11. – Mastrokostas, *Prakt.* 1963, 211, Pl. 186:1 and *Ergon* 1963, 137, Pl. 151.

225 Poliochni, Lemnos. Early Bronze Age axe with shaft hole and cylindrical neck, with angled profile at the lower end; broken, length 13.6 cm.; second half of third millennium B. C. – Bernabò-Brea, *Poliochni* I (1964), 671, Pl. 183:1 upper.

226 Troy II. Ceremonial axe with flaring blade, upper side facetted lengthwise; three relief rings on either side of the shaft hole, between them a wide ridge with three rows of bosses; length 26 cm. Also three other axes of similar type, lapis lazuli and nephrite. Staatl. Mus., Berlin, Abt. f. Vor- u. Frühgeschichte. – Schmidt, *Schliemanns Sammlung* (1902), 242 f., Nos. 6055–6058; Matz, *Kreta–Mykene–Troja*, Pl. 7.

227 Said to be from Crete. Finely polished axe with shaft-hole, wide neck and central rib; probably EM., length 13.7 cm. Mus. f. Kunst. u. Gewerbe, Hamburg, Inv. No. 1928, 46. – v. Mercklin, *AA.* 1928, 281, Fig. 10.

228 Fig. 19: Palaiopyrgi, Laconia. Fragment of a polished stone axe with shaft-hole (probably EH). – Waterhouse–Simpson, *BSA.* 55 (1960), 80, Fig. 6:12.

229 Fig. 19: Zerelia, Thessaly; Tomb F. Early / Middle Bronze Age shaft-hole axe of hard stone; length 6.5 cm. Also from the same site come three complete examples and nine fragments, all Late Neolithic-Early Bronze Age. – Wace–Thompson, *Prehist. Thess.* 161, 164, Fig. 111 f.

230 Fig. 19: Poliochni, Lemnos. Find No. N/4860: Butt of an early Bronze Age shaft-holed axe; non local green stone; surviving length 6.5 cm. (first half of third millennium B. C.). – Bernabò-Brea, *Poliochni* I (1964), 603, Pls. 100:3; 102:1.

231 Fig. 19: Crete. Fragment of a shaft-holed axe of Anatolian type (EM); length 10 cm., width 6 cm. Hole not bored right through to the top. Formerly Giamalakis Coll. Herakleion, Inv. No. 295. – Hutchinson, *PPS.* 16 (1950), Pl. 4:3; Buchholz, *Zur Herkunft der kretischen Doppelaxt* (1959), 21, Fig. 5 b, c.

232 Mallia, Crete. Ceremonial axe or sceptre head, in the form of a panther; grey-brown schist, length 15 cm. MM III/LM I (c. 1600 B. C.). Arch. Mus., Herakleion. – Chapouthier–Charbonneaux, *Et. Crét.* I (1928), Pl. 32:1–3; Zervos, *Crète*, 297, Fig. 424; Schachermeyr, *Die minoische Kultur des alten Kreta* (1964), 130, Fig. 62; Schachermeyr–Buchholz, *AA.* 1971, 309 and 317 f. (dating: new palace period).

233 Sesklo, Thessaly. Late Neolithic pear-shaped club-head, stone. – Tsountas, *DS.* 322 ff.; Wace–Thompson, *Prehist. Thess.* 71; Zervos, *Naissance* II, 348, Fig. 488 centre. Other stone clubs from Thessaly and Crete: Müller–Karpe, *Hdb. d. Vorgeschichte* II (1968), Pls. 134:27–29; 139; A4, 5; 140:A 22, 23.

234 Palaikastro, east Crete. Well polished marble hammer, length 8 cm.; LM I; identical form: Late Neolithic-Early Bronze Age example from Hagia Triada (Montelius, *La Grèce préclassique* [1924], Pl. 1:13; Zervos, *Crète*, 132, Fig. 103 right) and three examples from the Palace of Zakro (Platon, *Prakt.* 1963, Pl. 151a). Arch. Mus., Herakleion. – Zervos, op. cit., 356, Fig. 522.

235 Sesklo, Dimini, Marmariani, Thessaly. Late Neolithic
to egg-shaped sling stones; limestone, more frequently un-
237 fired clay. A large deposit of such missiles was found in Sesklo (cf. p. 14, Fig. 3, *6*, No. 5). – Zervos, *Naissance* II, 348, Fig. 487 a–c; Buchholz, 'Die Schleuder als Waffe im ägäischen Kulturkreis', in *Jahrb. f. kleinasiat. Forschung.* 3 (1965), 133 ff.

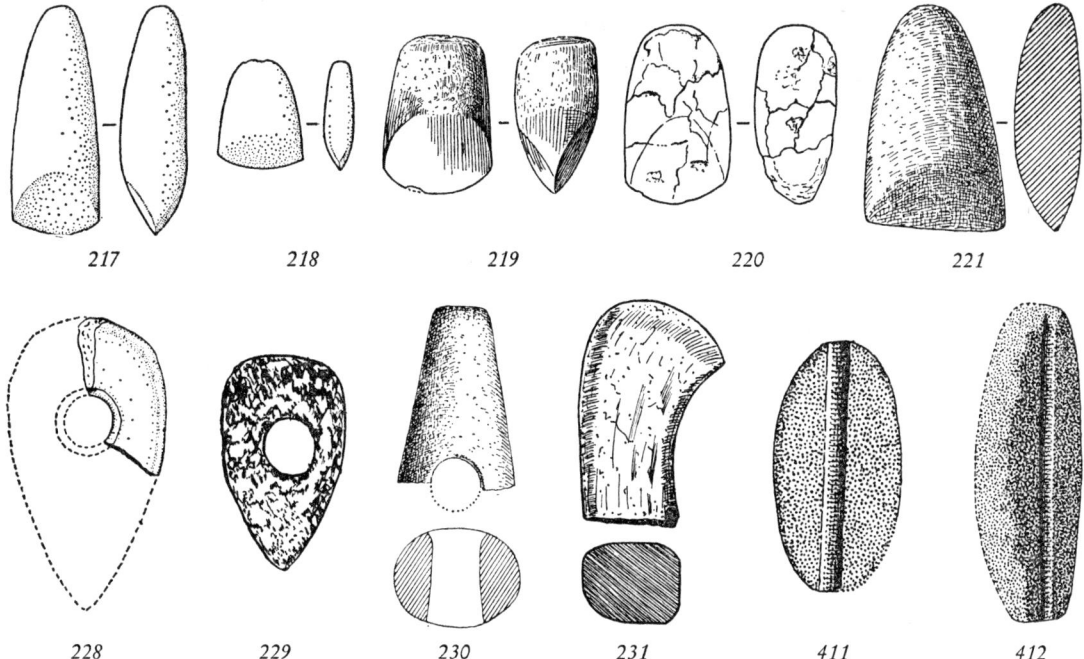

Fig. 19 Stone Age – Early Bronze Age stone hand-axes and axes. Sandstone arrow polishers

238 to 244 Tiryns, the Argolid. Obsidian implements (EH): four cores and three serrated sickle blades, length 5–10 cm.; cf. 337–347.

245 to 289 Leukas, Choirospilia Cave: Late Neolithic flint blades, points and scrapers, length 4–14 cm. – Dörpfeld, *Alt-Ithaka* (1927), 266 f., 330 ff. Suppl. 81 b; Valmin, *Das adriatische Gebiet in Vor- u. Frühbronzezeit* (1939), 70; Schachermeyr, *Die ältesten Kulturen*, 72.

290 to 308 Leukas, Choirospilia Cave. Flint blades and flakes (length 3–11.5 cm.) and arrowheads with tang; length 5 cm *(294, 295)*. – Velde, *ZfE*. 1912, 856, Fig. 8 (853, Fig. 5, ground plan of the cave).

309 to 336 Leukas, circular tombs in Nidri Plain; excavation 1910. Early Bronze Age obsidian implements from the deposit above the R tombs *(329–336)*. The rest from the large tomb R I, including two scraper flakes of flint *(318, 328)*. More than a dozen slender obsidian blades *(309 to 317, 319–327)* from a pithos burial under the floor of the chamber in R I (length 1.8–6.5 cm.). – Dörpfeld, *6. Brief über Leukas-Ithaka* (1911), 17; id. *Alt-Ithaka* (1927), Suppl. 63 c.

337 to 347 Tiryns, the Argolid. Large sickle blade, flint *(337*, length 8.5 cm.); flint and obsidian blades *(338, 340, 342–347)*; finely retouched arrowhead with tang, light flint *(341*, length 2.5 cm.); all EH (cf. *238–244)*.

348 to 351 Saliagos, small island near Antiparos. Neolithic obsidian implements: core, flat oval implement touched up on both sides, borer and slender point with careful touching up. During the excavations, over 1000 stone implements were found, of which 99% were of obsidian: they are the earliest artefacts hitherto identified on the Cyclades. – Evans-Renfrew, 'Excavations at Saliagos near Antiparos', in *BSA*. Suppl. V (1968), Pls. 34 above left; 36:1; 41:2; 35:1.

352 Analipsi, Kynouria. Tholos tomb: Whetstone with hole for attaching cord, length *c.* 8.7 cm., LH II. This implement appeared in the Aegean in the Early Bronze Age, at the same time as the metal implements, and was used to sharpen knives, sickles, etc. – Rhomaios, *Prakt.* 1954, 285, Fig. 18 c; Wiesner, *Grab u. Jenseits* (1938), 141 (whetstones as grave goods).

353 to 356 Mycenae, the Argolid, and Thebes, Boeotia. Arrowheads of flint. *353:* Tanged head (MH, length 5.7 cm., Mycenae). Nat. Mus., Athens, Inv. No. 1051. *354–356:* Heads with recessed base, Thebes, from LH III a chamber tombs. Arch. Mus., Thebes, unpublished.

357 to 376 Leukas, at the foot of Mount Skaros. Family tomb S – Burial 8: Arrowheads with recessed base, flint; length 2–4.6 cm. (MH. *384–387)*. – Dörpfeld, *Alt-Ithaka* (1927), Suppl. 70 right; Valmin, *Das adriatische Gebiet in Vor- u. Frühbronzezeit*, 211, Fig. 49:14, 15: Buchholz, *JdI*. 77 (1962), 34, No. 16 a, Figs. 5 q, r; 6 a–f.

377 to 383 Athens, south slope of Acropolis, and Asine, the Argolid. Arrowheads with tang, obsidian, length 1.5–3.4 cm. (EH/MH). *377–382:* Athens. – Skias, *Ephem.* 1902, 128, Fig. 3. *383:* Asine. – Persson, *Asine*, 243, Fig. 175:4; Buchholz, op. cit., 9, Fig. 5 j–p, and p. 33, Nos. 5, 10.

384 to 387 Leukas, at the foot of Mount Skaros. Family tomb S, Burial 8: Arrowheads with recessed base, flint (MH). Cf. *357–376*.

388 to 391 Leukas, at the foot of Mount Skaros. Family tomb S – Burial 4. Arrowheads with recessed base (Type III), flint (MH). – Dörpfeld, *Alt-Ithaka*, Suppl. 69, 5; Montelius, *La Grèce préclassique* II, 185 ff., Figs. 669–671, Buchholz, op. cit., 10, Fig. 6 g–i, and p. 35, No. 16 b.

392 to 400 Arrow-heads, crayfish-claw type (Type IV a), flint (LH I/II). *392, 400:* Thebes, Chamber Tomb. – Buchholz, op. cit., 40, No. 12. *393, 395:* Tholos A, Kakovatos, (cf. *158)*. – Loc. cit. 37, No. 4. *394:* Eutresis, Boeotia. – Loc. cit. 40, No. 13 b. *396, 397:* Chamber Tomb 515 and Shaft Grave IV, Mycenae. – Loc. cit. 39, No. 10 b, f. *398:* Chamber Tomb 8, Dendra. – Loc.

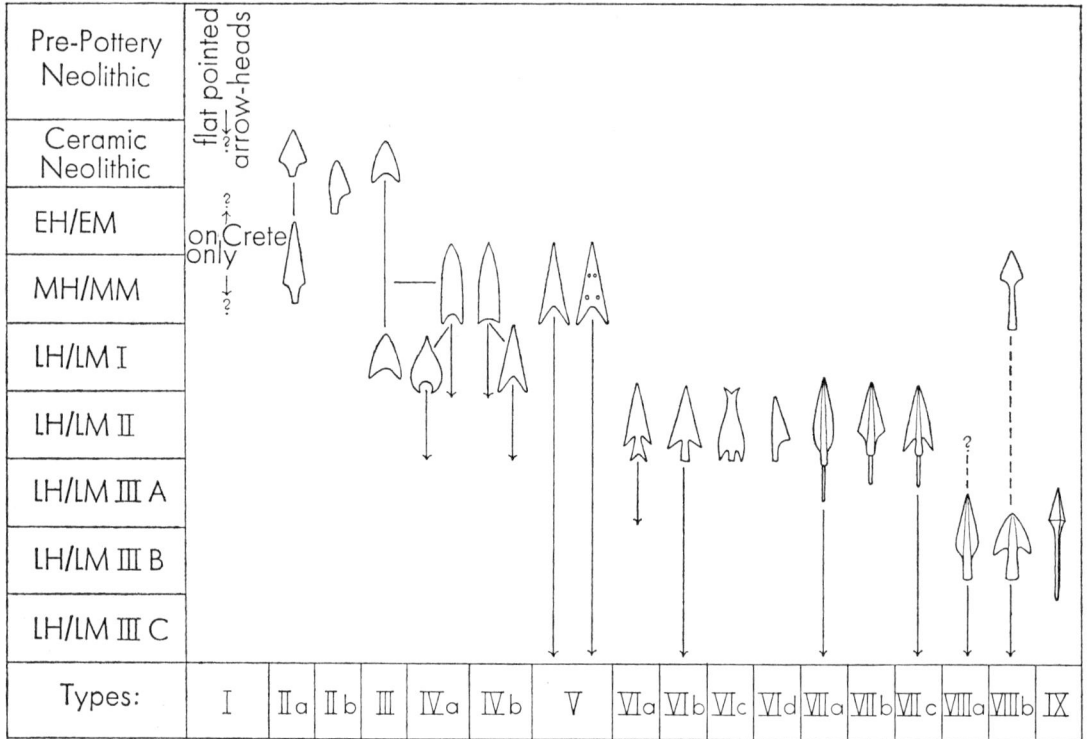

Fig. 20 410 Development of Aegean arrow-heads, diagram of types

cit. 38, No. 8. *399:* Malthi, Peloponnese. – Loc. cit. 38, No. 5 and p. 13, Fig. 9 i–q.

401 Arrowheads, crayfish-claw form (Type IV a), obsidian
to (LH I/II). *401:* Dendra, Chamber Tomb 8. – Buchholz,
409 42, No. 7. *402:* Prosymna, Tomb 34. – Loc. cit. 42, No. 8 d. *403, 404, 408, 409:* Pylos, Gouvalari, Tholos Tombs 1 and 2. – Loc. cit. 41, No. 2 c. *405, 406:* Mycenae, Chamber Tomb 515 and Shaft Grave IV. – Loc. cit. 43, No. 9 a, e. *407:* Dendra, Tomb 14. – Loc. cit. 42, No. 8 b and p. 15, Fig. 10 a–i.

410 Fig. 20: Development of Aegean arrowheads, diagram of types. – Buchholz, 11, Fig. 7.

411 Fig. 19: Malthi, Peloponnese. Arrow polisher, sandstone, length 6.5 cm.; nine examples in all (EH III– LH I). Wooden arrow shafts were smoothed in the groove between two implements of this kind. – Buchholz, 3, Fig. 1 h and p. 17.

412 Fig. 19: Asine, the Argolid. Arrow polisher, sandstone, length 10.5 cm. (EH/MH). – Persson, *Asine,* 248 f., Fig. 176:4; Buchholz, 3, Fig. 1 l and p. 17.

413 Dikeli Tash, west Thrace. Late Neolithic spindle whorls,
to clay; diam. 4.6 cm., 4.5 cm., 5.5 cm.; Arch. Mus., Ka-
415 valla *(413, 415)* and Nat. Mus., Athens *(414).* – Zervos, *Naissance* II, 394, Figs. 576, 578; for the Neolithic in Thrace, cf. Schachermeyr, *Die ältesten Kulturen,* 124 f.; Garasanin–Dehn, *JbZMusMainz* 10 (1963), 1 ff.

416 Troy II. Clay spindle whorl, ornaments on the upper side inlaid in white; flat on top, conical below; diam. 3.7 cm., height 2.4 cm. Buchholz Coll., Giessen. – For similar pieces, cf. Dörpfeld, *Troja u. Ilion* I (1902), Suppls. 47, 48; Schmidt, *Schliemanns Sammlung* (1902), Pl. 1, third row; Perrot–Chipiez VI (1894), 207, Fig. 56, and 907, Fig. 456.

417 Probably from Rhodes, origin not certain. Spindle whorl of white marble, upper side slightly rounded, lower side flat; diam. 4.1 cm., height 0.7 cm.; Late Bronze Age. Buchholz Coll., Giessen.

418 Region west of Hierapetra, east Crete. Three biconical
to and two conical spindle whorls. *418–420:* grey clay in
422 section, ochre brown hard clay outside; diam. 2 to 2.5 cm., height 1.7–2.2 cm., probably LM III. *421, 422:* grey-green, brown speckled diorite and light yellow limestone, well polished; diam. 2–2.2 cm., height 1.3 cm., LM III. *420* has a small, ribbed bead of grey stone beside it, diam. 9 mm. (no No.). Untied Coll., Hamburg.

423 Probably from Rhodes *(423–426);* Olympia *(427).* Five
to spindle whorls, or 'buttons'; all except *427* (pale green
427 marble) of grey-green steatite. Diam. 1.8–3.2 cm., height 0.8–1.7 cm. (LH III a/b). Pointed variants *(423–425),* flat spherical form *(426)* and conical form *(427).* Buchholz Coll., Giessen. For the typology, cf. Blegen, *Prosymna* II (1937), 147, Fig. 602; for the function of such objects, see recently Marinatos in *Arch. Hom. Lieferung A* (1967), 16 f., Fig. 1, d–h.

428 Phthiotic Thebes at the north edge of the plain of
429 Krokion, Thessaly. Two Late Neolithic loom-weights; clay, band painting, heights 4.5 and 7.5 cm. Arch. Mus., Volos. – Zervos, *Naissance* II, 344, Figs. 476, 477. For the site cf. Staehlin, *AM.* 31 (1906), 5 ff.; Wace–Thompson, *Prehist. Thess.,* 166 f.

430 Knossos, Crete. 15th Magazine: Weight with reliefs of cuttle-fish on all four sides (LM II). Red gypsum; similar in shape to loom-weights, but considerably larger (height 42.5 cm.); weight: 29 kg. Evans (*PM* IV, 651, Fig. 635), Bossert (*Altkreta*[3], No. 268) and others

have interpreted this as a Minoan royal standard unit of weight, corresponding to the ancient Babylonian talent. Rightly, there are doubts (cf. Buchholz, *PZ.* 37 [1959], 8); perhaps an anchor stone, similar to one from Tomb 27 in Ialysos (height 32 cm., Maiuri, *ASAtene* 6/7 [1923/24], 150, Fig. 72), which was wrongly interpreted as a 'sema tombali'. Arch. Mus., Herakleion. – Evans, *BSA.* 7 (1900/1901), 42, Fig. 12; Maraghiannis, *Ant. Crét.* III, Pl. 31; Zervos, *Crète,* 339, Fig. 495.

431 Rhodes. Two disc-shaped loom-weights (LH III a/b),
432 heights 5.5 cm. and 7.3 cm.; ochre-brown, coarsely sifted clay. Above the hole: groove for attaching a cord *(432).* Buchholz Coll., Giessen.

433 Rhodes. Two pyramidal loom-weights with square
434 bases (LH III a/b), heights 5.2 cm. and 5.5 cm.; finely sifted reddish yellow clay. Buchholz Coll., Giessen. Similarly, Dörpfeld, *Troja u. Ilion* I (1902), 410, Fig. 416 (*Troy* VII).

435 Mallia, Crete. Four loom-weights of the same type as
to *432* with one or two holes for cord, coarsely sifted
438 clay; height 5.5–7.5 cm. (LM I). – Pelon, *BCH.* 90 (1966), 579, Fig. 28.

439 Yiriza, Corinthia. Small EH settlement west of Gonia;
to Five pestles of coloured marble; characteristic EH and
443 Early Cycladic domestic utensils (variant form: *1132 b*). – Blegen, *Zygouries,* 196, Fig. 186.

444 Zygouries (for its position between Corinth and My-
to cenae, cf. Fig. 8, *107*). Five spool-shaped pestles of
448 coloured marble (EH). – Blegen, Pl. 22:16–20.

449 Mallia and Gournia, Crete. Horns of consecration, used
450 in sacred architecture (cf. *144* background, and Fig. 35, *1168* above right). *449:* Coarse clay, width 20 cm., LM I; Arch. Mus., Herakleion. – Zervos, *Crète,* 400, Fig. 596. *450:* Lime-sandstone, width 20.8 cm., LM I; Univ. Mus., Philadelphia, Inv. MS 4171. – Boyd Hawes, *Gournia* (1908), 48. Other fragments of horns of consecration have been found in Zakro (Platon, *Prakt.* 1966, Pl. 140 b), and also on the mainland, e. g. in the Palace of Gla; poros stone (*Ergon* 1960, 48, Fig. 58). For religious and historical significance, cf. Nilsson, *MMR*², 165 ff.

451 Berbati, the Argolid. Tombs I and II: Late Mycenaean
to flat tiles (40×64 cm., 36.5×50 cm., 40.7×54 cm.). –
453 Åkerström, *OpArch.* II (1941), 164 ff. and *6. internat. Kongr. f. Archäologie,* Berlin 1939 (1940), Pl. 20 b. For Mycenaean roof tiles and problems of roof covering, cf. also Smith, *AJA.* 46 (1942), 99 ff.; Dinsmoor, loc. cit., 370 ff.; Blegen, *AJA.* 49 (1945), 35 ff. – Mycenaean roof tiles also found in Gla and Peristeria.

454 Zygouries. Impressions of mats on the bases of vessels
a–h (EH); various weaving patterns; some of the mats must have been round. – Blegen, *Zygouries,* 116 f., Fig. 109.

455 Besika-Tepe, Troas. Impression of mat on Early Bronze Age sherd. – Dörpfeld, *Troja u. Ilion* II (1902), 546 f., Fig. 468.

456 Hierapetra, east Crete. Clay spiral of unknown function. Finely sifted, sandy grey clay with yellow, glossy slip; the open end broken; dimension 4.7 cm. Untied Coll., Hamburg.

457–464: MOULDS AND MATRICES

457 Mallia, Crete. Two-part mould for making double axes, stone, length 16 cm. (MM II). The notches were used for binding the two halves of the mould together. A plaster cast of the axe is shown (length 14.5 cm.). Arch. Mus., Herakleion, 2187. – Chapouthier–Demargne, *Et. Crét.* VI (1942), 56 f.; Zervos, *Crète,* 403, Fig. 610; Buchholz, *Zur Herkunft der kretischen Doppelaxt* (1959), 53, Pl. 13 a, d.

458 Kephala summit, near Knossos, Crete. Tholos tomb (LH I a/b; occupied till LH III a): Fragment of a matrix or mould, of green and red steatite for moulding gold or glass ornaments; dimensions, as preserved, 2.4×4 cm. – Hutchinson, *BSA.* 51 (1956), 80, No. 19, Pl. 12 e.

459 Eleusis, Attica. Mould stone (c. 4×6 cm.; LH) for making two oval bezels for signet rings (above: ritual scene of two women in flounced skirts; below: inverted bird and branch). The connecting holes at the corners show that a second leaf belonged to the complete mould. Steatite. Arch. Mus., Eleusis. Another mould stone of unknown provenance for gold ornament in the manner of round seals is in the Metropolitan Museum, New York, 26.31.392 (Richter, *Handbook of the Greek Collection* [1953], 17, Pl. 8 i). For Mycenaean finds in Eleusis, cf. Mylonas, *Eleusis and the Eleusinian Mysteries* (1962), 31 ff., 49 ff.

460 Mycenae. Mould (LH III b), both sides used for making ornaments; dark red steatite, the edges severely damaged; height 7.5 cm., width 7.4 cm., thickness 1.8 cm. Motifs include rosette and bee (cf. *1356*). Subsequently incised Linear B characters prove that even ordinary Mycenaean craftsmen used this script. Museum of Fine Arts, Boston, 66.194 (M. L. Smith Fund). – Vermeule, *Kadmos* 5 (1966), 144 ff., Pl. 2 and *BMusFA.* 65, No. 339 (1967), 19 ff., Figs. 1, 2 and p. 30, Fig. 11 (drawing), p. 31, note 4 (for list of other moulds cf. Megaw, *JHS.* 87 [1967], Arch. Rep. 9, Fig. 13, also from Mycenae, LH III b; cf. also Furtwängler–Löschcke, *Myken. Vasen.* 34, Fig. 22.

461 Knossos. Mould (LM II), steatite, top severely dam-
a, b aged; both sides used for making ornaments; length 9.5 cm., surviving height 4.3 cm. Ashmolean Mus., Oxford, 1910. 522. – Wace, *Archaeologia* 82 (1932), 192, note 6; Haevernick, *JbZMusMainz* 7 (1960), 39, Pl. 7; Vermeule, 23, Fig. 4.

462 Mycenae, excavations of 1932. Fragment of a mould
a, b (LH III a), steatite, both sides used for making ornaments; preserved length 9.5–9.8 cm. Arch. Mus., Nauplia, Inv. No. 2501.

463 Sitia, east Crete; site west of Palaiokastro and Epano Metochi (for the district, see Chalikiopoulos, *Sitia – die Osthalbinsel Kretas* [1903]). Mould of schist for making two decorative double axes (lengths 5.9 and 12 cm.); length of mould stone 22.5 cm., height 10 cm. (LM III). Arch. Mus., Herakleion. – Xanthoudides, *Ephem.* 1900, 26 ff., Pl. 4; Zervos, *Crète,* 451, Fig. 746; Buchholz, *Zur Herkunft der kretischen Doppelaxt* (1959) 54, No. 4, Pl. 13 f.

464 Sitia. Mould of schist for making wheel-shaped pendants and small figure of a goddess: the reverse also with hollowed out figure; length 22.5 cm., height 10 cm. (LM III). Arch. Mus., Herakleion. – Xanthoudides, op. cit., Pl. 3 a; Nilsson, *MMR*², 225, Fig. 12; Zervos, *Crète*, 450, Fig. 744.

465–516: BONE – HORN – IVORY

465 Souphli, Thessaly (magula). Bone awl, pre-pottery Neolithic period; length *c.* 8–10 cm. Arch. Mus., Volos. – Zervos, *Naissance* I, 159, Fig. 91.

466 Souphli (magoula). Bone hook with two holes for attaching a cord or sinew (after Mellaart, *Earliest Civilizations of the Near East* [1965], 115, Fig. 102 a, e, 'belt hook', according to Theocharis' 'fish-hook'; similar example of bone: Çatal Hüyük VI). Pre-pottery Neolithic period, dimension 9.8 cm. Arch. Mus., Volos. – Theocharis, *Thessalika* 1 (1958), Pl. 6:14; Zervos, 160, Fig. 96.

467 Poliochni, Lemnos. Early Bronze Age bone needles with
to eyes; length 6.2–10.5 cm. (mid-third millennium). –
479 Bernabò–Brea, *Poliochni* I (1964), 599, Pl. 89:28–40.

480 Poliochni, Lemnos. Early Bronze Age copper awl (bronze graver?) with bone handle, length 11.6 cm. – Riemann, *AA*. 1937, 163 f., Fig. 21; Bernabò–Brea, Pl. 86 c.

481 Tiryns. Bone implements – gravers, needles, spatulas –
to mostly in fragmentary state (EH). Arch. Mus., Nauplia.
492 For similar implements from Poliochni, cf. Riemann, 163 f., Fig. 20.

493 Leukas. Choirospilia Cave: Late Neolithic bone imple-
to ments and part of antler, perforated at the top. *494:*
498 Bone awl, length 8.3 cm. *497:* Hook, made from the pelvis of a sheep. Dörpfeld, *Alt-Ithaka* (1927), Suppl. 82 a.

499 Leukas. Choirospilia Cave: Late Neolithic bone dec-
500 orated by engraving (*500:* preserved length 8 cm.). – Dörpfeld, op. cit.; Velde, *ZfE*. 1912, 856 f., Fig. 7. Decorated Early Bronze Age bone tubes, similar to *501–505*, came to light in Circular Tomb 4 at Leukas Nidri: Dörpfeld, op. cit., Suppl. 66 b; Åberg, *Bronzezeitliche u. früheisenzeitliche Chronologie* III (1932), 152, Fig. 289.

501 Poliochni. Early Bronze Age bone tube (*c.* 2400 B. C.),
a, b with richly engraved decoration: seven zones with alternate empty and hatched triangles (cf. *502*), length 9 cm. – Bernabò–Brea, 457, 666, Pl. 178:12.

502 Cyclades. Early Bronze Age, richly decorated bone
to tubes; all in Nat. Mus., Athens. *502:* Syros, Tomb 174,
505 size 11.6 cm. – Tsountas, *Ephem.* 1899, Pl. 10.2; Montelius, *La Grèce préclassique* I (1924), 111, Fig. 329; Zervos, *Cycl.* 198, Fig. 262. *503:* Syros, fragment, size 6.4 cm. *504:* Syros, fragment, size 4.3 cm. – Zervos, op. cit. *505:* Syros, size 11 cm. – Zervos, op. cit. 35 such bone objects found in 30 tombs on Syros; cf. also: Naxos, Tomb 18; Nat. Mus., Athens, EM 8818; size 10.2 cm. – Papathanasopoulos, *Delt.* 17 (1961/62), *Meletai,* 126 f., Pl. 57 c. Apart from *500, 501,* there are similar pieces in Euboea and north Syria (Byblos, Qalaat-er-Rus, Ras Shamra, Qadesh and Hama); cf. Buchholz, *Hist. Zeitschr.* 201 (1965), 383; Hennessy, *The Foreign Relations of Palestine during the Early Bronze Age* (1967), Pl. 77.

506 Mycenae. Grave Circle A, Shaft Grave V (LH I): Part of an ivory implement; according to Karo, 'the end of a spoon handle'. Elaborately carved pointed elliptical shield with seven double circles on a latticed ground; length 4.3 cm. – Karo, *SchGr.* 145 f., No. 825, Fig. 62.

507 Mycenae. Grave Circle A, Shaft Grave V (LH I): Ivory implement with rich engraving of groups of circles and trefoil of wavy bands. According to Karo, it is a spoon (cf. *506*); Marinatos identifies it as a tool for inserting the weft into the weaving frame; but this is doubtful since Shaft Grave V has a male inventory. – Karo, *SchGr.* 145 f., No. 824, Fig. 62, Pl. 136; Marinatos in *Arch. Hom. Lieferung A* (1967), Pl. 7 a.

508 Perati, Attica. Chamber Tomb 152: Ivory spindle, length 13.6 cm. (LH III c). – Iakovidis, *Prakt.* 1963, Pl. 26 b; and *Delt.* 19 (1964), Chron., Pl. 90 f. A similar spindle was found in Tomb 65 (Daux, *BCH.* 83 [1959], 599, Fig. 33).

509 Mycenae. East wing of the palace: Ivory tools and fragments; sure signs of workshops *in situ* (LH III b). – Daux, *BCH.* 90 (1966), 778 f., Fig. 6.

510 Mycenae. Necropolis of Kalkani. Chamber Tomb 518: Reconstructed boar's tusk helmet. After LH I, little plates of tusk perforated on all four corners are often found in Mycenaean tombs. The accuracy of the reconstruction can be seen from portrayals *(716, 1286, 1288, 1289)*; description: Homer, *The Iliad* X, 260 ff.; cf. Hampe. *Gymnasium* 63 (1956), 12 f. – Wace, *Archaeologia* 82 (1932), 212 ff., Pl. 38 lower; and *Mycenae,* Pl. 78 a, b.

511 Mycenaean ivory and bone combs (cf. also *1279*). *511:*
to Mycenae. Grave Circle A, Shaft Grave IV (LH I):
516 Ivory, gold-plated, semi-circular, broken in many places; diam. 14.5 cm., height 2 cm.; ring cut from the upper end of a tusk. Concentric circles in zigzag pattern, burnt black; gold plating therefore secondary. Nat. Mus. Athens. – Karo *SchGr.,* Pl. 43, 310. *512:* Athens, Temple of Ares. Chamber tomb (LH II/III a, late fifteenth century B. C.): Ivory handle arranged in three zones of equal width, sculptural boss in the centre of the upper edge; width 5.7 cm., greatest height 4.1 cm. From the woman's burial V; Agora Mus., Athens, Inv. BI 665. – Vermeule–Townsend, *Hesperia* 24 (1955), 193, 215 f., No. 31, Fig. 8, Pl. 76:31. *513:* Mycenae. Bone, smooth handle with hole; width *c.* 6.5 cm. (LH). Nat. Mus., Athens (here taken from Schliemann's original photograph). – Schliemann, *Mykenae* (1878), 87, Fig. 130. *514:* Teichos Dymaion, Achaia (north-west Peloponnese). Ivory, handle divided into two, unadorned, more or less equally wide zones (LH III b). Arch. Mus., Patras. – Mastrokostas, *Ergon,* 1966, 163, Fig. 193. *515:* Perati, Attica. Chamber Tomb 5: Ivory, handle divided into two unadorned, unequally wide zones, width 4 cm., height 3.9 cm. (LH III c). *516:* Thebes, Boeotia. Chamber tomb near the town: Handle arranged in three smooth, equally wide zones (LH III a). Arch. Mus., Thebes, unpublished.

Fig. 21 *517* Distribution of Early Bronze Age metal finds

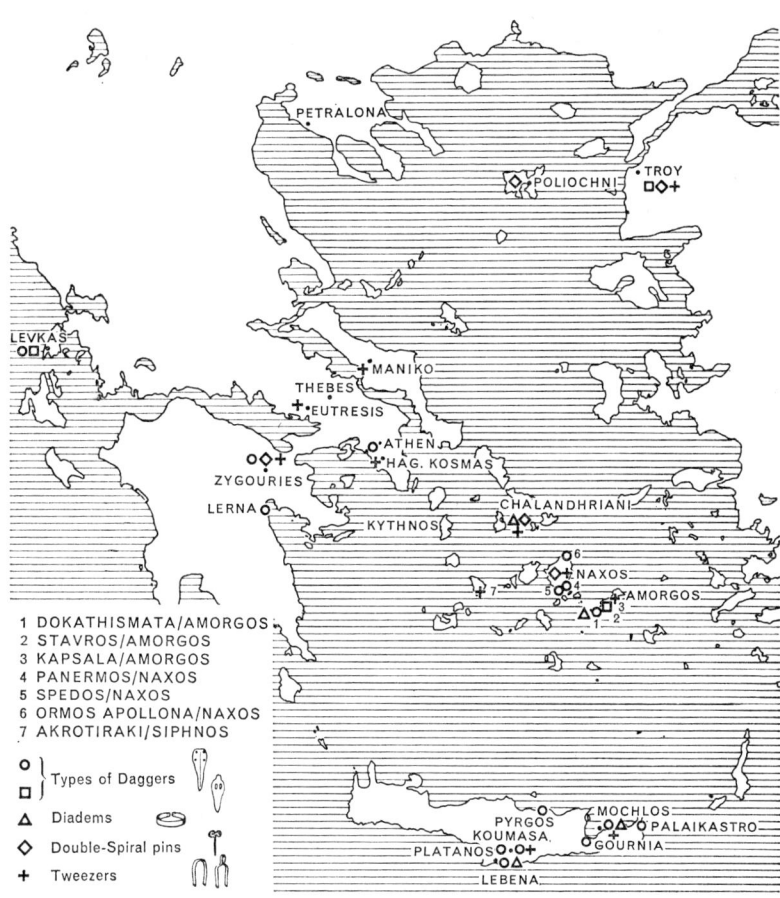

517–738: METAL

517 Fig. 21: Aegean, entire area. Map of distribution of selected Early Bronze Age metal types: daggers like *527* (Crete, Cyclades, Attica, the Argolid/Corinthia, Leukas); daggers like *537, 538, 542* (Cyclades, Leukas, Troy); diadems (Crete, Cyclades); ornamental pins with double-spiral head (Cyclades, Corinthia, Lemnos, Troy); tweezers (Crete, Cyclades, Attica, Corinthia, Boeotia, Euboea, Troy). – Renfrew, 'Cycladic Metallurgy and the Aegean Early Bronze Age', in *AJA*. 71 (1967), Pl. 11; cf. Branigan, 'Copper and Bronze Working in Early Bronze Age Crete', in *Studies in Mediterranean Archaeology*, 1968; and 'The Early Bronze Age Daggers of Crete', in *BSA*. 62 (1967), 211 ff.

518 Platanos, south Crete. Tholos tombs (EM III): Three
to copper daggers, lengths 21 cm., 15 cm. and 20.5 cm.
520 Arch. Mus., Herakleion. – Xanthoudides, *The Vaulted Tombs of Mesara* (1924); Pendlebury, *Arch. of Crete*, Pl. XI:3 d; Zervos, *Crète*, 170, Fig. 192; cf. also literature for *517*.

521 Tekes–Herakleion. Two copper or bronze daggers with
522 well-marked medial ribs (EM III); lengths 19.5 cm. and 20.5 cm. Arch. Mus., Herakleion. – Zervos, op. cit., 226, Figs. 290, 292.

523 Koumasa, south Crete. Three copper daggers (EM III);
to lengths 17 cm., 18.5 cm. and 17 cm. Arch. Mus., Hera-
525 kleion. – Pendlebury, 70 f., Pl. XI:3 c; Zervos, Fig. 291.

526 Amorgos, Cyclades. Seven Early Bronze Age daggers,
to Ashmolean Mus., Oxford. *526:* Inv. A E 252 (1893.60),
532 arsenical bronze, with weakly marked medial rib and five rivets; length 20 cm. – Renfrew, *AJA*. 71 (1967), 19, No. 59, Pl. 8. *527:* Inv. AE 239, arsenical bronze, weakly marked medial rib and four rivets, length 21.4 cm. – Loc. cit., No. 58. *528:* Inv. A E 240 (1898.17), copper, marked medial rib and four rivets, length 18.1 cm. – Loc. cit., No. 55. *529:* Inv. 1927.1360, copper, marked medial rib, four rivets, length 14.6 cm. – Loc. cit., No. 56. *530:* Inv. 1927.1359, arsenical bronze, with medial rib and four rivets, length 15.9 cm. – Loc. cit., No. 63. *531:* Inv. A E 230 (1893.61), copper with weakly marked medial rib and two rivets, length 17.1 cm. – Loc. cit., No. 57. *532:* Inv. A E 238, arsenical bronze, with strongly marked medial rib and four rivets, length 17.1 cm. – Loc. cit., No. 54.

533 Amorgos. Early Bronze Age daggers, Ashmolean Mus.,
to Oxford. *533:* Inv. 1927.1358, lead bronze, flat triang-
540 ular form, with four rivets, length 12.2 cm. – Renfrew, op. cit., 19, No. 62, Pl. 9. *534:* Inv. A E 229, flat triangle with four rivet holes; length 15.4 cm.; not analysed, probably copper. – Loc. cit., No. 61. *535:* Inv. A E 235, tinned bronze, with weakly marked medial rib, two rivets; length 16.6 cm. – Loc. cit., 20, No. 67, Pl. 9. – *536:* Inv. A E 234 (1893.64), copper,

flat, with four rivets; length 19.4 cm. – Loc. cit., 19 f., No. 66. *537:* Inv. A E 237 (1896.20), copper (5.1 % tin alloy), with medial rib and two slits; length 15.2 cm. – Loc. cit., 19, No. 47. *538:* Inv. 1927.1361, copper, with medial rib and two slits; length 19.5 cm. – Loc. cit., No. 48. *539:* Inv. A E 233, arsenical bronze, with two slits; length 20.5 cm. – Loc. cit., No. 52. *540:* Inv. A E 231, from Arkesine in Amorgos, arsenical bronze, thick blade, with short butt and four holes for attaching, length 23.5 cm. – Loc. cit., No. 53.

541 Amorgos. Two Early Bronze Age copper daggers with
542 bent tang, well marked medial rib, and two slits; lengths: 21.6 cm. and 19 cm. Nat. Mus., Athens. – Zervos, *Cycl.* 102, Fig. 103.

543 Kos, Asklepieion. Flat copper blade, from an Early Bronze Age pithos burial; Italian excavation 1940, Arch. Mus., Kos. Similar form: Riemann, *AA.*, 1937, 165 f., Fig. 23 upper (Poliochni, Lemnos).

544 Samos, Heraion. Copper or bronze blades of the third
to millennium B. C. *544:* Flat dagger with trapezoidal
548 tang; length 11 cm. *545:* Short, flat dagger blade, one rivet hole; length 6.5 cm.; found together with *544*. *546:* Slender knife blade, length 9.2 cm. *547:* Small razor; length 5 cm. *548:* Flat blade, short, broken-off tang, two rivet holes; length 18 cm. – Milojcic, *Samos* I (1961), 53, Nos. 4–8, Pl. 50:17–21 (drawing).

549 Chalandriani in Syros, the Cyclades. Early Cycladic copper knife with slightly curved back, rectangular butt, and two rivet holes, one rivet preserved; settlement find. Nat. Mus., Athens, 5244.

550 Amorgos, the Cyclades. Sickle knife, point missing, rectangular butt; length 23.5 cm.; tin-lead bronze. Ashmolean Mus., Oxford, Inv. 1927.1362. – Renfrew, *AJA.* 71 (1967), 19, No. 46, Pl. 9.

551 Fig. 22: Eutresis, Boeotia (House T; for its location, see Fig. 21). Copper knife (EH III), west Anatolian type, two rivet holes; length 16.5 cm. – Goldman, *Eutresis* (1931), 216, Fig. 286:7; Buchholz, *BJbV.* 7 (1967), 205, Fig. 3 e; p. 237, Analysis No. 86.

552 Fig. 22: Aila, Naxos. Early Cycladic saw, arsenical bronze; Nat. Mus., Athens, 6196. – Stephanos, *Congr. Internat. d'Arch., Athènes* (1905), 216; Buchholz, 203, note 78 and Fig. 3 f.

553 Teichos Dymaion, Achaea. Small flat axe with arm-like extensions (EH), copper or bronze; length 12.8 cm.; Arch. Mus., Patras, find No. 1451. Unusual for Greece in the third millennium; a similar one found at Tell Judaida (Maxwell-Hyslop, *Iraq* 15 [1953], 69 ff., Fig. 7:3). – Mastrokostas, *Prakt.* 1962. Pl. 138 d.

554 Kos, Seraglio. Bronze small flat axe with arm-like extensions, settlement find; length 15.3 cm., width 4.9 cm., LH II/III. Arch. Mus., Kos (Italian excavations 1940/43). Other axes of this type have been found at Lindos (Blinkenberg, *Lindos* I [1931], Pl. 3:27), Asine (LH III) and Dodona. – For the excavation of the Mycenaean settlement at Seraglio, cf. Hope Simpson, *Gazetteer and Atlas*, 1965, 187 f.

555 Kythnos, the Cyclades. Hoard find; three flat axes with
to holes and three slender, chisel-like flat axes, probably
560 copper. Brit. Mus., London. *555:* Inv. 66.2-7.1, length 19.8 cm. *556:* Inv. 66.2-7.2; length 19.9 cm. *557:* Inv. 66.2-7.3; length 17.1 cm. *558:* Inv. 66.2-7.4; length 21.7 cm. *559:* Inv. 66.2-7.5: length 18.6 cm. *560:* 66.2-7.6; length 16.2 cm. – Renfrew, *AJA.* 71 (1967), 7 ff., 19, Nos. 34–39, Pl. 6.

561 Fig. 22: Sesklo, Thessaly. Flat axe of copper; length
a, b 14.2 cm. (Chalcolithic). – Tsountas, *DS.* 351, Fig. 292; Buchholz, *BJbV.* 7 (1967), 205, Fig. 3 a.

562 Fig. 22: Eutresis, Boeotia. Two flat axes of copper and
563 lead bronze (6.1 % lead), lengths 13.3 cm. and 14.6 cm., EH II. – Goldman, *Eutresis* (1931), 217, Fig. 287:1,3 and p. 285; Buchholz, Fig. 3 b, c.

564 Paros and Amorgos, the Cyclades. Two chisel-like flat
565 axes, arsenical bronze and copper; lengths 12.8 cm. and 15.9 cm. Ashmolean Mus., Oxford, Inv. 1910.618 and 1927.1357. – Renfrew, op. cit., 19, No. 44 and 43, Pl. 9.

566 Naxos and Kythnos, the Cyclades. Three Early Bronze
to Age axe-adzes. *566 a, b:* Ashmolean Mus., Oxford, AE
568 86, tin bronze, oval shaft hole; length 14 cm. – Renfrew, 19, No. 41, Pl. 9. *567 a, b:* Ashmolean Mus., Oxford, AE 87, tin-lead bronze, oval shaft hole; length 17.9 cm. – Renfrew, No. 42, Pl. 9. *568 a, b:* Brit. Mus., London, 66.2-7.10, part of the Kythnos hoard (*555–560, 570, 572, 573*), probably copper, round shaft hole; length 11.6 cm. – Renfrew, 18, No. 30, Pl. 6.

569 Fig. 22: Eutresis, Boeotia. Axe-adze with round shaft
a, b hole, copper (EH II); length 9 cm. – Goldman, *Eutresis* (1931), 216 f., Fig. 287:2; Buchholz, *BJbV.* 7 (1967), 205, Fig. 3 d.

570 The Cyclades. Three Early Bronze Age axes with shaft
to holes. *570 a, b:* Brit. Mus., London, 66.2-7.7, part of
572 the Kythnos hoard (*555–560, 568, 572, 573*), probably bronze, round hole: length 15.8 cm. – Renfrew, 18, No. 31, Pl. 6. *571 a, b:* Ashmolean Mus., Oxford, 1927.2968; Amorgos, tin bronze, oval hole; length 14.5 cm. – Renfrew, 19, No. 40, Pl. 9. *572 a, b:* Brit. Mus., London, 66.2-7.8, part of the Kythnos hoard (cf. *570*), copper or bronze, round hole, knobbed neck; length 15.6 cm. – Renfrew, 18, No. 33, Pl. 6.

573 Kythnos. Hoard find (cf. *570*). Brit. Mus., London,
a, b 66.2-7.9; asymmetrical double axe, with round shaft hole, probably copper or bronze with weak tin alloy; length 10.6 cm. – Renfrew, 18, No. 32, Pl. 6; cf. Buchholz, *Zur Herkunft der kretischen Doppelaxt* (1957), 7, and Note 6.

574 Fig. 22: Niš, Yugoslavia. Double axe of copper,
a, b socket ring at upper end of round shaft hole; length c. 12.5 cm.; cf. similar examples: *575–577*, probably Chalcolithic-Early Bronze Age Balkan form. Considerably different are the South Aegean double axes (*716–738*); Nat. Mus., Belgrade, Inv. 7107. – Garasanin, *BerRGK.* 39 (1958), 49 f., Fig. 9:2 a, b.

575 Charadiatika, Leukas. Two copper double axes, curved
576 contour, flaring, rounded blades, round squat shaft hole, socket ring above; length 17 cm.; certainly Early Bronze Age (cf. *574*); Dörpfeld's view ('north Balkan form of historic period') is mistaken; Local mus., Nidri. – Dörpfeld, *Alt-Ithaka* 328 (see Suppl. 79 b for a similar example from Kechropoula-Palairos); Buchholz, *PZ.* 38 (1960), 41, Note 16 (others from Kertsch and the lower Danube).

577 Probably from Naxos. Copper double axe, wide type
a, b with oval hole and upper socket ring; length 18.1 cm. Nat. Mus., Copenhagen, 3159. – Buchholz, op. cit., 51, Fig. 6 a.

578 Leukas, Plain of Nidri; Family Tomb F, north-west of Steno. Burial 7 (1907): cist grave of stone slabs, containing a male skeleton in crouching position; among the grave goods: copper spearhead with special arrangement for attaching the shaft; length 18 cm. Local

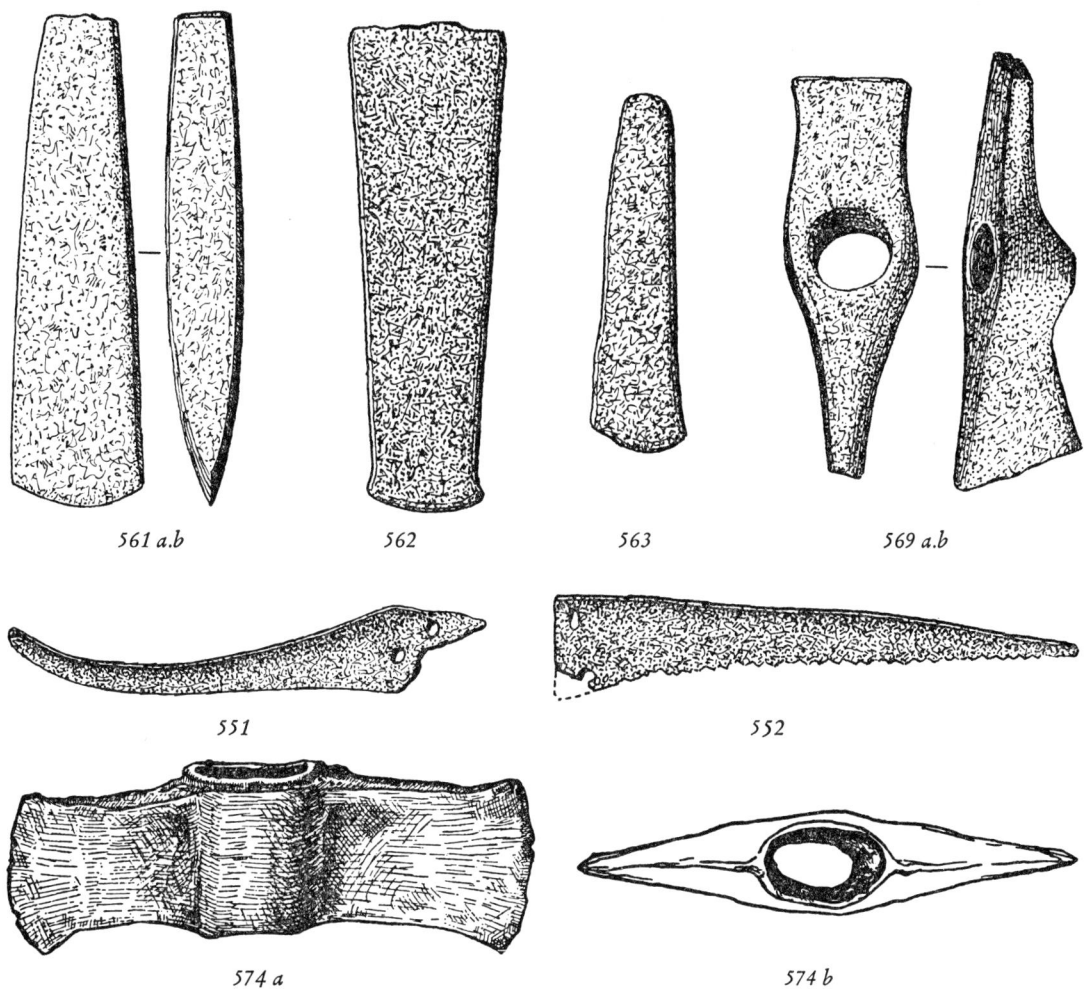

Fig. 22 Early Bronze Age implements of copper and arsenic bronze (574 a,b: Niš, Yugoslavia)

museum, Nidri. Similar type in Thessaly (Sesklo, where there was also a mould for such spearheads; Tsountas, *DS.* 334, 354, Pl. 4:10; for similar examples from Albania see Hammond, *Epirus* [1967], 337 f., Fig. 23 a–c); the latest possible chronological limit is given by an example from Shaft Grave IV at Mycenae (Karo, *SchGr.* 207, Pl. 102:463). – Karo, *AA.* 1908, 130, Fig. 1; Montelius, *La Grèce préclassique* I (1924), Pl. 15:13, 15; Dörpfeld, *Alt-Ithaka* (1927), 216, Suppl. 73, 16 and 74 a; id., *Alt-Olympia* I (1935), 307, Fig. 80.

579 Thebes, Boeotia. Two cast bronze lance-heads from a
580 Mycenaean chamber tomb near the town (1966/67). Lancet-shaped blade with wide medial rib; long, conical socket, with collar and holes for fastening below; lengths 18.5 cm. and 20 cm. Arch. Mus., Thebes, unpublished.

581 Messara, south Crete. Light bronze hunting spearhead, hammered socket with continuous slit. Galloping animal etched into the blade; length 11 cm. Metaxas Coll., Herakleion.

582 Archanes, Crete. Bronze socketed lancehead with rich spiral decoration. From the lower stratum of a tomb on Mount Phourni. Arch. Mus., Herakleion. – Sakellarakis, *Ergon.* 1966, 143, Fig. 166, and *Prakt.* 1966, 183, Fig. 153 a; Megaw, *JHS.* 87 (1967), Arch. Rep. 20, Fig. 35.

583 Perati, Attica. Chamber Tomb 123, metal grave goods:
to Socketed spearhead (length 22.5 cm.), tweezers (length
588 11.5 cm.), pin (length 13.1 cm.), 'razor' (length 21.5 cm.), chisel (length 16 cm.) and whetstone; LH III c. – Iakovidis, *Prakt.* 1961, 24, Pl. 8 a; and *Ergon* 1961, Fig. 16.

589 Ialysos, Rhodes. From Mycenaean chamber tombs: Six
to bronze lance- and spearheads of varying shapes and
594 sizes; slit, non-cast sockets, some terminating in a socket ring. Brit. Mus., London. – Walters, *Cat. Bronzes* 2, No. 20 (70.10–8.21, from Tomb 4; length 46.3 cm.; Furtwängler–Löschcke, *Myken. Vasen.* Pl. D 16). No. 24 (72.6–20.10; length 33 cm.; Furtwängler–Löschcke, Pl. D 14). No. 26 (72.6–20.12; length 25 cm; Furtwängler–Löschcke, Pl. D 15). No. 27, 2 (length 28.5 cm.). No. 19 (length 41.5 cm. Furtwängler–Löschcke, Pl. D 5). No 22 (length 32 cm.).

595 From the eastern Mediterranean, Cyprus or Rhodes. Bronze spearhead with marked medial rib and long slit socket; length 22.2 cm. Cypro-Mycenaean signs incised into one side of the blade. Nat. Mus., Copenhagen, Inv. 715. – Buchholz, *Minos* 3 (1954), 133 ff., Fig. 1.

596 Prosymna. Mycenaean necropolis at the Heraion of
597 Argos. Chamber Tombs 25 and 26: Two bronze lanceheads, LH II/III; lengths 25.7 cm. and 26.6 cm. Marked medial rib, socket with slit, *597* also with regular dents and a collar. Nat. Mus., Athens. – Blegen, *Prosymna*, 338 f., Pl.-Fig. 200:6; 214:4; 608.

598 Boeotia. From the region of Thebes. Bronze socketed spearhead, with marked medial rib and very curved outline; length 16.2 cm. LH III c; Ashmolean Mus., Oxford, Cat. No. 1918, 30. – Desborough, *Last Myc.*, Pl. 22 d; Snodgrass, *Early Greek Armour and Weapons* (1964), 119, No. 139; Hammond, *Epirus* 339, Fig. 24, 4; Catling, BSA. 63 (1968) 106.

599 Pylos. Palace, Room 60. Short bronze socketed head with well-marked medial rib and barbs; length *c*. 4 cm., LH III b. – Blegen–Rawson, *The Palace of Nestor at Pylos* I, 2 (1966), Pl.-Fig. 292; Buchholz, *JdI*. 77 (1962), 50, No. 14 a, Fig. 15 i.

600 Ialysos, Rhodes. Bronze arrowheads from Mycenaean
to tombs, excavated by Salzmann and Biliotti, 1868;
611 length 4–10.6 cm. Similar heads from Tomb L E 53 (Maiuri, *ASAtene* 6/7 [1923/24], 220, Fig. 142). Diagram of types: p. 48, Fig. 20. Brit. Mus., London. – Walters, *Cat. Bronzes* 3, Nos. 30–34 *(603:* 31; *608:* 30; *609:* Inv. No. 72.6–20.16); Buchholz, 49, No. 13 a–c.

612 Pylos. From a drain. Nine triangular arrowheads with
to deep concave base, made of thin bronze plate; length
620 *c.* 2 cm.; LH III a/b. – Blegen, *AJA*. 59 (1955). Pl. 25:8; Buchholz, 50, No. 14 b and Fig. 12 c–f.

621 Perati, Attica. Tomb 131, LH III c. Bronze fish-hook
622 with sharp barb, eyelet for cord broken off; preserved length 4.3 cm.; cf. fish-hooks from Crete: Metrop. Mus., New York: Richter, *Handbook of the Greek Coll.* (1953), Pl. 9 upper. *622:* Seventy-four net weights and ten fragments (of which forty-seven are illustrated); these are plummets grooved in such a way that net cords could be passed through the hollows. Important evidence of fishing in the Late Mycenaean Age. – Iakovidis, *Prakt.* 1961, 24, Pl. 8 b and *Ergon* 1961, 19, Fig. 19.

623 Dendra, the Argolid. Chamber Tomb 10: Silver spoon with repoussé ornament; found in a silver cup. Handle square in section, octagonal at the end, finial with three grooves; length 13 cm. Arch. Mus., Nauplia. – *AA*. 1940, 215 f., Fig. 52 right; Persson, *Dendra* II, 88 ff., No. 38, Figs. 99:4; 101.

624 Platanos, south Crete. Find from an EM circular tomb; copper spatula with widely flaring blade, hammered thin above and twisted into a spiral wire; length *c.* 7 cm. Arch. Mus., Herakleion. – Zervos, *Crète*, 170, Fig. 192.

625 Zapher Papoura, near Knossos. Shaft Grave 68: Bronze tweezers with wide arms; length 6.5 cm., LM II. Arch. Mus., Herakleion. – Evans, *Prehist. Tombs* 75, No. 68 d; Zervos, op. cit., 428, Fig. 698.

626 Zapher Papoura. Bronze mirror, diam. 18 cm., LM III a; probably from Chamber Tomb 14, in which were two other mirrors, not described; 12 mirrors in all in the necropolis; diam. 13–18 cm. Arch. Mus., Herakleion. – Evans, op. cit., 36.115.

627 Zapher Papoura. Shaft Grave 42: Two heavy cleavers
628 of the same shape and size, bronze, length 23. cm., LM III; this type of knife was in use from LM III a to LM III c; cf. Hood, BSA. 53/54 (1958/59) to Pl. 58 d (cleavers from chamber tombs of Knossos and Gypsades). Arch. Mus., Herakleion. – Evans, 60, No. 42 b, Fig. 63 and p. 115 f.; Zervos, 428, Fig. 698; Marinatos, *Arch. Hom. Lieferung B* (1967), 32, Pl. 5 d.

629 Dendra, the Argolid. Mycenaean chamber tomb 12:
630 Bronze knife with slightly curved back and four rivets in the haft; bronze mirror with two holes for attaching the handle made of perishable material, whose contour can be seen on the patina; 12.5 cm., LH II/III A. Arch. Mus., Nauplia. Verdelis, *AM*. 82 (1967), 44 ff. No. 6, 7 pl., 22 pp., 1–3 and 30, 3.

631 Kythera. Cave in the district of Leonti: Mycenaean grave find: Slim bronze knife with tang grip, LH III b (female grave goods, no No.: Bronze sewing needle, spindle whorl and beads). Nat. Mus., Athens, 1633. – Stais, *Delt*. 1 (1915), 191 ff. (*631* unpublished).

632 Dendra. Chamber Tomb 7: Bronze mirror with two
to holes for attaching the handle, traces of wooden handle
634 (diam. 11.6 cm.) and two cleavers similar to *627, 628;* blades considerably wider, grip very curved (both, length 25.5 cm.); LH III b (cf. also one example from Eleusis: Mylonas, *Prakt*. 1954, 52, Fig. 2). Arch. Mus., Nauplia. – Persson, *Dendra* II, 34 f., Fig. 35: 3–5.

635 Dendra. Chamber Tomb 8: Bronze knife with straight back, point missing, hilt with four rivets. Decorative groove parallel to the back; surviving length 24.5 cm.; LH II/III a. Arch. Mus., Nauplia. – Persson, op. cit., 44 f., Fig. 48:3.

636 Pylos, Messenia. Two bronze knives, LH III b. *636:*
637 Stratum above Rooms 89/90, straight back, handle with three rivets, pointed blade with deep blood channel; length 22.5 cm. Nat. Mus., Athens, 7794. *637:* Palace portico: back slightly bent, four rivet holes; length 21.8 cm., Nat. Mus., Athens, 7796. – Blegen–Rawson, *The Palace of Nestor at Pylos* I, 2 (1966), Pl. 274:5,6.

638 Perati, Attica. Chamber Tomb 38: Iron knife with rectangular grip, straight back and angled point, similar to a vine-dresser's knife; length, as restored, 17.3 cm.; LH III c. Important find, since it proves the use of iron in Late Mycenaean times for domestic utensils (cf. *675*) as well as for ornaments (cf. *1357*). Perhaps imported from Syria. – Iakovidis, *Delt*. 19 (1964), Chron. Pl. 90 e.

639 Fig. 23: Saw from Mallia, House Z beta, bronze, five rivet holes: length 1.41 m., LM I. – Deshayes–Dessenne, *Fouilles exécutées à Mallia* II (1959), 67, Pl. 21:1.

640 Fig. 23: Saw from Gournia, bronze, three rivet holes; length 45 cm.; ibid., another example and a fragment, LM. – Hawes, *Gournia*, 34, Pl. 4:1–3.

641 Fig. 23: Copper and bronze knives of the Late Bronze
to Age. 641: Hagia Triada; sickle-like knife, point miss-
664 ing, one rivet hole; length 18.2 cm.; Arch. Mus., Herakleion, 1240. – Deshayes, *Outils*, 147, No. 2787, Pls. 46:2 and 62:10. *642:* Knossos, slightly curved, two rivet holes, LM III c. – Hutchinson, BSA. 51 (1956), 79, Pl. 12 b. *643:* Karphi, Crete; sickle-like curved knife, one rivet hole; length 21.5 cm., sub-Minoan. – Davis, BSA. 38 (1937/38), 116, No. 232, Pl. 28:2. *644:* Mycenae, sickle-like curved knife, one rivet hole; length 20.2 cm., LH III. – Wace, BSA. 48 (1953), Pls. 2 b, and 49 (1954), 293, No. 405. *645:* Anthedon, Boeotia; curved, broken, one rivet hole; length 31 cm., LH III. – Rolfe, *AJA*. 6 (1890), 106, Pl. 15:12. *646:* Aspripetra Cave, Kos; slightly curved, three rivet holes, LH III. – Levi, *ASAtene* 8/9 (1925/26), 276, Fig. 61. *647:* Goulas, Crete, Strong cleaver-type knife with grip and

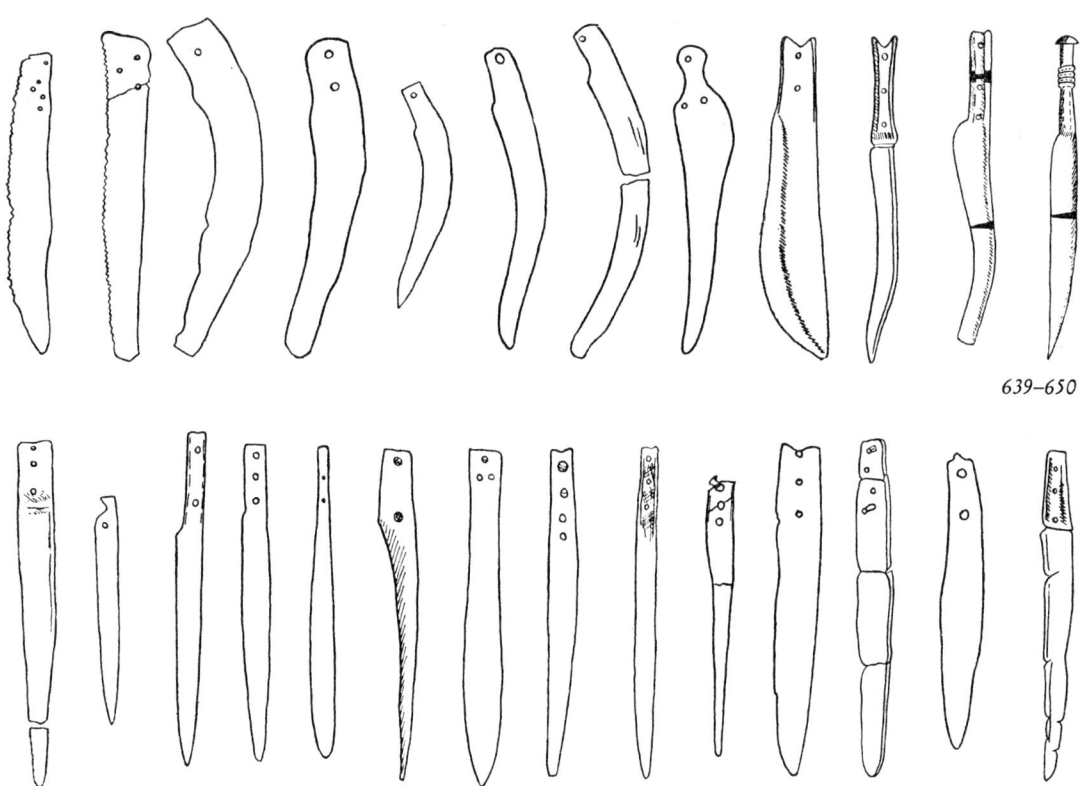

Fig. 23 Late Bronze Age saws and knives

two rivet holes; length 17.7 cm., LM III. – Sandars, *PPS*. 21 (1955), 195, Fig. 4:1. *648*: Cave of Psychro; slim blade, bent back, handle-flange with three rivet holes; length 21.1 cm., LM III a or later; Arch. Mus., Herakleion, 441. – Hogarth, *BSA*. 6 (1899/1900), 110, Fig. 43:2; Maraghiannis, *Ant. Crét.* I, Pl. 28:6; Boardman, *Cretan Coll.*, 22, Fig. 6 b. *649*: Mycenae; bent blade, handle-flange with three rivet holes, length 18.5 cm., LH III b. – Tsountas, *Ephem.* 1888, 173, Pl. 9:20. *650*: Mycenae; slim blade with straight cutting edge, solid handle; length 21 cm. – Sandars, *PPS.* 21 (1955), 194, Fig. 3:1. *651*: Knossos; point broken, three rivet holes, LM II–III. – Forsdyke, *BSA*. 28 (1926/27), 252 f., Fig. 6:4. *652*: Gazi, Crete; straight form, one rivet hole; length 17.5 cm., LM III a 2. – Chatzidakis, *Delt.* 4 (1918), 74, Fig. 17:6. *653*: Isopata, Crete; straight blade, handle-flange with two rivet holes, rivets with gold heads; length 30 cm., LM III a. Sandars, *PPS*. 21 (1955), 192, Fig. 2:1. *654*: Zapher Papoura, Crete; straight form, three rivet holes; two similar examples, lengths 20.4 cm. and 36 cm., LM III a/b. – Evans, *PTK*. 23, No. 4 b, 80, No. 80 b, Figs. 88, 113. *655*: Chania; elongated type, flaring towards the point, with two rivet holes; length 44 cm., LM III b. – Theophaneides, *Ephem.* 1948/49, Chron. 13, Fig. 23 b 1. *656*: Olous; blade very worn, two rivet holes; also two other smaller examples, LM III b/c. – Van Effenterre, *Nécropoles du Mirabello* (1948), 59, No. O 127–129, Pls. 22, 36. *657, 658*: Heraion of Argos; two examples of the straight type, with three or four rivet holes; lengths 25.8 cm. and 11.5 cm., LH III a/b. – Blegen, *Prosymna*, 344, 346, Figs. 299:1; 377:6. *659*: Dendra, the Argolid; straight slim type, handle-flange with three rivet holes; length 32 cm., LH III b. – Persson, *Dendra* I, 100, Pl. 32:5 lower. *660*: Argos; broken, very worn, three rivet holes, length 17.4 cm., LH III b. – Daux, *BCH*. 83 (1959), 771, Fig. 4 right. *661*: Palaiokastro, Kephalonia, wide, straight type with three rivet holes, blade broken, length 18 cm., LH III c. – Kyparissos, *Deltion* 5 (1919), 118, Fig. 35:1. *662*: Chalkis-Trypa, Euboea, straight type, four rivet holes, broken in several places; length 19 cm., LH III c 1. – Hankey, *BSA*. 47 (1952), 94, No. 536, Fig. 9. *663*: Metaxata, Crete; rounded type with two rivet holes; length 10 cm.; another similar example (length 8.5 cm.), LH III c 2. – Marinatos, *Ephem*. 1933, 93, Nos. A 9 and B. 10, Fig. 42. *664*: Troy VI, straight type, three rivet holes, broken in several places: length 23.3 cm. – Blegen, *Troy* III, 270, No. 37–780, Fig. 297. For further information on knife types in Crete, see Milojcic, *JbZMusMainz* 2 (1955), 153 ff.

665 Perati, Attica, Chamber Tomb 12, LH III c.: Knife with bird's-head handle cast in one piece, angled point like *638*, bronze; length 20.5 cm. – Iakovidis, *Prakt.*, 1954, 96 f., Fig. 6; and *Delt.* 19 (1964), Chron. 94, Pl. 90 a; Müller–Karpe, *Germania* 41 (1963), 9 ff. (corresponding mid-European types); Marinatos, *Arch. Hom., Lieferung B* (1967), 33, Fig. 12 a–c.

666 Zapher Papoura near Knossos. Chamber Tomb 80: Larnax burial; at the foot of the skeleton: heavy bronze cleaver with wide blade, curved cutting edge, and remains of the olive-wood hilt attached with seven

rivets; length of hilt 10 cm., length of blade 32 cm.; LM III (same type: 647). Arch. Mus., Herakleion. – Evans, *Prehist. Tombs*, 9, Fig. 4, p. 79, Fig. 88 and p. 114; Zervos, *Crète*, 439, Fig. 714.

667 Zapher Papoura. Two bronze daggers; Arch. Mus.,
668 Herakleion. *667*: Chamber Tomb 86: 'Peschiera dagger', slender leaf-shaped blade with continuous decorative grooves, both cutting edges curving inwards in the centre, one rivet at the upper end of the blade; cast grip with high flanges; entire length 23 cm., LM I/II. – Evans, *Prehist. Tombs*, 81 f., Fig. 90 and p. 113 f.; Zervos, op. cit., 439, Fig. 718; Milojcic, *JbZMusMainz* 2 (1955), 158, Fig. 2:1. *668*: Chamber Tomb 95; triangular blade with angular shoulders and handle-flange cast in one piece, and wide flaring pommel, and moulded rims, three rivets; length 37 cm., LM III b. – Evans, op. cit., 84 f., Fig. 94; Zervos, op. cit., 438, Fig. 715; Müller–Karpe, *Germania* 40 (1962), 270, Fig. 7:5.

669 Perati, Chamber Tomb 38: Bronze dagger with parallel cutting edges, decorative grooves in the middle and angular shoulders. Blade and hilt cast in one piece, the latter with wide pommel, flanged borders which overlap on to the blade, and six rivets; LH III c.

670 Dendra, the Argolid. Chamber Tomb 7: Bronze dagger, similar to *669*, but with wider blade and round shoulders; length 38 cm., LH III. Arch. Mus., Nauplia. – Persson, *Dendra* II, 34 f., Fig. 35:1.

671 Oxylithos–Paralia, Euboea. Bronze dagger with cast hilt with flanged rim broken off at the top, and round angles, large rivets and triangular, flat blade. The rather long, raised moulding in the middle of the blade at the end of the hilt covering is unusual; length 29 cm., LH II/III a. Probably from a tholos tomb. School Coll., Enoria (1964). – Sackett, *BSA*. 61 (1966), 74, Pl. 19 h.

672 Zapher Papoura. Chamber Tomb 14, 'Tomb of the Tripod Hearth' (other objects found here: *626, 1095 a to o*): pointed bronze dagger with medial rib, ivory covering of the hilt well preserved, as is the ivory pommel, eight decorative rivets; length 42 cm., LM III. Arch. Mus., Herakleion. – Evans, *Prehist. Tombs* 43, Fig. 39 a, b, Pl. 91:109; Zervos, *Crète*, 439, Fig. 716.

673 Dendra, the Argolid. Chamber Tomb 8: Two very
674 corroded bronze dagger blades, each with three silver rivets; lengths 24.5 cm., and 16.5 cm., LH II. Arch. Mus., Nauplia. – Persson, *Dendra* II, 43 ff., Fig. 48:1,2.

675 Perati. Chamber Tomb 28; Triangular iron dagger blade, preserved length 10.7 cm.; LH III c. Iron weapons are very rare in the Late Bronze Age (cf. *638* and iron knife with bronze rivets, Knossos–Gypsades, Tomb VII: Hood, *BSA*. 53/54 [1958/59], 248, No. VII, 12, Fig. 32, Pl. 60 a; also fragment of a sickle, Tiryns: Karo, *AM*. 55 [1930], 135 f., Fig. 6, and iron knife, Vrokastro, Chamber Tomb V: Hall, *Vrokastro*, 151, Pl. 21 a). – Iakovidis, *Prakt*. 1954, 98, Fig. 10.

676 Fig. 24: Hagia Triada, south Crete. Annexe of the small tholos: Bronze dagger with flanges on the shoulders, three rivets at the base of the blade and short, broken off handle-flange: length 32 cm., MM I/II. Arch. Mus., Herakleion, – Evans, *PM*. I, 195, Fig. 142 c; Sandars, *AJA*. 65 (1961), 22, Pl. 18:2.

677 Fig. 24: Mycenae, Grave Circle A, Shaft Grave VI: Bronze rapier with tang, severely oxidized, broken in several places: length 41 cm.; wooden haft attached with six gold plated rivets. LH I; Nat. Mus., Athens. – Karo, *SchGr*. 161, No. 905, Pl. 95; our drawing after: Sandars, Pl. 18:5 (one rivet missing).

678 Fig. 24: Kalbaki, Epiros. Bronze dagger with tang, hilt repaired in antiquity; length 35.2 cm.; found in a cist grave, LH III b; Arch. Mus., Johannina, – Dakaris, *Ephem*. 1958, 123 ff., Sandars, *AJA*. 67 (1963), 137, 151, Pl. 25:35; see also rapier of the same type from Epiros: Dakaris, *Delt*. 18 (1963), Chron. 153, Fig. 4, Pl. 187 e.

679 Fig. 24: Kastritsa near Johannina, Epiros. Bronze dagger with tang; length 38.5 cm., LH III b/c; Arch. Mus., Johannina. – Dakaris, *PPS*. 33 (1967), 30 ff., Pl. 1:2; Megaw, *JHS*. 87 (1967), Arch. Rep. 13 f., Fig. 21.

680 Babes near Olympia. Destroyed LH I tomb; the pottery is preserved in the museum at Olympia: Flat bronze dagger blade of slender pointed form with wide butt and four rivet holes (three rivets preserved), LH I, isolated find. New Museum, Olympia, Inv. BE 866. – Mentioned by Hood in *JHS*. 80 (1960), Arch. Rep. 11.

681 Mycenae. Grave Circle A, Shaft Grave V: Bronze dagger blade with pictorial inlays in electrum and niello; wild cats or leopards chasings ducks in a papyrus swamp by a winding stream with fish; length 16 cm., LH I; Nat. Mus., Athens. – Karo, *SchGr*. 138, No. 765, Pls. 93, 94; Perrot–Chipiez, VI, Pl. 17:1 (watercolour); Marinatos–Hirmer, Col. Pls. 35 above and 37 below.

682 Mycenae. Grave Circle A, Shaft Grave IV: Bronze dagger blade, severely eaten away at the edges, point broken off, four gold rivets. Decorative panels inlaid on both sides in dark non-ferrous metal alloy; figures cut from sheets of different electrum alloys hammered cold into roughened areas of the panels: lion hunt, animated scene. Reverse: five gazelles, pursued by a lion; length 23.8 cm., LH I; Nat. Mus., Athens. – Karo, *SchGr*., 95 ff., No. 394, Pls. 92, 93, 94; Perrot–Chipiez, VI, Pl. 18:3,4 (watercolour); Marinatos–Hirmer, Col. Pls. 35 middle and 36 lower; Mylonas, *Myc. and the Myc. Age*, Pl.-Fig. 140 (excellent photograph).

683 Mycenae. Grave Circle A, Shaft Grave IV: Bronze dagger blade, severely eaten away, only a remnant of the hilt survives and a large gold rivet. Ornamental panels: frieze of galloping lions, technique as in *682*; length 21.4 cm., LH I; Nat. Mus., Athens. – Karo, *SchGr*. 97, No. 395, Pls. 92, 93; Perrot–Chipiez VI, Pl. 19:6 (watercolour); Marinatos–Hirmer, Col. Pls. 35 lower and 37 upper.

684 Pylos. Tholos tomb: Bronze dagger with golden hilt with rich spiral decoration. Ornamental panels in gold and niello inlay: hunting leopards; length 32 cm., c. 1500 B. C. – Marinatos–Hirmer, Pl. 171 middle and lower, Col. Pl. 38 middle.

685 Mycenae. Grave Circle A, Shaft Grave V; Bronze dagger blade, very oxidized, one rivet at the top with gold-plated head. On both sides thin gold ornamental panel with engraved pattern filled with niello: elaborate spiral network with dot-rosettes; length 24.3 cm., LH I; Nat. Mus., Athens. Karo, *SchGr*, 135, No. 744, Pls. 91, 92; Perrot–Chipiez, VI (1894), Pl. 17:2 (watercolour); Marinatos–Hirmer, Pl. 170.

686 Mycenae. Grave Circle A, Shaft Grave IV: Bronze sword blade (detail; two fragments and half of the hilt survive). Frieze of large Minoan shields, framed on

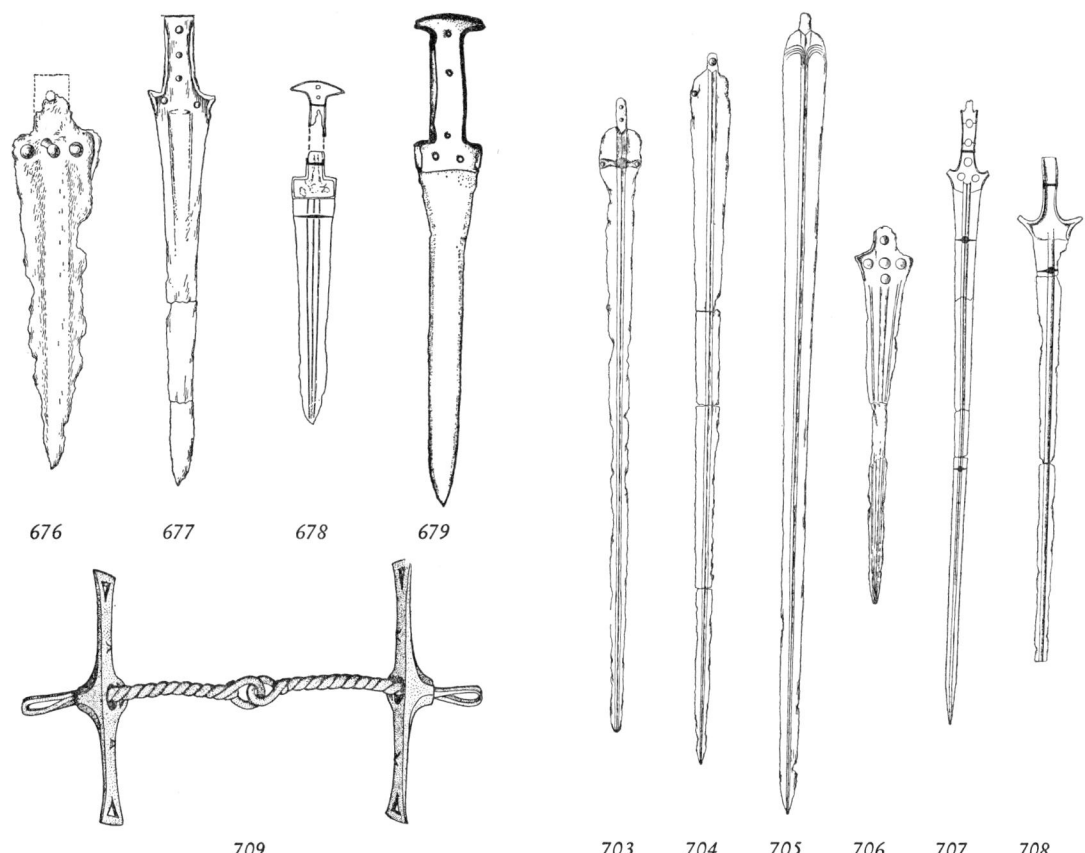

Fig. 24 Aegean bronze daggers and swords; cross bridoon from Mycenae

both sides by spiral bands; decoration formerly gilt: length 38.5 cm., LH I; Nat. Mus., Athens. – Karo, SchGr. 99, No. 404, Pl. 85.

687 Prosymna, the Argolid. Chamber Tomb 14: Bronze dagger blade with three large rivets at the upper end. In the middle of the blade an inlaid dolphin in gold, silver and niello; length 18.5 cm., LH II (c. 1450 B. C.), Nat. Mus., Athens. – Blegen, *Prosymna* I, 330 f., No. 1, Pl. 20 upper; Marinatos-Hirmer, Col. Pl. 38 lower.

688 Mycenae. Grave circle A, Shaft Grave V: Gold hilt of a much damaged bronze sword (surviving length 46 cm.). Hilt with hexagonal section consists of two symmetrical gold plates with rich ornament (length 11.8 cm.); pommel not illustrated (Karo, Nos. 690, 763). The upper gilt panelling of the sheath is preserved (length 12.2 cm.). Nat. Mus., Athens, – Karo, SchGr. 123, Nos. 634, 635, Pls. 83, 84.

689 Staphylos, Skopelos. From a severely damaged shaft grave: Gold sword hilt with pommel and rich engraving; ornaments arranged in zones; length of hilt incl. pommel: 24 cm., diam. of pommel: 13.8 cm.; LH II (c. 1500 B. C.). Nat. Mus., Athens. – Bakalakis, *6. internat. Kongress f. Archäologie, Berlin 1939* (1940), 309 ff., Pl. 17; Marinatos-Hirmer, Pls. 172, 173.

690 Zapher Papoura, near Knossos. 'Chieftain's Grave',
691 Shaft Grave No. 36 (a second sword near the corpse: 700): Golden hilt of a bronze rapier (length 61 cm.) with agate pommel; five large gold-plated rivets.

Engraving on the gold casing: lions and wild goats rushing impetuously. Rows of double spirals on medial rib of bronze blade and on flanges of tang. The blade shows impressions of weaving, probably from the lining of the sheath. *691:* like *690*, but pommel in gold; its lower part and the gold plate of the hilt covered with engraved spiral network; from a different burial. LM II; Arch. Mus., Herakleion. – Evans, *Prehist. Tombs*, 57 f., Figs. 59 and 110 b; Zervos, *Crète*, 437, Figs. 712, 713; Marinatos-Hirmer, Pls. 112, 113, and p. 98 f., Fig. 19.

692 Zapher Papoura. From Shaft Graves 42 and 44: Two
693 bronze tanged swords; lengths 58.5 cm. and 53 cm. Only the gold casing survives of the pommel of the first together with the gold-plated rivets; the second has round shoulders and a short, narrow tang: both with marked medial rib (*693* and *707* beside a skeleton). LH II/III a; Arch. Mus., Herakleion. – Evans, 60, 62, 107 ff., Fig. 111, Pl. 91:109; Zervos, 439, Fig. 717; Müller-Karpe, *Germania* 40 (1962), 265, Fig. 4:1.

694 Dendra, the Argolid. Chamber Tomb 7: Bronze rapier or dagger, blade and haft without shoulder angle, two ornamental grooves in middle of blade, five rivets; length 41 cm. (from the same tomb: 632–634, 670, 1112, 1113). LH III a/b; Arch. Mus., Nauplia. – Persson, *Dendra* II, 34 f., Fig. 35:2.

695 Corcyra, no precise details on site. Slender, pointed rapier or dagger with round shoulders, weak medial rib and very narrow, broken off tang (cf. *693*); length

36.8 cm.; LH III; Brit. Mus., London (from the Woodhouse Coll. in 1868). – Walters, *Cat. Bronzes*, 344, No. 2752; Hammond, *Epirus* (1967), pl. 20 m.

696 Skutari, Albania. Bronze sword with tang and sloping shoulders similar to swords 697 and 698 from Tiryns; length 57 cm., LH III. For Mycenaean swords and daggers outside Greece, cf. 699. Brit. Mus., London. – Walters, *Cat. Bronzes*, 344, No. 2754; Undset, *ZfE.* 22 (1890), 16, Fig. 26.

697 Tiryns. Hoard find, 1915: Two bronze swords with
698 tang and sloping shoulders, LH III b/c; Nat. Mus., Athens, 6228. 697: very oxidized, tang missing, otherwise intact; preserved length 55 cm. 698: Broken in several places, point missing, hilt plate with curved contour, length 81.3 cm. - Karo, *AM.* 55 (1930), 135, Suppl. 37. For the spread of this type in the eastern Aegean cf. Kos–Langada. Tomb 21: Morricone, *ASAtene* 27/28 (1965/66), 139 f., Figs. 123, 124.

699 Pelynt, Cornwall, England. Fragment of a Mycenaean dagger or rapier with tang, angular shoulders and flanged rim, bronze; preserved length 11 cm., LH III a/b. Noteworthy as an Aegean import, probably connected with the tin trade. County Museum, Truro (acquired: 1840/1850). Imported Mycenaean swords are slightly more frequent in the Balkans (list in Garašanin, *BerRGK.* 39 [1958], 124 f. – Childe, *PPS.* 17 (1951), 95, Pl. 2; Buchholz, *PZ.* 38 (1960), 55, Fig. 8 c; Sandars, *AJA.* 67 (1963), 152, Pls. 25, 44.

700 Zapher Papoura, near Knossos. 'Chieftain's Grave'. Shaft Grave 36 (cf. also 690): Bronze sword with tang and ivory pommel, horn-like shoulders and five large, gold-plated rivets: length 94.5 cm.; LM II/III a; Arch. Mus., Herakleion. – Evans, *Prehist. Tombs*, 55 ff., No. 36 h, Fig. 58, Pl. 91:109; Zervos, *Crète*, 436, Figs. 710, 711 right.

701 Mouliana, Crete. Tomb A: Bronze sword with tang; length 58.5 cm.; LM III b/c; Arch. Mus., Herakleion. – Xanthoudides, *Ephem.* 1904, 46 ff.; Zervos, 436, Fig. 709; Müller-Karpe, *Germania* 40 (1962), 266, Fig. 5:1. For an entirely similar, but already Protogeometric form, cf. Theatre of Elis, Tomb 1: Yalouris, *Ergon* 1963, 119, Fig. 124.

702 Perati, Attica. Chamber Tomb 12: Bronze sword with tang and curved hand guards, ornamental grooves parallel to the edges of the blade; considerable parts of the ivory casing of the hilt survive; LH III c. – Iakovidis, *Delt.* 19 (1964), Chron. 94, Pl. 90 b.

703 p. 57, Fig. 24: Mallia, Crete, earlier palace: Bronze long sword with round shoulders, medial rib and small, narrow tang with two rivet holes; length 81 cm.; 87.8 %, copper, 10.7 %, tin; MM II; Arch. Mus., Herakleion, 2284. – Chapouthier, *Et. Crét.* V (1938): Sandars, *AJA.* 65 (1961), 17, Pl. 17:1.

704 p. 57, Fig. 24: Kakovatos, west Peloponnese. Tholos Tomb B: Bronze sword like 703, broken in several places; ridged medial rib, rivets with gilt heads; length 92 cm., LH II a; Nat. Mus., Athens. – Müller, *AM.* 34 (1909), 298 f., Fig. 14; Sandars, 26, Fig. 17:2.

705 p. 57, Fig. 24: Arkalochori, Crete. Sacred cave: Bronze sword like 703; length c. 100 cm., MM III b; all the swords from this cave are without hilts, i. e. not yet ready for use. Arch. Mus., Herakleion. – Marinatos, *AA.* 1935, 249 f., Fig. 5; and *Kadmos* 1 (1962), 87 ff.; Evans, *PM.* IV Suppl. Pl. 68; Sandars, 17, Pl. 17:3.

706 p. 57, Fig. 24: Izmir, west Turkey. Found near the imperial forum; no Bronze Age context: Bronze sword with tang, top now missing and blade much damaged, marked central rib, four rivets preserved; surviving length 48 cm., LH III. Museum depot, Izmir. – Bittel, *AA.* 1943, 202 ff., Fig. 3; Sandars, op. cit., 27 f., Pl. 19:7.

707 p. 57, Fig. 24: Zapher Papoura, near Knossos, Crete. Shaft Grave 44: Bronze tanged sword with horn-like angular shoulders, broken in several places; length 91.3 cm., LM II/III a. Also near the skeleton: sword 693. Ashmolean Mus., Oxford, Inv. AE 462. – Evans, *Prehist. Tombs* 62, Fig. 66 and p. 106, Fig. 110 b, Pl. 91:109; Sandars, *AJA.* 67 (1963), 144, Pl. 21:1.

708 p. 57, Fig. 24: Knossos. 'Tomb of Acropolis', southwest of the aqueduct: Bronze tanged sword with weak central rib and hornlike angular shoulders, broken in several places; surviving length 69.4 cm., LM I/II. Ashmolean Mus., Oxford, Inv. AE 489. – Evans, *PM.* IV, 850, Fig. 832; Sandars, op. cit., 146, Pl. 23:12.

709 p. 57, Fig. 24: Mycenae. Bronze snaffle with bipartite twisted bit, part of the Tsountas hoard; LH III b. Nat. Mus., Athens, 2553. – Tsountas, *Ephem.* 1891, 25 ff.; Reichel, *Über Homerische Waffen*[2] (1901), 142, Fig. 90; Yalouris, *MusHelv.* 7 (1950), 30; Müller–Karpe, *JdI.* 77 (1962), 67, 115, Fig. 36 (badly drawn); Wiesner, *Arch. Hom., Lieferung F* (1968), 56 f., Fig. 14 a; Sandars, 135 f., Pl. 26:48.

710 Hagios Johannis, near Knossos. Warrior's Tomb 5: Conical helmet of sheet bronze, reconstructed from more than a hundred fragments; crowned by a moulded knob (Kymbachos), cheek-pieces, curved in front, rivetted to the helmet; holes for attaching a felt or leather lining: height 38.6 cm., LM II (1450–1425 B. C.); Arch. Mus., Herakleion. – Hood–De Jong, *BSA.* 47 (1952), 256 f., Pl. 50; Marinatos–Hirmer, Pl. 113 below; Hutchinson, *Prehistoric Crete* (1962), 255, Fig. 47; Snodgrass, *Arms and Armour of the Greeks* (1967), Pl.-Fig. 7; cf. bronze cheek-piece from LH III b tomb of Ialysos, Rhodes: Kukahn, *Der griechische Helm* (1936), 2; Müller–Karpe, *Germania* 40 (1962), 271. Pointed conical upper part of helmet from Cyprus: *1882*.

711 Kallithea, Achaea. Chamber Tomb A: Pair of bronze greaves, reconstructed from many fragments, hammered, divided up into sections by means of embossed fillets; with eyelets for threading bronze wires for attachment; height 25.5 cm., LH III c (cf. corresponding finds from Cyprus: *1880, 1881*), Arch. Mus., Patras. – Yalouris, *AM.* 75 (1960), 42 ff., Suppl. 28; Daux, *BCH.* 78 (1954), 124 f., Fig. 25; Van Merhart, *BerRGK.* 37/38 (1956/57), 113, Fig. 7:4; Hampe, *Gymnasium* 63 (1956), 14, Pl. 8 b; Vermeule, *Archaeology* 13 (1960), 71, Fig. 8, id., *AJA.* 64 (1960), 13, No. 48, Pl. 5, 35; Müller–Karpe, 275 f.

712 Dendra. 'Panoply Tomb' (Tomb 12, excavations 1960, 1962, 1963: Verdelis and Åström): Heavy bronze cuirass, consisting of neck guard, corslet for chest and back, shoulder-pieces and articulated protection for the lower body, LH II. Greaves also seem to have been found here. A 'helmet' (LH I/II: *AA.* 1940, 215 f., Figs. 49, 50; Persson, *Dendra* II, 43, 119 f.) dug up in Dendra earlier, now proves to be a shoulder-piece. Arch. Mus., Nauplia. – Verdelis, *Ephem.* (1957), Chron. 15 ff. and *Pepragmena tou 2. Diethnous Kretologikou Synedriou* I (1968, mod. Gk.), 128 ff., Pls. 7, 8; Van-

derpool, *AJA.* 67 (1963), 280 f., Pls. 62 and 63:8; Mylonas, *Myc. and the Myc. Age,* Pl.-Fig. 145; Snodgrass, Pl.-Fig. 9; Verdelis, *AM.* 82 (1967), I, 2, 2; 4–17 and 21.

713 Crete. Site unknown: Heavy double adze with round hole and protruding socket, bronze; length 33 cm., MM III/LM I. Arch. Mus., Herakleion, 1712. – Deshayes, *Outils* 109, No. 2092, Pl. 60:7.

714 Knossos, Crete. Two heavy double adzes like *713;*
a, b bronze, round hole and protruding socket; length *c.* 33
and cm., MM III/LM I. Ashmolean Mus., Oxford, Inv.
715 1910. 181 and 1924.12. – Catling, *Cypriot Bronzework*
a, b in the Myc. Age (1964), 90, Note 5, Pl. 7 d, e.

716 Fig. 25: Said to come from the region of Knossos: Bronze double axe, sheet metal, handle notched, broken off; length 9.4 cm., LM II/III. Formerly Giamalakis Coll., now Arch. Mus., Herakleion. – Buchholz, *Zur Herkunft der kret. Doppelaxt* (1959), 38, No. 15 j, Pl. 4 m. For much earlier double axes of a different type, see *574–577.* For their votive significance, cf. Nilsson, *Geschichte der griechischen Religion* I³ (1967), 275 ff.

717 Fig. 25: Said to come from Knossos; no more precise details. Solid cast bronze double axe with round shaft hole, length 18 cm., MM III–LM II. Noteworthy for the helmets engraved on both sides (cf. *510*). Formerly Giamalakis Coll., now Arch. Mus., Herakleion, Inv. 371. – Xenaki-Sakellariou, *BCH.* 77 (1953), 46 ff., Figs. 1–3; Deonna, *BCH.* 77 (1953), 46 ff., Figs. 1–3; Deonna, *BCH.* 78 (1954), 253 ff.; Buchholz, No. 15 h, Pl. 4 l; Borchhardt, *Homerische Helme* (1972), 148, Pl. 4, Nos. 5 and 6.

718 Said to be from Hagia Triada, Crete. Solid cast bronze double axe with curving cutting edges and oval shaft hole; length 16.1 cm., LM; Mus. f. Kunst u. Gewerbe, Hamburg, Inv. 1928. 47. – v. Mercklin, *AA* 1928, 280, Fig. 9; Buchholz, 36, No. 8 e, Pl. 3 b.

719 Vorou Monophatziou, Crete. Solid cast bronze double
a, b axe with round shaft hole; length 20.4 cm. Symbolic engravings on both sides. Arch. Mus., Herakleion, 2504. – Buchholz, *Kadmos* I (1962), 166 ff.; Fig. 1 a, b (Small, op. cit. 5 [1966], 103 ff. used weak arguments against my interpretation).

720 Probably from Pinakiano Kardamoutsa, Crete. Solid
a, b cast bronze double axe with round shaft hole; length *c.* 20 cm.; LM I. Noteworthy for the Linear A signs incised on either side of the hole. Brit. Mus., London, 1954.10–20.1. – Pope, *BSA.* 51 (1956), 132 ff., Fig. 1 a, Pl. 36 a, b; Buchholz, *Zur Herkunft der kret. Doppelaxt* (1959), 42, No. 27.

721 Seraglio, Kos. Settlement find: Bronze, solid cast
a, b double axe with oval shaft hole; length 14.8 cm., highly oxidized; LH III (Italian excavations 1940–43). Arch. Mus., Kos. – Buchholz, op. cit., 47, No. 10, Pl. 10 a. cf. *554* (bibliography on the excavation).

722 Kato Zakro, east Crete. Bronze, originally gilt, richly

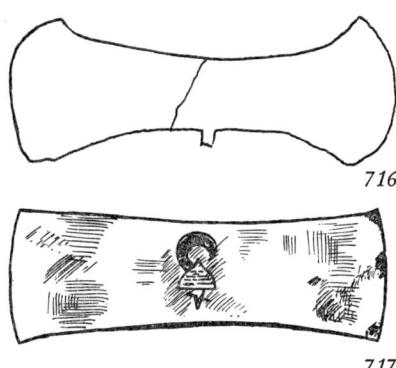

Fig. 25   Cretan double axes, bronze

decorated double axe with double-edged blades on either side; length 45 cm.; LM II, also a second, similar example. Arch. Mus., Herakleion. – Platon, *Prakt.* 1963, 182 f., Pl. 151 c; id., *Archaeologia Mundi: Crete* (1966), Fig. 53; Willetts, *Everyday Life in Ancient Crete* (1969), 165, Fig. 97.

723 Cave of Psychro, Crete. Twelve copper and bronze
to double axes; except for *732* and *733* (solid cast) they
734 are votive offerings not meant for practical use; thin sheet metal, length of illustrated examples: 4.6–18.2 cm., MM III/LM I; Ashmolean Mus., Oxford. – Buchholz, op. cit., 42 f., No. 29 a, b; Boardman, *The Cretan Coll. in Oxford* (1961), 42 ff., Fig. 19, Pl. 14:198, 199, 201; 15:200, 202–206, 208, 209; Milojcic, *JbZMusMainz* 2 (1955), 164, Fig. 3:12 (*730* wrongly identified as razor).

735 Galaxidi, near Delphi. Bronze double axe with very narrow centre, not a form for practical use; length 12 cm.; probably imported from Crete, LM III. Ontario Mus., Toronto, 918.3.109. – *Bull. Royal Ontario Mus.* 11 (March 1932), 6 f., Fig. 7.

736 Psorolithi, 2.5 km. east of Kalydon, Aetolia. Two
737 solid cast double axes; *736:* length 9.4 cm.; *737:* only half remains (length 7.7 cm.), probably LH III. From a hoard, which also includes flat axes, sickle blades, fragment of a dagger, spearhead and tripod. Arch. Mus., Agrinion, Inv. X 78 and 79. Also a chance find there from the neighbouring Chalkis: large solid cast double axe (Inv. X 146). – Mastrokostas, *Delt.* 20 (1965), Chron. 343 f., Pl. 410.

738 Cape Gelidonya, south Turkey. Underwater find, be-
a, b longing to the cargo of a ship wrecked *c.* 1200 B. C.: solid cast bronze double axe with oval shaft hole; length 17.5 cm. Mus., Bodrum. – Bass, *Cape Gelidonya-A Bronze Age Shipwreck* (1967), 94 ff., No. B 101, Figs. 107, 108. Aegean double axes spread to Rhodes, Kos *(721),* Lykia, Cyprus and Ras Shamra by way of the sea.

739–752: INGOTS (distribution map: p. 60, Fig. 26)

739 Kato Zakro, east Crete. Building G, Room E: 6 copper
to ingots in 'cushion form'. LM I. Early form of the so-
744 called 'Keftiu' ingots, i.e. the specifically Aegean Cypriot form of raw copper ready for delivery, as found in Egyptian representations of tribute, together with Minoan metal vessels (Fig. 34, *1100–1103*). Extremely important for information on the copper trade in the second millenium B.C. (cf. map Fig. 26). – Platon, *Archaeology* 16 (1963), 273; Buchholz, *Schweizer Münzblätter* 16, Sheet 62 (1966), 64, No. 16, Fig. 4.

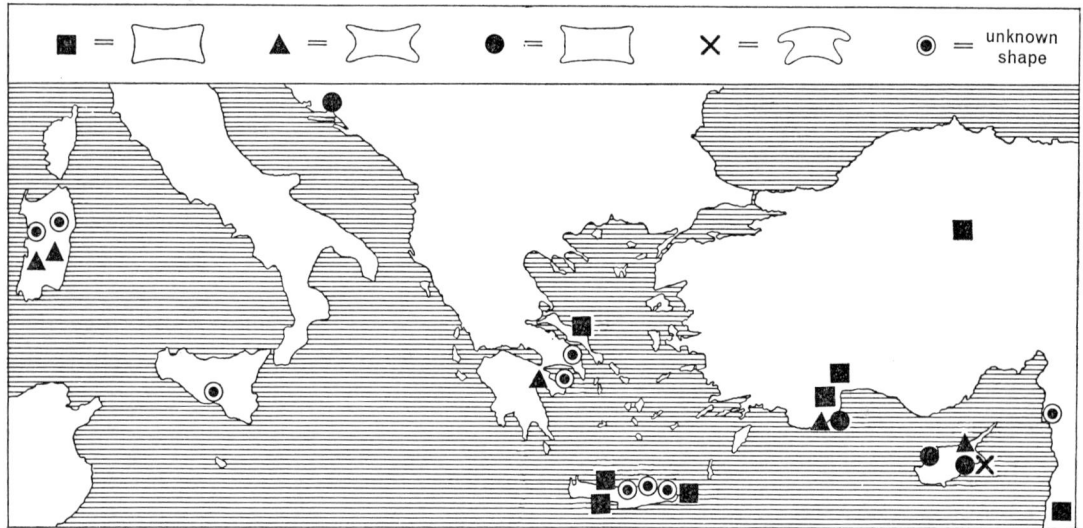

Fig. 26 Distribution of Eastern Mediterranean ingots; cf. *739–752 b* and *1898, 1899*

For ingots in general see in particular Buchholz, *PZ.* 37 (1959), 1 ff., and *Minoica, Festschrift zum 80. Geburtstag von J. Sundwall* (1958), 92 ff. Similar ingots found in great number in the Gelidonya shipwreck (cf. *738*).

745 to 749 Hagia Triada, south Crete. Hoard in the magazines of the palace: Nineteen copper ingots like *739–744*; weight 27–32 kg. LM. I. *745–748* show deeply cut marks (script-like signs). *749* shows a group of these ingots, *747* and *748* in front. Arch. Mus., Herakleion, Inv. 721–725, 726 a–m. – Buchholz, *PZ.* 37 (1959), 32 ff., Nos. 16–34, Pl. 4 and *Schweizer Münzblätter* 16, No. 62 (1966), 63 f., No. 11, Fig. 2 a. Analyses of the metal: id., *BJbV.* 7 (1967), 236 f., Nos. 60–76. *749* after Matz: *Kreta-Mykene-Troja*, Pl. 74 below.

750 751 From the sea near Kyme, Euboea. Two of seventeen copper ingots and two fragments (like *739–749*); weight: 5.35–17.64 kg. Surface very corroded by the sea water, LH I. Mus., Athens, Inv. 13051. – Svoronos, *Journ. Internat. d'Arch. Numism.* 1906, 168 ff., Pl. 3; Buchholz, *PZ.* 37 (1959), 36 f., Nos. 38–56, Pl. 5:3,4 and *Schweizer Münzblätter* 16, No. 62 (1966), 62, No. 7.

752 a,b Mycenae. Site directly west of the fortress: Copper ingots of more highly developed form than *739–751*, upper and lower side (cf. map Fig. 26 and *1898, 1899* [Cyprus]), show a deeply impressed mark (script-like sign), produced with the casting of the ingot; weight: 23.625 kg.; *Schweizer Münzblätter* 16, No. 62 (1966), No. 10 (with earlier literature).

Pottery

The general principles of the development of pottery applied without restriction to Greece too. The pre-ceramic Stone Age was followed by periods in which clay ware was formed by hand. The potter's wheel, with its rapid rotation, did not establish itself in the Aegean until early in the second millennium.

During the Stone Age and Bronze Age, painted ware predominated. Monochrome clay ware is also found, but it only achieved importance in the so-called 'Urfirnis' (glazed ware) and related types of the Early Bronze Age *(792—799, 801—829)*—except for the Neolithic black-polished ware *(753—756)* and Middle Helladic grey Minyan ware *(876—884)*. The third millennium, particularly the second half, brought the flowering of a monochrome, metallically lustrous ware to other cultural regions such as Anatolia, Cyprus (cf. below p. 144) and northern Syria. Presumably the occasional supersession of painted by monochrome ware was related to the return to metal vessels as models. On the early pottery of the islands of Samos, Kalymnos, and Chios, see Furness, *PPS.* 22 (1956) 173 ff.; and, on the black early Neolithic vessels, partly decorated with polished bands, *AA.* 1928, 625 ff., Figs. 19—22.

The independence of the Cyclades, in particular in the two-dimensional art of vase painting, lasted until the middle of the second millennium *(858—863)*; later the Cyclades also adopted the imitative tendencies of the Mycenaean *koine*, which spread throughout the Aegean. But, in the final phase, the artistic talent of the islands asserted itself again in the figurative style of the stirrup-jars of LH III c *(1030—1036)*.

Without a doubt the climax of ancient Aegean vase painting came in the Middle and Late Bronze Age. Here we find the highly refined, colourful 'egg-shell' ware of the early palaces of Crete *(885 ff.)*, which was in demand even in Cyprus *(1573)* and in northern Syria (Fig. 27, *897*), as well as the matt-painted ware of the mainland *(865 ff.)* which evolved into simple geometric patterns. Vessels *864 a* and *864 b* from Aegina are proof of the interactions between the Minoan and Helladic styles of painting in that period.

Extremely elegant vases were produced for the Court at the time of the later Cretan palaces (LM I and II). This is why the style of painting at the close of this period is described as the 'palace style.'

Vase painting is rightly considered very important, since it mirrored the pictorial motifs and stylistic characteristics of a larger-scale two-dimensional art—that of wall painting. Compare, for instance, the fragments of frescoes on landscape themes from Knossos and Hagia Triada *(1043, 1045—1047, 1050)* with the plant motifs on vases, or the fish fresco from Phylakopi *(1044)*, with the representation of marine life on vases, or the frieze of shields in the corridors of Knossos *(45)* with the shield symbols on Late Minoan vases *(903 a, b, 945 a, 946, 947)*.

Pictures of marine life, such as fish *(929)*, cuttlefish *(898, 935)*, snails, shells and seaweed *(900, 913 a—d, 914, 918, 943)*, were highly prized, as were representations of papyrus trees, grass and flowers *(916, 926, 927, 931, 933, 936 a, b)*. The stylized ivy leaf *(924, 954, 955)*, 'taenia' and 'cult knots' *(930)* had a special significance as religious symbols, like the figure-of-eight shields mentioned earlier, helmets *(938, 939)* and the sacred double axes *(902, 925, 928,* cf. *716 ff.)*.

The sense of form is most clearly expressed in the decoration of the vases, such as the spiral network covering the surface *(899, 932)*, the ornamental band rolled into a spiral *(920)*, the 'swaddling band' which, like the bands round mummies, was intended to veil the corporeality of the vessel *(937)*, and the central motif of the rosette and the star *(934)*. Together with the art of the tiny seal-stones, it was that of vase decoration which largely defines the basic formal character of ancient Aegean art. Vase decoration exemplified what has been described as 'torsion' and 'unceasing harmony' (Matz, 'Die kretisch-mykenische Kunst, Form und Entwicklung' in *Antike* 11 [1935], 171—210; and *Torsion, eine formenkundliche Untersuchung zur aigaiischen Vorgeschichte*, Diss., Mainz [1951]).

Thus the Minoan Cretans did not consider a vessel to be decorated as a segmented organism to be matched by a certain decorative order; their idea of perfection in this essentially two-dimensional art form lay in the interweaving of the patterns, in the vegetal covering of the surface. In contrast, the motive force in the decorative forms of the mainland was what has been described as the 'tectonic' element (Furumark, Matz). Here the decoration established definite emphases; it aimed at bringing out the corporeity and the axiality of the vase. Naturally, these two opposing tendencies in ancient Aegean art influenced each other; indeed, they resulted in that conflict which we experience as self-examination and the spiritual life.

At the end of the Bronze Age, a new figurative style appeared, as seen in vessels *944—1001* and *1025*. Stylized cuttlefish and fish join the beasts of the land to enliven the surfaces of stirrup-jars and cups from the workshops of the Cyclades and the western Anatolian coastal regions *(1030—1036)*.

Ancient Aegean trade and political relations in the second half of the second millennium can be traced through the distribution of Minoan and Mycenaean pottery: Egypt *(913 a—d)*, Cyprus *(1616—1648)*, North Syria *(973)* and southern Italy (Fig. 28, *1002—1020*).

Stubbings, *Mycenaean Pottery from the Levant* (1951), has been supplemented by Mrs. Hankey, 'Mycenaean Pottery in the Middle East, Notes on Finds since 1951' in *BSA.* 62 (1967), 107 ff. Catling and Karageorghis have told us about 'Minoika in Cyprus' in *BSA.* 55 (1960), 108 ff. Lord William Taylour has discussed *Mycenaean Pottery in Italy and Adjacent Areas* (1958).

The monumental works by Furumark, *The Chronology of Mycenaean Pottery* and *The Mycenaean Pottery, Analysis and Classification* (1941), remain fundamental studies; but see also the critique by Matz in *Gnomon* 19 (1943), 225 ff. Zois has recently made a comprehensive study of the earlier Cretan painted ware in *Der Kamares-Stil, Wesen und Werden* (1968). Desborough, on the other hand, has examined the close of the development in *The Last Mycenaeans and their Successors* (1964); this work has been discussed by Ålin in *Gnomon* 37 (1965), 723 ff. A post-palatial potter's workshop in Kydonia has been described by Tzedakis in *BCH.* 93 (1969), 396 ff. On the remains from the destruction-level at Knossos, see *Antiquity* 40 (1966), Figs. 3—5. Hood suggests a listing of 'knobbed pottery' from the end of the Mycenaean Age, in *Europa: Festschrift für Grumach* (1967), 120 ff. On the entire ancient Aegean ware there is also A. D. Lacy's *Greek Pottery in the Bronze Age* (1967), reviewed by Boardman in the *Burlington Magazine* (110 [1968], 468), and by Buck (*CW.* 6 [1968], 354 ff.), Guerrini (*Arch. Class.* 22 [1968], 408 f.), Kramer (*AAHG.* 21 [1968], 288 f.), Hackens (*AntC.* 37 [1968], 775 ff.), Popham (*AntJ.* 49 [1969], 142 f.), and Canciani (*Gnomon* 41 [1969], 829 ff.).

753–790: NEOLITHIC PERIOD – THRACE – THESSALY – BOEOTIA – ATTICA – AEGINA – ARCADIA – LEUKAS

753 Aegina. Hill of Kolonna. Neolithic, conical, straight-
754 walled bowls of local reddish clay, with black surface and burnished patterns resembling basketry; made without potter's wheel. Reconstructed from fragments; no sizes given. Arch. Mus., Aegina. – Welter, *AA.* 1937, 21 f., Figs. 1, 4; and *Aigina* (1938), 8 f., Figs. 3, 7; Müller-Karpe, *Hdb. d. Vorgesch.* II (1968), Pl. 138 E 2.

755 Aegina. Hill of Kolonna: Neolithic flat bowl, with incurved rim (cf. *756*); clay, technique and treatment of surface as *753*. Reconstructed from fragments; no sizes given. Arch. Mus., Aegina. – Welter, *AA.* 1937, 22, Fig. 6; and *Aigina* 8, Fig. 2; *Müller-Karpe, op. cit.,* Pl. 138 E 1. Other examples of black pottery with burnished groups of lines from the Argolid: Blegen, *Prosymna,* Pl.-Fig. 635; Holmberg, 'The Appearance of Neolithic Black Burnished Ware in Mainland Greece' (*AJA.* 68 [1964], 343 ff.); and Grundmann, *AM.* 57 (1932), Suppls. 24, 25.

756 Leukas. Chapel of Sotiros, Plain of Nidri: Sub-Neolithic, grey-brown, flat bowl with black burnished slip, external surface otherwise unadorned; form as *755,* but different decorative technique on the inside: below a simple border line, a large, triple curving band with radial axes, scored triangle suspended from the rim. Reconstructed from fragments; diam. c. 25–26 cm. Local museum in Dörpfeld's excavation house, Leukas. – Bulle, *AM.* 59 (1934), 185, Fig. 11 (photograph of the fragments; for some of them cf. Dörpfeld, *Alt-Ithaka* [1927], Suppl. 57 b), Pl. 13 (reconstruction).

757 Otzaki Magoula, near Larissa, Thessaly. Middle Neo-
a,b lithic bowl, red painted on light ground outside and inside; height 9 cm., diam. 22.2 cm., Sesklo style A 3 beta. Frequent form; cf. Wace-Thompson, *Prehist. Thess.* 92 f., Figs. 44 b, 45 (Tsangli); Müller-Karpe, Pl. 128:11, 12, 15, 24 (Otzaki), Pl. 130:25, 37 (Tsangli), Pl. 135 A 1 (Sesklo). Arch. Mus., Larissa. – Milojcic, *AA.* 1954, 10, Fig. 7; Zervos, *Naissance* I, 242 f., Figs. 267–269.

758 Gremnos Magoula, Thessaly. Fragment of a Neolithic, steep-walled amphora neck, as shown in Wace-Thompson, *Prehist. Thess.* Pl. 1 (Rachmani II, Type B 3 alpha). Spiral decoration completed diagrammatically (scroll-work; circumference of rim 33 cm.); Dimini period/Otzaki group. – Milojcic, *Neue deutsche Ausgrabungen* (1959), 230, Fig. 3 (photograph of the entire vessel).

759 Otzaki Magoula *(759, 761)* and Magoulitsa *(760,* after
to Theocharis, *Thessalika* 1 [1958], 41, Fig. 2): Middle
761 Neolithic sherds with so-called 'cardium prints', i. e. shell or finger-nail patterns (for their connections outside Greece cf. Schachermeyr, *Die ältesten Kulturen,* 59, Fig. 5; cf. also Grundmann, *AM.* 57, [1932], Suppl. Pl. 20). Arch. Mus., Larissa and Volos. – Zervos, *Naissance* I, 197, Figs. 169, 165, 166.

762 Souphli Magoula, Thessaly (German excavation di-
to rected by Milojcic): Middle Neolithic sherds, painting
764 combined with white-filled scratched and incised patterns; Arch. Mus., Volos. – Zervos, 199, Fig. 171 a–c.

765 Thessaly. Painted Neolithic sherds, width 4.3–8.4 cm.
to 765: light on dark: 768: monochrome, with moulded
771 spiral ornament; the remainder: B 3 alpha type, lattice pattern and small spiral hooks as in Rachmani II (cf. Wace-Thompson, *Prehist. Thess.,* 46, Fig. 2 [painted], 30, Fig. 9 [scratched]; also Tsountas, *DS.* Pls. 24: 7, 9; 27:6; 29:3, 4, 6). Origin and location of these sherds not known (photographs from the Grundmann estate).

772 Sesklo, Thessaly. Early Neolithic vase with funnel neck and conical foot; white linear painting on dark ground, Type A 3 alpha; height 17 cm. (the same shape of foot on monochrome Sesklo vessels: Matz, *Kreta u. frühes Griechenland,* 23 with Col. Pls.). Nat. Mus., Athens. – Tsountas, *DS.* 175, Fig. 83; Mylonas, *Neolith. Epoche.* 14, Fig. 5 a; Zervos, 219, Fig. 222.

773 Tsani Magoula, Thessaly. Middle Neolithic cup, with strap handle; red painting on white ground (Type A 3 beta). Bizarre stepped pattern, irregular triangles on rim and handle; height 10.5 cm. Arch. Mus., Volos. – Wace-Thompson, *Prehist. Thess.,* 140, Fig. 86 b; Zervos, 223, Fig. 232; Müller-Karpe, *Hdb. d. Vorgesch.* II, Pl. 131 B 4.

774 Balomenou Magoula–Chaironeia, Boeotia. Middle Neo-
775 lithic spherical pots with cylindrical neck and red geometric painting on white ground (Type A 3 beta, fourth millennium B. C.); heights 35 and 40 cm. Arch. Mus., Chaironeia. – *774:* Soteriadis, *Ephem.* 1908, Suppl.-Pl. 1; Mylonas, *Neolith. Epoche* 54, Fig. 59; Wace-Thompson, 198, Fig. 140 e; Weinberg, *AJA.* 51 (1947), Pl. 30 a; Zervos, I, 233, Fig. 251; Matz, *Kreta u. frühes Griechenland,* 24, Fig. 2 (drawing); Müller-Karpe, II, Pl. 131 A 11. *775:* Soteriadis, 79, Fig. 9; Weinberg, op. cit., Pl. 30 c; Zervos, 229, Fig. 242; Schachermeyr, *Die ältesten Kulturen,* 80 Fig. 12:1; Müller-Karpe, II, Pl. 131 A 13 (upper part only drawn).

776 Tsangli, Thessaly. From House T: Middle Neolithic vessel with funnel neck, restored bail handle, low suspension handles and off-set base. Red stepped frieze of lozenges in the manner of the stepped pattern on white-ground pottery (Type A 3 beta); height without

handle 13 cm. Arch. Mus., Volos. – Wace-Thompson, *Prehist. Thess.*, 89, Fig. 42 e (drawing); Zervos, I, 240, Fig. 262; Buchholz, *Jahrb. d. Hamburger Kunstsammlungen* 13 (1968), 18, Note 11; Müller–Karpe, *Hdb. d. Vorgesch.* II, Pl. 130:29; Grundmann, *JdI.* 68 (1953) 7, Fig. 8 (restored without handle).

777 Attica. Site unknown: Late or sub-Neolithic monochrome spherical pot without neck (pyxis), but with flat lid; two superimposed suspension eyelets respectively on vessel and lid. Dimensions unknown. Private collection, Athens. – Obviously there is a functional and structural connection with the pyxides of Early Cycladic I; cf. Lacy, *Greek Pottery in the Bronze Age* (1967), 242, Fig. 96 d.

778 Otzaki Magoula, Thessaly. Pot-bellied handled jug of the Middle Sesklo period, with dense brown zigzag pattern on reddish ground; inside of neck also painted; height 23.6 cm.; diam. of mouth 10.8 cm. Arch. Mus., Larissa. – Milojcic, *AA.*, 1955, 165 f., Fig. 4:3; id., *Neue deutsche Ausgrabungen* (1959), Col. Pl. 2 after p. 232; Zervos, I, 265, Fig. 315; Müller–Karpe, II, Pl. 128 A 10.

779 Lianokladi I, Thessaly. Early Neolithic handleless spherical pot, with offset rim and red painting, with the pattern of lines arranged so that the white ground is visible (Type A 3 delta); height 14.4 cm., diam. of mouth, 16 cm. Nat. Mus., Athens. – Wace and Thompson, *Prehist. Thess.* 175, Fig. 119 a; Mylonas, *Neolith. Epoche*, 50, Fig. 56 (left); Schachermeyr, *Die ältesten Kulturen*, Pl. 3:4; Zervos, *Naissance* I, 259, Fig. 302; and II, Col. Pl. after p. 520; Demargne, *Naissance de l'art grec* (1964), 30, Fig. 24 (Eng. trans., *Aegean Art* [1964]).

780 Cave of Pan, near Marathon, Attica. Late Neolithic spherical vessel, with conical neck and strap handle. Rim of mouth, handle, and body painted; Schachermeyr: 'Brown on brown, style of Arapi I'. Noteworthy are the functionally appropriate pendant ornaments under the handle and the few vertical bands with stepped double lines; height 34.5 cm. (cf. text to 2: Cave of Pan). In the depot of Brauron, Attica. – Daux, *BCH.*, 83 (1959), 589, Fig. 14; Schachermeyr, *AA.*, 1962, 171, Fig. 18; Zervos, II, 502, Fig. 843; Müller–Karpe, II, Pl. 138 B 3.

781 Orman Magoula, near Larissa, Thessaly. Late Neolithic bowl with scalloped rim on high, conical hollow pedestal, partly restored, perhaps a 'stand'; height 90 cm. Red decoration in the late Dimini style (Type B 3 alpha); two areas with horizontal and vertical borders, filled with a meander pattern running from top left to bottom right on the torsion principle. Inside and outside of bowl decorated with symmetrically arranged curves. – Grundmann, *AM.* 62 (1937), 65, Pl. 33; Schachermeyr, *Die ältesten Kulturen*, Pl. 6:3.

782 Col. Pl. 1, after p. 8: Arapi Magoula, near Larissa. Diagrammatic reconstruction of a multi-colour Late Neolithic pot-bellied bowl with short, steep neck and round base; handmade, Arapi style. – Milojcic, *Neue deutsche Ausgrabungen* (1959), Col. Pl. 3 after p. 232; Müller–Karpe, *Hdb. d. Vorgesch.* II (1968), Pl. 126 E 3.

783 Dimini, Thessaly. From Megaron A (Fig. 10, *12*): Late Neolithic spherical pot, with short cylindrical neck and two vertical handles. Dark brown and wine red decoration on light ground (Type B 3 gamma); height 25.5 cm. Nat. Mus., Athens. – Tsountas, *DS.* 226, Pl. 11; Mylonas, *Neolith. Epoche*, 30, Fig. 3; Zervos, *Naissance* II, 321, Fig. 421, and Col. Pl. after p. 552; Müller-Karpe, II, Pl. 135 A 7 (erroneously described as from Sesklo).

784 Sesklo, Thessaly. Late Neolithic bowl, with scalloped rim and very low vertical handle. Some cracks mended in ancient times; height 19 cm., diam. 35 cm. Decoration: blackish-brown spirals and meanders on reddish ground; the same inside (Type B 3 alpha). Nat. Mus., Athens. – Tsountas, *DS.*, Pl. 22; Zervos, II, 300 f., Figs. 385-387, and Col. Pl. B after p. 528; Müller-Karpe, II, Pl. 135 A 8.

785 Komotini, Thrace (excavation by Pelekanidis and Kyriakidis). Late Neolithic hemispherical sieve, assembled from coarse clay fragments; probable height 28 cm. (dimensions in Zervos: 82 cm.) Arch. Mus., Saloniki. – Zervos, II, 360, Fig. 507.

786 Gremnos Magoula, Thessaly. From a defensive trench: Late Neolithic, handmade, unpainted askos with fired colour effects on the surface ('mottled ware'). Arch. Mus., Larissa. – Milojcic, *AA.* 1959, 52, Fig. 6 (no dimensions).

787 Sesklo. Late Neolithic vessel with lateral opening, conical foot and wide stirrup handle; entirely covered in white-filled scratched and incised ornament (Type B 2; height 17 cm., length 19 cm.), perhaps imitation of woodcarving. The same type also in Kephala on Keos (Megaw, *JHS*, 87 [1967], Arch. Rep. 17, Fig. 26); for vase of comparable function, cf. Lacy, *Greek Pottery in the Bronze Age* (1967), 79, Fig. 34 c (MM vase from Knossos). Nat. Mus., Athens. – Tsountas, *DS.* 206 f., Pl. 16:3 a, b; Zervos, *Naissance* II, 298, Figs. 383, 384; Müller-Karpe, *Hdb. d. Vorgesch.* II, Pl. 134:21(erroneously described as from Dimini).

788 Choirospilia, Leukas. From the hard, grey second topmost layer in the south cave (1913 excavation): Sub-Neolithic askos jug with six wide blackish-brown diagonal bands; only half survives; ancient repair opposite the handle; height 8.5 cm. Local mus., Nidri. – Velde, *ZfE.* 45 (1913), 1156 ff., Fig. 3.

789 Asea, Peloponnese. Middle to Late Neolithic vessel of grey clay, with low bulge and tall steep-walled upper part; foot restored; greatest diameter 19 cm. Geometric patterns in brown lustre ('Neolithic Urfirnis') on reddish ground; several hatched lozenges and bands round the outside; asymmetrical arrangement of surface. – Holmberg, *The Swedish Excavations at Asea in Arcadia* (1944), 52 f., Fig. 54 b (without foot), Col. Pl. 3 b; Schachermeyr, *Die ältesten Kulturen*, 121, Fig. 28:2; Müller-Karpe, *Hdb. d. Vorgesch.* II, Pl. 137 C 18.

790 Asea. Middle to Late Neolithic vessel; base missing, probably round originally. Low bulge, steep-walled upper part, flaring mouth, and vertically drilled suspension eyelets; diam. 19 cm. Coarse grey pottery, with fine reddish slip and dark red painting ('coarse burnished patterned ware'). Decoration: rows of solid triangles, connected both horizontally and diagonally. – Holmberg, 47, Col. Pl. 2 a; Müller-Karpe, II, Pl. 137 C 17; Schachermeyr, *Ägäis und Orient* (1967), Pl. 10:43.

791 Thebes, Boeotia. City area of the town, Theodorou estate: Early Helladic askos jug of the Urfirnis-ware type with beak mouth; assembled from fragments. Decoration: horizontal white ornamental band, on which are painted dark, upright triangles. Arch. Mus., Thebes. – Daux, BCH. 90 (1966), 852, Fig. 3; Schachermeyr–Buchholz, AA. 1971, 394, with 83 pl.

792 Poliochni, Lemnos. Site 1129 (Find No. 4742). Early
a, b Bronze Age handmade conical bowl, with thickened rim (mid-third millennium); assembled from fragments. Shiny brown slip; scratched, white-filled chevrons outside and on the base; height 11.7 cm., diam. 24.3 cm. Bernabò-Brea, Poliochni 1 (1964), 459, Pl. 117 d, e.

793 Poliochni. Site 504 (Find No. 1139 a). Early Bronze Age tripod cauldron (mid-third millennium), with brown slip and round base; diagonal legs ending in a point, with ridged profile and front side extending up to the rim of the cauldron; high fluted handle above one of the legs; height 21 cm., diam. 21 cm. – Bernabò-Brea, 515, 578 ff., Pl. 71 a.

794 Tiryns, the Argolid. Central fortress: Early Helladic cooling vessel (psykter) of the Urfirnis-ware type with small ring base (diam. 17 cm.), red terracotta. A small pithos, with zigzag band on the rim and two small horizontal handles under the lip connected by a relief band, stands in the handleless bowl and was made in one piece with it. The fluid to be cooled – wine – was kept in the inner vessel, with the cooling water outside; height 51 cm., diam. 78 cm. Arch. Mus., Nauplia. – Karo, Führer durch Tiryns (²1934), 39, Fig. 14; Müller, Tiryns IV (1938), 33, 37, Fig. 34 (sectional drawing), Pls. 12:9; 13.

795 Boeotia. Early Helladic wide-mouthed Urfirnis-ware pot, with lateral tubular spout and low, steep rim; below the belly are horizontal lugs. Lower part largely reconstructed. Arch. Mus., Chaironeia, Inv. No. 3148. – Vessels with lateral spout are very rare on the mainland; cf. e. g. Goldman, Excavations at Eutresis in Boeotia (1931), 128, Fig. 173; Åberg, Chronologie IV (1933), 51, Fig. 87.

796 Poliochni. Site 611 (Find No. 6058): Early Bronze Age slender 'Troy goblet' (cf. 799) with two semi-circular, fragile, low-set handles; height 22.4 cm. – Bernabò-Brea, Bd'A. 42 (1957), 205, Fig. 19. – On pre-war finds of sherds of such cups, see Karo, AA., 1934, 185; Bittel, Kleinasiatische Studien (1942), 193.

797 Orchomenos, Boeotia. Chance find. EH goblet, like 796 and 799 (cf. also 1075, silver), but with stronger handles. Brownish-yellow terracotta; black to cherry-red slip, unglazed inside; handmade; height 17.5 cm. Nat. Mus., Athens, Inv. No. 5853. – Kunze, Orchomenos III (1934), 56, No. 45 and pp. 80, 94, Pl. 23:1.

798 Troy II. Staatliche Museen, Charlottenburg, Berlin.
799 798: Early Bronze Age vessel in the form of an animal, on three feet; grey polished slip; base, feet and lip of spout restored; animal head, tail and base of spout encircled by a double groove; small suspension eyelet on lower part of handle; height 22 cm. Schmidt, Schliemanns Sammlung 32, No. 608. 799: Grey-brown cup, like 796 and 797, but with larger dimensions; height 29.5 cm. – Schmidt, op. cit., 61, No. 1426; Matz, Kreta-Mykene-Troja, Pl. 4. This type of cup (796, 797, 799) occurs also in Tiryns, Samos, Syros (see Caskey, in Essays in Memory of K. Lehmann [1964], 63 ff., Fig. 8), west Anatolia (e. g. Aphrodisias: Kadish, AJA. 73 [1969], 49 ff., Pl. 25:18), central Anatolia and Cilicia as far as the Plain of Amuq; for maps of distribution, see Bittel, AA., 1944/45, 57 f., Fig. 7; and Renfrew, AJA. 71 (1967), Pl. 12; most recently: Spanos, Untersuchungen über den bei Homer 'depas amphikypellon' genannten Gefässtypus: I (1972), 6.

800 Tiryns. Early Helladic double-handled goblet painted with rows of black lines; handmade; light clay; height 16 cm., diam. of mouth 8 cm. Arch. Mus., Nauplia. – Müller, Tiryns IV (1938), 77 f., Pl. 32:5; Schachermeyr, Die ältesten Kulturen, 155, Fig. 40:42.

801 Raphina, east Attica. Handmade glazed bowl, with inverted rim and small offset base (EH); diam. of mouth c. 10 cm. Usual Early Bronze Age type (cf. Müller, Pl. 7). – Theocharis, Geras Keramopoullou (1953, mod. Gk.), 145, Pl. 10:2; and Prakt. 1953, 113 f., Fig. 7.

802 Askloupis, Kos. Vessels from Early Bronze Age pithos
to burials (Italian excavation 1943; 543 comes from this
805 source). Coarse, handmade monochrome ware: askoïd jug (803), pot-bellied vase with knob handles (804), handled cups (802, 805). For corresponding ware from Caria cf. Vermeule, Archaeology 17 (1964), 248, with Figs. Dimensions for 802–805 lacking. Arch. Mus., Kos. – Morricone, Bd'A. 35 (1950), 323 f., Figs. 98, 101, 102 (pithos burials). – cf. French, 'Anatolian pottery in the Aegean Area', AnatSt. 16 (1966), 49 f.

806 Eleusis, Attica. Handmade Early Helladic vessels, with
to scratched decoration: spherical pot with cylindrical
808 neck, height 19 cm. (806); pithos with low bulge and two horizontal handles, height 27 cm. (807): handled cup, with conical foot and two horizontal rows of holes; height 14 cm. (808). – Skias, Ephem., 1912, 15, Fig. 6:1–3.

809 Tiryns. Sherd of medium-sized EH vessel, with impressed vertical decoration after the manner of large hydriai, like 820; very lustrous, black, porous clay, fired hard; black outside with slightly shiny slip; surviving length 12.2 cm. According to Müller, 'imported from one of the islands'. Arch. Mus., Nauplia. – Müller, Tiryns IV (1938), 7, Pl. 2:2.

810 Orchomenos, Boeotia. Sherd of a small hydria (EH) with tubular horizontal suspension hole and rich incised decoration; clay ground inside; thin, grey-brown glaze outside; length of sherd 7 cm. Arch. Mus., Chaironeia. – Kunze, Orchomenos III (1934), 86, Pl. 29:6.

811 Orchomenos. Rim-fragments of a small bowl with regular vertical zigzags in incised work; between them wide, undecorated band. For EH decoration of this kind, see Holmberg, Swedish Excavations (1944), 81 ff., Figs. 83 f., 84 a. The sherd from Orchomenos was assigned to the Neolithic period by Kunze because it is polished black; it is shown in a photograph by the DAI., Athens, with a jug handle similarly polished (Kunze, Orchomenos II [1931], 45 and 53, Pl. 9:5) probably belonging to the early Helladic period. – Kunze, 12, 19 f., Pl. 5:1.

812 Orchomenos. EH sherds of fairly large vessels, with
to raised horizontal fillets decorated with diagonal in-
819 cised chip-cuttings *(815)*, cable-like bands *(814, 816, 819)* or profiles like overlapping discs *(817, 818)*. – Kunze, *Orchomenos* III, Pl. 6:3 h *(813:* hydria sherd), Pl. 28:1 a *(819:* sherd of a coarse hydria), 1 c, 2 d, 2 e *(816–818:* sherds of coarse bowls), Pl. 29:2 *(815:* with corresponding sherd, hydria or jug).

820 Orchomenos. Hydria of the Early Helladic Urfirnis-ware type, assembled from many fragments; well-fired clay, lustrous red slip, much mended in ancient times. Voluminous body, attractive flaring funnel mouth; four horizontally-drilled suspension loops on the belly; front emphasized by vertical incised decoration; height 66.5 cm. Nat. Mus., Athens, Inv. No. 5877. – Kunze, 19, No. 1, Pl. 1; Matz, *Kreta u. frühes Griechenland*, 49, with Col. Pl.; other examples, Blegen, *Korakou* (1921), 8, Fig. 8; Müller, *Tiryns* IV, Pl. 11:1, 2; for distribution and ethnic origins, see Fuchs, *Die griechischen Fundgruppen der frühen Bronzezeit u. ihre auswärtigen Beziehungen* (1937); and, for a critique of this, Bittel, *Germania* 23 (1939), 59 ff.

821 Orchomenos. Hydria from the latest Early Helladic Urfirnis-ware deposit, assembled from many fragments. Spherical body; base slightly flattened; short funnel mouth; two vertically pierced horizontal grips on the widest part of the body; brownish yellow clay, black, red and brown slip with dull lustre, on the upper part of the vessel only; height 33.5 cm. Arch. Mus., Chaironeia, Inv. No. 37. – Kunze, 21, No. 5, Pl. 3:2.

822 Orchomenos. From Section N, directly above the rock: Early Helladic beaked cup ('sauce-boat'), with high body and small base; fine, hard clay; inside and outside: light red slip; much restored, handle missing. Heights 15 cm. and 19.2 cm. Nat. Mus., Athens, Inv. No. 5860. – Kunze, 39, No. 27, Pl. 15:2.

823 Nidri, Leukas. Tomb R XV. Early Bronze Age small
824 suspension pyxis, with four vertically pierced eyelets for suspension (height 7.6 cm.); and beaked cup (height 24 cm.) of the same type as *822*. Local mus., Nidri. – Dörpfeld, *Alt-Ithaka* (1927), Pl. 65:1, 2; and *Alt-Olympia* I (1935), 306, Fig. 79; Bossert, *Alt Kreta*, ²No. 2 (³No. 114); Åberg, *Chronologie* III (1932), 147, Fig. 279. – The beaked cup is one of the major Aegean shapes of the Early Bronze Age, e. g. in silver and gold: *1082 a, b*; clay: Synoro Epidauria (*AA.*, 1940, 222, Fig. 55), Tiryns (Karo, *Führer durch Tiryns* [²1934], 38, Fig. 13; and Müller, *Tiryns* IV, Pls. 3, 4), Korakou (Blegen, *Korakou*, 6 f., Figs. 4, 6, Pl. 1:1), Lerna (Weinberg, *AntK*. 12 [1969], Pl. 3:1, 2), Phaleron (Fimmen, *Kret.-Myk. Kultur*, 136, Fig. 132), Raphina (Matz, *Kreta u. frühes Griechenland*, 46, with Col. Pl.), Asea (Holmberg, *Swedish Excavations at Asea in Arcadia* [1944], 70, Fig. 73 g), Olympia – Stadium – north wall (Kunze, *Delt.* 17 [1961/62], Chron. Pl. 122 a, b). Surveys of distribution: Fuchs, *Die griechischen Fundgruppen der frühen Bronzezeit u. ihre auswärtigen Beziehungen* (1937), and Renfrew, *AJA*. 71 (1967), 1 ff., Pl. 12.

825 Orchomenos. Handmade red monochrome bowl of hard thin clay, with straight finger-hold just below the rim (EH; height 8 cm. diam. 21.5 cm.). Arch. Mus., Chaironeia, Inv. No. 817. – Kunze, 68, No. 58, Pl. 27:3.

826 Orchomenos. Handmade wide-mouthed deep 'ring-handle pot', with round base and flared rim; handle and large parts of the side restored; a band under the rim and the whole inside are glazed reddish brown to black, otherwise unadorned; yellow clay, bluish grey at the core (EH; diam. 19 cm., height 9.5 cm.). Arch. Mus., Chaironeia, Inv. No. 822. – Kunze, 51, No. 35, Pl. 19:4.

827 Orchomenos. Early Helladic handled cup, with round base, high funnel neck and thick vertical handle. Damaged on the rim; thin reddish to grey clay; brownish black slip, with burnished bands, clay ground inside; height 7.5 cm. *827* and *828* come from the same site. Nat. Mus., Athens, Inv. No. 6438. – Kunze, 54, No. 42, Pl. 22:4.

828 Orchomenos. Early Helladic 'egg-cup' of reddish yellow clay, with red slip inside and out (height 8.1 cm.); typical form of the third millennium, even beyond the Aegean. Nat. Mus., Athens, Inv. No. 6439. – Kunze, 70, No. 62, Pl. 22:5.

829 Orchomenos. From Bothros N 11: Spherical glazed pot, with funnel neck, and tripartite suspension lugs, vertically pierced in three places, on the belly. Reddish clay, brown slip with glazed bands; height *c*. 12 cm. Nat. Mus., Athens, Inv. No. 5863. – Kunze, 37, No. 25, Pl. 14:1.

830 Lerna. Fourth settlement phase (EH III): 'Suspension amphora', with wide ornamental band on the shoulder, restored diagrammatically from sherds. Geometric patterns painted dark on light; height *c*. 29 cm. Arch. Mus., Argos, Find No. L 1461. – Caskey, *Charisterion eis Orlandon* 3 (1966, mod. Gk.) 151, Pl. 52:8.

831 Aegina. From Welter's excavations on the Hill of Kolonna: Glazed amphora; shape similar to *821*, but shoulder painted dark on light, as in *830*, with triangles filled with hatching. Sketched restoration; dimensions lacking. Arch. Mus., Aegina. Welter, *Aigina* (1938), 12, Fig. 10.

832 Aegina (cf. *831*). Ring vase, reconstructed from fragments, painted with groups of lines; with wide barb-handle, and standing on three small feet (EH). Vertical tubular spout, with diagonal beak mouth painted inside; dimensions lacking. Ring vessels are particularly common in the Early Bronze Age (Schmidt, *Schliemanns Sammlung*, No. 823; Zoïs, *Erevna peri tis Minoïkis Kerameikis* [1967, mod. Gk.], Pl. 34; and are also known from the later Bronze Age, e. g. from Troy VI/VII (Schmidt, No. 3246). Arch. Mus., Aegina. – Welter, 13, Fig. 11.

833–840: EARLY MINOAN PERIOD – CRETE

833 Kyparissi, near Kanli Kastelli, central Crete. Small cave tomb, from which we have some fifty supplementary vessels (EM I, cf. also *835*). Handled jug of typical pouch shape, with low bulge, diagonally rising mouth cut off on top, and vertical lines in matt paint; height 19 cm. Arch. Mus., Herakleion. – Alexiou, *Kret. Chron.* 5 (1951), 275 ff.; Zervos, *Crète*, 147, Fig. 133 (left); Marinatos–Hirmer, Pl. 5; Zois, *Der Kamares-Stil* (Diss. Tübingen, 1968), 55 ff.

834 Vitsilia Partira, central Crete. Cave tomb: Wide mouthed conical bowl (EM I) with marked conical foot and small, horizontal suspension lug on the rim; height 7 cm. Arch. Mus., Herakleion. – Zervos, *Crète*, Fig. 133 centre; Faure, *Fonctions des Cavernes crétoises* (1964), 29, n. 1, and 56, n. 1.

835 Kyparissi (cf. *833*). Handled jug with less exact contours than *833*, but also EM I; height 19 cm. Arch. Mus., Herakleion. – Marinatos–Hirmer, Pl. 5; Schachermeyr, *Die min. Kultur des alten Kreta* (1964), Pl. 6 c; Zervos, *Crète*, Fig. 133 (right).

836 Hagios Onouphrios, south Crete. Beaked jug, with spherical body and stripe decoration (EM I, height 20.5 cm. or, according to some authorities, 28 cm.). The round base is a sure mark of distinction between EM I and EM II jugs, according to Pendlebury; there are no stratigraphic observations from the place of origin. Arch. Mus., Herakleion. – Fimmen, *Kret.-myk. Kultur*, 129, Fig. 121; Evans, *PM.*, I, 62, Fig. 25; Karo, *Reallex. Vorgesch.* VII (1926), Pl. 56 a; Montelius, *La Grèce*. Pl. 52:24; Pendlebury, *Arch. of Crete*, 50, Pl. IX, 2 b; Zervos, 146, Fig. 132 (right); Matz, *Kreta–Mykene–Troja*, Pl. 18; and *Kreta u. frühes Griechenland*, 52 (Col. Pl.).

837 Vasiliki, east Crete. Beaked jug with mottled surface ('mottled ware', EM II, 2250 B. C.). Small protuberance under the diagonally rising rim of the mouth (plastic 'eye'); height 33.5 cm. Arch. Mus., Herakleion. – Seager, *Vassiliki*, 10, Pl. 34; Fimmen, *Kret. myk. Kultur*, 86, Fig. 68; Zervos, 148, Fig. 135 left; Matz, *Kreta–Mykene–Troja*, Pl. 18; Marinatos–Hirmer, Col. Pl. III; cf. Schiering, *JdI*. 75 (1960), 17 f., Fig. 1 (stones and painting in Minoan art).

838 Sphoungaras, near Gournia, east Crete (Zervos mistakenly locates the find in one of the two cave tombs of Hagia Photia on the isthmus of Hierapetra; also, Lacy, *Greek Pottery* [1967], 35, Fig. 8 b): EM II jug of bi-conical form with angular shoulder; narrow mouth; neckless; surmounted by a small beaked spout, and with loop handle on shoulder. The shape shows the influence of metal vessels; note the rows of dents imitating rivet holes. Surface mottled ('mottled ware'); height *c.* 12 cm. Arch. Mus., Herakleion. – Hall, *Excavations in Eastern Crete: Sphoungaras* (1912), 47, Fig. 21 c; Evans, *PM.* I, 79, Fig. 47 a; Pendlebury, *Arch. of Crete*, 68, Pl. X:2 a; Zervos, 148, Fig. 135 (right).

839 Mochlos. Region of the necropolis, but unconnected with the finds there. Beaked jug of the 'tea-pot' type (spout broken off), with sharp curve; bi-conical. Unpainted black slip, incised decoration on both sides of upper part; height 12 cm., diam. 17.5 cm.; transition between EM III and MM I. Arch. Mus., Herakleion. – Seager, *Explorations in the Island of Mochlos* (1912), 85, No. 75, Fig. 49; Zervos, 149, Fig. 137 (left).

840 Vasiliki. Jug with long, bizarre beak, 'tea-pot' type, with conical base (partly restored). White paint on dark glazing; height 20 cm.; EM III (*c.* 2100–2000 B. C.). Arch. Mus., Herakleion, Inv. No. 5299. – Seager, *Trans. Univ. Mus. Penns.* III, 2 (1906), 129, Fig. 13; Maraghiannis, *Ant. Crét.* 2, Pl. 25:12; Fimmen, *Kret. myk. Kultur*, 87, Fig. 69; Pendlebury, *Arch. of Crete*, Pl. XIII:3 d; Matz, *Kreta–Mykene–Troja*, Pl. 19 upper; Zervos, Fig. 137 (right); Schachermeyr, *Die minoische Kultur des alten Kreta* (1964), 57, Fig. 17 e; Zois, *Der Kamares-Stil* (Diss. Tübingen, 1968), 137 ff.

841–863: EARLY AND MIDDLE BRONZE AGE – THE CYCLADES

841 Thera. Two Early Cycladic bowls of conical form with
842 flat base and straight rim, emphasized outside and inside by bands of colour; *842* has a sketchily painted cross inside.

843 Thera. Two typical Early Cycladic asymmetrical jugs;
844 monochrome; *843* small and imprecisely formed.

845 Aegina. Early Cycladic imports. Two closed 'duck
a, b jugs', with pointed hump and lateral spout neck; small eye between body and neck, and others at the corners, suspension loops at widest part of body. *845 a*: only sherds survive; incised, white-filled spiral pattern. *845 b*: incised decoration on upper part only, consisting of horizontal bands filled with groups of lines. Arch. Mus., Aegina. – Welter, *Aigina* (1938), 14, Figs. 12 (*845 b*) and 13 (*845 a*).

846 Paros. Acropolis (excavation: Rubensohn): Early Bronze Age undecorated 'duck jug' of later type, with small hump and high, trumpet-like mouth. Type as *845 a, b*, but cruder and taller; very well fired; brick-red inside; height 17 cm. Nat. Mus., Athens, Find No. 1 – Rubensohn, *AM.* 42 (1917), 19, Fig. 8.

847 Thera. High, egg-shaped 'duck jug', with lateral spout, small stirrup handle on the hump and vertical stripes painted in pairs.

848 Syros. Early Cycladic 'sauce-boat', with high pedestal, vertical ribbed handle and three open spouts; perhaps a lamp; diam. 15.2 cm., height *c.* 12.5 cm. Nat. Mus., Athens. – Frankfort, *Studies in Early Pottery of the Near East* II (1927), Pl. 5:6; Åberg, *Chronologie* IV (1933), 86, Fig. 165; Zervos, *Cycl.*, 151, Figs. 185, 186; Lacy, *Greek Pottery*, 251, Fig. 100 d.

849 Chalandriani, Syros. Tomb 172. Early Bronze Age, glazed 'pedestal vase', with high pedestal (like *848*), squat spherical body, and low cylindrical neck. Middle of surface marked horizontally by deep incised lines, stamped ornaments and interwoven spirals; lines below

suspension holes; height 10 cm. Nat. Mus., Athens, Inv. No. 4972. – Tsountas, *Ephem.* 1899, 109, Pl. 9:19; Kahrstedt, *AM.* 38 (1913), Pl. 8:3; Bossert, *Altkreta*[3], No. 435; Åberg, 82, Fig. 151; Zervos, 157, Fig. 199; Bossert, *JdI.* 75 (1960), 5, Fig. 7:4 (drawing); Schachermeyr, *Die ältesten Kulturen*, Pl. 9:4.

850 Chalandriani. Early Bronze Age 'pedestal vase' with incised and impressed patterns (traces of white filling). This type, decorated also on the lower part, differs from *849* by its lower pedestal, its biconical basic shape with angular shoulder, and its slightly flaring mouth; height 10.5 cm. Nat. Mus., Athens, Inv. No. 5155. – Tsountas, 87, Pls. 8, 9; Kahrstedt, Pl. 8:4; Fimmen, *Kret.-Myk. Kultur*, 81, Fig. 64; Zervos, *Cycl.* 158, Fig. 202. – For other Early Cycladic 'pedestal urns', cf. Kahrstedt, Pl. 7; Fimmen, 135, Fig. 130; Åberg, 101 ff. (list); Zervos, 86 ff., Figs. 66, 73, 77; p. 158 f., Figs. 201, 203; p. 165 ff., Figs. 212–217; Bossert, *JdI.* 75 (1960), 3, Fig. 4; Schachermeyr, op. cit., Pl. 9:5; Lacy, *Greek Pottery in the Bronze Age* (1967), 242, Fig. 96 c.

851 Chalandriani Kastri, Syros. Settlement find. Early Bronze Age pot-bellied Cycladic pot of reddish clay with low funnel neck, the lustrous brown slip is rubbed away; three vertically pierced suspension eyes on the bulge. Lower part free of decoration; impressed and incised work on the upper part: wide zigzag band of incised pine-needles above two horizontal lines; in the upper apexes of the zigzag respectively one, in the lower, four, impressions of a round seal. The seal used was Egyptian (VII–VIII dynasty), according to Matz; height 11.5 cm.; diam. of the seal impressions 0.9 cm. Nat. Mus., Athens, Inv. No. 5080. – Tsountas, 122, Pl. 9:15; Zervos, *Cycl.*, 101, Fig. 101; Bossert, *JdI.* 75 (1960), 12 ff., Figs. 11, 12.

852 Cyclades. Early Bronze Age pot-bellied cauldron, with flaring mouth on neckless body. Two tripartite, vertically pierced suspension eyes above the widest part. Appliqué relief of a bearded goat facing left, with incised details on horns and back; the eye is indicated by a ring. Rare example of early Cycladic relief work; height 18 cm. Nat. Mus., Athens, Inv. No. 3524.

853 a, b Hagios Kosmas, near Athens. EH Tomb 12. Imported 'Cycladic frying-pan', with double-looped grip; grey clay with reddish brown slip. Concentric circular pattern: diagonally hatched band round the rim; connected spiral band further in, then thinner band of diagonal hatching; five-cornered star, with spiral in the centre (for this type of pan, particularly well known from Paros, cf. Montelius, *La Grèce Préclassique*, Pl. 89:8; Åberg, *Chronologie* IV, 78, Figs. 141, 142; Varoucha, *Ephem.*, 1925–26, 107, Fig. 9; Zervos, 172 f., Figs. 224, 225; Marinatos–Hirmer, Pl. 5; Bossert, *JdI.* 75 [1960], 4, Figs. 5, 6); diam. 17.5 cm. Nat. Mus., Athens. – Mylonas, *Aghios Kosmas* (1959), 92, No. 210; and p. 125, Pl. 148:210; cf. also Fig. 63.

854 Syros. Tomb 398: Early Bronze Age 'Cycladic frying-pan', with two rudimentary 'legs', above them an incised pudenda and white-filled stamped decoration: plain central circle, surrounded by a ring filled with impressions, in an eight-pointed star; height 27 cm. Nat. Mus., Athens. – Tsountas, *Ephem.*, 1899, 89, Pl. 9:4; Åberg, 77, Figs. 138, 139; Zervos, *Cycl.* 164, Fig. 211.

855 Syros. Tomb 174. Early Bronze Age 'Cycladic frying-pan', with two 'stump legs'; double rim of impressed zigzags and pudenda separated from the pictorial field in the same manner. Central motif: a many-oared Cycladic ship, with fish symbol, in a network of spirals; height 28 cm. Nat. Mus., Athens. – Tsountas, 86, Fig. 11; Fimmen, *Kret.-myk. Kultur*, 116, Fig. 107; Montelius, *La Grèce préclassique*, Pl. 90:13; Åberg, 77, Fig. 140; Bossert, *Altkreta*[3], No. 433; Matz, *Kreta–Mykene–Troja*, Pl. 12; Zervos, 170 f., Figs. 221–223; Schachermeyr, *Die ältesten Kulturen*, Pl. 9:2; Demargne, *Naissance de l'art grec* (1964), 44, Fig. 49 (Eng. trans., *Aegean Art* [1964]). – For ships on 'Cycladic frying-pans', cf. Karo, *AA*, 1915, 194, Fig. 7; Kunze, *Orchomenos* III, Pl. 29:3; Marinatos, *BCH.* 57 (1933), 170 ff. ('La Marine Créto-Mycénienne'); Barnett, *Antiquity* 32 (1958), 224, Fig. 3; for 'Cycladic frying-pans' as cult utensils, see Wiesner, *Grab und Jenseits* (1938), 134; cf. also *Delos* 18 (1938), Pl. 84:713.

856 Syros. Early Bronze Age 'Cycladic frying-pan', similar to *855*, but less well preserved; centrepiece consisting only of spiral network without rings; diam. 33.5 cm. Arch. Mus., Florence, Inv. No. 4333. – Milani, *Il R. Museo Archeologico di Firenze* (1912), Pl. 130:1.

857 Naxos. Early 'Cycladic frying pan'; 'feet' (i. e. handle) broken off. White-filled incised pattern: symbol of the sun in the middle surrounded by spiral quatrefoil, and outside, in each of its four quarters, a fish facing left; diam. 22 cm. Nat. Mus., Athens. – Frankfort, *Studies in Early Pottery of the Near East* II (1927), Pl. 6:2; Zervos, *Cycl.* 174, Fig. 228; Schachermeyr, *Die ältesten Kulturen*, Pl. 9:3.

858 Naxos. Necropolis of Spedos, Tomb 10: Early Cycladic 'triplet vase'; three connected bowls with bridge spouts rise from the dainty tripartite pedestal which has a ring-base below. Finely sifted yellow clay, painted with dark brown bands of hatching on the base and the inside rims of the bowls, and nested chevrons on the outside rims. Decoration on the little supporting columns much worn; height 18.9 cm.; identification as 'lamp' possible. Nat. Mus., Athens, Inv. No. 6108. – Stephanos, *Comptes Rendus Congr. Internat. Athènes* (1905), 221, Fig. 1; Frankfort, Pl. 5:2; Zervos, *Cycl.* 130, Fig. 154; Papathanasopoulos, *Delt.* 17 (1961–62), Pl. 49 a; Col. Pl. 1 after p. 116.

859 Thera. From 'Zahn's house' in the Potamos valley, near Akrotiri (cf. *860*, *861*): Tall, slender pithos, divided into six wide bands by horizontal ribs; on the front each band displays, in the same position, a blackish-brown disc symbol surrounded by rings flanked by semicircles. On the upper band, below the thick-lipped mouth, are two small lug handles; height 1.20 m. For the date, cf. *860*. Local mus., Thera. – Zahn, *Thera* 3 (1904), 43, Fig. 32 a; Åberg, op. cit., 134, Fig. 251.

860 Thera (for site, cf. *859*). Attractively formed pithos for fluids; with low spout, lug handles on the shoulder, low neck, and wide-rimmed mouth. Decoration in blackish brown, glaze-like colour: three superimposed circles, each filled with a cross and flanked on either side by a semicircle. Neck and mouth glazed; height 52 cm. Probably Middle Bronze Age, since the accompanying finds included much matt-painted ware and a sherd of imported Kamares ware. Local mus. Thera. – Zahn, Fig. 32 b; Åberg, 134, Fig. 252: Zervos, *Cycl.*, 256, Fig. 344.

861 Thera (for site, cf. *859*). Spherical vase, with loop handles, high conical pedestal, and short, cylindrical neck. Light slip with brown painting – probably matt painting – and superimposed white; rich vegetal patterns in hurried manner, but derived from MM III art of Crete; height 21.5 cm. Local mus., Thera. (Corresponding later Minoan ware, with conical foot from east Crete [Åberg, op. cit., 213, Figs. 293–295], are formally dependent on Cycladic prototypes; for dating and derivation, cf. Scholes, 'The Cyclades in the Later Bronze Age' in *BSA*. 51 [1956], 9 ff.; Lacy, *Greek Pottery*, 276, Fig. 110 c [Phylakopi]). – Zahn, 43, Fig. 32 d; Aberg, 136, Fig. 258; Zervos, *L'Art des Cyclades*, 243, Fig. 326.

862 Thera. Slender cylindrical vase, with parallel, sloping, loosely spaced floral decoration, 'dark on light matt painted' (Middle Cycladic III; cf. Lacy, 265); height 18.7 cm. Collection of the Ecole Française, Inv.-No. V. 47. – Zervos, 239, Fig. 322; Maffre, *BCH*. 96 (1972), 32 f. No. 66, Fig. 16 (with further bibliography).

863 Phylakopi, Melos. Detail of a fragmentary slender cylindrical vase (Middle Cycladic III). Decoration: four fishermen moving to the right, above dotted area and horizontal line; height 17 cm. The contour lines are traced in black; the bodies have a reddish brown lustre. Nat. Mus., Athens. – Edgar, *Excavations at Phylakopi in Melos* (1894), 123 ff., Fig. 95, Pl. 22; Zervos, 230 ff., Figs. 312–315; Lacy, 271, Fig. 109.

864–884: MIDDLE HELLADIC PERIOD – ATTICA – AEGINA – THE ARGOLID – BOEOTIA

864 Aegina. Two Middle Bronze Age belly-handled amphorae painted in several colours; graphic reconstruction (EM III/MM I). *864 a:* Cretan import; *864 b:* local imitation. Aegina Museum. – Welter, *Aigina* (1938), 16, Figs. 17, 18.

865 Boeotia. Pot-bellied storage jar, matt-painted with geometric motifs, convex neck and wide funnel mouth (MH). Arch. Mus., Chaironeia. – Welter, 18, Fig. 21. – Pieces of the same type from Drachmani and Eutresis: Soteriadis, *REG*. 25 (1912), 259, Fig. 5 = Wace and Thompson, *Prehist. Thess.* 198; Fig. 140 h = Montelius, *La Grèce préclass*. Pl. 102:6; Goldman, *Eutresis*, Pl. 13.

866 Orchomenos, Boeotia. Large matt-painted cup, with funnel mouth and wide, vertical strap handle (MH). Nat. Mus., Athens, Inv. No. 5861.

867 Aegina. Matt-painted cup, with low belly and thick round vertical handle. Ornament: horizontal row of filled circles linked by tangents (variant of spiral motif); MH. Aegina Museum. – Welter, *Aigina* (1938), 20, Fig. 23.

868 Orchomenos. Askos jug, with beaked mouth; matt-painted with geometric motifs (MH). Nat. Mus., Athens Inv. No. 5858. Hiller, Fisch oder Schiff (*Pantheon* 30 [1972], 439 ff.).

869 Aegina. Fragments of a large storage jar with matt-painted picture of man on ship's bow (MH). Survey of matt-painted pottery in Buck, *Hesperia* 33 (1964), 231 ff., Aegina Museum. – Welter, 19, Fig. 22; Vermeule, *Greece in the Bronze Age*, 76, Fig. 13; Marinatos, *Fourth Int. Congr. for Folk-Narr. Res. in Athens 1964* (1965), Pl. 17:4.

870 Lerna, the Argolid. Deposit V. Large matt-painted pithos, with low belly and horizontal lugs (cf. *871, 872*; MH). Arch. Mus., Argos.

871 Aegina. Two large thick-walled pithoi reconstructed
872 from fragments; both matt-painted with geometric motifs on upper part. Local Aeginaetan style; for this type from Aegina, see also *Ephem.*, 1895, Pl. 10:1–4 = Montelius, *La Grèce préclass.*, Pl. 117:10, 12–14; Fimmen, *KMK*, 142; Åberg, *Chronologie* IV, 42 f., Figs. 68–70 (Aegina and Korakou), and p. 32, Figs. 42, 43 (Eutresis); Blegen, *Korakou* (1921), 21, Fig. 28. On the lip of *872* are two pairs of holes for attaching a lid. Arch. Mus., Aegina. – Welter, *Aigina*, 17, Figs. 19, 20.

873 Mycenae. Voluminous belly-handled amphora, with matt-painted decoration as rows of lozenges. Two horizontal handles on the belly and two suspension eyes on shoulder (MH). Arch. Mus., Nauplia.

874 Argos. 'Aspis'. Wide-mouthed storage jar, with smooth base and lugs below the belly. Upper part painted matt with groups of chevrons and latticework; height 35 cm.; MH. Arch. Mus., Argos. – Vollgraff, *BCH*. 30 (1906), 20, Fig. 23.

875 Athens-Kerameikos. Region of Tomb of Hipparete. Tall handmade bi-conical handled cup with foot; 'light-on-dark' painting in the Cretan manner; zigzag ornament, dot rosettes. Clay reminiscent of Argive clay; thin blackish brown slip, matt white paint (MH). Kerameikos Mus., Athens, Inv. No. 645. – Kübler, *AA*. 1936, 205 f., Fig. 19.

876 Lerna, the Argolid. Handled bowl (height c. 11.8 cm.)
877 and sessile kantharos without foot (cf. *882, 883*); smooth grey Minyan ware (MH). Arch. Mus., Argos. – Caskey, *Festschr. f. Keramopoullos* (1953), 24 ff., Pl. 4; and *Hesperia* 23 (1954), Pl. 9 c (similar type to *876*, Blegen, *Korakou* 16, Fig. 22).

878 Argos. 'Aspis'. Elegant grey Minyan ware handled bowl with 'metallic' horizontal ribs and incised patterns of curves above the base (MH); similar vase from the 'Aspis' Argos in Fimmen, *KMK.*, 141, Fig. 141; *Reallex. Vorgesch.* 1 (1924), Pl. 9 c; *878:* Arch. Mus., Argos. – Vollgraff, *BCH*. 30 (1906), 13, Fig. 9.

879 Athens, Acropolis. Undecorated rather crude grey Minyan ware kylix, with two handles (MH III). Acropolis, Athens, Inv. No. 1961 Nak 194.

880 Orchomenos, Boeotia. Heavy grey Minyan ware goblet, with high ribbed foot and two small handles (MH). Similar type from Lianokladi in Fimmen, *KMK*. 141, Fig. 140 = Wace and Thompson, 187, Fig. 135 = Karo, *Reallex. Vorgesch.* I (1924), Pl. 9 b; cf. also Blegen, *Korakou*, 16, Fig. 20. *880:* Nat. Mus., Athens, Inv. No. 5854. – Biesantz, *Ullstein-Kunstgesch.* IV (1963), ill. suppl., 21.

881 Orchomenos. Grey Minyan ware goblet with foot, angular profile, and handles rising above the rim (MH). Nat. Mus., Athens, Inv. No. 5862.

882 Drachmani, Phokis. (excavated by Soteriadis; cf. *884*). Grey Minyan ware sessile kantharos; reconstructed from fragments (MH). Arch. Mus., Chaironeia.

883 Orchomenos. Low grey Minyan ware sessile kantharos; four grooves running round the belly. Nat. Mus., Athens.

884 Drachmani. Wide-mouthed grey Minyan ware bowl with foot, two horizontal handles on the belly and parallel ribs round upper part. Arch. Mus., Chaironeia. – cf. Soteriadis, *REG.* 25 (1912), 262, Fig. 10; Montelius, *La Grèce Préclass.*, 127 ff., Fig. 42.

885–897: MIDDLE MINOAN PERIOD – CRETE – EASTERN MEDITERRANEAN

885 Hagia Triada, south Crete. Three-handled painted jug studded with nipples; barbotine ware; height 15.5 cm., diameter 14.6 cm.; MM I–II (Banti), MM III/ LM I (Marinatos). Arch. Mus., Herakleion Inv. No. 5775. – Fimmen, *KMK.* 88, Fig. 71; Banti, *ASAtene* 13–14 (1930–1), 234 f., No. 338, Pl. 17 c; Zervos, *Crète*, 234, Fig. 311 left; Marinatos–Hirmer, Col. Pl. 4.

886 Gournia, east Crete. Small handled jug with mottled decoration; derived from Vasiliki ware (cf. *837*); height 12.2 cm.; MM I. Arch. Mus., Herakleion. – Marinatos–Hirmer, Col. Pl. 4.

887 Phaistos, south Crete. Steep-walled handled cup (height 7.5 cm.), with ornamental zone below the rim, colours: brown, red, and white. The remainder of the outside wall decorated with artificial shells in relief (MM II); for this cf. *Hesperia Art Bulletin* 20, No. 235; and Willetts, *Everyday Life in Ancient Crete* (1969), 117, Fig. 59. Arch. Mus., Herakleion, Inv. No. 5708. – Åberg, *Chronologie* IV, 188, Fig. 347; Zervos, *Crète*, 243, Fig. 331; Schiering, *JdI.* 75 (1960), 20 f., Fig. 7; id., *AntK.* 8 (1965), Pl. 3:5; Zoïs, *Ephem.* 1965, 108, Pl. 40.

888 Crete. Handled cup like *889* with painted marbled effect (MM). Arch. Mus., Herakleion. – Schiering, *JdI* 75 (1960), 20, Figs. 5, 6.

889 Crete. Handled cup with concave upper body (cf. *888*); stippled decoration in imitation of mottled natural stone; MM. Arch. Mus., Herakleion. – Schiering, loc. cit.

890 Col. Pl. 1: Phaistos, Old Palace. Handled Kamares ware cup; extremely thin 'eggshell' ware. Fine dense surface pattern in white and orange on black ground. Handle and mouth painted with groups of white lines; diam. 12 cm.; MM II (c. 1800 B.C.). Arch. Mus., Herakleion, Inv. No. 10570. – Matz, *Kreta u. frühes Griechenland*, 142 f. with col. ill.

891 Phaistos, Old Palace. Steep-walled bowl, with pointed spout and two lateral handles; rich polychrome painting; skilful stylized circular pattern; height 12.5 cm.; MM II. Arch. Mus., Herakleion. – Levi, *Bd'A.* 2 (1955), 144, Col. Pl.; Marinatos–Hirmer, Col. Pl. 5.

892 Phaistos, Old Palace. Bowl on low foot; polychrome picture inside with complex spiralled quatrefoil (torsion), interstices filled with bladder-like shapes; diam. 54 cm.; MM II. Arch. Mus., Herakleion. – Levi, *Bd'A.* 3 (1956), 248, Col. Pl. 2; Marinatos–Hirmer, Col. Pl. 13 and Pl. 23.

893 Phaistos, Old Palace. Richly painted Kamares-ware pedestal krater, with applied sculptural flowers and links. Imitation of metal elements; the artificial fragility was criticized by Higgins (*Min. and Myc. Art* [1967]; cf. on the other hand the appreciation by Zoïs, *Der Kamares-Stil, Werden u. Wesen*, [Diss., Tübingen 1968]); height 45.5 cm.; MM II. Arch. Mus., Herakleion. – Levi, 248, Col. Pl.; Marinatos–Hirmer, Col. Pl. 12; Schiering, *JdI.* 75 (1960), 21, Fig. 8; Schachermeyr, *Die min. Kultur des alten Kreta* (1964), Pl. 9 c.

894 Palaikastro, east Crete. Polychrome painted bowl with white-painted sculptured little bird inside; diam. 11.3 cm.; MM I. Arch. Mus., Herakleion. – Dawkins, *BSA.* Suppl. I (1923), 12, Pl. 6 d; Maraghiannis, I, Pl. 35:1 and II, Pl. 36:2; Zervos, *Crète*, 294, Fig. 262; Marinatos–Hirmer, Pl. 18; Demargne, *Naissance de l'art grec* (1964), 108, Fig. 138 (Eng. trans., *Aegean Art* [1964]); Zoïs, *Der Kamares-Stil*, 242.

895 Phaistos. Old Palace, Room LXIV. Dark pithos of rough, thickwalled clay, painted in white and brownish yellow; three handles. Ornaments: wavy lines and spirals, fish with bladderlike motif hanging from its mouth; height 50 cm.; MM (c. 1750 B.C.). Arch. Mus., Herakleion. – Levi, *ASAtene* 33/34 (1955/56), Pl. 3; Marinatos–Hirmer, Col. Pl. 11; Demargne, *Naissance*, 98, Fig. 124; Schachermeyr, op. cit., Pl. 9 d; Zoïs, *Ephem.* 1965, 106, Pl. 33 a, b.

896 Phaistos, Old Palace: Three-handled pithos painted in white and light red on dark ground. Rhythmic symmetrical decoration on surface; height 45.5 cm., Kamares style (MM II). Arch. Mus., Herakleion. – Levi, op. cit., 296 Fig. 11:1; Marinatos–Hirmer, Col. Pl. 10; Biesantz, *Ullstein – Kunstgesch.* IV (1963), Col. Pl. 2.

897 Fig. 27: Ras Shamra, north Syria. Fragment of an imported Cretan Kamares-ware cup (MM II, c. 1800 B.C., cf. Col. Pl. 1, *890*). Network of fine red-and-white decoration, similar in structure to *890*. – Schaeffer, *Syria* 18 (1937), 151, Fig. 16; and *JdI.* 52 (1937), 141, Fig. 1; id., *Ugaritica* I (1939), 56, Fig. 44; Bossert, *Altsyrien*, Fig. 727; Smith, *Interconnections in the Ancient Near East* (1965), Fig. 19 b.

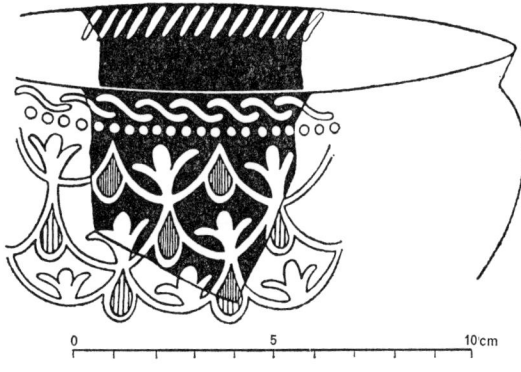

Fig. 27
897 Ras Shamra, fragment of a Kamares cup

898–903: LATE BRONZE AGE, PHASE I – CRETE – ATTICA – EGYPT

898 Palaikastro, east Crete. Two-handled vase (pilgrim flask), painted with an octopus, diagonal to the axis of the vessel. The motif organically combines natural forms and winding curves; height 28 cm., LM I (late sixteenth century B. C.). Arch. Mus., Herakleion. – Maraghiannis, *Ant. Crét.* I, Pl. 35:10; Bosanquet, *BSA.* Suppl. I (1923), Col. Pl. 18 a; Evans, *PM.* II, 509, Fig. 312 d; Zervos, *Crète*, 383, Fig. 561; Marinatos–Hirmer, Pl. 87; Matz, *Kreta u. frühes Griechenland*, 147, col. ill.; Schachermeyr, *Die minoische Kultur des alten Kreta* (1964), Pl. 15 a; Schiering, *AntK.* 8 (1965), Pl. 2:1.

899 Pseira, House D, Room 5. Pithos densely covered with spiral patterns; height 80 cm., LM I (late sixteenth century B. C.). Arch. Mus., Herakleion. – Seager, *Excavations on the Island of Pseira* (1910), 28, Fig. 9; Montelius, *La Grèce préclass.*, Pl. 71:2; Maraghiannis, *Ant. Crét.* II, Pl. 20; Åberg, *Chronologie* IV (1933), 216, Fig. 402:1; Bossert, *Altkreta*, Fig. 355; Kantor, *AJA.* 51 (1947), Pl. 2 n. See a similar vessel from Knossos in Evans, *PM.* II, 423, Fig. 245, and Marinatos–Hirmer, Pl. 80.

900 Egypt. Jug, richly decorated with marine life: nautilus, coral, seaweed. Narrow trefoil mouth with wide round rim; height 25 cm. Form based on metal models; similar to jug from the palace of Kato Zakro (cf. v. Matt, *Das antike Kreta* [1967], Pl. 174). LM I (sixteenth century). Mus. Chateau Boréli, Marseilles, Inv. No. 1043/113 (from the collection of Clot Bey, chief surgeon to the Egyptian viceroy). – Furtwängler, *Kl. Schriften* II, 120 f.; Perrot–Chipiez VI (1894), 926 f., Figs. 486, 488; Evans, *PM.* II, 509, Fig. 312 a; Kantor, Pl. 7 c; Matz, *KMT.* Pl. 73; Schachermeyr, op. cit., Pl. 16; *Les Trésors d'Art du Musée d'Arch. de Marseille: Chateau Borély* (1963), Fig. 12.

901 Knossos, Complex of houses outside the palace. Cup with high handle; for the decoration, cf. neck of *903*; height 16 cm.; LM I. – Zervos, *Crète*, 348, Fig. 509.

902 Pseira. Basket-like vase with two loop handles; only known example of this form; reconstructed from fragments. Decoration: continuous frieze of sacred double axes: height 19.8 cm.; LM I/II (c. 1500 B. C.). Arch. Mus., Herakleion, Inv. No. 5407. – Seager, op. cit., Fig. 12; Montelius, op. cit., Pl. 69:1 a, b; Maraghiannis, *Ant. Crét.* II, Pl. 21; Evans, *PM.* IV, 290, Fig. 226; Zervos, *Crète* 379, Fig. 557; Marinatos–Hirmer, Pl. 84; Karo, *Greifen am Thron* (1959), 107, Fig. 69; Willetts, *Everyday Life in Ancient Crete* (1969), 87, Fig. 40; Matz–Buchholz, *Arch. Hom.* Q (1970), Pl. 3 b.

903 Region of Vari, Attica. From a chamber tomb. Excel-
a,b lently preserved beaked jug; decoration on neck as *901*; four figure of eight shields on body (cf. *945, 946*); Cretan import; LM I. Private collection, Athens. – Photo DAI., Athens (1916).

904–907: UNPAINTED RELIEF PITHOI – CRETE AND MYCENAE (*906:* stone)

904 Knossos, West magazine of the palace (replaced *in situ*, without inv. no.): Thick-walled relief pithos; unarticulated barrel shape, only mouth differentiated. Four rows of suspension eyes corresponding to the four areas of relief with circular and linear motifs; height 1.60 m., LM II. – Karo, *Greifen* (1959), 109, Fig. 70.

905 Mallia. Thick-walled relief pithos, similar in form to *904*, but mouth more strongly differentiated and three relief zones: bands of wavy lines, spirals, horizontal bands with circular motifs. Early sixteenth century; replaced near north entrance to the palace; cf. *62, 64.* – Matz, *Kreta u. frühes Griech.* (1962), 100, ill. suppl. 10.

906 Knossos. Palace, Room of the 'Crocus Gatherer': Large storage jar with offset foot and lip; thick relief spirals; serpentine; height 49 cm.; MM or LM I/II. Arch. Mus., Herakleion, Inv. No. Stone 22. – Warren, *Minoan Stone Vases* (1969), 61, Fig. P 323..

907 Mycenae. Burial pithos richly decorated with relief ridges (cf. *187*); well-defined foot, very narrow mouth; height 1.70 m.; LH III c. Arch. Mus., Nauplia. – For bibliography, cf. *187*; also Furumark, *Myc. Pottery*, 75, Fig. 21:13; Lacy, *Greek Pottery in the Bronze Age* (1967), 218, Fig. 90 c; Matz–Buchholz, *Arch. Hom.* Q (1970), 29, Fig. 10 a.

908–1024: LATE BRONZE AGE, PHASE I–III – GREECE – NORTHERN AND EASTERN AEGEAN – CYCLADES – CRETE – SYRIA – EGYPT – ITALY

908 Samikon–Kleidi, Triphylia. Grave tumulus: Early Mycenaean pot-bellied, handled jug with steeply rising mouth, neatly cut off. Decoration: grotesque stylized flying bird; bichrome technique, emphatic contours; height 20.5 cm.; MH III/LH I. New Mus., Olympia., Find. No. Pi 49. – Yalouris, *Delt.* 20 (1965), Mel. 11, No. 3, Pl. 6 a; Col. Pl. 1; Vermeule, *Greece in the Bronze Age* (1964), Pl. 9 f.

909 Strephi near Olympia. Fragment of the rim of a Mycenaean krater. Decoration: bands of spirale, dark brown glaze; LH III a. New Mus., Olympia, Photo. No. 4549. — For the site see Yalouris, *Delt.* 17 (1961/62), Chron. 107.

910 Makrysia, near Olympia. Chamber Tomb A on the
a,b Alpheios, from the dromos: Krater fragments with freely painted goats between spiral bands on *910 a;* LH III. New Mus., Olympia, Finds Nos. P 241, P 241 b (Neg. No. 3885). – Yalouris, *Prakt.* 1954, 297, Fig. 12.

911 Knossos, House of Frescoes, Room H: Wide-mouthed vase on three moderately high feet, with two strong horizontal handles below the rim. Two zones of spirals separated by a wide band of glaze; height 28 cm.; MM III/LM I. Arch. Mus., Herakleion. – Evans, *PM.* II, 436, Fig. 253 c; Zervos, *Crète*, 368, Fig. 540; Schachermeyr, *Die min. Kultur des alten Kreta* (1964), Pl. 14 e.

912 Lower Egypt (exact site unknown; in Abbott Colln.,
a–d New York, in 1860). Pot-bellied beaked jug of light yellow clay, painted in glaze technique with marine animals and plants (for these, cf. *898, 900, 913, 917, 929, 935, 943, 944, 970, 975, 976, 1030, 1034, 1036*). Mainland-Mycenaean, according to Stubbings, but probably Cretan; cf. very similar piece from east Crete: Seager, *Pseira*, Fig. 13; Montelius, *La Grèce Préclass.*, Pl. 71:1. *912*: height 22 cm.; LM I b/II (fifteenth century). Brooklyn Mus., New York, Inv. No. 37, 13 E. – Murray, *AJA* 6 (1890), 437 ff., Pl. 22 upper; Perrot-Chipiez, VI (1894), 36, Fig. 105; and 869 Fig. 436 (drawing); Dussaud, *Civil. Préhell.*, 114, Fig. 85; *Cat. of Egypt. Antiq. of New York Hist. Soc.*, (1915), 6, No. 78; *Quart. of New York Hist. Soc.*, Jan. 1929; *Art and Techniques of Ceramics* (Brooklyn 1937), 44 with Fig.; Wace and Blegen, *Klio* 32 (1939/40), 146, No. D 1; Kantor, *AJA*. 51 (1947), Pl. 7 d; Stubbings, *Mycenaean Pottery from the Levant* (1951), 58; Caldwell and Gyles, *The Ancient World*, 1966, 119 with Fig.; *The Brooklyn Mus. Handbook* (1967), 108 f. and Fig.

913 Nirou Chani, north Crete. Wide-mouthed cylindrical vase with spout and two horizontal handles; painted with marine fauna and floral motifs (cf. *912*); height 18 cm., LM I. Arch. Mus., Herakleion. – Zervos, *Crète*, 381, Fig. 559.

914 Gournia. Double jug for cult purposes (cf. *915, 916*); striped decoration, sketchy horizontal wavy lines and wider ornamental strips on the belly with stipple-filled nautili (similar form of vase: Boyd-Hawes, *Gournia*, Pl. 9:9 = Maraghiannis, *Ant. Crét.* II, Pl. 27:1; and Montelius, *La Grèce préclass.*, Pl. 80:1 [Isopata, grave 6]); height 26 cm., LM I b (c. 1500). Arch. Mus., Herakleion. – Boyd–Hawes, Pl. J; Maraghiannis, Pl. 39:3; Montelius, Pl. 73:6; Zervos, *Crète*, 362, Fig. 531; Marinatos–Hirmer, Pl. 84 upper.

915 Katsamba (harbour area of Knossos, cf. *919, 938*). Grave A. Double vase; mouths almost completely stopped by clay slabs, two small sculptured birds on right-hand vase; painted with floral motifs; height 18 cm., width 26 cm.; LM II. Arch. Mus., Herakleion, Inv. No. 9556. – Alexiou, *Katsamba* (mod. Gk., 1967), 42 f., Pls. 7 a, b, 9 a; Zervos, Fig. 532.

916 Argive Heraion, Prosymna. Chamber Tomb 44: Composite cult vessel with stirrup handle (kernos), consisting of three painted, pot-bellied vases; put together from fragments; greyish green clay, yellow slip, blackish brown glaze; height, incl. handle, 8.4 cm.; LH III. Nat. Mus., Athens, Find No. 1029. – Blegen, *Prosymna*, 455, Figs. 530 and 727; Lacy, *Greek Pottery*, 211, Fig. 84 c.

917 Crete. Site unknown. Stirrup jar with three small stirrup handles painted with nautili; intact, one side erased; height 20 cm., diam 24.5 cm., LM I b/II. Private collection, Basel. – Schefold, 'Die Bedeutung der kretischen Meeresbilder', *AntK*. 1 (1958), 3 ff., Pl. 1:1, 2; and *Meisterwerke griech. Kunst* (1960), 116 f., No. 20.

918 Samikon–Kleidi, Triphylia. Grave tumulus, Grave I D (cf. *908*): Cup-like handled vase, with fairly narrow funnel mouth (for this type, cf. Evans, *PM*. II, Fig. 315). Decoration: hatched, bladder-like forms; height 7.5 cm., LH I. New Mus., Olympia, Find No. Pi 68, Photo No. 3792. – Yalouris, *Delt*. 20 (1965), Mel., 6 ff., 14, No. 16, Pl. 10 a.

919 Katsamba (cf. *915, 938*). Grave B: Long-necked beaked jug with red glaze applied (motifs: papyrus, nautilos); moulded figure-of-eight shield studded with bosses; height 49.5 cm., LM II (fifteenth century). Arch. Mus., Herakleion, Inv. No. 9540. – Alexiou, *Kret. Chron.* 6 (1952), 25 ff., Col. Pl. A; and *Katsamba*, (mod. Gk., 1967), 44, Pl. 5 a, b; Zervos, *Crète*, 430, Fig. 701; Marinatos–Hirmer, Pl. 95.

920 Palaikastro, east Crete. Handled jug. Decoration: spiralling tendrils and rosettes, tongue pattern on neck; form of handle based on metal models; height 24.5 cm.; early fifteenth century. Arch. Mus., Herakleion, Inv. No. 5172. – Dawkins, *BSA.* 11 (1904/05), 280, Fig. 11; Bosanquet, *BSA.* Suppl. I (1923), 46, Fig. 35; Montelius, *La Grèce préclass.*, Pl. 75:3; Marinatos–Hirmer, Pl. 83 upper; Matz, *Kreta u. frühes Griechenland* (1962), 143 and 145 with col. ill.; Schachermeyr, *Die min. Kultur des alten Kreta* (1964), Pl. 15.

921 Miletus, east of the Temple of Athene, excavated in 1957. Fragments of a fairly large, good-quality vase; regular pattern of dots on field (cf. *924*), then arcs (cf. *422*); LM/LH II (cf. similar sherds from Miletus: Weickert, *6. internat. Kongr. f. Archäologie, Berlin 1939* [1940], Pl. 24). Local mus., Miletus. – Weickert, *Istanbul Mitt.* 9/10 (1959/60), Pl. 35:3.

922 Thebes, Boeotia. Hagia Anna, Chamber Tomb 2:9
923 (*922*), and Kolonaki, Chamber Tomb 26:9 (*923*). Two bridge-spouted jugs of similar form, *923* slightly more squat (height 18 cm.); same pattern on neck. *922* (height 22 cm.) has curved stripes (cf. *921*), *923* a denser network pattern; LH II a. Arch. Mus., Thebes, Inv. Nos. 447 (*922*) and 436 (*923*). – Keramopoulos, *Ephem.* 1910, 225, Pl. 9:2; and *Delt.* 1917, 198, Fig. 143:2 (*923*); Montelius, *La Grèce Préclass.*, Pl. 104:3 (*922*).

924 Aegina. From a grave. Beaked jug of the same type as *921* and *923*, but taller and more globular. Stylized ivy leaves with swastika on field of dots. From Aegina, as indicated by clay and glaze. LH II a (Furumark), or LH III (Bossert). For Mycenaean chamber tombs in Aegina, see Harland, *Prehistoric Aigina* (1925), reviewed by Welter, *Gnomon* 1929, 185 ff. and 269. Arch. Mus., Aegina. – Welter, *AA.* 1925, 323 f., Fig. 6; and *Aigina* (1938), 23, Fig. 26; Bossert, *Altkreta*, Fig. 124; Furumark, *Myc. Pottery*, 270, Fig. 35 u.

925 Hagios Kosmas, Attica. House R. Mycenaean handled cup; yellow clay and slip, reddish-brown glaze; painted with double axes, with handles replaced by double wavy lines, separated by vertical rows of dots (cf. *928*, and Buchholz, *Zur Herkunft der kretischen Doppelaxt* [1959], 12 ff., esp. note 6); diam. of mouth: 10.5 cm., height 7 cm., LH I/II. Nat. Mus., Athens. – Mylonas, *Aghios Kosmas* (1959), 49 f., Pl. 135:72.

926 Region of Knossos. From a grave: Elegant three-handled storage jar in the Palace style, with floral ornament (LM III); height c. 30 cm. Arch. Mus., Herakl. – *A Land called Crete: Photographs*, No. XVII.

927 The Argolid. Three-handled storage jar with additional suspension eyes. Painted with papyrus and rosettes (same form of papyrus motif on sherds from the Tomb of Aegisthus, Mycenae: Wace, *BSA.* 25 [1921 to 1923], Pl. 51 b and *Myc.* [1949/1964], Fig. 61 b), LH II a. Arch. Mus., Nauplia. – cf. Furumark, *Myc. Pottery*, 261, Fig. 33:24.

928 Argive Heraion, Prosymna. Tomb 1, dromos: Ovoid rhyton with differentiated neck and ring handle; ochre-grey terracotta, yellow slip, blackish brown glaze. For the decoration of double axes cf. *925;* assembled from fragments; height 23 cm.; LH I. Nat. Mus., Athens. – Blegen, *Prosymna*, 406, No. 196, Fig. 670; Buchholz, *Zur Herkunft der kretischen Doppelaxt* (1959), 13, n. 6 b; Lacy, *Greek Pottery*, 187, Fig. 74 d.

929 Pseira, east Crete. Ovoid rhyton, more slender than *928* and *930*, with bulging collar and small ring handle; reconstructed from fragments. Decoration: fish in net. Exact counterpart from Pseira in Arch. Mus., Herakleion, Inv. No. 4508 (Seager, *Pseira*, Fig. 10; Maraghiannis, *Ant. Crét.* II, Pl. 21; Montelius, *La Grèce préclass.*, Pl. 71:3; Evans, *PM.* II, 509, Fig. 312 f.; Zervos, *Crète*, 384, Fig. 562; v. Matt, *Das antike Kreta* [1967], Pl. 156); height 27 cm., LM I b (1550–1500 B. C.). Univ. Mus., Philadelphia, Inv. No. MS. 4287. – Exhibition catalog, Smith. Coll. Mus. of Art, Northhampton, Mass.; *A Land Called Crete* (1967), No. 34.

930 Chalkis–Vromousa, Euboea. Chamber Tomb 5: Ovoid rhyton, probably Cretan import. Metallic collar at top of neck and ring handle; ochre-yellow terracotta, reddish brown glaze. Three friezes with tripartite motifs; height 23 cm., diam. 11.5 cm., LH II a. Arch. Mus., Chalkis, Inv. No. 401. – Furumark, *Myc. Pottery*, 333, Fig. 56, motif 38:1; Hankey, *BSA.* 47 (1952), 61 f., Fig. 1.

931 Knossos. Three-handled storage jar with papyrus decoration (cf. *927*, also Evans, *Prehist. Tombs*, Pl. 101) and rocky background (Marinatos: 'sand', cf. *938*); height 78 cm., LM II (c. 1430 B.C.). Arch. Mus., Herakleion. – Fimmen, *KMK.*, 140, Fig. 139; Schiering, *JdI.* 75 (1960), 27, Fig. 17; Matz, *KMT.* Pl. 72; and *Kreta u. frühes Griechenland* (1962), 146, 149 with col. ill.; Marinatos–Hirmer, Pl. 92; Schachermeyr, *Die min. Kultur des alten Kreta* (1964), Pl. 63 c; v. Matt, *Das antike Kreta* (1967), 88.

932 Dendra, the Argolid. Chamber Tomb 10: Three-handled storage jar with additional suspension eyes, decorated with a dense network of spirals; yellow terracotta, reddish brown glaze. Similar ornamental structure on corresponding vase from Kakovatos (Müller, *AM.* 34 [1909], Pl. 17; Fimmen, *KMK.* 91, Fig. 76; Montelius, *La Grèce préclass.*, Pl. 121); height 70 cm., diam. 52 cm., LH II. Arch. Mus., Nauplia. – Persson, *Dendra* II (1942), 64 ff., Fig. 77; Biesantz, *Ullstein-Kunstgesch.* IV (1963, ill. suppl. 22).

933 Phaistos, New Palace: Beaked jug with reed decoration (for this, cf. Popham, *BSA.* 62 [1967], 337 ff., Pl. 79 a, e, f; Furumark, *Myc. Pottery*, 281, Fig. 40, motif 16) in highly developed naturalistic floral style; put together from fragments; height 29 cm., LM I a (Zervos), LM I b (1550–1520 B.C. Marinatos). Arch. Mus., Herakleion, Inv. No. 3962. – Pernier-Banti, *Festòs* II, 175, Fig. 106, Pl. 2; Zervos, *Crète*, 349, Fig. 511; Karo, *Greifen am Thron* (1959), 97, Fig. 64; Marinatos–Hirmer, Pl. 79; Platon, *Crete*, Pl. 97; v. Matt, *Das antike Kreta* (1967), 115, col. ill.

934 Dictaean Cave, Crete. Fragmentary pilgrim flask with uncommon painted decoration: a twelve-cornered star in a circle (for this, cf. Zervos, *Crète*, 304, Fig. 441), a background of dots, with small reserved discs; LM III. Arch. Mus., Herakleion. – Unpublished (photo DAI. Athens).

935 Dictaean Cave. Late Minoan cup with lateral bridge spout; ingenious stylized octopus; chequered pattern (not visible here); height 16.5 cm., LM III. Arch. Mus., Herakleion. – Hogarth, *BSA.* 6 (1899/1900), 103, Figs. 31, 32; Maraghiannis, *Ant. Crét.* I, Pl. 30:2; Zervos, *Crète.* 443. Figs. 729, 730.

936 Chalkis–Trypa, Euboea. Chamber Tomb 8: Handled
a, b jug with straight mouth; ochre-yellow clay and slip, black glaze, some white body colour; put together from fragments. Decoration arranged in three panels: large stylized lilies. Height 32 cm., diam. 21 cm., LH II. Arch. Mus., Chalkis, Inv. No. 491. – Hankey, *BSA.* 47 (1952), 76, Pl. 24.

937 Vapheio, near Sparta. Tholos tomb (162). Large
a, b amphora-like storage jar; a sketched reconstruction from fragments; Palace style (LH II a). Dense interwoven decoration of bands encircling the vase; two antithetical rows of comma-shaped leaves on horizontal lip *(937 b)*; for the individual decorative motifs, cf. Furumark, *Myc. Pottery*, 281, Fig. 40, motif 17:5; 323, Fig. 54, motif 31:1; 333, Fig. 56, motif 38:7; 391, Fig. 68, motif 62:8. Height *c.* 1 m.; Nat. Mus., Athens. – Bosanquet, *JHS.* 24 (1904), 317 ff., Pl. 11.

938 Katsamba (harbour area of Knossos; cf. *915, 919*). Chamber Tomb Z: Three-handled storage jar. Decoration: zoned helmets lying on stony background (cf. Schiering, *JdI.* 75 [1960], 26, Fig. 16; and *931*); height 97 cm. (Alexiou, Zervos), 47.5 cm. (Marinatos, probably mistaken), LM II (c. 1450 B.C.). Arch. Mus., Herakleion, Inv. No. 10058. – Alexiou, *Antiquity* 28 (1954), 211, Pl. 8; id., *Prakt.* 1954, 375, Fig. 7; id., *Katsamba* (mod. Gk., 1967), 51, Pls. 18 a, b; 19 a–c; Hampe, *Gymnasium* 63 (1956), 12, Pl. 9; Zervos, *Crète* 435, Fig. 708; Marinatos–Hirmer, Pl. 94; Demargne, *Naissance*, 157, Fig. 210 (Eng. trans., *Aegean Art);* Schachermeyr, *Die min. Kultur des alten Kreta* (1964), Pl. 63 d.

939 Isopata, near Knossos. Polychrome painted conical vase with two double-ring handles; form based on alabaster models. Decoration: picture of a warrior's helmet (cf. *938*); height 28.5 cm.; MM III/LM I (Karo), LM II (Zervos): *c.* 1500 B.C.). Arch. Mus., Herakleion, Inv. No. 7702. – Zervos, *Crète*, 433, Fig. 705; Karo, *Greifen am Thron* (1959), 43, Fig. 60.

940 Vourvatsi, Attica. Bucket with bail handle, perforated base, rare form (LH III). For bail-handled vases in the Greek Bronze Age, cf. Buchholz, *Jahrbuch d. Hamb. Kunstsammlungen* 13 (1968), 13 ff.; and *AA.* 1969, 318 ff.; cf. Zervos, *Crète*, 443, Fig. 728 (vase of the same type from Nirou Chani). *940*: striped decoration; height *c.* 21 cm. Nat. Mus., Athens, prov. No. 192. – Stubbings, *BSA.* 42 (1947), 58, Pl. 18:6.

941 Aegina. Grave finds: Two squat, three-handled ala-
942 bastra with varying profiles. *941* has a dotted screen on the upper part above three horizontal lines; *942*: wavy line with low, filled-in loops (Furumark, *Myc. Pottery*, 373, Fig. 65, motif 53:2), LH II a/b. Local mus., Aegina. – Unpublished *(942);* Welter, *Aigina*, 24, Fig. 27 *(941).*

943 Greece. Site unknown. Beaked jug assembled from fragments. Decoration: very stylized nautili, with no relation to their natural form (cf. Furumark, 307, Fig. 50:6,9); richly decorated handle; pendant 'torsion' pattern of tongues on neck; height 27 cm.; LH II (first half of fifteenth century). Pomerance Coll., New York. – v. Bothmer, *Ancient Art from New York*

Private Collections (1961), 25, No. 99, Pls. 26, 31; *The Pomerance Colln. of Anc. Art* (1966), 72, No. 79.

944 Chalkis–Trypa, Euboea. Chamber Tomb 7. Beaked jug with even more abstract nautilus pattern than *943*; height 27.5 cm., diam. 20.8 cm., LH III a. Arch. Mus., Chalkis, Inv. No. 468. – Hankey, *BSA*. 47 (1952), 73, Pl. 24.

945 Kythera. Grave find 1915 (cf. *1161*): Low cylindrical
a, b askos with lateral suspension eyes, Minoan import. Decoration on shoulder: three figure-of-eight shields (cf. *903, 946, 947*) and floral motifs loosely arranged; LM II b. Nat. Mus., Athens, Inv. No. 6232. – Staïs, *Delt*. 1915, 193, Fig. 2; Furumark, op. cit., 44, Figs. 12, 195.

946 Chalkis-Trypa. Chamber Tomb 10: Globular stirrup jug with three handles. Decoration: figure-of-eight shields, like *903, 945, 947*; Cretan type; height 15.5 cm.; diam. 16.5 cm., LM II. Arch. Mus., Chalkis, Inv. No. 517. – Hankey, op. cit., 78 f., Fig. 4.

947 Crete or Greece. Site unknown. Squat, three-handled alabastron. Decoration: figure-of-eight shields (*903, 945, 946*) in a metope-like structured frieze; handles do not harmonize with figure-of-eight symbols; height 9.3 cm., diam. 22 cm.; LM/LH II a. Royal Ontario Mus., Toronto, Inv. No. 960.38,1. – Leipen, *Annual, Art and Archaeology Division of the Roy. Ont. Mus.*, 1961, 27 ff.; Heinrich, *Art Treasures in the Roy. Ont. Mus.* (1963), 93 with Fig.

948 Thera. Imported glaze-painted bottle, with round base; small ring handle now lost. Rare form, more Cretan than mainland. The festoon-like motif interspersed with networks of scales evolved from the rocky landscape motif. Local mus., Thera (from photo, DAI, Athens).

949 Hierapetra, south-east Crete. From a grave: Three-handled vase with slender tapering lower body; height 16.3 cm.; diam. 14.7 cm.; diam. of base 4.7 cm. Fine reddish brown clay, light yellow slip, blackish brown glaze, partly destroyed by acidity in the soil. Striped decoration, two close rows of vertical 'S' hooks on shoulder, narrow linear frieze at base of neck. LH III a/b. Untied Colln., Hamburg.

950 Chalkis–Trypa. Chamber Tomb 7. Cylindrical alabas-
a, b tron-pyxis with sharp bend at shoulder; unusually tall form; ochre-yellow clay and slip, dark reddish brown glaze. Decoration: uninterrupted pattern of horizontal stripes and rows of dots; ornament on base: double circle with four wavy double spokes attached to it; height 11.5 cm., diam. 13.5 cm.; LH I/II. Arch. Mus., Chalkis, Inv. No. 469 A. – Hankey, *BSA.*, 47 (1952), 73, Pl. 18.

951 Chalkis–Trypa. Chamber Tomb 10: Cylindrical alabastron-pyxis; ochre-grey clay and slip, dark brown glaze. Decoration: wavy landscape in two zones round the body and one on the shoulder. Base with furled spiral and four double spokes; height 10.5 cm., diam. 12 cm.; LH II a. Arch. Mus., Chalkis, Inv. No. 520 A. – Hankey, 80, Pl. 18.

952 Chalkis–Vromousa. Chamber Tomb 4: Squat alabastron
a, b with low cylindrical wall; ochre-grey clay, grey slip, lustrous brown glaze. Double zigzag on shoulder, wavy line on body, concentric circles on base; height 8 cm., diam. 13.5 cm.; LH III a. Arch. Mus., Chalkis, Inv. No. 451 B. – Hankey, 70, Pl. 18.

953 Chalkis–Trypa. Tomb 11. Squat three-handled alabastron; light yellow clay, dark yellow slip, lustrous reddish brown glaze. Decoration: wavy landscape, concentric circles on base; height 5.5 cm., diam. 15 cm.; LH III a. Arch. Mus., Chalkis, Inv. No. 523 E. – Hankey, 80, Pl. 15.

954 Chalkis–Vromousa. Chamber Tomb 2: Flat, three-handled alabastron; ochre-yellow clay and slip, opaque brown glaze. Decoration: ivy leaf on triple hooked stem, concentric circles on base; height 5.5 cm., diam. 20 cm.; LH III a. Arch. Mus., Chalkis, Inv. No. 438 B. – Hankey, 68, Pl. 15.

955 Chalkis–Vromousa. Chamber Tomb 2: Three-handled alabastron, ochre-coloured clay and slip, lustrous dark brown glaze. Decoration: hatched ivy leaves on triple stems and hook ornaments; concentric circles on base; height 6.5 cm., diam. 13 cm.; LH II/III. Arch. Mus., Chalkis, Inv. No. 438 A. – Fimmen, *KMK*., 91, Fig. 77; Furumark, *Myc. Pottery*, 299, Fig. 47:3; Hankey, 67, Pl. 15.

956 Areopagus, Athens. Mycenaean vases in a chamber tomb
a, b (p. 43, Figs. 17, *183*); *956 a*: as excavated; *956 b*: as reconstructed; length of dromos: 11 m.; width 2 m.; chamber 2.75×4×6 m. Among the grave goods: ivory box (cf. *1281 a-c*) and Palestinian monochrome imported amphora. Agora mus., Athens. – Shear, *Hesperia* 9 (1940), 274 ff., Fig. 15 (ground plan), Fig. 17 (position of finds); Lemerle, *BCH*. 63 (1939), 291, Fig. 5; Walter, *AA*. 1940, 155 ff., Fig. 26 (plan), Fig. 27 (position of finds); *The Athenian Agora: Guide to the Excav. and Mus.* (^{2}1962), 19, 78, 114, 145 (Myc. graves); Amiran, *Ancient Pottery of the Holy Land*, 1970, 142, Fig. 132; Travlos, *Bildlexikon zur Topographie des antiken Athen* (1971), 9 ff., Figs. 6–10.

957 Eleona, Kos. Grave 17 (excavated in 1943). *957*: Im-
958 ported pot-bellied handled jug; non-Greek, probably west Anatolian, form; slender neck, strong beaked mouth, dark brown clay micaceous in part. Decoration: three bosses in front on shoulder, three bands of wavy lines separated by grooves. *958*: Imported Mycenaean three-handled jar, slender below with hatched pattern on shoulder, light pink clay, light yellow slip, reddish brown glaze (similar type from Protogeometric Tomb 10, Seraglio, Kos: Morricone, *Bd'A* [1950], 319, Fig. 90 below, centre); heights 25.5 cm. and 19.3 cm.; LH III a/b. Arch. Mus., Kos, Inv. Nos. 376 and 367. – Morricone, *ASAtene* 27/28 (1965/66), 67 ff., Figs. 40, 41.

959 Aegina. From a grave: Wide-mouthed krater with vertical handles. Decoration: solid circles linked by double lines arranged in two rows; motif derived from network of spirals: cf. corresponding Minoan ware (MM III, Evans, *Prehist. Tombs*, 91, Fig. 102 a [larnax]; Furumark, *Myc. Pottery*, 403, Fig. 70, motif 66 a). LH III a. Arch. Mus., Aegina. — Åberg, *Chronologie* IV, 216, Fig. 403; Welter, *Aigina*, 26, Fig. 30.

960 Thera. Bronze Age monochrome rhyton, crude form; height without handle 26 cm. Local mus., Thera. – cf. Evans, *PM* II, Pl. 24:1.

961 Ialysos, Rhodes. From a grave: Pointed Mycenaean rhyton, handle lost; lustrous reddish brown stripe painting; two bands filled with chevrons on upper third. For the form, cf. *1629* (Cyprus); height 32.4 cm.; LH III a/b. Royal Ontario Mus., Toronto, Inv. No. 920.69,3. – Robinson, Harcum and Iliffe, *Catalogue of Greek Vases in the Royal Ontario Mus. of Arch.* (1930), 19, No. 74; Furumark, *Myc. Pottery*, 383, Fig. 67, motif 58:34.

962 Argive Heraion, Prosymna. Chamber Tomb 44. Wide-mouthed rhyton with ring handle on rim, put together from fragments; greenish yellow clay and slip; wide flat lip, thick walls. Hole in base; lower two fifths glazed in monochrome, with three rows of running spirals above; height 14.9 cm., diam. of mouth 7.6 cm.; LH I. Nat. Mus., Athens. – Blegen, *Prosymna*, 406, No. 1002, Pl.-Fig. 671.

963 Samikon–Kleidi, Triphylia. Grave Tumulus, Grave I B (cf. *908, 918*): Mycenaean conical rhyton, painted with dense stripes, reddish brown glaze; height without handle 24.8 cm., LH III a. New Mus., Olympia, Find No. Pi 70, Photo No. 3729. – Yalouris, *Delt.* 20 (1965), Mel. 31 f., No. 95, Pl. 22 a.

964 Thera. From a grave. Imported Mycenaean conical rhyton, found together with feeding bottles. Reddish brown glazed paint in wide and narrow stripes; in the centre a wide band with chevrons and semicircles; further up, below horizontal band, metope frieze with groups of bars and chevrons; LH III. Local mus., Thera (cf. comparable pot-bellied forms of rhyton: Furtwängler–Löschcke, *Myk. Vasen* [1886], Pl. 19,139 [Haliki, Attica]; Maraghiannis, *Ant. Crét.* I, Pl. 39:12 [Gournia]; Fimmen, *KMK.* 139, Figs. 135, 136 [Sitias and Mycenae]).

965 Argive Heraion, Prosymna. Chamber Tomb 3: Pot-bellied jug rhyton with thin walls; yellowish pink clay, yellow slip, reddish glaze on polished surface. Decoration: groups of horizontal stripes and two ornamental zones on shoulder with chevrons and stylized flowers (comparable pot-bellied rhytons: Furtwängler–Löschcke, *Myk. Vasen* [1886], Pl. 19:139 [Haliki, Attica]; Maraghiannis, *Ant. Crét.* I, Pl. 39:12 [Gournia]; Fimmen, *KMK.* 139, Figs. 135, 136 [Sitias and Mycenae]). Height, 14 cm., diam. 12 cm., diam. of mouth 6.1 cm.; LH III. Nat. Mus., Athens. – Blegen, op. cit., 454 f., No. 138, Pl.-Fig. 726.

966 Greece. Site unknown. Excellently preserved three-handled vase, slender below, densely hatched upper part. Main motif: two heads in profile with flying ribbons in hair and angular scaly wings (type missing in Furumark, *Myc. Pottery*, and Nilsson, *MMR.*; for Mycenaean winged beings, cf. *1069 a*); rosettes on left and right; pale yellow clay, thin light brown glaze; height 19 cm., LH III b. Antikensammlungen, Munich. – Hackl, *JdI.* 22 (1907), 101, No. 4, Pl. 2.

967 Greece. Site unknown. Excellently preserved jug. Decoration: three tendrils below handle, rim of handle and spout painted, stripes above the base and on neck; at beginning of neck: row of 'N' patterns; main motif: schematized lilies (similar jug: Thompson, *AA.* 1954, 109 f., Fig. 3 [Athens, Mycenaean grave under Attalos Stoa]). Private collection, Athens (here from photo, DAI., Athens).

968 Dendra, the Argolid. Chamber Tomb 10: Two three-
969 handled vases of varying profile. *968:* less pot-bellied, lower part concave; decoration of stripes and hooked spirals above wavy 'landscape' (similar vase: Thompson, *AA.* 1952, 165, Fig. 7 [Agora, Athens]); yellow clay, reddish brown glaze; height 25.2 cm., diam. 18 cm., *969:* bulky form; decorative stripes on lower part, upper part completely covered in network of scales (similar vase in Persson, *Dendra* II, 67, Fig. 79), reddish clay, reddish brown glaze; height 44 cm., diam. 35.5 cm.; LH III a/b. Arch. Mus., Nauplia. – Persson, op. cit., 67 ff., Fig. 81:1 *(968)*, 70 f., Fig. 83 *(969)*.

970 Origin unknown. Tall krater with vertical handles; large octopus on either side. Brit. Mus., London, No. 1959. 11–4.1. – For the octopus motif, cf. Wiesner, 'Die Hochzeit des Polypus' in *JdI.* 74 (1959), 35 ff.

971 Mycenae. Pot-bellied krater with vertical handles; pedestal partly restored. Decoration: high frieze of pairs of murex shells; LH III b. Nat. Mus., Athens, Inv. No. 1148. – Schliemann, *Mykenae*, 160, No. 213 a; Furtwängler–Löschcke, *Myk. Vasen*, Pl. 31,297; Montelius, *La Grèce préclass.*, Pl. 133:11; Collignon–Couve, *Cat. des Vases Peints du Mus. Nat. d'Athènes* (1904), No. 246.

972 Karphi, east Crete. Three-handled cult rhyton with moulded human face, large round eyes, body of vase glaze-painted; height 26 cm.; sub-Minoan. Arch. Mus., Herakleion. – Pendlebury, *BSA.* 38 (1937/38), 82, No. 256, Pl. 35:2,3; Schiering, *JdI.* 79 (1964), 3 f., Fig. 5 a, b.

973 Ras Shamra, north Syria (Excavated in 1963). Fragment of krater; griffin's head with long curved beak; dense reddish yellow clay, light yellow slip, dark brown glaze; length 9 cm., LH III a/b. Ibn Hani, expedition magazine.

974 Antissa, Lesbos. Kylix, grey clay and slip, unadorned; local imitation of Mycenaean undecorated type (local imitations also in e. g. Myrina, Lemnos: Fredrich, *AM.* 31 [1906], 61, No. 2, Fig. 5). Arch. Mus., Mytilene. – Lamb, *BSA.* 31 (1930/31), 170, 178, Pl. 28:2; Buchholz, *Methymna*, Pl. 17 a.

975 Mainland or islands. Site unknown. Mycenaean kylix with crude squid decoration: eyes beside the body! Broad stripes on foot and base; light grey clay, yellow slip, flaking light to dark brown glaze; height 18.4 cm., diam. 15 cm.; LH III a 2. Mus. f. Kunst u. Gewerbe, Hamburg, Inv. No. 1927,39. – v. Mercklin, *AA.* 1928 285 f., No. 14, Fig. 14; Furumark, *Myc. Pottery*, 305, Fig. 49:11 (curling tentacles inaccurately reproduced).

976 Origin unknown. Mycenaean kylix with very rudimentary squid. Some white applied over the glaze; one handle restored; LH III b; similar intrusive octopus form on kylix: Sieveking–Hackl, *Vasensammlung zu München* I, No. 17 (= Fimmen, *KMK.* 144, Fig. 145, and Bossert, *Altkreta*, Fig. 129). 976 from photo from the Grundmann bequest.

977 Greece. Site unknown (perhaps Rhodes). Mycenaean kylix with wide base; thin, light-to-middle brown glaze, finely sifted ochre-coloured clay and slip. Decoration: horizontal stripes and awkwardly painted running spirals (this form missing in Furumark); height, 18.5 cm.; incl. handle, 19.5 cm., diam. of mouth 14.8 cm., diam. of foot 8.5 cm.; LH III b. Mus. f. Kunst u. Gewerbe, Hamburg, Inv. No. 1919.133. – v. Mercklin, *Führer durch das Hamburgische Mus. f. Kunst u. Gewerbe* II: *Griechische u. Röm. Altertümer* (1930), 15, No. 20.

978 Origin unknown. Mycenaean kylix; decoration: stripes and stylized papyrus flowers (motif absent in this variant in Furumark, op. cit.); LH III a/b. From photo, Grundmann bequest.

979 Tiryns. Arch. Mus., Nauplia: Charcoal pan, or lamp, of clay, with long horizontal handle, pierced at the end; length incl. handle 32 cm.; LH III a/b. For this type, cf. Furumark, *Myc. Pottery*, 75 ff., Figs. 21:312, 321 a; also Deshayes, *Argos: les fouilles de la Deiras*

(1966), Pl. 53:4–7; similar charcoal pans also occurred in Crete: Demargne–Gallet de Santerre, *Et. Crét.* IX (1953), Pl. 42:6.

980 Samikon, near Olympia. Stirrup jug with concave lower part and sharp curve at the shoulder; striped decoration, dotted rosettes on shoulder, moderately lustrous brown glaze; diam. 12 cm., height 10 cm., LH III b. New Mus., Olympia, Inv. No. BE 1260; Yalouris, *Delt.* 20 (1965), Chron. 210, Pl. 233 b.

981 Stravo Kephalo, near Olympia. Small squat jug with vertical handle; striped decoration on shoulder; spout broken; from one of the Mycenaean chamber tombs; LH III b. New Mus., Olympia, Inv. No. P 619.

982 Makrysia, near Olympia. Askos bottle with base ring, socket spout and handle; glaze flaked away; length 10 cm., height 6.5 cm.; LH III a. From a grave. New Mus., Olympia. – Daux, *BCH.* 78 (1954), 129, Fig. 29, 2nd from left.

983 Kythera. From graves: Flat clay lamp with wick spout
984 and loop handle (diam., incl. spout and handle, c. 16 cm.; cf. Persson, *New Tombs at Dendra near Midea* [1942], 102 ff., Fig. 113, lamp variant missing; cf. also Matz and Buchholz, *Arch. Hom.* P. [1968], Pl. 6), and little flat bowl (diam. 15 cm.), clearly belonging with the stone vase *1164;* LH II/III. Nat. Mus., Athens. – Staïs, *Delt.* 1 (1915), 191 ff.

985 Perati, Attica. Grave 132: Slender, long-necked jug with vertical twisted handle; striped decoration; glaze partly flaked away; LH III c.

986 Stravo Kephalo, near Olympia (cf. *981*). Pot-bellied,
987 two-handled jar, with low cylindrical neck and lid fitting over it; from one of the Mycenaean chamber tombs; LH III b/c. New Mus., Olympia, Inv. No. P 354. – Matz and Buchholz, *Arch. Hom.* Q (1970), 40, Fig. 13 c (drawing).

988 Rhenia, near Olympia. Monochrome jug from one of the Mycenaean chamber tombs, with steep, broad, horizontally cut spout; LH III a/b. New Mus., Olympia. – Yalouris, *Delt.* 19 (1964), Chron. Pl. 183 c; Daux, *BCH.* 90 (1966), 828, Fig. 18.

989 Leukandi, Euboea. Large pot-bellied hydria, with tall base and narrow neck (restored); sparse striped decoration, 'S' spirals on shoulder; LH III c (corresponding in age and form to the 'Granary' hydriai from Mycenae: Wace, *BSA.* 25 [1921–23], Pl. 10 f.). – Daux, *BCH.* 90 (1966), 900 f., Fig. 7.

990 Stravo Kephalo. New Mus., Olympia, Inv. No. P 342. Small hydria of coarse clay painted with stripes and waves; LH III b/c; for Mycenaean hydriai, see Diehl, *Die Hydria* (1964), 223 f., and *AJA.* 71 (1967), Pl. 32:1.

991 Chalkis–Vromousa, Euboea. Property of Lembesi. From a grave: Beaker with tall foot and handle rising above the rim of the mouth, spiral decoration; height 9 cm.; incl. handle 12.3 cm.; LH I/II. For this form of beaker in Crete cf. *901.* Arch. Mus., Chalkis, Inv. No. 543. – Hankey, *BSA.* 47 (1952), 53, 84, No. 543, Pl. 20.

992 Chalkis–Trypa. Grave VIII (LH I, redocumented as LH II and III): Handled vase in 'teacup' form, with spiral decoration; height 6 cm., diam. 13.4 cm.; LH I. Arch. Mus., Chalkis, Inv. No. 493. – Hankey, op. cit., 77, No. 493, Pl. 20.

993 Chalkis–Vromousa. Property of Mantalou, Grave II (LH I–III): Handled cup of conical form, with concave contour (Vapheio cup) and modest decoration (mainly horizontal bands); height 9 cm., diam. 12 cm. (LH I/II). Arch. Mus., Chalkis, Inv. No. 440. – Hankey, op. cit., No. 440, Pl. 20.

994 Hagia Irini, Keos. Fragments of a Mycenaean figure-painted vase from the temple region (Find No. K 2071); frieze of roughly drawn male figures facing right, overlapping the striped decoration; LH III c. – Caskey, *Delt.* 19 (1964), Chron., Pl. 497 a (with dimensions); and *Hesperia* 33 (1964), Pl. 62 a.

995 Perati, Attica (excavated by Iakovidis, 1958; Find No. 615). Stirrup jar put together from fragments, with striped decoration; above this a roughly drawn crawling human figure, unnaturally composed in two dimensions, with double outline in places. – Daux, *BCH.* 83 (1959), 598, Fig. 32.

996 Tiryns (excavation of lower citadel by Verdelis, 1963). Fragment of a pinax with traces of a man facing right (head, long neck and chest); according to Verdelis, he wears a metal helmet of unknown type. Brick-red clay, orange slip, reddish brown paint; height 7.5 cm.; LH III b/c. Arch. Mus., Nauplia. – Verdelis, *AM.* 82 (1967), 28 f., No. 18, Pl. 2:3 (col.), and Suppl. 34:2.

997 Tiryns (excavation of lower citadel, Verdelis 1963). Fragment of krater of brick-red clay, with reddish slip and reddish brown paint; head, neck and shoulder area of warrior facing right; remains of spear behind the head; preserved height 4.5 cm.; LH III c. Arch. Mus., Nauplia. – Verdelis, 28, No. 16, Pl. 2:2 (col.) and Suppl. 33:4.

998 Mycenae. Krater fragment, with the picture of a linear, stylized stag facing right; preserved width 12.1 cm.; LH III b/c. Nat. Mus., Athens, Inv. No. 2654. – Buchholz–Karageorghis, *AAA.* 3 (1970), 388, Fig. 2.

999 Tiryns (excavations of lower citadel, Verdelis 1963). Arch. Mus., Nauplia. Three connected krater fragments, showing chariot frieze; four-spoked chariot with two drivers. Parts of the horses' bodies in solid silhouette, others in outline drawing. Technique of partly linear contours, partly solid areas also found on the islands: Daux, *BCH.* 90 (1966), 909, Fig. 8 (Naxos); Megaw, *JHS.* 87 (1967), Arch. Rep. 13, Fig. 18 (Leukandi, Euboea). LH III c. – Verdelis, 26 f., No. 15, Pl. 1 (col.) and Suppl. 34:3.

1000 Mycenae. Vase fragment. Part of warrior figure in armour and greaves, facing left (LH III c). Nat. Mus., Athens, Inv. No. 2580. – Tsountas, *Ephem.* 1891, 26 f., n. 4, Pl. 3:2; Lorimer, *Homer and the Monuments* (1950), Pl. 12:2; Verdelis, 25, No. 13, Suppl. 33:2.

1001 Mycenae. Fragment of a krater; height 9 cm.; picture of armed warrior facing left, leading a horse by the reins; an unusual feature is the gradation in depth of the two figures one behind the other (LH III c 1). Nat. Mus., Athens, Inv. No. 4691. – Rodenwaldt, *Der Fries des Megarons von Mykenai* (1921), 24, Fig. 14; Furumark, *Myc. Pottery,* 241, Fig. 26:9; Lorimer, op. cit., Pl. 12:1; Benson, *AJA.* 65 (1961), Pl. 108:39; Verdelis, 25, No. 12, Suppl. 33:1.

1002 Fig. 28: Scoglio del Tonno, near Taranto, south Italy.
to Important Bronze Age coastal centre of Aegean mari-
1023 time trade. Sherds of imported Mycenaean pottery (stirrup jars, kraters, skyphoi, three-handled pots), dating from 1400 to 1100 B.C.; LH III a *(1002–1008, 1010, 1013, 1014, 1023),* LH III a/b *(1015),* LH III b *(1009, 1011, 1018),* LH III b/c *(1016, 1020),* LH III c *(1012, 1019, 1021, 1022).* Decoration of fragment *1013*

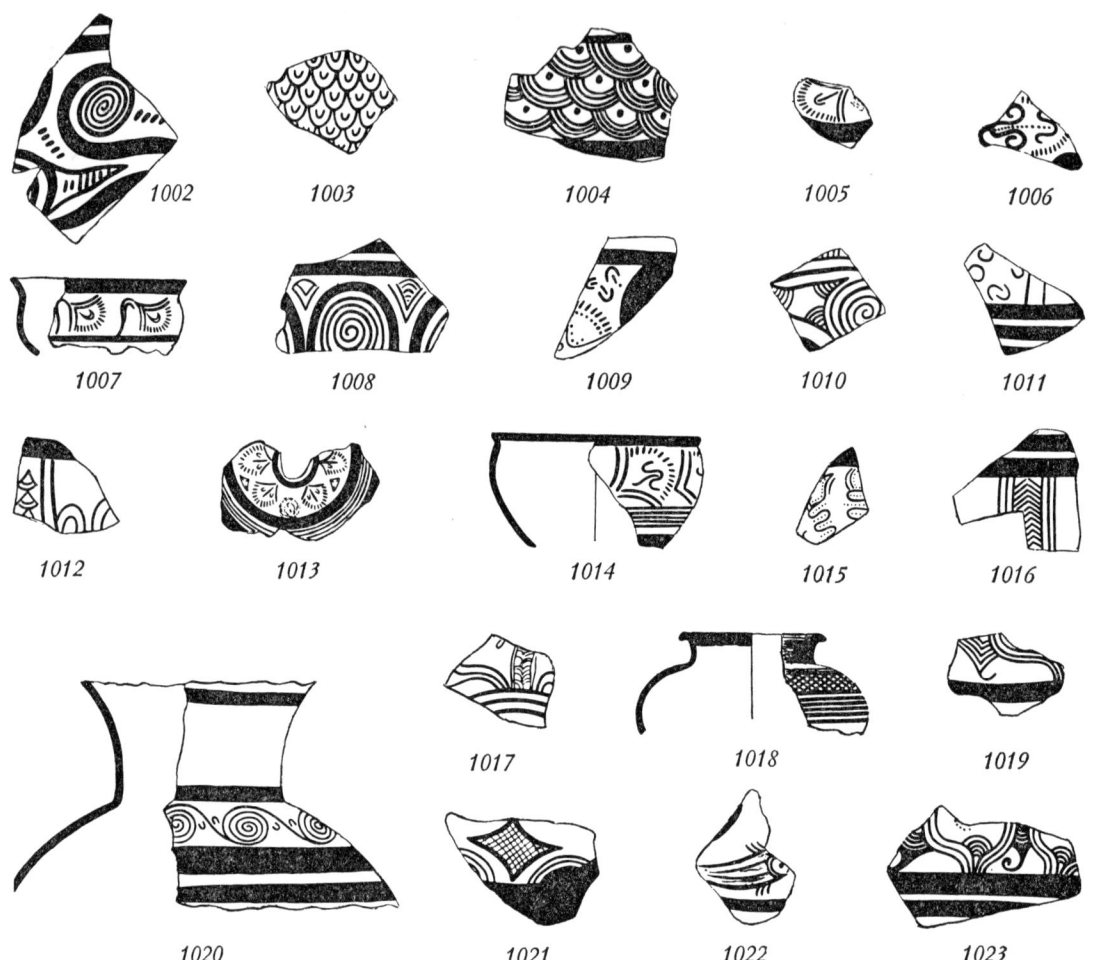

Fig. 28 1002–1023 Scoglio del Tonno, near Taranto, imported Mycenaean pottery

slightly altered in this drawing (after Müller–Karpe), compare photograph: *I Micenei in Italia* (1967), Pl. 10:46, and Lord W. Taylour, *Mycenaean Pottery in Italy and Adjacent Areas* (1958), Pl. 11:10. Mus. Naz., Taranto. – Taylour, 81 ff., Pls. 10–14; Biancofiore, 'La Ceramica Micenea dello Scoglio del Tonno e la Civiltà del Bronzo Tardo nell'Italia Meridonale', *Rivista dell' Ist. Naz. d'Arch. e Storia dell'Arte*, N. S. 7 (1958), 5 ff.; id., *Civiltà Micenea nell'Italia Meridoniale* (²1967); Staccioli, *Archeologia* 6, No. 42 (Rome 1967), 410 ff.; Müller–Karpe, 'Beiträge zur Chronologie der Urnenfelderzeit nördl. u. südl. der Alpen' (*RGF.* 22 [1959]), Pl. 13:20–41; Desborough, *The Last Mycenaeans and their Successors* (1964), 215. A recent survey by Buchholz of Mycenaean finds in the West is in *Arch. Anzeiger*. 1973.

1024 Berbati, the Argolid. Tall krater with two horizontal 'wishbone' handles; careful work, pictorial zone in upper half above three stripes: two fighting bulls, and between them a smaller bull falling. All animals richly painted inside the contours. Wishbone handle and pictorial style show close relation to Cypro-Minoan work; LH III b. Arch. Mus., Nauplia, Inv. No. 11628. – Furumark, *Myc. Pottery*, 244 ff., motif 3.

1025–1042: LATE BRONZE AGE – THE ARGOLID – ATTICA – KEOS – CRETE – EASTERN AEGEAN

1025 Mycenae. From the 'House of the Warrior Vase' *(90)*, directly south of Grave Circle A: Tall, richly painted krater, partially restored; height *c.* 40 cm.; LH III c 1. Horizontal horned-head handles, painted birds below the handles for similar 'hornedhead vase handles' in Greece and Cyprus, cf. Oakeshott, *JHS.* 86 [1966], 114 ff., Pls. 5–9. Famous as rare example of narrative picture (Warrior Vase). Six warriors setting out to war, with sacks of provisions on their lances, followed by a woman in attitude of mourning; on the other side: a row warriors with spiked helmets. Nat. Mus., Athens, Inv. No. 1426. – Schliemann, Mykenae (1878, 1964), 153, Fig. 213 and 161, No. 214; Tsountas-Manatt, *The Myc. Age*, Pl. 18; Perrot–Chipiez VI (1894), 935 f., Figs. 497, 498 (details); Furtwängler-Löschcke, *Myken. Vasen*, Pls. 42, 43; Hall, *The Civilization of Greece in the Bronze Age* (1928), 262, Fig. 338; Bossert, *Altkreta*, Figs. 133–135; Furumark, *Myc. Pottery*, 241, Fig. 26:1, Nos. 28, 29; Lorimer, *Homer and the Monuments* (1950), Pl. 3:1 a, b; Marinatos-Hirmer, Pls. 232, 233; Gray, *BICS*. 6 (1959), Pl. 5; Matz, *Kreta u. frühes Griechenland* (1962), 221, ill. suppl., 22; Schachermeyr, *Griechische Geschichte* (1960), Pl. 11 a; Yalouris, *AM*. 75 (1960), Suppl. 24; Müller-Karpe, 'Zur spätbronzezeitlichen Bewaffnung in Mitteleuropa u. Griechenland', *Germania* 40 (1962), 258, Fig. 1; Wace-Stubbings, *A Companion to Homer* (1962), Pl. 29 a; Wiesner, *Bilder zur abendländischen Kunst, 71. Lieferung* (1963), Fig. 352 b; Taylour, *The Mycenaeans* (1964), Pl. 7; Snodgrass, *Early Greek Armour and Weapons* (1964), 4,57 f., 85, 133, 170, 190, 192; and *Arms and Armour of the Greeks* (1967), Pl.-Figs. 10, 11; Oakeshott, *JHS*. 86 (1966), Pl. 5 a, b (details); Verdelis, *AM*. 82 (1967), 23 f., 34 f., 41, Suppl. 32:2; Marinatos, in Matz and Buchholz, *Arch. Hom. B* (1967), Pl. 3 d; Schuchhardt, 'Archäologisches zu Archilochos', *Opus Nobile: Festschr. zum 60. Geburtstag von U. Jantzen* (1969), 153 ff. (with further lit.).

1026 Hagia Irini, Keos. Temple, Room IV (Find No. K 2048, 1963): Upper part of an LH III c krater; diam. of mouth 18.4 cm. – Caskey, *Hesperia* 33 (1964), Pl. 62 b.

1027 Iria, Epidauria. Broad, wide-mouthed krater, put together from fragments, with two horizontal handles; metope zones on upper half, filled with stylized double axes near the handles; LH III c. Arch. Mus., Nauplia. – Gebauer, *AA*. 1939, 287, Fig. 15 and col. 294; id., *6. internat. Kongr. f. Archäologie, Berlin 1939* (1940), 299 ff.; cf. Jantzen, *AA*. 1968, 373.

1028 Knossos. Sub-Minoan pedestal krater (LM III c; diam. c. 42 cm., height c. 34.5 cm.), with unusual heraldic and similar birds to the right and left of the horns (similar example on krater from Phaistos: Maraghiannis, *Ant. Crét*. I, Pl. 14:5); there are connections with the so-called Philistine birds. Arch. Mus., Herakleion. – Popham, *BSA*. 60 (1965), 332, Fig. 9, and 341, No. 62, Pl. 84 a.

1029 Vrokastro, east Crete. Vault in rock near Room 36 (child's burial): Sub-Minoan krater, with two horizontal handles on the belly, high upper part with concave profile and debased painted linear motif; height 17 cm., diam. of mouth 18.5 cm. Arch. Mus., Herakleion. – Hall, *Excavations in Eastern Crete: Vrokastro* (1914), 118, 129, Pl. 29 b; Desborough, *Protogeometric Pottery* (1952), 262 ff.

1030 Eastern Aegean. Outstanding example of the richly painted figural stirrup jars of the Late Bronze Age (LH III c). Stylized octopus like *1031*; in interstices: rosettes and fish. Metrop. Mus., New York, No. 53.11.6 (height 26 cm.). – Hafner, *Geschichte der griechischen Kunst* (1961), 48, Fig. 45; *BMetrMus*. 1970, 133 with Fig.

1031 Attica. Similar to *1030*, perhaps from the same workshop; height 24.3 cm. For the fish, cf. Furumark, *Myc. Pottery*, 302 f.; Fig. 48:20, No. 9 (LH III c 1). Nat. Mus., Copenhagen, Inv. No. 13517. – Breitenstein, *Graeske Vaser* (1957), 7 f., Pl. 1; Vermeule, *Greece in the Bronze Age* (1964), 207, Pl. 45 c; Lacy, *Greek Pottery in the Bronze Age* (1967), 225, Fig. 94 e; National mus. Vejledninger, *Graekenland, Italien og Romerriget* (1968), 16 f. with Fig.

1032 Çandarli, Pitane, west Anatolia. Richly painted stirrup *a,b* jar of the same type as *1030* and *1031* (LH III c 1, height 20 cm.). Stylized octopus, with fish, land animals and birds between its tentacles (cf. stirrup jar from Kalymnos in Brit. Mus., London, A 1015). Arch. Mus., Istanbul, Inv. No. 2276. – Haussay, *RA*. 26 (1895), 1 ff., and 30 (1897), 81 ff.; Pottier, *RA*. 28 (1896), 24 ff.; Siret, *L'Anthropologie* 20 (1909), 148, Fig. 13; Perrot–Chipiez VI (1894), 923, and Figs. 489, 491; Oulié, *Les Animaux de la Crète préhell*., Fig. 49; Bossert, *Altkreta*, Fig. 454; id., *Altanatolien*, Fig. 7; Bittel, *Ist. Forsch*. 17 (1950), 21, Pl. 5; Stubbings, *Myc. Pottery from the Levant* (1951), 22; Desborough, *The Last Mycenaeans and their Successors* (1964), 161, 228, 272; Buchholz, *BJV*. 5 (1965), 78, No. 3, Fig. 4 g, and Pls. 14, 15.

1033 Athens–Dipylon. From the lowest foundation layer of Tower T in section w 3: Intact stirrup jar, with decorated, pointed stirrup handle, concentric semicircles on shoulder, and two highly stylized octopuses as main decoration in dull brown glaze; space between tentacles filled with rising scale pattern; height 18 cm.; LH III c 1–2. Clearly fell into the secondary layer from the tombs of the Pompeion (for this, see Styrenius, *Submycenaean Studies* [1967], cf. *1039*). Nat. Mus., Athens. – Noack, *AM*. 32 (1907), 157, 558, Pl. 25:1; Furumark, *Myc. Pottery*, 305, Fig. 49:29.

1034 Perati, Attica. Chamber Tomb 15 b: Stirrup jar in the 'fantastic figure-style' (Schachermeyr), with richly decorated pointed cap handle, rosettes on shoulder (cf. *1030)*, and with stylized octopus as main motif. Triangular hatched areas between tentacles, small fish above and flying bird on remaining surface; height 17.5 cm.; LH III c (Find No. 261). – Iakovidis, *Ergon* 1954, 11, Fig. 10; Benson, *JNES*. 20 (1961), Pl. 6:4; Desborough, op. cit., Pl. 6 d.

1035 Perati. Stirrup jar of the same style and period as *1034* (LH III c, Find No. 198). Curious ornaments: areas of chequered pattern, as though woven, arranged one above the other, between rosettes and wheel motifs, with stylized flowers above. – Iakovidis, *Delt*. 19 (1964), Chron. Pl. 87 b.

1036 Miletus. Southern section, 1957. Tankard with small handle and three ribbed feet. Very concave profile; curious painting on light ground, abstract but not at all rigid: fantastic fish, sea birds drawn with a few lines; 'Close Style', 'fantastic figure-style'; height 21 cm., LH III c. – Weickert, *Neue deutsche Ausgrabungen im Mittelmeergebiet u. im Vorderen Orient* (1959), 188, Fig. 8; Schiering, *Istanbul Mitt*. 9/10 (1959/60) 30, Pls. 16, 17; Cook, *The Greeks in Ionia and the East* (1962), 19, Fig. 1 (drawing); Vermeule, *Greece in the Bronze Age*, 315 (drawing).

1037 Kerameikos. Grave 106 north of Eridanos; Kerameikos mus., Athens, Inv. No. 503 (height 24 cm.): Sub-Mycenaean stirrup jar of elegant, severe form; large flange with knob; lower half glazed black, dense linear ornaments in bands above. This vase does not resemble the other Attic stirrup jars, and it shows signs of the later Protogeometric structure (eleventh century B. C.); similar decoration on stirrup jars from Salamis (cf. Müller-Karpe, *JdI.* 77 [1962], 114, Figs. 32, 33). – Kraiker-Kübler, *Kerameikos* I (1939), 47, Pl. 11 b.

1038 Mycenae. From the Granary region; Arch. Mus., Nauplia: Stirrup jar with frieze of birds (height 22 cm.). The areas of dense hatching on these birds correspond to the Close style of the frieze of birds on a wide-mouthed LH III c bowl from Mycenae (Wace, *BSA.* 25 [1921 to 23], Pl. 7 b; Taylour, *The Mycenaeans* [1964], 54, Fig. 14; Desborough, *The Last Mycenaeans and their Successors* [1964], Pl. 4 c). – Wace, op. cit., Pl. 10 g; Furumark, *Myc. Pottery,* 254 f., Fig. 31:7, No. 52; Wace, *Mycenae* (1949), Pl.-Fig. 75 a; Matz, *KMT.* Pl. 112 a.

1039 Athens Kerameikos. Grave 113; Kerameikos Mus.,

1040 Athens, Inv. Nos. 2162 and 2166: Two belly-handled amphoriskoi with high conical foot, glazed neck. Decoration: wavy line and concentric suspended semicircles (drawn freehand); sub-Mycenaean, twelfth to eleventh century B. C. The groups of sub-Mycenaean tombs in the Pompeion cemetery have been classified into five phases (Styrenius, *Submycenaean Studies* [1967]); Same applies for the other Attic LH III c vases; for the chronology of sub-Mycenaean amphoriskoi, cf. Kraiker-Kübler, *Kerameikos* I (1939), 64 ff., Pls. 16–20; Kübler, *Das neue Bild der Antike* I (1942), Fig. 14 after p. 48; Müller-Karpe, op. cit., 83 ff., Figs. 1:9, 2:11, 3:4, 4:14, 17, 5:18, 6:2.

1041 Palaikastro, east Crete. Street between Blocks beta and gamma: Handled cup (height 10.7 cm.; late LM III), with birds and rosettes painted in black on yellow slip (detail). Arch. Mus., Herakleion, Inv. No. 3268. – Dawkins, *BSA.* 9 (1902/03), 318, Fig. 17; Maraghiannis, *Ant. Crét.* II, Pl. 39:6; Bosanquet, *BSA.* Suppl. I (1923), 93, Fig. 17; Montelius, *La Grèce préclass.,* Pl. 82:1; Zervos, *Crète,* 449, Fig. 742.

1042 Gournia. Grave find. Pyxis (height 11.5 cm.); detail: bird with spread wings, front view! LM III. Arch. Mus., Herakleion. – Boyd-Hawes, *Gournia,* Pl. 10:40; Furumark, *Myc. Pottery,* 253, Fig. 30 m; Zervos, op. cit., 449, Fig. 741.

Wall-painting

There were no formative stages for the earliest known Cretan monumental painting (c. 1600 B.C.), apart from the monochrome tones and sparse ornamentation of earlier painted walls. In this the creative power of Minoan art found expression, although it did not, of course, develop entirely without outside stimuli (stucco painting in Mari on the Euphrates).

Preliminary sketches enabled the painters to apply their colours—red, blue, yellow, white, black, and occasionally green (cf. Lepik-Kopaczynska, 'Die Inkarnatsfarbe in der antiken Malerei,' *Klio* 41 [1963], 135 with Fig.)—flat on damp absorbent layers of plaster, thus creating true frescoes (Schneider-Franken, 'Die Technik der Wandgemälde von Tiryns,' *AM.* 38 [1913], 187 ff.).

The style of painting in the early phase in the sixteenth century B.C. can best be described as 'Cretan naturalism' *(1043, 1045, 1050;* cf. Schiering, 'Die Naturanschauung in der altkretischen Kunst,' *Antike Kunst* 9 [1965], 3 ff.). But later fresco painting, particularly on the Greek mainland, lost both its outward dynamism and its inner impetus (Figs. 30, 31, *1056—1060).* The attractiveness and novelty of the earliest wall-painting on Cretan soil arises from the fact that the artists did not set their figures against an empty background, but usually placed them in a colourful, apparently diffuse, setting, rich in forms and lines, that has been called 'landscape' in the sense understood in more recent art *(1045—1047, 1050;* cf. *1052, 1060).* In his essay 'Steine und Malerei in der minoischen Kunst' *(JdI.* 75 [1960], 17 ff., esp. 26 ff.), Schiering has shown just how far the 'landscape' effect of the surface compositions could be derived from the bizarre natural linear structures of the thinly ground alabaster plaques that were already used in the earlier palaces as wall cladding. There is no perspective or shading, in our sense of the words, in this two-dimensional art (cf. Walter, *ÖJh.* 38 [1950], 17 ff.). Colour is handled in the same way in the painted stucco reliefs *(1052)* as in the frescoes.

Fig. 29   *1055*   Knossos, chariot fresco

The first complete extant fresco, dating from the mid-millennium, was found in Thera in 1970. It covers a surface of fourteen square metres, and represents a spring motif. All the other wall decorations of this kind have been reconstructed from more or less small fragments. We also have very early wall-paintings of extremely high quality from Hagia Triada *(1043, 1045)*, a large number of frescoes spanning several centuries in the Great Palace of Knossos *(45, 48, 1046, 1055)*, and in various Minoan country houses in Crete (the white lilies from the Villa of Amnisos, MM III: Marinatos-Hirmer, Col. Pl. 22); the negative conclusions from the Small Palace of Knossos, in Mallia, and at Phaistos remain unexplained for the time being. Important hitherto unpublished examples from Hagia Irini, Keos, have now joined the fresco fragments from the Cyclades, Thera, and Melos *(1044)*. On the mainland we must note the wall-paintings of Mycenae, Tiryns *(1056, 1057, 1060)*, and Thebes *(1058)*; fragment *1058* is not from the palace, but from a chamber tomb. This art form came to an end with the frescoes from Pylos *(1059)*; they also include the painted stucco border of the round hearth in the royal megaron *(123 a, b)*.

There are excellent analyses of this fresco painting in Matz (*KMT.* 87 ff., 141 f.; *Kreta und frühes Griechenland* [1962], 111 ff., 206 ff.; Eng. trans., *Crete and Early Greece* [1962]). We must also note the attempts at an interpretation by Snijder with the help of eidetic (*Kretische Kunst*, 1936). Since 1967 we also have *A Catalogue of Plates in Sir A. Evans' Knossos Fresco Atlas*, compiled by Cameron and Hood (reviewed by Graham, *AJA.* 73 [1969], 81 f.). Cameron also wrote a doctoral thesis on *Minoan and Mycenaean Frescoes* at the University of Liverpool. His gleanings from the numerous fragments from Knossos proved fruitful (e.g. *1055*; and *Europa: Festschr. f. Grumach* [1967], 45 ff.); similarly Alexiou made discoveries among the old fragments in the archaeological museum of Herakleion (e.g. *1055*; and *Charisterion eis Orlandon* II [1966], 112 ff.).

Besides Schweitzer's 'Altkretische Kunst' (*Die Antike* 2 [1926], 291 ff.) with its comprehensive analytical approach, there are specialized studies such as 'Pflanzenbilder der minoischen Kunst' by Möbius (*JdI.* 48 [1933], 1 ff.). The works of Cretan wall-painting have been supplemented by studies of painting on the mainland by Rodenwaldt, in 'Die Fresken des Palastes' (*Tiryns* II [1912]), and *Der*

Fig. 30   *1056*   Tiryns, stag fresco

Fries des Megarons von Mykene (1921). Rodenwaldt's pupil, Reusch, wrote *Die zeichnerische Rekonstruktion des Frauenfrieses im böotischen Theben* (1956), following Rodenwaldt's 'Vorschlag zur Ordnung der Fragmente von Frauenfriesen aus Mykenai' (*AA*. 1953, 26 ff.). The frescoes of Pylos have been examined by Lang (*Archaeology* 13 [1960], 55 ff.), and she crowned her studies by the monumental study on 'The Frescoes' in *The Palace of Nestor at Pylos* II (1969).

Finally, we must note that Schadewaldt made a comparison between Cretan-Mycenaean wall-painting and Homeric imagery, in order to demonstrate the stark opposition between the two. Homer's nature has a quite different energy and dynamism; his images are dramatic, and so they are formed of a different material from the Minoan representations of nature (*Hermeneia: Festschrift O. Regenbogen* [1952], 9 ff., reprinted in *Von Homers Welt und Werk*, 3rd. ed. [1959], 130 ff.).

1043 Hagia Triada. Fresco fragments from a room beside the archives room (LM I): cat stalking pheasant; height 39.5 cm. Arch. Mus., Herakleion. – *Mon. Ant.* 13 (1903), Pl. 8; Bossert, *Altkreta*, Fig. 246; Pendlebury, *Arch. of Crete*, Pl. 32:2; Matz, *KMT*. Pl. 48 upper; Schiering, *Antike Kunst* 8 (1965), Pl. 1:1 (best photo of the state of preservation at the time).

1044 Phylakopi, Melos. Fresco fragments of a frieze, with flying fish; height 23 cm. – Phylakopi, *JHS*. Suppl. Paper IV (1904), Pl. 3; Bossert, Fig. 450; Lesky, *Thalatta* (1947), 42, Fig. 2; Matz, Pl. 49 above; Schadewaldt, *Von Homers Welt und Werk* (³1959), Pl.-Fig. 9; Schiering, Pl. 1:3.

1045 Hagia Triada. Fresco fragments from the same wall decoration as *1043*: trailing ivy, flowers and rocks; length 53 cm. – *Mon. Ant.* 13 (1903), Pl. 9; Bossert, Fig. 241; Matz, Pl. 48 lower; Schadewaldt, Pl.-Fig. 8.

1046 Knossos, House of Frescoes. Fragments of a frieze c. 80 cm. high, partly restored: blue ape in rocky parkland. – Evans, *PM*. II, 446 f., Pl. 10; Matz, Pl. 34 upper; Schiering, *JdI*. 75 (1960), 30, Fig. 20.

1047 Knossos. Bird fresco, detail. Arch. Mus., Herakleion; c. 1500 B.C. – Demargne, *Naissance de l'Art Grec* (1964), 141 Fig. 190 (Eng. trans., *Aegean Art* [1964]); Schachermeyr, *Die minoische Kultur des alten Kreta* (1964), Pl. 53 b; v. Matt, *Das antike Kreta* (1967), 79.

1048 Knossos. West wing, State Hall: Arch. Mus., Herakleion: Fresco fragment, height c. 25 cm., so-called 'little Parisienne' (detail of so-called 'folding-stool' fresco), c. 1500/1450 B.C. – Bossert, Fig. 226; Marinatos–Hirmer, Col. Pl. 16; Evans, *PM*. IV, 384 f., Fig. 319; Matz, Pl. 32; Schachermeyr, Pl. 23.

1049 Knossos. 'Queen's Megaron'. Fresco fragment from one of the pillars. Half life-size dancer; preserved height 37 cm., late sixteenth century. – Evans, *PM*. III, 70 f., Fig. 40, and Pl. 25 after p. 370; Bossert, Fig. 227; Matz, *Kreta und frühes Griechenland* (1962), 113, Col. ill.; Marinatos–Hirmer, Pl. 38 lower; Marinatos, *Arch. Hom. B* (1967), 9, Fig. 2 b.

1050 Knossos. Caravanserai of the palace: Partially restored frieze; height 28 cm. Partridges and hoopoe in rocky landscape; MM III/LM I. – Evans, *PM*. II, front.; Bossert, Fig. 230; Matz, *KMT.*, Pl. 34 centre.

1051 Knossos. Fresco, detail. Chief of the African guards running to the right, with horned hairstyle and two lances, followed by armed black warriors (not shown; for these, cf. Buchholz, *Jahrbuch f. Kleinasiat. Forsch.* 3 [1965], 140 f.); LM I/II. – Evans, *PM*. II, 756, Pl. 13; and IV, 886, Fig. 869; Bossert, Fig. 228; Marinatos, *Arch. Hom. B* (1967), 5, Fig. 1 b.

1052 Knossos. South wing of palace, upper storey: Stucco relief, preserved in fragments: 'Prince with the crown of feathers'; height *c.* 2.10 cm.; LM I. – Evans, *PM.* II, 2, Pl. 14 and front.; Bossert, Fig. 255; Karo, *Reallex. Vorgesch.* V (1926), s. v. 'Haartracht', Pl. 3; Matz, *KMT*. 89, Pl. 33.

1053 Knossos. South propylaeon: Large procession fresco. Almost life-size rhyton bearer; *LM* I (1500–1450 B. C.); light blue and yellow ground in broad wavy lines; flesh colour of youth: deep red; vase and jewelry: deep blue. Arch. Mus., Herakleion. – Evans, *PM.* II, 706 f., Pl. 12; Bossert, Fig. 231; Matz, op. cit., Pl. 38; Karo, *Greifen am Thron* (1959), 25, Fig. 12; Schiering, *JdI.* 75 (1960), 31, Fig. 23; and *Antike Kunst* 8 (1965), Pl. 4:3 Marinatos–Hirmer, Col. Pl. 15.

1054 Knossos. Small court in east wing of palace: Fresco restored from fragments; height *c.* 37 cm.; LM I (*c.* 1500 B. C.): One man and two women bull jumping. For bull sports, cf. Reichel, *AM.* 34 (1909), 85 ff. with Pl. 2; a bronze group of bull and acrobat, formerly in the Spencer–Churchill Colln., now in Brit. Mus., London, No. 1966. 3-28.1 (cf. Higgins, *JHS.* 87 [1967], Arch. Rep. 49 f., Fig. 11). – Evans, *PM.* III, 209 ff., Figs. 114, 145; Matz, Pl. 51 lower; Marinatos–Hirmer, Col. Pl. 17; Schadewaldt, op. cit., Pl.-Fig. 11.

1055 Fig. 29: Knossos. Fresco fragments; attempt at restoration. Chariot and bull; LM II/III a. – Alexiou, *AA.* 1964, 785 ff.; Cameron, *AA.* 1967, 330 ff., Fig. 12.

1056 Fig. 30: Tiryns. Fragments of wall-painting, probably hunting scene; stag fresco; LH III; thirteenth century (sketched reconstruction). – Rodenwaldt, *Tiryns* II (1912), Figs. 60–62, Pls. 15–17; Smith, *Interconnections in the Ancient Near East* (1965), 90, Pl.-Fig. 123.

1057 Fig. 31: Tiryns. Detail of frieze of woman, almost life-size; sketched reconstruction; LH III, thirteenth century B. C. Nat. Mus., Athens. – Rodenwaldt, op. cit., 80 ff., Pls. 7 and 8; Matz, *KMT*. Pls. 105, 106; Lorimer, *Homer and the Monuments* (1950), Pl. 28:2; Marinatos, *Arch. Hom. B* (1967), 11, Fig. 3 (cf. Marinatos–Hirmer, Pl. 226, and Col. Pl. 40).

1058 Thebes, Boeotia. Painted stucco from a chamber tomb; LH III a. Arch. Mus., Thebes. – Unpublished.

1059 Pylos. Throne Room. Fresco put together from fragments; detail of larger subject. Male lyre-player seated on a rock, so-called 'Orpheus'; height, incl. rock and upper pictorial frame, barely 50 cm.; LH III b. – Blegen, *AJA.* 60 (1956), Pl. 41:3; Reusch, in *Minoica und Homer* (1961), 37, Pl. 4 below; Vermeule, *Greece in the Bronze Age*, Pl. 30 a; Blegen and Rawson, *A Guide to the Palace of Nestor* (³1967), 11, Fig. 9; and *The Palace of Nestor at Pylos* I (1966), Pl.-Fig. 75; Lang, loc. cit. II (1969), Pls. 125, 126.

1060 Tiryns. Fresco, partially restored. Preserved width *c.* 43 cm. Boar hunt; LH III. – Rodenwaldt, *Tiryns* II (1912), Pl. 13; Bossert, *Altkreta*, Fig. 35; Matz, *KMT.*, 102, above; Schadewaldt, op. cit., Pl.-Fig. 12.

Fig. 31 *1057* Tiryns, wall fresco, detail of a frieze of women

Painted sarcophagi and stelai

Larnakes and tubs occur together here, although their functions were radically different despite the occasional similarity of forms. On the other hand, tubs of identical form were used both for bathing and for burial (cf. *1066, 1068*). The painted fish swimming on the inside walls of one of these tubs *(1068)* are particularly striking; they were meant to be seen through the refraction of moving water. Platon has discussed Minoan bathrooms, some of which had tubs of this kind, in this context (*Europa: Festschrift für Grumach* [1967], 236 ff.; cf. Graham, *AJA.* 65 [1961], 189 ff.). In the Mycenaean citadels of the mainland, the custom of using earthenware bath-tubs was continued (e.g. *125*); the Greek word for 'bath' (*asaminthos: Iliad* 10.578; *Odyssey* 3.468; 4.128; 10.361) came from a pre-Greek language.

There were larnax burials on Crete from the third millennium B.C. (EM; cf. Pini, *Beiträge zur minoischen Gräberkunde* [1968], 10 f., 52 ff.), although the question of their origin has still not been explained satisfactorily. In the LM III period larnax burials increased greatly in Crete (cf. maps 4 and 5 in Rutkowski, *Larnaksy Egejskie* [Polish, 1966]: Vasilika Anogeia; also Fimmen, *KMK.* 64, Fig. 55). The most famous example is the limestone sarcophagus of Hagia Triada *(1065 a, b)*; it has been illustrated so often and from so many angles that we decided to restrict our choice here to the principal picture on one of the long sides.

Outside Crete, clay sarcophagi have been found in Rhodes, Naxos, Kephallenia, Aegina, and the Greek mainland (Pylos, Dendra, Tiryns, Prosymna, Mycenae, Hagios Kosmas in Attica, Vrasti near Tanagra *[1069 a—c, 1070]*, and Thessaly); cf. the lists in Rutkowski, 126 ff. Recently the form of burial in Aegean types of coffin has also been found in Cyprus (Dikeleia, near Larnaka; Rutkowski, 127, No. 122).

Remains of wooden sarcophagi (Pini, op. cit., 54 f.) and the form of the chest-larnax *(1061—1063, 1065 a, 1067, 1069 a—c)* prove that the cult of the dead turned to types corresponding to the everyday furniture of the living (Laser, 'Hausrat', *Arch. Hom.* P, 1968, 68 ff.).

The large group of painted larnakes makes a considerable contribution to our knowledge of polychrome Minoan-Mycenaean painting. It shows relationships between vase painting and the various types of monumental painting; motifs and ornaments, such as cuttlefish *(1066)*, stylized papyrus plants *(1063)*, areas of network pattern *(1068)*, Maltese crosses *(1061)*, spiral bands *(1061, 1063)*, 'S' spirals *(1065 a)*, and chequer zones *(1069 a—c)*. Moreover, some paintings on sarcophagi give an insight into the ideas of the cult of the gods and of the cult of the dead, especially the sacrificial and mourning ceremonies (cf. *1065 b, 1069 a—c, 1070*). The important styles in art can easily be distinguished, thanks to sarcophagus painting (Crete: *1065 b*—Boeotia: *1069 a—c, 1070*); thus the warrior frieze on a grave stele painted in late Mycenaean times *(1071)* corresponds to the frieze on the so-called 'Warrior Vase' *(1025)*.

1061 Fig. 32: Pentamodi Malevyziou, Crete. Painted clay sarcophagus in the form of a chest with lid in the form of a pitched roof; LM III. Arch. Mus., Herakleion. – *Mon. Ant.* 1 (1890), 209 ff., Pl. 2; Schachermeyr, *Die minoische Kultur des alten Kreta* (1964), 289, Fig. 155 below; Rutkowski, *Larnasky Egejskie* (1966), 123, No. 72, Pl. 21:1; Erlenmeyer, *Europa: Festschrift f. Grumach* (1967), Pl. 7:6; Laser, *Arch. Hom.* P (1968), 71 ff., Fig. 13 a.

1062 Fig. 32: Knossos-Gypsades. Graves XIII and VI.
a, b Painted clay sarcophagus; form, incl. one preserved
1063 lid, and dating as *1061*. Arch. Mus., Herakleion. –
a, b Hood, Huxley and Sandars, *BSA.* 53/54 (1958/59), 230 ff., Figs. 24 b, 25; Rutkowski, 120, No. 52 b, Pl. 7:1,3.

1064 Fig. 32: Vorou Monophatsiou, central Crete. Chest sarcophagus, coarse clay, flat lid; numerous knobs and eyes for securing on exterior; MM/LM I. Arch. Mus., Herakleion. – *Delt.* 13 (1931), 137 ff.; Zervos, *Crète*, Fig. 420; Marinatos–Hirmer, Pl.-Fig. 25; Richter, *The Furniture of the Greeks, Etruscans and Romans* (1966), Pl.-Fig. 28; Rutkowski, 117, No. 14, Pl. 1:3; Laser, op. cit., 72, Fig. 12 a.

1065 Also Fig. 32: Hagia Triada. Limestone sarcophagus
a, b (LM III); Arch. Mus., Herakleion. Painted with cult scenes and ornaments; beautiful example of the chest sarcophagus form, lid missing; length 1.37 cm. On the long side (not shown): bull sacrifice; on the side illustrated: cult scenes in front of double axes on pillars and a tomb; according to Matz: two separate pictorial sequences! – Paribeni, *Mon. Ant.* 19 (1908), 6 ff.; Petersen, *JdI.* 24 (1909), 163 ff.; v. Duhn, *AfRW.* XII (1909), 278 ff.; Sitte, *ÖJh.* 12 (1909), 305 ff.; Harrison, *Themis* (1912), 158 ff.; Cook, *Zeus* II, 516 ff.; Schweitzer, *Gnomon* 4 (1928), 192; Bossert, *Altkreta*, Figs. 248–254; Nilsson, *MMR.*[2], 426 ff.; Matz, *KMT.*, Pls.

Fig. 32 Cretan clay and limestone sarcophagi

46, 47; id., *Göttererscheinung u. Kultbild im minoischen Kreta* (1958), 18 ff.; Buchholz, *Zur Herkunft der kretischen Doppelaxt* (1959), 17; Marinatos–Hirmer, Col. Pls. 27–30; Schachermeyr, *Die minoische Kultur des alten Kreta* (1964), Pls. 35, 36 a; Nauert, *Antike Kunst* 8 (1965), 91 ff., Pls. 24, 25; Mylonas, *Myc. and the Myc. Age*, Pl.-Fig. 134; Rutkowski, 126, No. 109, Pls. 3, 4; Nilsson, *Gesch. d. griech. Relig.* I (^{3}1967), 326 ff., Pl. 10.

1066 Episkopi Hierapetras, Crete. Tub sarcophagus of clay; stylized cuttlefish and geometric decoration. Arch. Mus., Herakleion. – Xanthoutides, *Delt.* 6 (1920/21), Parart. 158 f.; Levi, *ASAtene* 10–12 (1927–29), 628 ff; Zervos, *Crète*, Fig. 780; Nilsson, *MMR.*, 434; Rutkowski, 118, No. 29 a, Pl. 25:1.

1067 Kamilari near Phaistos, south Crete. Terracotta sarcophagus in chest form with flat lid. Arch. Mus., Herakleion. – Levi, *ASAtene* 29/30 (1961/62), 34, Fig. 31; Rutkowski, 120, No. 41, Pl. 18:4; Richter, *The Furniture of the Greeks, Etruscans and Romans* (1966), Pl.-Fig. 29.

1068 Pachyammos, east Crete. Tub larnax, clay. Outside painted with areas of network pattern; inside: fish, designed for viewing when tub is filled with water in motion; length 1.23 cm., LM III a (1400–1350 B. C.). Arch. Mus., Herakleion, Inv. No. 9499. – Alexiou, *Kretika Chronika* 8 (1954), 402; Zervos, *Crète*, Fig. 782; Marinatos–Hirmer, Pl. 126 upper; Karo, *Greifen am Thron* (1959), 111, Fig. 71; Rutkowski, 122 f., No. 68 b, Pl. 33:1.

83

1069 Vratsi, near Tanagra, Boeotia; Ludwig Colln., Aachen *a–c* (in Staatliche Kunstsammlungen, Kassel): Mycenaean terracotta sarcophagus in chest form; length 1.06 cm., width 30 cm., height 61–68 cm. Light brown, coarse clay, yellowish ground, matt wine-red to brick-red and black painting. Figurative shapes on both long sides and one narrow side: panels framed by chequer pattern, each with mourning woman painted in a stiff manner; LH III b. – Lullies, *Griechische Kunstwerke: Sammlung Ludwig, Aachen [catalogue]* (1968), 9 ff., with col. ills.; Vermeule, *Greece*, 210 ff., Pl. 34; and *JHS*. 85 (1965), 123 ff., Pls. 25, 26 a; Iakovidis, *AJA*. 70 (1966), 43 ff., esp. 46 ff., Figs. 3, 4; Rutkowski, 126, No. 110.

1070 Vratsi, Boeotia; Pomerance Colln., New York. Fragment of a Mycenaean terracotta sarcophagus like *1069*, from the same LH III b/c cemetery. Greyish yellow clay, dull black paint; mourning women and chequer pattern here also, but conceived in slightly different style of painting than *1069*; preserved height 33.3 cm., width 33.4 cm. – Vermeule, *Greece*, 212 f., Fig. 37 a, and 342 f., n. 13; id., *JHS*. 85 (1965), 129 ff., No. 4, Pl. 27 c; Iakovidis, op. cit., 46, 48; Wegner, *Arch. Hom. U* (1968), 84, Nos. 161–171.

1071 Mycenae. Grave stele of stone, with engraved ornaments that were covered with stucco and painted when the object was re-used. Two framed pictorial scenes, the upper showing a warrior frieze, the lower a hunting scene with animals; above them a hedgehog; LH III c. Nat. Mus., Athens, Inv. No. 3256. – Tsountas, *Ephem.* 1896, 1 ff., Pl. 1; Studniczka, *Die griechische Kunst an Kriegergräbern* (1915), Pl. 1:2; Bossert, *Altkreta*, Fig. 45; Furumark, *Myc. Pottery*, 449 f., 453; Lorimer, *Homer and the Monuments*, 229, Pl. 2:2; Wace–Stubbings, *A Companion to Homer* (1962), Pl. 29 b; Vermeule, *Greece*, 304, Fig. 47 a; Buchholz, *BJV*. 5 (1965), 71, Fig. 4 h, Pl. 13:5 (hedgehog); Verdelis, *AM*. 82 (1967), 24 and Suppl. 32:2 (detail); Andronikos, *Arch. Hom. W* (1968), 117, Fig. 9.

Metal vessels

For this, see the introductory text on p. 158 below, where I discuss the 'Metal vessels and implements of Cyprus.' The connection between Cypriot and Aegean metallurgy is reflected in the title of a work by Catling, *Cypriot Bronzework in the Mycenaean World* (1964); cf. also the material assembled in Montelius, *La Grèce Préclassique* (1924), Pls. 25—36.

The proportion of gold and silver vessels in the total metal production in the Aegean seems to have been considerably larger than in Cyprus (gold: *1072, 1073, 1079—1080, 1082, 1085—1087, 1089, 1104—1106, 1117*; silver: *1075, 1077, 1078, 1081, 1083, 1088, 1107, 1108*; electrum: *1074*). The wealth of silver of the early period (third millennium) suggests very close relations with Anatolia; the forms of some of the vessels point in the same direction: *1072—1075, 1079, 1080*. A highly developed metalwork flourished there in the third millennium (cf. Bittel, *JdI.* 74 [1959], 1 ff.). Early Cycladic metalwork seems to have had particular importance within the Aegean: *1077, 1084*; cf. also a lead boat *(1076)*, and Renfrew, 'Cycladic Metallurgy and the Aegean Early Bronze Age' (*AJA*. 71 [1967], 1 ff.).

Also noteworthy are a number of correspondences between metal vessels and their clay equivalents (cf. e.g. sauce-boat, clay: *822, 824*; gold: *1082 a, b*; two-handled Troy goblet, clay: *796, 797, 799*; silver: *1075*). There are also similarities with the typical Cypriot Late Bronze Age solid-cast wishbone handles: *1109—1112*; also Fig. 33 left, Knossos, Phaistos (Montelius, op. cit., Pl. 31: 2), and Kydonia (Jantzen, in Matz, *Forschungen auf Kreta*, 1942 [1951], Pl. 57: 2); also post-Minoan in Arkades, Crete (Levi, *ASAtene* 10—12 [1927—29], 473 f., Fig. 590 a 1, b 6); finally in Italy: Müller-Karpe, *Beiträge zur Chronologie der Urnenfelderzeit nördlich und südlich der Alpen* [1959], Pl. 68 a 1); clay, the Argolid: *1024*; metal, Cyprus: *1684*.

The care with which vase shapes were reproduced in Egyptian wall-paintings shows how sought after and wellknown Aegean metalwork was in the Nile valley (Fig. 34): *1100—1102* (Vapheio cups); corresponding archetypes in gold: *1104, 1105*. The jug (Fig. 34, *1103*) corresponds to the bronze original *1115*. Finally, Egyptian influence is evident in the end of the handle of a gold cup from Dendra (*1117 b*, cf. silver handles, Knossos: Montelius, op. cit., Pl. 29: 5).

Many more utilitarian vessels were made of copper than of bronze; the tongue of a copper cauldron handle from Mycenae has an incised check in Linear A script (pp. 118 and 121: *1411*). Clearly there were technical contacts between the different metalworkers who forged helmets and cauldrons (bronze

Fig. 33   1095 a–o   ›Grave of the Tripod Hearth‹ in Zapher Papoura near Knossos, Minoan metal ware

helmet, Knossos: 710). The sketch of the contents of a tomb in Knossos is impressive evidence of the wealth of metal in the Late Bronze Age (Fig. 33).

The notable achievements in chasing, soldering, riveting, and notching were exceeded only by a technical and artistic mastery in *repoussé* and embossed relief-work (1088, 1089, 1104—1106, 1117 a—c; for the technique of Minoan reliefwork in gold cf. Hudson, *Metallurgia* 32 [1945], 279 ff.). The ornamental reliefs on the rims and handles of a number of vessels (e.g. 1115, 1116), cast in 'lost wax,' are also remarkably accomplished.

One of the greatest achievements of this art is the silver vases with figurative inlays in gold and niello (1107, 1108, Cyprus: 1684). The raised birds on the handles of the 'Dove Cup' from Mycenae (1085, cf. the little bird on the rim of a bronze beaker from the hoard of Tiryns: Karo, *AM*. 55 [1930], 130 f., Suppl. 34, 1) are also very attractively modelled, and the large dogs' heads sculptured in the round on the handles of another gold vase from Mycenae (1087) are forceful and striking characterizations.

1072–1084:   GOLD – SILVER – LEAD – COPPER – EARLY AND MIDDLE BRONZE AGE

1072 to 1074 Troy II. Three gold and electrum vases from the great hoard of 1873, Schliemann's 'Hoard of Priam' (cf. *Trojanische Altertümer*, 298 ff. and *Ilios* 505 ff.); third millenium; formerly Staatl. Museen, Berlin (destroyed by war; now gold reproductions from plaster casts in Schloß Charlottenburg, Berlin). Inv. No. 5862 (1072): pot-bellied bottle with short narrow neck and flaring rim, hammered from a single piece of gold sheet, flanged at the mouth; weight 403 gr., height 14 cm. Inv. No. 5865 (1073) vertically facetted bell-shaped gold beaker, with separately worked ring foot, hammered work; weight 226 gr., height 8.9 cm., diam. of mouth 7.8 cm. Inv. No. 5864 (1074): small bell-shaped pedestal beaker, hammered from one piece of electrum sheet; curved contour, wide diagonal and parallel grooves; height 7.2 cm., diam. of mouth 6.3 cm.,

1075 Troas. Near Eastern Dept., Brit. Mus., London. Early Bronze Age silver beaker (third millennium) of a form frequently found in clay (cf. Caskey, in *Essays in Memory of K. Lehmann* [1964], 63 f.), which hardly deserves the Greek designation *depas amphikypellon* (cf. *1085*). – Barnett, *BMQ.* 27 (1963/64), 79, Pl. 29 b; Renfrew, *AJA.* 71 (1967), 16, Pl. 10 c.

weight 70 gr. – Schmidt, *Schliemanns Sammlung*, 230 f., Nos. 5862, 5864, 5865; Matz, *KMT.*, Pl. 5 upper.

1076 Naxos. Early Cycladic cist grave; Ashmolean Mus., Oxford, Inv. No. 1929.26: Small ship composed of three strips of hammered lead; not a vase, but a funerary offering made specifically for the cult of the dead; length 40.3 cm. – Renfrew, 18, No. 12, Pls. 1 (drawing) and 3 (various views); Thimme, *Frühe Randkulturen des Mittelmeerraumes* (1968), 10, Fig. 1.

1077 Kapros in Amorgos. Cist grave D; Ashmolean Mus., Oxford, Inv. No. AE 158: Wide-mouthed flat silver bowl with round base, short neck; undecorated; diam. 9.2 cm. – Dümmler, *AM.* 11 (1886), 15 f.; Renfrew, 6 f., 18, No. 17, Pls. 1 (drawing) and 10.

1078 Probably from Euboea or the Cyclades (cf. *1079–1081*); Metrop. Mus., New York, No. 46.11.1. Silver bowl, like *1077* but decorated on the belly: zone of dense vertical groups of lines and hatched triangles; diam. 6.25 cm., height 5.8 cm. – Segall, op. cit., 216, No. 1 b, Pl. 69; Richter, op. cit., 16, Pl. 11 i; Vermeule, *Greece*, Pl. 6 b; Renfrew, 7, note 76, Pl. 10 e.

1079 Euboea. Grave finds, site unknown; Benaki Mus., to Athens: Three of the most beautiful and best preserved 1081 gold and silver vases of the third millennium B.C. from the Aegean. Gold (*1079, 1080*, diam. 12.3 and 12.4 cm., heights 9 and 9.5 cm.; 560 and 468 gr.) and silver (*1081*, diam. 11.7 cm., height 4.9 cm.; 435 gr.). Strong resemblances to central Anatolian examples; perhaps imported from there. Characteristic features are the groups of parallel grooves, short flaring neck, round base, sometimes with inward rising omphalos (*1079*). – Segall, *Katalog der Goldschmiedearbeiten, Benaki-Mus.*, Athen (1938), 11 ff., 211 ff., Pl. 3 below,

Pls. 67, 69; Milojcic, *Germania* 31 (1953), 10; Richter, *Handbook of the Greek Coll.*, New York (1953), 16; Schachermeyr, *Die ältesten Kulturen*, 160, Fig. 41:1, Pl. 8:1–3; Demargne, *Naissance*, 34, Figs. 31–33 (Eng. trans., *Aegean Art*); Müller-Karpe, *Hdb. d. Vorgesch.* II (1968), 446 f., No. 105, Pl. 138:1–3.

1082 Said to be from Heraia, Arcadia. Louvre, Paris, Inv. a, b No. MNC 906 (1887). Important find from the third millennium (EH II); 'sauceboat' with ring foot made of 3 mm. thick hammered gold sheet and small solid rivetted gold handle decorated with chased chevrons; height 17 cm., length 14.4 cm. (incl. handle), weight 125.2 gr. Similar gold piece in Israel Mus., Jerusalem, Inv. No. BNAM. 2 (cf. below, Weinberg); similar types in clay, *822, 824*. – De Ridder, *Cat. sommaire des bijoux antiques du Louvre* (1924), Pl. 6, 1885; Childe, *JHS.* 44 (1924), 163 ff.; Karo, *Vorgeschichtliches Jahrbuch* 1 (1926), 105; Bossert, *Altkreta*, Fig. 147 (in damaged state); Schachermeyr, 183, Fig. 56:1; Demargne, *Naissance* 76, Fig. 98; Vermeule, *Greece*, 27, 40, Pl. 6 a; Renfrew, 16, Pl. 10 a; Weinberg, *Antike Kunst* 12 (1969), 3 ff., Fig. 1, Pl. 1:1–3.

1083 Gournia. From a grave. Arch. Mus., Herakleion: Kantharoslike silver vase, with acute shoulder, rim scalloped in four parts, and two handles; height c. 8 cm.; after 2000 B.C. (MM I). – Montelius, *La Grèce préclass.*, Pl. 29:4; Hall, *The Civilization of Greece in the Bronze Age* (1928), 75, Fig. 79 a; Åberg, *Chronologie* IV, 212, Fig. 391; Pendlebury, *Arch. of Crete*, 114, Pl. 18:4 c; Demargne, *Naissance*, 115, Fig. 151.

1084 From the sea, off the coast of Euboea; Mus. f. Kunst a–f und Gewerbe, Hamburg, Inv. No. 1966.109: Copper cauldron with basket-stirrup handle and socket spout, Cycladic origin; height, incl. handle, 25.7 cm., greatest width 25.7 cm., thickness of wall 4 mm. Analysis of copper: 0.8 %/₀ arsenic; tin, lead and silver in traces. Middle Bronze Age, c. 1700 B.C. – Buchholz, *Jahrb. d. Hamburger Kunstsammlungen*, 13 (1968), 13 ff.; and *AA.* 1969, 318 ff.

1085–1117: GOLD – SILVER – COPPER – BRONZE – LATE BRONZE AGE

1085 Mycenae. Grave Circle A, Shaft Grave IV; Nat. Mus., Athens: Gold cup with two handles of the Vapheio cup type, still attached to the stand. On each handle an embossed, moulded dove (so-called Dove Cup, or Cup of Nestor); diam., with handles, 14.5 cm.; LH I (sixteenth century). – Schliemann, *Mykenae* (1878), 272, Fig. 346 *(depas amphikypellon)*, cf. *1075*; Dussaut, *Civilis. préhell.* (1914), 147, Fig. 109; Montelius, op. cit., Pl. 26:2; Evans, *PM.* IV, 392, Fig. 327; Karo, *Schachtgräber*, Pls. 109, 412; Bossert, *Altkreta*, Fig. 148; Marinatos–Hirmer, Pl. 188; Mylonas, *Myc. and the Myc. Age*, Pl.-Fig. 85.

1086 Mycenae. Grave Circle A, Shaft Grave IV; Nat. Mus., Athens: Plain kantharos, hammered from thick gold sheet; height, with handles, 11.5 cm.; LH I (second half of sixteenth century). – Schliemann, 267, Fig. 339; Montelius, Pl. 26:3; Åberg, *Chronologie* IV (1933), 45, Fig. 74; Karo, *Schachtgräber*, Pls. 108, 440; Bossert, Fig. 150; Marinatos–Hirmer, Pl. 192 lower.

1087 Mycenae. Hoard south of Grave Circle A, discovered by Drosinos in 1877; Athens, Inv. No. 957: Detail of a gold vase; upper ends of handles in the form of dog's heads in the round; height of vase 13.7 cm.; LH I/II (early fifteenth century). – Schliemann 398, Fig. 528; Montelius, Pl. 27:5; Thomas, *BSA.* 39 (1938/39), 66, 68, Pls. 26 a, 27 b; Marinatos–Hirmer, Pl. 189; Demargne, *Naissance*, 194, Fig. 268 (Eng. trans. *Aegean Art*).

1088 Mycenae. Grave Circle A, Shaft Grave V (Schliemann's a, b no. I); Nat. Mus., Athens, Inv. No. 855. Silver jug, lower part grooved, upper part decorated with spiral band, neck hammered from separate piece; foot, round bar on shoulder, and rim of mouth lined with bronze. Traces of niello found during cleaning (*Ephem.* 1957,

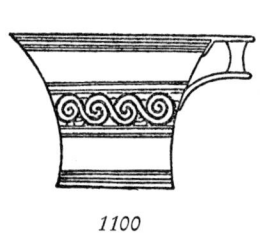  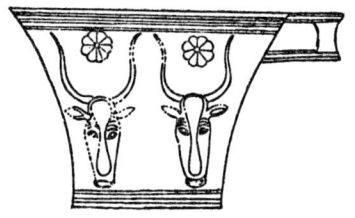 

1100   *1101*   *1102*   *1103*

Fig. 34   Minoan vases in Egyptian wall-paintings

Chron. Pl. 3 a); height 34.5 cm.; LH I (sixteenth century). – Schliemann, 362, Fig. 478; Montelius, Pl. 30:5; Evans, *PM*. II, Fig. 411; Bossert, op. cit., Fig. 122 d; Karo, *Schachtgräber*, Pls. 134, 855; Marinatos–Hirmer, Pl. 195.

1089 Mycenae. Grave Circle A, Shaft Grave V (Schliemann's no. I); Nat. Mus., Athens. Small hexagonal casket with lid, put together from fragments. Wood, coated with embossed gold plaques (length 9.4 cm.). Interesting example of Early Mycenaean two-dimensional composition in relief; LH I. – Schliemann, 354, Figs. 470, 471; Müller, *JdI*. 30 (1915), 294 f.; Bossert, Figs. 78, 80; Karo, Pls. 143, 144, 808–811; Marinatos–Hirmer, Pls. 198, 199 below; Mylonas, *Myc. and the Myc. Age*, Pl.-Fig. 139 a, b; Richter, *The Furniture of the Greeks, Etruscans, and Romans* (1966), Pl.-Fig. 32.

1090 Mycenae. Grave Circle A, Shaft Grave IV; Nat. Mus.,
a, b Athens, Inv. No. 604 a. Copper cauldron with concave profile on upper part, greatest diameter sharply profiled, and round base separately worked, rim folded over and attached with crude nails; two handles with large leaf-shaped attachments; height 40 cm., greatest diam. 56 cm.; LH I. – Karo, *SchGr.*, 118, 282, Fig. 124, Pls. 161, 604 a; Catling, *Cypriot Bronze Work* (1964), Fig. 18:5.

1091 Mycenae. Grave Circle A, Shaft Grave IV; Nat. Mus.,
to   Athens. Five copper cauldrons, partly repaired in an-
1094 cient times. *1411* (cf. p. 121) has a Linear A sign on one of the tongues of the handles. – Karo, Pl. 159; Catling, Fig. 18:3,4.

1095 Zapher Papoura, near Knossos. Grave 14 ('Grave of
a–o the Tripod Hearth'); Arch. Mus., Herakleion: Minoan bronze and copper vessels as grave goods; cups and basins, jugs and hydriai, tripod cauldron, ladle, lamp. Sketch of position of finds; in front the clay tripod hearth with remains of charcoal; LM III. – Evans, *Prehist. Tombs* (1906), 36, Fig. 33, Pl. 89; and *PM*. II, 634 ff., Fig. 398; Fimmen, *KMK*. 190, Fig. 185 (hydria); Montelius, *La Grèce préclass.*, Pl. 32:1–19; Yavis, *Greek Altars* (1949), 12, Fig. 5. – Lamb, *Greek and Roman Bronzes* (1929), 13 ff. (further Min.-Myc. bronze vessels); also p. 85, Fig. 33, above.

1096 Mycenae. Grave Circle A, Shaft Grave IV; Nat. Mus.,
to   Athens, Inv. Nos. 602, 604, 601: Copper hydriai, partly
1098 repaired in ancient times; *1099* similar but more squat, with shorter neck; heights 51, 55.5, 52 cm.; LH I, second half of sixteenth century. – Karo, *SchGr.*, Pls. 154:602, 155:604, 601; Bossert, *Altkreta*, Fig. 160; Catling, op. cit., 175 f., Nos. 16, 18, 15, Fig. 20:2.

1099 Probably from Dendra. In London art market since
a, b spring 1962; acquired by Brit. Mus. (No. 1963.7–5.1): Large, excellently preserved copper hydria of the early fourteenth century; only slightly bent at rim, recent pickaxe blow on neck! Several layers of mineralization: green encrustations on a basic brown tone, especially on base; height 54 cm. (?; subsequent measurement 52.5 cm.), inner diam. of mouth 11.5 cm., outside 15.5 cm., diam. of base 16.3 cm.; thickness of wall c. 1.5 cm. Hammered from four pieces of copper without seams (traces of hammer blows in horizontal rows on outside) and rivetted together (rivet heads inside). The base overlaps the next piece with the horizontal handle (thick 1.4 cm. square bar, both ends hammered flat and attached with two rivets); this overlaps the upper part of the vase, which in turn is overlapped by the neck piece. The vertical handle, 4.4 cm. wide, is attached on top, below the overhanging lip, with three rivets, the lower end at the shoulder with two rivets. – Higgins, *BMQ*. 28 (1964), 18 f., 112, Pl. 6; and *JHS*. 87 (1967), Arch. Rep. 49, Fig. 7; Catling, 176, No. 33 (cf. also No. 7 from Kydonia, LM III: Matz, *Forschungen auf Kreta*, 1942 [1951], Pl. 57:1).

1100 Fig. 34. Aegean vase types on Egyptian wall-paintings,
to   details from the Keftiu paintings in the Tomb of Sen-
1103 mut in Thebes, northern Egypt. *1100, 1102;* Vapheio cups like *1104–1105; 1103:* Metal jug like *1115; 1101:* Pithos with suspension eyes and rosettes and figure-of-eight shield decoration, similar form in clay: *927*. First half of fifteenth century. – Wainwright, *Liv. Ann.* 6 (1913/14), Pl. 13:101,102; Fimmen, *AM*. 38 (1913), 191 f.; id., *KMK*. 181 ff., Figs. 176, 182, 184; Malten, *JdI*. 43 (1928), 127, Fig. 63; Evans, *PM*. II, 534, Fig. 338 and p. 737, Fig. 470; Bossert, *Altkreta*, Figs. 536, 537; Kantor, *The Aegean and the Orient in the Second Millennium B. C.* (1947), Pl. 9 c–e; Vercoutter, *L'Egypte et le monde égéen préhellénique* (1956), 203 ff., Nos. 67–69, Pls. 1, 2; Hutchinson, *Prehist. Crete*, 280, Fig. 54; Schachermeyr, *Die min. Kultur des alten Kreta* (1964), 112, Fig. 55; Smith, *Interconnections in the Ancient Near East* (1965), Fig. 90.

1104 Vapheio, Laconia; Nat. Mus., Athens. Embossed gold
a, b cup from a tholos tomb (LH II, c. 1500 B. C.). Form of vase faithfully reproduced on Egyptian wall-paintings (cf. Fig. 34); belongs with *1105;* diam. of mouth 10.8 cm. Impressive relief frieze: bringing home captured wild bulls *(1104 a)*. – Tsountas, *Ephem.* 1889, Pl. 9 (also *1105*); Riegl, *ÖJh.* 9 (1906), 1 ff.; Müller, *JdI*. 30 (1915), 325, Pls. 9–11 (also *1105*); Fimmen,

KMK. 189, Fig. 183; Montelius, *La Grèce préclass.*, Pl. 28:2; Bossert, *Altkreta*, Figs. 71, 73, 75; Matz, *KMT*. Pl. 64 lower; Marinatos–Hirmer, Pls. 182–185; Schadewaldt, *Von Homers Welt u. Werk* (^{3}1959), Pl.-Fig. 16; Mylonas, *Myc. and the Myc. Age*, Pl.-Fig. 120.

1105 Vapheio. Gold cup (belonging together with and almost same dimensions as *1104*), with relief picture of bull caught in net. – Montelius, Pl. 28:1 a, b; Bossert, Figs. 70, 72, 74; Mode, *Die indischen Frühkulturen u. ihre Beziehungen zum Westen* (1944), 71, Fig. 156; Matz, Pl. 65 upper; Marinatos–Hirmer, Pls. 178–181; Schadewaldt, Pl. 17; Schiering, *Antike Kunst* 8 (1965), Pl.3:1. Cf. also *1104*. The form, esp. of the handle, is also found in bronze; cf. Catling, *Cypriot Bronzework*, 179, Fig. 21:2. Clay imitations appeared in central Europe: Nienhagen, cf. Pl. 1 b. Mötefind, *AA*. 1912, 99 ff.; Buchholz, *PZ*. 38 (1960), 49 and Fig. 9 a.

1106 Probably from Aegina (from a hoard or grave; cf. *1305*). Embossed gold bowl with central rosette and spiral quatrefoil; contrasting fluted rim with rivet holes (attachment for grip); diam. 9.7 cm.; LM/LH I. Brit. Mus., London, Cat. No. 768. – Evans, *JHS*. 13 (1892/93), 196 f., Fig. 1 a, b; Higgins, *BSA*. 52 (1957), 54, Pl. **14**.

1107 Pylos. Propylon and ramp 59. Eleven bearded heads in profile, inlays of gold and niello on silver; all parts of silver cup similar to *1108*; LH III b. – Blegen, *AJA*. 59 (1955), Pl. 23, and 66 (1962), Pl. 61:8; Hampe, *Gymnasium* 63 (1956), Pl. 15 a; Marinatos–Hirmer, Pl. 204 below; Blegen–Rawson, *The Palace of Nestor at Pylos* I (1966), 58, 62, 237, Pl.-Fig. 261; and *A Guide to the Palace of Nestor* (^{3}1967), 32, Fig. 34.

1108 Mycenae. From a chamber tomb; Nat. Mus., Athens: Silver cup like *1107*, also with frieze of inlaid bearded heads facing left (hair at nape of neck in separate locks; cf. Marinatos, 'Haartracht', *Arch. Hom*. B [1967], 25, Pl. 2 c); diam. of mouth 16 cm., height without handle 6.2 cm.; LH II/III a (Bossert: still sixteenth century). – Tsountas, *Ephem*., 1888, Pl. 7:2; Perrot–Chipiez, VI, 813, Fig. 381; Montelius, *La Grèce préclass.*, Pl. 30:1 a–c; Bossert, *Altkreta*, Figs. 153–155; Zervos, *L'Art en Grèce* (1937), Fig. 39; Marinatos–Hirmer, Pl. 196 above; Taylour, *Mycenaeans* (1964), Pl. 52.

1109 Argive Heraion (Prosymna). Grave 10; Arch. Mus.,
1110 Nauplia: Two bronze wishbone handles (LH III) belonging to cauldrons or lekanai (like *1111* and *1112*). Comparable pieces above, p. 84, and Persson, *New Tombs at Dendra near Midea* (1942), 36, No. 15. – Blegen, *Prosymna* (1937), 353, Fig. 610; Catling, *Cypriot Bronzework*, 172, No. 26.

1111 Dendra, the Argolid. Grave 7; Arch. Mus., Nauplia:
1112 Two squat cauldrons or lekanai with wishbone handles (like *1109*, *1110*); height 13 cm. *(1111)* and 15 cm. *(1112)*, LH III b. Persson, 35 f., Nos. 14, 15, Fig. 35:6,7; Catling, 172, Nos. 23, 24.

1113 Tiryns. Part of great treasure of 1916 *(1114, 1307, 1378 to 1380)*; Nat. Mus., Athens. Three handled copper cauldron, with round base and lip for pouring on rim; comparable pieces according to Catling only; LM/LH I. – Karo, *AM*. 55 (1930), 119 ff.; Catling, Fig. 18:2.

1114 Tiryns (cf. *1113*). Copper cauldron with sharp bend at shoulder; two vertical ribbed handles, with wide horizontal attachment above and end rounded lower; height 30 cm., diam. of mouth 37 cm.; LH III c. – Karo, 133, Pl. 34:2; Catling, 168, Form 3 b, No. 2, Fig. 18:6.

1115 Dendra. So-called 'Panoply Tomb' (Tomb 12, cf. *629*,
a, b *630, 712, 1099*); Arch. Mus., Nauplia: Slender copper jug ('piriform oinochoe'), made in two parts. Connecting zone covered by cast metal collar decorated in relief; angular strap handle similarly decorated in relief; height 33 cm.; LH II/III a. This form not found in Crete; similar pieces in Mycenae, Asine, and Dendra, Chamber Tomb 2 (Persson, *The Royal Tombs at Dendra near Midea* [1931], Pl. 31:1–3). – Hood, *JHS*. 81 (1961), Arch. Rep. 9, Fig. 8; Catling, 178, No. 6, Fig. 20:6; Verdelis, *AM*. 82 (1967), 48 ff., No. 9, Figs. 13, 14, Suppls. 24, 26:1.

1116 Argive Heraion, Prosymna. Grave 29; Arch. Mus., Nauplia. Lamp in the form of a flat pan, with almost vertical handle; leaf ornament on rim produced during castings; bronze; diam. 11.3 cm., length of handle 7 cm.; LH III a/b. – Blegen, *Prosymna* (1937), 352 f., Fig. 609; Catling, 184, Form 28 b, No. 13.

1117 Dendra. Burial Shaft I of Chamber Tomb 10 (Find
a–c No. 19); Arch. Mus., Nauplia: Gold cup, hammered in one piece, with offset base and rim scalloped in eight places *(1117 a)*. The separately worked handle is attached to the vase with two rivets on top and one rivet below, where the vase is decorated with suspended double papyrus motifs. On the body, relief strips of stylized ivy leaves between two transversely ribbed fillets. Lip and edges of handle reinforced with bands of beading. Height 5 cm.; incl. handle, 7.5 cm., diam. without handle 13 cm.; c. 1450 B. C. – Persson, *6. internat. Kongr. f. Archäologie, Berlin 1939* (1940), Pl. 19; id., *New Tombs at Dendra near Midea* (1942), 74 f., Fig. 88, and p. 142, Fig. 118:5, Pl. 4; cf. *AA*. 1940, 215 f., **Fig. 51**.

Stone vessels and reliefs

These groups of remains occupy a dominant position in ancient Aegean arts and crafts (cf. the survey of Cypriot stone vessels on pp. 155 f., and the bibliography there). Recently Peter Warren (*Minoan Stone Vases* [1969]) has described more than 3,500 Aegean stone vases from typological aspects, examining problems of chronology, and discussing the materials employed, their provenance, and their treatment.

These works of stone tell us much about their function—for example, as cult objects—and also with respect to their importance to trade or significance to art history. Thus the name of Pharaoh Userkaf on an imported little marble bowl from Kythera points to the range of trade relations in the third millennium B.C. and the value attached to such vessels (Fifth Dynasty; Nat. Mus., Athens, Inv. No. 4578; cf. Smith, *Interconnections in the Ancient Near East* [1965], Fig. 10).

The material for making a mortar *(1132)*—or perhaps the finished vessel—must have been imported into Attica in the third millennium B.C., since andesite of this kind does not occur naturally there. Similarly an Early Cycladic marble vessel *(1134)*, found on the west coast of Anatolia, is characteristic evidence of trade within the Aegean, while the famous lid inscribed with the name of Chian *(1142)* and an amphora of Egyptian alabaster with the name of Thutmose III in hieroglyphics *(1140)* indicate Cretan-Egyptian trade connections in the second millennium B.C. (cf. also *1141 a, b*).

Mortars such as *1159* were imported from Syria (cf. Buchholz, *JdI.* 78 [1963], 1 ff.). But an example found in Thera shows that foreign tripod bowls were already being imitated in the Aegean in the middle of the second millennium B.C.; the unpublished bowl from Thera is made of brilliant white island marble. Richly decorated tripod bowls of steatite represent the Cypriot variants of this type, and occur as imports in Rhodes and east Attica *(1160)*.

Marble predominated in the earliest production in Crete and the islands. Steatite, which was easier to work, was popular in many areas and in all periods. Porphyry and alabaster were used less frequently as raw material for Cretan stonework and with no historical uniformity. Even more rare was the use of obsidian (natural volcanic glass) and rock crystal *(1156)*, or *lapis lacedaemonius* of any considerable size *(1157)*. Andesite and basalt *(1132, 1159)* served as materials for everyday utility vessels for grinding or pulverizing certain foods, spices, drugs, pigments, etc.

Hand lamps of steatite *(1126)*, low stone lamps *(1143, 1158)*, and splendid lighting appliances on tall pedestals *(1149—1151)* show that we are dealing here with equipment used by a sophisticated courtly culture. Often the stone vessels also served votive uses in shrines or as grave goods *(1119, 1122—1126, 1134, 1140, 1141, 1143, 1156, 1160, 1161)*; this does not, however, prove that they were used exclusively for this purpose. Considered as a vessel, the model of a seven-celled granary *(1122)* is undoubtedly a kernos, a container for sacrifices (cf. the clay ring kernos *1271*). But, in terms of their primary function, other so-called 'house' models could be regarded quite differently; e.g. a Cycladic pyxis: Bossert, *Altkreta*, Fig. 402, and Zaphiropoulou, 'A Prehistoric House Model from Melos,' *AAA.* 2 (1969), 406 ff. In the case of many precious vessels from the Late Bronze Age, we must assume their use to have been ritual, particularly in the case of libation vases of stone *(1157, 1165)*, cf. also animal head rhyta *(1234, 1237)* and chalice-goblets *(1152—1155)*.

With regard to the sacred function of steatite vessels and—if they are decorated with reliefs—their religious content *(1162—1167, 1235,* small steatite fragment with cuttlefish tentacles in relief) see Nilsson, *The Minoan-Mycenaean Religion and its Survival in Greek Religion* (^{2}1950).

The storage vessel *906* (pp. 70, 310) is so closely reminiscent of the malleability of clay in form and in the doughy softness of its relief spirals that this stone vessel serves to demonstrate the influence of the potter's art.

A pot-bellied jug with lovely marbling in concentric circles (p. 311, *1146;* cf. similar circular effects: *1130 a)* also shows the relationship between clay and stone forms; the shape of this jug was developed in terracotta and imitated in stone. The reverse also occurs (cf. Schiering, *JdI.* 75 [1960], 17 ff.), and we find formal relationships in the production of metalwork and stone vases; cf. Warren, 'The Relation of Stone Vases to Clay and Metal Works,' *Minoan Stone Vases* (1969), 168 ff. At least some of the steatite relief vessels were originally gilded, and must have looked like solid gold to a naïve observer (cf. traces of gilding on *1163* and on a fragment from east Crete: Bosanquet-Dawkins, 'The Unpublished Objects from the Palaekastro Excavations' [1923], 137, Fig. 118 [in Bossert, *Altkreta*, Fig. 68, wrongly described as 'Vapheio?'], new photograph: Kyrieleis, *MarbWPr.* 1968, Pl. 3, centre); for the gilding of steatite vessels, see Buchholz, *OLZ.* 61 (1966), 131 f.

Mycenaean grave stelai *(1170, 1171)* were discussed in detail by Heurtley (*BSA.* 25 [1921—23], 126 ff.; also Mylonas, *AJA.* 55 [1951], 134 ff.), even before the final discussion by Karo of the Shaft Graves. Mylonas discussed the stelai in Grave Circle B at Mycenae, and so did more recently Marinatos (*AAA.* 1 [1968], 175 ff.; cf. Andronikos, 'Totenkult,' *Arch. Hom.* W [1968], 114 ff.); and Kyrieleis, 'Eigenart spätminoischer Reliefarbeiten' (*MarbWPr.* 1968, 5 ff.). Besides the larger-format stelai *(1168—1171)* and the tiny stone reliefs on seals, the vessels with figurative and ornamental decoration also are important evidence of an animated, imaginative and comparatively original planar art *(1162—1166).*

1118–1167: VASES (cf. also *906, 1236*)

1118 Thessaly. From a magoula near Larissa. Fragment of *a, b* a Neolithic marble vase; Private colln., Athens. – Grundmann, *AM.* 57 (1932), 107, Suppl. 22; Buttler, *Marburger Studien* (Festschrift v. Merhart, 1938), 29, Pl. 13 b 5.

1119 Mochlos. Grave I. Pyxis lid of green steatite (chlorite), with dense incised ornament, concentrically arranged, and grip in the form of a reclining long-legged dog (cf. *Prakt.* 1963, Pl. 154 b); pairs of holes at opposite sides of rim for attachment; height 3 cm., diam. 11 cm., EM II/III (c. 2400–2200 B.C.). Arch. Mus., Herakleion, Inv. No. 1282. – Seager, *Explorations in the Island of Mochlos* (1912), 20 f., Figs. 4, 5; Maraghiannis, *Ant. Crét.* II, Pl. 4:8; Hall, *The Civilization of Greece in the Bronze Age* (1928), 51, Fig. 46; Pendlebury, *Arch. of Crete*, Pl. 11:2; Marinatos–Hirmer, Pl. 6; Karo, *Greifen am Thron* (1959), 35, Fig. 18; Demargne, *Naissance*, 66, Fig. 83; Schachermeyr, *Älteste Kulturen*, 211, Fig. 71; id., *Die minoische Kultur des alten Kreta* (1964), Pl. 7 a; Willetts, *Everyday Life in Ancient Crete* (1969), 35, Fig. 15; Warren, *Minoan Stone Vases* (1969), 82, Figs. P 457 and D 250; Branigan, *The Foundations of Palatial Crete* (1970), Pl. 12 a.

1120 Monastiraki, north-west Crete; region of Rethymna. From the store rooms of an Early Bronze Age settlement: Lid of vase with knob; light green steatite; incised pattern of five-pointed star, in a circle, with interstices containing hatching; height 0.6 cm., diam. 4.2 cm.; from the transitional period EM/MM; cf. stone lid from the Cave of Trapeza, Lasithi (*AA.* 1936, 168 f., Fig. 20), and steatite lid with seven-pointed star from Melos (*Excav. at Phylakopi* [1904], Pl. 38:18). – Grundmann, in Matz, *Forschungen auf Kreta 1942* (1951), 69 (not illustrated).

1121 Cyclades. Exact origin unknown. Pyxis lid of green steatite; diam. 6.1 cm.; pairs of holes on opposite sides of rim for attachment (cf. *1119*). Slightly concave underneath, very abraded incised decoration in concentric circles: inner and outer circle densely hatched; EM II (c. 2300 B.C.); similar form in Goldman, *Eutresis* (1931), 183, Fig. 254. Mus. f. Kunst u. Gewerbe, Hamburg, Inv. No. 1925,47. – v. Mercklin, *AA.* 1928, 277, No. 6, Fig. 6.

1122 Melos, Cyclades. Composite vase, formed of seven individual hollows and one irregular central one, in the form of a house or granary; greyish green steatite; length 12 cm., height 10 cm.; *c.* 2000 B.C. Antikensammlung, Munich, Inv. No. 1983 W 112. – Dümmler, *AM.* 11 (1886), 18, Suppl. 1; Lubbock, *Prehistoric Times*[3], 52, Fig. 77; Perrot–Chipiez VI (1894), 910, Fig. 461; Montelius, *Archiv. f. Anthrop.* 23 (1895), 464, Fig. 44; Tsountas–Manatt, *The Myc. Age* (1897), 259, Fig. 133; Winter, *Kunstgesch. in Bildern*, 83, Fig. 10; Pfuhl, *AM.* 30 (1905), 337, Fig. 1; Bulle, *Orchomenos* I (1907), 45, Fig. 11; Schuchhardt, *SB.* 1914, 289; Montelius, *La Grèce préclass.*, Pl. 43:6 a, b; Karo, *Reallex. Vorgesch.* V (1926), 224, s. v. 'Haus', Pl. 73 d; Oelmann, *AM.* 1925, 20, Fig. 1; id., *BJb.* 134 (1929), 6, Fig. 5; Zschietzschmann, *RE.* XV (1931), 572 f., s. v. 'Melos'; Åberg, *Chronologie* IV (1933), 73, Fig. 133; Bossert, *Altkreta*, Fig. 403, and Fig. in text 16 (with additional references); Schachermeyr, *Älteste Kulturen*, Pl. 12:5; Zervos, *Cycl.* 64, Figs. 28, 29; Matz, *Kreta u. frühes Griechenland* (1962), 36, 47, 91, Fig. 20 (wrongly: Nat. Mus., Athens); Vermeule, *Greece in the Bronze Age*, Pl. 8 d; Simon, *Die Götter der Griechen* (1969), 106, Fig. 98.

1123 Mochlos. Pot-bellied wide-mouthed vase, with flanged rim, several parallel grooves on shoulder, and two horizontal lugs; greyish brown, fine-grained stone (basalt?); height 8.1 cm. Not identifiable in Seager, *Explorations in the Island of Mochlos* (1912), but origin can be established from collective photograph of DAI., Athens (Karo). Minoan imitation of Egyptian model; Pendlebury, *Aegyptiaca* (1930), 30. Stone vases from Mochlos show resemblances to Egyptian productions of the Old Kingdom, but in no cases are they true imports. Arch. Mus., Herakleion, Inv. No. 353. – Warren, 74, Fig. P 396.

1124 Mochlos. Grave 19: Slender pedestal vase of attractive proportions; excellent metal-grey steatite (serpentine); height 9 cm., diam. 5 cm.; EM II (c. 2400 B.C.). Arch. Mus., Herakleion. – Seager, 71, No. XIX, 2, Fig. 4, Pl. 9; Pendlebury, *Arch. of Crete*, Pl. 10:3h; Montelius, *La Grèce préclass.*, Pl. 37:4; Warren, 73, Fig. P 373.

1125 Mochlos. Pot-bellied bowl with low belly, torus rim, and below it several decorative grooves; height *c.* 12 cm. Arch. Mus., Herakleion. Not identifiable in Seager (cf. *1123*), but so similar to an example from Hagia Triada it may be identical (LM I; Inv. No. 346; Warren, 25, Fig. P 145).

1126 Mochlos. Cist Grave 12: Hand-lamp of dark grey serpentine, with socket spout, strong grip, decorated with three grooves at the end; notched pattern on rim; base ring; height 3.2 cm., length with grip 12.3 cm. This type occurs in LM I/II houses in Pseira (Maraghiannis, *Ant. Crét.* II, Pl. 19:14; Willetts, *Everyday Life in*

Ancient Crete [1969], 117, Fig. 61; Warren, 60, Fig. P 316) and in Hagia Triada; date of Mochlos example MM III/LM I. Arch. Mus., Herakleion, Inv. No. 1279. – Seager, 62, No. XII a, Fig. 47, Pl. 9; Maraghiannis, op. cit., Pl. 4:3; Montelius, op. cit., Pl. 38:9; Warren, 59, Fig. D 174.

1127 Crete. Stone vase with careful relief (cult vase, MM/LM I) of the so-called 'blossom-bowl' type, evolved from the 'bird's nest' type (e. g. Inst. of Art, Detroit, No. 66.43; Montelius, op. cit., Pl. 43:1,2; Fimmen, *KMK*. 103, Fig. 91 [fragment from Troy, after Schmidt, *Schliemanns Sammlung*, 290, No. 7905 with ill.]; Schefold, *Meisterwerke griech. Kunst* [1960], 115 ff., Nos. 18, 19; Warren, 14 ff., Figs. P 59–64 and D 19,20; detailed assessment of type: Münzen und Medaillen, Basel, *Auktion XXII* [13. 5. 1961], 7, No. 8); diam. 16.2 cm., height 8.8 cm. Mus. f. Kunst u. Gewerbe, Hamburg, Inv. No. 1927, 318. – v. Mercklin, *AA.* 1928, 277 f., No. 7, Fig. 7.

1128 Crete (perhaps Pseira). Steatite vase like *1127*, with lid; height 8.7 cm., diam. 13.2 cm.; probably MM. Mus. of Fine Arts, Boston, No. 57.138. – Exhibition catalogue: Smith Coll. Mus. of Art (Northampton, Mass.), *A Land called Crete* (1967), No. 13 with Fig. (cf. Maraghiannis, *Ant. Crét.* II, Pl. 19:13).

1129 Crete. Said to come from Mirabello. Stone vase like *1127*; relief: fine steeply rising ribs, lid lost, greyish green steatite; height 5–5.1 cm., diam. 10.5 cm.; MM I (after v. Mercklin: LM II; for dating, cf. also Warren, 32, Fig. P 182). Mus. f. Kunst u. Gewerbe, Hamburg, Inv. No. 1927,145. – v. Mercklin, *AA.* 1928, 278 ff., No. 8, Fig. 8.

1130 East Crete. Flat marble bowl (EM); colourful greyish white effect due to grinding the layers in the form of eccentric circles; vertical lug on either side of chip-carved rim; not quite circular, diam. 17.7–18.3 cm. Mus. f. Kunst u. Gewerbe, Hamburg, Inv. No. 1931,273. – v. Mercklin, *AA.* 1935, 71 ff., No. 1, Figs. 1, 2.

1131 Tiryns. Upper citadel. Early Helladic stone vase, with vertical lug and animal head protome sculptured in the round. Deep groove for the (lost) lid with two holes on each side for attaching it; height 2.5 cm., length incl. handle and protome 4.7 cm., diam. 3.2 cm. Arch. Mus., Nauplia.

1132 Hagios Kosmas, Attica. Early Helladic mortar, care-
a,b fully ground, with two horizontal lugs (EM III); porous andesite, rim damaged; diam. 45 cm., inner diam. 37 cm., height 9.1 cm. Pointed conical pestle belonging to it, with hole at upper end (length c. 22 cm., *1132 b*). – Mylonas, *AJA.* 38 (1934), 267, Fig. 10; id., *Aghios Kosmas* (1959), 92 f., No. 48, p. 145, Fig. 169; Bossert, *Altkreta*, Fig. 63.

1133 Crete. Beautifully shaped conical beaked cup of slate-grey steatite; horizontal lug behind, below the rim; long open spout; incised hatching in triangular fields, rim notched in parallel lines; base also hatched in four fields of parallel lines; height 3.7 cm., diam. 11 cm., diam. of base 2.6 cm.; EM II. Similar types, but with high foot, in Chalandriani, Syros, Tomb 325: Tsountas, *Ephem*. 1899, 98, Fig. 27; without foot, variegated limestone, in Mochlos: Seager, Pl. 6, No. 3; and Evans, *PM*. I, 90, Fig. 58; others: Warren, *Minoan Stone Vases*, 93 ff., *1133*. East Cretan product (Marinatos wrote as follow on a stylistically similar pyxis from Maronia [*AA. 1937, 228, Fig. 7*]: 'probably not Cycladic, but with strong Cycladic influences'). Formerly in art market. – Münzen und Medaillen, Basel, *Auktion XXII* (13.5.1961), 7, No. 7.

1134 Iasos, Carian coast. In Chalcolithic burial. Marble vase of conical 'flower-pot' form, with flat base and two long vertical lugs pierced in the upper third. Early Cycladic type; cf. *Ephem*. 1989, Pl. 10:18 (= Åberg, *Chronologie* IV, 67, Fig. 113, Despotikos, Grave 129); Schefold, *Meisterwerke griech. Kunst* (1960), 114 f., No. 14 (Basel, private colln.); Zervos, *Cycl.*, 51 f., Figs. 1, 2; and Thimme, *Kunst der Welt: Frühe Randkulturen des Mittelmeerraumes* (1969), 16 with col. ill. (Badisches Landesmuseum, Karlsruhe). – Levi, *ILN*. Arch. Sect. 2229 (7. 8. 1965), 27, Fig. 6.

1135 Cyclades. Exact origins unknown. Three Early Bronze
a–c Age suspension eye vases, with high conical foot and steep neck, marble. *1135 a*: Twin vase, height 8 cm.; *1135 b*: height 15.5 cm.; *1135 c*: height 9 cm. Müller Colln., Solothurn, Switzerland. – Racz, *Antikes Erbe* (1965), Fig. 6; Jucker, *Antike Kunst aus Privatbesitz Bern – Biel – Solothurn Exhibition 1967*, 14, Nos. 43, 44.

1136 Cyclades (*1136:* Paros; *1137:* Naxos). Early Bronze
to Age marble vases, each with four vertical salient
1139 pierced lugs. Conical feet of varying heights, high conical necks, more or less squat bodies. *1136:* height 17.8 cm.; white island marble with large crystals. Mus. f. Kunst u. Gewerbe, Hamburg, Inv. No. 1928,44 (v. Mercklin, *AA.* 1928, 274 f., No. 3, Fig. 3). *1137:* Nat. Mus., Athens. *1138:* Brooklyn Mus., No. 35.761. *1139:* Antikensammlung, Munich, Inv. No. 10367 KM 1990. This kind of distinctly marked suspension vase, for the most part carefully worked in white marble, is a key form of the Early Cycladic period and occurs very frequently; cf. e. g. *Ephem*. 1898, Pl. 10:16 (Paros, Grave 24; also Åberg, *Chronologie* IV, 67, Fig. 112); Hall, *The Civilization of Greece in the Bronze Age* (1928), 58, Fig. 61 (Ashmolean Mus., Oxford); Bossert, *Altkreta*, Fig. 428, (formerly Antikenabt., Berlin); Inst. of Arts, Detroit, No. 65.81 (unpublished?); Richter, *Handbook of the Greek Collection Metr. Mus., New York* (1953), Pl. 8 a; Thimme, *Kunst der Welt: Frühe Randkulturen des Mittelmeerraumes* (1969), 15 with col. ill. (Badisches Landesmuseum, Karlsruhe); Zervos, *Cycl.*, 54 f., Figs. 6–8.

1140 Katsamba, harbour area of Knossos. Chamber Tomb II. Imported Egyptian alabaster vase with hieroglyphic inscription of the name Thutmose III (1504–1450 B. C.). Slender, egg-shaped amphora on high foot, with low funnel mouth and torus rim; height 29 cm. Of great importance for dating the other finds here; first half of fifteenth century. Arch. Mus., Herakleion., Inv. No. 2409. – Alexiou, *KChron*. 1952, 12 ff., Figs. 1, 3; id., *Hysterominoikoi Taphoi Limenos Knosou-Katsamba* (mod. Gk., 1967), 46, Pl. 10 a, b; cf. Hutchinson, *Prehistoric Crete* (1962), 268, Fig. 50; Demargne, *Naissance*, 16, Fig. 14 (Eng., *Aegean Art*); Smith, *Interconnections*, 79.

1141 Isopata, near Knossos. Royal tomb: Imported Egyp-
a,b tian alabaster vases; small bag-shaped vase of variegated stone, one side broken, and jug with long cylindrical neck, vertical strap handle, and low, conical foot; coarse-grained stone; height 7.4 cm. and 25.3 cm.; Eighteenth Dynasty (second half of fifteenth

century B.C.). Arch. Mus., Herakleion, Inv. Nos. 603 and 600. – Evans, *Prehistoric Tombs* (1906), 146 ff., Nos. 2, 5, Fig. 125, nos. S2 and S5; Maraghiannis, *Ant. Crét*. III, Pl. 33; Fimmen, *KMK*. 172, Fig. 168; Montelius, *La Grèce préclass.*, Pl. 42:6,8; Pendlebury, *Aegyptiaca* (1903), 23 ff., Nos. 35, 32, Pl. 3; Demargne, *Naissance*, 181, Fig. 252; Warren, *Minoan Stone Vases* (1969), 112 f., Figs. P 611, P 618. – There is also a limestone rhyton (Arch. Mus., Herakleion, Inv. No. 2393) which may be an imitation of an Egyptian alabaster vessel (Demargne-Gallet de Santerre, *Et. Crét*. IX [1953], Pl. 43:6,7).

1142 Knossos. Egyptian imported vase lid with hieroglyphic inscription of the Hyksos king Chian (Fifteenth Dynasty, c. 1730 B.C.); alabaster, rim broken, found near north-west Lustral basin in deposit dated MM III a (1630 B.C.); diam. c. 11.5 cm. Arch. Mus., Herakleion, Inv. No. 263. – Evans, *PM*. I, 419, Fig. 304 b; Fimmen, *KMK*. 172, Fig. 167 (inverted); Karo, *Reallex. Vorgesch*. VII (1926) s. v. 'Kreta', Pl. 42 a; Hall, *Civilization of Greece*, 123; Pendlebury, *Aegyptiaca* (1930), 22, No. 30, Pl. 2; Demargne, *Naissance*, 16, Fig. 13; Schachermeyr, *Die minoische Kultur des alten Kreta* (1964), 86, Fig. 37; id., *Ägäis u. Orient* (1967), Pl. 30:15; Warren, 113.

1143 Old Peoples' Home, Thebes, Boeotia. From a Mycenaean chamber tomb (excavated in 1966/67): Flat stone lamp broken in two, with two socket spouts cut off cleanly; elegant relief on rim; length incl. socket 15.7 cm. Arch. Mus., Thebes. – Unpublished.

1144 South-east Crete. Bought in the region of Hierapetra: Cylindrical stone vessel, tapering slightly towards the bottom, with smooth base; ground into conical shape inside; grooves from grinding visible, base rounded off inside. External wall and base polished. Greyish black variegated limestone, mottled with brown; unbroken, hardly damaged; height 5.3 cm., diam. of base 6.1 cm., diam. of mouth 6.6 cm.; MM/LM I. Untied Colln., Hamburg, Inv. No. 6. – Unpublished. For this type, cf. Warren, 41, Fig. P 238.

1145 Crete. Attractively variegated alabaster vase in conical beaker shape, with torus rim and lugs; height 11 cm., diam. 8.7 cm., EM II (c. 2500–2200 B.C.). Mus. of Fine Arts, Boston, No. 09.18. – Vermeule, *The Class. Coll. of the Mus. of Fine Arts* (1963), Fig. 1; id., *Greek, Etruscan and Roman Art* (³1963), 19, Fig. 19.

1146 p. 311: Knossos. Pot-bellied jug with spout, wide strap handle, and low neck. Attractive, concentrically variegated light and dark grey limestone; height 20 cm.; LM I or later. Arch. Mus., Herakleion, Inv. No. 50. – Zervos, *Crète*, 338, Fig. 494; Warren, 48, Figs. P 281, D 166.

1147 Knossos, Mavro Spilio. Grave 3, Squat, egg-shaped rhyton of variegated black and light grey limestone or marble, similar in type to *1148* but more compact; height 23 cm., diam. 15.35 cm.; probably LM I. Arch. Mus., Herakleion, Inv. No. 2141. – Forsdyke, *BSA*. 28 (1926/27), 254, 290, Fig. 42; Zervos, 337, Fig. 493; Warren, 88, Fig. P 488 b; Evans, *PM*. II, Pl. 21 c.

1148 Knossos. Central Treasury. Rhyton with sixteen vertical leaf-shaped flutes, of variegated whitish grey and orange limestone; height 38.2 cm., diam. 15.15 cm.; large areas restored; LM I b (similar type, Alexiou, *Führer durch das Archäolog. Mus. v. Herakleion* [1969], Pls. 8 a und 19 a). Arch. Mus., Herakleion, Inv. No. 42. – Evans, *BSA*. 6 (1899/1900), 30 ff.; id., *PM*. II, 822, Fig. 537 b; Maraghiannis, *Ant. Crét*. III, Pl. 29 a; Bossert, *Altkreta*, Fig. 371 c; Pendlebury, *Arch. of Crete*, Pl. 38:1; Zervos, 337, Fig. 492; Warren, 86, Fig. P 481.

1149 Palaikastro, east Crete. Lamp with tall foot, porphyry-like stone *(rosso antico)*, with thick base and ivy-leaf relief in the middle of the shaft; oil container also decorated with ivy leaves; height 46.15 cm., probably LM I. For the typology of lamps with tall foot, see Persson, *New Tombs at Dendra near Midea* (1942), 105 ff., Fig. 113:21-29 (25 = *1149*), and Matz–Buchholz, *Arch. Hom. P* (1968), Pl. 6 (e.g. Nirou Chani: Xanthoudides, *Ephem*. 1922, 14, Fig. 11). Arch. Mus., Herakleion, Inv. No. 616. – Bosanquet–Dawkins, *The Unpublished Objects from the Palaikastro Excav.* (1923), 139 f., Fig. 121 a; Zervos, *Crète*, 322, Fig. 466; Warren, 58.

1150 Knossos. South-east House. Column of porphyry *(rosso antico)*, probably stand of lamp with tall foot; the upper half was worked separately and is missing; the spreading foot, decorated with relief foliage, is partly missing. Egyptian derived bands of ivy leaves wind diagonally round the shaft ('torsion'); preserved height 46 cm.; MM III b, or a little later. Arch. Mus., Herakleion, Inv. No. 66. – Evans, *PM*. I, 344 f., Fig. 249; and II, 481, Fig. 228; Bossert, *Altkreta*, Fig. 216; Persson, op. cit., Fig. 113:24; Karo, *Greifen am Thron* (1959), 73, Fig. 44; Marinatos–Hirmer, Pl. 114 lower; Zervos, *Crète*, 323, Fig. 468; Alexiou, op. cit., Pl. 8 b; Warren, 57.

1151 Knossos. Later Palace, 'Room of the Lotus Lamp' N. of central court: Stone lamp, with rich relief; on high pedestal in the form of a bundle of papyrus, freely copied from an Egyptian capital; foot restored; height c. 45–55 cm., preserved height 38 cm., diam. 28 cm.; red porphyry-alabaster *(rosso antico)*. MM III b/LM I (c. 1600 B.C.). Arch. Mus., Herakleion, Inv. No. 27. – Evans, *BSA*. 6 (1899/1900), 44; id., *PM*. II, 521 ff., Fig. 325; III, 26, Fig. 14 a; Pendlebury, *Arch. of Crète*, Pl. 38:3; Matz, *KMT.*, Pl. 68 lower; Karo, Fig. 44; Marinatos–Hirmer, Pl. 114 lower; Zervos, *Crète*, 322, Fig. 467; Schachermeyr, *Ägäis u. Orient* (1967), Pl. 56,209 left; Alexiou, Pl. 8 b; Warren, 57.

1152 Kato Zakro, east Crete. Palace Treasury. Cult chalice of mottled polychrome limestone (cf. *1155*; for similar types of chalice in alabaster and obsidian, cf. *Prakt*. 1963, Pl. 149 b, c), with narrow fluting round it horizontally; base worked separately; height 30 cm.; LM I (c. 1500 B.C.). Arch. Mus., Herakleion, Inv. No. 2726. – Platon, *Prakt*. 1963, Pl. 149 a; id., *Crete* Fig. 49; v. Matt, *Das antike Kreta*, Pl. 191; Sakellariou, *Europa: Festschr. f. Grumach* (1967), 292 f., Pl. 28; Kyrieleis, *MarbWPr*. 1968, 12, Pl. 3 left; Warren, 36.

1153 Thera. Cult chalices with conical upper part, profiled
1154 intermediate plate, concave pedestal, and profiled base (for this, cf. Karo, *Schgr.*, Nos. 600 and 854; Sakellariou, Pl. 27:4; similar form in silver in Persson, *The Royal Tombs at Dendra near Midea* [1931], 51, Fig. 30, Pl. 17), variegated marble and Egyptian alabaster, height, 22.6 cm. and 20.5 cm. (these dimensions throw doubt on the possible identity of the two pieces; Zervos: 19.8 cm.); MM III/LM I. Nat. Mus., Athens, Inv. No. 3964. — Åberg, *Chronologie* IV, 75, Fig. 137, (cf.

Renaudin, *BCH.* 46 [1922], 127, Fig. 16); Zervos, *Cycl.* 56, Fig. 9; Demargne, *Naissance,* 46, Fig. 53; Warren, 37.

1155 Kato Zakro. Palace Treasury (cf. *1152*). Four-lobed cult chalice, extremely thinly ground with carefully gradated demarcation between cusp, foot, and similarly worked base; fine-grained light-grey to black veined limestone, giving the impression that the material can be folded like paper; restored from numerous fragments; height 32.5 cm.; LM I (c. 1500 B.C.). Arch. Mus., Herakleion, Inv. No. 2734. – Platon, *ILN.* 7.3.64, Fig. 13; Sakellariou, op. cit., 293, Pl. 27:3; Warren, 36.

1156 Mycenae. Grave Circle B; Grave Omicron: Oval vase back, sculptured in the round; rock crystal; length 13.2 cm. Crouching animals with head turned back are frequent in Egyptian and ancient Oriental art (cf. *1737*); originally they were foreign to Greece, but note steatite weight in the form of a sea bird with head turned back from Crete (Ars Antiqua, Lucerne, *Sale Catalogue,* June 1966, No. 106, Pl. 18) and ivories (Frödin-Persson, *Asine* [1938], 391, Fig. 254). Nat. Mus., Athens. – Mylonas, *Anc. Myc.,* 139, 146, Figs. 49, 60, 61; and *Myc. and the Myc. Age,* Pl.-Fig. 99 a, b; Marinatos–Hirmer, Pl. 212 lower; Biesantz, *Ullstein-Kunstgesch.* IV (1963), 90, Pl.-Fig. 47; Schachermeyr, *Ägäis u. Orient,* Pl. 56,208.

1157 Mycenae. Rhyton Well: Fragment; lower part of a rhyton decorated with vertical fluting; preserved height 20 cm. Material comparatively rarely used: blackish green mottled with yellowish green *lapis lacedaemonius* (cf. *BSA.* 55 [1960], 106 f.; Buchholz, *Hist. Zeitschr.* 200 [1965], 362 f.). MM III/LM I import in LH III environment. Arch. Mus., Nauplia, Inv. No. 8352. – Wace, *BSA.* 24 (1919–21), 201, Pl. 11; id., *Mycenae* (1949), Pl.-Fig. 86; Warren, *Minoan Stone Vases,* 86,133.

1158 Midea, the Argolid. Lamp with rich relief decoration and low base; steatite. Arch. Mus., Nauplia. For this type, see Persson, *New Tombs at Dendra near Midea* (1942), 107, Fig. 113:19. – 'Midea' is not mentioned by Warren, 52 ff.; perhaps confusion of site for museum?

1159 Midea. N. boundary of acropolis: Tripod bowl of grey basalt (with wrongly restored side spout); diam. c. 35 cm., height 13 cm., LH III; probably Syrian import. Arch. Mus., Nauplia. – Persson, op. cit., 10 f., Fig. 8; Åström, *Opusc. Athen.* IV (1962), 298, note 4; Buchholz, *JdI.* 78 (1963), 8, No. A 13, Fig. 2 g.

1160 Charvati, east Attica. From a grave: Imported Cypriot tripod bowl of steatite, with rich geometric incised decoration and bull's head protome; diam. 13 cm., height 7.5 cm.; LH III b/c. Stathatos Coll., Athens. – Buchholz, 4, No. A 2, Figs. 1 a, 9 l, 10 g (for further references, see Schachermeyr, *Anz. f. d. Altertumswiss.* 6 [1953], 218; and *Ägäis u. Orient* [1967], Pl. 57,211; Bisi, *Oriens Antiquus* 5 (1966), Pl. 6:2).

1161 Kythera. Mycenaean chamber tomb: Globular pyxis, with four vertically pierced suspension eyes; steatite; height 8.7 cm., diam. 10.5 cm. The incised spiral pattern, esp. on upper part, corresponds to decorative motifs on stelai from Mycenae *(1170)* and Early Cycladic vases (Nat. Mus., Athens, Inv. No. 5358: Åberg, *Chronologie* IV, 74, Fig. 135); relief work not completed; the same applies to the notched zigzag bands: Cycladic work, LH I/II (but Kantor: Early Cycl. III vessel in LH III tomb). Nat. Mus., Athens, Inv. No. 6231 (1628). – Staïs, *Delt.* 1 (1915), 192, Fig.; Heurtley, *BSA.* 25 (1921–23), 137; Evans, *PM.* II, 208, Fig. 117 b (drawing); Åberg, op. cit., 75, Fig. 136; Kantor, *AJA.* 51 (1947), 8, Pl. 4 d.

1162 Hagia Triada, south Crete. Black rhyton of steatite or serpentine, put together from many fragments, the so-called 'Boxer Rhyton' (detail: boxers in action); height without handle 46.5 cm., LM I (1550–1500 B.C.). Upper section: wrestling match; second section: bull sports; third and fourth sections: boxing match between helmeted and unhelmeted fighters. Forceful, animated drawing; thematically significant (similar figure on steatite fragment from Knossos: Pendlebury, *Arch. of Crete,* Pl. 37:4; Warren, *Minoan Stone Vases,* Fig. P. 472). For the form and cult use of such rhytons, cf. Egyptian alabaster imitation in Brit. Mus., London (Forsdyke, *JHS.* 31 [1911], 117, Fig. 5; Hall, *Civilization of Greece,* 222, Fig. 292); *960–965* and *1629* (clay); and *1671* (faience, also Egyptian imitation in Brit. Mus., London, No. 22.731. Hall, 222, Fig. 291; Evans, *PM.* II, Pl. 24:20; Bossert, *Altkreta,* Fig. 569); also in electrum, Ras Shamra (Schaeffer, *AfO.* 21 [1966], 131 f., Figs. 8–10). Arch. Mus., Herakleion, Inv. No. 342.498.676; – Müller, *JdI.* 30 (1915), 247 f.; Hall, 159, Fig. 196; Evans, *PM.* III, 224, Fig. 157; IV, 20 f., Fig. 10; Dussaud, *Civilis. préhell.* (1914), 67, Figs. 46, 47; Montelius, *La Grèce préclass.,* Pl. 40:1; Oulié, *Décoration égéenne,* Pl. 38; Bossert, *Altkreta,* Figs. 271–275; Lorimer, *Homer and the Monuments* (1950), Pl. 15:5; Matz, *KMT.,* Pl. 69; Marinatos-Hirmer, Pls. 106, 107; Warren, 85, Fig. P 469; Schachermeyr, *Die minoische Kultur des alten Kreta* (1964), Pls. 28, 49 a.

1163 Kato Zakro, east Crete. From the Minoan Palace, Rooms Ee and Psi: Detail of a rhyton made of brown chlorite, originally gilt, with relief picture of religious and historical significance: mountain-top shrine with reclining ibexes; on reverse: leaping ibex in rocky landscape. Height without neck 31.1 cm., diam. 13.85 cm., LM I (c. 1500 B.C.). Arch. Mus., Herakleion, Inv. Nos. 2764 and 2722 (neck). – Platon, *Ergon* 1963, 174, Fig. 187; id., *Prakt.* 1963, 185, Pls. 152–154; Daux, *BCH.* 88 (1964), 843, Fig. 13; V. Matt, *Das antike Kreta* (1967), Pls. 192–194; Kyrieleis, *MarbWPr.* 1968, 16, n. 34:10; Simon, *Die Götter der Griechen* (1969), 152, Fig. 140; Alexiou, *AAA.* 2, 1969, 84 ff. (for the shrine); Warren, 87.

1164 Knossos. Fragment of a serpentine vase (rhyton): Bearded archer; rather indefinite workmanship. Background of figure indistinct, the line behind the back foot could be the edge of a boat or a cord leading diagonally upwards. LM I/II. Arch. Mus., Herakleion, Inv. No. 257. – Evans, *BSA.* 7 (1900/1901), 44, Fig. 13; id., *PM.* III, 106, Fig. 59; Pendlebury, *Arch. of Crete,* 271, Pl. 37:4; Lorimer, *Homer and the Monuments* (1950), 279, Fig. 35; Buchholz, *JdI.* 77 (1962), 2; Smith, *Interconnections,* Fig. 87 b; Warren 85, Fig. P 473.

1165 Hagia Triada. Upper part of an egg-shaped libation vase of dark steatite, so-called 'Harvester Vase' (detail), showing harvest procession (olive harvest?): the leader, wearing a scale-patterned cloak, is followed by a procession of men with pitchforks with knife blades

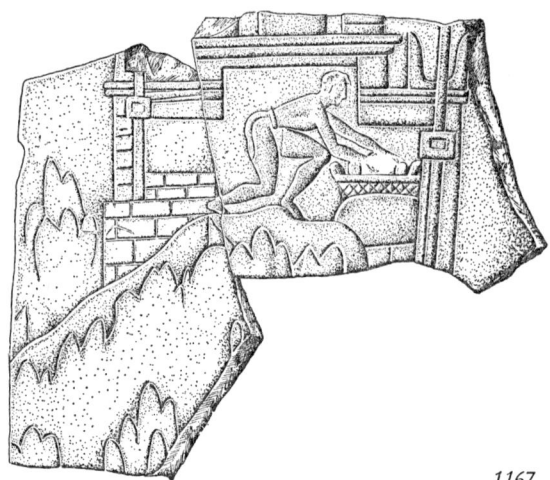

1167

Fig. 35 Interlocking fragments of a steatite vase with figural relief-work, Knossos

attached, and four singers, the leader waving a sistrum (sacred rattle); preserved height 9.6 cm., greatest diam. 11.5 cm., LM I (sixteenth century B.C.). Arch. Mus., Herakleion, Inv. No. 184. – Savignoni. *Mon. Ant.* 13 (1903), Pls. 1–3; Harrison, *JHS.* 24 (1904), 241 ff.; Müller, *JdI.* 30 (1915), 242; Evans, *PM.* II, 47; IV, 218; Hall, *Civilization of Greece,* 156 f., Fig. 193; Bossert, *Altkreta,* Figs. 276–281; Zervos, *L'Art en Grèce* (³ 1937), Figs. 25, 26; Forsdyke, 'The Harvester Vase of Haghia Triada', *Journal of Warburg and Courtauld Insts.* 17 (1954), 1 ff.; Marinatos-Hirmer, Pls. 103–105; Matz, *KMT.* Pl. 67; id., *Kreta u. frühes Griechenland* (1962), Pl.-Figs. 15, 16; Schachermeyr, *Die minoische Kultur d. alten Kreta* (1964), Pl. 29; Schiering, *Antike Kunst* 8 (1965), Pl. 3:2; id., in Matz-Buchholz, *Arch. Hom.* H (1968), 154 f., Pl. 3; Willetts, *Everyday Life,* 122, Fig. 69 and front.; Warren, 88.

1166 Hagia Triada. Almost completely preserved conical
a, b steatite vase, so-called 'Chieftain Cup', or 'Prince Cup'. *1166 a, b:* details. Height 11.5 cm.; upper diam. 9.9 cm. Interpretations of the picture vary: 'presentation of a delegation' (Matz), 'Children playing' (Marinatos, also wrong identification of sword sheath held against the officer's left shoulder). The figures are adapted to the surface of the conical vase; contrast between reserved background and animated attitudes of the figures; according to Marinatos, there is a deliberate awkwardness (the prince is allegedly too stiff, the officer too melodramatic!). LM I (second half of sixteenth century). Arch. Mus., Herakleion, Inv No. 341. – Müller, *JdI.* 30 (1915), 242; Evans, *PM.* II, 742 ff., 790 ff.; Hall, op. cit., 158, Figs. 194, 195; Bossert, *Altkreta,* Figs. 269, 270; Marinatos-Hirmer, Pls. 100–102; Matz, *KMT.,* Pl. 66; id., *Kreta u. frühes Griechenland* (1962), 127 ff., Col. Pl.; Schachermeyr, op. cit., Pl. 51 a; Willetts, 121, Fig. 68; Warren, 37, Fig. P 197.

1167 Fig. 35: Knossos. Region of Hogarth's houses on the Gypsades hill. Two adjacent fragments of serpentine from a vase decorated in relief (height of fragments 5.9 cm.). Mountain shrine; worshipper setting down a basket with sacrificial bread. Smith (*Interconnections,* Fig. 93) suggested the addition of a procession fragment to the same scene (Evans, *PM.* II, 752, Fig. 486; Schachermeyr, *Die minoische Kultur,* 137, Fig. 67; Warren, Fig. P 474); LM I. Arch. Mus., Herakleion, Inv. No. 2397. – Platon, *KChron.* 5 (1951), 154 ff.; Alexiou, *KChron.* 13 (1959), 346 ff., Pl. 34; Schachermeyr, *AA.* 1962, 150, Fig. 15; and *Die minoische Kultur,* Pl. 32 a; Warren, 85, Fig. P 476.

1168–1171: RELIEFS

1168 Hyria Dramesi, Boeotia. Weathered fragment of an anta-block with incised pictures of ships; LH III. – Blegen, *Hesperia-Suppl.* VIII (1949), 41 f., Pl. 7:6.
1169 Hagia Irini, Keos (excavated by Caskey). Piece from a marble tablet with carefully incised drawing of a Mycenaean warrior's head: 'zone helmet' with cheek-pieces and crest; LH I/II. – Daux, *BCH.* 89 (1965), 858, Fig. 13; Borchhardt, *Homerische Helme* (1972), Pl. 7, 7.
1170 Mycenae. Grave Circle A: Grave stelai decorated in
1171 relief, limestone, in separate rectangular panels: spiral ornaments and pictures of scenes of war (chariot and human figures); *1171* originally stood over Grave V; height 1.34 cm.; LH I. Nat. Mus., Athens. – Schliemann, *Mykenae* (1878/1964), 91, Fig. 140 and 97, Fig. 141; Karo, *Schachtgräber,* Pls. 5–8; Heurtley, 'The Grave Stelai', *BSA.* 25 (1921–23), 126 ff.; Bossert, *Altkreta,* Figs. 66, 67 (inverted); Lorimer, *Homer and the Monuments* (1950), Pl. 24; Mylonas, *The Figured Mycenaean Stelai'* in *AJA.* 55 (1951), 134 ff.; Matz, *KMT.,* Pl. 95; Andronikos, in Matz-Buchholz, *Arch. Hom.* W (1968), 114 ff., Pl. 7 d, e; Taylour, *Mycenaeans,* Pl. 20.

Sculpture in the round

For Cypriot sculpture in stone, terracotta, and metal, cf. below, pp. 159 ff. See also the essay by Nikolaou on Mycenaean terracottas in the Cyprus Museum (*OpAth.* 5 [1965], 47 ff., Pls. 1—8). For similarities with figured metal and stone reliefs, see ornaments *(1303)*, gold *(1104, 1105)* and steatite vessels *(1162—1166)*, the Lion Gate at Mycenae *(83, 155)*, several grave stelai *(1170, 1171)* and the representation of octopuses on a large perforated gypsum stone from Knossos *(430)*. The Early Cycladic picture of a bearded goat *(852)* and a Cretan 'head vase' *(972)* are examples of clay reliefs. In Greek relief work, figured decorated ivory implements occupy a very important place *(1273, 1278, 1279, 1282, 1284, 1285—1290)*. We need hardly stress the importance of the tiny but distinctive relief pictures on seals (pp. 112 ff.), and of the moulds and matrices with which the decorative reliefs on metal, glass and faience were created (e.g. *459, 461 a, 464*).

Besides the examples of creativity in sculpture mentioned here, there are also the little ram's head on an Early Helladic stone vessel from Tiryns *(1131)* and the reclining dog placed off-centre in the circle of an Early Minoan steatite lid *(1119)*. A ceremonial axe from Mallia in the form of a panther is an example of Cretan stylistic tendencies in stone sculpture in the round before the middle of the second millennium B.C. *(232)*. A duck's head protome on a Mycenaean rock-crystal vessel *(1156)* seems inspired by Egypt, while Cypriot influences inform the bull's head protome on a stone tripod bowl from Attica *(1160)*. The clay dove in the cavity of a bowl *(894;* also a male figure in a bowl: Bossert, *Altkreta*, Fig. 292) shows the close connection between pottery and sculpture, as do the fragile terracotta flowers and blossoms *(893)* found on Cretan Kamares ware.

Finally, the fully sculptural ornaments on the handles of gold and silver vessels give evidence of refined taste and careful observation of animals; again we find doves *(1085)* and dogs' heads *(1087)*. The forms of the figured handles of implements from the Late Bronze Age *(665)* suggest the influence of Central European urn decoration. However, Grundmann has shown that figured images had already appeared in the Neolithic period concomitantly with the development of pottery in northern and central Greece: *JdI.* 68 (1953), 1 ff.

Cult vessels in the form of female busts *(1193)*, animal and animal-head vessels—predominantly pottery again—tell of the strong ancient Aegean-Cretan-Mycenaean desire to give lifelike form to inanimate objects: *798* (Troy), *1190* (Melos), *1238* (Naxos), *1239* (Karpathos), *1242* and *1271* (Rhodes), *1214, 1220—1222, 1236, 1237* (Crete), *1240* (Argolid), *1254* (Attica), *1257* (Boeotia). That most of these vessels really are ritual 'animal-head rhyta' has been proved by Grumach with the aid of the clay tablets of Hagia Triada (in *Charisterion eis Orlandon* III [mod. Gk. 1966], 388 ff.); cf. also Tuchelt, 'Tiergefäße in Kopf- und Protomengestalt,' *IstForsch.* XXII (1962). A small Mycenaean animal-head rhyton in a private collection in Basel was published by Schefold (*Meisterwerke der griechischen Kunst* [1960], 120, No. 30 with Fig.).

The general survey by V. Müller, *Frühe Plastik in Griechenland und Vorderasien* (1929), still offers the most comprehensive material, although oriented entirely to typology. Of the meagre detail in Higgins' *Greek Terracottas* (1967), 6 ff., the sections on the earliest periods and the Bronze Age alone concern us. With regard to Stone Age idols, see in particular Weinberg, 'Neolithic Figurines and Aegean Interrelations,' *AJA.* 55 (1951), 121 ff.; cf. also Bass, 'Neolithic Figurines from Thespiai,' *Hesperia* 28 (1959), 344 ff.; Daux, *BCH.* 83 (1959), 681, Fig. 13; and Goldman, 'Typology of the Mother-Goddess Figurines,' *Ipek* 20 (1960—63), 8 ff. Too little attention has been paid to the early sculptural fragments which Walker Kosmopoulous published in *The Prehistoric Inhabitation of Corinth* (1948). Schachermeyr has noted the fine quality idols in stone and clay recently found in Crete (*AA.* 1962, 109 ff., Figs. 1 a, b; 2 a, b; 4). Müller-Karpe collected drawings of sculpture from Argissa in Thessaly (*Hdb. d. Vorgesch.* II, Pls. 126 ff.) cf. also a steatopygous statuette in Cambridge from Avaritza, Thessaly (Dussaud, *Civil. Préhell.* 191, Fig. 142 = Bossert, *Altkreta*, Fig. 85). A well-preserved Neolithic Thessalian clay figure of a woman, with traces of paint, in private hands is remarkable for the wide gap between the legs (Schefold, *Meisterwerke griechischer Kunst* [1960], 110, No. 1). Fresh prehistoric idol finds have also been made from the Thracian north of Greece (cf. *Prakt.* 1967, Pl. 69 b).

A piece from Malta made of Pentelic marble, formerly in the Middleton collection, is related in type to, if not from the same workshop as, Neolithic idols such as *1181a—c, 1182, 1183 a, b* (J. Evans, in *Bosch-Gimpera en el Septuagésimo Aniversario de su Nacimiento* [Mexico 1963], 161 ff.).

In the third millennium, island marble became the favourite material for idols. The workshops founded in the Cyclades also supplied Crete and the mainland as far as Katakolon in Elis (Daux, *BCH*. 83 [1959], 651, Fig. 7). It has still not been decided whether the idols of white marble—geometric symbols of the human form—found in Sardinia also derive from the Cyclades (Fuhrmann, *AA*. 1940, 548 ff., Figs. 57, 58; Pesce-Lilliu, *Sculture della Sardegna Nuragica* [1949], 31, Nos. 1, 2; Levi, *Studi Sardi* 10/11 [1952/53], 48 f.).

'What is physiognomically remarkable about the Cycladic idols is the elongated form which ... is reflected in the length of the neck, the high oval of the face and the long ridge of the nose. This and the receding brow are typical of the later Minoan image of man. We will have to consider them as characteristics of the ancient Aegean people as such. After the direct naturalism of their Neolithic ancestors, the schematization and articulation of isolated parts is striking... That modern artists should feel attracted by such works seems to be due to the abstract, transcendental nature of this form' (Matz).

The most recent general studies are: Höckmann, 'Zu Formenschatz und Ursprung der schematischen Kykladenidole,' (*BJbV*. 8 [1968], 45 ff.) and Renfrew, 'The Development and Chronology of the Early Cycladic Figurines' (*AJA*. 73 [1969], 1 ff.). See also Doumas, *The N.P. Goulandris Collection of Early Cycladic Art* (1968). Thimme paid particular attention to questions of authenticity (*AA*. 1969, 89 ff.) and interpretation ('Die religiöse Bedeutung der Kykladenidole,' *AntK*. 8 [1965], 72 ff.). In his reply to this work, Schefold ('Heroen und Nymphen in Kykladengräbern,' loc. cit., 87 ff.), listed the following as certain with regard to interpretation: the spiritualization of the figures as against the powerful Neolithic forms; and the gesture of the head thrown back, which he saw as signifying enthusiasm.

In Late Bronze Age terracotta sculpture the difference in formal concepts and techniques are striking, in spite of the extreme uniformity of female idols. Besides representations of all kinds of objects, e.g. shoes *(1248 f)* and thrones *(1249 a, b)*, crude hand-formed, solid 'phi' idols *(1259 a, b—1262 a, b, 1264)*, 'tau' *(1263)* and 'psi' idols *(1258 a, b)* were the main finds. Sometimes they are adapted to active figures, such as an enthroned goddess *(1248 d)*, a driver *(1248 c)*, a horsewoman *(1248 b)*, and reclining *(1248 e)* and working *(1248 a)* figures. Technically this type also embraces animal figures such as cattle and dogs *(1251, 1252)*. There are also statuettes of mother and child (e.g. Mycenae: *Ephem*. 1888, Pl. 9: 16 = Perrot-Chipiez VI, 745, Fig. 338) and richly painted women with large round eyes and artistic head-dresses (Wiesner, *AA*. 1937, 252 ff., Fig. 7). For the chronology of Late Helladic terracotta figurines, cf. Furumark, *The Chronology of Mycenaean Pottery* (1941), 86 ff.

The Minoan origin and the development of Mycenaean idols have been discussed by Laviosa (*ASAtene* 41/42 [1963/64], 7 ff. and *Akten des 2. Kretologen-Kongr*. I [1968], 374 ff., Pls. 123—124) and by E. Wace-French (*The Development of Mycenaean Terracotta Figurines, with special Reference to unpublished Material from Mycenae* [thesis, London 1962], see now *BSA* 1972); cf. also Furtwängler, *Aigina*, 370 ff., Pl. 109. We can see the virtuosity and also the weakness of Minoan art in the curious terracotta group of a girl on a swing from Hagia Triada (Nilsson, *MMR*. 332, Fig. 153); this figure goes beyond the actual figurative potential of sculpture.

In Keos, at least twenty-four female terracotta statues were found, considerably larger than any known hitherto from the Late Bronze Age; this again raised the question of the existence of massive images of the gods and of the earliest forms of the sub-Minoan goddesses with raised arms *(1267—1269;* Caskey, *Hesperia* 33 [1964], 326 ff.; Vermeule, *Greece in the Bronze Age*, Pl. 40 a, b; Simon, *Die Götter der Griechen* [1969], 290, Fig. 281; cf. also V. Müller, 'The Beginnings of Monumental Sculpture,' *Metr. Mus. Studies* V [1934—36], 157 ff.).

The Keos finds include local wheel-made figures of bulls of a kind hitherto known only among sub-Mycenaean finds (Hafner, *JdI*. 58 [1943], 183 ff.; cf. a horse of this type from Amyclae in Nat. Mus. Athens: Zervos, *L'Art en Grèce* [³1937], Figs. 41, 42; also *1266* [Rhodes]. With regard to wheel-made sculpture, excavations carried out from 1966 by Taylour in 'Wace's Citadel House' at Mycenae also revealed new aspects: on the female and occasionally male statuettes, c. 16—60 cm. tall, even the heads are made on the wheel, and only eyes, nose, ears, and mouth are modelled by hand by the application of fine clay. The majority of figures are painted in monochrome red or black, sometimes with ochre yellow areas on the face. One figure has painting of the LH III a/b-transitional pottery (Taylour, *Antiquity* 43 [1969], 91 ff., Pls. 11—13; id., *ILN.* 27, XII. 1969, 24 f.; Ervin, *AJA.* 73 [1969], 346, Pl. 88: 18—22). The sculptured coiled snakes also found are of enormous importance for the history of religion (Taylour, Pl. 9).

A word on the preferred materials of early Aegean sculpture in the round: in the Stone and Bronze Ages, clay and stone predominated (limestone, marble, steatite); cf. p. 159 (Cyprus). One rare piece of Mycenaean stone sculpture is a little head from Naxos which served as handle for an implement (Cook, *JHS.* 71 [1951], 250, Pl. 46 c). Stucco has only rarely been found (*1245* and Wace, *Mycenae*, 83, Pl. 104 b); faience was somewhat more popular (*1233*), but at first only imported from abroad (for Cyprus and Egypt, cf. p. 157; also Noble, 'The Technique of Egyptian Faience' in *AJA.* 73 [1969], 435 ff.; and von Bissing, 'Zeit und Herkunft der in Cerveteri gefundenen Gefäße aus ägyptischer Fayence und glasiertem Ton,' *SBMünchen* 1941, II, No. 7, and Stone-Thomas, 'The Use and Distribution of Faience in the Ancient East and Prehistoric Europe,' in *PPS.* N.S. 22 [1956], 37 ff.).

The use of metal as a working material was confined to a short period of time around the middle of the second millennium (LM I/II). Silver and lead from Asia Minor were very rare: a rhyton in the form of a stag made of a silver and lead alloy, found by Schliemann in Grave Circle A at Mycenae (Karo, *SchGr.* 94, No. 388; Marinatos-Hirmer, Pl. 177), is considered an Anatolian import. The silver statuette of a warrior with conical helmet, long hair, and loin-cloth from the Thessalian-Macedonian border area is allegedly Mycenaean work (Ashmolean Mus., Oxford; *AA.* 1901, 165). A tholos tomb at Kampos, Laconia, has yielded lead statuettes of youths and women imported from Crete (Tsountas, *Mykenai* [mod. Gk.], Pl. 11; Bossert, *Altkreta*, Figs. 88—91; Marinatos-Hirmer, Pls. 224, 225; Taylour, *The Mycenaeans* [1964], Pl. 53).

We can obtain an idea of the artistic importance and variety of Minoan-Mycenaean solid metal-casting by the *cire perdue* method from the bronze work, mostly statuettes of men and women in an attitude of prayer (*1224 a—d, 1225 a, b, 1226 a, b, 1229—1232*; Furtwängler, *Kl.Schr.* II, 453 ff. = Bossert, Fig. 317 a—c). Ample and soft fluid forms seem characteristic here. The heads, in particular, are formed with deliberate imprecision. But the artists always took great care in rendering the hair, although without subsequent cold working ('chasing'). The freedom and directness of movement is astonishing. 'The modern observer is inclined at first sight to admire this as a free-moving and mature naturalism. But he soon notices that the spiral pose of the arms and the three-dimensional fulfilment of this form guarantee character, expression and clarity. It is impossible to overlook the relation to the inner centre here...' (Matz, *Göttererscheinung und Kultbild im minoischen Kreta*, Diss., Mainz [1958], No. 7, 428; cf. also Sakellariou, *Proceedings of the 2nd Congress of Cretology* I [mod. Gk. 1968], 247 ff., Pls. 48—51; Nat. Mus., Athens., Inv. Nos. 8913, 8914, 6284).

The same applies to the animation and vividness of Minoan bronze figures of animals (*1227, 1228;* also bronze bull in Mus. of Art, Toledo, USA, No. 63, 41); note the very animated bull-jumping group in the Spencer-Churchill Collection recently acquired by the British Museum (Karo, *Reallex. Vorgesch.* VII [1926]; s. v. Kreta, Pl. 71; Lamb, *Greek and Roman Bronzes* [1929], 27, Pl. 6; Hutchinson, *Prehistoric Crete* [1962], Pl. 16; cf. text of *1054*).

Forgeries continually confuse the assessment of Greek sculpture. For instance, we must hesitate before the statuette of a youth from Griviglia, near Rhethymnon (Marinatos-Hirmer, Pl. 121), and the Stanford worshipper (I. Raubitschek, in *Atti e Memorie del 1. Congr. Internaz. di Micenologia* [Rome 1967]). For questions of dating and, at times, re-dating to the Geometric period, cf. U. Naumann, 'Subminoische und protogeometrische Bronzeplastik von Kreta' (thesis, Hamburg 1967) and in *Opus Nobile: Festschr. zum 60. Geburtstag von Jantzen* (1969), 114 ff.

1172 Athens–Patissia. Early Neolithic marble idol; crouching woman, highly stylized, with crossed legs and arms resting on belly; height 8.6 cm. or 11.5 cm. (contradictory notes). Ashmolean Mus., Oxford, No. 1895.166, AE 148. – Hogarth, *Essays in Aegean Arch. pres. to ... Evans* (1927), Pl. 7 b; Weinberg, *AJA*. 55 (1951), 122 f., No. 3, Pl. 1 c (and other idols of the same type); Zervos, *Naissance* I, 187, Fig. 145 (wrongly described as 'with child in her arm'); Müller–Karpe, *Hdb. d. Vorgesch.* II, Pl. 136 c; Renfrew, *AJA*. 73 (1969), Pl. 1 b.

1173 Sesklo, Thessaly. Fragment of a seated fat, female figure with well-marked fold on abdomen. Head, hands, and parts of arms and legs lost; light yellow clay; height 4.7 cm.; Neolithic I b. Nat. Mus., Athens. – Tsountas, *DS*., 294, Pl. 33:6; Zervos, 179, Fig. 130; Müller–Karpe, Pl. 133:12.

1174 Magoula Balomenou, near Chaironeia. Red-painted
a, b Neolithic terracotta idol; head lost; female figure with fat buttocks, bulky legs, hands resting below the breasts; Style A 3 B; preserved height 12.7 cm. Arch. Mus., Chaironeia. – Soteriades, *Ephem*. 1908, Pl. 1 a; V. Müller, *Frühe Plastik* 15, Pl. 3:55; Franz, *Ipek* 8 (1932/33), Pl. 9:1 a; Zervos, 226 f., Figs. 238,239; Müller–Karpe, Pl. 131 a 1.

1175 Attica. Site unknown. Early Neolithic female idol, with very elongated neck, well-defined backbone, and exaggerated buttocks; decorative lines on neck, right hand raised to the head; pentelic marble; height 22.5 cm. Arch. Mus., Eleusis. – Zervos, I, 210 f., Figs. 203, 204.

1176 Thessaly. Region of Larissa. Late Neolithic, ithyphallic seated man, red terracotta. Decorative lines on the neck, the right hand raised to the head, the partly broken left hand over the genitals. Crude work; height 38 cm. (Zervos: 49 cm.); Late neol. (Karo, Matz), EH (Bossert, Möbius). Nat. Mus., Athens. – Wace–Thompson, *Prehist. Thess.*, 56 f., Fig. 30; Hoernes, *Urgeschichte der bildenden Kunst in Europa*[2], 314; Karo, *Religion des ägäischen Kreises* (1925), VI; Bossert, *Altkreta*, Fig. 84; Matz, *Hdb. Arch.* II, i, 185; Möbius, *AA*. 1954, 207 ff., Fig. 1; Zervos, *Naissance* II, 354 f., Figs. 501, 502.

1177 Origin unknown (Sesklo?). Torsoes of Neolithic, thick-
1178 bodied female idols with marked buttocks; stone and clay. – Photos: Grundmann Bequest.

1179 Neighbourhood of Sparta. Neolithic female idol, white
a, b limestone; height 15 cm. Characteristic example of type with large buttocks, protruding belly, short thick legs, disproportionate arms and head, elongated neck. Hands restings below breasts (for this posture, cf. *1172, 1174, 1181, 1182, 1183, 1191*). Roll on head; ear or earring in relief; tattooing on upper arms. Nat. Mus., Athens, Inv. No. 417 (formerly Colln. of Arch. Soc., Athens, Inv. No. Lith. 3069). – Wolters, *AM*. 16 (1891), 52 f., Fig. 1; Perrot–Chipiez VI (1894), 741, Fig. 334; V. Müller, *Frühe Plastik* 15, Pl. 3:56; Zervos, *L'Art en Grèce* (1946), Fig. 13; and *Naissance* I, 170 f., Figs. 113, 114; Renfrew, *AJA*. 73 (1969), 28, Fig. 4 above.

1180 Sesklo. Enthroned mother-goddess and child (kourotrophos), richly painted in black and red; put together from fragments, head missing; terracotta; height 16 cm.; Neolithic (Dimini period). Nat. Mus., Athens (formerly coll. of the Arch. Soc.). – Tsountas, *DS*. 290, Fig. 31:2 a, b; V. Müller, 19, Pl. 3:70,71; Schachermeyr, *Die ältesten Kulturen*, Pl. 7:1 a, b; Zervos, *Naissance* II, Col. Pl. C; Higgins, *Greek Terracottas* (1967), 7, Pl. 2 e; Müller–Karpe, *Hdb. d. Vorgesch.* II, Pl. 133:16.

1181 Aegina. Surface find in the valley of Alones, south of
a–c the Temple of Aphaia: Neolithic female statuette, white stone; height 10.6 cm. Similar workmanship as *1172*. – Welter, *AA*. 1954, 40, Figs. 3–5.

1182 Aegina (contradicted by Welter: surface find from Vagia, west of the ridge of Aphaia, or the Colonna hill near the town of Aegina; inventory entry: 1908, from Athens art dealer). Neolithic female statuette like *1181, 1183 a, b*; grained shell (according to Ohly: not marble, as indicated in earlier publications); height 7.5 cm. Staatl. Antikensammlungen, Munich, Inv. No. 10.060. – Sieveking, *Münchner Jahrbuch* 1909, 74, I, No. 1, with Fig. 1; and *AA*. 1910, 48, II, No. 2, with Fig. 1; Welter, *Aigina* (1938), 10, Fig. 8; Müller–Karpe, Pl. 138 E 4.

1183 Neighbourhood of Sparta (according to DAI. Photo
a, b Archive, Athens, 'from Sparta'). Two Neolithic idols like *1181* and *1182*: white limestone; height 7.2 and 7 cm. Nat. Mus., Athens (formerly coll. of Arch. Soc., No. Lith. 3066). – Wolters, *AM*. 16 (1891), 52, Fig. 2, drawing; followed by V. Müller, Pl. 3:57, and Valmin, *Das adriatische Gebiet in Vor- u. Frühbronzezeit* (1939), 221, Fig. 54:2; Zervos, *Naissance* I, 174 f., Figs. 119, 120; and 185, Fig. 139; Weinberg, *AJA*. 55 (1951), 125, Pl. 3 b; Thimme, *Frühe Randkulturen des Mittelmeerraumes* (1968), 20, Fig. 2.

1184 Probably from Crete. Site unknown. Small crouching monkey of yellow steatite, with knees drawn up and feet crossed; eating with both hands, elbows supported on knees; hole between the feet for attachment to base; height 3.2 cm., EM II (second half of third millennium). Comparable pieces from Crete: Evans, *Prehist. Tombs*, 152, Fig. 131 a, b (little monkey; lapis lazuli pendant; MM); id., *PM* I, 118, Fig. 87:1 (crouching monkey); Marinatos–Hirmer, Pl. 12 (ivory seal in the form of a crouching baboon, EM III, formerly Giamalakis Coll.); Warren, *Minoan Stone Vases*, 104, Fig. P 587 (stone vase in the form of a monkey). Staatl. Antikensammlungen, Munich, Inv. No. 10.369. – Vierneisel, *Münchner Jahrbuch* 1966, 227, Fig. 9.

1185 Trapeza Cave, Lasithi, east Crete. Grave offering of person buried there. Ivory stamp-seal crowned with a little crouching monkey, sitting straighter than *1184*; height 4.4 cm., diam. 1.6 cm.; EM III (Pendlebury, Demargne, Willetts), MM I (2000–1800 B. C., Matz). Arch. Mus., Herakleion, Inv. No. 1570. – Karo, *AA*. 1936, 163 f., Fig. 18; Pendlebury, *Arch. of Crete*, Pl. 13:2; Bossert, *Altkreta*, Fig. 400 a; Matz, *Kreta u. frühes Griechenland* (1962), 32, 62, 70 and 66 with col. ill.; Demargne, *Naissance*, 74, Fig. 89; Willetts, *Everyday Life in Ancient Crete* (1969), 28, Fig. 6; Platon, *CMS*. II, i (1969), 516, No. 435.

1186 Syros. Early Cycladic vase, in the form of a bear sitting on its hind legs holding a bowl in its front paws. Clay, painted in stripes; height 10.8 cm., late third millennium. Nat. Mus., Athens. – Frankfort, *Studies in Early Pottery of the Near East* II (1927), Pl. 5:8; Zervos, *Cycl.* 180 f., Figs. 238, 239; Demargne, *Nais-*

sance, 45, Fig. 50; Higgins, *Greek Terracottas* (1967), 6, Fig. 3; Thimme, *Frühe Randkulturen des Mittelmeerraumes* (1968), 22, ill. suppl. 14.

1187 Panormos, Naxos. Monochrome vase in the form of
a, b a quadruped (perhaps a bear or pig) standing on its hind legs, holding a vessel in its front feet, like *1186;* curiously shaped eyes. Private colln., Athens. – Photo DAI., Athens.

1188 Orchomenos, Boeotia. Monochrome fragment of a vase protome: sculptured animal-head with disc-shaped eyes and curved neck (horse?); EH. – Kunze, *Orchomenos* III (1934), Pl. 29:5.

1189 Said to be from Vari, Attica. Crude animal, executed in Urfirnis technique (EH). For animal-head protomes and entire animal vases of the Early Bronze Age, cf. Tuchelt, 'Tiergefäße in Kopf- u. Protomengestalt' (*Ist-Forsch.* XXII, 1962) and Weinberg, *AntK.* 12 (1969), 6 f., Figs. 3–6, Pl. 3:5,6 (Tiryns and Zygouries). Private colln. (?). – Photo DAI., Athens.

1190 Phylakopi, Melos. Early Cycladic monochrome vase in the form of an animal; spout with wide rim in place of head; ridge and two loops on back; incised zigzag decoration on both sides, double line at base of neck, incised lozenges on chest; length 13.1 cm., height 11.4 cm. Nat. Mus., Athens. – Zervos, *Cycl.* 99, Figs. 96–98; Mallowan, *Ugaritica* VI (1969), 541 ff., Fig. 2.

1191 Lerna, the Argolid. Late Neolithic statuette of a
a, b woman, clay; head and both feet missing. Naked goddess with hands resting below the breast; slim and well proportioned; preserved height 18.2 cm. Arch. Mus., Argos. – Caskey, *Hesperia* 25 (1956), 175; Schachermeyr, 'Das ägäische Neolithikum', *Stud. in Mediterr. Arch.* VI (1964), 15, Fig. 11; Zervos, *Naissance* II, 274 f., Figs. 334, 335; Müller–Karpe, *Hdb. d. Vorgesch.* II, Pl. 137 B 1; Higgins, op. cit., Pl. 2 c, d.

1192 Thera. Crudely formed, ill-proportioned female clay
a, b statuette, with steatopygia, moulded breasts and disc eyes. All signs indicate prehistoric work; within post-Bronze Age art, according to V. Müller, *Frühe Plastik* 64:87 and 171 to Pl. 19,270: 'early dating'; cf. *Thera* II, 307, Fig. 494 b.

1193 Mallia. Necropolis: Vase in the form of the bust of a woman; height 16.4 cm., no sculptured differentiation of details; diagonal sloping shoulders, stump arms, small head; breasts represented as spouts. White-painted on dark ground. EM III (2200–2000 B. C.); cf. rhyton from Mochlos in the form of a bust, which Marinatos considered male (Arch. Mus., Herakleion, Inv. No. 5499. Evans, *PM.* I, 116, Fig. 84; Marinatos–Hirmer, Pl. 10 upper). *1193:* Arch. Mus., Herakleion. – *Mélanges Glotz* (1932), Pl. 1; Demargne, *Naissance*, 78, Fig. 100.

1194–1212: EARLY CYCLADIC STONE SCULPTURE AND RELATED WORK

1194 Amorgos. Large Early Bronze Age marble head with
a–c long neck, high oval face, ridge nose, and oval schematic mouth; Parian marble; red and black vertical stripes of colour on left cheek represent tattooing; eyes also were painted; height 29 cm., second half of third millennium. Nat. Mus., Athens, Inv. No. 3909. – Zervos, *Cycl.* 146 f., Figs. 177, 178; Matz, *Kreta u. frühes Griechenland* (1962), 60 f., with col. ill.; Thimme, *Frühe Randkulturen des Mittelmeerraumes* (1968), 31 with col. ill.

1195 Cyclades. Female marble figure of rigid form; upper
a–c body bent forward from the hip, round shoulders, deep groove on spine, arms folded in front of body (cf. *1197–1199, 1204*); head and feet missing. Brooklyn Mus., New York, No. 35.812.

1196 Amorgos. Marble head with well-defined profile and well differentiated details. Indication of short hair by parallel grooves, neck broken (deceptive retouching at base); height 9.5 cm. (11.8 cm., Bossert), Later Cycladic culture (Hall). Ashmolean Mus., Oxford, Inv. No. AE 147. – Wolters, *AM.* 16 (1891), 46; Hall, *Aegean Archaeology* (1915), Pl. 14; Bossert, *Altkreta,* Figs. 414, 415; Zervos, *Cycl.* 254 f., Figs. 342, 343; Renfrew, *AJA.* 71 (1967), 6.

1197 Cyclades. Female marble idol, surface very abraded
a–c and corroded; with round shoulders, arms folded, wide cleft between legs; feet missing (cf. *1195, 1198, 1199, 1204*). Brooklyn Mus., New York, No. 35.734.

1198 Cyclades. Completely preserved slender marble idol like *1197;* crude work. Brooklyn Mus., New York, No. 35.733.

1199 Paros. Female idol with round shoulders, arms folded, and long unstructured abdomen (type and date as *1197*); coarse-grained white marble with reddish-yellow patina; height 16.9 cm. Mus. f. Kunst u. Gewerbe, Hamburg, Inv. No. 1927.135. – v. Mercklin, *AA.* 1928, 274 ff., No. 2, Fig. 2.

1200 Cyclades. Early Bronze Age headless marble fiddle-idol, with very elongated neck, moulded breasts and incised neck ornament in the form of a double 'v'; flat, broken in the middle; height 18.5 cm. For this type, cf. V. Müller, *Frühe Plastik,* Pl. 2:45–48; and Zervos, *Cycl.* 80 ff., Figs. 53–58. Private colln., Switzerland. – Schefold, *Meisterwerke griechischer Kunst* (1960), 110, No. 6; Rácz, *Antikes Erbe* (1965), Fig. 1; Jucker, *Kunst der Antike aus Privatbesitz Bern – Basel – Solothurn Exhibition 1967,* 13, No. 39.

1201 Amorgos. Early Cycladic idol, so-called 'Artemis'; very distinct from the other types; ears in the form of round pegs, hair drawn back in strands on the nape, right hand stylized in triangular form, or dagger; small, widely spaced breasts, legs closed (cf. *1206, 1207*), apron indicated by protuberance, and shoulder belt (for the latter, cf. also Zervos, op. cit., 193, Fig. 253); marble; height 22.8 cm. Staatl. Kunstsammlungen, Dresden, Skulpturenabt. Inv. No. Z. V. 2595 (2967). – W. Müller, *AA.* 1925, 143 f., No. 92, Fig. 38; Majewski, *Figuralna Plastyka Cycladzka* (1935), No. 248, Pl. 71 b; Renfrew, *AJA.* 73 (1969), Pl. 8 d.

1202 Cyclades. Early Bronze Age female fiddle-idol (cf. *1200*), with tall headdress; more natural ears, eyes, nose, mouth, and navel; long neck, spindly arms, prominent hips and calves; height 18 cm.; white marble, right leg repaired in ancient times; late third millennium. For this type, cf. Demargne, *Naissance*, 52, Fig. 65 (Ashmolean Mus., Oxford); Richter, *Handbook of the Greek Coll.* [Metrop. Mus., New York] (1953), 165, Pl. 5 b; similarly, Bossert, *Altkreta*, Fig. 410. *1202:* Private colln., Switzerland. – Rácz, op. cit., Fig. 2; Jucker, op. cit., 12, No. 35.

1203 Paros. Early Cycladic female double figurine, surface very corroded, yellowish marble; height 21.6 cm. Badisches Landesmuseum, Karlsruhe, Inv. No. B 839. – Gerhard, *Abh.* Pl. 44:3; Perrot–Chipiez VI (1894), 740, Fig. 332; Bossert, *Altkreta*, Fig. 411; Zervos, *Cycl.*, 237, Fig. 319; Vermeule, *Greece in the Bronze Age,* Fig. 7 d; Thimme, *AntK.* 8 (1965), Pl. 21:2; id., *Frühe Randkulturen des Mittelmeerraumes* (1968), 44 with col. ill.

1204 Cyclades. Complete Early Cycladic female marble figurine, with roundish oval face disc and round shoulders like *1198;* height 19 cm.; second half of third millennium. Staatl. Antikensammlungen, Munich, Inv. No. 10.368. Vierneisel, *Münchner Jahrbuch* 1966, 227, Fig. 7.

1205 Syros. Complete large female figurine, with angular shoulders and triangular face disc; Parian marble; height 46 cm. Nat. Mus., Athens, Inv. No. 6174. – Zervos, *Cycl.*, 191, Fig. 251; Renfrew, *AJA.* 73 (1969), Pl. 5 d.

1206 Cyclades. Early Bronze Age female figurine, with short closed legs, very broad angular shoulders, and triangular face plaque; very flat, very corroded; height 17.4 cm. Mus. f. Kunst u. Gewerbe, Hamburg, Inv. No. 1924. 181. – v. Mercklin, *AA.* 1928, 273, No. 1, with Fig.

1207 Naxos. Fragment of Early Bronze Age female marble figurine, with angular shoulders; interesting because shoulders rise instead of slope; very elongated neck. Nat. Mus., Athens.

1208 Knossos–Tekke, Crete. Double idol on single base; Cycladic type with folded arms (EM II, 2400–2200 B. C.); green steatite; height 5 cm. Arch. Mus., Herakleion, Inv. No. 288. – Marinatos *AA.* 1933, 299 ff.; Marinatos–Hirmer, Pl. 11; Demargne, *Naissance*, 49, Fig. 61; Renfrew, *AJA.* 73 (1969), Pl. 9 b.

1209 Knossos–Tekke. Seated female figure, with thin folded arms, seated on backless stool like *1210,* marble; height 8.3 cm.; EM II (Bossert: made in Thera). Arch. Mus., Herakleion, Inv. No. 287. – Marinatos, *AA.*, 1933, 301, Figs. 10, 11; Bossert, *Altkreta*, Figs. 418, 419; Marinatos–Hirmer, Pl. 11; Richter, *The Furniture of the Greeks, Etruscans and Romans* (1966), Pl..–Fig. 35; Renfrew, op. cit., Pl. 9 a; Willetts, *Everyday Life*, 116, **Fig. 56.**

1210 Thera. Early Bronze Age statuette of seated harpist; feet, part of instrument, and right arm missing; height 17.3 cm. or 16.7 cm. (Schefold: 15 cm.), late Early Cycladic (Renfrew: *c.* 2000–1900 B. C.). For the backless stool, cf. Laser, *Arch. Hom. P* (1968), 55, Fig. 9 b. Badisches Landesmus., Karlsruhe, Inv. no. B 864 (other harpists: Zervos, op. cit., 234, Fig. 316; and Schefold, *Meisterwerke griechischer Kunst* [1960], 110, No. 4; also *1211 b–d* and Metrop. Mus., New York, No. 47.100.1: Richter, *Handbook of the Greek Coll.*, 15, Pl. 6 a, b). – Koehler, *AM.* 9 (1884), 159, Pl. 6; V. Müller, *Frühe Plastik,* 14, Pl. 1:24; Bossert, Pls. 412 b, 413 b; Zervos, 235, Fig. 317; Thimme, *Frühe Randkulturen des Mittelmeerraumes* (1968), 33, with col. ill.; Renfrew, Fig. 4 penultimate row.

1211 Keros, Cyclades. Early Bronze Age statuette of a standing pipe player, with legs splayed and bent at the knees; base unfinished; marble; height 20 cm. Another Early Cycladic syrinx-pipe player in Badisches Landesmuseum, Karlsruhe, (Thimme, 38 f., with col. ill.). Nat. Mus., Athens. – Perrot–Chipiez, vol. cit., Fig. 357; Bossert, Figs. 420, 422; Zervos, 223, Fig. 302.

1212 Keros. Early Bronze Age statuette of a harpist on
a–c skilfully executed throne (for this, cf. Laser, op. cit., 55, Fig. 9 i); yellowish-white marble; height 22.5 cm. Most beautiful and unusual example of Cycladic sculpture of the third millennium. Nat. Mus., Athens, Inv. No. 3908. – Koehler, *AM.* 9 (1884), Pl. 6; Perrot–Chipiez, vol. cit., 761, Fig. 358; and Dussaud, *Civil. Préhell.*, 363, Fig. 268 (old state, right foot missing); Herbig, *AM.* 54 (1929), suppls. 57, 58; Bossert, Fig. 421 (with further references); Zervos, 248, Figs. 333, 334; Schefold, *Frühgriechische Sagenbilder* (1964), Fig. 1; Thimme, 47, col. ill.; Simon, *Die Götter der Griechen* (1969), 235, Fig. 222.

1213–1223: MINOAN TERRACOTTAS (MM/LM)

1213 Palaikastro, east Crete. Votive gift. Deep, handle-less clay bowl filled with tiny sculptured figures: a shepherd and his flock, almost 160 animals. Unique composition; although a few animals are lost, their distribution in the round shows a sense of asymmetry and tension. Exterior: lattice pattern painted in red and white on black glaze ground; height 3.9 cm., diam. 19.5 cm.; MM I. Arch. Mus., Herakleion, Inv. No. 5806. – Bosanquet–Dawkins, *Palaikastro Excav.* (1923), 12, Pl. 7; Evans, *PM*. I, 180 f., Fig. 130; Marinatos–Hirmer, Pl. 18 upper; Rodenwaldt, in *Essays in Honour of Sir Arthur Evans* (1927), 100, Pl. 17; Karo, *Greifen am Thron* (1959), 85, Fig. 53; Schiering, *AntK*. 8 (1965), Pl. 3:4; Branigan, *The Foundations of Palatial Crete* (1970), Pl. 8 b.

1214 Koumasa, south Crete. From a family grave in the Mesara. Clay rhyton in the form of a bull; three tiny acrobats hold on to the horns and head of a three-legged animal; originally glazed in the Urfirnis technique (on this, cf. p. 60); length 20.5 cm.; MM I. Arch. Mus., Herakleion, Inv. No. 4120. – Reichel, *AM*. 34 (1909), 92, Fig. 11 (drawing); Karo, 44, Fig. 24; Willetts, *Everyday Life*, 168, Fig. 99; Branigan, Pl. 11 a.

1215 Crete, various sites. Little heads and busts of female
to statuettes, with richly worked hair; terracotta. *1215:*
1217 large headdress of horizontal bands; curls on brow and temples (MM); *1216, 1217:* large spiral curl falling on left shoulder only (LM). Metaxas Colln., Herakleion (*1215:* Alexiou, *Delt*. 18 [1963], Chron. Pl. 360 a, b, probably from Kophina); v. Matt, *Das antike Kreta* (1967), 45.

1218 Piskokephalon, east Crete. From a hill shrine: Clay statuette of praying woman, with sophisticated hair knot, heavy long bell skirt, and coiled belt; right hand on left shoulder, left hand on right hip; height 26.4 cm.; MM II (Zervos: MM III). Arch. Mus., Herakleion. – Marinatos–Hirmer, Pl. 17; Zervos, *Crète*, 279, Figs. 396, 397; Marinatos, *Arch. Hom.* A (1967), 28, Pl. 1 d.

1219 Phaistos. Female terracotta figure, with long bell skirt
a, b and high hair style with ornamental plaques attached to it; right arm stretched forward, left arm broken; MM. Arch. Mus., Herakleion. – Levi, *ASAtene* 39/40 (1961/62), 396, Fig. 35; Marinatos, *Arch. Hom.* B (1967), 20, Fig. 5 a, b.

1220 Pachyammos, east Crete. Clay rhyton in the form of a strong bull with well-marked dewlap, fairly straight back, and bushy tail; length 17.2 cm., LM I (second half of sixteenth century B. C.). Brooklyn Mus., N. Y., No. 35.753 (formerly Seltmann Colln.). – Williams, *The Brooklyn Mus. Quarterly* 22 (1935) 105 ff.

1221 Pseira, east Crete. Clay rhyton in the form of a bull, painted with network pattern; straight back, short head, sturdy legs, well-marked dewlap; length 26 cm.; LM I Arch. Mus., Herakleion. – Zervos, *Crète*, 334, Fig. 487; Marinatos–Hirmer, Pl. 90 lower.

1222 Pseira. Clay rhyton in the form of a bull; humped neck, short sturdy legs, well-marked dewlap; yellowish clay, thinly painted; put together from many pieces; length 25 cm. MM III/ LM I (Karo), second half of sixteenth century B. C. (Marinatos, Matz), 1500–1450 B. C. (Higgins). Arch. Mus., Herakleion, Inv. No. 5412. – Zervos, *Crète*, 335, Fig. 448; Karo, *Greifen am Thron* (1959), 45, Fig. 25; Matz, *Kreta u. frühes Griechenland* (1962), ill. suppl. 8; Marinatos–Hirmer, Pl. 90 upper; Higgins, *Greek Terracottas* (1967), 11 f., Pl. 5 a.

1223 Kamilari, near Phaistos, south Crete. From a tholos: Terracotta group of the sixteenth century B. C.; small model of a building with two pillars, cultic scene of great interest to the history of religion: sacrifice before the heroicized dead. For the site, cf. *133*. Arch. Mus., Herakleion. – Levi, *ILN*. 6469 (27. 7. 1963), 137, with Fig. 16; id., *ASAtene* 39/40 (1961/62), 124, Fig. 170 a; Schachermeyr, *Die minoische Kultur des alten Kreta* (1964), Pl. 38 a; id., *AfO*. 21 (1966), 188, Fig. 69; v. Matt, *Das antike Kreta* (1967), 120; Levi, *Atti e Memorie del 1. Congr. Internaz. di Micenologia*, Rome 1967 (1968), 195, Pl. 5:9 a, b.

1224–1233: CRETAN BRONZE AND FAIENCE SCULPTURE (MM/LM)

1224 Said to be from Troas. According to Karo: 'Site un-
a–d known' (1926): Good quality bronze statuette of a Minoan female worshipper, with right hand raised to brow (gesture of prayer, Matz; of adjuration, Karo). Flounced skirt, bare breast, complex hairstyle (for this cf. Marinatos, *Arch. Hom.* B [1967], 8 f., Pl. 1 f, g); height 18.4 cm.; bronze, solid cast; LM I. Antikenabt. d. Staatl. Mus., Berlin, Inv. No. Misc. 8092 (similar piece: Hagia Triada; height 7.8 cm.; MM III b, Arch. Mus., Herakleion, Inv. No. 761; Karo, *Greifen am Thron* [1959], 67, Fig. 40). – Perrot-Chipiez, VI (1894), 754 f., Figs. 349, 350; Furtwängler, *Aigina* (1906), 371, Fig. 296; Karo, *Reallex. Vorgesch.* V (1926), 26, s. v. 'Haartracht', Pl. 2; V. Müller, *Frühe Plastik*, 40, 51, 54, Pl. 12,226; Lamb, *Greek and Roman Bronzes* (1929), 26, Pl. 27 a; Evans, *PM*. IV, 176, Fig. 138; Bossert, *Altkreta*, Figs. 314 and 315; Neugebauer, *Die minoischen und archaisch griechischen Bronzen*, Berlin (1931), 1, No. 1, Pl. 1; Matz, *Die Antike* 11 (1935), 187, Pl. 14; id., *KMT*. 95, Pl. 58; id., *Göttererscheinung u. Kultbild im minoischen Kreta* (1958), 31, 48, Fig. 18; Gehrig-Greifenhagen-Kunisch, *Führer durch die Antikenabt.* (1968), 25, Fig. 8; Schweitzer, *Die geometr. Kunst Griechenlands* (1969), Pl.-Fig. 105.

1225 Tylissos. Bronze statuette of a strong man praying,
a, b with very hollow small of back and slightly spread legs; leaning forwards; right hand at brow (cf. *1224–1226, 1231, 1232*); base with pegs; height, without pegs, 25 cm.; LM I (c. 1550 B. C.). Arch. Mus., Herakleion. – Hazzidakis, *Ephem.* 1912, Pl. 17; Dussaud, *Civilis. préhell.* 58, Fig. 37; Evans, *PM*. III, 449, Fig. 313; V. Müller, *Frühe Plastik*, Pl. 14,240; Lamb, 22 f., Pl. 5 c, d; Bossert, *Altkreta*, Fig. 320 a, b; Demargne, *Naissance*, 162, Fig. 220.

1226 Tylissos. Praying youth in characteristically rigid pose,
a, b with hollow small of back and right hand raised to

brow (for the interpretation of this gesture, cf. *1224*; recently Karo: representation of man dazzled by the appearance of the deity); belted loin-cloth, necklace, soft shoes, and gloves, as demanded by cult; height 15.2 cm. (Zervos: 16.5 cm.); solid cast bronze; MM III b (Karo, LM I (sixteenth century; Matz). 1500 B. C. (Marinatos, Demargne). Arch. Mus., Herakleion, Inv. No. 1831. – Hazzidakis, *Et. Crét.* III (1934), 95, Pl. 26; Lamb, 23, Pl. 8 a; Zervos, *Crète*, 345, Figs. 502, 503; Karo, *Greifen am Thron* (1959), 69, Fig. 41; Matz, *Göttererscheinung u. Kultbild im minoischen Kreta* (1958), 31, Fig. 17 a, b; and *Kreta u. frühes Griechenland* (1962), 127, 151, ill. suppl. 6; Marinatos–Hirmer, Pl. 108; Demargne, 163, Fig. 222; Schweitzer, Pl.-Figs. 107, 108.

1227 Kato Zakro, east Crete. Standing stag; bronze; length 7.5 cm.; LM I (Zervos), Geometric (U. Naumann). Arch. Mus., Herakleion. – Zervos, *Crète*, 327, Fig. 474; Naumann, *Festschr. zum 60. Geburtstag v. Jantzen* (1969), 118, n. 13 q.

1228 Hagia Triada, south Crete. Recumbent ibex; bronze; length 4.5 cm., LM I. Arch. Mus., Herakleion. – Zervos, 332, Fig. 484 right; Willetts, *Everyday Life*, 65, Fig. 28.

1229 Crete. Site unknown. Seated man with garland and belt; arms and legs partly missing; arm gesture to be completed like *1230*; preserved height 6.7 cm.; bronze; LM I (Zervos), Geometric (Naumann, cf. *1228*). Arch. Mus., Herakleion. – Zervos, 342, Fig. 498.

1230 Said to be from the neighbourhood of Phaistos, south Crete. Bronze figure of praying youth, with small of back very hollow; calves and feet lost; wide-brimmed hat, rolled belt, short apron and codpiece. Bossert concluded from the position of the arms that he was a flautist! Preserved height 13.8 cm.; LM I. Rijksmus. van Oudheden, Leiden, Inv. No. I 104/2.1. – Van Hoorn, *JdI.* 30 (1915), 65 ff., Pl. 1; Glotz, *La Civilisation Egéenne* (1923), 376, Fig. 64; V. Müller, *Frühe Plastik*, 47, 215, Pl. 14:241; Lamb, *Greek and Roman Bronzes*, 23, Pl. 8 c; Bossert, *Altkreta*, Figs. 318, 319; Schweitzer, op. cit. Pl.-Fig. 106.

1231 Anatoli near Hierapetra, south Crete. Praying man with right hand on brow, left hand on left thigh, upper body naked; long, wide-belted apron, base with peg; height 19.5 cm.; incl. base, 22 cm.; solid cast bronze, MM III (c. 1600 B. C.) Lamb, LM I (1550–1500 B. C.) Zervos, Brit. Mus., London, Reg. No. 1918.1-1.114. – Spratt, *Travels and Researches in Crete* I, 290; Pryce, *JHS.* 41 (1921), 86 ff., Pl. 1; Lamb, 22 f., Pl. 5 a, b; V. Müller, 48, Pl. 14:242; Zervos, Figs. 496, 497.

1232 Phaistos. Small, block-like worshipper on thick base; bronze, c. 1500 B. C. Arch. Mus., Herakleion. – Demargne, *Naissance*, 162, Fig. 221.

1233 Knossos. From the treasure of the shrine in W. wing of Palace. Large snake goddess of multicoloured faience, with smooth, horizontally striped skirt; above this, an apron-like garment richly patterned and incised, tightly laced bodice, breasts free, heavy headdress; height 34.2 cm.; MM III (earlier than 1600 B.C.). – Arch. Mus., Herakleion, Inv. No. 63. – Maraghiannis, *Ant. Crét.* III, Pl. 16; Dussaud, *Civilis. préhellén.* 59, Fig. 38 (drawing); Evans, *PM.* I, 500 and col. ill.; and IV, 177, Fig. 139; Bossert, *Altkreta*, Fig. 289; Karo, *Relig. d. ägäischen Kreises* (1925), Fig. 35; Nilsson, *MMR.* 84; Karo, *Greifen am Thron* (1959), 58, Fig. 34; Matz, *Göttererscheinung u. Kultbild im minoischen Kreta* (1958), 32, Fig. 19; Marinatos–Hirmer, Pl. 70.

1234–1242: LATE BRONZE AGE ANIMAL SCULPTURE, ESPECIALLY ANIMALHEAD RHYTA

1234 Argive Heraion, Prosymna. Grave III: Figurine of hippopotamus or elephant, flat at the back; head, front foot, and tail broken; amulet or magic object; cornelian, length 4 cm., height 2 cm.; LM/LH III; perhaps Egyptian import. Nat. Mus., Athens. – Blegen, *Prosymna*, 292, Fig. 600.

1235 Knossos. Fragment of a steatite vase, with relief decoration (for this, cf. *1162–1167*). Octopus under stones; preserved length 9 cm.; LM I a. Arch. Mus., Herakleion. – Pendlebury, *Arch. of Crete*, Pl. 37:4; Zervos, *Crète*, 351, Fig. 515; Schiering, *AntK.* 8 (1965), Pl. 3:3; Kyrieleis, *MarbWPr.* 1968, Pl. 3 right.

1236 Knossos. From the Small Palace: Bull's head rhyton, with inlet hole on neck and spout on mouth. Greyish black steatite or serpentine with inlays of limestone and rock crystal; horns of gilt wood; restored. Neck closed by flat steatite lid, decorated by the hand of the artist: sketch of head from the front: example unique in Minoan art! Height of brow 20 cm. (height 45 cm., after Bossert, *Altkreta*, Fig. 308); LM I (Karo, Matz, Marinatos); LM II/III a (Warren). (Fragments of similar steatite rhyta from Mycenae: Fimmen, *KMK.* 187, Fig. 178; Wace, *Mycenae* [1949/1964], 68, Pl.-Fig. 26 a, b; 27 a, b). Arch. Mus., Herakleion, Inv. Nos. 1368 and 1550. – Maraghiannis, *Ant. Crét.* III, Pl. 27; Evans, *PM.* II, 527 f., Fig. 330; Karo, *Greifen am Thron* (1959), 43, Fig. 23; Marinatos–Hirmer, Pl. 98; Matz, *Kreta u. Frühes Griechenland* (1962), 125, 174 and with col. ill.; Warren, *Minoan Stone Vases* (1969), 98, Fig. P 489.

1237 Knossos. Central Treasury: Rhyton in the form of the head of a lioness, of translucent yellowish-white limestone; eyes and nostrils of differently coloured material now missing; traces of red jasper. Almost completely reconstructed from fragments; round inlet hole on neck; diam. of rear 17 cm.; length 29.5 cm.; c. 1500 B.C. Arch. Mus., Herakleion, Inv. No. 44. – Maraghiannis, Pl. 28; Fimmen, *KMK.* 187, Fig. 179; Evans, *PM.* II, 827 f., Fig. 542 a, b, Pl. 31 a; Bossert, *Altkreta*, Fig. 309; Karo, 51, Fig. 29; Marinatos–Hirmer, Pl. 99; Demargne, *Naissance*, 161, Fig. 219; Warren, 90, Type E.

1238 Naxos Town. Harbour region: Richly painted rhyton in the form of a ram's head; put together from fragments; greyish yellow clay; funnel spout above, handle behind; height 12.9 cm., LH III. Arch. Mus., Naxos, Inv. No. 1000. – Doumas, *Delt.* 19 (1964), Chron. 412; and *AA.* 1968, 374 ff., Figs. 1–5.

1239 Karpathos. Painted clay bull's head rhyton, LH III. Brit. Mus., London, Cat. No. A 971. Forsdyke, *Cat.*

of Greek and Etruscan Vases I, 2 (1925), 177 f., No. A 971; CVA. Great Britain, Brit. Mus., Fasc. 7, Pls. 10:11; Bossert, op. cit., Fig. 466; Vermeule, Greece in the Bronze Age, Pl. 42 c; Doumas, AA. 1968, 381, Fig. 10.

1240 Tiryns, the Argolid. Painted rhyton, in the form of the head of a fox or dog; LH III. Ashmolean Mus., Oxford, Inv. No. AE 298. – Evans, 'The Tomb of the Double Axes', Archaeologia 65 (1913/14), 89; Maximova, Les Vases Plastiques dans l'Antiquité (1927), 76, Fig. 7; Karageorghis, Nouveaux documents pour l'étude du bronze récent à Chypre (1965), 228 f., Pl. 22:6; Lacy, Greek Pottery in the Bronze Age (1967), 216, Fig. 85 c; Doumas, 384 f., Fig. 19.

1241 Ras Shamra, north Syria. Mycenaean animal-head rhyton painted in lustrous red on light slip; clay (goat's head or schematized bull's head); height 22 cm.; LH III. Louvre, Paris, Inv. No. AO 19932. – Schaeffer, Ugaritica II (1949), 222 f., Fig. 93:5–7; Karageorghis, 226, Fig. 21:5,6; Doumas, 384 f., Figs. 16–19.

1242 Ialysos, Rhodes. From the Mycenaean necropolis: Painted bull's head rhyton; clay; originally surmounted by a knob between the horns, handle behind; height c. 15 cm. (similar rhyta: Karo, JdI. 26 [1911], 259 ff., Figs. 11, 12). Arch. Mus., Rhodes. – Maiuri, Clara Rhodos 1 (1928), 63, Fig. 44; Bossert, op. cit., Fig. 467; Doumas, 380, Figs. 6–8.

1243–1265: MYCENAEAN GOLD MASKS – CLAY AND STUCCO SCULPTURE – ANIMAL FIGURES

1243 Mycenae. Grave Circle A, Shaft Graves V and IV:
1244 Gold funeral masks. *1243:* so-called 'Agamemnon'; height 31.5 cm., also side view: Taylor, The Mycenaeans (1964), Pl. 16; *1244:* height 30.3 cm., LH I (sixteenth century). Nat. Mus., Athens, Inv. Nos. 624 and 259. – Schliemann, Mykenae (1878/1964), 256, Fig. 332 and 332 Fig. 474; Karo, SchGr. Pl. 52:624 and Pls. 49, 50:259; Marinatos–Hirmer, Pls. 162, 166; Blegen, AJA. 66 (1962), Pl. 62:4,6; Matz, KMT. Pl. 87; id., Kreta u. frühes Griechenland (1962), 165, col. ill., and ill. suppl. 18.

1245 Mycenae. Acropolis; excavated by Tsountas, 1896: Painted stucco female head (goddess or sphinx); headdress: light and dark blue; eyes, eyebrows, curls on temple, side-burns, hair on back of head: bluish black; lips and circlet: red. Tattooed dotted red rosettes on brow, chin, and cheeks; height 16.8 cm., LH II/III (Bossert), LH III b/c (Matz). Nat. Mus., Athens, Inv. No. 4575. – Tsountas, Ephem. 1902,1 ff., Pls. 1, 2; Hall, The Civilization of Greece in the Bronze Age (1928), 273, Fig. 349; Evans, PM. III, 519 f., Fig. 364; Bossert, Altkreta, Fig. 87 a, b; Zervos, L'Art en Grèce (³1937), Figs. 33–35; Curtius, Die Antike Kunst II (1938/1959), 63, Fig. 58; Matz, KMT. 131, Pl. 107; Marinatos–Hirmer, Col. Pls. 41, 42; Vermeule, Greece in the Bronze Age, Pl. 40 c.

1246 Amyklae. Excavation by Tsountas in the region of the Mycenaean settlement Hagia Kyriaki, Shrine of Apollo Amyklaios: Fragment of head of slightly under-life-size human figure of clay; brow, headdress with moulded waves, and parts of both eyebrows preserved; traces of glaze paint; preserved width 14 cm., height 9.5 cm. Arch. Mus., Sparta. – Unpublished.

1247 Amyklae (cf. *1246*). Remarkably fine left hand, hold-
a, b ing the foot of a kylix; structure and firing certainly point at Mycenaean clay; relatively lustrous brown glaze; preserved length 4.5 cm., height without remains of vessel 2.6 cm., LH III b. Arch. Mus., Sparta. – Unpublished.

1248 Greece. Site unknown. Mycenaean statuette of female
a bread baker at the trough; bright red clay with brown glaze; height barely 10 cm., diam. of through 6 cm.; basic form of phi idols (cf. *1259–1262*); LH III b. Similar type: Perrot–Chipiez VI (1894), 810, Fig. 379 (Tiryns). *1248 a:* Private colln., Athens. – Blegen, ASAtene 8–10 (1946–48), 13 ff., Figs. 1–4; Bruns, in Matz–Buchholz, Arch. Hom. Q (1970), Pl. 7 a.

1248 Charvati, east Attica. Horsewoman in high side-saddle;
b basic form of psi idols (cf. *1258*); with stripe decoration and wide headdress; LH III b/c. Stathatos Colln., Athens. – Levi, in Studies Pres. to D. M. Robinson I (1951), 108 ff., Pl. 4 c; Amandry, Coll. Stathatos III, Pl. 2:6; Vermeule, Greece in the Bronze Age, Pl. 41 f.; Mylonas, Mycenae and the Myc. Age (1966), Pl.-Figs. 118, 119; Wiesner, in Matz–Buchholz, Arch. Hom. F (1968), 117, Fig. 21 e.

1248 Argive Heraion, Prosymna. Grave XXII: Mycenaean
c highly stylized two-horse chariot; reconstructed from thirteen fragments; grey clay, yellow slip, brownish glaze; stripe decoration, in part probably to resemble harness. Nat. Mus., Athens. Similarly: Vermeule, op. cit., Pl. 41 d (also Prosymna); height 7.3 cm., length 7.2 cm.; LH III b. – Blegen, Prosymna 365 f., No. 416, Fig. 618.

1248 Mycenae. Enthroned goddess, terracotta, LH III. For
d the seated-woman type, cf. Möbius, Über Form u. Bedeutung der sitzenden Gestalt in der Kunst d. Orients u. d. Griechen; AM. 41 (1916), 119 ff., esp. 152; Mylonas, 'Seated and Multiple Mycenaean Figurines', Festschrift für Goldmann, 110 ff. *1248 d:* Nat. Mus., Athens. – Richter, The Furniture of the Greeks, Etruscans and Romans (1966), Pl.-Fig. 12.

1248 Site unknown. Mycenaean terracotta group. Two fig-
e ures reclining on a bed, probably a sacred marriage; stripe decoration, LH III. Mus. of Fine Arts, Budapest. – Szilagyi-Castiglione, Führer durch das Mus. d. bildenden Künste, Griech.-röm. Sammlung (1957), Pl. 2:2; Richter, Pl.-Fig. 24; Higgins, Greek Terracottas (1967), 15, Fig. 7.

1248 Voula, Attica. Mycenaean libation vessel, in the form
f of a winged, pointed shoe, with typical textile patterns; height c. 13 cm. (There is a second example, as yet unpublished, from Attica. Nat. Mus., Athens.) – Marinatos–Hirmer, Pl. 236; Marinatos, in Matz–Buchholz, Arch. Hom. A (1968), 33, Pl. 6 f.

1249 Argive Heraion, Prosymna, the Argolid. Small model
a, b of a three-legged chair with high back; height 13.6 cm.; brown glaze decoration: stripes, irregular interwoven lines, quadruple running spirals; LH III. Nat. Mus., Athens. – Blegen, Prosymna II, 151, Fig. 619; Higgins, Greek Terracottas (1967), Pl. 4 c; Laser, in Matz–Buchholz, Arch. Hom. P (1968), 55, Fig. 9 k.

1250 Troy VI/VII. Small sculpture in the form of a pig; hollow interior, thrown on the wheel; micaceous yellow clay, lustrous red glaze, made probably in the Greek islands; height 4.5 cm., length 8.5 cm.; LH III b. Staatl. Mus., Berlin; Vor- u. Frühgeschichtl. Abt., Inv. No. Sch. 3563. – Schmidt, *Schliemanns Sammlung* (1902), 171, No. 3563; Buchholz, *BJbV*. 5 (1965), 77, Pl. 11:2–4.

1251 Site unknown. Mycenaean statuette of a reclining dog; yellow clay, orange-red stripe-and-dot decoration; height 6.3 cm., length 10.4 cm.; LH III (c. 1300 B. C.). Mus. of Fine Arts, Boston, No. 65.1339. - *Early Art in Greece: Emmerich Gallery, New York* (1965), 27 f., No. 73 with Fig.; Vermeule, *Class. Journ.* 62 (1966), 100 f., Fig. 6.

1252 Eastern Mediterranean. Site unknown, probably exported from a production centre in the Argolid. Mycenaean figurine of a bull, put together from fragments; points of horns and front legs restored. Yellow clay, fine yellowish slip, light brown stripe painting; height 9 cm., length 11.5 cm. Buchholz Colln., Giessen. – Unpublished.

1253 Argive Heraion, Prosymna. From Graves XI and XXI.
a, b Two handled vases, decorated with stripes, in the form of hedgehogs; LH III. Nat. Mus., Athens. – Blegen, *Prosymna*, 245 and 453 f., Fig. 725:29; Buchholz, *BJbV*. 5 (1965), 77, Pl. 13:4.

1254 Vari, Attica. Animal-shaped vase (hedgehog or pig) on four stump feet, with tall spout and handle; indication of hide or spines by rows of regular lines. Nat. Mus., Athens, Inv. No. 5813. – Fabricius, *AM*. 11 (1886), 142; Collignon-Couve, *Cat. des vases peints du Mus. Nat. d'Athènes* (1904), No. 104, Pl. 7; Buchholz, 77, Pl. 13:1.

1255 Greece or Cyprus. Site not traceable. Mycenaean hedgehog vase, with stump feet, dolphin-type head, funnel, and handle on back; brown glaze decoration in regular wavy lines; eyes: concentric circles; LH III. Akad. Kunstmus., Bonn, Inv. No. 1641. – Karo, *JdI*. 26 (1911), 264; Maximova, *Les Vases plastiques dans l'antiquité* (1927), 63, Pl. 7:24; Buchholz, 77, Pl. 13:3.

1256 Greece. Site unknown. Mycenaean vase in the form of a hedgehog, almost completely rolled up, with spines indicated by regular rows of dots; on the back: handle and funnel; LH III. Glyptothek, Munich (formerly Arndt Colln.). – Sieveking-Hackl, *Die königl. Vasensammlung zu München* I (1912), No. 48, Pl. 5; Buchholz, 77, Pl. 16:1.

1257 Boeotia. Vase in the form of a ram; dark slip with light dots; broad strap handle on back; inlet hole in front on the neck; length c. 18.5 cm. Bronze Age date uncertain; for similar pieces described either as Mycenaean, cf. Nat. Mus., Athens, Inv. No. 12248 (similar type but with LH III c feet and decoration); also Vermeule, *Greek, Etruscan and Roman Art; Boston, Mus. of Fine Arts* (^{3}1963), 26, Fig. 17 (Inv. No. 87.415), or as Boeotian–Archaic: Münzen und Medaillen, *Auktion 34* (6. 5. 1967), 49, No. 103, and Pl. 27; and Canciani, *AA*. 1968, 131, Fig. 12 (Würzburg, Inv. No. H 5061). *1257*: Nat. Mus., Athens, Inv. No. 12247. Photo DAI., Athens.

1258 Tiryns, the Argolid. Necropolis at Hagios Elias, from
a, b old excavations: Mycenaean female idols of the psi
to type *(1258 a, b)* and phi type *(1259 a, b–1262 a, b)*; clay
1262 with glaze decoration. In all cases, sculptural indication
a, b of breasts; on *1260 a, b* and *1261 a, b* also clearly visible indication of arms. Height 10–14.5 cm.; LH III. Arch. Mus., Nauplia. Biesantz, 'Die kret.-myk. Kunst', *Ullstein-Kunstgesch*. IV (1963), Pl.-Fig. 46 *(1258 a, 1259 a, 1260 a)*.

1263 Greece. Site unknown. Mycenaean female idol of the tau type, with arms folded in front of chest; terracotta, stripe decoration; height 10.8 cm.; LH III a (fourteenth century) Metrop. Mus., New York, No. 35.11.16. – *BMetrMus*. 31 (1936), 68 with Fig.; Alexander, *Early Greek Art* (1939), Fig. 4; *BMetrMus*. N. S., 3 (1944/45), 238, 241 with Fig.; Jucker, *Festschr. Schefold* (1967), 141, Pl. 50:4.

1264 Lipari. Acropolis. Fragment of a phi-type idol; ochre-coloured clay, lustrous reddish brown stripe decoration; preserved height 5 cm.; LH III a; from deposit of the Milazzese culture; import from the Aegean. Local mus., Lipari. – Bernabò-Brea and Cavalier, *Bull. Paletnol. Ital*. N. S., 10 (1956), 60, Fig. 41; Taylour, *Myc. Pottery in Italy* (1958), 43, Pl. 8:3 a, b; Fuchs, *AA*. 1964, 688 f., Fig. 10.

1265 Mycenae. Female figure, thrown cylindrically on the wheel and highly stylized; head and arms crudely modelled freehand. Broken on top; hands folded on chest; details in glaze: horizontal stripes on skirt; breasts; necklace and armlets, eyes and mouth. Indications of broken-off handle on back; height 18.5 cm. Similar figures from Mycenae and Pylos: *1266* (horse); also Winter, *Die Typen der figürlichen Terrakotten* I, 3 (1903), 4; cf. Higgins, *Greek Terracottas* (1967), 15, Fig. 9 (drawing); Zervos, *L'Art en Grèce* (^{3}1937), Fig. 82. *1265*: Arch. Mus., Nauplia. – Daux, *BCH*. 87 (1963), 740, Fig. 7; Jucker, op. cit., 141, Pl. 50:5; Mylonas, *Myc. and the Myc. Age* (1966), Pl.-Fig. 128 a–c.

1266–1271: LATE BRONZE AGE TERRACOTTA SCULPTURE – CRETE AND RHODES

1266 Ialysos, Rhodes. Hollow terracotta figure of a loaded horse; body, legs, and head thrown on the wheel, and highly schematized. Painted in the 'close style'; height 24 cm.; LH III c (twelfth century). Arch. Mus., Rhodes. – Jacopi, *ASAtene* 13/14 (1930/31), 293 ff., Figs 35, 39 and col. ill.; Vermeule, *Greece in the Bronze Age*, Pl. 42 a; Higgins, op. cit., Pl. 5 b; Benson, *AJA*. 72 (1968), 206, Pl. 66:4.

1267 Karphi, in the Diktaean mountains, and Gazi, west of
1268 Herakleion, Crete. Two large hollow terracotta statues: goddess in the 'epiphany' attitude, with raised arms. Superficial modelling of upper body and head; lower body undifferentiated and cylindrical. Details of the Karphi goddess: plaited hair, bald patch (originally covered in real hair), symbolic head ornament. Poppy Goddess of Gazi: hair indicated by incisions, circlet with three poppy-headed knobs; height c. 87 cm. (Karphi), 77.5 cm. (Gazi, Marinatos), or 79 cm. (Zervos); sub-Minoan (twelfth to eleventh centuries B. C.). Arch. Mus., Herakleion, Inv. Nos. 11042 and 9305. – Alexiou, 'Die minoische Göttin mit erhobenen Händen', *Kret. Chron*. 12 (1958), 179 ff.; Zervos, *Crète*, 466 f.,

Figs. 773–775; 803–807; Matz, *KMT.*, Pl. 59; Marinatos–Hirmer, Pls. 130, 131; Higgins, 16, Pl. 5 d; Marinatos, in Matz–Buchholz, *Arch. Hom.* B (1968), 14, Pl. 1 a, b.

1269 Knossos, Palace. Shrine of the Double Axes: Terracotta idol of a goddess, with a dove on her head, raised hands, and cylindrical lower body like *1267, 1268;* height 21 cm. For this type and its interpretation, cf. Alexiou, op. cit., and Matz, *Göttererscheinung u. Kultbild im minoischen Kreta* (1958), 29, Fig. 15; LH III (late thirteenth century B. C.). Arch. Mus., Herakleion. – Maraghiannis, *Ant. Crét.* I, Pl. 50; Evans, *PM.* II, 337 ff., Fig. 193 a; V. Müller, *Frühe Plastik*, Pl. 12,228; Nilsson, *MMR.*, 78 ff.; Zervos, op. cit., Fig. 767; Marinatos–Hirmer, Pl. 132; Demargne, *Naissance*, 226, Fig. 315; Brandt, *Gruß u. Gebet* (1965), Pl. 2:3.

1270 Karphi. From Room 27: Rhyton in the form of an ox-drawn cart, with three wheels and driver; animals reproduced sketchily as heads only. Technical explanation of the unusual form of cart by Wiesner, in Matz–Buchholz, *Arch. Hom.* F (1968), 34 and Fig. 3 c; sub-Minoan (twelfth to eleventh centuries B. C.); height 50 cm. Arch. Mus., Herakleion. – Zervos, op. cit., 483, Fig. 802; Seiridaki, *BSA.* 55 (1960), 28, Pl. 13 a–c; Treue, *Achse, Rad u. Wagen* (1965), 119; Demargne, 304 f., Figs. 396, 397.

1271 Probably from Rhodes or Cyprus. Site unknown. Terracotta ritual ring kernos, hollow, with attached jugs little bowl, dove and bull's head in the round. Glaze decoration in dense patterns. LH III b/c (late thirteenth century B. C.). Mus. of Fine Arts, Boston, No. 35.735. – Caskey, *AJA.* 40 (1936), 312, Fig. 10; Vermeule, *Greek, Etruscan and Roman Art*, Boston (1963),[3] 25, Fig. 15; Vermeule-Townsend, *Archaeology* 13 (1960), 69, Fig. 4; Vermeule, *Greece in the Bronze Age* (1964), Pl. 42 d.

Ivories

Bone, horn, tusks, and antlers have served as important basic working materials since Palaeolithic times (Neolithic, *465, 466, 493—500, 1835*; Chalcolithic, *1838, 1839*). In the Aegean, ivory manifestly joined these during the third millennium, predominantly for more sophisticated, precious work, e.g. seals *(1185, 1367—1369)*, although the use of bone did not cease in Early Helladic times *(467—492* and *501—505)* or later *(1911 a, b*, Late Cypriot styli).

In the second millennium, ivories included—apart from cult figurines and mountings on weapons (e.g. pommel: *700*; also Vermeule, *Greece in the Bronze Age*, Pl. 13 a [Mycenae, Grave Circle B, Delta])—spindle whorls *(1844, 1852, 1853)*, ornaments *(1810)* and ladies' toilet articles such as combs *(511—516*, LH I—III c), cosmetic jars *(1272, 1281, 1283*; Cypriot: p. 163 and *1743)*, jewel- and gaming-caskets *(1749 a, b)* and mirror handles (p. 165; *1747, 1748*; also Marinatos-Hirmer, Pls. 220—222; recognizable from the impression in the metal: *626, 630, 632*).

For Cypriot finds besides those included here, see p. 163. From the Shaft Grave period until LH III c *(508)*, there was no demonstrable increase or decrease in the production of ivories in Greece, which is to say that the channels of supply for this precious material remained intact. Workshop sites have been traced in Mycenae *(509)*.

In later times the ivory carver was called 'Elephanteus,' 'Elephantomos', or 'Elephantourgos.' The Mycenaean-Greek word 'Elephas/Elephant' (cf. Ventris-Chadwick, *Documents in Myc. Greek* [1956], 393) clearly derives from an oriental language (cf. Ugaritic *lahpa-*).

Beside the import of untreated raw material from Syria and presumably also Africa—not just individual pieces, but at times even whole tusks: Daux, *BCH.* 87 (1963), 835, Fig. 15, and Schachermeyr, *AnzAW.* 19 (1966), 1 (Kato Zakro, east Crete) —finished works of art were already imported to the Aegean in the third millennium. A little ivory head with inlaid shell eyes from the Trapeza Cave (EM III) is an import from Syria (Pendlebury, *Arch. of Crete*, 90, Pl. 13:2). On the other hand, the motifs and techniques of Cretan-Mycenaean ivory ornaments demonstrably influenced this art form in south-east and central Europe, as shown by horn and bone carvings from Vršac in Yugoslavia and from Blučina in Moravia (Werner, 'Mycenae-Siebenbürgen-Skandinavien,' in: Atti 1. Congr. Internaz. Preist. e Protost. Mediterranea 1950 [1952], 299, Fig. 5; Tihelka, 'Kommission für das Äneolithikum und die ältere Bronzezeit', Nitra 1958 [1961], 91 f., 106, Pl. 8: 1—3; Piggott, *Ancient Europe* [1965], 135, Fig. 72, Pl. 18 b). The modest selection given here shows the quality and variety of Minoan-Mycenaean ivories and the adoption, elaboration, and transmission of their forms and motifs. In spite of the perishable nature of the material, new finds constantly come to light. Thus we may note an ivory relief pyxis which Alexiou found in Katsamba (*Prakt.* 1963, Pls. 156, 157; *Delt.* 19 [1964], Chron., Pl. 517:2; *Hysterominoikoi Taphoi Limenos Knosou* [mod. Gk.,

1967], Pls. 30—33 and frontispiece; L. von Matt, *Das antike Kreta* [1967], Fig. 95). It represents a highly animated hunting scene. Important ivory carvings were also brought to light by Sakellarakis in Archanes, central Crete *(Atti e Memorie del 1. Congr. Internaz. di Micenologia*, Rome 1967 [1968], 245 ff.; cf. Megaw, *JHS.* 87 [1967], Arch. Rep. 20 f., Fig. 34). Taylour found an exceptional little head the size of a fist, together with other ivories, dating from the second half of the thirteenth century in Mycenae (*ILN.* 10. i. 1970, 26 f.).

There is an interpretation of the mentions of horn and ivory in Homer by Amory ('The Gates of Horn and Ivory,' *Yale Classical Studies* 20 [1966], 3 ff.). The investigations of Mrs. Freyer-Schauenburg are of immense value to the comparison of Bronze Age with later Greek ivories (*Elfenbeine aus dem samischen Heraion* [1966]), as is the study by Miss Marangou (*Lakonische Elfenbein- und Beinschnitzereien* [1969]).

General studies: W. F. Albright, 'Ivory and Apes of Ophir', *Americ. Journ. of Semitic Languages and Literature* 37 (1920/21), 144 ff.; Lorimer, 'Gold and Ivory in Mythology, in Greek Poetry and Life,' *Essays pres. to Gilbert Murray* (1936); Wace, 'Obsidian and Ivory,' *Bull. of the Faculty of Arts, Univ. of Alexandria* 1 (1943), 6 ff.; Kantor, 'Ivory Carving in the Mycenaean Period,' *Archaeology* 13 (1960), 14 ff. (further refs. on p. 25); Jantzen, 'Elfenbein' (*Lex. d. Ant. Welt*, 804 f.); Gallis, 'Mycenaean-Minoan Ivories' (unfinished thesis; cf. *BICS.* 13 [1966], 123).

1272 Mycenae. Remains of a curved piece of elephant tusk (detail), tapering towards the top. Delicate lotus and lily blossom relief adapted to the central perpendicular of a voluted column. According to Vermeule, also reclining goats; above them, flying bird (libation horn, import from Syria?). Lower diam. 7.2 cm., preserved height 25.9 cm.; LH II. Nat. Mus., Athens, Inv. No. 2916; Curtius, *Die antike Kunst* II, 116, Fig. 185; Vermeule, *Greece in the Bronze Age*, Pl. 39 c; Mylonas, *Myc. and the Myc. Age* (1966), Pl.-Fig. 143; Staïs, *Coll. Myc.*, 117.

1273 Menidi, Attica. Tholos tomb: Eight-stringed ivory harp, with figuratively decorated rectangular sounding-board (motif of relief: central column, balanced groups of winged griffins), and relief-decorated crossbar (another reconstruction: Aign, *Die Gesch. d. Musikinstrumente d. ägäischen Raumes bis um 700 v. Chr.* [1963], 82 f., Figs. 45, 46). LH III a/b; Nat. Mus., Athens, Inv. Nos. 1972 and 1974. − Lolling, *Das Kuppelgrab bei Menidi* (1880), Pl. 8:6; Staïs, *Coll. Mycén.*, 166 ff.; Deubner, *AM.* 54 (1929), *196;* Lorimer, *HM.*, 456; Wegner, *MGG.* V (1956), 866, Fig. 9; Platon, *Charisterion eis Orlandon* III (mod. Gk., 1966), 221, Fig. 11 (drawing), Pl. 70.

1274 Mycenae. Two small end-pieces of ivory plaques with
a, b double volutes in flat notched relief; widths 3.7 and 3.9 cm. LH I/II. Nat. Mus., Athens. − From group photo, DAI., Athens.

1275 Mycenae. Fragments of two ivory relief bands; ivy
1276 leaves and running spirals. *1275:* preserved length 11 cm., width 3.5 cm. *1276:* preserved length 11.7 cm., width 4.3 cm.; therefore they do not belong together. LH I/II. Nat. Mus., Athens. − From group photo, DAI., Athens.

1277 Mycenae. Ivory lid of a pyxis, with relief of calf sunk on its knees and head turned back; a lot of detailed inner drawing; diam. 6.5 cm.; LH II/III. Nat. Mus., Athens. − Bossert, *Altkreta*, Fig. 62.

1278 Pylos-Routsi, Messenia. Tholos Tomb 2: Ivory comb with teeth on one side and separately worked damaged handle (slightly bent in photo). Flat linear relief style: animated scene, wild cats chasing wild ducks. LH II (early fifteenth century B.C.). Nat. Mus., Athens. − Hood, *JHS.* 77 (1957), Arch. Rep. 14 f.; Marinatos–Hirmer, Pl. 222; Smith, *Interconnections,* 77, Fig. 105 b; Marinatos, in Matz-Buchholz, *Arch. Hom. B* (1967), 30, Pl. 3 c.

1279 Argive Heraion, Prosymna. Chamber Tomb 51: Ivory statuette of a woman, with richly decorated flounced skirt and open bodice; careful carving in the Minoan style, very corroded; height 11.8 cm.; put together from ten fragments. Since she has no attributes, it is uncertain whether she is a goddess. LH/LM III. Nat. Mus., Athens. − Blegen, *Prosymna,* 461 ff., Pl. 191; 729–731; Nilsson, *MMR.,* 313, Fig. 151, and *Gesch. d. griech. Relig.* I, Pl. 23:2; Vermeule, *Greece in the Bronze Age* (1964), Pl. 39 a.

1280 Mycenae. Excavated in 1939, at the great northern
a, b retaining wall of the Archaic Temple. Sculptured ivory group: divine child, watched over by two crouching mothers, one of whom has her arm round the other; the women are also linked by their shared cloak (Simon: Demeter, Kore, Pluto); height 7.3 cm. LH II (fifteenth century B.C.; Taylour: LH III). Nat. Mus., Athens, Inv. No. 7711. − Wace, *JHS.* 59 (1939), 210 ff.; Blegen, *AJA.* 43 (1939), 698, Fig. I; Lemerle, *BCH.* 63 (1939) Pl. 57; Wace, *Mycenae* (1949/1964), 83 f., Figs. 101–103; Nilsson, *MMR.* 313 f., note 20; Marinatos–Hirmer, Pls. 218, 219; Mylonas, *Eleusis and the Eleusinian Mysteries* (1961), 51 f.; and, *Anc. Myc.*, Figs. 129, 130; Wace-Stubbings, *A Companion to Homer* (1962), Pl. 27 a; Vermeule, Pl. 38; Taylour, *The Mycenaeans* (1964), Pls. 12, 13; Wace–Williams, *Mycenae Guide*, 4th ed. (1966), Pl. 5 a; Simon, *Die Götter der Griechen* (1969), 94 f., Figs. 90, 91.

1281 Athens. From a Mycenaean chamber tomb by the Areo-
a–c pagus *(956 a, b).* Ivory pyxis decorated in relief, with lid *(1281 a, c);* height of pyxis 16 cm., diam. 11.2 cm.; LH III a (c. 1400 B.C.). Agora Mus., Athens. − Shear, *AJA.* 43 (1939), 583 ff., Figs. 12–14; Lemerle, *BCH.* 63 (1939), 291 f., Fig. 6; Pl. 55 (roll-out of relief frieze); *JHS.* 59 (1939), Pl. 14 a; Shear, *Hesperia* 9 (1940),

286 ff., Figs. 27–29; Walter, *AA.* (1940), 161 f., Figs. 28, 29; Picard, *MonPiot* 40 (1944), 113 f., Figs. 1, 2; Broneer, *Antiquity* 30 (1956), 9 ff., Pl. 6; Kantor, *Archaeology* 13 (1960), 15, Fig. 3; *The Athenian Agora: A Guide to the Excav. and Mus.* (²1962), 146, Pl. 11; Vermeule, Pl. 36 b, c; Mylonas, *Myc. and the Myc. Age* (1966), Pl.-Fig. 141; Schachermeyr, *Ägäis u. Orient* (1967), Pl. 21:79.

1282 Mycenae. Ivory relief plaque; winged griffin reclining among flowers; careful work; height 6.5 or 6.8 cm., width 7 or 7.1 cm.; probably 1400 B. C. (Bossert, *c.* 1500). Nat. Mus., Athens. – Fimmen, *KMK.* 205, Fig. 198; Bossert, *Altkreta* Fig. 53; Vermeule, Pl. 37 a.

1283 Pylos-Routsi, Messenia. Tholos Tomb 2: Ivory pyxis with relief decoration, careful Early Mycenaean work under Minoan influence. Alternating vertical spirals and bands of foliage; handle in the form of a small figure-of-eight shield; height 16 cm., LH II (*c.* 1500 B. C.). – Marinatos, *ILN.* 6. IV. 1957, 543, Fig. 21; Marinatos-Hirmer, Pl. 223; Taylour, *The Mycenaeans* (1964), Pl. 61.

1284 Spata, east Attica. From a chamber tomb. Rectangular ivory plaque, with recumbent sphinx facing right; schematic indication of wings, curls, and crown. Clearly from a small casket or piece of furniture; LH III b (thirteenth century B. C.); cf. similar ivory relief from Mycenae: Kantor, *Archaeology* 13 (1969), 18, Fig. 9 b = Bossert, *Altkreta*, Fig. 56 a. *1284:* length *c.* 6 cm. Nat. Mus., Athens, Inv. No. 2053. – Haussoullier, *BCH.* 2 (1878), 185 ff., Pl. 17; Marinatos-Hirmer, Pl. 216; Demargne, *Naissance,* 242, Fig. 338.

1285 Spata. Chamber Tomb 1: Rectangular ivory plaque with delicate relief picture of a falling bull attacked by a lion; length *c.* 6 cm., LH III b (thirteenth century B. C.). Nat. Mus., Athens, Inv. No. 2045. – Haussoullier, 185 ff., Pl. 17; Kantor, 20, Fig. 13 (drawing); Marinatos-Hirmer, Pl. 216; Demargne, *Naissance,* 245, Fig. 339.

1286 Mycenae. From a chamber tomb in the lower town. Warrior's head with boar's tusk helmet, facing right; ivory, reverse plain. Similar pieces: Taylour, op. cit., Pl. 62; Wace, *BSA.* 49 (1954), Pl. 35 b, c; Wace-Stubbings, *A Companion to Homer* (1962), Pl. 32 b (Mycenae); Murray, *Excav. in Cyprus* (1900), 9, Pl. 2,1340 (Enkomi). Similar helmet incised on leg of a clay tripod: Wace, *BSA.* 25 (1921–23), Pl. 37 = Gray, *BICS.* 6 (1959), Pl. 9. *1286:* height 8.5 cm. (Bossert: 9.8 cm.); LH III a, b (*c.* 1300 B. C.; Bossert: *c.* 1500 B. C.). Nat. Mus., Athens, Inv. No. 2468.2470. – Tsountas, *Ephem.* 1888, Pl. 8:12; Perrot-Chipiez, VI, 811, Fig. 380; Rodenwaldt, *Fries v. Mykenai,* Fig. 30; Bossert, *Altkreta,* Fig. 57; Persson, *Dendra* I, 64, Fig. 42; Evans, *PM* IV, 870, Fig. 861; Mylonas, *AJA.* 55 (1951), 143, Fig. 7 b; Marinatos-Hirmer, Pl. 214; Demargne, 242, Fig. 337; Staïs, *Coll. Myc.* 90 f.

1287 Spata. Warrior's head, like *1286;* profile facing left, wearing a boar's tusk helmet; nail hole in lower zone of helmet; reverse flat, therefore piece probably meant as decorative inlay; height 7.4 cm.; LH III b (thirteenth century B. C.; Bossert: fifteenth century B. C.). Nat. Mus., Athens. – Haussoullier, *BCH.* 2 (1878), 185 ff., Pl. 18:2; Perrot-Chipiez, VI, 776, Fig. 366; Bossert, Fig. 60; Marinatos-Hirmer, Pl. 215; Demargne, *Naissance,* 245, Fig. 340; Korres, *Ephem.* 1966, 119 ff., Figs. 2, 3 (reverse!).

1288 Knossos. Small zoned helmet, with rows of rosettes and cheek-piece; ivory carving; reverse flat, so piece intended as inlay; height 5.5 cm., LM I. Arch. Mus., Herakleion. – Zervos, *Crète,* 427, Fig. 695.

1289 Delos. Artemision. Ivory plaque from a piece of furniture put together from many fragments. Muscular warrior with 'wasp waist' facing right; boar's tusk helmet, mitra, figure-of-eight shield, and lance; height 11.8 cm., perhaps Cypro-Levantine work; LH III b (mid-thirteenth century B. C.). Nat. Mus., Athens, Inv. No. B 7069. – Gallet de Santerre, *BCH.* 71/72 (1947/48), 148 ff., Pl. 25; Hampe, *Gymnasium* 63 (1956), 12, Pl. 10; Kantor, *Archaeology* 13 (1960), 22, Fig. 20; Wace-Stubbings, *A Companion to Homer* (1962), Pl. 27 b; Kirk, *The Songs of Homer* (1962), Pl. 2 c; Taylour, *The Mycenaeans* (1964), Pl. 64; Vermeule, Pl. 39 b; Demargne, 223, Fig. 311; Snodgrass, *Arms and Armour of the Greeks* (1967), Pl.-Fig. 5; Schweitzer, *Die geometr. Kunst Griechenlands* (1969), 157, Pl.-Fig. 180.

1290 Minet-el-Beda, near Ras Shamra, north Syria. Round ivory relief lid, crumbled at the sides. Detail of picture of seated goddess, with Semitic features, in Cretan dress, with ears of corn in her hands, between two standing wild goats; height 13.7 cm.; LH III. Louvre, Paris. – Schaeffer, *Syria* 10 (1929), Pl. 56; Bossert, *Altkreta,* Fig. 503; Kantor, *AJA.* 51 (1947), 86 ff., Pl. 22 j; Wace-Stubbings, *A Companion to Homer* (1962), Pl. 38 b; Taylour, 131, Fig. 49 (drawing); Harden, *The Phoenicians* (²1963), Pl.-Fig. 60; Samuel, *The Mycenaeans in History* (1966), 92, Fig. 31; Schachermeyr, *Ägäis u. Orient* (1967), Pl. 22:83; Marinatos, in Matz-Buchholz, *Arch. Hom.* B (1967), 14, Pl. 3 b; Wiesner, *Frühe Randkulturen des Mittelmeerraumes* (1968), 179, 181, col. ill.; Mallowan, *Ugaritica* VI (1969), 541 ff., Fig. 2.

Relief from ivory pyxis, Katsamba, Crete

Jewellery

We have made observations that also apply to articles of jewellery in the Ancient Aegean below, pp. 165 f., as preface to the corresponding section on ancient Cyprus. For the Early Minoan period, see the recent work by Keith Branigan, *The Foundations of Palatial Crete* (1970), 147 ff., while Middle Minoan is discussed by Demargne in 'Bijoux Minoens de Mallia,' *BCH.* 54 (1930), 404 ff.

Recognizable imports found in the necropolis at Perati come from Syria-Palestine *(1350—1352)*; there are close formal relations between the violin-bow fibulae from Attica and Cyprus *(1353—1355, 1819, 1820)* and jewellery in the form of figure-of-eight shields in Greece and Cyprus *(1348, 1789, 1790)*.

On questions of enamel inlay and granulation, cf. Rosenberg, *Geschichte der Goldschmiedekunst auf technischer Grundlage* II (1921) and III (1918). Lotus and melon beads were examined by Eisen (*AJA.* 34 [1930], 20 ff.); the distribution of faience beads is the subject of a study by Stone and Thomas (*PPS.*, N.S. 22 [1956], 37 ff.; cf. also Van der Sleen, 'Ancient Glass Beads', *Journ. Royal Anthrop. Inst. of Great Brit. and Ireland* 88 [1958], 203 ff.).

Glass was very widely used by the Mycenaeans as a material for jewellery (e.g. Schefold, *Meisterwerke griech. Kunst* [1960], 308 f., Nos. 552, 553); Haevernick has studied glass ornaments (*JbZMus Mainz* 7 [1960], 36 ff.; cf. also Beck, 'Glass before 1500 B.C.', *Ancient Egypt and the East* I [1934]; Mond-Myers, *Cemeteries of Armant* I [1937], 83).

Late Helladic fibulae are discussed in Blinkenberg, *Fibules Grecques et Orientales* (1926), ornamental pins in Jacobsthal, *Greek Pins and their Connections with Europe and Asia* (1956). Mötefindt has examined Early Bronze Age pins, such as *1295*, in 'Zur Geschichte der Löttechnik in vor- und frühgeschichtl. Zeit,' *BJb.* 123 (1916), 164 and Fig. 23.

For general works see in particular Marshall, *Catalogue of the Jewellery, Greek, Etruscan and Roman in the British Museum* (1911); Becatti, *Oreficerie Antiche, dalle Minoiche alle Barbariche* (1955); Higgins, *Greek and Roman Jewellery* (1961), and Bielefeld, 'Schmuck', in Matz-Buchholz, *Arch. Hom.* C (1968).

1291–1305: EARLY BRONZE AGE – MIDDLE BRONZE AGE – SHAFT GRAVE PERIOD – SEMI-PRECIOUS STONES AND GOLD

1291 Kapros, in Amorgos. Early Cycladic cist grave (Dümmler's Grave D; cf. *1077, 1362 a–c*). Five Early Bronze Age green and brown long stone beads; length 2.4–3.8 cm. Ashmolean Mus., Oxford, Inv. No. AE 162. – Renfrew, *AJA.* 71 (1967), 18, No. 23, Pl. 4.

1292 Nidri, on Leukas. From Grave Circles R I/1908 (58
1293 beads as grave goods in pithos burial: *1292*), and R XII/1910 (41 beads as grave goods in pithos burial: *1293*): Two Early-Middle Bronze Age gold necklaces of hammered bi-conical hollow beads and flattened spheroids, enlarging towards the middle of the necklace. Present location unknown (after Dörpfeld, *6. Brief über Leukas–Ithaka* [1911], Pl. 4: Mus. of Nidri). – id., *Alt-Ithaka* (1927), 287 f., suppl. 60:1,2; and *Alt-Olympia* I (1935), 305, Fig. 78 (drawing).

1294 From the Thyreatis, north Laconia. Grave find. Artistic gold necklace; the individual links consist of multiple circles of wire and hollow spheroids round the axis of the thread; suspended from them are twenty-three little chains with pendant triangular gold rattles; EH III (triangular tin pendants are typical EM II, e. g. Mochlos: Bossert, *Altkreta*, Fig. 375 c, e; Schachermeyr, *Die min. Kultur d. alten Kreta* [1964], 53, Fig. 14; also Troy II: Schmidt, *Schliemanns Sammlung*, Nos. 5878–5880). Antikenabt. d. Staatl. Mus., Berlin–Charlottenburg, Inv. No. 30987,1. – Higgins, *Greek and Roman Jewellery* (1967), Pl. 1; Bielefeld, in Matz-Buchholz, *Arch. Hom.* C (1968), 16, Pl. 3 a.

1295 The Troad. Site unknown. Early Bronze Age gold ornamental pin, bent at the bottom; rectangular ornamental plaque soldered on top, framed below and above by laterally rolled-up fillets; the front is divided into four fields filled with spirals; the whole surmounted by six partially damaged small long-necked jugs. Comparable piece from Troy: Schmidt, No. 6133; Matz, *KMT.* Pl. 6; Schachermeyr, *Die ältesten Kulturen*, Pl. 11:1; *1295*: Univ. Mus., Philadelphia, USA. – Bass, *Expedition* 8 (1966), 29 with Fig.; Bielefeld, 38, 60, Pl. 4 b.

1296 Mallia–Chrysolakkos. Grave find (first quarter of second millenium). Precious gold pendant, hammered work with granulation (filigree appliqué); the hollows in the wings and pendant rattles originally held inlays, perhaps of glass paste; width 4.9 cm.; EM III (c. 2000 B. C., Marinatos), MM I a (Branigan), MM I (Matz, Bossert, Karo). Two hornets suck at a granulated honeycomb (Bossert and Matz: bees). For the symbolism of honey gatherers and robbers, cf. *1356.* Arch.

1338   1339   1340   1341   1342   1343   1344   1345

Fig. 36 Mycenaean glass ornaments, Museum of Fine Arts, Boston

Mus., Herakleion, Inv. No. 559. – Demargne, *BCH.* 54 (1930), Pl. 19; id., *Et. Crét.* VII (1945), Pl. 66; Evans, *PM.* IV, 75, Fig. 48; Bossert, *Altkreta*, Fig. 381; Deubner, 'Mordwespen', *AA.* 1937, 308 f.; Karo, *Greifen am Thron* (1959) 21, Fig. 10; Marinatos–Hirmer, Pl. 13 lower; Matz, *KMT*., Pl. 55; id., *Kreta u. frühes Griechenland* (1962), 135 with col. ill., and p. 140; Schachermeyr, *Die minoische Kultur d. alten Kreta* (1964), Pl. 39 a; Bielefeld, Col. Pl. 1 a; Branigan, *The Foundations of Palatial Crete* (1970), Pl. 13 c.

1297 Mycenae. Grave Circle A, Shaft Grave III: Early
1298 Mycenaean large ornamental pins with rock crystal heads, LH I; according to Karo: hair pins; according to Jacobsthal: dress pins. *1298:* length 27.7 cm. Nat. Mus., Athens. – Schliemann, *Mykenae*, 232, Figs. 309, 310; Karo, *SchGr.* 186 f., Pl. 31:102, 103; K. Müller, *JdI.* 30 (1915), 300 and *AM.* 43 (1918), 153 ff., Fig. 1; Jacobsthal, *Greek Pins* (1956), 37, No. 140 *(1298)*; Bielefeld, 38, Pl. 4 e, and Marinatos, ibid., B 26 f.

1299 Mycenae. Grave Circle A, Shaft IV: Four dia-
to dems of stamped gold foil, each with a wire loop at
1302 the tapering ends; lengths 38.2–52 cm.; LH I (sequence of Figs.: *1299:* = Inv. No. 234, *1300* = 235, *1301* = 233, *1302* = 232). Five skeletons and nine gold diadems were found in this grave (cf. also Taylour, *The Mycenaeans* [1964], Pl. 27). Nat. Mus., Athens. – Karo, *SchGr.*, 71 ff., 286 f., Nos. 232–235, Pl. 36; Bielefeld, 15, Pl. 6 a–d.

1303 Mycenae. Grave Circle A, Shaft Grave III: Stamped ornamental gold plaque; miniature representation of a tripartite cult shrine with cult horns, columns, and doves; holes for attachment at the corners; height 7.5 cm., width 6.9 cm., LH I (sixteenth century B. C.). In all, five plaques stamped with the same matrix were found: two in Grave III, three in Grave IV. Nat. Mus., Athens. – Schliemann, *Mykenae* 306, Fig. 423; Fimmen, *KMK.* 67, Fig. 57; Hall, *The Civilization of Greece in the Bronze Age*, 277, Fig. 355; Bossert, *Altkreta*, Fig. 189; Karo, *SchGr.* 48, No. 26 and p. 74 f., Nos. 242–244, Pls. 18 and 27; Yavis, *Greek Altars* (1949), 31, Fig. 17; Marinatos–Hirmer, Pl. 205, centre; Wace-Stubbings, *A Companion to Homer* (1962), 468, Fig. 41 (drawing, followed by Taylour, op. cit., 72, Fig. 22).

1304 Aegina (cf. *1305*). Gold pendant, open work; central motif: opposing dogs, below them monkeys back to back. Moulded siren birds and carnelian beads suspended on little chains. Diam. of main ring 6.5 cm.; total height 10.3 cm.; MM III (seventeenth century B. C.). Brit. Mus., London, No. 92.5-20.13. – Marshall, *Brit. Mus. Cat. Jewellery* (1911), No. 765; Higgins, *BSA.* 52 (1957), Pl. a, b; id., *Greek and Roman Jewellery* (1961), 65, Pl. 4 b; Hopkins, *AJA.* 66 (1962), Pl. 51.

1305 Probably from Aegina. Treasure of Aegina (cf. *1106*). Pendant stamped from gold foil; Master of the Animals walking; Egyptian-derived form, on a base ending in lotus flowers on either side. In each hand he grasps a goose, around each of which curves a double 'snake-frame'. Five small pendant plaques are attached; eye for threading above; height 6 cm. (seventeenth century). Brit. Mus., London, No. 92.5-20.8. – Marshall, No. 762, Pls. 6, 7; Bossert, *Altkreta*, Fig. 186 a; Nilsson, *MMR.* 367, Fig. 177; Higgins, Col. Pl. B 1 after p. 64, and Pl. 3 b; Hopkins, *AJA.* 66 (1962), Pl. 52:3.

1306–1358: LH II AND LH III – GOLD, BRONZE, IRON, SEMI-PRECIOUS STONES, FAIENCE, GLASS

1306 Olous, Gulf of Mirabello, east Crete. Grave find. Gold earring, with granulated pendant in the form of a bunch of grapes; similar pieces exist that look like mulberries or bull's heads: Hutchinson, *BSA.* 51 (1956), Pl. 12 a (tholos, Kephale Hills, near Knossos); v. Matt, *Das antike Kreta* (1967), Fig. 87 (Mavro Spilio, near Knossos; cf. Zervos, *Crète* 407, Fig. 623; Marinatos–Hirmer, Pl. 120 right: 'something between a bucrane and a bunch of grapes'; cf. also Higgins, *Greek and Roman Jewellery*, Pl. 11 c). A mould indicates that it was produced in Crete (v. Matt, Fig. 84 lower); but originally it was a Cypriot form of decoration: Murray, *Excavations on Cyprus*, Pl. 8 upper right; Schaeffer, *Missions en Chypre* (1936), Pl. 36:1; L. Åström, *Arts and Crafts of the Late Cypriot Bronze Age* (1967), 30, Nos. 8, 9. *1306:* fourteenth to thirteenth century B. C. Arch. Mus., Herakleion. – Van Effenterre, 'Nécropole du Mirabello', *Et. Crét.* VIII, Pl. 47 above left.

1307 Tiryns. Hoard 1915 (LH III): Group of articles of
a–e jewellery (reduction in scale approx 1:2). Nat. Mus., Athens. Inv. No. 6212 *(1307 a):* Four necklaces, total weight 372 gr., modern threading, 71, 72, and 75 are solid gold beads; diam. 0.4 cm. – 0.7 cm.; the fourth necklace consists of 172 smaller beads; diam. 0.2–0.3 cm. One of the necklaces has a non-Aegean gold pendant with granulation. Inv. No. 6213 *(1307 b):* Seventeen granulated, tubular beads; lengths 0.6–1.2 cm.;

Fig. 37 Forms of Mycenaean jewellery

total weight 52 gr. Inv. No. 6215 *(1307 c):* Cylindrical bead of smooth red carnelian; length 2.8 cm. Inv. No. 6216 *(1307 d):* Olive-shaped bead of red carnelian; length 2.1 cm. Inv. No. 6223 *(1307 e):* Glass beads of various shapes and sizes. Karo, *AM.* 55 (1930), 124 ff., Pl. 4.

1308 Thebes, Boeotia. Palace. Cylindrical and olive-stone
a–c shaped beads of banded agate, from about three necklaces. Agate was much loved in Mycenaean times (cf. Persson, *Dendra* I, Pl. 25:2). LH III a/b. Arch. Mus., Thebes. – Touloupa. *Kadmos* 3 (1964), Fig. 3, after p. 26; id., *Delt.* 20 (1965), Chron. Pl. 276 a.

1309 Argive Heraion, Prosymna. Grave III: Necklace made of 54 squat round glass beads, smaller variegated glass beads towards the back of the neck; diam. up to 2 cm.; LH III a. Nat. Mus., Athens. – Blegen, *Prosymna,* 298, Figs. 464:6 and 601.

1310 Said to be from Aigion, north Peloponnese. From Mycenaean chamber tombs. LH ornaments of dark blue glass; 28 ornamental links, embossed, reverses flat.

Motifs: spirals, large double figure-of-eight shields, pendant lily blossoms; height of individual beads: 1.2–2.7 cm. Mus. f. Kunst u. Gewerbe, Hamburg, Inv. No. 1908,95. – v. Merddin, *AA.* 1928, 286 ff., No. 15 with comparative lit.; suppl.: *AA.* 1935, 139 f.

1311 Said to be from Attica. Grave find: Little ornamental necklace, length 28 cm.; openwork blue glass rosettes and small lentoid spacer beads of faience; moulded; LH III a/b (1450–1200 B.C.). Mus. of Art, Toledo, USA, No. 53.139. – Riefstahl, *Mus. News: The Toledo Mus. of Art*, N. S., 4, No. 2 (1961), 29 with Fig.; *A Land Called Crete* (exhibition cat.), Smith Coll., Mus., of Art, Northampton, Mass. (1967), No. 55.

1312 Ialysos, Rhodes. Grave find: Three large eight- to
to fifteen-leaved capsular rosettes stamped with a matrix,
1314 some with holes for attachment; gold, diam. 2.8–3 cm.; LH III. Mus. f. Kunst u. Gewerbe, Hamburg, Inv. No. 1927.285 a–c; – v. Merddin, *AA.* 1928, 283 ff., No. 13, Fig. 13; Hoffmann-v. Claer, *Antiker Gold- u. Silberschmuck* (1968), 3 ff., Nos. 1, 2 with Fig.

1315 Thebes, Boeotia. From Mycenaean chamber tombs near
1316 the Old Peoples' Home: Two glass pendants, cast in a mould; reverse flat, front ornamented. *1315* with linear motif like *1320*, but rolled inwards (cf. Shear, *Hesperia* 9 [1940], 290, Fig. 32 [gold]); *1316:* alternating boar's tusk helmets, the middle one inverted. LH III a. Arch. Mus., Thebes. – Unpublished.

1317 Fig. 37. Late Helladic pendants, necklace links, and
to beads moulded from glass, frequently gold plated.
1337 Usual motifs: plants, marine fauna, also architectural and geometric elements *(1323, 1329, 1332, 1333)*, miniature pictures of figure-of-eight shields *(1324,* cf. *1348* with other examples). – Bielefeld, op. cit., 28 ff., 31, Fig. 4; cf. also Higgins, *Greek and Roman Jewellery* (1961), 77 f.

1338 Fig. 36. Probably from a grave in Attica or the east
to Peloponnese. Eight Mycenaean necklace spacers, dark
1345 blue translucent glass, colour well preserved. Eyes above on each piece, also eyes below on *1341* and *1342;* moulded motifs: figure-of-eight shield *(1338,* cf. Fig. 37, *1324),* pomegranate *(1339),* blossoms *(1340, 1341, 1344),* suspended lily blossoms *(1345,* cf. Fig. 37, *1320, 1326, 1328);* LH III a/b. Mus. of Fine Arts, Boston (from Athens art market, formerly Warren Coll.). – Furtwängler, *KlSchr.* II, 428, with Fig.

1346 Stravokephalo, near Olympia. From a Mycenaean chamber tomb: Glass diadem *in situ.* The individual elements represent stylized little curls, like Fig. 37, *1336–1337* and Fig. 36, *1343*. LH III b. New Mus., Olympia. – Yalouris, *Delt.* 18 (1963), Chron. 103, Pl. 38 c; Vermeule, *BMusFA.* 65 (1967), 28, Fig. 9.

1347 Pylos, Messenia. From Tholos Tomb D: Reverse of a flattened cylindrical seal, with diagonal network pattern, granulation, gold; length 2.7 cm.; obverse: reclining griffin; LH III b. Nat. Mus., Athens, Inv. No. 7986. – Blegen, *AJA.* 58 (1954), Pl. 9:15; Matz, *CMS.* I (1964), No. 293 (further refs.).

1348 Pylos. From a tholos tomb (cf. *1347).* Miniature figure-of-eight shield; for similar shields cf. *45, 682, 719 b, 903, 945–947, 1289, 1324, 1338, 1789, 1790, 1348;* height 4.2 cm., gold; LH II (c. 1450 B.C.). Nat. Mus., Athens. – Blegen, Pl. 9:14; Hampe, *Gymnasium* 63 (1956), Pl. 7 a; Taylour, *The Mycenaeans,* Pl. 63; cf. also Amandry, *Coll. Stathatos* I, 24, No. 29 f., Pl. 8, with parallels.

1349 Perati, east Attica. Grave 147: Necklaces of beads of various types: gold, carnelian, glass; diam. of outer chain 14 cm.; length of cylindrical agate bead above left 2 cm.; LH III c. – Iakovidis, *Prakt.* 1963, Pl. 26 a.

1350 Perati. Grave 147. Three imported gold amulets. *1350.*
to *1351:* round repoussé plaques with eye and star pattern;
1352 diams. 1 and 1.3 cm.; cf. Goldman, *AJA.* 42 (1938), 46, Fig. 37 a; Petrie, *Ancient Gaza* IV (1934), Pls. 17, 18:112; Möbius, *Studia Varia* (1967), 14 ff. *1352:* pendant half moon with eye; width 1.5 cm. Similar import, unrecognized: Furtwängler, *Aigina,* 421, No. 214, Pl. 116 (silver, inverted!); cf. similar pieces from Gezer and Shechem: Thiersch, *AA.* 1909, 359, Fig. 5; Galling, *Biblisches Reallexikon* (1937), 259 f., Fig. and 27 f., Fig. 15; also one example in Mus. f. Kunst u. Gewerbe, Hamburg. – *1350–1352:* Iakovidis, Pl. 25 b.

1353 Perati. Bronze fibulae (LH III c). Grave 74: *1353;*
to length 6.2 cm., with bow turned in on itself; cf. Blegen,
1355 *Korakou* (1921), 108, Fig. 133:6 (Iakovidis, *Delt.* 19 [1964], Chron. Pl. 90 c). Grave 155: *1354;* length 6.9 cm., with angular bow; cf. Morricone, *ASAtene* 27/28 (1965/66), 134, Fig. 119, Kos–Langada, Grave 20 (Iakovidis, *Prakt.* 1963, Pl. 27 b). Grave 65: *1355,* length 7 cm., regular, flat form; cf. *Et. Crét.* XI (1956), Pl. 51:8, Mallia, House E; LM III b (Iakovidis, *Delt.* 19 [1964], Chron. Pl. 90 d). For the types of fibula in the Aegean Late Bronze Age, cf. Müller–Karpe, *JdI.* 77 (1962), Fig. 33 after p. 144; and Desborough, *Last Myc.,* Pl. 21.

1356 Thebes, Boeotia. From Mycenaean chamber tombs, near the Old Peoples' Home. Gold finger-ring, with soldered-on bee in the round; unusual and excellent work; length of bee 1.2 cm.; inner diam. of hoop, barely 2 cm.; LH III. Arch. Mus., Thebes. Unpublished. – For the symbolic value of ornaments in the form of bees, wasps, hornets, crickets, cf. *1296,* also: Cook, 'The Bee in Greek Mythology', *JHS.* 15 (1895), 1 ff.; Murray, *Excavations in Cyprus,* Pl. 8 upper left, and Pl. 11,397.398 (Enkomi); Telfer, 'Bees in Clement of Alexandria', *Journ. of Theol. Stud.* 28 (1927), 167 ff.; Ramsay, 'Wolf-Priests, Goat-Priests, Ox-Priests, Bee-Priests', *Asianic Elements in Greek Civilization* (1927), Ch. VII; Ransome, *The Sacred Bee in Ancient Times and Folklore* (1937); Elderkin, 'The Bee of Artemis', *AJPh.* 60 (1939), 203 ff.; Schefold, *Meisterwerke griechischer Kunst* (1960), 186, No. 199 (bronze, Attic-Archaic, cricket), 310, No. 566 (gold, fifth century B. C. from Patras, bee); Marinatos, *Ergon* 1962, 116, Fig. 140 (gold bees; Peristeria, tholos tomb; cf. Bielefeld, in Matz–Buchholz, *Arch. Hom.* C [1958], 29); Vermeule, *Greece in the Bronze Age,* Pl. 5:3,5 (bees on EH Lerna seals; bees or spider-like insects also on EH seal impressions: Frödin–Persson, *Asine* [1938], 235, Fig. 172:5). Also: Mus. f. Kunst u. Gewerbe, Hamburg, Inv. No. 1966.85 a, b (gold earrings, eighth to seventh centuries B. C., Iran, crickets); Böhme, 'Unsterbliche Grillen', *JDI.* 69 (1954), 49 ff.; Higgins, *Greek and Roman Jewellery,* Pl. 24 b (bee or cricket, silver, Louvre).

1357 Thebes. From Mycenaean chamber tombs near the Old Peoples' Home. Plain finger-ring of iron, finger bone still inside!, very corroded; width 2.5–3 cm.; LH III a/b; extremely precious during Bronze Age; cf., for iron, *638* and *675,* and, for iron jewelry in Late Mycenaean times, Bielefeld, in Matz–Buchholz, *Arch. Hom.* C (1968), 34 f., 47.

1358 Perati. Grave 74: Finger-ring of bronze, with soldered double spiral; length 2.8 cm., inner width of ring: barely 2 cm., LH III c (similar rings also in Yugoslavian Macedonia and central European tumulus graves; cf. Müller-Karpe, *JdI.* 77 [1962], 87, Fig. 5:16; Desborough, *PPS.* 31 [1965], 224; Bouzek, *Homerisches Griechenland* [1969], 95, Fig. 37 map, 98, Fig. 36:18). – Iakovidis, *Perati* I, 85, No. M 115, II, 293, Fig. 127, Pl. 27 b.

Seals and signet rings

This group of finds is among the most important examples of ancient Aegean small-scale art—including, not only two-dimensional art, but in many cases also sculpture in the round *(1185)*; it can also count as 'jewellery' or 'insignia of honour,' according to the manner of wearing the article and its function. Matz shed much light on Minoan art structures by establishing the foundations of a systematic analysis of seals (*Die frühkretischen Siegel* [1928]). His pupil Biesantz carried on his work (*Kretisch-mykenische Siegelbilder* [1954]), and studied the question of 'right' and 'left' in the pictures, i.e. the question of the 'intention' of the artists—original seal or impression? Finally, we owe to the initiative of the master, Matz, the monumental, but as yet incomplete, *Corpus der minoischen und mykenischen Siegel*, of which eight volumes have appeared to date.

Besides the work by Xenaki-Sakellariou, *Les Cachets Minoens de la Collection Giamalakis* (1958), summarized in 'Die mykenische Siegelglyptik,' *Stud. Mediterr. Arch.* IX (1964), another essential work for the study of seals is Kenna, *Cretan Seals* (1960; cf. Buchholz's review in *OLZ.* 61 [1966], 123 ff.). Furtwängler laid the groundwork in 1900 with his work *Antike Gemmen.*

For Cypriot glyptic, cf. pp. 164 f., where we also trace the interconnection between the art of cutting seal-stones in the Aegean and in the Eastern Mediterranean, including the East. Their formal development was influenced by imports (cf., e.g., cylinder seals in Greece and Crete: *1374—1380*).

Matz has also shown how some seals serve as outstanding evidence of old beliefs: 'Göttererscheinung und Kultbild im minoischen Kreta' (Diss., Akad. Mainz, 1958; cf. *1384*). Reichel had already examined the iconography on large gold rings in his work *Über vorhellenische Götterkulte* (1897); cf. Persson, *Religion of Greece in Prehistoric Times* (1942); and Nilsson, *Minoan-Mycenaean Religion* (2nd ed., 1950). The motifs we have chosen for illustration are: a priestess at the altar: *1397*, divinities: *1381, 1385, 1400*, and cult vessels: *1406*.

We have some knowledge of artistic impressions of the external and internal appearance of the male face from funeral masks *(1243, 1244)* and an unusual group of Minoan gems *(1398, 1399)*. These portraits seize upon the characteristic points in profile view; the representation of rank and dignity, the personality and temperament of the person depicted, seems so individual as to suggest that here we have the first achievement of genuine portraiture in Europe; cf. Biesantz, *MarbWPr.* 1958, 9 ff.; Marinatos, in *Festschrift Wegner zum 60. Geburtstag*; Blegen, *AJA.* 66 (1962), 245 ff., and Buchholz, *In Memoriam Bossert* (1965), 139 ff.

1359-1374: NEOLITHIC PERIOD – EARLY BRONZE AGE – MIDDLE BRONZE AGE

1359 to 1361 Sesklo, Thessaly. Early and late Neolithic stamp-seals of clay; heights 4.8 cm., 3.2 cm., and 4.4 cm. On oval and round seal surfaces: maze motifs, dotted circles, and groups of chevrons. Possibly used for stamping on body; similar seals: Giannopoulos, *AM.* 38 (1913), 29 f.; Theocharis, *Thessalika* 2 (1959), 64, Fig. 28 (from Pyrasos and Philia); Schachermeyr, *Ägäis u. Orient* (1967), Pl. 9:36,37. *1359-1361*: Nat. Mus., Athens, Inv. Nos. 6013, 6012, 6016. – Tsountas, *DS.* 340 f., Figs. 271–273; Zervos, *Naissance* I, 256, Figs. 296, 297; Kenna, 'Two Ancient Trade Routes', *AAA.* 1 [1968], 278 ff. *[1361]*; Müller-Karpe, *Hdb. d. Vorgesch.* II, Pl. 133:31, 29, 30; Matz, *CMS.* I, 4 ff., Nos. 1–3.

1362 a-c Kapros in Amorgos. Dümmler's Early Cycladic Cist Grave D (cf. *1077, 1291*). Cylinder seal with loop; ornament on cylinder: concentric groups of circles, tangents, and chevrons; underneath also patterned (chevrons); height 4.4 cm.; without eye 3.3 cm.; greenish marble. Ashmolean Mus., Oxford, Inv. No. AE 159. – Dümmler, *AM.* 11 (1886), 20, Pl. 1 D 6; Renfrew, *AJA.* 71 (1967), 18, No. 19, Pl. 4; Buchholz, in Bass, *Cape Gelidonya* (1967), 152, No. 3 (earlier lit.).

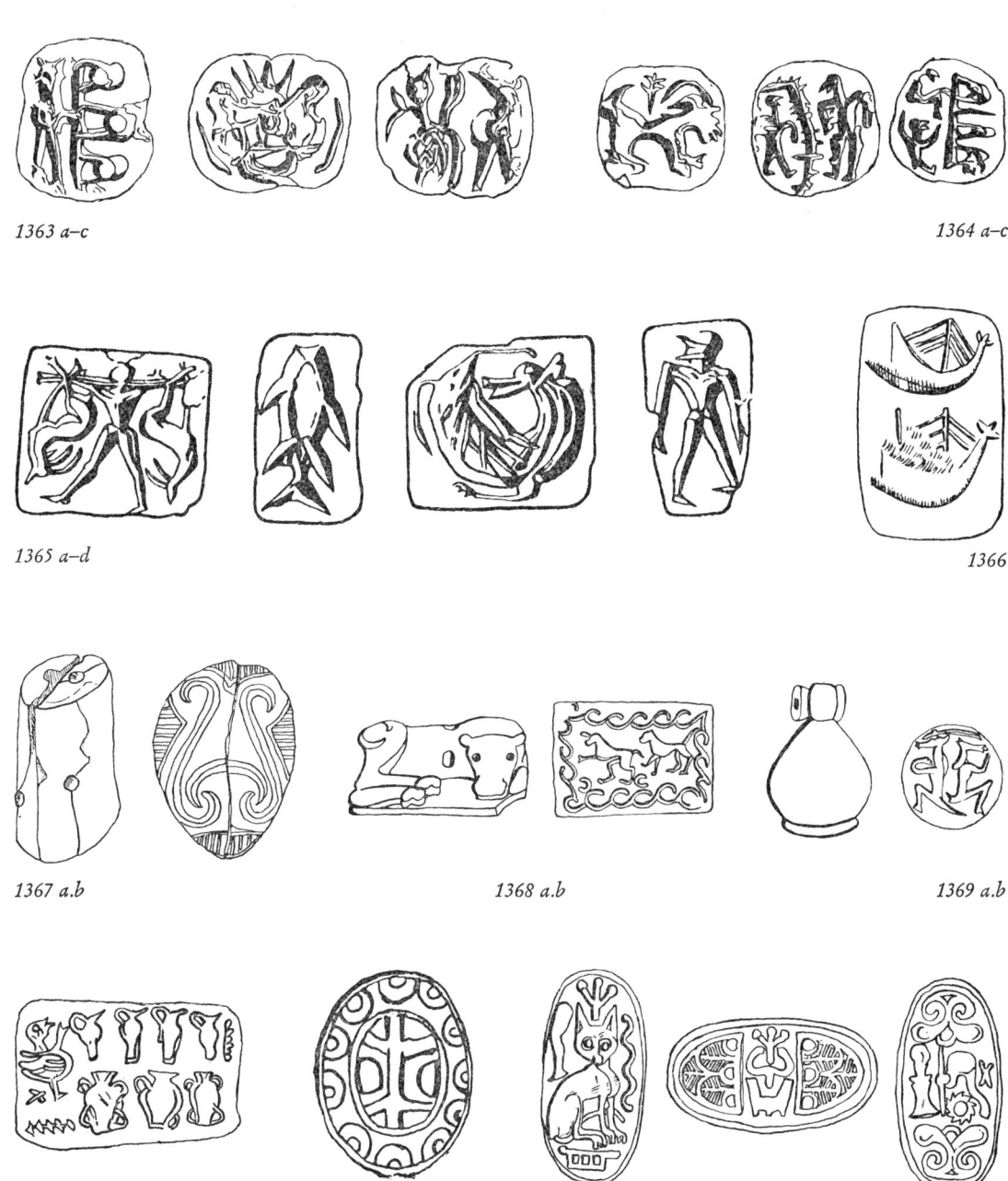

1363 a–c Fig. 38: Crete. Place of origin unknown. Three-sided prism bead of yellow steatite; length 2.3 cm.; EM. Side *a*: man carrying vases by a pole; side *b*: perhaps lion mask; side *c*: insect and front part of animal. Ashmolean Mus., Oxford, Inv. No. 1938.742. – Kenna, *Cretan Seals* (1960), 87, No. 1, Pl. 1; id., *AA*. 1964, 918, No. 4 a–c.

1364 a–c Fig. 38: Crete. Place of origin unknown. Three-sided prism bead of green steatite; length 1.8 cm.; EM. Side *a*: wild goat; side *b*: two figures with implement; side *c*: two seated men and vessels suspended from pole. Ashmolean Mus., Oxford, Inv. No. 1938.743. – Kenna, *Cretan Seals*, 87, No. 2, Pl. 1; id., *AA*. 1964, 918, No. 5 a–c.

Fig. 38 Early Cretan seals

113

1365 Fig. 38: Mallia. Four-sided rectangular bead of yellow
a–d steatite; length 1.4 cm.; EM. Side *a:* hunter with prey; side *b:* tunny; side *c:* quadruped, very contorted; side *d:* man with splayed legs. Ashmolean Mus., Oxford, Inv. No. 1938.763. – Kenna, *Cretan Seals,* 92, No. 36, Pl. 2.

1366 Fig. 38: Crete. Place of origin unknown. Three-sided prism bead of white steatite; length 1.4 cm.; EM. Two ships with masts; on the other two sides (not shown): horse and three crouching men. Ashmolean Mus., Oxford, Inv. No. 1938.757. – Evans, *PM.* I, 120, Fig. 89, and IV, 620, Fig. 462; Kenna, 94, No. 50, Pl. 3.

1367 Fig. 38: Mochlos. Grave II: Ivory seal with palmette
a, b motif on stamp side; height 3.5 cm.; EM II; repaired with bronze rivet. Arch. Mus., Herakleion, Inv. No. 743. – Seager, *Explorations in the Island of Mochlos* (1912), 34 f., No. II, 41, Fig. 12, and p. 108; Evans, *PM.* I, 94; Kenna, 18, Figs. 25, 26; id., *AA.* 1964, 917, Fig. 1 a, b; Platon, *CMS.* II, 1 (1969), 563, No. 472 (with refs.).

1368 Fig. 38: Platanos, Messara. EM round grave: Ivory
a, b seal, in the form of a reclining ox; stamp surface: two baboon-like lions in spiral frame (impression: facing left); length 3 cm.; EM II. Arch. Mus., Herakleion, Inv. No. 1044. – Kenna, *Cretan Seals,* 23, Fig. 33; id., *AA.* 1964, 925, Fig. 12 a, b; Matz, *Kreta u. frühes Griechenland* 63, with col. ill.; Platon, 289, No. 253.

1369 Fig. 38: Mochlos. Grave II (cf. *1367*). Ivory seal;
a, b stamp surface: two dog-monkeys, back to back; height 1.8 cm., diam. 1.2 cm.; EM II. Arch. Mus., Herakleion, Inv. No. 744. – Seager, op. cit., 33 f., No. 42, Fig. 11, and p. 108 f.; Kenna, *Cretan Seals,* 18, Figs. 27, 28, and *AA.* 1964, 918, Fig. 8 a, b; Platon, 564, No. 473 (with bibl.).

1370 Fig. 38: Mallia. Stamp-seal, with loop and rectangular stamping surface, steatite; length 2.6 cm.; EM III. Seal picture: bird, four jugs, three amphorae and branches. Arch. Mus., Herakleion, Inv. No. 1399. – Chapoutier, *BCH.* 70 (1946), 79, and *Et. Crét.* VI, 69, Fig. 45; Kenna, 22, Fig. 32, and *AA,* 1964, 925, Fig. 13 b.

1371 Fig. 38: Palaikastro, east Crete. Trial excavation in N 7, under LM I b – floor. Oval scarab impression (1.7 × 2 cm.) on handle of vessel of yellow clay with brown insertions; EM III/MM I. Arch. Mus., Herakleion. – Sackett–Popham, *BSA.* 60 (1965), 301, Fig. 18 and p. 304, No. 21.

1372 Fig. 38. Lasithi district, east Crete (Kenna, following
a–c Evans: central Crete, 1898). Three-sided reddish brown carnelian bead with long oval stamping surfaces; length 1.8 cm.; MM II; probably royal seal. Hieroglyphs, side *a:* cat and silphium, leg and snake, lattice; side *b:* throne, fork, silphium in framed panel; side *c:* two implement symbols, toothed wheel, and capital 'X'. Ashmolean Mus., Oxford, Inv. No. 1938.791. – Evans, *Scripta Minoa* I (1909), 153, No. 23, Pl. 2 and *PM.* I, 277, Fig. 207 a; Grumach, in *Minoica: Festschr. zum 80. Geburtstag v. Sundwall* (1958), 162 ff., Fig. 1 a–c; Kenna, *Cretan Seals,* 113, No. 174, Fig. 74, Pl. 8; id., *AA.* 1964, 918, Fig. 2.

1373 Crete. Site unknown. Three-sided prism of dark brown steatite, rounded corners; length 1.4 cm.; MM I. Side *a:* walking man; side *b:* wild goat; side *c:* diagonally grooved amphora (original and impression). Private colln., England. – Matz, *CMS.* VIII (1966), 127, No. 100.

1374 Herakleion. West border of town. Imported Babylonian cylinder seal of haematite; god in slit coat and worshippers, cuneiform inscription: 'Awel Ishtar' (or 'Apillum'), 'son of Mardukmushalim, servant of Nabu'. Hamurapi period. Arch. Mus., Herakleion, Inv. No. 132. – Evans, *PM.* II, 265 f., Fig. 158; Kenna, *AJA.* 72 (1968), 328, Pl. 106:9; Buchholz, in Bass, *Cape Gelidonya* (1967), 154, No. 22 (with bibl.).

1375–1408: LATE BRONZE AGE

1375 Thebes, Boeotia. Palace: Hoard find of numerous cyl-
to inder seals of various dates and origins, including Cas-
1377 site seals (Brinkman, *Zeitschr. f. Assyriologie* 59 [1969], 231 ff. for seal inscribed: 'Meli-Sihu/Shipak'). Arch. Mus., Thebes. – Touloupa, *Kadmos* 3 (1964), 25 f., Figs. 6–8; Buchholz, 157 f., No. 61 ff. (with bibl.); cf. also Opificius, *Ugarit-Forschungen* 1 [1969], 109, No. 77).

1378 Tiryns. Hoard 1915 (cf. *1307*). Imported northern
a, b Syrian cylinder seal; haematite; height 2.8 cm. Antithetical group: two demons with tails, hoofs, and animal ears hold staff crowned by bud, above this winged sun; bearded heads facing forward. Beside this group are two pictorial zones; above: reclining wild goats and griffins; above this an eagle; below it a band of circles; below this a tree of life between two kneeling wild goats; fifteenth/fourteenth century B. C. Nat. Mus., Athens, Inv. No. 6214. – Philadelpheus–Karo, *Delt.* 2 (1916), Appendix 17, Fig. 6; Karo, *AA.* 1916, 146, Fig. 3; id., *AM.* 55 (1930), *126, Pl. 2:6;* Buchholz, 158, No. 100 (complete bibl.).

1379 Mycenae. Kalkani Necropolis, Chamber Tomb 517: Cylinder seal of faience; height c. 2.3 cm. Man in long robes, hands on chest, between tree of life and leaping wild goat; linear, threadlike style; LH I/II; sixteenth to fourteenth centuries B. C. (Wace and Schaeffer), eleventh century B. C. (Hogarth). Origin disputed: Cicilian (Wace), Cypriot (Hall), Syrian (Hogarth, Schaeffer, Porada); style not determinable (Nilsson). Nat. Mus., Athens. – Wace, 'Chamber Tombs', *Archaeologia* 82 (1932), 73, No. 32, Fig. 28, Pl. 35:32; id., *Mycenae* (1949/64), Pl.-Fig. 110 b; Buchholz, 157, No. 52 (complete bibl.).

1380 Perati, east Attica. Chamber Tomb 142, Find No. 267: Cypriot cylinder seal, haematite; height 3.4 cm.; LH III c. Setting: enthroned Egyptian god; in front and below him: Cypro-Minoan script symbols; flying bird, other beings with animal heads and wings. Excellent workmanship. – Buchholz, 157, No. 55 (with refs.); also Iakovidis, *Prakt.* 1962, 20 f., Pl. 10 a; id., *Festschr. f. Grumach* (1967), 143 ff.; Iakovidis–Kenna, in *Charisterion Orlandos* II, 324 f., Pl. 66 c; Daux, *BCH.* 87 (1963), 714, Fig. 26.

1381 Tiryns. Hoard find 1915 (cf. *1307, 1378*): Two gold
a, b rings with oval shield and partial loop; lengths of
1382 shields 5.7 cm. *(1381)* and 3.4 cm. (1382); gilt overfilling of other metal, perhaps lead. Motifs hammered, not cast. Picture on large ring: procession of genii with libation jugs before enthroned goddess. Small ring: mythical scene, ship, and palace. Nat. Mus., Athens, Inv. Nos. 6208 *(1381),* 6209 *(1382).* – For refs., cf. *1378*; also, Schweitzer, *Herakles,* 27, Fig. 3 *(1382);* V. Müller, *JdI.* 42 (1927), 1 ff., Fig. 1 *(1381);* v. Salis, *Theseus u. Ariadne,* 27 ff., Figs. 29–31 *(1382);* detailed: Karo, *AM.* 55 (1930), 121 ff., Pls. 2,3, Suppl. 30; Evans, *PM.* IV, 460, Fig. 385; Marinatos–Hirmer, Pl. 207 above; Ventris–Chadwick, *Documents in Myc. Greek* (1956), 333, Fig. 21; and Taylour, *Mycenaeans,* 73, Fig. 23 (drawing, *1381*); Mylonas, *Myc. and the Myc. Age* (1966), Pl.-Fig. 123:16; Matz, *CMS.* I, 202 ff., Nos. 179, 180 (with extensive bibl.).

1383 Mycenaean. Grave Circle A, Shaft Grave IV: A large gold signet ring with oval bezel, found near a female skeleton; diam. of shield 3.5 cm. Battle scene (so-called 'Battle in the Glen'), left and right as original, not impression; LH I (sixteenth century B. C.). Nat. Mus., Athens, Inv. No. 241. – Karo, *SchGr.* 73,306, Pl. 24; Biesantz, *Kret.-myk. Siegelbilder* (1954), Pl. 1:1 a, b; Hafner, *Gesch. d. griech. Kunst* (1961), 31, Fig. 15; Matz, *Kreta u. frühes Griechenland* (1962), 171 with col. ill.; id., *CMS.* I, 27 f., No. 16 (with refs.).

1384 Isopata, near Knossos. Royal tomb: Gold ring with cult scene of woman in ecstatic dance and epiphany of the gods; right and left as original; length of shield 2.6 cm.; MM III (Karo), LM II (Zervos), late LM I (1550–1530 B. C.). Arch. Mus., Herakleion, Inv. No. 424. – Evans, *Archaeologia* 65 (1914), 10, Fig. 16; Biesantz, Pl. 1:3 a, b; Zervos, *Crète,* 411, Fig. 632; Karo, *Greifen am Thron* (1959), 30 Fig. 15; Marinatos–Hirmer, Fig. 111 upper; Matz, *Kreta u. frühes Griechenland,* 135, col. ill.; and, *Göttererscheinung und Kultbild im minoischen Kreta* (1958), Fig. 3; Brandt, *Gruß u. Gebet* (1965), 5, Pl. 1:1; Simon, *Die Götter der Griechen* (1969), 271, Fig. 260.

1385 Crete. Site unknown. Gold signet ring; length of bezel 2.2 cm., width 1.5 cm.; lower side hollow; hoop hammered; 9.05 gr. Female worshipper with flowers before seated goddess with mirror; behind: shrine. Thematically comparable seal: worshipper before enthroned goddess: Matz, *CMS.* I, 117, No. 101; Brandt, op. cit., Pl. 1:3. *1385:* LM I/II. Antikenabt., Staatl. Museen, Berlin-Charlottenburg, Inv. No. FG 1. – Furtwängler, *Die antiken Gemmen* I (1900), Pl. 2:21 and II, 10; Evans, *JHS.* 21 (1901), 190, Fig. 64; Mylonas, *Myc. and the Myc. Age* (1966), Pl.-Fig. 127:4; Bielefeld, in Matz–Buchholz, *Arch. Hom.* C (1968), Pl. 2 a.

1386 Probably from Crete. Site unknown. Gold ring with low relief on oval, cast bezel: antithetical group (bulls, for this motif cf. Matz, *CMS.* I, 74, No. 58); length 2.3 cm., weight 7.46 gr. LH II/III (fifteenth century B. C.). Mus. f. Kunst u. Gewerbe, Hamburg, Inv. No. 1924, 176. – v. Mercklin, *AA.* 1928, 281 f., No. 11, Fig. 11; Hoffmann v. Claer, *Antiker Gold- u. Silberschmuck* (1968), 171, No. 107.

1387 Mycenae. Grave Circle A, Shaft Grave III: Lentoid gem; motif: spiral rosette formed of ten small circles linked by tangents and a larger central ornament; brown onyx, diam. 2.4 cm. Nat. Mus., Athens, Inv. No. 118. – Karo, *SchGr.,* Pl. 25,118; Hafner, *Gesch. d. griech. Kunst* (1961), 41, Fig. 31; Matz, *CMS.* I, 25, No. 14.

1388 Fig. 39: Mycenae. Grave Circle A, Shaft Grave III: Rectangular gold spacer, with relief of a duel. The 'object hard to interpret' belonging to the assailant and running parallel to the spear of the victim is the empty sword sheath on his shoulder strap! 1.8×1.2 cm. Nat. Mus., Athens, Inv. No. 35. – Karo, *SchGr,* Pl. 24:35; Hampe, *Gymnasium,* 63 (1956), 13, Fig. 8; Matz, *CMS.* I, 22, No. 11 (with bibl.).

1389 Fig. 39: Region of Knossos. Cushion-shaped flat cylinder of bronze, length 0.5 cm. Ship with patterned sail; spiral hook on right in front of ship; very delicate work, LM I a. Ashmolean Mus., Oxford, Inv. No. 1938.957. – Evans, *PM.* II, (1928), 243, Fig. 140; Kenna, *Cretan Seals,* 122, No. 228, pl. 9; id. Marb-WPr. 1968, 2, Fig. 1; Schachermeyr, *Die minoische Kultur des alten Kreta* (1964), 205, Fig. 118.

1390 Fig. 39: Neighbourhood of Knossos. Amygdaloid gem with picture of sailing boat; black stone with red veining; length c. 2.6 cm.; LM I. Formerly Evans Colln. – Fimmen, *KMK.* 114, Fig. 103; Evans *PM.* IV, 828, Fig. 807; Schachermeyr, *Ägäis u. Orient* (1967), 61 f., Pl. 62,228.

1391 Fig. 39: Knossos. Small Palace: Fragment with two superimposed seal impressions of ship and horse, LM II. Arch. Mus., Herakleion. – Evans, *PM.* IV. 827, Fig. 805; Schachermeyr, *Anthropos* 46 (1951), 723; Kenna, *Cretan Seals,* 58, Fig. 121; and *AA.* 1964, 917, Fig. 3; Wiesner, in Matz–Buchholz, *Arch. Hom.* F (1968), 36 f., Fig. 5 a.

1392 Fig. 39: Mirabello, east Crete. Lentoid gem of olive-green jasper with mottling; diam. 1.6 cm. Motif: three swans on rippled water; fine harmonious composition; LM II. Ashmolean Mus., Oxford, Inv. No. 1938.971. – Evans, *PM.* IV, 492, Fig. 426; Kenna, *Cretan Seals,* 131, No. 297, p. 61, Fig. 131, Pl. 12 and 23; id., *AA.* 1964, 938, Fig. 24.

1393 Fig. 39: Kalyvia near Phaistos, Messara. Grave IX,
a, b near the head of the skeleton: Three-sided prism; LM III a. Side *a:* contorted lion; side *b:* two hippopotamus-genii facing each other; side *c:* not reproduced. Length c. 1.7 cm. Arch., Mus., Herakleion. – Savignoni, *Mont. Ant.* 14 (1904), 519 f., Fig. 10 b, c; Kenna, AA. 1964, 945 ff., Fig. 30 a, b.

1394 Fig. 39: Knossos. Lentoid gem of rock crystal; excellently cut lion, adapted to the circular contour of the gem (torsion); diam. 2 cm.; LM II. Ashmolean Mus., Oxford, Inv. No. 1938.1058. – Evans, *PM.* IV, 588; Fig. 583; Kenna, 938, Fig. 26; and *Cretan Seals,* 55, Fig. 115, No. 315, Pl. 12.

1395 Fig. 39: Hagia Triada, south Crete. Impression of a metal signet ring: horses and wagon facing right (on this theme, cf. Alexiou, 'Neue Wagendarstellungen aus Kreta', *AA.* 1964, 785); impression of the same signet ring also in Sklavokampo (Marinatos, *Ephem.* 1939–41, 90, No. 8, Pl. 4:8; Marinatos–Hirmer, Pl. 111 lower; and Schachermeyr, *Die minoische Kultur des alten Kreta*

1396 Fig. 39: Isopata. Royal tomb, near Knossos: Seal of light blue chalcedony set in gold; cushion-shaped, flattened cylinder. Two men and huge dog facing right (here facing left, impression); length 2.7 cm.; LM III a/b. Arch. Mus., Herakleion, Inv. No. 900. – Evans, *Tomb of the Double Axes*, 9, Fig. 14; and *PM*. II, 766, Fig. 496; Bossert, *Altkreta*, Fig. 396 c; Kenna, *Cretan Seals*, 66, Fig. 143; and *Festschr. f. Matz* (1962), 9 with Fig. and Pl. 1; Matz, *Kreta u. frühes Griechenland*, 138 with col. ill.

1397 Pylos–Routsi, Peloponnese. Tholos Tomb II, latest burial: Lentoid gem of carnelian; diam. 1.7 cm.; excellently preserved; picture here is from impression (original motif faces right): woman in cult skirt with two lilies in her left hand, before an altar with cult horns and branches; LH II (fifteenth century B.C.). Nat. Mus., Athens, Inv. No. 8323. – Marinatos–Hirmer, Fig. 208:4; Marinatos, in Matz-Buchholz, *Arch. Hom. B* (1967), 5, Fig. 1 a; Matz, *CMS*. I, 315, No. 279.

1398 Knossos. Small Palace: Lentoid gem of black steatite; diam. 1.5 cm.; head of bearded man in left profile (here: impression) crafty Oriental; engraving on reverse: bull's head. MM III/LM I. Arch. Mus., Herakleion, Inv. No. 1419. – Evans, *PM*. IV., 216 ff., Fig. 167 b; and p. 489, Fig. 419, Pl. 54 k; Matz, *KMT*. 68, Pl. 50:1; Zervos, *Crète*, 416, Fig. 646 centre; Biesantz, *MarbWPr*. 1958, 1, Pl. 10:3; Marinatos–Hirmer, Pl. 118:5; Marinatos, *Festschr. f. Wegner zum 60. Geburtstag* (1962), 9 ff., Fig. 2; Kenna, *Festschr. f. Matz*, (1962), 5 f., with Fig.

1399 Mycenae. Grave Circle B, Grave Gamma: Lentoid gem with bearded head in profile, very expressive 'portrait'; amethyst; diam. 1 cm.; MH III (Biesantz), beginning of LM I. Nat. Mus., Athens, Inv. No. 8708. – Mylonas, *Anc. Myc.*, 139, Fig. 49; and, *Myc. and the Myc. Age*, Pl.-Fig. 98; Biesantz, *MarbWPr*. 1958, Pl. 10:4; Blegen, *AJA*. 66 (1962), Pl. 61:7; Marinatos–Hirmer, Pl. 212; Marinatos, *Festschr. f. Wegner zum 60. Geburtstag*, 9 ff.; Kenna, loc. cit., 6, Pl. 1:1; Matz, *CMS*. I, 13, No. 5.

1400 Knossos. Warrior Tomb III, near the new hospital: Lentoid onyx, with goddess between two winged griffins; crown of snakes with double axe on head of female figure (for this pictorial type, cf. Reusch, *Minoica-Festschr. z. 80. Geburtstag v. Sundwall* [1958], 354); height 3.4 cm., width 1.3 cm.; LM II (1450 to 1400). Arch. Mus., Herakleion. – Hood-de Jong, *BSA*. 47 (1952), 272 f., No. III, 20, Fig. 16, Pl. 54 c; Zervos, *Crète*, 410, Fig. 629; Buchholz, *Zur Herkunft der kretischen Doppelaxt* (1959), 18, n. 11; Spartz, 'Das Wappenbild des Herrn u. der Herrin der Tiere in der min.-myk. u. frühgriech. Kunst' (thesis, Munich 1962), 13 f., 100, No. 11; Demargne, *Naissance*, 177, Fig. 243.

1401 Phaistos, south Crete. Lentoid seal stone, with bull-man in violent contortions, adapted to the shape of the seal; 'minotaur'; meteorite; after 1500 B. C. Arch. Mus., Herakleion, formerly Giamalakis Colln. – Xenaki-Sakkelariou, *Les Cachets Minoens de la Coll. Giamalakis* (1958), 63, No. 379; Marinatos–Hirmer, Pl. 119:3.

1402 Greece or Crete. Site unknown. Lentoid gem of red jasper diam. 2.1 cm. Lion attacking antelope; forceful composition, adapted to the circular shape. LM/LH III a (c. 1400 B. C.). Mus. d'Art et d'Histoire, Geneva, Inv. No. 1965–20304. – Vollenweider, *Cat. des Sceaux, cylindres et intailles* I (1967), No. 197, Pl. 76:1–4.

1403 Perati, east Attica. Grave 142: Modern impression from a lentoid gem, with three overlapping delicate roebucks; excellent work, certainly earlier than the grave (LH III c); diam. 2.1 cm. – Iakovidis, in *Charisterion Orlandos* II (1966), 320 ff., Pl. 66 b; and *Prakt*. 1962, Pl. 10 b.

1404 Perati. Grave 128, Find No. 258: Amygdaloid gem with engraved picture of a chamois, facing right, falling to its knees, and with head turned back; length 2.2 cm.; LH III. – Iakovidis, *Charisterion Orlandos* II, Pl. 65 c; and, *Prakt*. 1961, Pl. 7 a.

1405 Phylakopi, Melos. Necropolis: Amygdaloid gem of dark green jasper; length 1.9 cm.; symmetrical vase-like design of six deep lunettes and central circle; LM II. Staatl. Kunstsammlungen, Kassel. – Zazoff, *AA*. 1965, 9 ff., No. 4, Fig. 1:4; and *Antike Gemmen in Deutschen Sammlungen, Kassel*, 188, No. 4, Pl. 85 (with earlier lit.).

1406 Arcades–Aphrati, southern part of the Cretan eparchy Pediados. Amygdaloid gem of red and white agate; length 2 cm., width 1.5 cm.; reproduced here from impression. Two cult jugs and branches. LM I. Arch. Mus., Herakleion, Inv. No. 891. – Nilsson, *MMR*. 263, Fig. 128; Kenna, *Cretan Seals*, 68, n. 2; id., *Stud. Mediterr. Arch.* XXIV (1969), 14, Pl. 3:11.

1407 Crete. Place of origin unknown. Amygdaloid gem, dark green jasper, with brownish veining; length 2 cm.; octopus with six tentacles formed from lunettes, highly stylized; LM III. Mus. f. Kunst u. Gewerbe, Hamburg, formerly Jantzen Colln. – Zazoff, *AA*. 1963, 42 ff., No. 1, Fig. 1:1.

1408 Perati. Grave 147: Lower side of imported scarab, with Egyptian hieroglyphic inscription; 1.5 × 1.1 cm. Other scarabs from Perati: *Delt*. 19 (1964), Chron. Pl. 89; and *BCH*. 83 (1959), 509, Figs. 34, 35; scarabs from other Aegean sites: Fimmen, *KMK*. 176 ff.; unusual inscribed scarabs: formerly Spencer–Churchill Colln., now in Brit. Mus. (No. 1966.3–28.23); Higgins, *JHS*. 87 (1967), Arch. Rep. 52, Fig. 17; *Kadmos* 2 (1963), 1 ff. *1408*: Iakovidis, *Prakt*. 1963, 37, Pl. 25 a.

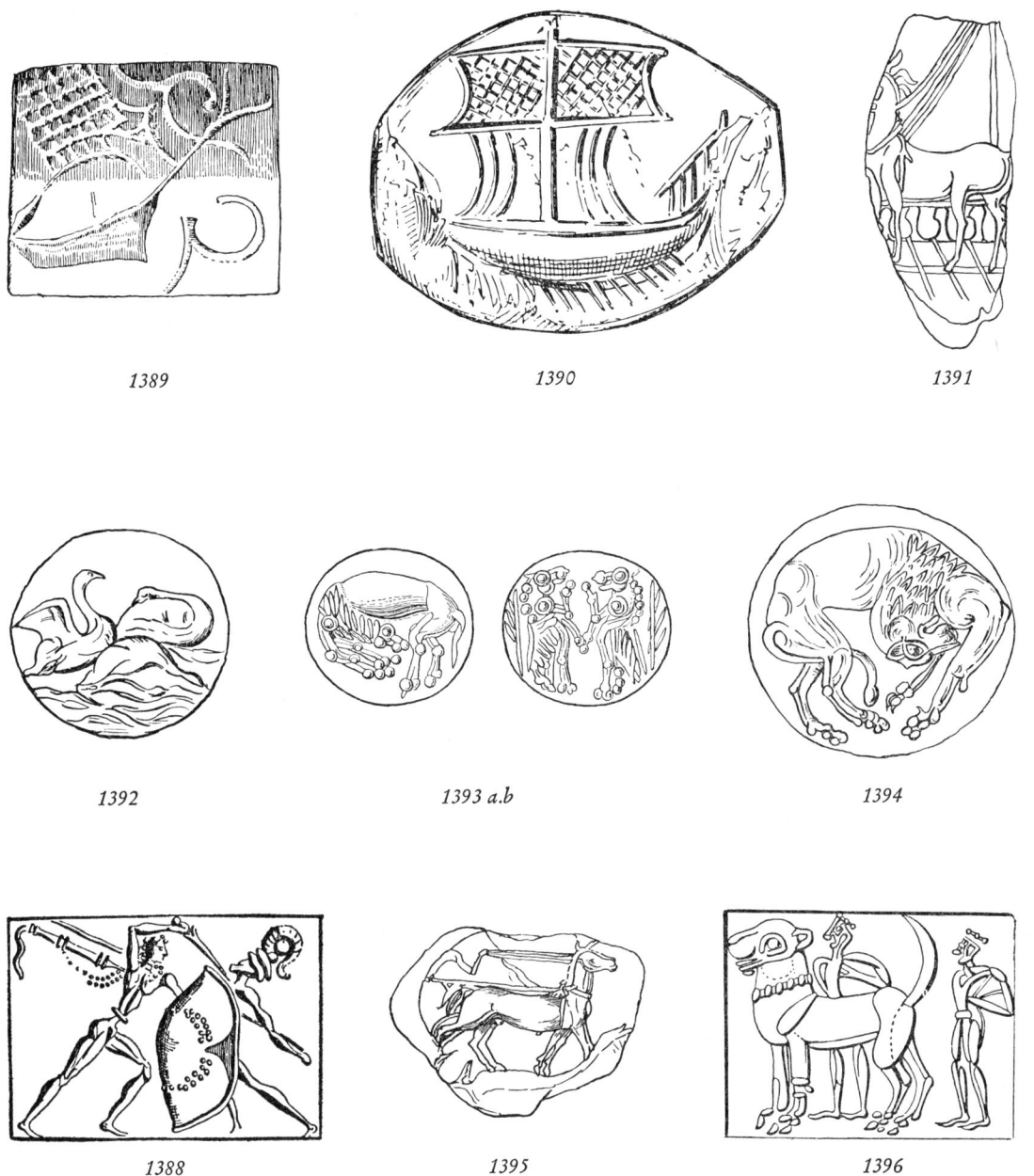

Fig. 39 Cretan-Mycenaean seals, spacer, impressions

Written remains

The symbols that appear during the Stone Age as body painting or tattooing *(1179, 1180)* cannot be regarded as a script. But during the Early Bronze Age the use and differentiation of incised potter's marks increased to such an extent that we must ask whether contacts with the outside world, e.g. Anatolia and Cyprus (cf. below, p. 172), did not lead here to the first attempts at writing in the Aegean civilization.

From the beginning of the second millennium B.C. (MM I), a pictographic script is found in Crete, in which we can detect several direct borrowings from Egypt, as well as several forms very similar to signs of the Hittite hieroglyphic script. Yet the origins of the Cretan script remain obscure.

Besides this hieroglyphic-pictographic type of script, which has survived almost exclusively as titles or proper names on seals, and in which the signs hardly changed over 400 years because of religious conservatism, several other systems of writing are classified as 'Minoan' or 'Cretan-Mycenaean' script, and they penetrated to the rest of the Aegean islands and the Greek mainland (Pylos: *1415, 1420*; Mycenae: *460, 752, 1411*; Thebes: *1413, 1414*; Orchomenos: *1412*). From the middle of the second millennium, they extended their influence to Cyprus (cf. below, pp. 172 f.; *595, 1382, 1898–1910*) and northern Syria (Ras Shamra).

The Phaistos disc *(1409 a–d)*, with a spiral inscription on each side, is an isolated find from the late seventeenth century B.C., and reproduces none of the known script types. The groups separated by radial lines show forty-five different signs stamped into the soft clay. A bronze double axe from Arkalochori shows a further variant of the ancient Cretan pictographs related to the script on the disc; a third variant has been found on a stone block in Mallia.

These different types of script coincide only in part with the Cretan hieroglyphs, which were accompanied also by a 'protolinear system'. Consequently, in later times a number of local types were evolved from the primary protolinear script; they are described as 'Linear A' (e.g. *1410*. The cult bowl, from Troullos-Archanes, proves the religious use of this script). The signs on a bronze double axe from Crete must probably also be regarded as votive inscriptions *(720)*. Stonemasons', potters' and ingot marks *(745–749)* prove the use of such signs in crafts. An incised sign on a copper cauldron found in Mycenae *(1411)* indicates how Linear A reached the Greek mainland.

In contrast to earlier stages in the history of writing, all the 'A' scripts appearing at the start of MM III have in common a simplification of the symbols. The most important Linear A archive was found in Hagia Triada. The texts on the tablets consist of introductory formulae followed by rows of ideograms, together with signs of numbers and dimensions; some of these rows of ideograms are subdivided by further introductory formulae. This script runs from left to right. The three hundred-odd surviving Linear A documents originate from some twenty Cretan sites, also from Melos, Kythera, Thera, Siphnos, Naxos and Keos and a few from the mainland *(1411*, presumably also *1412)*.

Linear B (Fig. 43, *1422*) has been described as 'the Palace calligraphy of Knossos', for this script is not found elsewhere in Crete—apart from a few inscriptions on vases recently discovered in the west of the island. Nor does it seem to have been unknown in artisan circles, as shown by auxiliary signs in this system on a mould *(460)*. Linear B had clearly taken over some signs, absent from Linear A, from pictographic hieroglyphic script—another indication of the long coexistence of the earlier script forms and systems. In structure, the texts show a definite sense of order and clarity; this was achieved by marking out lines (Fig. 41, *1419, 1420*) and differentiating between groups of main and subordinate words, numerical signs and ideograms, by remarkably relative orders of magnitude (e.g. ingot and scales ideograms: *1417, 1418*; vase ideograms: *1420* and Fig. 42, *1421*).

Linear B was also used in the court chancelleries of the mainland palaces in Pylos *(1415, 1420)*, Mycenae, Tiryns, and Thebes *(1414)*. The script on large stirrup jars from Orchomenos *(1412)* and Thebes *(1413)*, for example, is very distinct from Linear B. Not all its special features are derived from the technique of writing with brush and colour—unlike the incised Linear texts—which is why Sundwall drew some connections between the 'stirrup jar script' and Linear A.

The tripod tablet from Pylos (Fig. 41, *1420*) provided the key for deciphering the script, for its ideograms have exact counterparts in the syllabic script groups belonging to them, if one interprets them

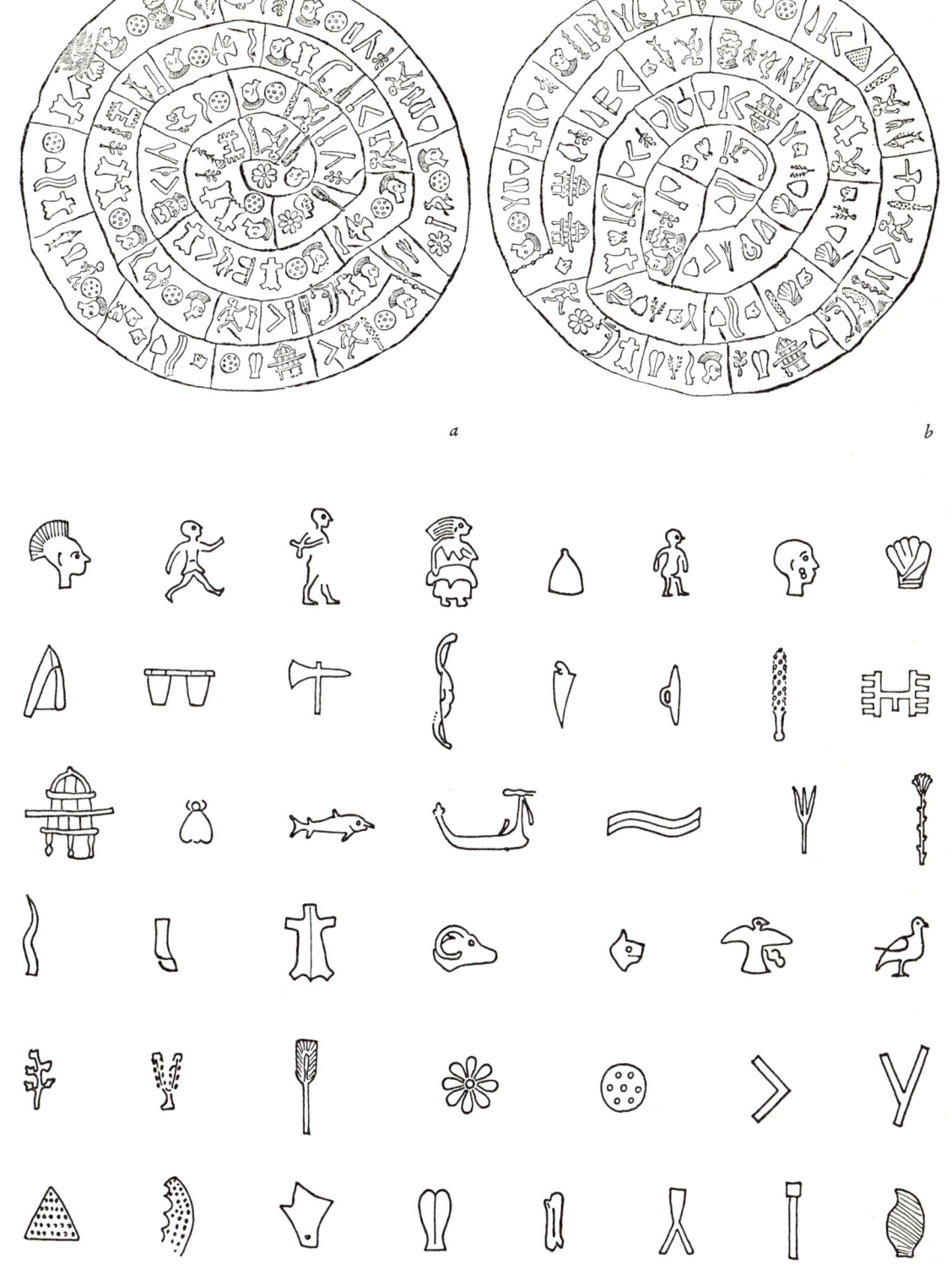

Fig. 40 1409 a–c Phaistos Disc

Fig. 41 Inscribed Linear B tablets

1416

1417
1418

1419

1420

in Greek (cf. Fig. 42, *1421*); but recently there has been strong criticism of the decipherment by Ventris and Chadwick: Eckschmitt, *Die Kontroverse um Linear B* (1969).

Foreign script systems became known to the Bronze Age inhabitants of the Aegean through inscriptions on imported objects; for instance, Egyptian hieroglyphs as early as the Hyksos period (*1142*: vase lid of Chian, Knossos) in the fifteenth century B.C. (*1140*: alabaster vase, Katsamba) and at the end of the Bronze Age (*1408*: inscribed scarab, Perati), and finally the Mesopotamian cuneiform script and Cypro-Minoan signs on cylinder seals (*1374, 1376, 1382*).

Bibliography: Grumach, *Bibliographie der kretisch-mykenischen Epigraphik* (1963) and Supplement I (1967); especially Ventris-Chadwick, *Documents in Mycenaean Greek* (1956); Chadwick, *The Decipherment of Linear B* (1958); Palmer-Boardman, *On the Knossos Tablets* (1963); Heubeck, *Aus der Welt der frühgriechischen Lineartafeln: eine kurze Einführung in Grundlagen, Aufgaben und Ergebnisse der Mykenologie* (1966); Grumach, 'Die kretischen und kyprischen Schriftsysteme', in Hausmann, *Handbuch der Archäologie* I (new ed., 1969), 234 ff.; Buchholz, 'Die ägäischen Schriftsysteme und ihre Ausstrahlung in die ostmediterranen Kulturen', in *Frühe Schriftzeugnisse der Menschheit* (1969); Kerschensteiner, *Die mykenische Welt in ihren Schriftzeugnissen* (1970); Hiersche, *Grundzüge der griechischen Sprachgeschichte bis zur klassischen Zeit* (1970). — See also more literature given on pp. 182 f.

Fig. 42
1421 Mycenaean vase ideograms and their interpretations

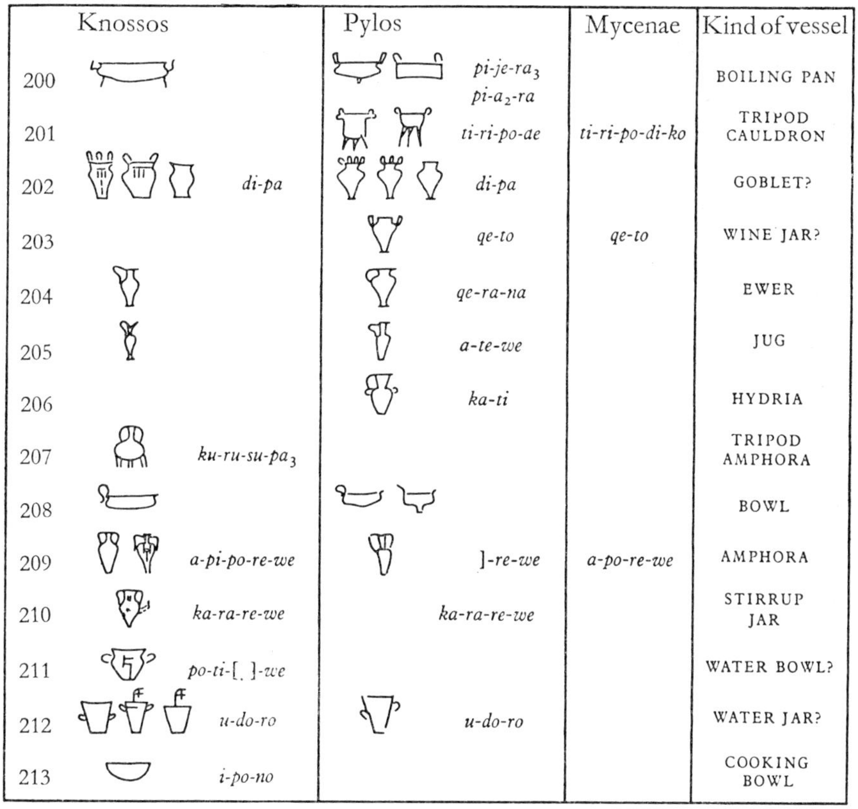

	Knossos		Pylos		Mycenae	Kind of vessel
200				pi-je-ra₃ pi-a₂-ra		BOILING PAN
201				ti-ri-po-ae	ti-ri-po-di-ko	TRIPOD CAULDRON
202		di-pa		di-pa		GOBLET?
203				qe-to	qe-to	WINE JAR?
204				qe-ra-na		EWER
205				a-te-we		JUG
206				ka-ti		HYDRIA
207		ku-ru-su-pa₃				TRIPOD AMPHORA
208						BOWL
209		a-pi-po-re-we		]-re-we	a-po-re-we	AMPHORA
210		ka-ra-re-we		ka-ra-re-we		STIRRUP JAR
211		po-ti-[ ]-we				WATER BOWL?
212		u-do-ro		u-do-ro		WATER JAR?
213		i-po-no				COOKING BOWL

1409 Also Fig. 40: Phaistos. Clay disc with spirally ar-
a–d ranged bands of script on either side, so-called Phaistos disc; diam. 16 cm.; stamped with forty-five different ideograms (Fig. 40); late seventeenth century B.C. (for late date, cf. Jeppesen, *Kuml* 1962, 157 ff.). Arch. Mus., Herakleion. – Grumach, *Bibliographie der kretisch-mykenischen Epigraphik* (1963), 23; and Suppl. 1 (1967), 8 f.; also *AJA*. 15 (1911), 234, 556; Burton-Brown, *The Coming of Iron to Greece* (1955), 70, 77 ff., 150; Neumann, *Gnomon* 34 (1962), 574 ff. (review of Davis, *The Phaistos Disk* [1961]); id., *Kadmos* 7 (1968), 27 ff. – For the spiral arrangement of the script, cf. Karo, *PZ*. 23 (1932), 351, n. 4, and Budge, *Amulets and Superstitions* (1930), 283 ff., Figs. 1–4.

1410 Troullos–Archanes. Little libation bowl ('spoon') of white, fine-grained marble, with fairly long Linear A text, no doubt of religious significance; length 9 cm., width 7 cm.; MM III. Arch. Mus., Herakleion, Inv. No. 1545. – Bossert, *Altkreta*, Fig. 519; Brice, *Inscriptions in the Minoan Linear Script of Class A* (1961), 14 f., Pl. 20, I, 16 (complete bibl.); Warren, *Minoan Stone Vases* (1969), 49.

1411 Mycenae. Grave Circle A, Shaft Grave IV: Copper cauldron of the sixteenth century B.C. (shown in full: below p. 345; cf. text to *1091*); Linear A sign deeply incised on one of the tongues of the handle. Nat. Mus., Athens. – Grumach, *Kadmos* 1 (1962), 85 f.; Vermeule, *Greece in the Bronze Age* (1964), 41, Fig. 6 t.

1412 Orchomenos, Boeotia. Detail of a stirrup jar with painted inscription; LH III. Nat. Mus., Athens. – Bulle, *Die Woche* 1904, Issue 5, 216, Fig. 4; Evans, *Scripta Minoa* I, 57, Fig. 31; and, *PM*. IV, 739, Fig. 723; Bossert, *OLZ.* 1931, 321, Fig. 10; Buchholz, *Minos* 3 (1954), 149 f., Figs. 10, 11; Jensen, *Die Schrift in der Vergangenheit und Gegenwart* (²1958), 116, Fig. 92 (inverted); MacKendrick, *The Greek Stones Speak* (1962), 89 f.; Grumach, *Bibliographie der kretisch-mykenischen Epigraphik* (1963), 78.

1413 Thebes, Boeotia. Stirrup jar with fairly long, painted linear text; LH III. Arch. Mus., Thebes. – Raison, *Les Vases à inscriptions peintes de l'âge mycénien* (1968); Grumach, op. cit., 78 f.; Catling–Millett, 'A Study of the Inscribed Stirrup Vases from Thebes', *Archaeometry* 8 (1965), 1 ff., 69, Pl. 10 a.

1414 Thebes. Fragment of a clay leaf-shaped tablet with Linear B signs; LH III. Arch. Mus., Thebes. – Touloupa, *Kadmos* 3 (1964), 25 ff., Fig. 9; Ktistopoulos, ibid., 28; cf. Grumach, op. cit., Suppl. I, 25 f.

1415 Pylos. Room 4: Reconstructed fragments of a Linear B tablet, with vase ideograms from the archives of the Palace of Nestor; LH III b. – Blegen, *AJA*. 58 (1954), 29, Pl. 7:8.

1416 Fig. 41: Knossos. From the armoury of the palace (discovered 1904). Leaf-shaped Linear B tablet, the upper line written after the lower one; representing chariots (cf. ideogram above right); LM III. Arch.

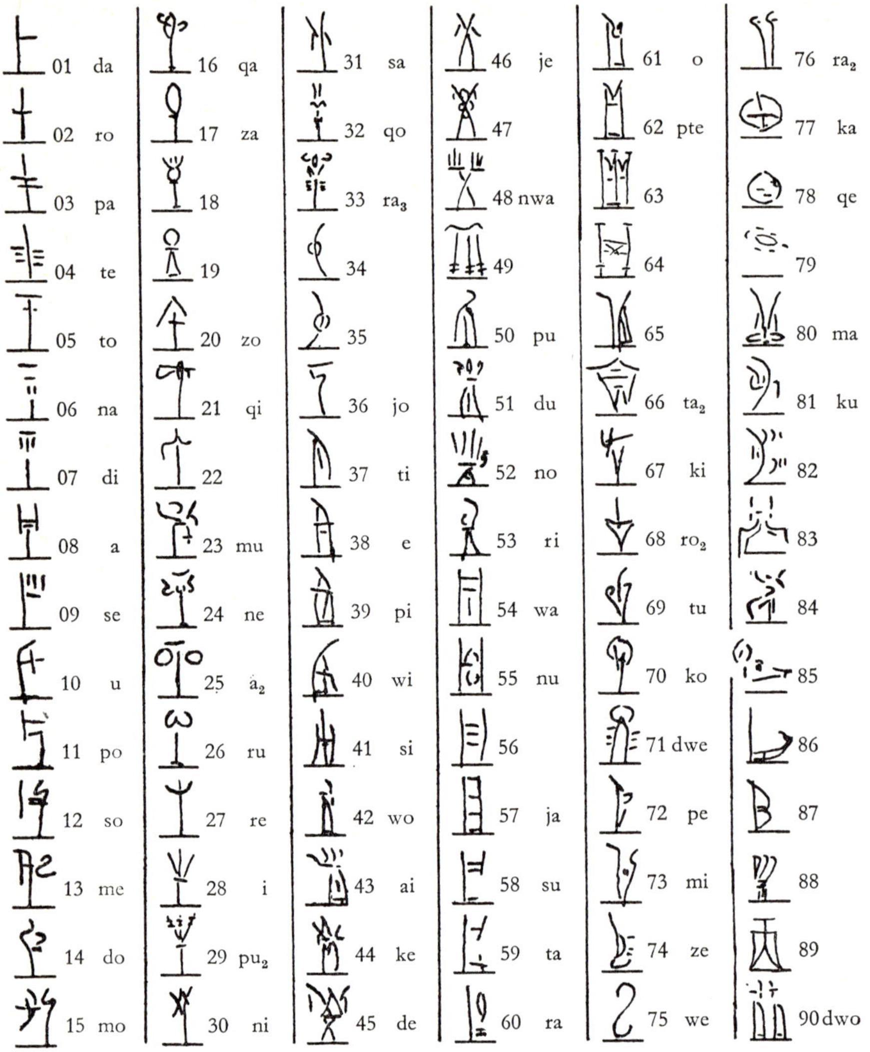

Fig. 43
1422 Linear B, list of signs

01 da	16 qa	31 sa	46 je	61 o	76 ra_2		
02 ro	17 za	32 qo	47	62 pte	77 ka		
03 pa	18	33 ra_3	48 nwa	63	78 qe		
04 te	19	34	49	64	79		
05 to	20 zo	35	50 pu	65	80 ma		
06 na	21 qi	36 jo	51 du	66 ta_2	81 ku		
07 di	22	37 ti	52 no	67 ki	82		
08 a	23 mu	38 e	53 ri	68 ro_2	83		
09 se	24 ne	39 pi	54 wa	69 tu	84		
10 u	25 a_2	40 wi	55 nu	70 ko	85		
11 po	26 ru	41 si	56	71 dwe	86		
12 so	27 re	42 wo	57 ja	72 pe	87		
13 me	28 i	43 ai	58 su	73 mi	88		
14 do	29 pu_2	44 ke	59 ta	74 ze	89		
15 mo	30 ni	45 de	60 ra	75 we	90 dwo		

Mus., Herakleion, Inv. No. Sd 0403. – Ventris–Chadwick, *Documents in Mycenaean Greek,* 12, Fig. 2, and p. 365 f. (translation).

1417 Fig. 41: Knossos. Two fragments of clay leaf-shaped
1418 tablets with entries in Linear B; metal ingots, notations of numbers, and weight ideogram *(talanton = scale)*. These ingot ideograms relate to actual ingots like *752 a, b;* LM III. Arch. Mus., Herakleion. – Fimmen, KMK. 123, Fig. 115 *(1418);* Myres, *Scripta Minoa* II (1952), No. 246/Nj 82, Pl. 29 *(1417),* No. 730/Oj O1, Pl. 51 *(1418);* Buchholz, PZ. 37 (1959), 16 f., Fig. 8; Forbes, in Matz–Buchholz, Arch. Hom. K (1967), 25, Fig. 13 g, h.

1419 Fig. 41: Knossos. Clay leaf-shaped tablet; Linear B; according to the introductory group, two rows of ideographic representations of objects (rams and ewes), with accompanying details. LM III. Arch. Mus., Herakleion, Inv. No. Dd 1150. – Grumach, 'Der ägäische Schriftenkreis', *Studium Generale* 18 (1965), 745, Fig. 1; cf. Ventris–Chadwick, op. cit., 201.

1420 Fig. 41: Pylos. Palace of Nestor. Tripod tablet (Inv. No. Ta 641), that serves to confirm Ventris's proposed decipherment (cf. above, p. 120); the inventory lists vases, including tripod cauldrons; LH III b. – Ventris-Chadwick, 336 f., No. 236, Pl. 3 b; Ventris, *Acta Congressus Madvigiani: Copenhagen 1954* I (1958), 78 f.; Chadwick, *The Decipherment of Linear B* (1958), 99 ff.; Grumach, *Propyläen-Weltgeschichte* III (1962), 101; Blegen-Rawson, *A Guide to the Palace of Nestor* ([3]1967), 7, Fig. 4; Eckschmitt, *Die Kontroverse um Linear B* (1969), 107 ff.; Pl. 7 c.

1421 Fig. 42: Knossos, Pylos, and Mycenae. List of vase ideograms on Linear B tablets. – Ventris–Chadwick, 324, Fig. 16; Chadwick, *Linear B,* 142, Fig. 16.

1422 Fig. 43: Linear B, list of signs with notation of phonetic values after Ventris' decipherment. Standard numbering of signs after the Wingspread Colloquium, 1962.

ANCIENT CYPRUS

Introduction

Although Cyprus covers only a modest area of 6,093 sq. km., an important prehistoric culture developed on the island, thanks largely to its geographic location (cf. Figs. 44, 45). Its position lies at the point of intersection of the cultural channels from Anatolia, Egypt and the Aegean. These influences are reflected in the development of Cypriot civilization; but the island succeeded more or less in safeguarding its cultural independence by continually modifying the foreign elements to its own character, so that the style even of its prehistoric art is clearly Cypriot.

Fig. 44 Sites of Stone and Bronze Age finds in Cyprus (English excavations brought to light another important settlement on the north coast, not far from Troulli, in 1969, which is not shown on this map)

THE STONE AGE

The earliest period to be determined archaeologically on the island to date is the Neolithic period. It began early in the sixth millennium, according to radiocarbon measurements, and it lasted some three millennia. It can be divided into two main periods: an early phase, Neolithic I (c. 5800—4950 B.C.), and a late phase, Neolithic II (c. 3500—3000 B.C.). Stone, chiefly andesite, was used for making vessels *(1657—1661)* and idols in the sixth millennium *(1690—1694, 1696, 1697* and Fig. 62). In these little figurines, which are basically abstract and anthropomorphic, we can trace an artistic development which continued far into the succeeding periods *(1689—1697)*. The same applies to the andesite bowls, some of which have incised or relief decoration. Implements of daily use were made of the same material, as well as of flint and bone *(1828 ff.)*.

Fig. 45 Sphere of influence of the Aegean civilization in the Eastern Mediterranean

The main characteristic of the late Neolithic period is the birth of fired painted pottery *(1485 ff.* and Fig. 62). The terracotta ware of this period, which generally belongs to the 'combed ware' class, is in the form of bowls and large jugs. The surface is covered with a thick brown slip, which was treated before firing and while still wet with a comb-like instrument, so that the light brown clay ground became visible in wavy stripes *(1486, 1487* and Fig. 62).

The best evidence of Neolithic I architecture is in Khirokitia (Fig. 46). The houses of this farming settlement were built near a spring on the slope of a hill. They are tholoi *(1426 ff.)*—i.e., buildings with a conical, beehive-like roof on a circular substructure. This upper structure of sun-dried mud bricks rested on walls of river gravel. The dimensions of the tholoi varied, the largest having a diameter of ten metres. Occasionally up to three of these round houses were grouped into farms (Figs. 47—49). Later, in the second phase of the Neolithic period, best represented in Sotira near the south coast, houses with two or more square rooms were built (Figs. 50, 51).

In the Stone Age the inhabitants of Khirokitia formed a community of farmers, who tilled the land and already bred domestic animals, including sheep and pigs. They knew how to prepare wool, to spin, weave and knit; they made clothes and wore ornaments of stones and shells *(1767 ff.).* Their highly developed religious life centred around the cult of the dead, whom they buried in their houses or in the immediate vicinity *(1463—1475),* and to whom they offered libations.

THE CHALCOLITHIC PERIOD

Important evidence of the Chalcolithic period (c. 3000—2300 B.C.) was found in Erimi, also on the south coast of Cyprus; this was the transitional period between the Neolithic and the Bronze Ages. Chalcolithic pottery shows the emergence of new forms. The predominant decoration is now red painted on a white ground, with a variety of linear and floral ornaments *(1489—1493* and Fig. 62). At the same time, we find a great number of idols of steatite or terracotta; most of the latter represent a mother goddess *(1699—1703).*

Fig. 46 *1425* Plan of the Early Stone Age settlement of Khirokitia

The pit-like sunken houses of Kalavassos (Fig. 52), constructed at the end of the Neolithic period and during the transitional phase of the Copper Age, are a new form, probably derived from southern Palestine. A copper chisel was found in the upper strata of Erimi. This metal played a decisive part in the cultural life of the island from the early third millennium B.C. Although this earliest metal find was probably imported, it proves that the Erimi culture has rightly been designed 'Chalcolithic.' Buchholz has discussed it in 'Kulturhistorische Aspekte der kyprischen Stein- und Kupferzeit', *Archaeologia Viva* (1969).

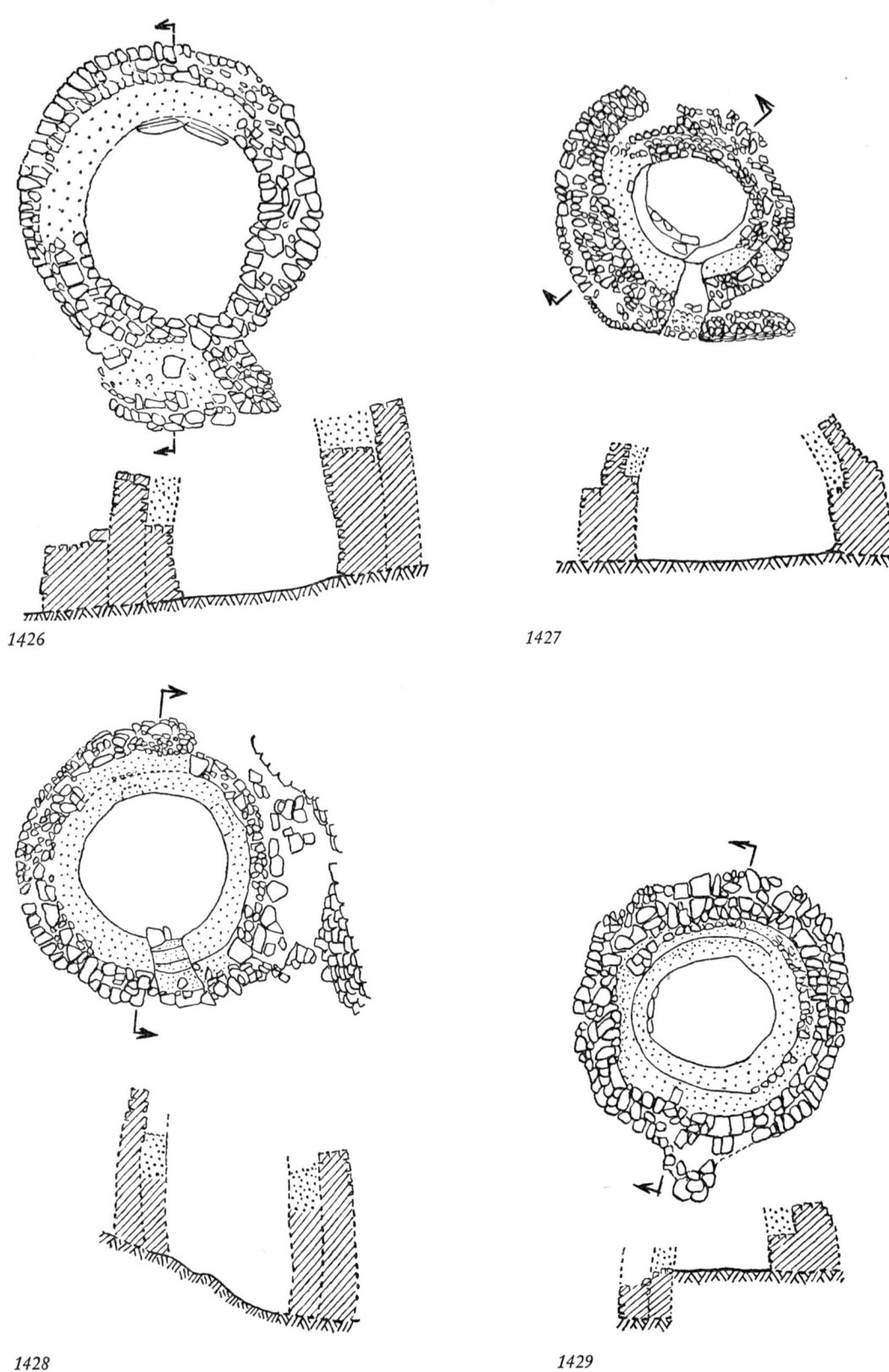

1426

1427

1428

1429

Fig. 47 1426–1429 *Khirokitia*, ground plans of Early Stone Age buildings

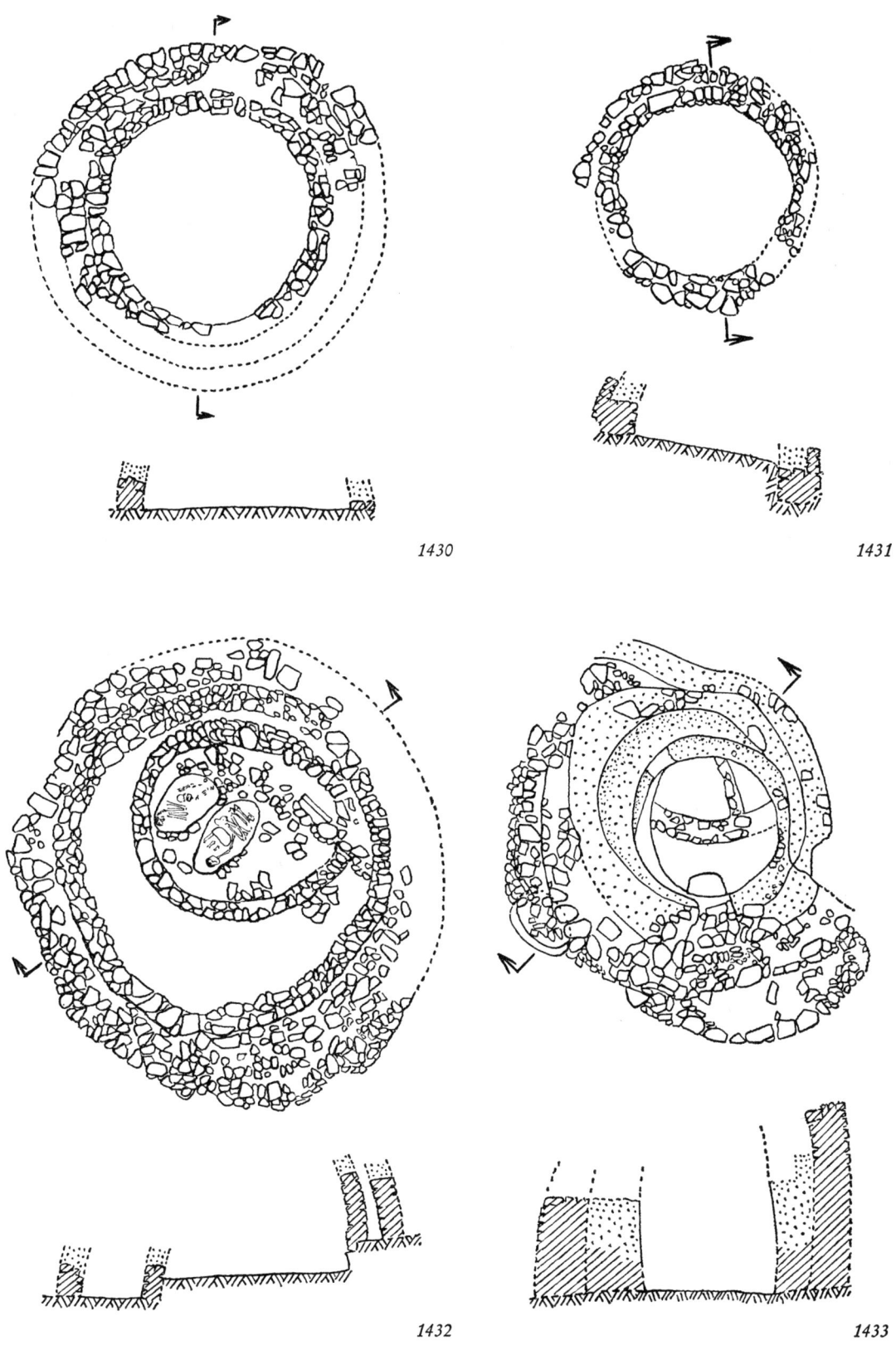

Fig. 48   1430–1433   Khirokitia, ground plans of early Neolithic buildings

127

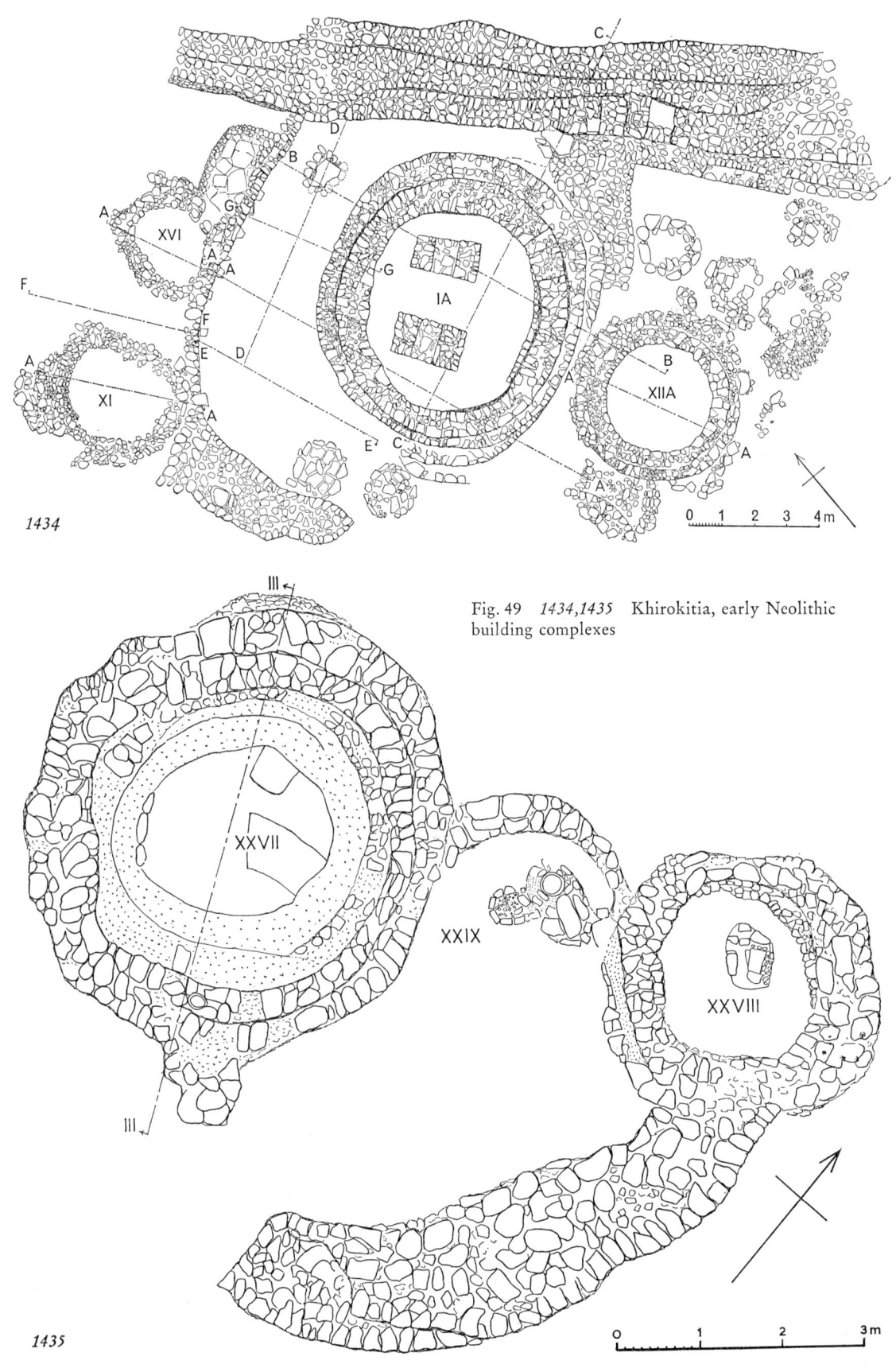

Fig. 49 *1434, 1435* Khirokitia, early Neolithic building complexes

1441

1442

1443

1444

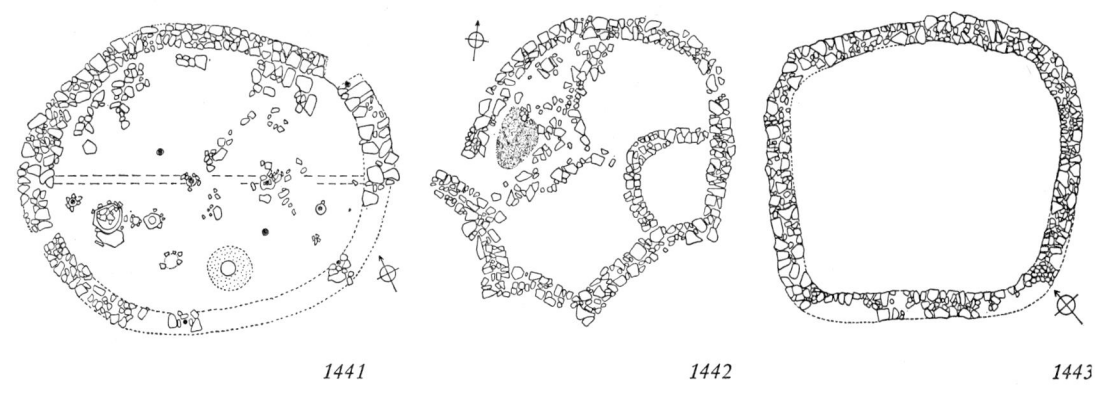

Fig. 50 *1441–1443* Sotira, types of early Neolithic house, Houses 8, 11, and 7 of settlement phases II and III. *1444* Overall plan of the Stone Age settlement

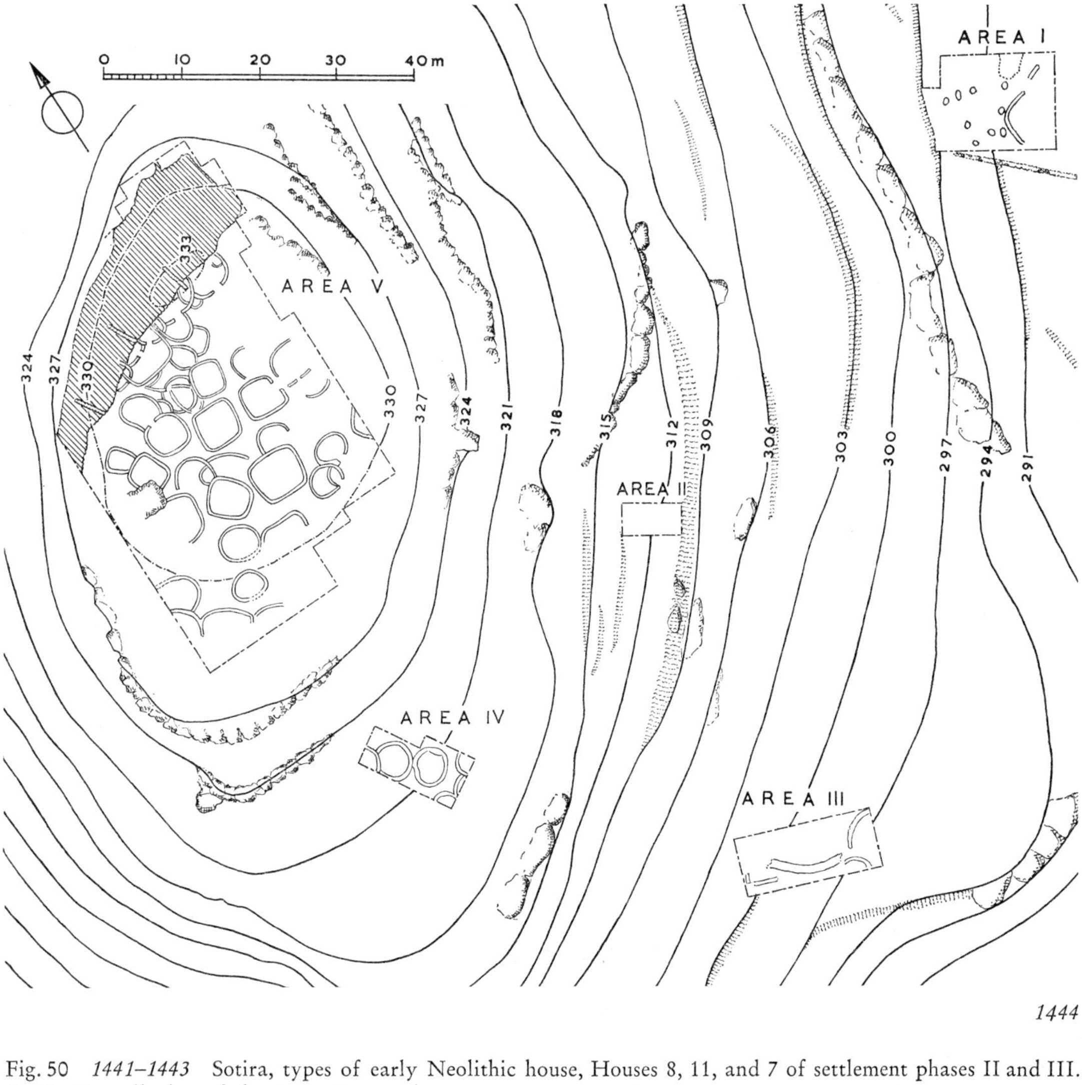

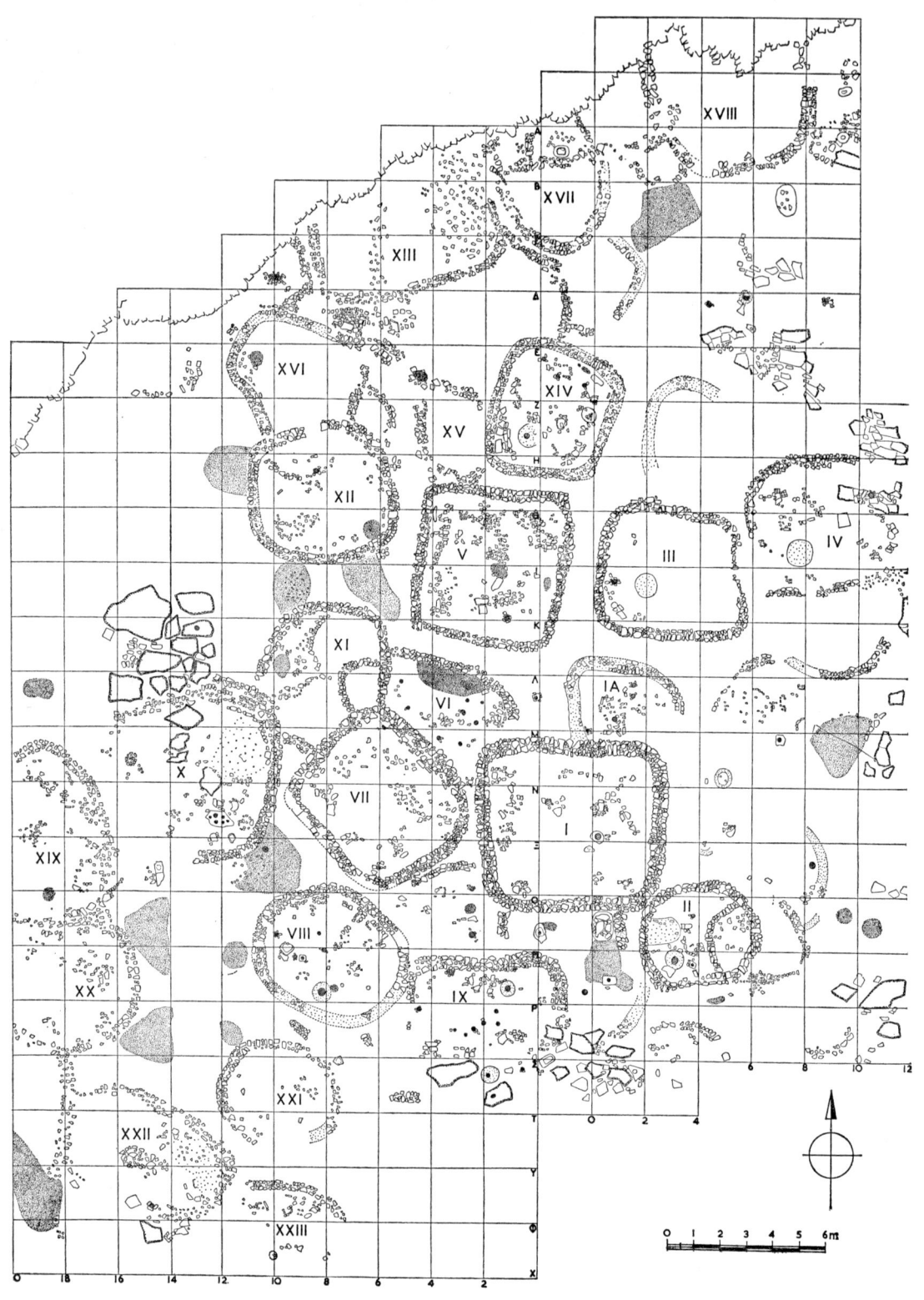

Fig. 51 *1445* Sotira, Excavation Area V (cf. Fig. 50, *1444*)

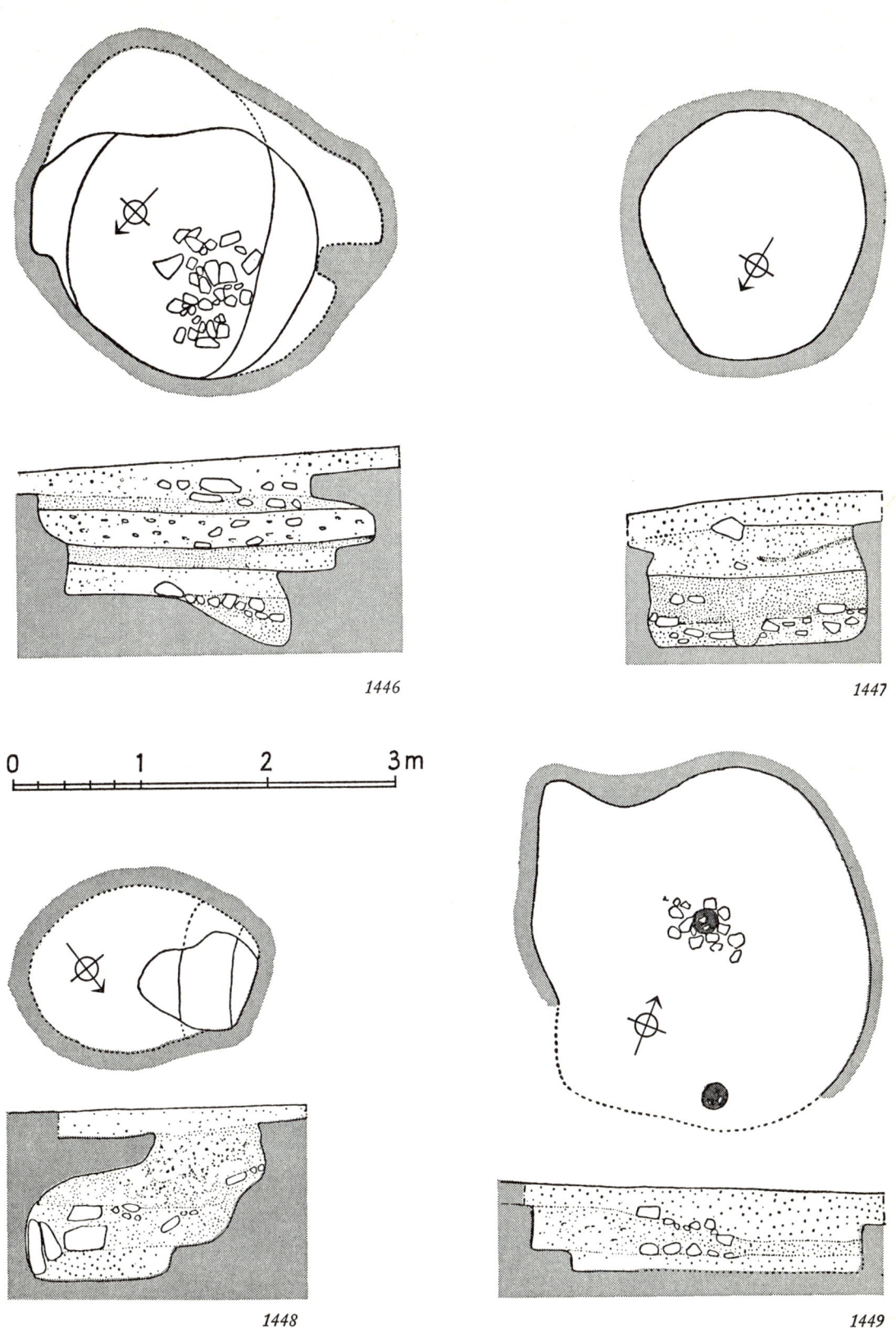

Fig. 52 *1446–1449* Sunken Neolithic dwellings in Kalavassos

EARLY BRONZE AGE

In the Early Bronze Age Cyprus was a densely populated and economically flourishing country, in close contact with its neighbours. Yet excavators have found no signs of settlement in this period, except for one house in Alambra and another in Ambelikou (Fig. 53). The Cypriots now began to construct cemeteries outside the areas of settlement, with chamber tombs richly furnished with pottery and bronzes (Fig. 61, and *1479 a, b*). The pottery is generally of the Red-Polished type, with a warm glow, and decorated with reliefs or incised patterns *(1494—1527)*. At first the Cypriot potters drew their inspiration from the art of south-west Anatolia; for, after the catastrophe which befell this region in the second phase of the Early Bronze Age in Anatolia, new settlers came to Cyprus. But the local artisans soon learnt to adapt the foreign influences to their own style. They also gained in technical skill, and developed an excellent sense of form and decoration and an incomparable sense of humour.

The northern coastal region is the location of the great necropolis of Vounous, which we have to thank for most of the finds that have survived from this period (cf. map, Fig. 44). One of the important finds is a terracotta model of a miniature temenos *(1705)*; it provides a lively record of the religious customs of the Early Bronze Age in Cyprus, which were concentrated on the cycle of life and death.

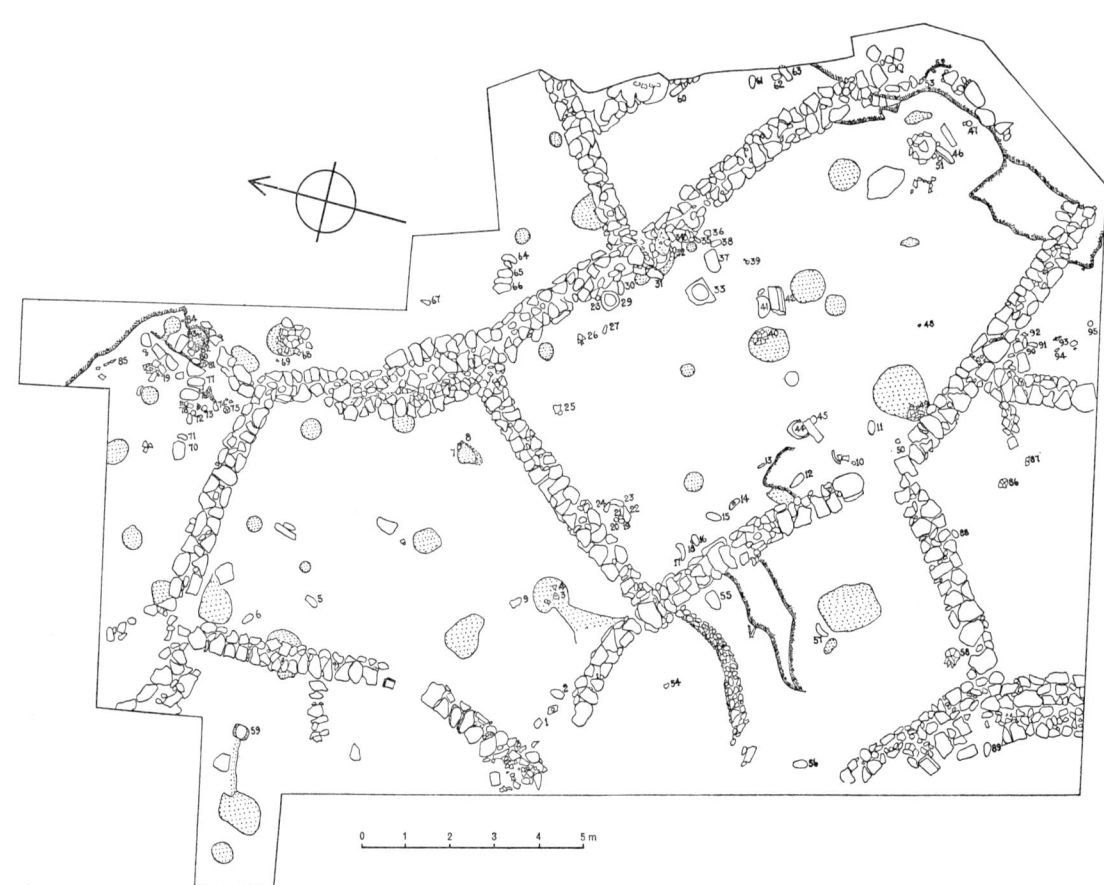

Fig. 53   *1451*   Ambelikou, ground plan of an Early Bronze Age building

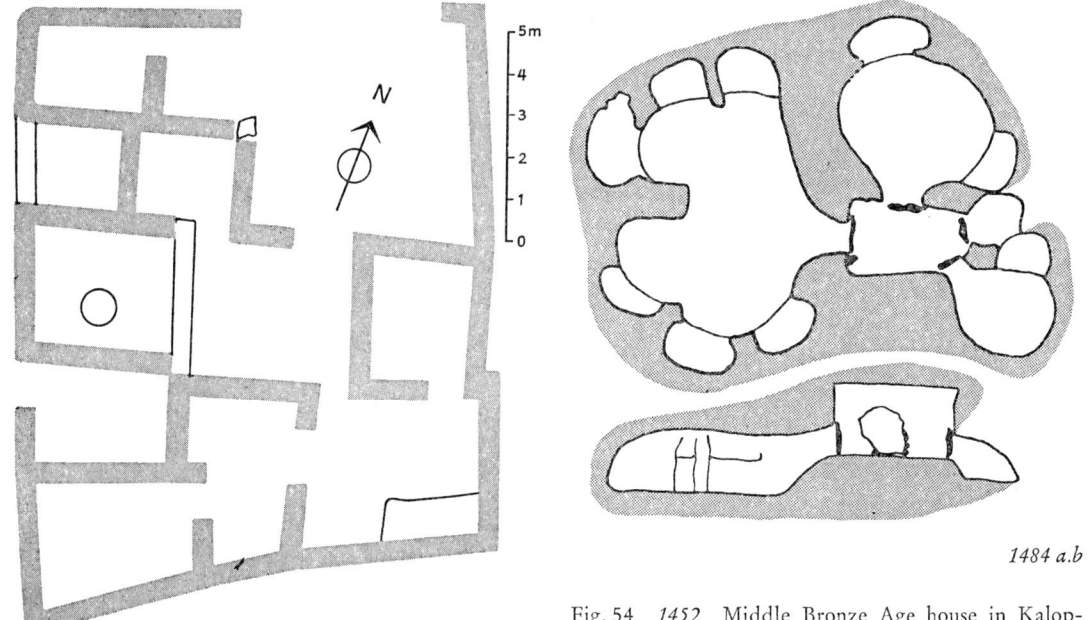

Fig. 54 *1452* Middle Bronze Age house in Kalopsida *1484* Middle Bronze Age Tomb 313 in Lapithos

MIDDLE BRONZE AGE

The Middle Bronze Age (c. 2000—1600 B.C.) can be understood as an independent period almost exclusively through the tomb finds. No dwelling houses have been traced apart from a large house in Kalopsida (Fig. 54, *1452*), but fairly detailed information on Cypriot military fortifications has been gleaned. An entirely new phenomenon on the island, they were erected towards the end of the period, in the seventeenth century, as protection against invasions by the Hyksos; impressive examples are the fortresses of Krini in the northern part of Cyprus, Hagios Sozomenos in the centre of the island, and Nitovikla on the Karpass peninsula. The architecture of Nitovikla shows traces of Anatolian elements, and recalls the fortifications of Boğazköy; directly adjacent to the massive walls surrounding a rectangular court lay barracks whose flat roofs served as sentry posts. Two square towers flanked the entrance to the fortress (Fig. 55).

Richly furnished chamber tombs dating from this period have been uncovered throughout Cyprus, particularly on the north coast at Lapithos and Karmi (cf. Fig. 54, *1484*) and near Kalopsida to the east. In pottery, the search for new means of expression had begun, and the technique of Red-Polished ware was gradually abandoned. Pottery painted on a white ground now predominated; occasionally there were sculptural additions, which gave some vessels an anthropomorphic or theriomorphic appearance (e.g. *1556*). In this period we also find Red-on-Black painting *(1538—1541)* and Black Slip pottery (e.g. *1551, 1552*). In addition, there is evidence of imported vessels and bronzes from Minoan Crete *(1572, 1573, 1877)* and from the Syrian and Palestinian coast (e.g. *1876*). But indigenous Cypriot metalwork reached a high standard, as is proved by a large number of implements and weapons from tombs.

The Middle Bronze Age marks the transition from the Early Bronze to the Late Bronze Age. The island became very wealthy during this transitional phase, as a result of continually growing trade with its neighbours in the Near East. The unrest resulting from the Hyksos invasions to which the rest of the eastern Mediterranean was exposed does not seem to have had any adverse effects on the cultural and economic development of Cyprus (for this period, cf. van Seters, *The Hyksos* [1966]).

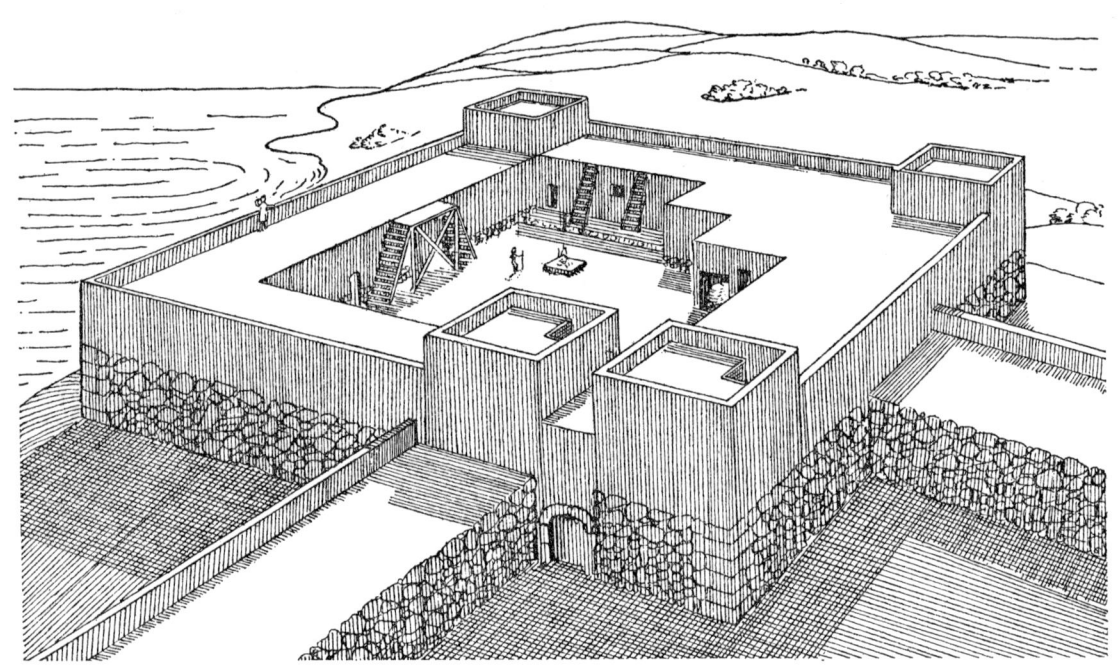

Fig. 55 *1453* Diagrammatic reconstruction of the Bronze Age fortress of Nitovikla. It was built at the end of the Middle Bronze Age, and restored at the beginning of the Late Bronze Age

LATE BRONZE AGE

The middle of the second millennium marks a turning-point in the history of the eastern Mediterranean and, in particular, of Cyprus. Mycenaeans from the Greek mainland and the Aegean islands conquered Minoan Crete, and eventually made their way to the Near East, establishing close trade relations; so the break between the Middle and the Late Bronze Ages is primarily a change in the internal evolution of Cyprus. However, the character of Cypriot culture at this time (1600—1050 B.C.) was also largely determined by the emergence of the new Mycenaean power. The Mycenaeans settled in the ports of the east and south coasts of Cyprus, whence they established trade relations with the opposite Syrian and Palestinian coast. It is highly probable that artists and craftsmen also settled in these centres, and that the style which has been called 'Levanto-Aegean' was born there. This development becomes particularly evident in vase painting, which used Aegean motifs, assembling them into richly figurative scenes on large kraters; there are chariot and ship scenes, designs with bulls and birds, and friezes with human figures *(1620, 1621, 1623—1627, 1630)*.

Ivory carving *(1742—1749)*, glyptic *(1750—1760)*, and works of gold and silver *(1773—1803)* display the same mixture of Aegean and Eastern motifs. A very large number of artefacts of this kind was found during excavations at Enkomi and Kition. A faience rhyton of the thirteenth century B.C. found recently at Kition is a splendid example of this new hybrid Eastern and Aegean style, with its inlaid pictorial decoration, bulls, human figures and vertically arranged spirals *(1671 a—d, Col. Pl. 3 and dust jacket)*.

At the same time, a script described as 'Cypro-Minoan' came into use in Cyprus *(1900—1910)*. Several inscribed clay tablets, of which the earliest can be dated *c.* 1500 B.C., have survived. Should they ever be deciphered, we may find that a kind of literature existed at this time too, as well as the works of art we have described. This happy and fruitful association offered new impulses to Aegean and Eastern art, which was to experience a severe set-back in its development in the first millennium. Six hundred years later, this same phenomenon of a union between East and West was repeated in the Orientalizing phase of Greek art; once again the island of Cyprus was to play the role of an intermediary.

The peaceful settlement of traders and artists in Cyprus during the fourteenth and thirteenth centuries was followed by waves of immigrant Achaean settlers c. 1200 B.C., who occupied the most important towns and ruled the entire island for a long time. Mycenaean pottery of the LH III c 1 type *(1646—1648)* records their presence: introduced by them, it almost entirely superseded the old Cypriot ware. This process marked a decisive change in Cypriot history. For almost five millennia Cyprus had lain in the sphere of Eastern influence, whereas henceforth the island was to be part of the Greek world. This had lasting effects on the historical development of the island: the Greek element became the basis of all its later culture. The Greek gods now entered Cyprus—for instance, Apollo Kereatas from Arcadia, who was revered in Enkomi-Alasia as Apollo Alasiotas, and of whom a marvellous bronze statue has been found in a temple built of ashlar masonry *(1740)*. His forcefully moulded body and refined features anticipate the great age of archaic Greek art.

Its economic and cultural relations with the Near East and the Aegean increased the island's activity. Houses (Fig. 56, *1454*) and fortresses were constructed with more care during the Late Cypriot period than hitherto. We find houses of several rooms, grouped on three sides round an open courtyard, which was used as a place of burial. For the first time we can speak of true monumental architecture and public buildings: temples with sacrificial altars, built of regular ashlar blocks, and palaces for the princes and noblemen, the most impressive of which have been found in Enkomi (Fig. 57, *1455*, also *1457*). In the town, streets intersecting at right angles formed a regular grid, and the entire town was surrounded by a kind of Cyclopean wall, whose foundations consisted of two rows of large stones, topped by mud bricks *(1456)*. A similar structure is the fortification wall of Palaiokastro-Maa

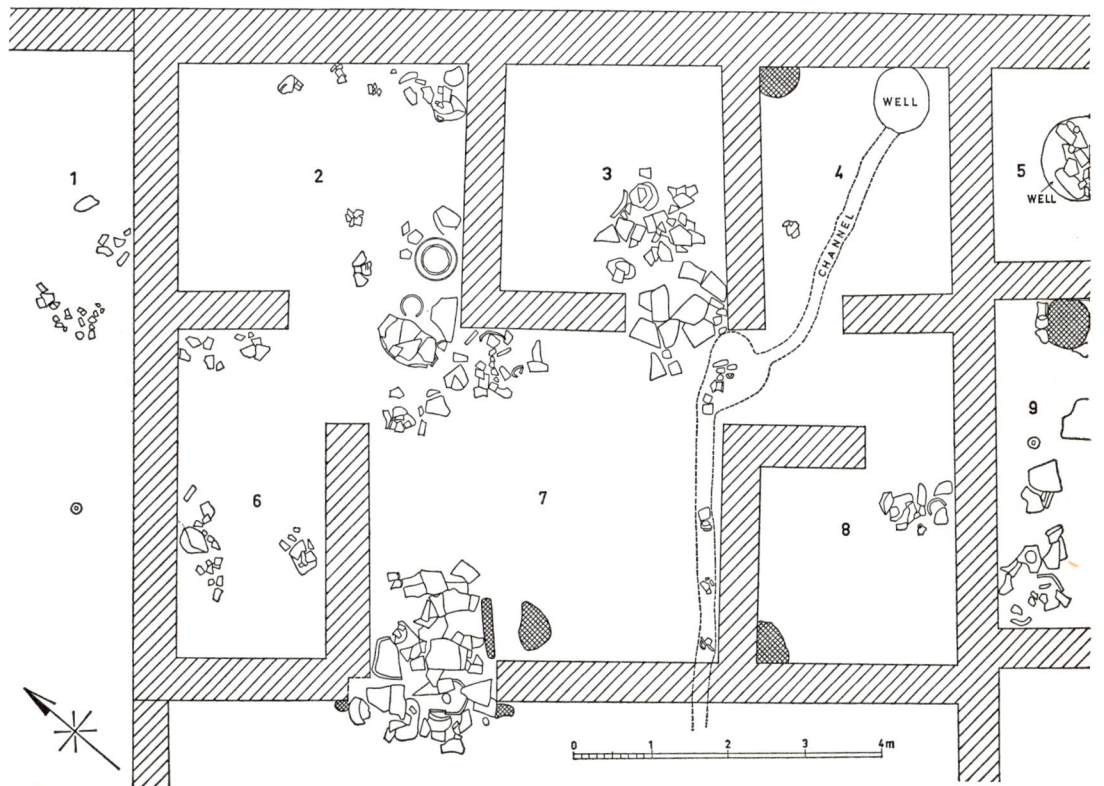

Fig. 56 *1454* Late Bronze Age house in Pyla Kokkinokremos

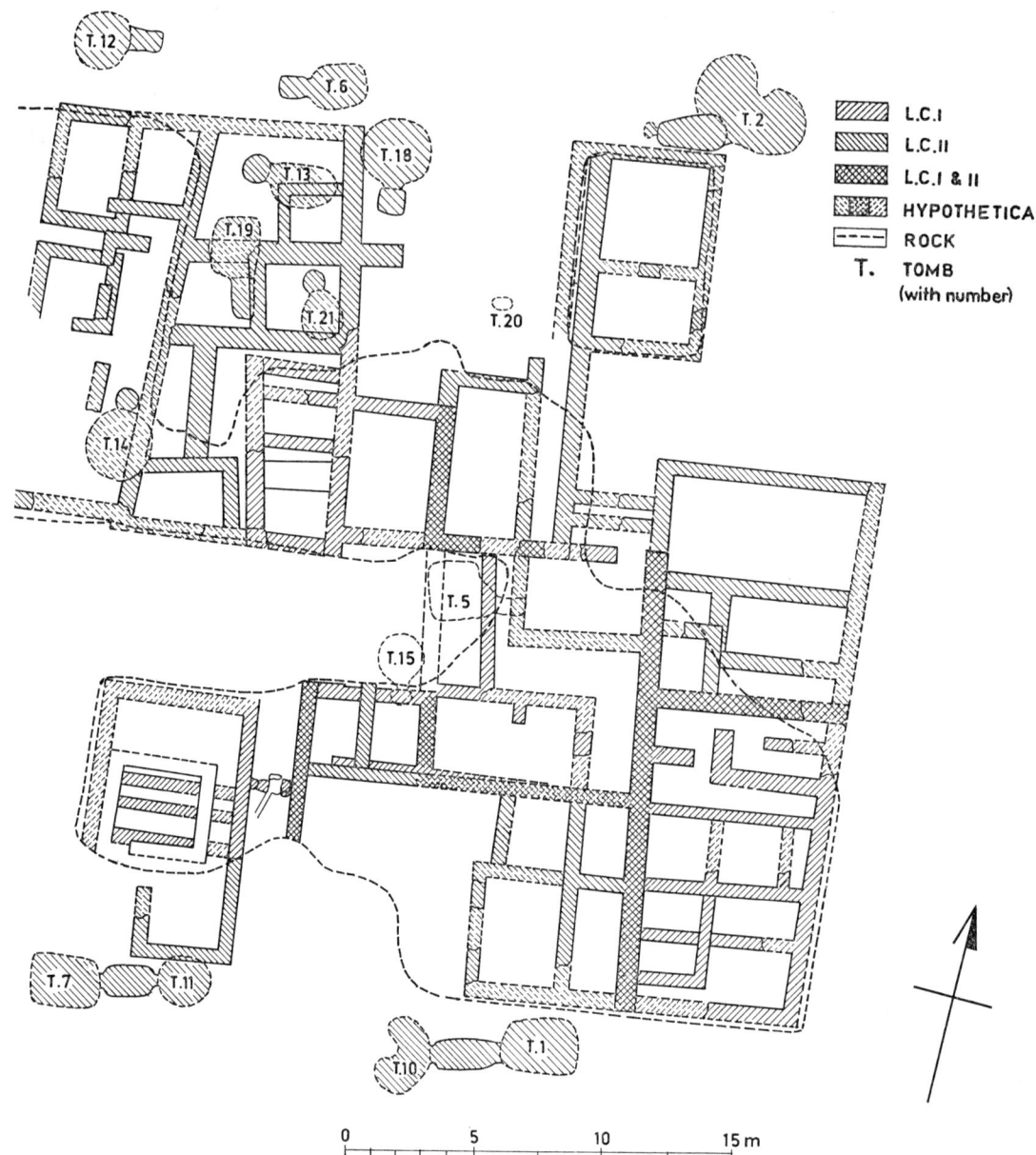

Fig. 57 *1455* Enkomi, Excavation Area I

in the west of the island (Fig. 58, *1462 a*, cf. *1462 b*). In Kition, by contrast, rectangular bastions were set at intervals directly in front of the town wall (Fig. 58, *1461*, cf. *1458—1460*). This was a time of unrest, in which the so-called 'Sea Peoples' rendered unsafe the coasts of the eastern Mediterranean.

Late Cypriot tombs consisted of a chamber hewn into the rock with an entrance (dromos) in front of the stomion. In addition, tombs with rectangular chambers were built from regular blocks of stone, as well as tholos tombs of fired mud bricks, examples of which have recently been found in Enkomi.

As we have mentioned, Enkomi is the largest and most thoroughly studied Late Bronze Age town; its splendid public buildings of ashlar masonry are masterpieces of architecture. However, in Enkomi, as in Kition, there are also numerous proofs of an extensive destruction which must have taken place soon after the general reconstruction work inspired by the arrival of the first Achaean colonists. Similar contemporary destructions have been observed in other Cypriot towns, and are usually considered to have resulted from the invasions by the Sea Peoples. Although the impressive ashlar buildings were restored and inhabited again, the town appears to have lost the brilliance of earlier days. Even the new settlers from the Levantine coast and those from the Aegean area, who fled from the Dorian invasions and brought with them the pottery of the LH III c 2 type, did not manage to bring about a new awakening. In about 1075 B.C. an earthquake destroyed Enkomi entirely, as it did most of the Late Bronze Age towns of Cyprus. The inhabitants of Enkomi turned to the sea, and founded Salamis at the mouth of the Pediaios; this new port was destined to become the capital of the island. The towns must have coexisted for a space of about twenty or twenty-five years, as shown by the discovery of early eleventh-century remains in Salamis, but finally, around mid-century, Enkomi was abandoned completely. A further reason for this may have been the silting-up of the Bronze Age harbour. Enkomi shared this fate with most of the well-known towns of the second millennium, with the exception of Kition, which was rebuilt and experienced a stimulus from the Early Iron Age settlement there until the end of the eleventh century.

For five millennia early Cypriot history was characterized by constantly changing forms of expression in its political and cultural life; although influenced by the great neighbouring cultures, it was indigenous cultural factors that played the decisive part in the emergence of a lively and rich, typically Cypriot, art.

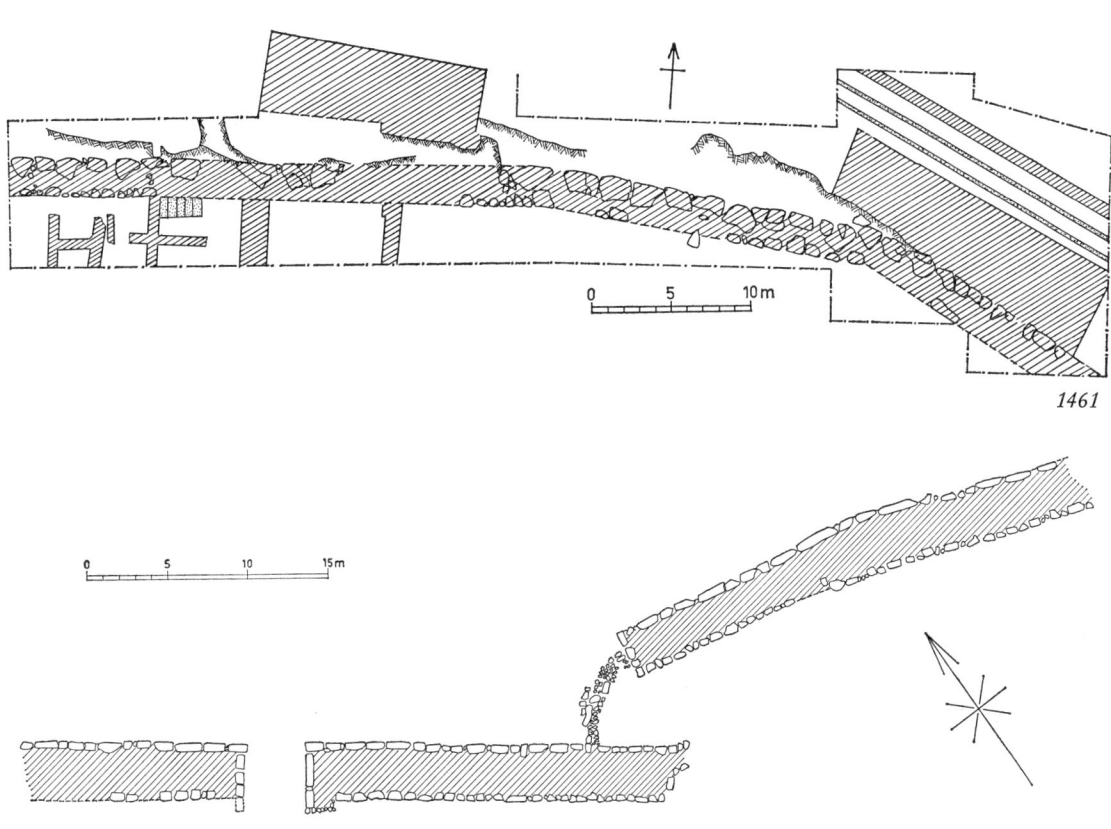

Fig. 58 Late Bronze Age fortification walls *1461* Kition *1462 a* Palaiokastro Maa

Cypriot chronology

The dates now generally accepted for the Stone and Bronze Ages in Cyprus are based partly on radiocarbon measurements and partly on observations of synchronisms with foreign cultures from the study of imports and exports (see the chronological table of Early Aegean cultures on pp. 29 f.). The chronological periods noted largely correspond to those which Dikaios established in the third edition of his *Guide to the Cyprus Museum* (1961), and to those in the recently published sections of *The Swedish Cyprus Expedition*. The chronology of the Late Bronze Age presented is based in part on the author's own excavations and research, described in *Cyprus, Archaeologia Mundi* (English ed. 1969), 103 ff., 233 ff. The chronological table should be read from below upwards, as should the grouping of pottery in Fig. 62. Note the synchronism of the dating given by Sjöqvist, Schaeffer, Furumark and Åström in: Dikaios, *Enkomi* I (1969), p. 438.

Periods		Approx. dates B. C.	Historical reference points	Sites
Late Bronze Age 'Late Cypriot Period'	III C:	1150–1050	Destruction of Late Bronze Age towns by earthquake	Enkomi, Sinda, Pyla Kokkinokremos, Kition, Kourion, Bamboula, Kouklia, Palaiokastro Maa, Myrtou Pigades and Myrtou Stephania
	III B:	1190–1150	So-called 'Sea Peoples migrations'	
	III A:	1230–1190	Achaean colonization	
	II B:	1300–1230		
	II A:	1400–1300	Extension of trade; much Mycenaean pottery in Cyprus and Near East	
	I B:	1450–1400	First appearance of Cypro-Minoan script (c. 1500)	
	I A:	1600–1450		
Middle Bronze Age 'Middle Cypriot Period'		2000–1600	Late 17th century: threat to Cyprus by Hyksos	Kalospida, Karmi, Lapithos; fortresses of Nitovikla, Krini and Hagios Sozomenos
Early Bronze Age 'Early Cypriot Period'	III:	2100–2000		Vounous B, Kourion Phaneromeni
	II:	2200–2100		Vounous A
	I:	2300–2200		Vasilia
Chalcolithic	II:	2500–2300		Ambelikou, Philia Drakos
	I:	3000–2500		Kalavassos B, Erimi, Lapithos Kythrea
Neolithic	II:	3500–3000		Kalavassos A, Sotira
Unexplained gap				
Neolithic	I B:	5250–4950	First appearance of pottery	Troulli
	I A:	5800–5250	Pre-pottery Late Stone Age	Khirokitia, Petra tou Limniti. Maria Tenta, Phrenaros

CATALOGUE

Excavated sites—architecture

For the history of archaeological discoveries, see the survey in Karageorghis, *Cyprus, Archaeologia Mundi* (English ed. 1969). For the sites of the most important finds, see the map, Fig. 44. The Stone and Copper Age settlements of Cyprus have been well catalogued and charted by Nikolaou in *Kypriakai Spoudai* 31 (1967), 37—52. Dikaios has written a brief 'Conspectus of Architecture in Ancient Cyprus,' *Kypriakai Spoudai* 24 (1960), 1—30, Pls. 1—60; for prehistoric architecture, see the remarks in our introduction (p. 124: Neolithic; p. 125: Chalcolithic; p. 132: Early Bronze Age; p. 133: Middle Bronze Age; pp. 134 ff.: Late Bronze Age).

The early round buildings of Khirokitia (*1425—1438*, Figs. 46—49) are as noteworthy as the pit houses of Kalavassos (Fig. 52, *1446—1449*). The art of fortified architecture reached its first culmination during the Middle Bronze Age (Fig. 55, *1453*); then, during the Cypriot Late Bronze Age, we find surprising achievements in the sphere of town planning and great technical skill in the art of fortified building in Enkomi and Kition (Fig. 57, *1455*; Fig. 58, *1461*; cf. *1456—1460*).

1423–1450: NEOLITHIC AND CHALCOLITHIC SETTLEMENTS AND BUILDINGS

1423 Troulli, north coast. Early Neolithic settlement, from the south-east. – Dikaios, *SCE.* IV/1A, Pl.-Fig. 20.

1424 Rocky hill with temple site of Aphrodite Akraia, on the east cape of the Karpass peninsula. Early Neolithic settlement from the south-west. – Karageorghis, *BCH.* 86 (1962), 372 ff., Fig. 61 (62–64: Neolithic small finds).

1425 Fig. 46: Overall plan of the early Neolithic settlement of Khirokitia, in a loop of the river Maroniou. – Dikaios, *Khirokitia* (1953), Pl. 1.

1426 Fig. 47: Khirokitia. Ground plans and elevations of
to several early Neolithic round buildings (tholoi). *1426:*
1429 Tholos V; external diam. 4.50 m. – Dikaios, 57 ff. *1427:* Tholos XLVII; external diam. c. 7 m. – Ibid., 172 ff. *1428:* Tholos III, external diam. 4.30 m. (cf. *1437*). – Ibid., 43 ff. *1429:* Tholos XXVII, with outer stone wall 1.20 m. thick and adjacent inner wall of dry masonry (width 40–60 cm.; cf. Fig. 49, *1435*). – Ibid., 147 ff.

1430 Fig. 48: Khirokitia. Ground plans and elevations of
to several Neolithic tholoi. *1430:* Tholos VII; internal
1433 diam. 3 m. – Dikaios, 65 ff. *1431:* Tholos X (I). Upper building of at least four erected on the same place; internal diam. 2.70 m. – Ibid., 73 ff. *1432:* Tholos VIII (I–II). Two round buildings erected one after the other; diam. of earlier one (II) 2.80 m., internal diam. of later one (I) 4.40 m.; two graves in the middle. – Ibid., 69 ff. *1433:* Tholos XV (II–III), only the walling in the middle belongs to the earliest building (III), cf. *1437*. – Ibid., 86 ff.

1434 Fig. 49: Khirokitia. Plan of early Neolithic Tholoi IA, XI, XIIA and XVI, south of the main road (at the upper edge of the plan); Tholos IA: *1438*. – Dikaios, 14 ff., Pl. 3.

1435 Fig. 49: Khirokitia. Plan of the complex of early Neolithic Tholoi XXVII, XXVIII and XXIX. Tholos XXVII also Fig. 47, *1429*. – Dikaios, 148, Fig. 75.

1436 Khirokitia. Early Neolithic Tholos XVII; platform inside with two graves (cf. *1473 a, b*). – Dikaios, Khirokitia, Pls. 25 a, 26 b; and *SCE.* IV/1A, Pl.-Fig. 4:2.

1437 Khirokitia. Complex of early tholoi XV (II), X (II), III, and IV. – Dikaios, *Khirokitia,* Pl. 20 a; and *SCE.* IV/1A, Pl.-Fig. 4:5.

1438 Khirokitia. Tholos IA; external diam. 8.75 m.; two huge stone pillars inside. – Dikaios, *Khirokitia,* 18 ff., Pl. 11 a; and *SCE.* IV/1A, Pl.-Fig. 3:3.

1439 Sotira. Phase II. Late Neolithic House 1, Floor 3, from the south-west. – Dikaios, *Sotira* (1961), 21 ff., Pl. 39 c; and *SCE.* IV/1A, Pl.-Fig. 24:1.

1440 Sotira. Phase II. Late Neolithic House 5, Floor 3, from the west. – Dikaios, *Sotira,* 41 ff., Pl. 43 b; and *SCE.* IV/1A, Pl.-Fig. 24:3.

1441 Fig. 50: Sotira. Phase III: Late Neolithic round-oval House 8, with door in the east; numerous post-holes and hearth (cf. Fig. 51). – Dikaios, *Sotira,* 67 ff., Pl. 24 a.

1442 Fig. 50: Sotira. Phase III. Late Neolithic polygonal House 11 (cf. Fig. 51). – Dikaios, 74 ff., Pl. 25 b.

1443 Fig. 50: Sotira. Phase II. Late Neolithic square house 7, with rounded corners (cf. Fig. 51). – Dikaios, 50 ff., Pl. 21.

1444 Fig. 50: Sotira. Overall plan of Late Neolithic settlement, with Excavation Areas I–V. Tomb region, Area I: Fig. 60, *1476*. Main living quarters, Area V: Fig. 51, *1445*. – Dikaios, Pl. 4.

1445 Fig. 51: Sotira. Excavation Area V (cf. Fig. 50, *1444*). Houses 8, 7 and 11 (*1441–1443*) west of the centre. – Dikaios, Pls. 8, 10.

1446 Fig. 52: Kalavassos, Settlement A. Late Neolithic pit
to houses, with round or irregular oval ground plan, dug
1449 into the soft limestone. *1448* is cavelike; the others have central wooden posts to support the roof. – Dikaios, *SCE.* IV/1A, 106 ff., Pl.-Fig. 52.

1450 Erimi. Early Chalcolithic Round House 9 a; grave in foreground. – Dikaios, loc. cit., 113 ff., Pl.-Fig. 35:3.

139

1451 Fig. 53: Ambelikou-Alatri, north-west Cyprus. Ground plan of Early Bronze Age groups of rooms; part of a settlement with copper-smelting equipment. – Dikaios, *ILN.* 2, 3, 1946, 245, Fig. 17; and *Kypriakai Spoudai* 24 (1960), 8, Pls. 3 b (photograph), 29 c (plan).

1452 Fig. 54: Kalopsida, east Cyprus. Ground plan of a Middle Bronze Age house, with eleven rooms grouped round an inner court. The two rooms in the north-west recall megaron architecture. Mud-brick walls on foundations of rubble. Middle Cypriot III. – Gjerstad, *Studies on Prehistoric Cyprus* (1926), 27 ff.; Dikaios, loc. cit., 8, Pl. 29 b; Åström, *The Middle Cypriote Bronze Age* (1957), 1 ff., Figs. 1, 2.

1453 Fig. 55: Nitovikla, Karpass peninsula. Sketched reconstruction of a Middle Bronze Age fortress, probably built as a defence against Hyksos attacks (seventeenth century B. C.). – Sjöqvist, *SCE.* I, 371 ff.; Dikaios, 8 f., Pls. 4 a (photograph), 33 a, b (reconstruction and ground plan).

1454 Fig. 56: Pyla-Kokkinokremos. Excavation Area II: Building with several small rooms; rubble walls, Late Cypriot III. – Dikaios, 12, Pls. 5 b (photograph), 36 a (plan).

1455 Fig. 57: Enkomi. Complex of buildings in Excavation Area I. Late Cypriot I and II.

1456 Enkomi. Northern section of the foundations of the town wall built of Cyclopean masonry, originally surmounted by superstructure of sun-dried bricks. Late Cypriot III. – Dikaios, *Kypriakai Spoudai* 24 (1960), 12, Pl. 4 b.

1457 Enkomi. View over the town centre from the north-west, with remains of the ashlar building known as the Sanctuary of the Horned God. Late Cypriot III *(1740:* 'Horned God'). – Dikaios, *ILN.* 27, 8, 1949, 316 f.; id., *Kypriakai Spoudai* 24 (1960), 12 f., Pl. 5 a; and *AA.* 1962, 10, Fig. 6.

1458 Kition. Northern section of the Cyclopean substructure
1459 of the town wall *(1459:* from the east). Late Cypriot III; cf. also Fig. 58, *1461.* – Karageorghis, *BCH.* 91 (1967), 317 ff., Figs. 104, 108.

1460 Kition. Rectangular Bastion B in the northern section of the town wall. Late Cypriot III. – Karageorghis, 318, Fig. 106.

1461 Fig. 58: Kition. Plan of the northern section of the town wall, including bastions in front of it. Late Cypriot III.

1462 Fig. 58: Palaiokastro–Maa, Paphos district. Plan of the
a fortification wall built for the defence of a peninsula settlement. Cyclopean substructure in the manner of the fortresses of Enkomi and Kition; filled with pebbles between inner and outer shell of wall. Late Cypriot III. – Dikaios, *Kypriakai Spoudai* 24 (1960), 13, Pl. 37 b; and *Enkomi* (1969), Pl. 295:2 a, 3, 4.

1462 Palaiokastro-Maa. Fortification wall with north gate
b (cf. *plan 1462 a*). Late Cypriot III. – Dikaios, loc. cit., Pl. 6 a (different view).

Tombs

Originally, Cypriot tombs were simple pits, each containing a single skeleton lying on its side with knees drawn up *(1463—1478)*. From the Early Bronze Age, bodies were interred in larger, cave-like sites *(1479 a—1483)*; in the Middle Bronze Age, the rock tomb, which had several main and numerous side-chambers, predominated (Fig. 54, *1484*). We know of the special forms of tombs in the Late Bronze Age from Enkomi. While the earliest burials were always in individual graves, family or dynastic tombs became more common from the Early Bronze Age. Thus we find large necropoleis outside the settlements; yet interment beneath the floor of the dwelling house was so much a part of the most ancient Cypriot tradition (cf. e.g. *1436, 1450*), that we still encounter this custom at the end of the Bronze Age at Enkomi.

Dikaios deals also with the changing forms of tomb architecture in 'A Conspectus of Architecture in Ancient Cyprus', *Kypriakai Spoudai* 24 (1960), 3 ff.; there are further details in Wiesner, *Grab und Jenseits* (1938), in Pini, *Beiträge zur minoischen Gräberkunde* (1968), and in the literature listed there. For tombs in the Aegean see above, pp. 39 ff.

1463–1478: NEOLITHIC BURIALS

1463 Fig. 59: Khirokitia. Early Neolithic types of burial in
to the tholoi of a settlement; cf. Dikaios, *Khirokitia*
1473 (1953), 215 ff., Pl. 145 a–k. *1465 a, b:* Sketch and photo-
b graph of the skeleton of a young man in Tomb 6, Tholos V. – Dikaios, *Khirokitia* (1953), 62, Pl. 16 a; and *SCE.* IV/1A, Pl.-Fig. 5:4. *1473 a, b:* Sketch and photograph of the skeleton of an eight-year-old child in Tomb 2, Tholos XVII. – Dikaios, *Khirokitia*, 106, Pl. 26 a; and *SCE.* IV/1A, Pl.-Fig. 6:4.

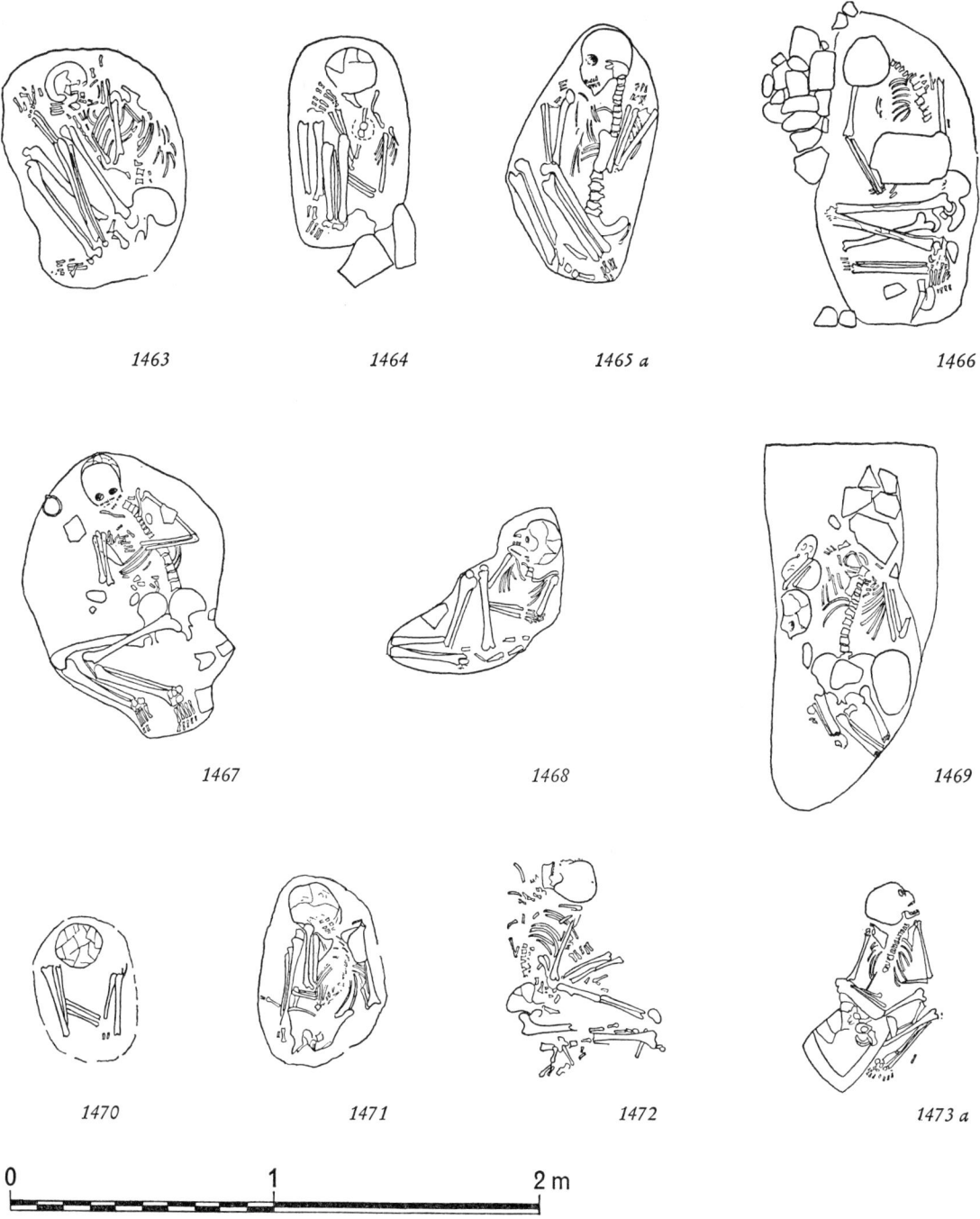

Fig. 59 1463–1473 a Khirokitia, Stone Age tombs

1474 Khirokitia. Tomb 1, early Neolithic Tholos XVIII. – Dikaios, *Khirokitia*, Pl. 28 c; and *SCE*. IV/1A, Pl.-Fig. 8:1.

1475 Khirokitia. Tomb 16 in early Neolithic Tholos XV, Building Phase II. – Dikaios, *Khirokitia*, Pl. 23 d, and *SCE*. IV/1A, Pl.-Fig. 6:3.

1476 Fig. 60: Sotira. Plan of Excavation Area I, with site of late Neolithic tombs; cf. overall plan of Sotira: Fig. 50, 1444. – Dikaios, *Sotira* (1961), 139 ff., Pl. 5.

1477 Sotira. Area I, Tombs 12 and 5: Neolithic II. – Di-
1478 kaios, *Sotira*, Pl. 57 f, c; and *SCE*. IV/1A, Pl.-Fig. 27:4, 6.

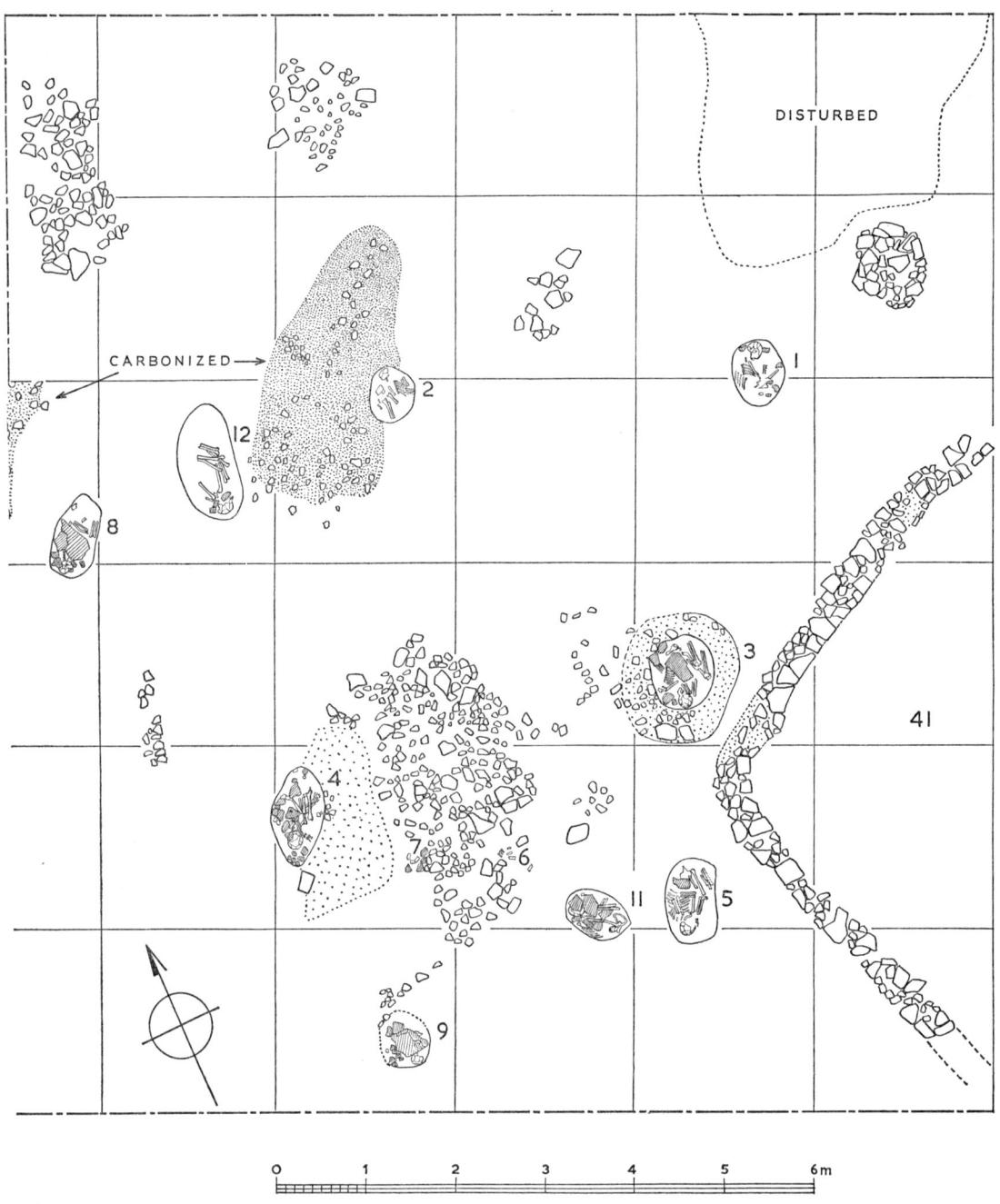

Fig. 60 1476 Sotira, Excavation Area I with Neolithic tombs

1479–1484: EARLY AND MIDDLE BRONZE AGE TOMBS

1479 Philia–Vasiliko. Chamber Tomb 1: Remains of skeleton
a–c and grave goods *in situ*. Fig. 61: Plan and section of the burial chamber. Early Cypriot I (*c.* 2250 B. C.). – Dikaios, *SCE*. IV/1A, 160 ff., Fig. 75, and Pl.-Fig. 49:2, 5.

1480 Vounous. Tomb 32: Dromos with sealed door *in situ* Early Cypriot III. – Dikaios, *Archaeologia* 88 (1940), Pl. 5 a.

1481 Vounous. Tombs 35, 41, 36: Grave goods *in situ*. Early to Cypriot III. – Dikaios, *Archaeol.* 88, Pls. 5 c; 6 c;
1483 5 d.

1484 Fig. 54: Lapithos, north coast. Chamber Tomb 313,
a, b ground-plan and section. Date of occupation: Middle Cypriot I–II. – Gjerstad, *SCE*. I, 88, Fig. 43; Dikaios, *Kypriakai Spoudai* 24 (1960), 9, Pl. 31 a; Stewart, *SCE*. IV/1A, 390 (dating); Pini, *Beiträge zur minoischen Gräberkunde* (1968), Fig. 19 (ground-plan).

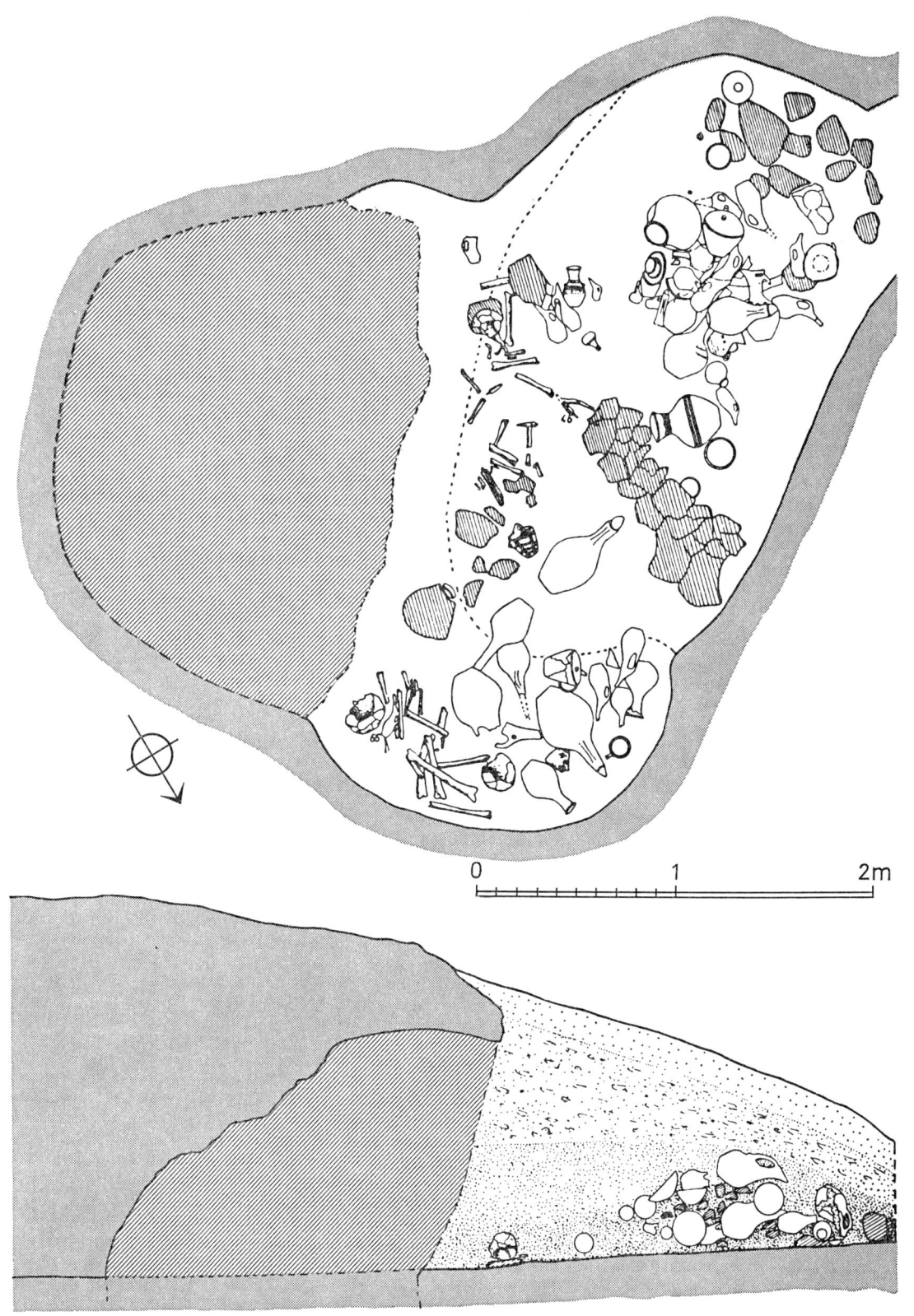

Fig. 61 *1479 c* Philia Vasiliko, Early Bronze Age Tomb I

Pottery

Pottery is one of the most important types of archaeological find, as it allows one to establish a good chronological framework; it enables the archaeologist to date the strata of finds and tomb inventories. However, the earliest cultural period hitherto ascertained on the island, Neolithic I A, has yielded us no pottery as yet (cf. Fig. 62 and table, p. 138). The pottery of the following period was made carefully by hand, without the potter's wheel; from the very beginning it displayed highly developed forms (Neolithic II and Chalcolithic: *1485—1493* and Fig. 62). Monochrome red pottery predominated in the Early Bronze Age *(1494 ff.)*, while numerous new types appeared during the Middle Bronze Age and the variety of forms also increased *(1528 ff.)*. At the same time, here and there we find imported vessels on the island.

In terms of the periods that concern us here, the Late Bronze Age is particularly rich in elaborately painted vases *(1620 ff.)*. One of the major problems in the study of Late Cypriot pottery is the origin of the so-called 'Cypro-Helladic' ware. According to some scholars, it was imported from the Peloponnese; others believe it was made by Mycenaean settlers in Cyprus (cf. pp. 60 ff.).

Gjerstad, in *Cypriot Pottery* (1932), suggests a rather more sophisticated system of classification of Cypriot ware than that which Myres and Ohnefalsch-Richter attempted in their *Catalogue of the Cyprus Museum*; in his earlier *Studies on Prehistoric Cyprus* (1926), 88 ff., he starts from the Early Bronze Age pottery. The essay by Dikaios in *SCE*: IV/1A (1962) is informative on the earlier ware; our Fig. 62 is based on it, although Watkins has recently put forward divergent views on the development of early pottery. The pottery of the Middle Bronze Age has received exemplary treatment in Åström, *The Middle Cypriot Bronze Age* (1957), 11—134.

For Late Bronze Age pottery, see the works listed in the bibliography (pp. 176 ff.)—in particular Sjöqvist, *Problems of the Late Cypriot Bronze Age* (1940); Coche de la Ferté, *Essai de Classification de la Céramique Mycénienne d'Enkomi* (1951); Stubbings, *Mycenaean Pottery from the Levant* (1951); Karageorghis, *Nouveaux Documents pour l'Etude du Bronze Récent à Chypre* (1965) and, for polychrome painted ware, Epstein, *Palestinian Bichrome Ware* (1966). There are also studies by Merrillees, 'Cypriot Bronze Age Pottery found in Egypt,' *Stud. in Mediterr. Arch.* XVIII (1968), and by Hocking, 'Ceramic Style in Prehistoric Cyprus,' *Man* 80 (1963), 65 ff.

In *Bei Töpfern und Töpferinnen in Kreta, Messenien und Zypern* (1962), Hampe and Winter impressively proved that prehistoric conventions and practices in the manufacture of pottery still survive in Cyprus today.

1485–1493: NEOLITHIC AND CHALCOLITHIC PERIOD

1485 Sotira. Area V, Phase III, House 13, Floor II: Jug of the late Neolithic red-on-white type, with plain pattern of 'combed' lines; spherical, smooth base, narrow, cylindrical neck, flat rim. Wide vertical bands of colour decorated with comb-strokes alternating with vertically superimposed rings surrounding coloured discs; height 39 cm. Cyprus Mus., Nicosia. – Dikaios, *SCE.* IV/1A, Pl.-Fig. 29:7; and *Sotira* 89, No. 284, Pl. 74.

1486 Sotira. Area V, Phase III, House 27, Floor II: Jug of the late Neolithic combed-ornament type; shape as *1485*. Vertical bands of combed ornament on neck and body of vessel; height 37 cm. Univ. Mus., Philadelphia. – Dikaios, *SCE.* IV/1A, Pl.-Fig. 28:2; and *Sotira* 122, No. 195, Pls. 66, 86.

1487 Khirokitia. Late Neolithic hemispherical bowl, with open spout and plain base. Wavy bands in comb-stroke technique inside and out; height 15 cm., diam. 32.5 cm. Cyprus Mus., Nicosia. – Dikaios, *SCE.* IV/1A, Fig. 21, No. 496; and *Khirokitia*, Pls. 71, 135; Karageorghis, *Cyprus*, Pl. 24.

1488 Sotira (site as *1485*). Small late Neolithic jug of the red-on-white type; spherical with plain base; neck missing. Decoration: wide vertical bands and zigzag lines; surviving height 16.5 cm. Cyprus Mus., Nicosia. – Dikaios, *SCE.* IV/1A, Pl.-Fig. 29:8; and *Sotira* 89, No. 305, Pls. 77, 87.

1489 Erimi. Early Chalcolithic steep-walled vessel of the red-on-white type, with plain base. Decoration: wide, diagonally arranged pairs of bands and painted rim; height 20.5 cm., diam. 23 cm. Cyprus Mus., Nicosia. – Dikaios, *RDAC.* 1936, Pl. 15:2, No. 403, and *SCE.* IV/1A, Pl.-Fig. 36:2.

1490 Erimi. Early Chalcolithic steep-walled vessel of the red-on-white plain base. Decoration: wide, diagonally arranged pairs of bands and painted rim; height 20.5

cm., diam. 23 cm. Cyprus Mus., Nicosia. – Dikaios, *RDAC.* 1936, Pl. 15:2, No. 403, and *SCE.* IV/1A, Pl.-Fig. 36:2.

1491 Erimi. Early Chalcolithic steep-walled vessel, like *1490*. Decoration: three diagonally running double zigzag lines and painted rim; height 15 cm., diam. 16 cm. Cyprus Mus., Nicosia. – Dikaios, *RDAC.* 1936, Pl. 16:1, No. 414, and *SCE.* IV/1A, Pl.-Fig. 36:3.

1492 Erimi. Early Chalcolithic, large, pithos-like vessel of the red-on-white type, with convex walls and flattened base; cylindrical handle below the rim. Decoration: two wide vertical bands and a narrower stripe encircling the vessel horizontally, filled artistically with geometric patterns; also two diagonally-arranged stepped bands and U-shaped ornaments (perhaps abstract representations of the arms of the human body); height 53 cm., diam. 38 cm. Cyprus Mus., Nicosia. – Dikaios, *RDAC.* 1936, 30, No. 162, Fig. 4, Pl. 15:3, 4; id., *SCE.* IV/1A, Pl.-Fig. 36:4; id., *Iraq* 7 (1940), Pl. 8:10; and *Guide,* Pl. 2:5; Karageorghis, *Cyprus,* Pl. 26.

1493 Hagios Epiktetos. Early Chalcolithic deep bowl of the red-on-white type, with convex walls, flattened base and tubular, lateral spout. Decoration: below the rim a frieze of upright rectangles; height 13 cm., diam. 18.5 cm. Cyprus Mus., Nicosia, Inv. No. R.R. 305.

1494–1527: EARLY BRONZE AGE

1494 Philia–Vasiliko. Tomb 3, Nos. 8, 9: Early Cypriot handled jug of the first Early Bronze Age phase (Red-Polished Ware I), with ovoid body decorated with incised work, and long narrow neck. Diagonally rising spout, cut straight above; two smaller jugs of the same type on the shoulder of the big one, on either side of the handle; height 36 cm. Cyprus Mus., Nicosia. – Dikaios, *SCE.* IV/1A, Pl.-Fig. 51:11, Fig. 80:23.

1495 Philia–Vasiliko. Tomb 1, No. 4. Early Cypriot, red-polished jug with ovoid body, smooth base, long concave neck, and mouth with spout; horn-like pegs in place of handle. Incised decoration below mouth and on shoulder; height 30 cm. Cyprus Mus., Nicosia. – Dikaios, Pl.-Fig. 51:2, Fig. 82:4.

1496 Philia–Vasiliko. Tomb 1, No. 30: Early Cypriot tall cup, in the form of the upper part of a jug like *1494* (type and date of pottery as *1494*); smooth base, handle between rim of vessel and lower third of body; height 13.5 cm. Cyprus Mus., Nicosia. – Dikaios, Pl.-Fig. 51:7, Fig. 82:18; Karageorghis, *Cyprus,* Pl. 36.

1497 Philia–Vasiliko. Tomb 1, No. 64. Early Cypriot bottle with spherical body, long concave neck and flaring rim, flat base (type and date of pottery as *1494*); height 24 cm. Cyprus Mus., Nicosia. – Dikaios, Pl.-Fig. 55:1, Fig. 82:2.

1498 Philia–Vasiliko. Tomb 1, No. 12: Early Cypriot handled jug with ovoid body, long slim beak neck and flat base (type and date as *1494*); height 36 cm. Cyprus Mus., Nicosia. – Dikaios, Pl.-Fig. 51:5, Fig. 82:25; and *Guide,* Pl. 3:6; Karageorghis, *Cyprus,* Pl. 35.

1499 Philia–Vasiliko. Tomb 1, No. 50: Early Cypriot small basket with basket handle; red-on-white type of the first Early Bronze Age phase; flat base, spouts below the rim. Surface decorated with horizontal and vertical stripes; height 16.8 cm. Cyprus Mus., Nicosia. – Dikaios, *SCE.* IV/1A, Pl.-Fig. 50:5, Fig. 83:18; and *Guide,* Pl. 3:1; Karageorghis, *Cyprus,* Pl. 44.

1500 Philia–Vasiliko. Tomb 1, No. 17: Early Cypriot small bowl with spouts and flat base. Decoration: chevrons and other linear motifs (type and date as *1499*); height 8 cm., diam. 13 cm. Cyprus Mus., Nicosia. – Dikaios, *SCE.* IV/1A, Pl.-Fig. 50:9, Fig. 83:17.

1501 Philia–Vasiliko. Tomb 3, No. 15: Early Cypriot tall bowl with spout (type and date as *1500*); height 9 cm. Cyprus Mus., Nicosia. – Dikaios, Pl.-Fig. 50:7, Fig. 83:15.

1502 Lapithos. Tomb 322, Chamber D, No. 1: Kernos-like red-polished multiple vessel; three small hemispherical bowls, with sockets and suspension eyes, on a ring with three feet. Incised decoration on ring and feet; height 20 cm., diam. 19.5 cm. Early Cypriot III/Middle Cypriot I. Cyprus Mus., Nicosia.

1503 Limassol. Tomb 83, No. 15: Red-polished jug in the shape of a squat bird, with short 'tail', concave neck, beak spout and vertical handle; suspension eyes at base of neck and at either side of upper end of handle; Early Cypriot III. District Mus., Limassol, Inv. No. 38. – Karageorghis, *BCH.* 91 (1967), 307, Fig. 88 (sketch).

1504 Episkopi. Deep bowl with lugs and three long, cylindrical feet; height 24 cm., diam. 16 cm. (type and date as *1503*). Cyprus Mus., Nicosia, Inv. No. 1933, XII-28.4.

1505 Lapithos. Tomb 7 (1917): Multiple vessel made up of three connected cups, with incised decoration, on three cylindrical feet, and basket handle; height 14 cm. (type and date as *1503*). Cyprus Mus., Nicosia, Inv. No. A 444.

1506 Kalavassos. Tomb 5, No. 36: Conical bowl, with high conical foot and unilateral handle rising steeply from the rim. Incised decoration on wall and foot; height 10.5 cm., diam. 17 cm. (type and date as *1503*). District Mus., Larnaka. – Karageorghis, *RDAC.* 1940–48, 136, Fig. 18, Pl. 10 g.

1507 Larnakas tis Lapithou, Kyrenia District. Tomb 1, No. 38: Large bowl with round base, tubular spout close under rim and connected to it by a bridge; opposite, a short round lug, also wide strap handle on either side. Impressed circular ornaments below the rim, on handles and spout; encircling zigzag ridge; height including spout 39 cm., diam. 57 cm. (type and date as *1503*). Cyprus Mus., Nicosia, Inv. No. 1963, XII-23.1. – Karageorghis, *BCH*. 88 (1964), 312, Fig. 34.

1508 Lapithos. Tomb 322, Chamber D, No. 6: Red-polished multiple vessel, consisting of hollow conical body, with flat base, surmounted by beaked jug; four hemispherical bowls at the point of attachment. The whole densely covered with white filled incised patterns; height 42.5 cm. Early Cypriot III/Middle Cypriot I. Cyprus Mus., Nicosia. – Gjerstad, *SCE*. I, Pl. 102:6; Bossert, *Altsyrien*, No. 180.

1509 Cyprus. Provenance unknown. Ladle with long handle, consisting of two parallel cylindrical rods, connected at the end and in the middle by cross pieces and a small hemispherical bowl; length 34 cm. (type and date as *1503*). Cyprus Mus., Nicosia, Inv. No. A 465.

1510 Denia. Tomb 1: Spherical amphora, with high neck and three pointed feet; flat strap handles between mouth and shoulder. Applied zigzag fillets on shoulder and neck; height 56 cm., diam. 25 cm. (type and date as *1503*). Cyprus Mus., Nicosia.

1511 Vounous. Tomb 164, Chamber A, No. 45: Ovoid handled jug with small, flat base and long neck, ending in a beak spout cut straight; ridge at base of neck. Circular and linear decoration on shoulder and neck, decorative bosses on neck and handle; height 77.4 cm. Early Cypriot II, Red-Polished Ware. Cyprus Mus., Nicosia. – Stewart, *Vounous*, Pl. 50 b; Karageorghis, *Treasures*, Pl. 7.

1512 Vounous. Tomb 19, No. 67: Multiple vessel, consisting of three gourd-shaped vessels with long necks surmounted by another gourd jug with handle and beak mouth; also three small jugs with two or three beaks between the lower vessels; all parts are interconnected; height 83 cm. (type and date as *1503*). Cyprus Mus., Nicosia. – Dikaios, *Archaeologia* 88 (1940), Pl. 32 c; and *Guide*, Pl. 4:4; Karageorghis, *Treasures*, Pl. 8; and *Cyprus*, Pl. 41.

1513 Denia. Large bowl, with flat base and lugs on the rim. Relief decoration: bucrania, vertical ribs, and diagonal notched zigzag ridges; height 24.3 cm., diam. 47.5 cm. (type and date as *1503*). Nicosia Survey, No. CS. 992/5. – Karageorghis, *BCH*. 90 (1966), 302, Fig. 9.

1514 Margi. Large, handled bowl (lower part lost) with two tubular spouts, connected to the rim of the vessel by a bridge. Circle of sculptured human figures below the rim facing the inside of the bowl with outstretched arms; one small figure is riding an unidentifiable quadruped; height 26.2 cm., diam. 35.7 cm. (type and date as *1503*). Cyprus Mus., Nicosia, Inv. No. 1942.X-17.1. – Karageorghis, *RDAC*. 1940-48, Pl. 11 a, c.

1515 Cyprus. Provenance unknown. Handled jug with spherical body, rounded base, long tubular spout and three cylindrical necks. Several decorative ridges and wide lips; rich linear incised decoration; height 30 cm. (type and date as *1503*). Cyprus Mus., Nicosia, Inv. No. 1933.I-31.1.

1516 Denia. Tomb 1, No. 92: Spherical handled jug with rounded base and long cylindrical neck, suspension eye at base of neck opposite handle. Relief decoration: four stylized goats on shoulder, vertical serpentine motifs on neck; height 48.5 cm. (type and date as *1503*). Cyprus Mus., Nicosia.

1517 Vounous. Tomb 15, No. 50: Multiple vessel, consisting of three small, egg-shaped bodies with a single long neck; small vertical handle on upper back of neck. Linear incised patterns and concentric circles cover the entire surface; height 47 cm. (type and date as *1503*). Cyprus Mus., Nicosia. – Dikaios, *Archaeologia* 88 (1940), Pl. 31:6; Karageorghis, *Cyprus*, Pl. 40.

1518 Vounous. Multiple vessel, consisting of two beaked jugs, the smaller superimposed on the larger, both equipped with handle and mouth; sculptured birds at the base of each neck and at the upper end of the handle of the lower jug. Incised decoration over the entire body of the vessel; height 26 cm. (type and date as *1503*). Cyprus Mus., Nicosia, Inv. No. 1933.VI-7.7. – Dikaios, Pl. 14 a.

1519 Denia. Black-polished ovoid amphoriskos, with long neck flaring outwards at the mouth, and two suspension handles at the base of the neck. Rich incised and stippled decoration on body and neck; height 28 cm. Early Cypriot III. Cyprus Mus., Nicosia, Inv. No. 1961.IX-9.3. – Karageorghis, *BCH*. 85 (1961), 305, Fig. 57.

1520 Vounous. Tomb 2, No. 91: Squat spherical pyxis with flat lid; plank-shaped modelled statuettes on either side of mouth, one with a child in its arm. Incised parallel lines on body of vessel and on figurines. Greatest diam. 22 cm. (type and date as *1503*). Cyprus Mus., Nicosia. – Dikaios, *Archaeologia* 88 (1940), Pl. 36 a.

1521 Limassol-Katholiki. Spherical pyxis and accompanying flat, rectangular lid with doubly pierced lug; four suspension eyes on shoulder. Decoration: incised, white-filled parallel lines and bars; height 15.2 cm. (type and date as *1503*). District Mus., Limassol, Inv. No. 235. – Karageorghis, *BCH*. 88 (1964), 325, Fig. 54.

1522 Vounous. Tomb 160, Chamber B, No. 12: Red-polished votive vessel (Early Cypriot Phase II), with flat base and 'sword pommel' grip; two bulls' heads, a bird's head, and two pairs of two spoon-like shapes alternating on the rim. Incised and dotted patterns on the body of the vessel, the grip and the sculptural protomes. Height 18.2 cm., diam. 17 cm. Cyprus Mus., Nicosia. – Stewart, *Vounous*, Pls. 91 b, 92 a; Karageorghis, *Cyprus*, Pl. 39.

1523 From the Pyla region. Terracotta statuette, representing a quadruped with elongated body and long, almost horizontal neck, and with a container on its back; incised decoration: parallel zigzag lines; height 11 cm., length 21 cm. (type and date as *1503*). Cyprus Mus., Nicosia, Inv. No. 1962.IV-17.3. – Karageorghis, *BCH*. 87 (1963), 341, Fig. 23.

1524 Cyprus. Provenance unknown. Theriomorphic vessel with elongated hollow body, four stump legs, long

---

opposite: Fig. 62 Development of Cypriot pottery from the Neolithic period to the Early Bronze Age

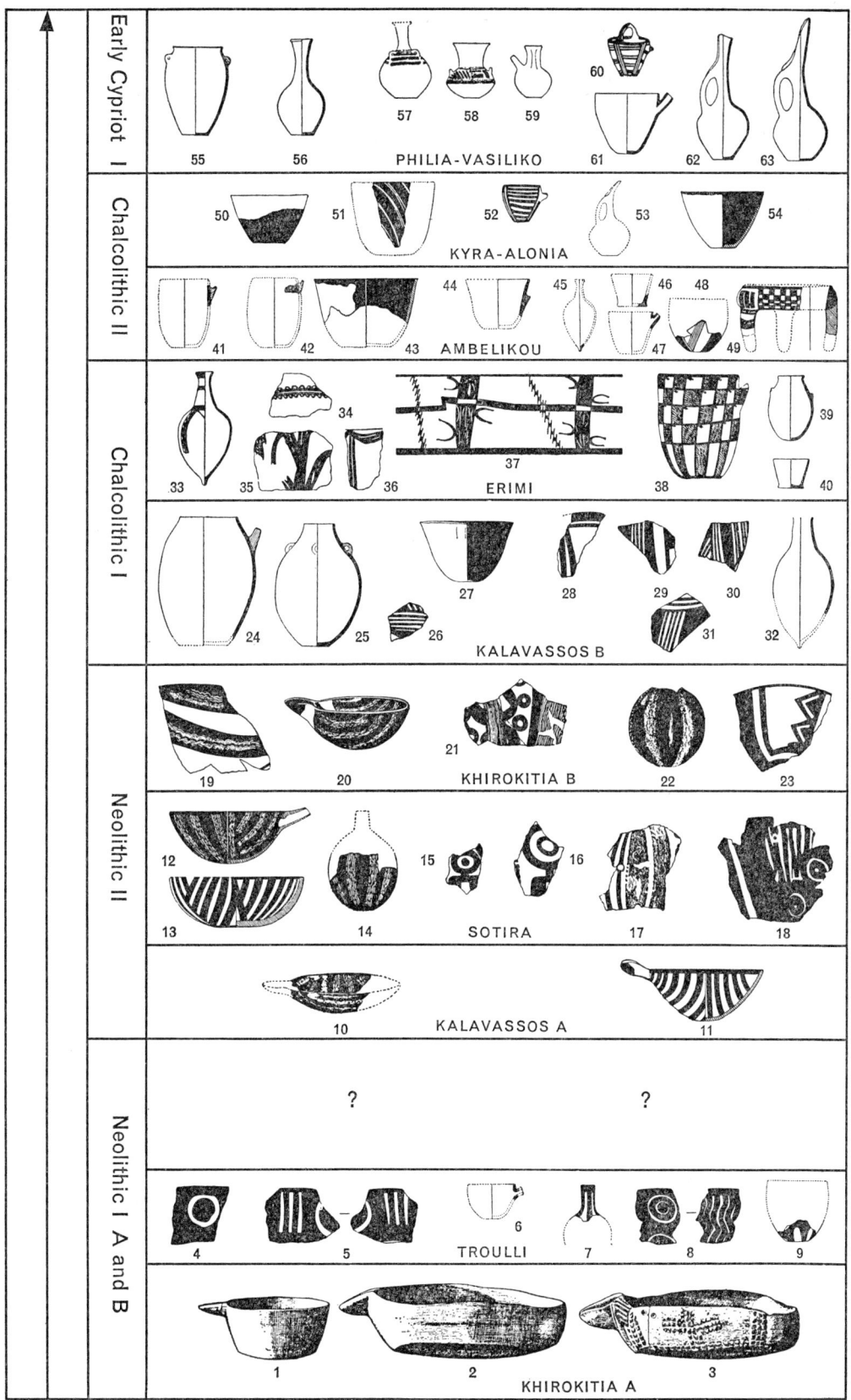

neck, and large ass-like head; the mane is suggested by a diagonally grooved ridge. Suspension handle on the back; neck and body incised with bars and zigzag lines; height 16 cm., length 21 cm. (type and date as *1503*). Cyprus Mus., Nicosia, Inv. No. A 474.

1525 Soloi. Vessel in the form of a bull, with plump, cubical body, four stump legs, and large horns pointing diagonally forward; suspension eye on neck. Wealth of zigzag and bar patterns in incised work on body, brow and horns; height 13 cm., length 17.5 cm. (type and date as *1503*). Cyprus Mus., Nicosia, Inv. No. 1943.I-20.1. – Karageorghis, *Cyprus*, Pl. 48 right.

1526 Cyprus. Provenance unknown. Theriomorphic vessel with ovoid body on four stump legs; long neck, small head and little tail; loop handle on neck and suspension eye on lower side of body. Dense pattern of bars, zigzags and lozenges in incised technique on head, neck, handle and body; height 15.3 cm., length 19 cm. (type and date as *1503*). Cyprus Mus., Nicosia, Inv. No. A 445. – Karageorghis, Pl. 48 left.

1527 Cyprus. Provenance unknown. Theriomorphic vessel; date, ceramic type, and form similar to *1526*; also small jug on the neck; height 14 cm., length 15.2 cm. Cyprus Mus., Nicosia, Inv. No. A 472.

1528–1656: MIDDLE AND LATE BRONZE AGES

1528 Cyprus. Find-spot unknown. Middle Cypriot bottle, curved like a horn, with black slip (Black Slip III); flat base, funnel-like mouth and small vertical handle at beginning of neck. Fine dense incised decoration: latticed or hatched lines, triangles and zigzag bands; height 29.9 cm. Cyprus Mus., Nicosia, Inv. No. A 599.

1529 Arpera. Tomb 1, Chamber A, No. 16: Middle Cypriot small jug (Black Slip III, imitation of Tell el-Yahudiye Ware). Ovoid body with short, slender neck, sharply profiled round mouth, handle attached below rim and 'button' base. Ochre-yellow clay, surface unpainted; vertical bands filled with dots; height 14 cm. Cyprus Mus., Nicosia.

1530 Cyprus. Find-spot unknown. Middle Cypriot small jug (type as *1528*). Ovoid body, short neck and 'button' base; horn-like bosses in three zones on body. Rich incised decoration; height 11.3 cm. Cyprus Mus., Nicosia, Inv. No. A 621.

1531 Cyprus. Provenance unknown. Middle Cypriot small jug (type as *1528*). Ovoid body with high, conical 'button' base; short neck, trefoil mouth and handle attached on the shoulder. Incised decoration: groups of horizontal bars, with stippled horizontal and zigzag bands; height 10.5 cm. Cyprus Mus., Nicosia, Inv. No. A 613.

1532 Cyprus. Provenance unknown. Middle Cypriot handled jug (type as *1528*). Bi-conical squat body with flat base, long narrow neck, and funnel-like, profiled mouth; incised decoration: zigzag groups; height 10.5 cm. Cyprus Mus., Nicosia, Inv. No. A 609. – Gjerstad, *Studies on Prehistoric Cyprus*, 146, No. 2.

1533 Cyprus. Find-spot unknown. Middle Cypriot handled jug of Tell el-Yahudiye Ware type. Ovoid body; neck narrowing in the middle; round, profiled mouth, flattened base. Large stippled triangles on body; height 27 cm. Cyprus Mus., Nicosia, Inv. No. A 1440. – For this type of vessel in Cyprus, cf. also Fimmen, *Kret.-myk. Kultur*, 158 ff.

1534 Cyprus. Find-spot unknown. Middle Cypriot small handled jug of the Tell el-Yahudiye Ware type with ovoid body, short narrow neck, round profiled mouth, and 'button' base; decoration: stippled bands; height 12 cm. Cyprus Mus., Nicosia, Inv. No. A 1442.

1535 Milia. Tomb 10, No. 60: Middle Cypriot small handled jug of the Tell el-Yahudiye Ware type. Bi-conical form, short, narrow neck, round profiled mouth, and 'button' base; stippled bands above and below the widest diameter (undecorated); height 11.5 cm. Cyprus Mus., Nicosia. – Westholm, *QDAP.* 8 (1939), Pl. 1, No. 26.

1536 Cyprus. Find-spot unknown. Middle Cypriot small handled jug of Tell el-Yahudiye Ware type; similar to *1535*, buth with round body; height 14.5 cm. Cyprus Mus., Nicosia, Inv. No. A 1441.

1537 Cyprus. Find-spot unknown. Middle Cypriot small handled jug of Tell el-Yahudiye Ware type. Cylindrical body with markedly offset rounded base and equally offset sloping shoulder; short narrow neck, round profiled mouth; stippled chevrons on body; height 12.5 cm. Cyprus Mus., Nicosia, Inv. No. A 1448.

1538 Cyprus. Find-spot unknown. Middle Cypriot handled jug of the red-on-black type, with spherical, squat body, flat base, long wide neck, and small knob on upper end of handle. Frieze of cross-hatched lozenges on shoulder; horizontal and vertical bars on neck and body; height 26 cm., diam. of mouth 12.5 cm. Cyprus Mus., Nicosia, Inv. No. A 960.

1539 Cyprus. Find-spot unknown. Middle Cypriot pot-bellied vessel of the red-on-black type with short cylindrical neck, rounded base, and large loop handle set diagonally on shoulder; decoration: vertical bars; height 12 cm., diam. 10 cm. Cyprus Mus., Nicosia, Inv. No. A 944.

1540 Cyprus. Find-spot unknown. Middle Cypriot pot-bellied vessel, with rounded base, wide neck and flaring mouth; two diametrically opposed holes below the rim; decoration: horizontal and vertical bars (type as *1539*); height 13.5 cm., diam. 10.3 cm. Cyprus Mus., Nicosia, Inv. No. A 968.

1541 Cyprus. Find-spot unknown. Middle Cypriot shallow bowl with round base, small open spout on rim, opposite a vertical loop handle; inner and outer decoration in vertical bars (type as *1539*); height 9 cm., diam. 28.2 cm. Cyprus Mus., Nicosia, Inv. No. A 939.

1542 Galinoporni. Tomb 2, No. 144: Middle Cypriot multiple vessel of Phase II, consisting of two small spherical jugs with common neck and vertical handle. Sculptured female figure in curved aperture between the two vessels, opposite the handle. Painted vertical and horizontal bars (type as *1539*); height 18.5 cm. Cyprus Mus., Nicosia, Inv. No. 1956.III-7.6.

1543 Cyprus. Find-spot unknown. Multiple vessel, three small jugs with common neck and vertical handle (type and date as *1539*); vertical and horizontal bars on body and neck; height 19.5 cm. Cyprus Mus., Nicosia, Inv. No. A 973. – Åström, *Opusc. Ath.* 5 (1965), 61, Fig. 1.11.

1544 Cyprus. Find-spot unknown. Middle Cypriot multiple vessel, Phase III (White-Painted V); three spherical jugs with common neck and long vertical handle; painted decoration: wavy lines and groups of lines; height 14 cm. Z. D. Pierides Coll., Larnaka.

1545 Morphou. 'Toumba tou Skourou': Askos in form of bird (date: Late Cypriot I; type as *1544*); tubular spout with beak-like mouth on one side; on the other, bird's head protome; large loop handle between the two; decoration: bars and stripes; height 12 cm. Cyprus Mus., Nicosia, Inv. No. 1963.XI–18.1(4). – Karageorghis, *BCH.* 88 (1964), 313, Fig. 35 a.

1546 Morphou. 'Toumba tou Skourou': Handled jug with ovoid, squat body and flat base; animal protome with horns opposite handle; painted stripes on body, neck, and protome (type and date as *1545*); height 12 cm. Cyprus Mus., Nicosia, Inv. No. 1963.XI–18.1(2). – Karageorghis, op. cit.

1547 Angastina. Tomb 2, No. 8: Multiple vessel (type and date as *1545*), four small spherical jugs with a common neck, against which a sculptured female figure leans; decoration: lattice-work pattern of stripes and triangles; height 13 cm. Cyprus Mus., Nicosia. – Nikolaou, *JHS.* 86 (1966), Arch. Rep. 29, Fig. 2.

1548 Morphou. 'Toumba tou Skourou': Spherical, handled jug with simple, flat base (type and date as *1545*); diagonally set, cut-away spout, horn-like decorative modelling opposite handle on shoulder. Decorative bars and bands; height 13 cm. Cyprus Mus., Nicosia, Inv. No. 1963.XI–18.1(6). – Karageorghis, op. cit.

1549 Cyprus. Find-spot unknown. Vessel with egg-shaped body, small, flat base and short funnel neck; two small vertical handles with button-like bosses between base of neck and low-set bulge. Bulge decorated with vertical bars; zone decoration from the middle upwards, including the neck. The various wide, horizontal bands are filled with zigzag lines and cross-hatched triangles; height 27.5 cm. Middle Cypriot III (White-Painted V). Cyprus Mus., Nicosia, Inv. No. A 845.

1550 Cyprus. Find-spot unknown. Bowl with offset foot, marked bulge, smooth rim, vertical handle and tubular spout on shoulder. Also on shoulder: frieze of cross-hatched triangles; wide band of colour below this, vertical bars on lower part; height 16.5 cm. (type and date as *1549*). Z. D. Pierides Coll., Larnaka.

1551 Cyprus. Find-spot unknown. Handled jug with squat, ovoid body, rounded base and long cylindrical neck with decorative bosses; upper end of handle extends above the mouth like a horn. Additional small suspension handle in front, at beginning of neck. Horizontal incised lines on body and neck; height 43.5 cm. Middle Cypriot II (Black Slip II). Cyprus Mus., Nicosia, Inv. No. A 572. – Gjerstad, *Studies on Prehistoric Cyprus*, 139; Dikaios, *Guide*, Pl. 7:3.

1552 Cyprus. Find-spot unknown. Amphora with squat circular body, round base, wide cylindrical neck, and widely flaring rim; two small handles at base of neck, rising to a point, each pierced twice. The middle of the wall of the body is stressed vertically by a row of small decorative sculptural bosses. Incised decoration: horizontal zones filled with zigzags separated by parallel lines; height 24.5 cm. (type and date as *1551*).

Cyprus Mus., Nicosia, Inv. No. A 586. – Gjerstad, 140.

1553 Cyprus. Find-spot unknown. Askos with elongated, cylindrical body on three short feet; open beak-like spout at the end of the body, and upright animal protome at the opposite end; small basket handle on the middle of the back. Decoration: vertical and horizontal bands, filled with cross-hatched patterns or wavy lines; height 13 cm., length 15.5 cm. Late Cypriot I (White-Painted V). Cyprus Mus., Nicosia, Inv. No. A 924.

1554 Lapithos, Tomb 50, No. 272. Ring kernos on four small
a, b feet, 'string-loop type'; tubular spout and large basket handle. Decoration: zones of lattice-work, horizontal bars and zigzag lines; height 11.7 cm. Middle Cypriot III (White-Painted III–V). Cyprus Mus., Nicosia, Inv. No. A 908. – Gjerstad, op. cit., 160.

1555 Cyprus. Find-spot unknown. Askos in bird form with elongated body and flat base; tubular spout with wide flaring beak; on the opposite side a tail-like peg; high basket handle on the back; decoration on body: carefully engraved zigzag lines and parallel lines; height 9 cm., length 15.5 cm. Late Cypriot I (Black Slip III). Cyprus Mus., Nicosia, Inv. No. A 622. – Gjerstad, 146.

1556 Lapithos. Tomb 21, No. 107: Multiple vessel, 'suspension-eye type', consisting of two small round jugs, each on three feet. The two vessels are connected by a human figure, whose widely spread legs adjoin the lower joints of the handles, while the hands rest on their upper ends. Pierced ears, recessed eyes. Painting: bars and chequer pattern; height 11.5 cm. (type and date as *1554*). Cyprus Mus., Nicosia, Inv. No. A 907. – Gjerstad, 160.

1557 Cyprus. Find-spot unknown. Askos in form of bird with elongated body on a high base. Bird's head protome at one end, tubular spout with lidded mouth at the other; basket handle on the back. Painted with bars and wavy lines; height 12 cm., length 13.3 cm. Probably Middle Cypriot III (White-Painted V). Cyprus Mus., Nicosia, Inv. No. A 1945.

1558 Pendagia. Tomb 1, No. 57: Theriomorphic askos (Black Slip III; Late Cypriot I). The cylindrical body, carefully decorated with chevrons, has four feet, an animal protome at one end, and at the other a tubular spout with mouth compressed into a point and a ring handle on the back; height 9.5 cm., length 12 cm. Cyprus Mus., Nicosia. – Karageorghis, *Nouveaux Documents,* Fig. 10, No. 57.

1559 Denia. Jug with spherical body (White-Painted III; Middle Cypriot II), round base, long, narrow neck with marked lip; small handle between lower part of neck and shoulder; painting: horizontal and vertical zones with hatched lozenges, squares and triangles, also zigzag stripes and chequer pattern; height 25 cm. Nicosia, Survey No. CS. 992/6. – Karageorghis, *BCH.* 90 (1966), 303, Fig. 10.

1560 Probably from Hagia Paraskevi. Middle Cypriot terracotta statuette, with child in its arms (White-Painted Ware). Cylindrical body and long cylindrical neck, ears pierced, eyes indicated by depressions. Diagonal bands on the chest; horizontal stripes on neck and body; feet missing; surviving height 20.5 cm. Z. D. Pierides Coll., Larnaka. – Karageorghis, *BCH.* 91 (1967), 313, Fig. 99.

1561 Cyprus. Find-spot unknown. Multiple vessel (White-Painted IV; Middle Cypriot II/III), consisting of two connected little bowls with round bases and flared rims, painted with stippled triangles. Tall loop handle above the joint, crowned by fishtail ornament; height 15 cm. Cyprus Mus., Nicosia, Inv. No. A 1973.

1562 Vounous. Tomb 64, No. 138: Boat-shaped pyxis (White Painted I; Early Cypriot III), with round base and 'ear handle' on either side of mouth. Horse protome with rider in front and at back of the body, painted with cross-hatched and chequered patterns in horizontal zones; hatching and stripes on horses and riders; height 23.5 cm., length 39.5 cm. Cyprus Mus., Nicosia. – Schaeffer, *Missions en Chypre* (1936), Pl. 22:2; Dikaios, *Guide*, Pl. 6:6; Karageorghis, *Cyprus*, Pl. 54.

1563 Trikomo, east Cyprus. Gourd bottle (White-polished; Early Cypriot III), with squat ovoid body, round base, and long neck narrowing toward the top; horizontal and zigzag stripes in incised technique, with intermittent patches of red paint; height 32.2 cm. Cyprus Mus., Nicosia, Inv. No. 1938.XI-15.5. – Stewart, *SCE*. IV/1A, Pl.-Fig. 154:20; Dikaios, *RDAC*. 1937-39, Pl. 41:5; Karageorghis, *Cyprus*, Pl. 42.

1564 Hagia Paraskevi necropolis, Nicosia: Bottle of the
a,b suspension-eye type (White-Painted III-V; Middle Cypriot II); slender ovoid body, with flat base, long narrow neck, tubular spout, and lateral opening; small handle and, immediately below it, three pairs of suspension eyes on either side of body and neck. The entire bottle is densely painted with broad bands dividing it up into zones filled with latticed chequer patterns; height 24 cm. Cyprus Mus., Nicosia, Inv. No. 1958.I-17.4.

1565 Cyprus. Find-spot unknown. Spherical handled jug (type and date as *1566*), with round base and long neck flared like a funnel towards the mouth, and densely covered in sketchy rippled bands. Decoration: densely hatched triangles on the shoulder, above a double horizontal wavy band; the white area below is sparely divided up by vertical rippled lines; height 18.2 cm. Z. D. Pierides Coll., Larnaka.

1566 Cyprus. Find-spot unknown. Handled cup with high pedestal (White-Painted V; Middle Cypriot III). Decoration: horizontal zones with diagonal parallel lines; height 9.2 cm., diam. 6.5 cm. Cyprus Mus., Nicosia, Inv. No. 1952.III-18.7.

1567 Cyprus. Find-spot unknown. Spherical handled jug (type and date as *1565*), with round base and narrow neck, the upper part anthropomorphic; mouth severely damaged; decoration: horizontal and vertical friezes of latticed lozenges; height 27 cm. Cyprus Mus., Nicosia, Inv. No. A 689.

1568 Achera. Tomb 1, No. 12: Handled jug (White-Painted V; Late Cypriot I). Pentagonal body with rounded edges, flat base and offset shoulder; cylindrical neck with diagonally rising beak mouth; an animal protome leans against the front of the neck. Painting in zones: hatched zigzag bands, lozenges and rippled lines; height 24.8 cm. Cyprus Mus., Nicosia, Inv. No. 1960.IX-27.1. – Karageorghis, *Nouveaux Documents*, Pl. 7:3; and *Cyprus*, Pl. 53.

1569 Achera. Tomb 1, No. 11: Handled jug with hexagonal body; height 20 cm. (type, date, decoration and form as *1568*). Cyprus Mus., Nicosia, Inv. No. 1960.IX-27.1. – Karageorghis, *Nouveaux Documents*, Pl. 7:4.

1570 Cyprus. Site unknown. Handled jug (White-Painted V; Middle Cypriot II), with ovoid body and flat base; two necks stem from a diagonally rising beak spout. Richly painted with stripes, latticed triangles, chevrons and bars; height 19.2 cm. Z. D. Pierides Coll., Larnaka.

1571 Kythrea. Tomb 1: Spherical handled jug (White-Painted V; Middle Cypriot III), with round base, narrow neck, and steeply rising beak spout. Animal protome on shoulder in front; short sculptured tail under handle. Decoration: hatched vertical bands, latticed frieze of lozenges and zigzag lines; horizontal stripes on neck and mouth; height 20.5 cm. Cyprus Mus., Nicosia, Inv. No. A 911.

1572 Lapithos. Tomb 406, Chamber A, No. 16: Vessel imported from Crete (MM I/Early Cypriot III), with open spout and two small loop handles on the shoulder; bi-conical shape, marked bulge; lower third monochrome, horizontal lines above it, and nested chevrons on the shoulder; height 16 cm., diam. 15 cm. Cyprus Mus., Nicosia. – Grace, *AJA*. 55 (1940), 10 ff.; Catling-Karageorghis, *BSA*. 55 (1960), 109 f., No. 1, Fig. 2 (with further refs.); Karageorghis, *Cyprus*, Pl. 52.

1573 Karmi, District of Kyrenia. Tomb of the Seafarer: Im-
a,b ported Cretan, steep-walled conical cup with handle (Middle Minoan Kamares Ware; MM II/Middle Cypriot I); flat flared base, angular profiled, vertical handle, markedly offset steep rim; hard-fired thin terracotta (egg-shell ware), with black slip inside and out, painted over with white and dark red; height 9 cm., diam. 8.5 cm. Cyprus Mus., Nicosia. – Stewart, *Op.Ath*. 4 (1963), 197 ff., Pl. 7; Karageorghis, *Cyprus*, 134, Col. Pl. 55.

1574 Denia. Tomb 1, No. 27: Handled jug (Late Cypriot I); wheel-turned ware with ring base; spherical body, short neck and flared rim; wide strap handle from rim to shoulder. Painted with stripes and fish in bichrome technique; height 28.2 cm. Cyprus Mus., Nicosia. – Epstein, *Palestinian Bichrome Ware* (1966), Pl. 9:2.

1575 Hagia Irini. Spherical handled jug with round base (Late Cypriot I); wheel-turned ware, cylindrical neck, sharply-profiled wide mouth. Painted in bichrome technique, with stripes crossing diagonally, horizontal and vertical bands, and images of birds and fish; height 24.7 cm. Cyprus Mus., Nicosia, Inv. No. 1964.X-12.18. – Karageorghis, *BCH*. 89 (1965), 247, Fig. 25.

1576 Cyprus. Find-spot unknown. Ovoid handled jug with base ring (Late Cypriot I); wheel-turned ware, painted in bichrome technique: stripes and bands on the belly, shoulder, handle, and neck; sharply profiled wide mouth; handle from middle of neck to shoulder; height 43 cm. Cyprus Mus., Nicosia, Inv. No. 1938.IX-21.2. – Epstein, op. cit., Pl. 12:5.

1577 Achera. Tomb 1, No. 1: Theriomorphic vessel (Late Cypriot I); wheel-turned ware; bichrome linear painting of bands and fields. Cylindrical body on four stump feet; loop handle on back; head broken off. Cyprus Mus., Nicosia. – Karageorghis, *Nouveaux Documents*, Pl. 7:1; Epstein, Pl. 20:3.

1578 Hagia Irini. Tankard made on potter's wheel, with low base ring (Late Cypriot I); squat body, with pronounced bulge, short shoulder, wide neck, and flared rim; handle between rim and shoulder; painted on neck and shoulder in bichrome technique with bars, horizontal bands, and friezes of metopes (bird motifs, geometric patterns); height 21 cm. Cyprus Mus., Nicosia, Inv. No. 1965.X-8.2. – Karageorghis, *BCH.* 90 (1966), 304, Fig. 12.

1579 a,b Enkomi. Tomb 12. Water bottle (Red-Lustrous Wheel-made ware; Late Cypriot II); round body, narrow neck, lip thickened; suspension eye to right and left of thick handle; height 23 cm. Cyprus Mus., Nicosia, Inv. No. A 1408. – Schaeffer, *Missions en Chypre 1932–1935* (1936), 88, Fig. 36.

1580 Hagia Irini. Spindle-shaped handled bottle (Late Cypriot II), with base ring, long conical neck and wide-rimmed mouth. Surface covered in white glaze; shape imitating such jugs as *1581–1585*; height 23.2 cm. Cyprus Mus., Nicosia, Inv. No. 1965.X-8.6. – Karageorghis, *BCH.* 90 (1966), 305, Fig. 15.

1581 1582 Enkomi. Tomb 8, No. 8; and Tomb 12, No. 13: Two handled bottles of similar type, in exaggerated slender spindle shape (type and date as *1579*) with long conical neck, wide-rimmed mouth, and handle running from middle of neck to shoulder; height *c.* 32 cm. Base and lower third restored on *1581; 1582* has a mark incised underneath the base before firing. Louvre, Paris. – Schaeffer, op. cit., 80, Figs. 33:8, and p. 88, Fig. 36.

1583 1584 Cyprus. Site unknown. Two spindle bottles (type and date as *1581*); heights 36 cm. and 25 cm. Z. D. Pierides Coll., Larnaka.

1585 Enkomi. Tomb 2, No. 2. Large spindle bottle with wide flaring base (type and date as *1581–1584*); height 79 cm. – Schaeffer, *Enkomi–Alasia* I, 122, Fig. 42, No. 12.

1586 Enkomi. Tomb 69 (1896): Arm-shaped votive implement (type and date as *1581*), pierced at the rear. The elongated implement narrows at the beginning of the neck; the hand grasps a cup; length 62 cm. Cyprus Mus., Nicosia, Inv. No. A 1423. – Murray, *Excavations in Cyprus,* 40, Fig. 68, No. 1108; Bittel, *Boğazköy* III (1957), 37 ff., Pl. 28:7.

1587 Cyprus. Find-spot unknown. Multiple vessel assembled from two similar jugs (Late Cypriot I; Base Ring I ware), with common strap handle. The jugs are spherical, with conical hollow feet, long conical necks with decorative ridges, and funnel spouts; height 11 cm. Cyprus Mus., Nicosia, Inv. No. A 1233. – Gjerstad, *Studies on Prehistoric Cyprus,* 186.

1588 Cyprus. Find-spot unknown. Jug (type and date as *1587*), with spherical body, round base, conical narrow neck, and funnel mouth; the handle starts below the funnel on the neck, which is encircled by a small ridged ring at that point; spiral reliefs on shoulder, on either side of handle; height 16.5 cm. Cyprus Mus., Nicosia, Inv. No. A 1042.

1589 Kazaphani. Tomb 2 b, No. 126: Small, handled jug (type as *1587*; Late Cypriot I/II), with egg-shaped body on three small feet; long conical neck, funnel-like mouth. Long tubular spout on shoulder, opposite vertical strap handle, ending in a bull protome; height 14 cm. District Mus., Kyrenia. – Karageorghis, *BCH.* 88 (1964), 335, Fig. 68 a–b.

1590 Cyprus. Site unknown. Multiple vessel (basic form, type, and date as *1587*), with common horizontally set loop handle; double line of decorative ridges on the bulge; height 13.5 cm. Cyprus Mus., Nicosia, Inv. No. 1946.XII–14.1.

1591 Cyprus. Find-spot unknown. Handled jug (type and date as *1587*) with flaring high pedestal, ovoid body, conical neck, funnel-shaped mouth and vertical strap handle. Decorative ridge on neck; height 15.2 cm. Cyprus Mus., Nicosia, Inv. No. A 1146.

1592 Cyprus. Find-spot unknown. Ovoid, handled jug (type as *1587*; Late Cypriot I/II) with long, cylindrical neck, large beak mouth, and wide, flared conical foot; applied relief fillets and scrolls on body, horizontal ridges on neck; height 44.5 cm. Cyprus Mus., Nicosia, Inv. No. A 1156. – Dikaios, *Guide,* Pl. 7:4; Karageorghis, *Treasures,* Pl. 13:1; and *Cyprus,* Pl. 69.

1593 Cyprus. Find-spot unknown. Askos Base Ring Ware; Late Cypriot I), with spherical squat body, conical foot, and two spouts; one spout in the form of a bull protome, with long, cylindrical neck; the other in the form of a biconical cup; linked by a basket handle; height 16 cm. Cyprus Mus., Nicosia, Inv. No. A 1244.

1594 Cyprus. Find-spot unknown. Conical cup (type and date as *1593*) with ring base, offset concave rim, and wish-bone handle; vertical relief stripes on body; height 14.2 cm. Cyprus Mus., Nicosia, Inv. No. A 1016.

1595 Cyprus. Find-spot unknown. Conical cup (type and date as *1593*). Base ring, concave receding lower part, steep offset rim, and wishbone handle rising above the lip. Vertical ribs on body; height 13.2 cm., diam. 16 cm. Cyprus Mus., Nicosia, Inv. No. 1933.IV–14.2.

1596 Cyprus. Find-spot unknown. Conical cup (type and date as *1593*) with conical foot, receding offset rim, wish-bone handle rising above the lip; height 10 cm., diam. 10.5 cm. Cyprus Mus., Nicosia, Inv. No. A 1018.

1597 Cyprus. Find-spot unknown. Conical cup (Base Ring II; Late Cypriot II) with base ring, concave, receding side walls, low, offset steep rim and wish-bone handle in 'S'-shaped curve; height 10.5 cm., diam. 18 cm. Cyprus Mus., Nicosia, Inv. No. A 1023.

1598 Cyprus. Find-spot unknown. Pot-bellied jug (Base Ring II ware; Late Cypriot II), with narrow neck and bull protome on shoulder. Bull's head connected to rim of mouth by a handle; white linear patterns; height 13 cm. Cyprus Mus., Nicosia, Inv. No. A 1242.

1599 Cyprus. Find-spot unknown. Biconically shaped cup (type and date as *1598*) with broad, conical foot, wide neck narrowing above, and wide flared rim; 'fishtail' peg on upper end of handle; white linear patterns; height 20.5 cm., diam. 10.5 cm. Cyprus Mus., Nicosia, Inv. No. A 1193.

1600 Cyprus. Find-spot unknown. Ring kernos on three small feet (type and date as *1598*). Vertical tubular spout on one side; on the other an animal protome with small horns and long cylindrical neck (wild goat?); wide strap-like handle between protome and spout; white linear pattern; height 12.5 cm. Z. D. Pierides Colln., Larnaka.

1601 Cyprus. Find-spot unknown. Lidded pyxis, with squat biconical body and flat base (type and date as *1598*). Short neck and flaring rim, high basket handle, pointed grip peg in the middle of the lid. Decoration: white stripes and dots; height 10.5 cm. Rare form; cf. Merrillees, *Op.Athen.* 6 (1965), 148, Pl. 2:9. Z. D. Pierides Coll., Larnaka.

1602 Cyprus. Find-spot unknown. Bowl (painted Apliki ware; Late Cypriot II), with hemispherical body on three small feet; loop handle beginning on the plain rim, leading to the middle of the wall; painting: white stripes and dots; height 7.5 cm., diam. 13.5 cm. Cyprus Mus., Nicosia, Inv. No. 1938.XII–21.5.

1603 Cyprus. Find-spot unknown. Miniature pot with flat base, squat bi-conical body, short neck flaring outwards, and three small vertical suspension handles on the shoulder (Base Ring II Ware; Late Cypriot II); decoration: white zigzag lines; height 5.8 cm. Cyprus Mus., Nicosia, Inv. No. A 1229.

1604 Cyprus. Find-spot unknown. Amphora (Grey Bucchero ware; Late Cypriot III). Ovoid body and base ring, short neck narrowing toward mouth, cable handle crowned by horn-like pegs; rich relief decoration: diagonal and horizontal bands with notched patterns; height 20.5 cm. Cyprus Mus., Nicosia, Inv. No. 1954. III–5.2. – Megaw, *JHS*. 75 (1955), Arch. Rep. 30, Pl. 3 e.

1605 Cyprus. Find-spot unknown. Ovoid jug with base ring (Base Ring II ware; Bucchero, Late Cypriot II). Short concave neck, flanged rim, strap handle from rim to shoulder. Relief fillet at beginning of neck; ribs running vertically down the body; height 15.5 cm. Cyprus Mus., Nicosia, Inv. No. A 1291.

1606 Cyprus. Find-spot unknown. Bucchero jug turned on the wheel (Late Cypriot III), with ring base, vertical strap handle, spherical body, neck narrowing at the top and flanged rim; relief fillet at beginning of neck; widely spaced vertical ribs on belly of vessel; height 15.5 cm. Cyprus Mus., Nicosia, Inv. No. A 1282.

1607 Pendagia. Deep bowl, with flat base, open spout, and horizontal loop handle (White Slip I ware; Late Cypriot I); height 11.6 cm., diam. 17 cm. Cyprus Mus., Nicosia, Inv. No. 1963.VII–27.1. – Karageorghis, *BCH*. 88 (1964), 314, Fig. 36.

1608 Cyprus. Find-spot unknown. Hemispherical bowl, with round base and wish-bone handle (Proto-White Slip ware; Late Cypriot I); height 9.5 cm., diam. 12 cm. Cyprus Mus., Nicosia, Inv. No. 1963. VII–18.17.

1609 Achera. Tomb 1, No. 88: Bowl with wish-bone handle (shape as *1608*, type and date as *1607*); height 8 cm., diam. 13.5 cm. Cyprus Mus., Nicosia. – Karageorghis, *Nouveaux Documents*, Pl. 8:1.

1610 Cyprus. Find-spot unknown. Deep bowl with offset rim and flat base; pierced in two places below the rim (type and date as *1607*); height 6.7 cm., diam. 12 cm. Cyprus Mus., Nicosia, Inv. No. 1953.V–12.1.

1611 Cyprus. Find-spot unknown. Small bowl with flared rim and flat base; pierced in two places below the rim (White Slip II ware; Late Cypriot II); height 7 cm., diam. 9.5 cm. Cyprus Mus., Nicosia, Inv. No. A 1370.

1612 Cyprus. Find-spot unknown. Tankard with squat body, wide neck, narrowing towards the top, and flared rim; 'fishtail' peg crowns upper part of handle (White Slip II ware; Late Cypriot II); height 27.5 cm., diam. 11.5 cm. Cyprus Mus., Nicosia, Inv. No. A 1395. – Karageorghis, *Treasures*, Pl. 13:2.

1613 Cyprus. Find-spot unknown. Tankard (type, date and shape as *1612*); horn-like protome in front on shoulder; height 23 cm., diam. 12.5 cm. Cyprus Mus., Nicosia, Inv. No. A 1390. – Dikaios, *Guide*, Pl. 8:5.

1614 Cyprus. Find-spot unknown. Amphora (type and date as *1612*). Squat spherical body; flat base, wide low neck, and flaring rim; handles set at either side of neck, ending on shoulder; decoration: latticed bands on lower part and on the bulge, scale pattern on neck in Mycenaean manner; height 15.5 cm., diam. 12.5 cm. Cyprus Mus., Nicosia, Inv. No. A 1993.

1615 Cyprus. Find-spot unknown. Handled jug with flat base, spherical body, long concave neck, and trefoil mouth (type and date as *1612*); height 20.5 cm. Cyprus Mus., Nicosia, Inv. No. 1381. – Gjerstad, *Studies on Prehistoric Cyprus*, 195.

1616 Milia, east Cyprus. Tomb 10, No. 22. Kylix with high pedestal and vertical handles; Mycenaean type LH III a; decoration: encircling frieze of stylized ivy leaves and flowers; height 14.5 cm., diam. 15.5 cm. – Westholm, *QDAP*. 8 (1939), Pl. 5:1; Stubbings, *Myc. Pottery from the Levant* (1951), 26 f., Fig. 2 a.

1617 Enkomi. Tomb find 1896. Squat alabastron, with narrow mouth and three small loop handles on the shoulder (type as *1616*); decoration: stripes, battlement pattern and dotted circles; height 7.5 cm., greatest diam. 9.8 cm. Cyprus Mus., Nicosia, Inv. No. A 1709. – Karageorghis, *CVA. Cyprus* I, Pl. 24:3–4.

1618 Maroni. Tomb 23 (1897): Small, three-handled jug (LH II b/III a 1); floral decoration: sketchy, stylized grass or reeds; height 8.9 cm., diam. of mouth 5.5 cm. Cyprus Mus., Nicosia, Inv. No. A 1651 a. – Karageorghis, *CVA. Cyprus* I, Pl. 17:1 (earlier literature).

1619 Cyprus. Find-spot unknown. Flattened squat alabastron (LH III a 1), with three small loop handles on the shoulder; decoration: stylized ivy; height 5.3 cm., greatest diam. 15.3 cm. Cyprus Mus., Nicosia, Inv. No. 1950. XII–6.2. – Karageorghis, *CVA. Cyprus* I, Pl. 23:7–8.

1620 Enkomi. Tomb 10, No. 200: Pot-bellied krater (LH III a), with two vertical strap handles, glazed foot and neck; groups of three horizontal stripes on lower part, and picture-frieze on shoulder: leaping bulls against rocky background; human figures on one side; height 43.5 cm., diam. 31.7 cm. Cyprus Mus., Nicosia. – Dikaios, *Guide*, Pl. 37:3; id., *Enkomi* III 2 (1969), Pls. 204, 205, 224.

1621 Enkomi. Tomb 17, No. 1: Krater (LH III a), with two vertical handles, glazed foot, and stripes painted on handles and neck. The pictorial zone covers almost the entire wall space; one side is dominated by a large octopus, the other shows a chariot scene. A figure in long robes with a scale in its hand stands in front of the horses, perhaps 'Zeus with the scales of fate'; below this a bull, below the horses a warrior, also a flying bird and stylized trees; height 37.5 cm., diam. 26 cm. Cyprus Mus., Nicosia. – Sjöqvist, *SCE*. 1, Pl. 120:3–4; Karageorghis, *Treasures*, Pl. 14; Nilsson, *Gesch. d. griech. Religion* I ^{3}(1967), 366 f., Pl. 25:1; Karageorghis, *Myc. Art*, Pl. 1:2.

1622 Pyla–Vergi. Tomb 1, No. 37: Pot-bellied krater (LH III a 1), with two vertical handles. Almost the entire surface of the vessel is divided by vertical bands, the sections filled alternately with slanting lines, 'S' spirals, and parallel chevrons; a wavy band encircles the neck; the foot is glazed, apart from two stripes of light horizontal lines; height 43 cm., diam. 34.5 cm. Cyprus Mus., Nicosia, Inv. No. 1952.IV–12.1. – Dikaios, *Guide*, Pl. 37:1; and *Enkomi* III 2 (1969), Pl. 232.2.

1623 Probably from the region of Kition. Tall krater (LH III b), with vertical handles; pairs of boxers in the shoulder zone between the handles, separated by sketchily painted birds; foot and neck glazed, lower part undecorated; height 41 cm., diam. 27.5 cm. G. G. Pierides Colln., Nicosia, Inv. No. 35. – Karageorghis, *CVA. Cyprus* II, Pls. 2:1–4, 3; and *Syria* 34 (1957), 89 ff., Figs. 10–12; and *Myc. Art,* Pl. 5:1–2.

1624 Cyprus. Find-spot unknown. Tall krater (LH III b), with two vertical handles, glazed foot and neck. Horizontal stripes on lower part and pictorial frieze on shoulder zone: two antithetical pairs of bulls, flanking a stylized tree of life. Bird under each handle; character from the Cypro-Minoan syllabic script on the base; height 43 cm., diam. 26 cm. Cyprus Mus., Nicosia, Inv. No. A 1647. – Karageorghis, *CVA. Cyprus* I, Pl. 5:1–2; id., *Myc. Art,* Pl. 7:3.

1625 Probably from the region of Kition. Bell krater (LH III b). Pictorial frieze between the horizontal handles: bull and human figure, possibly bull fight (side A); two bulls walking to the right (side B); height 28 cm., diam. 30 cm. G. G. Pierides Coll., Nicosia, Inv. No. 234. – Karageorghis, *CVA. Cyprus* II, Pl. 4:1–3; id., *Myc. Art,* Pl. 6:1.

1626 Probably from the region of Kition. Bell krater (LH III b). Pictorial friezes between the horizontal handles: bull and wheel motif (side A), and bull chasing bird (side B); height 26 cm., diam. 27.7 cm. G. G. Pierides Coll., Nicosia, Inv. No. 42. – Karageorghis, *CVA. Cyprus* II, Pl. 5:1–3; and *Myc. Art,* Pl. 6:2.

1627 Enkomi. Tomb 82 (1896): Bell krater (LH III b); pictorial friezes between the horizontal handles, each showing three stags running to the right; large rosettes in the spaces between; height 28 cm., diam. 30.5 cm. Cyprus Mus., Nicosia, Inv. No. A 1546. – Karageorghis, *CVA. Cyprus* I, Pl. 10:1–3; and *Myc. Art,* Pl. 9:4.

1628 Probably from the region of Kition. Handled jug (LH III b), with ovoid body, tall concave neck, and round profiled mouth; eight fish on the shoulder zone, horizontal bands on lower part, bulge and neck; height 26 cm. G. G. Pierides Coll., Nicosia, Inv. No. 38. – Karageorghis, *CVA. Cyprus* II, Pl. 8:1–4; and *Myc. Art,* Pl. 10:2.

1629 Maroni. Tomb 18 (1897): Conical rhyton (LH III b), with high loop handle on the rim. The surface of the body is encircled by dense horizontal rings, except for the glazed lower part and one wider ring above. On the exterior, a large mark from the Cypro-Minoan script in matt red; height 34.5 cm., diam. 10 cm. (Corresponding rhytons from the Aegean: *960–964.*) Cyprus Mus., Nicosia, Inv. No. A 1733. – Karageorghis, *CVA. Cyprus* I, Pl. 33:1.

1630 Shemishin, between Kellia and Aradippou. Tall krater (LH III b), with two vertical handles. Glazed foot and neck, unpainted lower part, and three horizontal stripes on the belly; pictorial zones at the shoulder: two pairs of antithetically opposed quadrupeds (lions?) on either side of a stylized tree, and large rosettes; height 41.5 cm., diam. 31.5 cm. Cyprus Mus., Nicosia, Inv. No. A 1648. – Stubbings, *Myc. Pottery from the Levant* (1951), Pl. 11:1; Karageorghis, *CVA. Cyprus* I, Pl. 10:4–5; and *Myc. Art,* Pl. 7:2.

1631 Probably from the region of Kition. Handled jug (LH III b); neck sharply offset from body; trefoil mouth; decoration: bull moving to the right on the shoulder zone; large rosettes and lozenges in the field; stripes and frieze of large rosettes on lower part of vessel; height 27.5 cm. G. G. Pierides Coll., Nicosia, Inv. No. 34. – Karageorghis, *Syria* 34 (1957), 82 ff.; id., *CVA. Cyprus* II, Pl. 6:1–3; and *Myc. Art,* Pl. 8:1.

1632 Cyprus. Find-spot unknown. Water bottle (LH III b), with round body, short neck, flanged rim, and two small handles; painted on both sides of body: concentric circles of varying width and density; height 15.5 cm. Cyprus Mus., Nicosia, Inv. No. 1933.V–6.6. – Karageorghis, *CVA. Cyprus* I, Pl. 31:2, 4.

1633 Enkomi. Tomb 68 (1896): Three-handled vessel (LH III b), with flat base, pear-shaped body, and narrow, high neck. Areas between the handles decorated with scale patterns; characters from the Cypro-Minoan syllabary incised on two handles after firing; height 34.5 cm. Cyprus Mus., Nicosia, Inv. No. A 1650. – Karageorghis, *CVA. Cyprus* I, Pl. 19:6, and p. 48, Pl. 3:20 (marks).

1634 Cyprus. Find-spot unknown. Three-handled vessel (LH III b), similar to *1633* but more pot-bellied; small dotted circles in the areas between the handles; two identical Cypro-Minoan signs incised on two of the handles after firing; height 33.3 cm. Cyprus Mus., Nicosia, Inv. No. A 1650 a. – Karageorghis, Pl. 19:5 and p. 48, Fig. 3:19 (marks).

1635 Cyprus. Find-spot unknown. Handleless goblet on tall pedestal (LH III b), with concave contours and sharp profiled angle at the junction of pedestal and body; wide strip of glaze below the rim, above a frieze of identical bull protomes and – also on the pedestal – horizontal stripes; height 24.5 cm., diam. 10.2 cm. British Mus., London, loan from M. Sikes. – Karageorghis, *BSA.* 52 (1957), Pl. 8 a; and *Nouveaux Documents,* Pl. 19:5.

1636 Cyprus. Find-spot unknown. Drinking bowl with high pedestal and two horizontal handles on rim (LH III b). Painted inside and out with horizontal bands and lines; height 11.2 cm., diam. 18.1 cm. Cyprus Mus., Nicosia, Inv. No. A 1643. – Karageorghis, *CVA. Cyprus* I, Pl. 32:5–6; and *Nouveaux Documents,* 211, Fig. 49:4.

1637 Cyprus. Find-spot unknown. Hemispherical cup, with ring base and wish-bone handle (LH III b); band of chevrons encircles the vessel horizontally at the line of the handle; height 9.5 cm., greatest diam. 16 cm. Mycenaean product, but imitation of Cypriot White Slip ware. Cyprus Mus., Nicosia, Inv. No. 1955.IV–14.3. – Karageorghis, *CVA. Cyprus* I, Pl. 31:5–6; id., *Nouveaux Documents,* 207, Fig. 48:3, Pl. 15:1–2; and *Myc. Art,* Pl. 17:1.

1638 Cyprus. Site unknown. Tall cup with receding lower part, wish-bone handle, straight base, stripes painted on inside and out in LH III b technique. Like *1637,* this piece imitates Cypriot Base Ring ware; height 7 cm., diam. 12.6 cm. Cyprus Mus., Nicosia, Inv. No. 1951.III–7.5. – Karageorghis, *CVA. Cyprus* I, Pl. 31:7–8; id., *Nouveaux Documents,* 207, Fig. 48:2, Pl. 15: 5–6; and *Myc. Art,* Pl. 17:3.

1639 Kition. Tomb 9, No. 12: Cup with curving side walls, wish-bone handle and flat base (LH III b); frieze of stylized flowers below rim; lower part covered with dense horizontal stripes; height 7.6 cm., diam. 12.9 cm. Manner of making, firing and painting Mycenaean; shape and handle local Cypriot form (cf. Base Ring cups: *1595, 1597,* and text to *1637, 1638*). Cyprus Mus., Nicosia. – Karageorghis, *Nouveaux Documents,* 207, Fig. 48:1, Pl. 15:3–4; id., *Myc. Art,* Pl. 17:2; and *Cyprus,* Pl. 58.

1640 Probably from the region of Kition. Flat bowl with two handles (LH III b; typical Levanto-Helladic style). Interior picture: two wild goats with heads turned back facing in opposite directions round the centre (torsion motif); height 4.5 cm., diam. 18 cm. G. G. Pierides Coll., Nicosia, Inv. No. 44. – Karageorghis, *CVA. Cyprus* II, Pl. 10:1–2; and *Myc. Art*, Pl. 11:2.

1641 Kition. Tomb 9, upper burial No. 90: Flat bowl with two handles (LH III b). Interior decoration: latticed frieze of lozenges in the outer zone, then a stripe with zigzag pattern, then a wider stripe with four fish, one of which is differentiated by the delineation of its bones; height 5 cm., diam. 18 cm. Cyprus Mus., Nicosia. – Karageorghis, *BCH.* 88 (1964), 349, Fig. 84; id., *Myc. Art*, Pl. 10:1; and *Cyprus*, Col. Pl. 73 left.

1642 Probably from the region of Kition. Flat bowl with two handles (LH III b). The picture inside is in a circular area with eleven identical bird protomes; height 5.3 cm., diam. 19 cm. G. G. Pierides Coll., Nicosia, Inv. No. 55. – Karageorghis, *CVA. Cyprus* II, Pl. 10:4–5; and *Myc. Art*, Pl. 11:3.

1643 Kition. Tombs 4 and 5, No. 132: Flat bowl with two handles (LH III b). Inner picture: concentric bands and area with seven swallows flying in a circle; height 6 cm., diam. 19.2 cm. Cyprus Mus., Nicosia. – Karageorghis, *BCH.* 88 (1964), 347, Fig. 80; id., *AA.* 1967, 166, Fig. 5; *Myc. Art*, Pl. 12:2; and *Cyprus*, Col. Pl. 73. – For this method of depicting swallows, cf. Kyrieleis, *Antiken aus dem Akademischen Kunstmuseum Bonn* (1969), 92, No. 104, Pl.-Fig. 65.

1644 Cyprus. Find-spot unknown. Wide-mouthed broad krater (LH III b) with horizontal handles, decorated in the so-called Rude Style; pictures of bulls between the handles on either side; height 22 cm., diam. 22.1 cm. Cyprus Mus., Nicosia, Inv. No. A 1758. – Gjerstad, *Studies on Prehistoric Cyprus*, 222, Fig. 'Crater 1'; Karageorghis, *CVA. Cyprus* I, Pl. 14:1–2; and *Nouveaux Documents*, Pl. 27:5–6.

1645 Enkomi. Tomb 78 (1896): Krater (LH III b) in the 'Rude style' with stripe decoration round the base, middle and mouth; otherwise undecorated save for sketchy running spirals; height 23.4 cm., diam. 21.5 cm. Cyprus Mus., Nicosia, Inv. No. A 1550. – Karageorghis, *CVA. Cyprus* I, Pl. 13:8; and *Nouveaux Documents*, Pl. 27:8.

1646 Cyprus. Find-spot unknown. Pot-bellied jug with sieve spout on shoulder, narrow tall neck, and lateral strap handle; two areas of typical LH III c 1 decoration on upper part of body; height 26.2 cm. Cyprus Mus., Nicosia, Inv. No. A 1749 a. – Karageorghis, *CVA. Cyprus* I, Pl. 35:1–2.

1647 Cyprus. Find-spot unknown. Deep bowl (LH III c 1), c. 1190 B.C.; decorated with horizontal bands and running spirals; one of the two loop handles missing; height 8.5 cm., diam. 10.7 cm. Cyprus Mus., Nicosia, Inv. No. A 1931. – Karageorghis, Pl. 34:6.

1648 Sinda (Swedish excavation, 1948). Deep bowl (LH III c 1), with two horizontal loop handles; on either side, a latticed lozenge between two antithetical linear formations; height 11.5 cm., diam. 14.5 cm. Cyprus Mus., Nicosia. – Young, *AJA.* 52 (1948), 531, Pl. 58 a; Furumark, *Op.Ath.* 6 (1965), Pl. 1 lower (similar piece); Karageorghis, *Cyprus*, Pl. 96.

1649 Enkomi. Vessel in the form of a bird on disc base (local ware, Late Cypriot III); spout and handle on back of animal; wings indicated by painting, also stripes of paint on head, neck and back; length 27 cm., height 17 cm. Cyprus Mus., Nicosia, Inv. No. 1935.XII–24.2. – Dikaios, *RDAC.* 1935, 26, Pl. 9:4; Karageorghis, *CVA. Cyprus* I, Pl. 34:1.

1650 Probably from Enkomi. Ring kernos with three miniature vases and one bull protome. All parts sketched in painted stripes (local ware, Late Cypriot III); height 10 cm., diam. 22 cm. This kind of ring kernos was used for cultic purposes; cf. *1271* and Nilsson, *MMR.²*, 135 ff., 450 ff., Cyprus Mus., Nicosia, Inv. No. 1935. XII–24.1. – Dikaios, op. cit., Pl. 9:1; Karageorghis, op. cit., Pl. 34:3–4; and *Myc. Art*, Pl. 18:2.

1651 Kouklia (Palaipaphos). Tomb 9, No. 7. Kalathos
a, b (Proto-White Painted; c. 1100 B.C.), with slender lower part and upper walls flaring outward; two horizontal loop handles set low under mouth; decoration outside: vertical fields with vaguely human figures, a palm, zigzag stripes and latticed lozenges; decoration inside: fields with figurative and ornamental filling, e. g. lyre player, wild goat, birds, palm, rosette, swastikas and linear motifs in rich variety; height 15 cm., diam. 27 cm. Cyprus Mus., Nicosia. – Karageorghis, *RDAC.* 1967, Pl. 1; id., *Myc. Art*, Pl. 16:1; and *Cyprus*, Pl. 66.

1652 Probably from the region of Kition. Large stirrup jar (Proto-White Painted), with complex, hatched triangle motifs on the shoulder; stripes and scale patterns on the bulge, base, handles and spout; height 24.5 cm. Z. D. Pierides Coll., Larnaka. – Karageorghis, *CVA. Cyprus* II, Pl. 22:1–4; Desborough, *Last Mycenaeans*, Pl. 18 a.

1653 Idalion, Hagios Georgios. Tomb 2, No. 1: Ring kernos (Proto-White Painted), with stirrup handle on a transverse fillet; animal protome and miniature vase on the ring; decoration: parallel chevrons; height 8.3 cm., diam. 19.7 cm. For ring kernoi, cf. also *1650*. Cyprus Mus., Nicosia. – Karageorghis, *Nouveaux Documents*, 189, Fig. 46:1, Pl. 14:1–2.

1654 Lapithos. Askos (Proto-White Painted), with cylindrical body and marked bulge; small base and steeply rising shoulder; tubular spout, animal protome, and double basket handle on the side; painting: triangle patterns, stripes and bars; height 17 cm. Cyprus Mus., Nicosia, Inv. No. A 1776. – Karageorghis, *CVA. Cyprus* I, Pl. 35:3–4.

1655 Cyprus. Find-spot unknown. Small handled jug (Proto-White Painted), with small offset base, concave cylindrical body, sharp bend at shoulder, narrow neck and funnel mouth; painting: stripes, latticed and diagonally hatched triangles, and segments of concentric circles; height 16 cm. Cyprus Mus., Nicosia, Inv. No. A 1750. – Karageorghis, I, Pl. 36:9.

1656 Kouklia (Palaipaphos). Tomb 9, No. 21; cf. *1651 a, b*. Horn-shaped bottle (Proto-White Painted), with two pierced lugs on the upper side for attaching a string; decorative bands with linear motifs surround the conical body; length 18.5 cm. Local mus., Kouklia. – Karageorghis, *RDAC.* 1967, Pl. 3.

Stone vessels and conical stones

The Egyptians were considered past masters and superb teachers in the art of making durable vessels of hard stone (Lucas, *Ancient Egyptian Materials and Industries* [3][1959], 480 ff.). But increasing research on the 'pre-ceramic Neolithic,' i.e. the time before the discovery of pottery, makes it ever clearer that other peoples also developed astonishing skill in working stone. In technical and aesthetic terms, the Cypriot andesite bowls of the sixth millennium deserve great attention *(1657—1661)*. The forms and engravings on small conical stone amulets *(1662—1664)* show how familiar the Cypriot craftsmen were with this volcanic material.

While the stone work of Cyprus displays an unmistakable character of its own in these earliest times, in the second millennium the influence of Egypt—probably stimulated by imported works *(1665)*—became noticeable. The preferred stones were now local *(1667)*, together with Egyptian types of alabaster *(1665, 1666)*, and in particular soapstone, which was easy to cut (steatite: *1668—1670*). This stone facilitated the imitation of metal models, as can be seen in the flat wide lower ends of the handles of an amphora, and in the rivet head *(1669 b)*. The spiral motif on the rim of a soapstone cup, however, derives from Aegean influences *(1670)*.

In Greece and Crete in the third and second millennia, local industries in the production of stone vessels flourished (cf. *1119—1167*). But imported steatite vessels have also been found in Rhodes and Athens which come from twelfth-century Cypriot workshops *(1160)*. So we may assume that there was a lively interaction among the stylistic centres of the eastern Mediterranean in this branch of craftsmanship too. There is a general survey in Lena Åström, *Studies on the Arts and Crafts of the Late Cypriot Bronze Age* (1967), 64 ff., 128 ff.

1657–1664: NEOLITHIC PERIOD

1657 Khirokitia. Tholos XVII, grave good. Early Neolithic flat bowl of dark grey andesite, almost rectangular, with flat base and open spout on one narrow side; relief decoration outside; prehistoric repair on one side; maximum height 10 cm., length 30.5 cm., greatest width 27.5 cm. Cyprus Mus., Nicosia. – Dikaios, *Khirokitia* (1953), 108 f., No. 813, Fig. 52, Pls. 56, 122; and *SCE*. IV/1A, 25, Fig. 11, No. 813, Pl.-Fig. 11:8; Karageorghis, *Cyprus*, Pl. 31.

1658 Khirokitia. Tholos XVIII: Early Neolithic round flat bowl of grey andesite, with smooth, slightly convex, base and horizontal loop handle; polished decoration but without relief; restored from fragments; height 9 cm., diam. 27 cm. Cyprus Mus., Nicosia. – Dikaios, *Khirokitia*, 111 f., No. 927, Fig. 54, Pls. 46, 109; and *SCE*. IV/1A, 17. Fig. 6:927, Pl.-Fig. 10:1.

1659 Khirokitia. Early Neolithic bowl of grey andesite, almost rectangular, with flat base and open spout; suspension eye below spout, and on opposite narrow side; length 20 cm. (including spout), height 5 cm. Cyprus Mus., Nicosia, Inv. No. 1939.I-4.1. – Dikaios, *Khirokitia*, 406, No. 1276, Pls. 57, 123; and *SCE*. IV/1A, 25, Fig. 11:1276, Pl.-Fig. 10:10.

1660 Khirokitia. Early Neolithic bowl of diabase stone; largely restored with the use of a large fragment; smooth base; incised decoration on the outside: vertical and diagonal parallel lines; height 5 cm., diam. 13 cm. Cyprus Mus., Nicosia. – Dikaios, *Khirokitia*, 346, No. 103, Pls. 46, 109; and *SCE*. IV/1A, Pl.-Fig. 9:14.

1661 Khirokitia. Small Early Neolithic bowl of diabase stone, shaped rather long, with slightly rounded base and open spout; pair of vertical ribs on outside in relief; height 4.5 cm., diam. 9 cm. Cyprus Mus., Nicosia. – Dikaios, *Khirokitia*, 356, No. 362, Pls. 54, 120; and *SCE*. IV/1A, 23, Fig. 10:362, Pl.-Fig. 11:4.

1662 Khirokitia. Early Neolithic conical stone of andesite, with incised network of vertical and horizontal lines; latticed incised decoration on base also. Purpose unknown, but probably with religious significance (cf. *1663, 1664*); height 5.8 cm., diam. 6 cm. Cyprus Mus., Nicosia. – Dikaios, *Khirokitia*, 342, No. 12, Pls. 89, 138; and *SCE*. IV/1A, 37, Fig. 19:12, Pl.-Fig. 13:11.

1663 Khirokitia. Surface find. Early Neolithic conical stone with mushroom shape, of porous andesite; oval base; 'head' and 'foot' separated from one another by deep groove; incised chevrons on 'head'; height 5.3 cm., diam. 7 cm. Cyprus Mus., Nicosia. – Dikaios, *Khirokitia*, 357, No. 386, Pls. 89, 138; and *SCE*. IV/1A, 37, Fig. 19:386, Pl.-Fig. 13:12.

1664 Khirokitia. Tholos XXXIV: Early Neolithic flat conical stone of weathered andesite; incised decoration over entire surface, consisting of dense chevrons; height 3 cm., diam. 8 cm. Cyprus Mus., Nicosia. – Dikaios, *Khirokitia*, 155 f., No. 1071, Fig. 81, Pl. 89, 138; and *SCE*. IV/1A, 37, Fig. 19:1071.

1665 Cyprus. Find-spot unknown. Amphora (Late Cypriot III) of Egyptian alabaster, with pot-bellied body and wide cylindrical neck. The two vertical handles, affixed at the middle of the neck, rest on ibex protomes below to appear as horns; shoulder: incised hanging lotus blossoms; height 34 cm., diam. 18 cm. Egyptian import. Cyprus Mus., Nicosia, Inv. No. A 218. – Dikaios, *Guide,* Pl. 32:4.

1666 Kition. Tomb 9, No. 238, upper burial: Amphora (Late Cypriot II) of Egyptian alabaster; badly proportioned, the cylindrical neck very wide, and high in relation to the body. Two small, horizontal loop handles on shoulder; undecorated; height 21.5 cm., diam. 14.5 cm. Cyprus Mus., Nicosia.

1667 Kition. Tomb 3, No. 8: Amphoriskos (Late Cypriot III) of local alabaster; slender ovoid body, and high cylindrical neck; two horizontally pierced suspension eyes on the shoulder; incised decoration: entire surface covered in latticed and hatched bands and in rectangular and triangular unspaced areas; height 25 cm., Cyprus Mus., Nicosia. – Karageorghis, *BCH.* 84 (1960), 544, Figs. 60, 61; and *Cyprus,* Pl. 90.

1668 Larnaka, Kition. Amphoriskos (Late Cypriot III), of
a, b dark grey steatite; low conical foot, ovoid body rising from a calyx of leaves in relief, and short cylindrical neck offset from sculptured rib; a bull's head in relief on either side of shoulder; above, vertically pierced suspension eyes; height 11.7 cm. Cyprus Mus., Nicosia, Inv. No. 1938. VI–23.5. – Dikaios, *RDAC.* 1937–39, 202, Pl. 42:4.

1669 Enkomi. Tomb 406, No. 68 (1934): Late Cypriot am-
a, b phoriskos of dark, greyish-green steatite; pleasing shape derived from metal vessels; ovoid body, short cylindrical neck, and flat vertical handles; decoration on body: foliage ornament bordered by deep double grooves; neck: opposing hatched and notched triangles; height 8.5 cm. Cyprus Mus., Nicosia. – Schaeffer, *Missions en Chypre* (1936), Pl. 35:3.

1670 Cyprus. Find-spot unknown. Small, hemispherical bowl with ring base, small suspension eye, and flat rim (Late Cypriot III), of grey-green steatite; diam. 7.2 cm. Careful work; incised and engraved decoration on exterior: three ornamental bands alternating with empty fields; at the top, running spirals (i. e. compass circles with 'S' tangents); in the middle, a frieze of hanging stippled triangles; below, a simple stippled horizontal band. Cyprus Mus., Nicosia, Inv. No. W 21.

Faience and glass

The discovery of faience is attributed to the Egyptians. This knowledge spread from the Nile to Syria, Cyprus, and the Aegean in the latter half of the second millennium (Evans, *PM* IV, 779 ff.). At the time of the eighteenth dynasty, we even find Mycenaean stirrup jars made of faience (evidence in Hall, *The Civilization of Greece in the Bronze Age* [1928] passim; Kantor, *The Aegean and the Orient in the Second Millennium B.C.* [1947] 80, note 10; cf. unpublished pieces in the Akad. Kunstmus., Bonn; also a summary in Maximova, *Les Vases Plastiques dans l'Antiquité* I [1927], 178 ff.); on the faience stirrup jars painted in the tomb of Ramses III and actual examples in the Nat. Mus., Cairo, see Fimmen, *KMK*, 208 f., Figs. 201, 202.

The basic material was silica sand, which could be worked after mixing with small quantities of clay. Pure potter's clay could not be used, because it did not fuse with alkaline flux (soda and potash). Faience was fired twice: first the object was fired in the normal way, and then glazed.

The main colour of the mixture—i.e. of the crushed sand and the alkaline flux—was green or blue; the linear drawing was usually applied in black. After the eighteenth dynasty, faiences were also produced in white, yellow, and red, besides the traditional colours.

There is an excellent survey in the articles 'Fayence' and 'Glas,' in Galling, *Biblisches Reallexikon* (1937), 154 ff., 198 ff. Mycenaean glass has been dealt with by Haevernick, 'Mykenisches Glas,' *JbZMusMainz* 7 (1960), 36 ff.; see also 'Glazed Ware' by Lucas in *Ancient Egyptian Materials and Industries* ³(1959), 178 ff. For the origins of the Enkomi faiences, see Marinatos, *AA*. 1928, 533 ff.

1671 Also Col. Pl. 3, after p. 160: Kition, excavated in 1962.
a–d Conical faience rhyton (Late Cypriot II); point and handle lost; coated inside and out with blue enamel; exterior arranged in three zones: upper zone, jumping bulls and wild goat with head turned back; middle zone: group of hunters chasing animals; below, vertically arranged running spirals; branches and stylized flowers fill the free spaces in the upper and middle zones; figures executed in black outlines filled with yellow colour or inlaid red enamel; height 27 cm. Cyprus Mus., Nicosia. – Karageorghis, *BCH*. 87 (1963), Pl. 8; Åström, *Arts and Crafts*, 54, Fig. 68; Karageorghis, *Myc. Art*, Col. Pl. 39; and *Cyprus*, Pls. 76, 77.

1672 Cyprus. Find-spot unknown. Little faience jug (Late Cypriot II), with squat, spherical body, short concave neck, flanged rim, and strap handle running from rim to shoulder; glazed surface of the body decorated with black and yellow bands; large black dots on the shoulder; height 10.3 cm. Cyprus Mus., Nicosia, Inv. No. G 64. – Åström, Fig. 70:30; Karageorghis, *Myc. Art*, Pl. 40:2.

1673 Cyprus. Find-spot unknown. Faience jug (Late Cypriot II); body squat and spherical, with base ring, vertical handle, and wide cylindrical neck; black paint on light blue glaze: frieze of slender triangles on neck, stripe of adjacent circles on body; height 8.5 cm. Cyprus Mus., Nicosia, Inv. No. 1957.III–1.8. – Åström, Fig. 70:32.

1674 Cyprus. Find-spot unknown. Little faience bowl (Early Cypriot II), with vertical ribs, sharply offset shoulder, high conical pedestal, two rectangular suspension handles, vertically pierced, on the rim, and light blue glazed surface; height 7.5 cm., diam. 13.5 cm. Cyprus Mus., Nicosia, Inv. No. G 65. – Åström, Fig. 70:23; Karageorghis, *Myc. Art*, Pl. 40:4.

1675 Cyprus. Find-spot unknown. Blue faience vessel (Late Cypriot II), with conical body, straight walls, sharp bend at shoulder, and short cylindrical neck; originally two handles, one of which is missing; attachment-points of the handles functionally decorated in the form of 'rivet heads'; height 9 cm., diam. 6.5 cm. Cyprus Mus., Nicosia, Inv. No. G 82. – Åström, Fig. 70:27.

1676 Kition. Tomb 9, No. 14, lower burial: Fragment of a
a, b faience water bottle (Late Cypriot II). Lentoid form, short conical neck, flanged rim; two small handles starting at the neck and ending on the side of the shoulder. Thickly applied blue-green glaze, interspersed on the main sides by cross stripes, at the neck by vertical strokes, and on the narrow sides by a ladder pattern in light green glaze; height 13 cm., diam. 11 cm.

1677 Kition. Tomb 9, No. 294, upper burial: Ovoid faience bottle (Late Cypriot II), with cylindrical neck and funnel mouth; surface covered in green glaze, much faded; height 10 cm.

1678 Enkomi. Tomb 43; excavated in 1896: Faience bottle in the form of a pomegranate (Late Cypriot II); decoration: wide horizontal running bands of zigzags in brown, on white ground, produced by the sand-core method; height 7 cm. Cyprus Mus., Nicosia, Inv. No. G 91. This kind of vessel is more frequently of glass and usually occurs in Late Cypriot II tombs (references in Åström, 52, Type 5, 121, Fig. 70:25). – Karageorghis, *Myc. Art*, Pl. 40:3.

1679 Cyprus. Find-spot unknown. Flat faience bowl, with blue glazing (Late Cypriot II). Linear decoration of human figures, birds, and fish in very Egyptian style in centre, surrounded by ornamental stripe; height 4.2 cm., diam 13.2 cm. Cyprus Mus., Nicosia, Inv. No. G 63. – Dikaios, *Guide*, Pl. 33:5.

1680 Kition. Tomb 9, No. 230, upper burial. Small faience bowl (date as *1674*, but without high pedestal); light blue glazed surface and vertical ribs on lower part; compact, pyxis-like shape with sharp bend at shoulder, and two rectangular handle-plates, vertically pierced, for attaching the lost lid; height 7 cm., diam. 15.2 cm. Cyprus Mus., Nicosia. – Karageorghis, Pl. 40:1.

1681 Arpera; excavated by the Cyprus Museum, 1915. Long slender bottle of coloured glass (Late Cypriot II), crowned at the upper end by a sculptured pomegranate; height 22.2 cm. Cyprus Mus., Nicosia. – Åström, 58, Fig. 71:4; Karageorghis, Pl. 28:3.

Metal vessels and implements

Copper—a word cognate with the name 'Cyprus'—was the most important export in the Bronze Age and succeeding periods. The raw metal was exported in the form of ingots *(739—752* and *1698, 1699*; cf. *1900)*. Moreover, there were flourishing processing industries in large economic centres such as Enkomi and Kition, as is proved by the slag residues.

Works of a high technical, and occasionally also artistic, level were produced in the metal workshops of Cyprus. For instance, the casting in *cire perdue* of a bronze statue measuring 54.2 cm. was an outstanding technical feat of its time. The cauldron-stands with open-work reliefs *(1685, 1686)* are also great achievements in metallurgy, as are the rod tripods decorated with sculptured bull's heads *(1687)* and the bronze vessels and implements *(1682, 1683, 1688)*. The cup from Enkomi *(1684)* is considered a masterpiece of the technique of polychrome ornamental inlay in silver developed in the Cretan-Mycenaean cultural milieu; it has a counterpart in the Argolid. It follows that there are different theories about the origins of such works, and it has been suggested, with reference to the rich relief work on the cauldron-stands, that they may have come from workshops outside Cyprus.

Buchholz discusses metals in 'Analysen prähistorischer Metallfunde aus Zypern,' *BJbV* 7 (1967), 189 ff. Technical questions of Cypriot metallurgy are dealt with by Forbes, 'Bergbau, Steinbruchtätigkeit und Hüttenwesen', *Arch. Hom. Lieferung K*, 1967. Again we recommend L. Åström, *Studies on the Arts and Crafts of the Late Cypriot Bronze Age* (1967) for the material the author has assembled. The most important general work on Cypriot metallurgy is Catling, *Cypriot Bronzework in the Mycenaean World* (1964).

1682 Enkomi. Tomb 47: Ovoid bronze jug (Late Cypriot III), with flat base, long conical neck, and beak spout; strap handle, attached at the rim by a transverse attachment hammered flat, rises in an elegant curve high above the mouth; rivetted below on shoulder; height 30.8 cm. British Mus., London, No. 1897.4–1. 1533. – Catling, *Cypriot Bronzework*, Pl. 19 h.

1683 Enkomi. Bronze cup (Base Ring ware; Late Cypriot II b/III a), with sharp carination; the lost handle was attached to the rim with three rivets; height 5.8 cm., diam. 15.3 cm. British Mus., London, No. 1897.4–1. 1528. – Catling, Pl. 19 d.

1684 Also Col. Pl. 4. Enkomi. Tomb 2, No. 4207: Four-
a–c teenth-century silver cup with inlays in gold and niello on the exterior; hemispherical form with slightly concave base; wishbone handle with button top (cf. *1110–1113)*; decoration: frieze of six bulls' heads alternating with lotus blossoms; below this, a pattern of arcades filled with rosettes; row of dots along rim; height 6 cm., diam. 15.7 cm. Similar piece in a tholos tomb near Dendra, the Argolid, perhaps imported from Cyprus. Cyprus Mus., Nicosia. – Schaeffer, *Enkomi-Alasia* I (1952), 380 ff., Pl. 116, Col. Pls. C, D; Karageorghis, *Treasures*, Pl. 40:3; Buchholz, 'Analysen prähistorischer Metallfunde aus Zypern', *BJbV*. 7 (1967), 236, No. 39, Pl. 1 d.

1685 Probably from Larnaka, Kition. Four-sided bronze
a, b wheeled cauldron-stand (Late Cypriot III); pictorial areas: two pairs of sphinxes in open-work relief, arranged antithetically on either side of a column; small birds in the round sit on the four corners; the stand is crowned by a cast ring, with double spirals in open-work relief; height 34 cm., diam. of ring 17 cm. Staatl. Museen, Berlin, Inv. No. 8947. – Catling, op. cit., Pl. 36 a; Karageorghis, *Myc. Art*, Pl. 25.

1686 Cyprus. Find-spot unknown. Four-sided bronze wheeled cauldron-stand (Late Cypriot III); four pictorial areas show different representations, each in two zones; among others, sphinx, lion, chariot scene, human figures, birds and fish; ring crowning it on top decorated with an animal frieze in relief; bird in the round on each of the four corners; bud-shaped pendants suspended from the lower edge of each pictorial field; height 31 cm., diam. 15 cm. Four six-spoked wheels, as in *1685*. British Mus., London, No. 1946.10–17.1. – Catling, Pl. 35.

1687 Kourion–Episkopi, district of Kaloriziki, Tomb 40, No. 19: Rod tripod of bronze (Late Cypriot III); feet worked in the form of bovine feet and end above in volute capitals. Sculptured bull's head on the outside of each leg; height 39.5 cm., diam. 26.5 cm. Cyprus Mus., Nicosia, Inv. No. L 299. – McFadden, *AJA*. 58 (1954), 141 f., Pl. 27:37; Catling, Pl. 28 c–e.

1688 Enkomi; French excavations 1936. Round bronze table *a, b* (Late Cypriot III), with low turned-up rim and round, bowl-like depression in the centre. Four large, rivetted looped feet consisting of wide bronze bands; height 22.5 cm., diam. 65.5 cm. Cyprus Mus., Nicosia. – Schaeffer, *Missions en Chypre* (1936), Pl. 40; Buchholz, *JDI*. 83 (1968), 601, Fig. 1 d (with complete bibliography).

Sculpture in the round

The Neolithic and Early Chalcolithic idols represent a first attempt on the part of the island culture to produce works of art. At first volcanic andesite was preferred, then soapstone, because it was easier to work (steatite and steatite vessels: *1668—1670*). The characteristic form of these early sculptures was partly determined by the material. When andesite was used, we find block-like or violin-like abstractions of the human frame, with no indications of sex and very economic modelling of the limbs and face, reducing naturalism in the characteristics of man and animal to the minimum.

In west Cyprus in particular, after the transition from the Stone Age to the Copper Age (Chalcolithic), marked progress was made in the sculpture of idols. The plasticity of steatite made it possible to imitate more closely the forms given by nature, and to model details in relief. So we now find eyebrows, eyes, and nose—even neck ornaments—*(1699)* carefully noted. Yet, by comparison with the traditional early forms, the overlong neck, the legs with drawn-up knees *(1699—1703)*, and the board-like outstretched arm stumps express a high degree of deliberate stylization. In some cases the cruciform shape of these idols is carried so far that, instead of the transverse cross of the outstretched arms of the main figure, we find a second human figure, whose trunk represents the horizontal arm of the cross *(1700*; also Karageorghis, *Cyprus*, Col. Pl. 33; for a general survey of Neolithic and Chalcolithic stone sculpture see Buchholz, *Archaeologia Viva: Cyprus* [1969]).

The Stone Age already saw the first attempts to make free-standing terracotta sculptures *(1698)*. Stone was completely abandoned as a working material during the Early Bronze Age. At that time, activity in sculpture became the domain of the potter; pottery itself proves this by its composite forms and sculptured additions such as reliefs *(1513)* and figurative protomes *(1514, 1520, 1522)*. As an art form, vessels in the shape of animals belong as much to pottery as to sculpture *(1523—1527)*. Clay imitations of daggers, dagger sheaths, brushes and combs, and spindles *(1706—1712)* certainly owe their existence to the practices of particular cults, but they also bear witness to the sculptural skill and sense of form of the Cypriots in the third millennium. The most beautiful examples of this love of making figures from kneaded clay are two contemporary figurative groups from Vounous— one a ploughing scene, the other a cult scene *(1704, 1705)*.

The tendency towards exaggerated stylization and abstraction we have observed in the idols of the Chalcolithic period degenerated into works that were formally entirely sterile—the 'board-shaped' idols *(1713—1716)*. The carefree naïvete and freshness we find in the animated figurative sculpture of the Middle Bronze Age seems like a new beginning *(1718)*. Late Bronze Age votive sculpture and idols reflect the influences of ancient indigenous forms (e.g. Base-Ring bulls: *1724—1726*) and, in particular, of north Syrian *(1722, 1723)*, Mycenaean *(1729, 1730)*, and Cretan *(1731)* forms. Besides statuettes of bulls *(1730*; cf. *1252)*, Late Helladic votive sculpture in Cyprus mainly concentrated on female figurines, such as we find throughout the sphere of Mycenaean influence, from Lipari *(1264)* to Ras Shamra and to the land of the Philistines.

The bronze sculpture of Cyprus *(1732–1741)*, whose development is very illuminating in many respects to archaeologists, partly followed the traditional development of terracottas *(1734)*, and also continued to show itself indebted to the style of the north Syrian workshops *(1732, 1733, 1741)*. A very great metallurgical achievement is the 'Horned God' of Enkomi *(1740)*: in terms of size alone (54.2 cm.), this work seems strange compared to the usual bronze casts, which were much smaller. Over and above this, it achieves inner stature, true monumentality.

1689–1703: NEOLITHIC AND CHALCOLITHIC PERIOD – STONE AND CLAY

1689 Hagia Mavri, region between Kithasi and Salamiou, Paphos District. Idol of dark andesite (Neolithic II); round flat head; eyes, nostrils and mouth represented by depressions, hair by grooves; rudimentary arms and legs; height 16 cm. District Mus., Paphos, Inv. No. 1503. – Karageorghis, *BCH*. 87 (1963), 349, Fig. 36; id., *AA*. (1963), 506, Fig. 2; Nikolaou, *Kypriakai Spoudai* 31 (1967), 52, No. 78.

1690 Omodos, west Cyprus. Andesite head in flat circular shape (probably Neolithic II); eyebrows and nose indicated by relief ridges, eyes by depressions; long cylindrical 'neck', intact below; height 13.7 cm. Cyprus Mus., Nicosia, Inv. No. 1948.5–17.2. – Dikaios, *Khirokitia*, Pl. 97.

1691 Khirokitia. Tholos XLVII: Animal protome (Neolithic I) of diabase stone in flat form; nostrils and mouth indicated by grooves, contrasting ridge on throat; height 9.8 cm. Cyprus Mus., Nicosia. – Dikaios, *SCE*. IV/1A, 48, Fig. 25, No. 1252; id., *Khirokitia*, 186, No. 1252, Pls. 97, 143.

1692 Khirokitia. Animal protome (lioness?; Neolithic I), of diabase stone; ears modelled in relief; mouth and eyes shown by depressions; preserved length 11 cm. Cyprus Mus., Nicosia. – Dikaios, *SCE*. IV/1A, 48, Fig. 25, No. 561, Pl.-Fig. 14:3; id., *Khirokitia*, 365, No. 561, Pls. 97, 143.

1693 Khirokitia. Andesite idol (Neolithic II), with flat, cubical body, cylindrical neck, and round head; eyes and mouth recessed; hair on back of head indicated by scoring. Legs separated by vertical groove; height 19 cm. Cyprus Mus., Nicosia. – Dikaios, *SCE*. IV/1A, 48, Fig. 25, No. 967, Pl.-Fig. 14:2; id., *Khirokitia*, 391, No. 967, Pls. 95, 143; Karageorghis, *Treasures*, Pl. 2:1.

1694 Hagios Thomas, near Palaiomylos. Andesite idol (Neolithic II); head missing; flat oval body; arms and other limbs indicated by grooves; waist marked by horizontal groove; short radial notches on lower part of idol, also deep incision representing female genitals; height 14 cm. District Mus., Limassol, Inv. No. 94.8.

1695 Sotira. Limestone idol in 'violin form' (Neolithic II). Legs separated by deep incision; head represented by curve; extreme abstraction in remainder; height 16.5 cm. Cyprus Mus., Nicosia. – Dikaios, *SCE*. IV/1A, 96, Fig. 48, No. 106, Pl.-Fig. 31:1; id., *Sotira*, 201 f., Pl. 91:106.

1696 Khirokitia. Tholos LI: Head of Neolithic andesite idol, with eyebrows and nose in relief, eyes represented by round depressions; pointed chin and holes broken out on the edge, perhaps for earrings; preserved height 7.5 cm., width 8.5 cm. Cyprus Mus., Nicosia. – Dikaios, *SCE*. IV/1A, 48, Fig. 25, No. 1068, Pl.-Fig. 14:6; id., *Khirokitia*, 394, Pls. 96, 144.

1697 Khirokitia. Surface find. Head of Neolithic andesite idol in flat round form, with eyes, eyebrows, and nose in relief; cylindrical neck broken off; preserved height 11 cm. Cyprus Mus., Nicosia. – Dikaios, *SCE*. IV/1A, 48, Fig. 25, No. 1404, Pl.-Fig. 14:7; id., *Khirokitia*, 407, No. 1404, Pls. 96, 143.

1698 Khirokitia. Tholos XLVII. Head of Early Neolithic idol of unfired clay; eyes tightly shut; mouth and nose represented naturalistically, scoring on brow and back of head to indicate hair; disproportionately thick neck; height 10.5 cm. Cyprus Mus., Nicosia. – Dikaios, *SCE*. IV/1A, 48, Fig. 25, No. 1063, Pl.-Fig. 15:4, 5; id., *Khirokitia*, 183, Pls. 98, 144; Karageorghis, *Treasures*, Pl. 2:2.

1699 Probably from Pomos, Paphos District. Chalcolithic idol of grey steatite; carefully worked, polished, and highly stylized; cruciform body, with round flattened head, long neck, and arms stretched horizontally to the side like boards; legs separated by vertical incision; knees angled; no details on feet; relief work: details of face and pendant on neck in the form of an idol; height 15.3 cm. Cyprus Mus., Nicosia, Inv. No. 1934. III–2.2. – Dikaios, *RDAC*. 1934, 16, No. 10, Pl. 6:1; Karageorghis, *Treasures*, Pl. 3:2.

1700 Salamiou–Anephani. Early Chalcolithic double idol of grey steatite. Two human figures, a male and a female, are joined together in cruciform shape in such a way that the body of each is a substitute for the arms of the other; basic form similar to *1699*. Breasts represented on main figure; height 10.5 cm. Cyprus Mus., Nicosia, Inv. No. 1959. XI–3.6. – Karageorghis, *BCH*. 84 (1960), 244, Fig. 2; Nikolaou, *Kypriakai Spoudai* 31 (1967), 52, No. 76; Karageorghis, *Cyprus*, Col. Pl. 33.

1701 Cyprus. Find-spot unknown. Early Chalcolithic idol
a, b of grey steatite in cruciform shape, with small angular flattened head, very elongated neck, and stumpy arms outstretched horizontally; angular body and knees drawn up; deep groove separating legs; details of face in relief; hair represented by scoring; incised decoration on both arms: hatched diagonal lines; height 13.5 cm. Cyprus Mus., Nicosia, Inv. No. W 290. – Karageorghis, *Treasures*, Pl. 3:1; id., *Cyprus*, Fig. 32.

1702 Cyprus. Site unknown. Two Early Chalcolithic cruci-
1703 form idols of dark grey and green steatite, both of the same type, with mushroom-shaped heads, no facial details, long necks and horizontally outstretched board-like arms; outline of body triangular, legs drawn up and separated by incisions; height 6.6 cm. *(1702)*, and 7.6 cm. *(1703)*. Z. D. Pierides Coll., Larnaka.

1726 Rhyton in the form of a bull, Base-Ring II Ware, from Enkomi

1671 c and d Figurative details on a faience rhyton from Kition

Colour plate 3

1704–1716: EARLY BRONZE AGE – TERRACOTTA

1704 Vounous, north Cyprus. Early Cypriot terracotta model of a ploughing scene, in the technique of Red Polished ware; two ploughmen and two sculpturally modelled teams of oxen drawing a hook plough are on a flat rectangular table with five legs; two other human figures hold a trough with grain, while a third drives an animal; width 19 cm., length 41 cm. Cyprus Mus., Nicosia (Vounous, Special Series 1). – Dikaios, *Archaeologia* 88 (1940), Pls. 9, 10 a; id., *Guide*, Pl. 5:4; Karageorghis, *Treasures*, Pl. 10; id., *Cyprus*, Col. Pl. 47.

1705 Vounous. Tomb 22, No. 26: Terracotta model of circular open votive temenos, with surrounding walls and gate (Early Cypriot III); human figures stand or sit on benches, one seated on a throne, another kneeling before the relief of three human or divine beings which stand on a low platform by the back wall; they wear bull masks and hold snakes in their outstretched hands. One can also recognize sacrificial animals and a figure with a child in its arms; one figure is trying to climb over the wall in order to observe the action inside the temenos; this motif has a comic and realistic effect, but also shows that the cult represented had the character of a mystery. Height 12 cm., diam. 37 cm. Cyprus Mus., Nicosia. – Dikaios, *Archaeologia* 88 (1940), Pls. 7, 8; id., *Guide*, Pl. 5:3; Karageorghis, *Treasures*, Pl. 9; id., *Cyprus*, Col. Pl. 49.

1706 Vounous. Tomb 45, No. 15. Model of a dagger sheath, with relief and incised decoration (Early Cypriot III; Red Polished ware); length 29 cm. Cyprus Mus., Nicosia. – Dikaios, *Archaeologia* 88 (1940), Pls. 29 a, 56:7.

1707 Vounous. Tomb 45, No. 14. Model of a dagger (Early Cypriot III; Red Polished ware), with flat triangular shaft, decorated with incised work, and blade with medial rib; length 22 cm. Cyprus Mus., Nicosia. – Dikaios, Pls. 29 a, 56:8.

1708 Vounous. Tomb 29, No. 51 (Red Polished ware; Early
1709 Cypriot III). Model of a dagger, similar to *1707*, but more indefinite in outline and less richly decorated; length 26.5 cm. 1709: Model of a dagger blade similar to *1706*; length 20.5 cm. Cyprus Mus., Nicosia.

1710 Cyprus. Find-spot unknown. Model of a large brush or comb, with incised patterns (Red Polished ware; Early Cypriot III); height 10 cm. Cyprus Mus., Nicosia, Inv. No. A 63.

1711 Vounous. Tomb 9, No. 27: Model of a large brush or comb (form, type, and date as *1710*); with long handle, pierced above; height 14.5 cm. Cyprus Mus., Nicosia. – Dikaios, op. cit., Pls. 38 c, 56:5.

1712 Vounous. Tomb 29, No. 52: Model of a spindle, with rich incised decoration; length 20.3 cm. Type and date as *1710*. Cyprus Mus., Nicosia. – Dikaios, ibid., Pl. 56,6; Pieridou, *RDAC*. 1967, 27, Fig. 1.

1713 Vounous. Tomb 48, No. 2: Multiple vessel (Early Cypriot III; Red Polished ware), consisting of four small hemispherical bowls with a common, vertical handle; a board-shaped female idol with child in its arms; 'body' with three 'windows' and incised decoration; height 46 cm. Cyprus Mus., Nicosia. – Dikaios, op. cit., Pls. 27 d, 30 b.

1714 Lapithos. Tomb 18, No. 206 (excavated in 1913: Red Polished, board-shaped idol (Early Cypriot III), with two long necks and two heads on an ungainly rectangular body; noses sculptured, and eyes indicated by concentric circular incisions; besides horizontally incised bands on body and head, the neck is richly ornamented with rows of dots and bars; height 24 cm. Cyprus Mus., Nicosia, Inv. No. A 4. – Myres, *BSA*. 41 (1940–1945), 83, Fig. 5:18, Pl. 26:2, No. 18.

1715 Lapithos. Tomb 21 (excavated in 1913): Board-shaped idol (type, date, and form similar to *1714*); rich incised decoration, especially on body, with lozenge patterns filled with hatching; height 29 cm. Cyprus Mus., Nicosia, Inv. No. A 12. – Myres, 83, Fig. 5 (top row, third from left).

1716 Denia. Tomb 1, No. 6: Board-shaped idol (type and date as *1714*, *1715*); two engraved lines and concentric semicircles represent arms and hands; horizontal band of hatched triangles on the body, other linear patterns on upper body and heads; height 30 cm. Cyprus Mus., Nicosia, Inv. No. 1943.IV–13.4.

1717–1731: MIDDLE AND LATE BRONZE AGES – TERRACOTTA

1717 Akaki. Terracotta idol with flat body, arms and legs indicated crudely; eyebrows and nose modelled; engraved 'necklace'; height 22.2 cm. (Red Polished IV ware; Middle Cypriot I). Cyprus Mus., Nicosia, Inv. No. 1938.II–14.1. – Dikaios, *RDAC*. 1937–39, 201, Pl. 41:3; Åström, *Middle Cypriote Bronze Age*, 154, No. 5, Fig. 16:9.

1718 Cyprus. Find-spot unknown. Clay model of a ship with crew (White Painted II ware; Middle Cypriot I); deeply concave like a bowl, with flat base, also pierced on both sides on the rims; crew of eight human figures, in animated motion on the edge of the ship; also two sculptured birds; figures and exterior of ship painted with linear patterns; height 17 cm., length 25 cm., width 7 cm. Louvre, Paris, Inv. No. AM 972. – Pottier, *CVA. France*, 5, Pl. 4:7,9; Bossert, *Altsyrien* (1951), Fig. 111; Åström, 153, Fig. 16:13.

1719 Kazaphani, north Cyprus. Tomb 2 b, No. 377: Terracotta model of a boat (Late Cypriot II); attachment for mast in centre; holes around edge for rigging; length 45 cm., height 23 cm. Cyprus Mus., Nicosia. – Karageorghis, *BCH*. 88 (1964), 337, Fig. 70 a, b; Nikolaou, *JHS*. 85 (1965), Arch. Rep. 1965/66, 29 f., Fig. 3 a, b.

1720 Cyprus. Find-spot unknown. Clay model of a boat (Proto-White Painted ware; Late Cypriot III); three small feet on the underside, basket handle on top; richly painted with lozenges, triangles, chevrons and zigzag bands; length 31 cm., height 12.4 cm. Cyprus Mus., Nicosia, Inv. No. 1943.V-29.1.

1721 Lapithos. Tomb P 74, No. 108: Clay model of a boat (Proto-White Painted ware; late Cypriot III), similar to *1720;* length 28 cm., height 13 cm. Cyprus Mus., Nicosia. – Pieridou, *RDAC.* 1965, Pl. 10:9.

1722 Hagios Theodoros Soleas, Alonia. Tomb 2: Terracotta figurine (Base Ring ware; Late Cypriot II). Naked female figure with bird's head, holding a child in her left arm (kourotrophos). The overlarge ears are pierced for earrings, disc-shaped eyes, pointed, modelled breasts, scored lines on neck and especially on pubes; height 18.5 cm. Cyprus Survey, Nicosia, No. 1484.II-1. – Karageorghis, *BCH.* 90 (1966), 317 f., Fig. 48; Åström, *Arts and Crafts,* 41 f., No. 3.

1723 Cyprus. Find-spot unknown. Terracotta figurine, with child in its arms, like *1722* (Late Cypriot II); height 14 cm. Cyprus Mus., Nicosia, Inv. No. 1964.IX-8.8. – Karageorghis, *BCH.* 89 (1965), 244, Fig. 19; Åström, op. cit.

1724 Tamassos–Politiko. Tomb 6, No. 51: Rhyton in form of a bull (Base Ring II ware; Late Cypriot II). Originally painted with white stripes; basket handle begins on neck behind main opening and leads to middle of back; rings in relief for eyes; pointed horns; bronze ring in mouth; height 11.5 cm., length 18.8 cm. Cyprus Mus., Nicosia. – Karageorghis, *RDAC.* 1965, 18, No. 51, Pl. 4.

1725 Cyprus. Find-spot unknown. Rhyton in the form of horse and rider (Base Ring II ware; Late Cypriot II); loop handle on neck immediately in front of rider; height 11.5 cm., length 15 cm. Damage on front legs, mouth and ears. Cyprus Mus., Nicosia, Inv. No. 1935.III-1.8.

1726 Col. Pl. 3 after p. 160: Enkomi. Tomb 55; English excavation, 1896. Vessel in form of a bull (Base Ring II ware; Late Cypriot II); long cylindrical body; strong neck; small head; pointed horns; eyes modelled sculpturally by ridged discs; ear broken, otherwise excellently preserved; stirrup handle on back; painted in white with pine-branch pattern; height 10.7 cm., length 15.4 cm. Cyprus Mus., Nicosia, Inv. No. A 1258.

1727 Katydata. Tomb 28: Terracotta figurine of a seated naked woman (Late Cypriot II); eyes, nose and breasts modelled sculpturally; both arms laid against the body; legs stretched almost straight out before it; seat reproduced in simplified form by vertical supports; incised lines and painting on lower part of body, also band of colour on neck; height 9.5 cm. Cyprus Mus., Nicosia, Inv. No. A 39. – Åström, *Arts and Crafts,* 57, Fig. 70:5; Karageorghis, *Cyprus,* Col. Pl. 79.

1728 Kition; excavated in 1963. Little painted terracotta head of warrior with helmet; height 2.5 cm. (Late Cypriot III). Cyprus Mus., Nicosia.

1729 Cyprus. Find-spot unknown. Upper part of small Mycenaean terracotta figurine (probably LH III b). Unusually ugly; wide mouth, angular chin, and large jutting nose; painting on head and breast; height 7.3 cm. Cyprus Mus., Nicosia, Inv. No. A 30. – Nikolaou, *Op.Ath.* 5 (1965), 49, No. 4, Pl. 4:4; Karageorghis, *Myc. Art,* Pl. 35:2.

1730 Cyprus. Find-spot unknown. Mycenaean terracotta bull with rider, who holds on to the horns with both hands; stripes painted on bull and man; height 10 cm., length 11 cm. (similar figurine without rider, *1252*). Cyprus Mus., Nicosia, Inv. No. A 32. – Nikolaou, Pl. 6; Karageorghis, Pl. 36.1.

1731 Enkomi. On wall-platform in a sanctuary; French excavation, 1962. Large terracotta figure, eleventh century B. C., in the form of a centaur with two human heads; cylindrical body, pierced in front and behind, and four cylindrical legs with flaring bases; painting in the east Cretan Vrokastro style in matt orange; height 30.5 cm. Cyprus Mus., Nicosia. – Karageorghis, *Charisterion eis A. K. Orlandon* II (1964, mod. Gk.), Pl. 21 a.

1732–1741: LATE BRONZE AGE – METAL

1732 Probably from Enkomi. Bronze statuette of a standing god in walking position (Late Cypriot II); right arm raised in the manner of the Syrian god Reshef, left reaches forward (cf. *1741*); conical head covering; remains of gilding on head and chest; pegs for securing on both feet; height 12.2 cm. Cyprus Mus., Nicosia, Inv. No. 1945.V-26.1. – Dikaios, *Guide,* 157.

1733 Enkomi. Bronze statuette (Late Cypriot III) of seated male figure, with flat body in long robe; folds reproduced by scored lines; height 7.5 cm. Cyprus Mus., Nicosia, Inv. No. 1949.II-24.1. – Catling, *Cypriot Bronzework,* Pl. 45 a, b.

1734 Nicosia. Bronze statuette (Late Cypriot III) of standing naked female figure; right arm and both feet missing; eyes represented as on clay figures *(1722, 1723, 1727)*; curls and breasts modelled sculpturally; long necklace with pendant; height 10.5 cm. Cyprus Mus., Nicosia, Inv. No. 1936.VI-18.1. – Catling, Pl. 44 j.

1735 Hagios Jakovos, District of Dima. Sanctuary No. 36:
a, b Bronze statuette (Late Cypriot II) of squatting lion; mane reproduced in relief; eyes and mouth notched; height 5.5 cm. Medelhavsmus. Stockholm. – Sjöqvist, *SCE.* I, Pls. 66:2; 144:4; Catling, Pl. 43 a.

1736 Myrtou–Pigades. Shrine. Bronze statuette of a standing bull (Late Cypriot III, early twelfth century); very long disproportionate legs, parts of front legs restored; height 8.8 cm., length 9.3 cm. Cyprus Mus., Nicosia, Inv. No. 1949.III-8.1. – Catling, 250, No. 6, Pl. 43 g, h; Karageorghis, *Myc. Art,* Pl. 21:4; Åström, *Arts and Crafts,* 4, Fig. 60:12 (drawing).

1737 Kition. Excavation 1963. Bronze weight in the form of a reclining quadruped (goat?), with head turned back (Late Cypriot II); height 3 cm., length 5 cm. Cyprus Mus., Nicosia. – Karageorghis, Pl. 21:3.

1738 Region of Enkomi. Bronze weight in the form of a reclining bullock (Late Cypriot II). Apart from concavity filled with lead on the underneath, cast solid; height 3.7 cm., length 6.5 cm., weight 172.9 g. Cyprus Mus., Nicosia, Inv. No. 1963.X–19.2. – Karageorghis, *BCH*. 88 (1964), 310, Fig. 31.

1739 Cyprus. Find-spot unknown. Bronze weight in the form of a reclining bullock (Late Cypriot II); careful work, naturalistic representation; cast hollow, filled with lead; marking on one side of body in the form of four parallel bars; height 3.5 cm., length 5.2 cm. Cyprus Mus., Nicosia, Inv. No. C 966. – Catling, *Cypriot Bronzework*, 251 f., Pl. 44 d; Karageorghis, *Myc. Art*, Pl. 21:2.

1740 Enkomi. Central shrine, excavated in 1948 (Dikaios). Bronze statue of a young horned god (Late Cypriot III), cast solid; details such as border of apron finely chased. Most important Cypriot metal statue of second millennium, not only for its size. Erect stance, left arm with clenched fist held against chest; short apron and conical horned cap; height 54.2 cm. Cyprus Mus., Nicosia. – Dikaios, *Guide*, Pl. 24; id., *AA*. 1962, 2 ff., Figs. 14, 18–22; Catling, Pl. 46; Karageorghis, *Cyprus*, Pl. 95; Dikaios, *Enkomi* III, 2 (1969), Pls. 138–144.

1741 Enkomi. French excavation, 1963, No. 16.15 (for site cf. *1731*). Bronze statuette of bearded god with horned helmet (Late Cypriot III), cast solid; repairs on legs below apron; attachment on the back for pegs to fasten it to wall; stand peg below; base in form of copper ingot (cf. *1898, 1899*). Apart from its horned, conical helmet and greaves (?), the figure carries a small round shield and a spear; also close-fitting vest and apron; height 35 cm. Cyprus Mus., Nicosia. – Schaeffer, *AfO*. 21 (1965), 59 ff.; Karageorghis, *BCH*. 88 (1964), Pl. 16; and *Myc. Art*, Pl. 19:1; id., *Cyprus*, 142 f., Pl. 65.

Ivories

Like horn, antlers and bone, ivory has been extensively used as a material for precious carvings in Egypt, the Near East, Cyprus and the Aegean. In every region where there were no elephants in antiquity, ivory was a foreign import. Here, conditions were so similar for Cyprus and the Minoan-Mycenaean civilization that we can refer back to pp. 105 ff. See also ivory spindle-whorls: *1844, 1852* and *1853*.

1742 Kition. Tomb 9, No. 354, upper burial: Miniature bath tub of ivory (toilet box; Late Cypriot II). Slightly receding slanting side walls; attachment on one narrow side for securing the lid; two small suspension handles on each long side; height 5 cm., length 32 cm. (cf. Mycenaean tub sarcophagi: *1066, 1068*; similar miniature tub of steatite in District Mus., Paphos). Cyprus Mus., Nicosia. – Karageorghis, *BCH*. 88 (1964), 348 f., Fig. 86; Åström, *Arts and Crafts*, 81, No. 5; 83, Fig. 77.

1743 Kition. Tomb 3, No. 9: Cylindrical bone pyxis (Late Cypriot III), with slightly concave sides; lid and base missing; two superimposed holes in upper part; decoration: horizontal grooves and scale patterns engraved on exterior (cf. LH III b ivories from Minet el Beida: Kantor, *The Aegean and the Orient* [1947], Pl. 24 f.; from Hama: Riis, *Hama* II; 3, 181, Fig. 230 h); height 11.8 cm., diam. 3.4 cm. or 3.9 cm. Cyprus Mus., Nicosia. – Karageorghis, 543, Figs. 62, 63.

1744 Kition. Tombs 4 and 5, No. 235: Fragments of an ivory disc (Late Cypriot II), flat and pierced in the middle. Carefully executed engraving in linear and volute pattern on upper side; diam. 8.5 cm. Cyprus Mus., Nicosia.

1745 Kition; excavated in 1962. Ivory purse (Late Cypriot III); flat, in the form of a capital or a stylized flower; deeply incised horizontal fluting on the front; length 5.6 cm. Cyprus Mus., Nicosia. – Karageorghis, *Myc. Art*, Pl. 42:3.

1746 Kition. Tomb 9, No. 132, upper burial: Thick ivory pin (Late Cypriot II); scale pattern on upper part of shaft (cf. *1743*; also vases, *923, 969*, Fig. 28, *1004*); pinhead in form of pomegranate; length 23 cm. Cyprus Mus., Nicosia. – Karageorghis, Pl. 28:1.

1747 Enkomi. Tomb 24 (1896): Ivory mirror handle (Late Cypriot III); relief picture on upper part: on one side, warrior fighting griffin (perhaps Arimasp motif; cf. Bolton, *Aristeas of Proconnesus* [1962], Pl. 2); on the other, lion attacking bull; stylized foliage vertically arranged on the shaft, and band of rosettes at the junction with the plate to which the metal disc was attached; length 20 cm. British Mus., London, No. 97.4–1.872. – Murray, *Excavations in Cyprus* (1900), Pl. 2; Schäfer, *AM*. 73 (1958), 73 ff., Suppl. 61, 62; Higgins, *Minoan and Myc. Art*, Figs. 165, 166.

1748 Kouklia, Old Paphos, Evreti District. Tomb 8, Find No. 7.26.34: Ivory mirror handle (Late Cypriot III); carving in high relief: on either side a warrior fighting a lion; height 21.5 cm. Cyprus Mus., Nicosia. – Catling, *Cypriot Bronzework*, Pl. 1 c; Karageorghis, *Treasures*, Pl. 41:1; id., *Myc. Art*, Pl. 42:1.

1749 Enkomi. Tomb 58 (1896): Rectangular ivory casket, a, b with relief decoration, on four feet (Late Cypriot III a); both long sides show hunting scenes with chariot; pairs of animals on short sides; linear carving on lid, which served as gaming table; length 29 cm., width 7.5 cm., height 8.5 cm. British Mus., London. – Murray, *Excavations in Cyprus*, Pl. 1, No. 996; Singer-Holmyard, *History of Technology* I (1955), 677, Fig. 476 a; Kantor, *The Aegean and the Orient*, Pl. 26 a; Lorimer, *Homer and the Monuments* (1950), Pl. 11:1; Laser, *Arch. Hom.*, Lfg. P (1968), 76, Fig. 14 a; Åström, *Arts and Crafts*, 82 ff., Fig. 78 (with further references).

Seals

In spite of their small size, seals are of prime archaeological and historical importance. In the case of the Aegean at least (cf. *1359 ff.*), this is clear from numerous studies by Matz. The types of seal, the material, and, in particular, the pictures and ornaments tell us much about the ideas and ability of the stone cutters and their patrons, about trade and cultural relations, and about larger-scale art forms, which the pictures and ornaments of glyptic usually reflect in miniature.

The known materials are steatite, haematite, semi-precious stones, faience, ivory, lead and bronze. The types of seal most frequently found in Cyprus in the Bronze Age are cones on a round base, lentoid stones *(1759 a, b)*, scarabs, and cylinder seals *(1750—1758, 1773)*. The typically Near Eastern cylinder seal reached Greece in both its North Syrian and its Cypriot form (Perati, *1382*); details by Buchholz can be found in Bass, *Cape Gelidonya* (Transact. of the Amer. Philos. Soc. 57, Part 8, 1967, 148 ff.).

The style of a number of cylinder seals proves the influence of pictorial ideas and formal elements from all the cultural regions with which the island had relations. Accordingly, we have described the pieces *1750* and *1753* as Cypro-Aegean (cf. *1758*: Aegean); *1751* belongs to the 'Cypro-Mitannic hybrid style.' Sometimes there are also Egyptian influences *(1752)*, and we occasionally find imported Babylonian cylinder seals *(1773)*. A unique 'Philistine seal' from Enkomi *(1760)* is of the greatest historical interest; the existence of Anatolian Hittite relations is proved by a silver seal from Tamassos inscribed with the Hittite hieroglyphic script (Ashmolean Mus., Oxford, Inv. No. 1896.1908; cf. Hogarth, *Hittite Seals* [1920], No. 191, Pl. 7; further references in Masson, *BCH.* 88 [1964], 204 f., note 7, Fig. 6 a, b).

For the specifically Cypriot elements of indigenous glyptic (e.g. *1754—1757*), see H. Frankfort, *Cylinder Seals* (1939), 303 f.; Porada, *AJA* 52 (1948), 178 ff.; idem, in *Vorderasiatische Archäologie: Festschrift für Moortgat* (1964), 234 ff.; and *AJA* 73 (1969), 244.

1750 Kition. Tomb 9, No. 16. Impression of a haematite seal (Late Cypriot II); pictures arranged in two superimposed zones, representing seated or kneeling figures, fabulous beings, and animals; Cypro-Aegean style; height 3.1 cm. Cyprus Mus., Nicosia. – Kenna–Karageorghis, *Studi Micenei ed Egeo-Anatolici* 3 (1967), 95, Fig. 1; Karageorghis, *Cyprus*, Fig. 62.

1751 Probably from Pyla. Impression of a haematite seal (Late Cypriot II). Scenes and motifs of different kinds arranged in various pictorial groups: gods, sphinxes, and animals; particularly noteworthy is the sacred tree; Cypro-Mitannic hybrid style; height 2.9 cm. Cyprus Mus., Nicosia, Inv. No. 1950.VI-1.1.

1752 Kition. Tomb 9, No. 205. Impression of a haematite seal (Late Cypriot III). Antithetical groups of human figures and monkeys in three adjacent vertical pictorial fields; also large band of guilloche; Egyptianizing style; height 2.4 cm. Cyprus Mus., Nicosia. – Kenna–Karageorghis, *Studi Micenei ed Egeo–Anatolici* 3 (1967), 95, Fig. 2; Karageorghis, *Cyprus*, Fig. 61.

1753 Enkomi; excavated in 1934. Trial Trench 37, No. 2: Impression of a haematite seal (Late Cypriot II, fifteenth to fourteenth century B.C.); symmetrical picture: standing human figure in short chiton with outstretched arms in the middle – the 'Master of Animals', holding two lions by the ears; to his left and right are genies with water pitchers, and above this birds and griffins; Cypro-Aegean style; height 3.5 cm. Cyprus Mus., Nicosia. – Schaeffer, *Missions en Chypre*, 89 f., 112 f., Figs. 48, 49; Karageorghis, *Treasures*, Pl. 45:1; Spartz, 'Das Wappenbild des Herrn u. der Herrin der Tiere in der minoisch-mykenischen u. frühgriechischen Kunst' (thesis Munich 1967), 104, No. 35 (bibliography); Gill, *AM.* 79 (1964), 20, No. 46, Pl. 6:2; Schachermeyr, *Ägäis u. Orient* (1967), 54, Pl. 53:193.

1754 Dekelia, Steno. Tomb 3, No. 53: Impression of a seal of yellowish faience (Late Cypriot II); frieze of helmeted figures, with staffs in their hands, moving to the left; Cypriot style; height 2.7 cm. District Mus., Larnaka. – Karageorghis, *AA.* 1963, 531, Fig. 15.

1755 Achera. Tomb 3, No. 29: Steatite cylinder seal (Late Cypriot II) and impression; seal picture in Cypriot style; seated human figure on either side of an altar, holding weapons; height 2.5 cm., diam. 1 cm. Cyprus Mus., Nicosia. – Karageorghis, *Nouveaux Documents*, Pl. 10:3.

1756 Achera. Tomb 2, No. 35: Steatite cylinder seal (Late Cypriot II), and impression; seal picture in Cypriot style; seated lions antithetically arranged, with raised front paws, between them a stunted tree; god or 'hero' behind, holding a lion by the tail on his left and right; height 2.6 cm., diam. 1.9 cm. Cyprus Mus., Nicosia. – Karageorghis, Pl. 10:1.

1757 Achera. Tomb 2, No. 30: Cylinder seal of light-coloured glass paste (Late Cypriot II) and impression; two human figures, separated by vertical lines, and a stag, with head turned back; above and below, deep pictorial frame lines; height 1.8 cm., diam. 0.8 cm. Cyprus Mus., Nicosia. – Karageorghis, Pl. 10:2.

1758 Analiondas, Paliekklisia District, 23 km. SSW. of Nicosia. Pithos fragment with Bronze Age impression of a cylinder seal (Late Cypriot II); hunting scene with hunter on war chariot drawing his bow, preceded by fleeing animals, and followed by two runners; Aegean style; height of impression 3 cm. Cyprus Mus., Nicosia, Inv. No. 1953. IX-3.6. – Catling–Karageorghis, *BSA.* 55 (1960), 122, Pl. 30 a, b; Karageorghis, *Myc. Art,* Pl. 38:5.

1759 Enkomi. Lentoid seal of light steatite; Cypriot style a, b (Late Cypriot II); front: seated goddess with long scaly – i. e., flounced – dress; to her left and right, two animals turning away; rosettes in free space; reverse: the same goddess with Minoan apron running to the right; with one hand she grasps a ram, the other holds a sword; diam. 2.5 cm. Cyprus Mus., Nicosia, Inv. No. 1965.VI–1.1. – Karageorghis, *RDAC.* 1965, Pl. 2:1–4; id., *Myc. Art,* Pl. 37:1, 2; id., *Cyprus,* Fig. 64.

1760 Enkomi. Rubble deposit in the temple of the 'Horned God', excavated by Dikaios 1950. Find No. 184: Oval seal surface of a stamp seal (Late Cypriot III). Black steatite, from an alabaster impression; bearded Philistine warrior, with characteristic crown of reeds and large embossed shield; height 1.5 cm., width 1 cm. Cyprus Mus., Nicosia. – Dikaios, *AA.* 1962, 18, Fig. 11; Kenna, *BCH.* 92 (1968), 145, Fig. 1:12, and 147, Fig. 2:21; Dikaios, *Enkomi* I (1969), frontispiece.

Ornaments and toilet articles

During the Stone and Bronze Ages, the inhabitants of Cyprus did not differ from the members of other civilizations in their desire for ornament. So we cannot describe their necklaces of shells and round beads *(1767—1772)* as 'characteristically Cypriot'. However, the early appearance of manufactured glass beads does seem noteworthy *(1770—1772)*; there were no glass ornaments in the Aegean world until the Mycenaean Age *(1310, 1311, 1315, 1316, 1346)*.

Silver jewellery is remarkably rare *(1827 a, b)*, whereas we find a wealth of gold in the island in the latter half of the second millennium *(1773 ff)*. The high quality of native goldsmithing in this period is evident from the knowledge of granulation *(1780)*, embossing, chasing, soldering, plaiting with fine gold wire *(1774, 1776)*, and, above all, in the technique of enamel inlay *(1785—1788)*. The poorer inhabitants wore bronze ornaments instead of gold or silver (cf. *1868*, bracelet).

Apart from the fact that one of the objects represented in our illustrations—the gold sceptre with the pair of falcons *(1788)*—was not an ornament but a badge of rank, we must note that many types of ornament also doubled as amulets; for example, the Neolithic stone fish *(1761)* and the group of Chalcolithic steatite idols *(1699—1703)* which, as shown by *1699*, were worn on a necklace to bring good fortune. Pendants and beads, in the shape of poppy seeds or pomegranates *(1772, 1773, 1780)*, were fertility symbols; they were valued as much for their magic properties as for their purely aesthetic appeal. Gold necklace beads in the form of figure-of-eight shields *(1789, 1790)* follow directly in the Minoan tradition and also have a religious significance.

The existence of an inherent relationship between seals, amulets, and ornaments is revealed by the fact that cylinder seals frequently appear in Cypriot tombs as necklace pendants *(1773, 1791)*. The many gold diadems and mouth-plates often found in Late Cypriot burials *(1793—1803)* can also be explained partly in terms of the ritual of the dead; they too had a religious significance, and cannot simply be considered ornaments in our sense of the word. The same applies to the diadems found in the shaft graves of Mycenae *(1299—1303;* cf. Bielefeld, *Arch. Hom. Lieferung C* [1968], 14 ff.).

But, in spite of the religious, ritual, or magical aspect of ornaments, we must not forget that they often owed their existence to practical needs. They include the dress pins which appeared in great variety during the Cypriot Bronze Age *(1804—1818, 1858, 1859;* cf. Aegean pins: *1295, 1297, 1298)*, and, later, the fibulae constructed according to the principle of the safety pin *(1819, 1820;* cf. *1353—1355)*.

The care of the body reached a degree of sophistication during the Late Bronze Age, as we can deduce from miniature models of bath tubs *(1742)* and from the toilet articles found in contemporary tombs. Round metal mirrors were indispensable articles *(1822;* cf. *626, 630, 632)*. The richly carved ivory mirror-handles from Enkomi and Kouklia *(1747, 1748)* are luxuries among toilet articles (Schäfer, 'Elfenbeinspiegelgriffe des 2. Jahrhunderts', *AM.* 73 [1958], 73 ff.). Ointments and cosmetics were kept in precious ivory containers *(1743)*. There were bronze, and sometimes silver, tweezers *(1821, 1865;*

cf. *584, 624, 625)* and razors *(1823, 1824)* for the removal of individual hairs or the entire beard; for hair and beard styles, cf. Marinatos, *Arch. Hom. Lieferung B* (1967). Finally, ivory and wooden combs (which we have not illustrated) have been found in Cyprus, particularly in Enkomi and Apliki; some of them derive from Mycenaean tradition *(511—516, 1279)*. A recent study is A. Pierides, *Jewellery in the Cyprus Museum* (1971).

1761–1772: STONE, SHELL AND GLASS PASTE

1761 Khirokitia. Surface find. Early Neolithic fish amulet of stone, described as 'picrolith'; horizontally pierced; length 4 cm. Cyprus Mus., Nicosia. – Dikaios, *Khirokitia*, 306, Figs. 107, 408, No. 1476, Pl. 68 a; id., *SCE.* IV/1A, Pl.-Fig. 16:3.

1762 Khirokitia. Early Neolithic dress pin of andesite, with flat round head, pierced in middle, and with 'V' shaped notch on edge; length 4 cm. Cyprus Mus., Nicosia. – Dikaios, *Khirokitia*, 365, No. 564, Pls. 100, 141; id., *SCE.* IV/1A, Pl.-Fig. 17:1.

1763 Khirokitia. Early Neolithic amulet in the form of a pin or club (?); material as *1761;* long pointed shaft and bi-conical head; length 4.1 cm. Cyprus Mus., Nicosia. – Dikaios, *Khirokitia*, 378 f., No. 762, Pls. 100, 141; id., *SCE.* IV/1A, Pl.-Fig. 17:3.

1764 Khirokitia. Early Neolithic dress pin of calcite, with semicircular head and two parallel points; length 2.4 cm. Cyprus Mus., Nicosia. – Dikaios, *Khirokitia*, 392, No. 1009, Pls. 100, 142; and *SCE.* IV/1A, Pl.-Fig. 17:4.

1765 Khirokitia. Early Neolithic amulets in the form of
1766 pins or clubs (?); heads pierced, point of *1766* missing; lengths 3.3 and 2.5 cm. Cyprus Mus., Nicosia. – Dikaios, *Khirokitia*, 392, Nos. 1006, 1007, Pls. 100, 141; and *SCE.* IV/1A, Pl.-Fig. 17:3.

1767 Khirokitia. Tholoi XVII *(1769)*, XVIII *(1768)* and
to XIX *(1767)*. Neolithic necklaces of alternate groups of
1769 dentalium shells and carnelian beads; *1767* is linked by flat, rectangular pieces of picrolith, beads of the same material on *1768* (Neolithic II). Cyprus Mus., Nicosia. – Dikaios, *Khirokitia*, 108 f., No. 560, Fig. 52 *(1769* here); 111 f., No. 928 a, Fig. 54 *(1768);* 118 f., No. 1485, Fig. 58 *(1767* here), Pls. 68 a, 99; and *SCE.* IV/1A, Fig. 16:1 *(1769),* 2 *(1767),* 4 *(1768).*

1770 Kalavassos. Tomb 5, No. 16: Necklace with 108 round beads of light blue glass paste (Early Cypriot III); diam. of individual beads 0.8–1.5 cm. District Mus., Larnaka. – Karageorghis, *RDAC.* 1940–48, Pl. 10 d.

1771 Kalavassos. Tomb 5, No. 20: Long necklace of two rows of tiny beads; dark red and black cylindrical stone beads, and white or bluish-green flat beads of glass paste (Early Cypriot III). District Mus., Larnaka. – Karageorghis, op. cit., Pl. 10 c.

1772 Kition. Tomb 9, No. 306, upper burial: Necklace of 197 beads (Late Cypriot II); most of the small round beads made of black glass paste, and several larger round and long beads of a bluish colour, and two polished 'bottle-shaped' carnelians, certainly imitations of poppy seeds symbolizing fertility; length 32 cm. Cyprus Mus., Nicosia.

1773–1803: GOLD

1773 Hagios Jakovos. Dima District, Nos. 3, 4 and 27: Gold necklace (Late Cypriot II), of seven hollow beads in the shape of pomegranates, six large and two small date-shaped hollow beads, and a Babylonian cylinder seal of haematite in a solid gold setting as a bead; length of entire necklace 19.8 cm. Cyprus Mus., Nicosia. – Sjöqvist, *SCE.* I, Pl. 147:9; Karageorghis, *Cyprus,* Col. Pl. 81.

1774 Enkomi. Tomb 17, No. 82: Gold ornamental pin (Late Cypriot II), with gold wire ring attached to middle; lower half smooth, upper plaited from many interwoven loops; plated gold spherical head on a similar terminal of blue glass paste; length 14 cm. Cyprus Mus., Nicosia. – Sjöqvist, *SCE.* I, Pl. 145:4; Åström, *Arts and Crafts,* 37, Fig. 65:7; Karageorghis, *Myc. Art,* Pl. 32:9; and *Cyprus,* Col. Pl. 83.

1775 Enkomi. Find No. 4202: Late Bronze Age oval gold pectoral, pierced at both ends. Decoration in embossed work: stylized plant, flanked on either side by a winged sphinx facing inwards; above and below are punched rosettes, along the rim a row of small bosses; length 17.5 cm., width 10 cm. Cyprus Mus., Nicosia. – Schaeffer, *Enkomi-Alasia* I, Pl. 24; Karageorghis, *Myc. Art,* Pl. 30:1; and *Cyprus,* Col. Pl. 87.

1776 Hagios Jakovos. Dima District, No. 5. Pair of gold
a,b earrings (Late Cypriot II) of twisted and interwoven wire, in flat crescent shape; diam. 4.7 cm. Cyprus Mus., Nicosia. – Sjöqvist, *SCE.* I, Pl. 115:8; Karageorghis, *Myc. Art.,* Pl. 33:8.

1777 Cyprus. Find-spot unknown. Pair of gold crescent-
a,b shaped earrings (Late Cypriot II), formed of twisted bands with thinly hammered overlapping ends; diam. 3 cm. Cyprus Mus., Nicosia, Inv. No. J 67. – Åström, *Arts and Crafts,* 37, Fig. 65:10; Karageorghis, Pl. 33:6.

1778 Kition. Tomb 9, No. 134: Pair of gold pendant ear-
a,b rings (Late Cypriot II) in the form of thin rings, with overlapping ends and bull's head pendants; length 2.7 cm. Cyprus Mus., Nicosia. – Åström, *Arts and Crafts,* 37, Fig. 65:12 (further examples); Karageorghis, *Cyprus,* Col. Pl. 82.

1779 Kition. Tomb 9, No. 210: Pair of gold earrings (Late
a,b Cypriot II) in the form of an oval, with one end

overlapping; length 2 cm. Cyprus Mus., Nicosia. – For this form, cf. Åström, op. cit., 29, No. 4 (further examples); Karageorghis, *Myc. Art*, Pl. 33:5.

1780 Enkomi. Pendant (Late Cypriot II) in the form of a pomegranate, with small triangles of granulation; height 4.7 cm., diam. 3.2 cm. Cyprus Mus., Nicosia, Inv. No. 1954.III–24.1. – Karageorghis, *Treasures*, Pl. 41:3; *Myc. Art*, Pl. 32:7; and *Cyprus*, Col. Pl. 81.

1781 Kition. Tomb 9, No. 249, upper burial: Cast gold finger-ring (Late Cypriot II), with smooth hoop and flat oval ornamental bezel showing a bull between stylized trees; diam. 1.8 cm. Cyprus Mus., Nicosia. – Karageorghis, *RDAC*. 1963, Pl. 2:4; id., *BCH*. 88 (1964), 348, Fig. 85; and *Myc. Art*, Pl. 32:2.

1782 Kition. Tomb 9, No. 10: Cast gold finger-ring (Late Cypriot II), with smooth hoop and flat oval ornamental bezel; decoration: bird with outstretched wings and a character in the Cypro-Minoan syllabary; diam. 1.9 cm. Cyprus Mus., Nicosia.

1783 Kition. Tomb 9, No. 291, upper burial: Gold ring with round undecorated hoop (Late Cypriot II), having gold wire twisted round the ends and stone in the form of a ram's head, made of dark blue glass paste; it is set in gold, and is attached to the ring so that it can be turned axially; diam. 2.3 cm. Cyprus Mus., Nicosia. – Karageorghis, *Myc. Art*, Pl. 32:3; and *Cyprus*, Col. Pl. 82.

1784 Enkomi. Tomb 18, No. 62 (Late Cypriot II). Bronze finger-ring with gold plating, in the form of a horseshoe, with flat oval ornamental relief bezel depicting lion with head turned back moving to the right; mane, ribs and other details indicated in relief; diam. 2.6 cm. Cyprus Mus., Nicosia. – Sjöqvist, *SCE*. I, Pls. 88:2; 145:21–23.

1785 Kouklia–Evreti (Old Paphos, cf. *1748*). Tomb 8: Gold to finger-rings (Late Cypriot III); ornamental bezels with
1787 areas divided up by gold fillets and multi-coloured enamel inlays; diam. 2.2 cm. Cyprus Mus., Nicosia. – Karageorghis, *Treasures*, Pl. 41:2; Higgins, *Minoan and Mycenaean Art*, Fig. 223; Bielefeld, *Arch. Hom. Lieferung C* (1968), Col. Pl. 1 b; Karageorghis, *Cyprus*, Col. Pl. 80.

1788 Also Col. Pl. 4 after p. 168. Kourion–Kaloriziki. Shaft
a–d grave without dromos (twelfth to eleventh century B. C.). Sceptre of gold and enamel: tubular rod of thin gold plate, surmounted by a sphere decorated with gold fillets and covered in enamel scales, and crowned by a similarly worked pair of falcons; the areas divided up by the gold fillets are filled with white, green and light violet enamel; height 16.5 cm. Cyprus Mus., Nicosia, Inv. No. J 99. – Casson, *Ancient Cyprus* (1939), Pl. 5; Westholm, *Arkeologiska Forskningar och Fynd* (1952), 82 ff., 449 f., Fig. 1; McFadden, *AJA*. 58 (1954), 141, Pl. 18:2; Deonna, *Coll. Latomus* XVIII (1955), Pl. 7; Hampe, *Gymnasium* 63 (1956), 56, Pl. 16; Åström, *Arts and Crafts*, 27, 93, 95, 149; Higgins, *Minoan and Mycenaean Art*, Fig. 222; Karageorghis, *Treasures*, Pl. 40:1; and *Cyprus*, Col. Pl. 89.

1789 Enkomi. Tomb No. 604: Gold necklace (Late Cypriot II), consisting of sixteen large beads in the form of figure-of-eight shields, which are pierced horizontally in four places, and form rows with smaller beads between them; in the middle of the necklace are six large almond-shaped carnelians and more small beads; length of gold shield beads 3.5 cm. British Mus., London. – Murray, *Excavations in Cyprus*, Pl. 6:604; Higgins, *Minoan and Mycenaean Art*, Fig. 218; Karageorghis, *Myc. Art*, Pl. 29.2.

1790 Enkomi. Tomb 18, No. 20: Gold necklace (Late Cypriot II), formed of ten hollow beads in the form of figure-of-eight shields and eleven smaller triple coiled tubes as spacers; length 31.7 cm. Cyprus Museum, Nicosia. – Sjöqvist, *SCE*. I, Pl. 147:8; Karageorghis, *Treasures*, Pl. 40:2; and *Cyprus*, Col. Pl. 86.

1791 Kition. Tomb 9, No. 293 (Late Cypriot II). Seven small gold beads of different shapes, and cylinder seal of hammered gold over a stone or faience core as pendant; engraved decoration: birds, snakes, fish, human figure and sacred tree; length of seal 2.8 cm. Cyprus Mus., Nicosia. – Kenna–Karageorghis, *Studi Micenei ed Egeo-Anatolici* 3 (1967), 96, Fig. 3; Karageorghis, *Myc. Art*, Pl. 32:4.

1792 Kition. Tomb 9, No. 201: Gold pendant formed of circular disc (diam. 1.4 cm.) with eye; through it passes an elliptical ring that can be turned, which also has a horizontal eye; height of both parts 3 cm. Cyprus Mus., Nicosia.

1793 Kition. Tomb 9, No. 295 (Late Cypriot II). Ribbon-like gold diadem with row of seven embossed bucrania; both ends pierced; length 11.5 cm., width 2.5 cm. Cyprus Mus., Nicosia. – Karageorghis, *Myc. Art*, Pl. 31:4.

1794 Kition. Tomb 9, No. 22 (Late Cypriot II). Ribbon-like gold diadem with impressed decoration: three horizontal rows of small rosettes; three holes at either end; length 26 cm., width 4 cm. Cyprus Mus., Nicosia. – Karageorghis, *RDAC*. 1963, Pl. 2:2; and *Myc. Art*, Pl. 31:1; id., *Cyprus*, Col. Pl. 88.

1795 Kition. Tomb 9, No. 309 (Late Cypriot II). Wide gold diadem, with five large many-leaved rosettes in embossed work; two holes at either end; length 26 cm., width 5.5 cm. Cyprus Mus., Nicosia. – Karageorghis, *RDAC*. 1963, Pl. 2:1; and *Cyprus*, Col. Pl. 88.

1796 Kition. Tomb 9, No. 179, upper burial (Late Cypriot II). Gold diadem with pierced corners; two long decorative fields in embossed work, the upper with groups of bars, the lower with a frieze of arrow-like symbols; length 25.5 cm., width 3 cm. Cyprus Mus., Nicosia.

1797 Kition. Tomb 9, No. 1, upper burial (Late Cypriot II). Gold diadem with rounded corners and lattice pattern in chased work; perforated at either end; length 23.5 cm., width 4 cm. Cyprus Mus., Nicosia.

1798 Kition. Tomb 9, No. 129, upper burial (Late Cypriot II). Gold diadem with rounded corners; two holes for securing at either end; decoration: five large foliage rosettes, roughly executed in repoussé work; length 19 cm., width 4 cm. Cyprus Mus., Nicosia.

1799 Kition. Tomb 9, No. 127, upper burial (Late Cypriot II). Gold oval mouthpiece, with ends pointed and pierced; irregular chevron pattern in chased work; length 10.5 cm., width 3.2 cm. Cyprus Mus., Nicosia.

1800 Kition. Tomb 9, No. 276, upper burial (Late Cypriot II). Gold diadem with rounded corners and two holes for securing on either end; decoration in embossed work: three stylized trees among rows of bosses; length 13.6 cm., width 3 cm. Cyprus Mus., Nicosia. – Karageorghis, *RDAC*. 1963, Pl. 2:3.

1801 Kition. Tomb 9, No. 242, upper burial (Late Cypriot II). Gold oval mouthpiece, with three threading holes on either end. Decoration in chased work: horizontal lines; length 10.3 cm., width 3.8 cm., Cyprus Mus., Nicosia.

1802 Kition. Tomb 9, No. 146, upper burial (Late Cypriot II). Gold oval mouthpiece shaped as lips, with one hole at each end; length 6.8 cm., width 2.7 cm. Cyprus Mus., Nicosia.

1803 Kition. Tomb 9, No. 297, upper burial (Late Cypriot II). Gold diadem, pointed and perforated at the ends; decoration: three horizontal rows of impressed bosses; length 10.5 cm., width 1.7 cm. Cyprus Mus., Nicosia.

1804–1820: BRONZE AND BONE DRESS PINS AND FIBULAE (cf. also 1858, 1859)

1804 Lapithos. Tomb 18, Chamber B, No. 7: Middle Cypriot dress pin of bronze, with button-like head; length 39.8 cm. Cyprus Mus., Nicosia.

1805 Cyprus. Find-spot unknown. Middle Cypriot thick dress pin of bronze, with conically widening head; length 25 cm. Cyprus Mus., Nicosia.

1806 Lapithos. Tomb 201, No. 46: Bronze dress pin (Early Cypriot III–Middle Cypriot), with oval shaft and button-like head; length 28.8 cm. Cyprus Mus., Nicosia. – Catling, *Cypriot Bronzework*, Fig. 5:18.

1807 Cyprus. Find-spot unknown. Middle Cypriot bronze
1808 dress pins, with disc-like head; length 25.5 cm. and 29.5 cm. Cyprus Mus., Nicosia.

1809 Cyprus. Find-spot unknown. Middle Cypriot bronze
1810 dress pins, with eye (toggle pins), button-like head (1809), and mushroom head (1810); lengths 20.4 cm. and 17.8 cm. Cyprus Mus., Nicosia.

1811 Lapithos. Tomb 27, No. 8: Middle Cypriot bronze dress pin, with eye and button head; length 10 cm. Cyprus Mus., Nicosia.

1812 Cyprus. Find-spot unknown. Probably Middle Bronze Age looped pin, bronze, length 6 cm. Cyprus Mus., Nicosia. – For this type of pin, cf. Bittel, 'Die kyprischen Schleifennadeln', *Marburger Studien* (1938) 9 ff.

1813 Cyprus. Find-spot unknown. Bronze dress pin (prob-
a, b ably Late Cypriot III), with eye, large fluted head, channelled shaft, and 'guard disc'; length 9.4 cm. Cyprus Mus., Nicosia. – Catling, *Cypriot Bronzework*, Fig. 6:8.

1814 Cyprus. Find-spot unknown. Late Cypriot dress pin of
a, b bronze, with large eye, fluted head, and spirally channelled shaft; length 9.5 cm. Cyprus Mus., Nicosia. – Catling, *Cypriot Bronzework*, Fig. 6:6.

1815 Cyprus. Find-spot unknown. Middle Cypriot (?) thick dress pin of bronze, with eye, conical head, and transverse channels on shaft; length 14.3 cm. Cyprus Mus., Nicosia.

1816 Pendagia. Tomb 1, No. 10: Small Late Cypriot dress pin of bone, with eye, pointed conical head, and engraved lines on shaft; length 8.5 cm. Cyprus Mus., Nicosia. – Karageorghis, *Nouveaux Documents*, 40, Fig. 15:10.

1817 Cyprus. Find-spot unknown. Middle Cypriot dress pin of bronze with eye; flat end above; length 10.5 cm. Cyprus Mus., Nicosia.

1818 Cyprus. Find-spot unknown. Middle Cypriot dress pin of bronze, with hook-like curving head; length 12.7 cm. Cyprus Mus., Nicosia.

1819 Cyprus. Find-spot unknown. Fragmentary bronze fibula of the 'violin bow' type; length 8 cm.; probably Late Cypriot III. Cyprus Mus., Nicosia. – Catling, *Cypriot Bronzework*, Pl. 42 e.

1820 Cyprus. Find-spot unknown. Bronze fibula with raised bow curving downwards at forearm; decorated with herring-bone pattern; length 11.8 cm. Late Cypriot III. Cyprus Mus., Nicosia. – Catling, Fig. 22:26, Pl. 42 b.

1821–1824: BRONZE TOILET ARTICLES

1821 Cyprus. Find-spot unknown. Bronze tweezers with narrow loop and spoon-like flared arms; length 13.9 cm. Middle Cypriot/Late Cypriot. Cyprus Mus., Nicosia.

1822 Cyprus. Find-spot unknown. Round bronze mirror with short peg shaft and one rivet hole; diam. 16 cm. Probably Late Cypriot III. Cyprus Mus., Nicosia.

1823 Probably from Lapithos. Bronze razor (Early Cypriot III/Middle Cypriot I), with short wide blade, triangular tang, and one rivet hole; length 14 cm. Cyprus Mus., Nicosia, Inv. No. L 47. – Catling, op. cit., Fig. 5:5.

1824 Cyprus. Find-spot unknown. Bronze razor (Early Cypriot III/Middle Cypriot I); rectangular blade with narrow tang and rivet hole; length 13.5 cm. Cyprus Mus., Nicosia.

1825–1827: GOLD, SILVER AND BRONZE HAIR-GRIPS

1825 Lapithos. Tomb 6, Chamber A, Nos. 24, 25: Hair
a, b ornament (Early Cypriot III) of thin, triangular gold plate, rolled up in tubular form and decorated with dots and zigzag lines in repoussé technique; length 5.5 cm. Cyprus Mus., Nicosia. – Grace, *AJA*. 44 (1940), 44, Nos. 24, 25, Pl. 12; Karageorghis, *Syria* 42 (1965), 142 f., Fig. 1:4–7.

1826 Kalavassos. Tomb 5, Nos. 14, 15, 17: Ornamental
a–c bronze hair pieces (Early Cypriot III) of tubular plate, decorated with rows of dots. Two of them (a pair, length 8.5 cm.) are one inside the other; length of individual piece 13 cm. Cyprus Mus., Nicosia. – Karageorghis, *RDAC*. 1940-48, 126, Nos. 14, 15, Fig. 7, Pl. 10 a; id., *Syria* 42 (1965), 142 f., Figs. 1:11–12 and 3:2.

1827 Lapithos. Tomb 322, Chamber A, No. 38: Fragments of
a, b hair ornaments (Middle Cypriot I), of thin tubular rolled-up silver plate in triangular form; above (left in picture) with narrow rim; decoration in chased work: rows of bosses, circles and zigzag lines; length 9 cm. Cyprus Mus., Nicosia. – Gjerstad, *SCE*. I, Pl. 35:2; Karageorghis, *Syria* 42, Figs. 1:8–9 and 3:1.

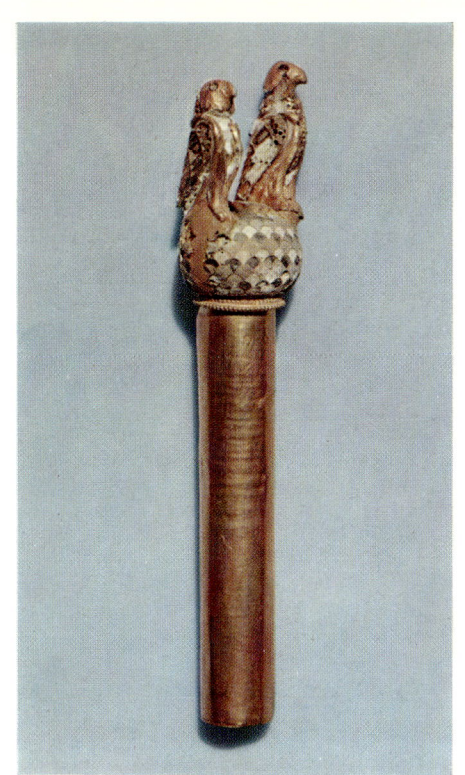 

1788 c and d Gold sceptre from Kourion (Kaloriziki)

1684 c Silver cup with gold and niello inlays from Enkomi

Colour plate 4

Tools—lamps—weapons—ingots

For purposes of comparison we can consider Aegean stone hand-axes, axes, clubs *(217—234)*, flint and obsidian implements *(238—351)*, bone tools *(467 ff.)*, whorls, weaving weights, and 'spools' *(413—488)*. From the mass of general literature, we particularly recommend, because of its modernity of outlook, Åström, *Studies on the Arts and Crafts of the Late Cypriot Bronze Age* (1967). For information on methods of lighting, including a bibliography, see Jantzen-Tölle, in *Archaeologia Homerica, Lieferung P* (1968), 83 ff.

The Cypriot metal ware illustrated here can be compared with implements from the Aegean such as knives and saws *(549, 550, 627—629, 631, 633—665)*, adzes and axes *(553—573, 575—577, 713, 715)*, double axes *(716—738)*, and fishing implements *(621—622)*. Late Bronze Age metallurgy in Cyprus (including ingots: *1898, 1899*, cf. *739—752*) is dealt with expertly by Catling, *Cypriot Bronzework in the Mycenaean World* (1964); for analyses of metals, see Buchholz, *BJbV* 7 (1967), 189 ff. (cf. also above, p. 44).

A consideration of the Cypriot offensive and defensive weapons illustrated here must also take into account the arms of prehistoric Greece: daggers and swords *(518—548, 666—702)*, spear- and lanceheads *(578—583, 589—598)*, arrowheads of stone and metal *(353—410, 599—620)*, as well as armour, greaves and helmets *(510, 710—712)*. Besides the work by Catling mentioned above, see Snodgrass, *Early Greek Armour and Weapons* (1964) for Cypriot weapons (see *Gnomon* 1969, 393).

1828–1839: STONE AND BONE

1828 Erimi. Find No. 905: Chalcolithic sickle blade of brownish-yellow flint, with sparse retouching of edge; length 10 cm. Cyprus Mus., Nicosia. – Dikaios, *RDAC*. 1936, Pl. 27:3.

1829 Khirokitia. Find No. 395: Early Neolithic curved sickle blade of grey flint; both edges serrated; length 7.7 cm. Cyprus Mus., Nicosia. – Dikaios, *Khirokitia*, Pl. 86:395.

1830 Karavas. Neolithic symmetrical arrowhead of light-brown flint, with small tang for shaft; length 4.5 cm. Cyprus Mus., Nicosia, Inv. No. 1962.I-17.1. – Karageorghis, *BCH*. 84 (1960), 298, Fig. 77; for this type, cf. Buchholz, *JdI*. 77 (1962), 11, Fig. 7 II a (here p. 48, Fig. 20, *410*).

1831 Khirokitia. Find No. 908: Early Neolithic arrowhead of dark brown flint with tang for shafting, crudely flaked; length 6.7 cm. Cyprus Mus., Nicosia. – Dikaios, op. cit., Pl. 86:908.

1832 Phrenaros. Find No. 30 (1926): Early Neolithic long slender flint blade of brownish colour; length 16.5 cm. Cyprus Mus., Nicosia. – Gjerstad, *Antiq. Journal* 6 (1926), Pl. 7:30.

1833 Khirokitia. Finds Nos. 407, 270: Early Neolithic blades
1834 of dark obsidian, imported volcanic glass; not found in natural form in Cyprus (cf. Aegean obsidian implements *238—244, 309—351*); length 4.5 cm. and 4.4 cm. Cyprus Mus., Nicosia. – Dikaios, op. cit., Pls. 86:407 and 270.

1835 Kalavassos. Site A, Find No. 2: Late Neolithic polished andesite axe-head, with straight blade, in a bone sheath which comes to a point toward the top; lost shaft probably of wood; length of both parts 17 cm. Cyprus Mus., Nicosia.

1836 Erimi. Find No. 178: Early Chalcolithic polished triangular andesite axe-head with pointed neck and straight blade, sharpened on one side; length 10.3 cm. Cyprus Mus., Nicosia.

1837 Khirokitia. Find No. 277: Early Neolithic polished andesite axe-head with pointed neck, tapering sides and round blade, whetted on one side; length 15 cm. Cyprus Mus., Nicosia. – Dikaios, op. cit., Pls. 83, 136.

1838 Erimi. Finds Nos. 509 and 445: Early Chalcolithic
1839 bone needles with eye; lengths 7.5 cm. and 4.2 cm. Cyprus Mus., Nicosia. – Dikaios, *RDAC*. 1936, Pl. 27.

1840–1856: TERRACOTTA – IVORY – STEATITE

1840 Katydata. Find No. 104: Red Polished terracotta whorl
a,b of biconical form (Early Cypriot III); concave base, rounded contours; incised decoration: zigzag lines and rows of dots on body, stippled vertical lines on base, concentric circles on top; height 3.8 cm., diam. 4.7 cm. Cyprus Mus., Nicosia.

1841 Cyprus. Find-spots unknown. Middle Cypriot terra-
a,b cotta whorls of the Red and Black Polished ware type;
and both bi-conical, *1841* with abraded outline, *1842* with

1842 slightly concave base; incised decoration: hatched ver-
a,b tical bands and other linear patterns; heights 4 cm. and 3.2 cm. Cyprus Mus., Nicosia, Inv. No. A 140 and 1941.III-21.5.

1843 Kyrenia. Tomb 3, No. 7: Middle Cypriot Red Polished
a,b terracotta whorl; biconical, with low bulge and flat bottom. Incised decoration with white filling consisting of four groups of vertical zigzag stripes; height 2.5 cm. diam. 3 cm. Cyprus Mus., Nicosia.

1844 Cyprus. Find-spot unknown. Undecorated ivory whorl
a b (Late Cypriot); conical, with flattened top and flat base; height 1.4 cm., diam. 3.5 cm. Cyprus Mus., Nicosia, Inv. No. W 262.

1845 Cyprus. Site unknown. Early Cypriot steatite whorl,
a, b half-domed shape, with slightly concave base. Incised decoration and deep groove encircling it directly above the base; height 1.5 cm., diam. 2.6 cm. Cyprus Mus., Nicosia, Inv. No. W 264.

1846 Probably from Lythrodontas. Middle Cypriot steatite
a, b spindle whorl; biconical with low belly and flat base. Ring-shaped drilled lines round base, middle of body, and top; height 1.8 cm., diam. 2.1 cm. Cyprus Mus., Nicosia, Inv. No. 1966.VIII–25.2.

1847 Leuka. Late Cypriot hemispherical steatite whorl with
a, b flat base; decoration: incised zigzag pattern, concentric circles on base; height 1.9 cm., diam. 3 cm. Cyprus Mus., Nicosia, Inv. 1933.XII–29.3.

1848 Cyprus. Site unknown. Middle Cypriot conical clay
a, b whorl, with slightly convex base; no decoration; height 2.7 cm., diam. 3.4 cm. Cyprus Mus., Nicosia, Inv. No. W 12.

1849 Cyprus. Find-spos unknown. Late Cypriot conical
a, b steatite spindle whorls of varying heights; flat bases
to and rich incised decoration in the form of zones be-
1851 tween deep horizontal grooves filled with concentric
a, b semicircles *(1849, 1851)*, and circles with centre-point and dotted patterns *(1850)*. *1849:* height 1.2 cm., diam. 4.5 cm. *1850:* height 1.6 cm., diam. 3.4 cm. *1851:* height 1 cm., diam. 3.2 cm. Cyprus Mus., Nicosia, Inv. Nos. W 7, W 3, and D 2950.

1852 Cyprus. Find-spots unknown. Late Cypriot flat ivory
a, b whorls of conical and hemispherical shape, with flat
and base; careful incised decoration: ten-leaved rosette with
1853 dots in the interstices and frieze of circles with centre-
a, b point marked. *1852:* height 1 cm., diam. 2.5 cm. *1853:* height 0.7 cm., diam. 2.4 cm. Cyprus Mus., Nicosia, Inv. Nos. Y 176 and 1933.II–13.25.

1854 Enkomi. Tomb 8, No. 61: Terracotta lamp (Middle Cypriot III); bowl with compressed spout and smooth base; length 13 cm., height 4.5 cm. Cyprus Mus., Nicosia. – Sjöqvist, *SCE.* I, Pl. 80:1.

1855 Kalopsida. Site Area 'Kouphos', No. 254: Fragment of clay lamp (type and date as *1854*); length 12 cm., height 5 cm. Cyprus Mus., Nicosia. – Åström, *Excav. at Kalopsidha and Ayios Iakovos* (1966), 111, Fig. 107.

1856 Apliki, north-west Cyprus. Torch-holder of clay (Late Cypriot III); flat wall bracket, pierced in upper part for suspension; bowl below with right-angled curves and three angular projections; zigzag line on wall bracket, engraved before firing; height 37.5 cm., length of bowl 17 cm. Cyprus Mus., Nicosia. – DuPlat Taylor, *Antiq. Journal* 32 (1952), Pl. 26 e.

1857–1899: COPPER AND BRONZE

1857 Cyprus. Site unknown. Torch-holder like *1856* but bronze (Late Cypriot III); flat wall bracket with scalloped contour, pierced for suspension and with low holder; fully three-dimensional bull's head attached to the upper part of the wall bracket with three rivets; height 30 cm, length of holder 14 cm. Cyprus Mus., Nicosia. – Catling, *Cypriot Bronzework*, Pl. 25 b, c.

1858 Lapithos. Tomb 18, Chamber B, No. 8 (1913): Bronze pin (Middle Cypriot I), with oval thickening in the middle of the shaft and small button-like head; length 36 cm. Cyprus Mus., Nicosia. – Myres, *BSA*. 41 (1940–45), Pl. 25:3 right; Catling, 72.

1859 Lapithos. Tomb 29, No. 132: Middle Cypriot dress pin of bronze with eye and mushroom head; length 22.8 cm. Cyprus Mus., Nicosia. – Myres, Pl. 25:2.

1860 Cyprus. Find-spot unknown. Early Cypriot flat axe-head of copper or bronze with triangular flared neck and slightly concave sides; length 20.5 cm. Cyprus Mus., Nicosia, Inv. No. L 10.

1861 Lapithos. Tomb 322, Chamber A/1: Early Cypriot bronze chisel; rectangular cross-section; bone shaft; length 25.5 cm. Cyprus Mus., Nicosia. – Gjerstad, *SCE.* I, Pl. 35; Catling, Fig. 4:10.

1862 Lapithos. Tomb 29, No. 153. Middle Cypriot bronze chisel; rectangular cross-section; length 27.2 cm. Cyprus Mus., Nicosia. – Myres, op. cit., Pl. 24:3.

1863 Cyprus. Find-spot unknown. Bronze daggers (Early
1864 Cypriot III), with willow-leaf shaped blade, weak medial rib *(1863* only), narrow tang, and round *(1863)* or angular *(1864)* shoulder; lengths 14.6 cm. and 18.5 cm. Cyprus Mus., Nicosia, Inv. Nos. L 168 and 178.

1865 Lapithos. Tomb 47, No. 21: Middle Cypriot bronze tweezers, with arms flaring at ends; length 14.3 cm. Cyprus Mus., Nicosia. – Myres, op. cit., Pl. 25:1.

1866 Lapithos, Tomb 21, No. 123: Middle Cypriot meat hook of bronze, with shaft socket and three bent prongs; length 8.2 cm. Cyprus Mus., Nicosia. – Myres, Pl. 24:3; Catling, *Cypriot Bronzework*, Pl. 4:7.

1867 Probably from Vasilia. Flat axe-head with straight blade (Early Cypriot I); rounded neck pierced; stamped symbol of script character on blade; length 19 cm. Cyprus Mus., Nicosia, Inv. No. 1959.IV–20.1. – Karageorghis, *BCH*. 84 (1960), 244, Fig. 3.

1868 Probably from Vasilia. Bronze bracelet (Early Cypriot I); almost round in section; much corroded; diam. 10.5 cm. Cyprus Mus., Nicosia, Inv. No. 1959.IV–20.4. – Karageorghis, loc. cit.

1869 Probably from Vasilia. Bronze awl (Early Cypriot I); rectangular in section, flat at the neck; opposite end pointed; stamped symbol of script character, cf. *1867*; length 26 cm. Cyprus Mus., Nicosia, Inv. No. 1959.IV–20.2. – Karageorghis, loc. cit.

1870 Probably from Vasilia. Bronze spearhead or dagger (Early Cypriot I; for type, cf. *1871–1873*), shaped as willow-leaf with medial rib; point bent, long tang, rectangular in section, bent at the top, with button head; length 36.5 cm. Cyprus Mus., Nicosia, Inv. No. 1959.IV–20.3. Karageorghis, loc. cit.

1871 Cyprus. Find-spot unknown. Middle Cypriot bronze dagger shaped as willow-leaf, with sloping round shoulders, marked medial rib, and tang bent at top; length 47 cm. Cyprus Mus., Nicosia.

1872 Vasilia. Bronze dagger (Early Cypriot I). Short willow-leaf blade with broad medial rib and angular shoulders; strong, long tang, square in section, with bent button terminal; length 30.2 cm. Cyprus Mus., Nicosia, Inv. No. 1937.III–31.2. – Catling, *Cypriot Bronzework*, Fig. 1:1, Pl. 2 b.

1873 Cyprus. Site unknown. Bronze dagger in the shape of a willow-leaf (probably Early Cypriot III) with angular shoulders, marked medial rib, and long tang with bent button terminal; length 45 cm. Cyprus Mus., Nicosia, Inv. No. 1946.XI–30.4.

1874 Katydata. Tomb find. Late Bronze Age (I) bronze dagger of Syrian type, with cast tongue for the hilt; rim for attaching rivetted handguard; length 27 cm. Cyprus Mus., Nicosia, Inv. No. 1957.I–17.1 (27). – Catling, op. cit., Pl. 15 j; Karageorghis, *AA*. 1963, 537 f., Fig. 20 b.

1875 Katydata. Tomb find (together with *1874*). Late Bronze Age (I) bronze dagger of Syrian type, with twelve rivets; length 30.5 cm. Cyprus., Nicosia, Inv. No. 1957.I–17.1 (26). – Catling, Pl. 15 i; Karageorghis, loc. cit., 537, Fig. 20 a.

1876 Cyprus. Find-spot unknown. Middle Cypriot 'Byblite' dagger blade of bronze, with broken short tang and three rivet holes; converging grooves on either side of blade; length 19.2 cm. Cyprus Mus., Nicosia. – Catling, Fig. 3:19, Pl. 2 c.

1877 Lapithos. Tomb 18, Chamber B, No. 2 (1913): Middle Minoan or Byblite dagger blade with accompanying Middle Cypriot I finds; bronze; four rivet holes; converging grooves on both sides; length 23.5 cm. Cyprus Mus., Nicosia. – Catling–Karageorghis, *BSA*. 55 (1960), Pl. 25 c; Branigan, *AJA*. 70 (1966), 123 ff.

1878 Cyprus. Find-spot unknown. Middle Cypriot bronze
1879 axes, with cylindrical ribbed haft socket and long slender blade; length 19 cm. Cyprus Mus., Nicosia, Inv. Nos. 1967.III–10.1 and 1958.II–18.1. – Both unpublished; similar example: Richter, *Greek, Etruscan and Roman Bronzes* (Metrop. Mus. of Art, New York 1915), 433, No. 1632, with Fig.

1880 Enkomi. Tomb 15: Bronze greave with lacing (Late Cypriot III); two parallel relief lines in repoussé technique strengthen the folded edge; height 16.7 cm. (cf. *711;* also Verdelis – Åström, *AM*. 82 [1967], 35 ff., 59, 62). British Mus., London, No. 1897.4–1.1531. – Catling, *Op.Ath.* 2 (1955), 25, Fig. 5; Hampe, *Gymnasium* 63 (1956), Pl. 8 a; Catling, *Cypriot Bronzework*, Pl. 18 c.

1881 Enkomi. Chamber of Tomb 18, No. 129: Lower part of bronze greave (Late Cypriot II b); traces of fixtures for lacing visible, also modelled reinforcements on the edges; surviving height 22.5 cm. Cyprus Mus., Nicosia. – Catling, *Op.Ath.* 2 (1955), 21 ff.; *Cypriot Bronzework*, Pl. 18 a.

1882 Enkomi. Tomb 10, No. 299: Part of a conical bronze helmet (Late Cypriot II b); at the tip is a tube for attaching the plume; height 42.5 cm. Cyprus Mus., Nicosia. – Catling, Pl. 17 a, b.

1883 Enkomi. Bronze sword of Naue II type (late Cypriot III); tang hilt with eight rivets; sloping shoulder; strong cast edges; pommel ending in fishtail shape; blood channels on the blade; length 47 cm. District Mus., Famagusta. – Catling, *Antiquity* 35 (1961), 115 ff., Pl. 16; id., *Cypriot Bronzework*, Pl. 12 j.

1884 Cyprus. Find-spot unknown. Bronze sword (type and date as *1883*); five rivets; length 55.5 cm. Cyprus Mus., Nicosia, Inv. No. 18. – Catling, *PPS*. 22 (1956), Pl. 9 a; id., *Cypriot Bronzework*, Pl. 12 i.

1885 Cyprus. Find-spot unknown. Late Cypriot bronze lance-head, with long slit socket, rivet hole, blade in the shape of a willow-leaf, and well-marked medial rib; length 32.2 cm. Cyprus Mus., Nicosia.

1886 Lythrangomi. Bronze lance-head like *1885* (Late Cypriot III); length 25.7 cm. Cyprus Mus., Nicosia, Inv. No. 1966.III–11.1.

1887 Cyprus. Find-spot unknown. Late Cypriot bronze spear-head shaped as a willow-leaf, with flat medial rib and slit socket; holes for two rivets; length 20 cm. Cyprus Mus., Nicosia, Inv. No. 1949.X–24.1.

1888 Cyprus. Find-spot unknown. Late Cypriot bronze lance-head (like *1886*), with marked medial rib and fragmentary socket; surviving length 18.7 cm. Cyprus Mus., Nicosia.

1889 Cyprus. Find-spot unknown. Late Cypriot lancet-shaped spear- or lance-head of bronze, with conical slit socket and ridged medial rib; cf. *590, 595, 596;* length 25.5 cm. Cyprus Mus., Nicosia.

1890 Cyprus. Find-spot unknown. Late Cypriot bronze spear-head of conical form, without cutting edges; rectangular section and slit socket; two holes for rivets; length 16.6 cm. Cyprus Mus., Nicosia. – Catling, *Cypriot Bronzework*, Fig. 16:18.

1891 Cyprus. Find-spot unknown. Late Cypriot fragmentary bronze spear-head. Willow-leaf shape; cutting edges eroded; wide flattened medial rib; broken socket; surviving length 19.4 cm. Cyprus Mus., Nicosia.

1892 Enkomi. Hoard find. Bronze ploughshare (Late Cypriot III), with short slit socket and blade flaring towards the rounded tip. Three impressed syllabic characters; length 24 cm.; width 7.7 cm. Cyprus Mus., Nicosia, Inv. No. 1958.VI–24.9 (from the Stylianou Coll.). – Karageorghis, *BCH*. 83 (1959), 338, Fig. 2; Catling, op. cit., Pl. 4 e.

1893 Enkomi. Hoard find (cf. *1895, 1896*). Bronze shovel (Late Cypriot III), with long slit socket, wide blade, corroded at the edges, on which are stamped two syllabic characters; length 31.5 cm., width 18.3 cm. Cyprus Mus., Nicosia, Inv. No. L 35 (from the Gunnis Coll.). – Catling, Fig. 7:1, Pl. 3 a.

1894 Cyprus. Find-spot unknown. Bronze pick (Late Cypriot III), with short slit socket and solid working piece, round in section; length 33 cm. Cyprus Mus., Nicosia. – Catling, op. cit., Pl. 53 c.

1895 Enkomi. Hoard find (cf. *1893, 1896*). Bronze axe-adze with round shaft hole (Late Cypriot III); length 14 cm. Cyprus Mus., Nicosia, Inv. No. R 370 (from the Gunnis Collection). – Catling, *Cypriot Bronzework*, Pl. 8 c.

1896 Enkomi. Hoard find (cf. *1893, 1895*). Bronze double adze with two transverse cutting blades (Late Cypriot III), with round shaft hole, syllabic character impressed on the lower side; length 16 cm. (similar adzes from Crete: *713–715*). Cyprus Mus., Nicosia, Inv. No. L 38 (from the Gunnis Coll.). – Catling, op. cit., Fig. 9:4, Pl. 7 f.

1897 Meniko. Surface find. Bronze double adze (probably Late Cypriot III); length 31.3 cm. Cyprus Mus., Nicosia, Inv. No. 1953.IX–3.3. – Catling, Pl. 7 a.

1898 Probably from Enkomi. Copper ingot of the so-called 'ox-hide' type (Late Cypriot III), with large sign stamped on it (probably Cypro-Minoan syllabic character, cf. *752*); length 72 cm., width 42.3 cm., thickness 3.9 cm., weight 39.18 kg. Cyprus Mus., Nicosia, Inv. No. 1939.VI-20.4. – Dikaios, *RDAC*. 1937–39, Pl. 42:5; Buchholz, *PZ*. 37 (1959), 29, No. 2, Pl. 3:2; Catling, Pl. 49 a, b.

1899 Enkomi. Copper ingot like *1898* (Late Cypriot III); length 69.8 cm., width 40.6 cm., thickness 5 cm., weight 37.02 kg. British Mus., London, No. 1897.4.–1.1535. – Buchholz, *Schweizer Münzblätter* 16 (1966), 65 f., No. 24, Fig. 5 (with complete bibliography); Catling, Pl. 49 c.

Texts in syllabic script and writing implements

As a meeting-point between East and West, Cyprus has always occupied a notable position (cf. map, Fig. 45). In the context of the history of scripts also, the island was exposed to foreign influences. Apart from Egyptian hieroglyphic documents, we find a few isolated Hittite hieroglyphs (silver seal from Tamassos, cf. map, Fig. 44, p. 123) and documents of cuneiform writing, mainly in the form of imported cylinder seals.

Besides this, simple linear signs, derived from local tradition, appear from the third millennium. They were chiefly used as craftsman's marks in the pottery trade (Stewart, *Vounous* (1950), 391, Figs. 279, 280; Åström, *A Corpus of Pot-Marks in Excavations at Kalopsidha and Ayios Iakovos in Cyprus* [1966], 149 ff.).

Occasionally the Early Bronze Age metal workers and their later trade associates used such marks *(1867, 1869)*. There also appear to have been numerical signs in Cyprus, in the form of simple parallel notches (e.g. weight: *1739*). Since these and other signs have a geometric basis (line, cross, circle, star, T), they sometimes coincide with elements from foreign scripts, such as the linear systems of the Aegean, which reached Cyprus from the middle of the second millennium. It has become established practice to call the special forms of these scripts 'Cypro-Minoan', they appear as metal marks on ingots *(1898, 1899)*, agricultural implements *(1892, 1893)*, and heavy double adzes *(1896)*, as incised or painted signs on pottery *(1582, 1624, 1629, 1633, 1634, 1903, 1904)*, and sometimes in the form of texts of up to six signs *(1901, 1902)*.

It also seems likely that this Late Bronze Age script was used in cult practices, judging from the inscribed votive gifts, soothsayers' balls, and similar objects *(1900, 1907—1910)*. Perhaps the explanation of an isolated character with the picture of a bird in flight on the bezel of a finger ring *(1782)* also lies in the religious sphere. Interesting use is made of the Cypro-Minoan script in connection with pictorial compositions of a religious nature; the spread of such texts far beyond the narrow confines of the island is also noteworthy (Perati, *1382*).

The earliest document in the Cypro-Minoan script *(1905)* already has a continuous text, so it cannot merely be a record of trade or list of miscellaneous objects. The most complete of the Enkomi tablets *(1906)* must convince even the most obstinate sceptic of the high level of this writing system, which was obviously sophisticated enough to express an involved text (contract or letter). No doubt the few surviving documents of this kind represent only a small fragment of what once existed; for even the Ancient Cypriots 'wrote on wood' (cf. Bossert, *Minoica: Festschrift zum 80. Geburtstag von Sundwall* [1958], 67 ff.).

In his monumental work *Les Inscriptions Chypriotes Syllabiques* (1961), Masson enabled us to gain greater insight into the complicated conditions; he sketched out the history of research into the script, compiled a body of inscriptions and a bibliography, and established the connection between the Bronze Age script and the Cypriot syllabic script, which was in use until the age of Alexander the Great.

For the origins of the script, see Buchholz, 'Zur Herkunft der kyprischen Silbenschrift', *Minos* 3 (1954), 133 ff. See also above, p. 134, and examples of ancient Aegean scripts: *1409—1422*.

1900 Probably from Enkomi. Miniature copper ingot (type and date as *1898, 1899*), with two stamped Cypro-Minoan characters separated by a vertical stroke (for the position of the marks, cf. Buchholz, *Minoica: Festschr. zum 80. Geburtstag von Sundwall* [1958], 105 ff., Fig. 4 a, b); length 9.4 cm., width 3.5 cm. Cyprus Mus., Nicosia, Inv. No. 1936.VI-19.1. – Dikaios, *RDAC.* 1936, 112, Pl. 34:2; Masson, *Minos* 5 (1957), Pl. 7:26; Buchholz, *PZ.* 37 (1959), 20, Fig. 9; Catling, op. cit., Pl. 49 h.

1901 Enkomi (1913). Sherd of large clay pithos (Late Cypriot II), with five Cypro-Minoan characters incised after firing; dimensions of sherd: width 22.8 cm., height 14 cm. Cyprus Mus., Nicosia, Inv. No. A 1507. – Masson, op. cit., Pl. 4:14; Dikaios, *Guide,* Pl. 10:1.

1902 Arpera. Tomb 5, No. 5 (1914). Fragment of large pithos (Late Cypriot II), with rippled and linear decoration incised before firing and six signs; dimensions of sherd: width 16 cm., height 13 cm. Cyprus Mus., Nicosia, Inv. No. A 1508. – Masson, Pl. 3:7.

1903 Enkomi (1927). Jug handle (so-called 'Plain White ware'; Late Cypriot II), with two Cypro-Minoan characters engraved one above the other after firing; height of fragment 10.5 cm. Cyprus Mus., Nicosia, Inv. No. A 1502. – Masson, Pl. 5:17.

1904 Enkomi. Tomb 68 (1896): Detail of an amphoroid krater (LH III b). Four Cypro-Minoan characters on lower part of body in matt red (three of them on our photograph, 'Y' is adjacent on the right). Cyprus Mus., Nicosia, Inv. No. A 1646. – Masson, *RA.* 47 (1956), 20 ff.; Karageorghis, *CVA. Cyprus* I, 50, Fig. 3:13, and Pl. 8:1–2.

1905 Enkomi. Find No. 1885 (1955): Fragment of a small clay tablet (Late Cypriot I), with three straight guidelines and large linear Cypro-Minoan characters; height 5.5 cm., width 7.5 cm. Cyprus Mus., Nicosia. – Dikaios, *Antiquity* 30 (1956), 40 ff., Pl. 9; Masson, *Minos* 5 (1957), Pl. 6:25; Dikaios, *Kadmos* 2 (1963), 39 ff., Fig. 3; id., *Enkomi* I (1969), Pl. 190:1; Karageorghis, *Cyprus,* Col. Pl. 91.

1906 Enkomi. Find No. 1687 (1953); Fragment of a small terracotta tablet (Late Cypriot II). Closely inscribed on both sides before firing in continuous lines with characters of the Cypro-Minoan script; height 10 cm., width 9 cm. Cyprus Mus., Nicosia. – Dikaios, *Antiquity* 27 (1953), 233 ff., Pl. 4:5; Masson, Pl. 6:24; Karageorghis, *Treasures,* Pl. 20; Dikaios, *Kadmos* 2 (1963), 39 ff., Fig. 6; id., *Enkomi* I (1969), Pl. 190:2; Karageorghis, *Cyprus,* Col. Pl. 91.

1907 Enkomi. Find No. 255. Terracotta ball i (probably Late Cypriot III), with four characters in the Cypro-Minoan script incised before firing. Louvre, Paris. – Schaeffer, *Enkomi-Alasia* I, 404, Fig. 133; Masson, 22, Fig. 22.

1908 Enkomi. Find No. 254: Terracotta ball h (like *1907*), with five characters. Louvre, Paris. – Schaeffer, 403, Fig. 130; Masson, Fig. 21.

1909 Enkomi. Find No. 252: Terracotta ball f (like *1907*), with three marks. Louvre, Paris. – Schaeffer, 401, Fig. 124; Masson, Fig. 19.

1910 Enkomi. Find No. 253. Clay ball g (like *1907*), with eight marks. Louvre, Paris. – Schaeffer, 403, Fig. 129; Masson, Fig. 20.

1911 Enkomi. Find No. 807. Bone stylus (Late Cypriot II), *a, b* pierced in the upper part, and sharpened at the point; length 21.3 cm. Cyprus Mus., Nicosia. – Karageorghis, *Cyprus,* Col. Pl. 91.

LIST OF FIGURES IN THE TEXT AND SOURCES OF PLATES

Colour Plate 1: *782* and *890* 9
Colour Plate 2: *78* and *177* 41
Colour Plate 3: *1671* and *1726* 161
Colour Plate 4: *1684 c* and *1788 c, d* 169

Black and white illustrations (photographs) . . 189–508

Figures in the text

1 Aegean, survey of sites mentioned 12
2 Crete, survey of sites mentioned 13
3 Sesklo and Dimini (ground plans: *6, 7*) 14
4 Thermi, Lerna, Orchomenos, and Poliochni (ground plans: *24–28*) . . . . 16 f.
5 Thermi, Vasiliki, and Aegina (ground plans: *29–31*) 18
6 Knossos (ground plan and reconstruction: *41, 42*) 21
7 Mycenae (ground plans: *94–96 a*, section: *96 b*) . 24
8 Argolid, Tiryns, and Athens (ground plans: *106 a, b*, map: *107*, section: *108*) 25
9 Mycenaean sites of finds in the eastern Aegean (*129*) and Rhodes (*130*) 28
10 Stone Age buildings (ground plans: *8–13*) . . . 32
11 Thermi (herringbone masonry: *21*) 33
12 Phaistos, palace (plan: *53*) 34
13 Mallia, environs and houses (plan: *67*, ground plans: *68, 69*) 36
14 Mallia, palace (ground plan: *70*) and Kato Zakro palace (ground plan: *75*) 37
15 Gla, Boeotia (plan: *120*), and Pylos, Messenia (ground plan of palace: *121*) 38
16 Tombs in Hagios Kosmas, Attica (sections and views from above: *136–140*), Knossos, Temple-Tomb (view from above and section: *141, 142*) . 41
17 Tholos (schematic diagram: *180*), Athens, chamber tomb (section: *183*), Mycenae, Grave Circle B (view from above: *153*) 43
18 Macedonia, Epiros, and Samos, stone implements (*193–216*) 45
19 Stone shaft-hole axes and normal stone axes (*217–221, 228–231*), arrow polishers (*411, 412*) . . . 47
20 Aegean arrow-heads (survey of types and development: *410*) 48
21 Early Bronze Age metal finds (map of distribution: *517*) 51
22 Implements of copper and arsenical bronze (*551, 552, 561 a–563, 569 a, b, 574 a, b*) 53
23 Copper and bronze saws and knives (*639–664*) . 55

24 Aegean bronze daggers and swords (*676–679, 703–708*), bridoon from Mycenae (*709*) 57
25 Cretan double axes (*716, 717*) 59
26 Copper ingots (map of distribution) 60
27 Ras Shamra, fragment of a Kamares cup (*897*) . 69
28 Scoglio del Tonno, near Taranto, imported Mycenaean pottery (*1002–1023*) 76
29 Knossos, chariot fresco (*1055*) 79
30 Tiryns, stag fresco (*1056*) 80
31 Tiryns, frieze of women, detail (*1057*) 81
32 Cretan clay and limestone sarcophagi (*1061–1065 a*) 83
33 'Grave of the Tripod Hearth', Zapher Papoura, near Knossos, Minoan metal vessels (*1095 a–o*) . . 85
34 Minoan vases in Egyptian wall-paintings (*1100–1103*) 87
35 Interlocking fragments of a steatite vase with figural relief-work, Knossos (*1167*) 94
Relief from ivory pyxis, Katsamba, Crete 107
36 Mycenaean glass ornaments, Museum of Fine Arts, Boston (*1338–1345*) 109
37 Forms of Mycenaean jewellery (*1317–1337*) . . . 110
38 Early Cretan seals (*1363 a–1372 c*) 113
39 Cretan-Mycenaean seals, spacers, impressions (*1388–1396*) 117
40 Phaistos Disc (*1409 a–c*) 119
41 Inscribed Linear B tablets (*1416–1420*) 120
42 Mycenaean vase ideograms (*1421*) 121
43 Linear B, list of signs (*1422*) 122
44 Cyprus, sites of finds (index map) 123
45 Aegean civilization and the Eastern Mediterranean (index map) 124
46 Settlement of Khirokitia (plan: *1425*) 125
47 Khirokitia (ground plans: *1426–1429*) 126
48 Khirokitia (ground plans: *1430–1433*) 127
49 Khirokitia (building complexes: *1434, 1435*) . . 128
50 Sotira (types of house, ground plans: *1441–1443*; total plan: *1444*) 129
51 Sotira, Excavated Area V (*1445*) 130
52 Dwellings in Kalavassos (ground plans and sections: *1446–1449*) 131
53 Ambelikou (ground plan of house: *1451*) . . . 132
54 Kalopsida (ground plan of house: *1452*), Lapithos (tomb, view from above, and section: *1484 a, b*) . 133
55 Nitovikla (diagrammatic reconstruction of the fortress: *1453*) 134
56 Pyla Kokkinokremos (ground plan of house: *1454*) 135
57 Enkomi, Excavation Area I (*1455*) 136
58 Kition and Palaiokastro Maa, fortification walls (*1461, 1462 a*) 137
59 Khirokitia, tombs (*1463–1473 a*) 141
60 Sotira, tombs (*1476*) 142
61 Philia–Vasiliko, tomb (view from above and section: *1479 c*) 143
62 Earliest Cypriot pottery development 147

PHOTOGRAPHS:

Prof. Å. Åkerström, Emeritus, Univ. Göteborg, Sweden: *451–453*

American School of Classical Studies, Athens, Agora-excavation: *1281 a–c*

Prof. G. Bass, Philadelphia, USA: *738 a, b. 1295*

Dr. H. Bauer, Marburg, presently Rome: *167*

Berlin, Staatl. Museen; Charlottenburg, Antikenabt. & Museum f. Vor- u. Frühgeschichte: *226. 798. 799. 1072–1074. 1224 a–d. 1250. 1294. 1385.* – Museumsinsel, Antikenabt.: *1685 a, b*

Dr. B. v. Bothmer, New York, Brooklyn Mus.: *912 a–d. 1138. 1195 a–c. 1197. 1198. 1220*

Dr. W. Brice, Manchester: *1410*

British Museum, London, Trustees of the Museum: *555–560. 568 a, b. 570 a, b. 572 a, b. 573 a, b. 589–594. 600–611. 695. 696. 720 a, b. 970. 1075. 1099 a, b. 1239. 1304. 1305. 1682. 1683. 1686. 1747. 1789. 1794 a, b. 1880. 1899*

Prof. H.-G. Buchholz, Gießen: author's photos: *1 a, b. 18. 19. 33. 37–40. 43. 72. 74. 83. 93. 103 a, b. 115. 126–128. 131. 156. 158. 179. 973.* Private archive: *2. 3. 5. 22. 46. 76. 77. 86. 88. 89. 91 b. 92. 122. 125. 134. 135. 151. 152. 166. 168. 170. 181. 187. 192 a–c. 222. 225. 232–237. 352. 413–415. 428–430. 435–438. 449. 450. 457. 458. 463. 464–480. 501 a, b. 509. 510. 512. 518–525. 541. 542. 550. 569. 581. 596. 597. 599. 612–620. 624–628. 636. 637. 666–668. 672. 684. 687. 689–693. 699–701. 710. 711. 713. 719 a, b. 735. 739–752. 772. 773. 783–785. 787. 791–793. 801. 806–808. 833–836. 838–840. 853 a, b. 862. 863. 870. 873. 874. 888. 889. 891. 893–895. 898. 899. 901. 902. 906. 911. 913–917. 919. 920. 925. 926. 929. 932. 933. 938–940. 943–947. 961. 962. 965. 966. 974. 989. 1028. 1031. 1038. 1041. 1042. 1050–1052. 1066–1068. 1070. 1071. 1078. 1082 a, b. 1083. 1107. 1119. 1128. 1132–1135. 1140–1142. 1145–1152. 1155. 1156. 1160. 1163. 1164. 1168. 1173. 1175. 1176. 1185. 1193. 1200. 1202. 1214. 1218. 1219 a, b. 1221. 1223. 1225–1228. 1231–1235. 1241. 1242. 1248 a, b, d. 1248 f. 1249 a, b. 1263–1269. 1285. 1288–1291. 1296–1298. 1306. 1308 a–c. 1311. 1347. 1348. 1375–1377. 1402. 1409. 1411. 1412*

Prof. & Mrs. J. Caskey, Cincinnati & Athens: *150. 223. 876. 877. 994. 1026. 1169. 1191 a, b*

Dr. H. W. Catling, Oxford, Ashmolean Museum: *461 a, b. 526–540. 564–567. 571. 598. 714 a, b. 715 a, b. 723–734. 1076. 1077. 1196. 1240. 1362 a–c*

Dr. S. Charitonides, late Ephor of the Argolid: *907*

Cyprus Museum, Nicosia: *1423–1671 a, b. 1671 c, d* (Col. Pl.3). *1672–1681. 1684 a, b. 1684 c* (Col. Pl. 4). *1687–1717. 1719–1725. 1726* (Col. Pl. 3). *1727–1734. 1736–1746. 1748–1788 a, b. 1788 c, d.* (Col. Pl. 4). *1790–1793. 1795–1879. 1881–1898. 1900–1911 b*

Dr. A. Delivorrias, late Ephor in Sparta: *1246. 1247 a, b.*

Deutsches Archäologisches Institut; Archiv der Zentraldirektion, Berlin: *921.* – Archive of the Department in Athens: *34 a, b. 159. 160. 161. 186. 238–347. 353. 357–376. 459. 462 a, b. 481–500. 502–507. 511. 513. 544–549. 575. 576. 578. 623. 629–635. 670. 673. 674. 685. 688. 694. 697. 698. 712. 757 a, b. 774–779. 786. 788. 794–797. 800. 809–829. 832. 841–852. 854. 855. 857–861. 866–869. 871. 872. 875. 879–884. 903 a, b. 908. 924. 927. 934. 935. 941. 942. 945 a, b. 948. 956 a, b. 959. 960. 964. 967–969. 971. 979. 983. 984. 996–1001. 1027. 1033. 1037. 1039. 1040. 1048. 1049. 1079–1081. 1085–1098. 1104 a, b. 1105. 1108–1117 a–c. 1123–1126. 1131 a, b. 1137. 1153. 1154. 1157–1159. 1161. 1162. 1165. 1170–1172. 1174 a, b. 1180. 1183 a, b. 1186–1190. 1192 a, b. 1194 a–c. 1205. 1207–1209. 1211–1213. 1222. 1229. 1236. 1237. 1245. 1254. 1257. 1258–1262 a, b. 1272–1277. 1279. 1282. 1284. 1286. 1287. 1292. 1293. 1299–1303. 1307. 1378 a, b. 1381–1383. 1387. 1414. 1415.* – Archive of the Department in Istanbul: *1032 a, b. 1036.* – Archive of the Department in Rome: *856*

Dr. Ch. Doumas, Athens: *1238*

Dresden, Staatl. Kunstsammlungen, Skulpturenabt.: *1201*

Prof. J. D. Evans, Director, Inst. Arch., London Univ.: *17. 348–351*

Prof. P. R. Franke, Saarbrücken: *45. 51. 58 a*

Dr. H. v. Gall, scientific adviser DAI., Istanbul: *16. 32 a, b. 50. 52. 54. 55. 58 b. 60 b. 61 b. 62. 63. 84. 102. 105. 123 a, b. 124. 132. 143–149. 162. 171. 172. 174–176*

K. Grundmann, late of DAI., Berlin: *759–771. 780. 781. 976. 978. 1118 a, b. 1120. 1177. 1178. 1179 a, b. 1181 a–c*

Mrs. V. Hankey, Westerham, Kent, England: *671. 922. 923. 930. 936 a, b. 944. 946. 950–955. 991–993*

Photographer D. A. Harissiades, Athens: *1270*

M. Heinrich, Tübingen: *416. 417. 423–427. 431–434. 1252*

Prof. N. Himmelmann-Wildschütz, Bonn: *1255*

Prof. M. Hirmer, Munich: *885. 886. 892. 896. 1025. 1047. 1116 a, b. 1280 a, b. 1283*

Dr. H. Hoffmann, Director of Antikenabt., Mus. f. Kunst u. Gewerbe, Hamburg: *227. 718. 975. 977. 1084 a–f. 1121. 1127. 1129. 1130 a, b. 1136. 1199. 1206. 1310. 1312–1314. 1386*

Holle-Verlag, Baden-Baden: *890* (Col. Pl. 1)

Prof. Dr. S. Iakovidis, Athens: *110. 188–191. 508. 515. 583–588. 621. 622. 638. 665. 669. 675. 702. 985. 995. 1034. 1035. 1349–1355. 1358. 1380. 1403. 1404. 1408*

H. Kraft, editor, Berlin: *78* (Col. Pl. 2). *97. 177* (Col. Pl. 2)

Dr. Krien-Kummerow, adviser at DAI., Berlin: *49. 73. 81. 82. 112. 165. 173. 904. 905*

W. Kühne, late actor in Berlin: *4. 14. 15. 20. 23. 35 a, b. 36. 56. 57. 59. 60 a. 61 a. 65. 66. 71. 79. 80. 85. 91 a. 98. 100. 101. 104. 109. 111. 113. 114. 116–119. 155. 157. 164. 1413*

Leiden, Netherlands, Rijksmuseum van Oudheden: *1230*

Louvre, Département des Antiquités Orientales, Paris: *1718*

Prof. R. Lullies, Staatl. Kunstsammlungen, Kassel: *1069 a–c*

Marburg, Foto-Marburg: *44. 47. 48. 99. 169. 681–683. 837. 900. 931. 1053. 1054. 1065 b. 1243. 1244*

Prof. Sp. Marinatos, Athens: *1278. 1397*

Euth. Mastrokostas, formerly Ephor in Patras: *178. 224. 514. 553. 736. 737*

Photographer L. v. Matt, Buochs, Switzerland: *1215–1217*

Prof. F. Matz, Marburg (corpus of seals): *1359–1361. 1373 a, b. 1374. 1379. 1384. 1398. 1401. 1406*

Dr. L. Morricone, Rome: *543. 554. 721 a, b. 802–805. 957. 958*

Munich, Staatl. Antikensammlungen (Prof. D. Ohly and Dr. K. Vierneisel; photographers: C. H. Krüger-Moessner & G. Wehrheim): *1122 a, b. 1139. 1182. 1204. 1256*

Olympia, photo-archive of the New Museum (Dr. N. Yalouris & Dr. P. G. Themelis): *184. 185. 680. 909. 910. 918. 963. 980–982. 986–988. 990. 1346*

Epimelet N. Pharaklas, formerly Thebes, Boeotia: *354–356. 516. 579. 580. 1058. 1143. 1315. 1316. 1356. 1357*

Dr. I. Pini, Marburg: *133*

Prof. P. J. Riis, Copenhagen: *577 a, b. 595*

Prof. W. Schiering, Göttingen: *887. 972*

Dr. J. Szilágyi, Fine Arts Museum, Budapest: *1248 e*
Stockholm, Medelhavsmuseet: *1735 a, b*

Dr. J. Thimme, Badisches Landesmuseum, Karlsruhe: *1203. 1210*

Dr. N. M. Verdelis, late Director of the Acropolis museum, Athens: *1024*

Dr. & Mrs. C. C. Vermeule, Boston: *460. 1251. 1271*

J. Wieland & K. Untied, both Hamburg: *418–422. 456. 949. 1144*

Fräulein K. Winkelmann, Berlin-Dahlem: *87. 90. 154*

Verlag Ph. v. Zabern, Mainz: *64. 163. 1030*

Dr. P. Zazoff, Hamburg: *1405. 1407*

DRAWINGS AND WATERCOLOURS:

after C. Blegen, Zygouries, Fig. 109, Fig. 186 & Pl. 22: *439–448* u. *454 a–b*

Prof. H.-G. Buchholz, Gießen, private archive: *8–13* (Fig. 10). *31* (Fig. 5). *41* (Fig. 6). *53* (Fig. 12). *67–69* (Fig. 13). *70 & 75* (Fig. 14). *95 & 96 a, b* (Fig. 7). *107 & 108* (Fig. 8). *121* (Fig. 15). *130* (Fig. 9). *180 & 183* (Fig. 17). *193–216* (Fig. 18). *217–221 & 228–231* (Fig. 19). *517* (Fig. 21). *574 a, b* (Fig. 22). *582. 709* (Fig. 24). *722. 878. 928. 937 a, b* (after watercolour by J. H. Marshall). *1029. 1055* (Fig. 29). *1056* (Fig. 30). *1059. 1060* (after watercolour by Piet de Jong). *1095 a–o* (Fig. 33). *1167* (Fig. 35). *1248 c. 1253 a, b. 1309. 1338–1345* (Fig. 36). *1363–1372* (Fig. 38). *1388–1396* (Fig. 39). *1409 a–c* (Fig. 40). *1416–1420* (Fig. 41). *1421* (Fig. 42). *1422* (Fig. 43).

Prof. J. Caskey, Cincinnati & Athens: *25 & 26* (Fig. 4). *830*

Cyprus, Archive of the Department of Antiquities, Nicosia: Fig. 46–62

Deutsches Archäologisches Institut, Archive of the Department in Athens: *106 a, b* (Fig. 8). *753–755. 831. 864 a, b. 865. 1044. 1045*

after W. Dörpfeld, Troja u. Ilion II (1902), Fig. 468: *455*

after A. Evans, JHS. 13 (1892/93), 196 f., Fig. 1: *1106*

O. Flor, Kiel (technical assistant, University): *716 & 717* (Fig. 25)

Prof. G. Gruben, Munich: *30* (Fig. 5). *42* (Fig. 6)

K. Grundmann, late of DAI., Berlin: *129* (Fig. 9). *377–409. 410* (Fig. 20). *411 & 412* (Fig. 19). *551 & 552* (Fig. 22). *561–563 & 569 a, b* (Fig. 22). *756. 758. 782* (Col. Pl. 1). *1057* (Fig. 31). *1317–1337* (Fig. 37). Fig. 26 (map)

Frau G. Hecker, Berlin (member of technical staff of the Berlin Museums): *182. 1061–1064 & 1065 a* (Fig. 32)

M. Heinrich, Tübingen: *6 & 7* (Fig. 3). *27 & 28* (Fig. 4). *31* (Fig. 5). *94* (Fig. 7). *120* (Fig. 15). *136–140* (Fig. 16). *153* (Fig. 17). *639–664* (Fig. 23). *676–679* (Fig. 24). *703–708* (Fig. 24)

after E. J. Holmberg, Asea, Col. Pl. 2 a & 3 b: *789. 790*

after G. Karo, Schachtgräber, Pl. 85,404: *686*

Marburg, Foto-Marburg: *1043. 1046*

after H. Müller-Karpe, Beiträge zur Chronologie der Urnenfelderzeit nördl. u. südl. der Alpen (1959), Pl. 13: *1002–1023* (Fig. 28)

after C. F. A. Schaeffer, JdI. 52 (1937), 141, Fig. 1: *897* (Fig. 27)

Frau K. Vischer, Berlin (member of the technical staff of Archaeologia Homerica): Fig. 1 (map). Fig. 2 (map). Fig. 44 (map). Fig. 45 (map). *141 & 142* (Fig. 16). *1100–1103* (Fig. 34).

Verlag Wasmuth, Tübingen, archive: *21* (Fig. 11). *24* (Fig. 4). *29* (Fig. 5)

BIBLIOGRAPHICAL NOTES

BIBLIOGRAPHIES – REPORTS ON EXCAVATIONS AND RESEARCH – SUMMARIES – NATIONAL CUSTOMS

Comprehensive bibliographical details are in E. VERMEULE, Greece in the Bronze Age (1964); cf. also bibliographies, such as B. E. MOON, 'Mycenaean Civilization, Publications since 1935' (Univ. of London, Inst. of Classical Studies, Bulletin Suppl. 3) (1957) and 'Publications 1956–1960', ibid., Suppl. 12 (1961).

Reports on literature, research, and excavations: F. SCHACHERMEYR, Klio 33 (1940), 103 ff.; 35 (1942), 115 ff.; 36 (1943), 117 ff.; Anzeiger f. d. Altertumswiss. 4 (1951), 5 ff.; 6 (1953), 193 ff.; 10 (1957), 65 ff.; 14 (1961), 129 ff.; 19 (1966), 1 ff.; AA. 1962, 105 ff.; cf. also the annual reports by G. DAUX and V. KARAGEORGHIS in BCH., by KARAGEORGHIS in Annual Report of the Director of the Department of Antiquities, A. K. ORLANDOS in Ergon, M. S. F. HOOD and A. H. S. MEGAW in the Arch. Rep. of JHS., by N. PLATON in Kret. Chron., and by P. DEMARGNE in REG.

R. HOPE SIMPSON, A Gazetteer and Atlas of Mycenaean Sites (Univ. of London, Inst. of Classical Studies, Bulletin Suppl. 16) (1965).

AEGEAN *General:*

N. Åberg, Bronzezeitliche u. früheisenzeitliche Chronologie IV – Griechenland (1933)

St. Alexiou, Minoan Culture (modern Greek, 1965); id., Guide to the Archaeological Museum in Herakleion (1969); id., Ancient Crete (1969)

T. D. Atkinson, Excavations at Phylakopi in Melos: JHS. Supl. IV (1904)

L. Banti, Il Sentimento della Natura nell'Arte Minoica e Micenea: Geras A. Keramopoullou (1953) 119 ff.

L. Banti - G. Pugliese Carratelli - D. Levi, Arte Minoica e Micenea: Enciclopedia dell'Arte Antica Class. e Orient. V (1963) 42 ff.

H. Biesantz, Die kretisch-mykenische Kunst: Ullstein Kunstgeschichte IV (1963) 57 ff.

K. Bittel, Grundzüge der Vor- u. Frühgeschichte Kleinasiens (^{2}1950)

H. Th. Bossert, Altkreta – Kunst u. Handwerk in Griechenland, Kreta u. in der Ägäis von den Anfängen bis zur Eisenzeit (^{3}1937)

H. Boyd Hawes, Gournia (1908)

R. M. Burrows, The Discoveries in Crete (1908)

F. Chapouthier - P. Demargne, Mallia: Etudes Crétoises, I ff. (1928 ff.)

J. Charbonneaux, L'Art Egéen (1929)

P. Demargne, Naissance de l'Art Grec (1964)

R. Dussaud, Les Civilisations Préhelléniques dans le Bassin de la Mer Egée (^{2}1914)

A. J. Evans, The Prehistoric Tombs of Knossos (1906); id., The Palace of Minos at Knossos I–IV (1921–1936/1964)

P. Faure, Fonctions des Cavernes Crétoises (1964)

E. Fiechter, RE. VII (1912) 2523 ff. s. v. Haus

D. Fimmen, Die kretisch-mykenische Kultur (^{2}1924)

E. J. Forsdyke, Minoan Art (1929)

G. Glotz, La Civilisation Minoenne (1921/1952)

E. Hall, The Decorative Art of Crete in the Bronze Age (1907)

H. R. Hall, The Civilization of Greece in the Bronze Age (1928)

W. A. Heurtley, Prehistoric Macedonia (1939)

R. Higgins, Greek and Roman Jewellery (1961); id., Greek Terracottas (1967) 6 ff.; id., Minoan and Mycenaean Art (1967). Review by J. E. Coleman, Archaeology 23 (1970) 68

R. G. Hoegler - O. Keverdin, Kreta – Mutterland der Kultur Europas (1960)

E. J. Holmberg, The Swedish Excavations at Asea in Arcadia (1944)

M. S. F. Hood, The Home of the Heroes – The Aegean before the Greeks (1967); id., The Minoans, Crete in the Bronze Age (1971)

R. W. Hutchinson, Prehistoric Crete (1962)

A. Ippel, Das griechische Kunstgewerbe, in: H. Th. Bossert, Geschichte des Kunstgewerbes aller Zeiten u. Völker IV (1930) 164 ff.

H. J. Kantor, The Aegean and the Orient in the 2nd Millenium B. C. (1947)

G. Karo, RE. XI 2 (1922) 1718 ff. s. v. Kreta; id., Reallex. Vorgesch. VII (1926) 63 ff. s. v. Kreta; loc. cit. VIII (1927) 380 ff. s. v. Mykenai; loc. cit., VIII (1927) 389 ff. s. v. Mykenische Kultur; id., RE. XVI 1 (1933) 1015 ff. s. v. Mykenai; id., RE. Suppl. VI (1935) 584 ff. s. v. Mykenische Kultur; id., Greifen am Thron – Erinnerungen an Knossos (1959)

G. v. Kaschnitz-Weinberg, Die mittelmeerischen Grundlagen der antiken Kunst (1944)

D. Mackenzie, Cretan Palaces and Aegean Civilization: BSA. 11 (1904/05) 181 ff.; loc. cit. 12 (1905/06) 216 ff.; loc. cit. 13 (1906/07) 423 ff.; loc. cit. 14 (1907/08) 343 ff.

G. Maraghiannis, Antiquités Crétoises I–III (1908–1915)

Sp. Marinatos, Zum Symbolismus in der kretisch-mykenischen Kunst: Prakt. Akad. Athen 31 (1956) 400 ff.

Sp. Marinatos - M. Hirmer, Kreta u. das mykenische Hellas (1959)

L. v. Matt, Das antike Kreta; in collaboration with St. Alexiou, N. Platon & H. Guanella (1967)

R. Matton, La Crète Antique (1959/60)

F. Matz, Torsion – Eine formenkundliche Untersuchung zur aigaiischen Vorgeschichte (1952); id., Die Ägäis: Handbuch d. Archäologie II (1954); id., Kreta–Mykene–Troja, die minoische u. homerische Welt (1956); id., Kreta u. frühes Griechenland (1962)

M. Möbius, Pflanzenbilder der minoischen Kunst. JdI. 48 (1933) 1 ff.

O. Montelius, La Grèce Préclassique I–II (1924/1928)

K. Müller, Frühmykenische Reliefs aus Kreta u. vom griechischen Festland: JdI. 30 (1915) 242 ff.

J. L. Myres, The Geographical Background of the Aegean Civilization: Archiv Orientální 17 (1949) Parts 3 & 4, 196 ff.

R. Naumann, Architektur Kleinasiens (2nd edition 1971)

M. P. Nilsson, Das frühe Griechenland von innen gesehen: Historia 3 (1954/55) 257 ff.

M. Oulie, Décoration Egéenne (n. d.); id., Les Animaux dans les Peintures de Crète Préhistorique (n. d.)

J. D. S. Pendlebury, A Handbook to the Palace of Minos with its Dependencies (1933/^{5}1954); id., The Archaeology of Crete (1939/reprint 1963)

L. Pernier - L. Banti, Il Palazzo Minoico di Festòs I–II (1935/1951)

G. Perrot - Ch. Chipiez, Histoire de l'Art dans l'Antiquité VI – La Grèce Primitive - L'Art Mycénien (1894)

I. Pini, Beiträge zur minoischen Gräberkunde (1968)

N. Platon, Crete, in the series ›Archaeologia Mundi‹ (1966)

C. Renfrew, The Emergence of Civilization: The Cyclades and the Aegean in the Third Millennium B. C.

D. M. Robinson, RE. Suppl. VII (1940) 224 ff. s. v. Haus

G. Rodenwaldt - K. Müller, Tiryns I–IV (1912–1944)

F. Schachermeyr, Die minoische Kultur d. alten Kreta (1964)

F. Schachermeyr and others, Forschungsbericht über die Ausgrabungen und Neufunde zur ägäischen Frühzeit: AA. 1971, 295 ff.

H. Schliemann, Mykenae (1878/1964); id., Tiryns – Der prähistorische Palast der Könige von Tiryns (1886)

H. Schmidt, H. Schliemann's Sammlung trojanischer Altertümer (1902)

B. Schweitzer, Altkretische Kunst: Antike 2 (1926) 291 ff.

G. A. S. Snijder, Kretische Kunst (1936)

Studi Micenei ed Egeo-Anatolici I ff. (1966 ff.)

Ch. Tsountas - J. I. Manatt, The Mycenaean Age (1897/1969)

E. Vermeule, Greece in the Bronze Age (1964)

A. J. B. Wace, The History of Greece in the 3. and 2. Mill. B. C.: Historia 2 (1953) 74 ff.

P. Warren, Minoan Stone Vases (1969)

J. Wiesner, Vor- u. Frühzeit der Mittelmeerländer, I (1943)

C. Zervos, L'Art de la Crète – Néolithique et Minoenne (1956); id., L'Art des Cyclades du Début à la Fin de l'Age de Bronze – 2500–1100 avant notre ère (1957)

CYPRUS *General:*

D. Alastos, Cyprus in History (1955)

S. Casson, Ancient Cyprus (1937)

P. Dikaios, A Guide to the Cyprus Museums (^{1}1947, ^{2}1953, ^{3}1961); id., A Conspectus of Architecture in Ancient Cyprus: Kypriakai Spoudai 24 (1960) 1 ff.

W. H. Engel, Kypros (1841)

E. Gjerstad, Studies on Prehistoric Cyprus (1926)

G. F. Hill, A History of Cyprus I (1940)

D. G. Hogarth, Devia Cypria (1889)

V. Karageorghis, Ten Years of Archaeology in Cyprus 1953–62; *AA*. 1963, 498 ff.; id., Cyprus: Archaeologia Mundi (1969); id. Mycenaean Art from Cyprus (1968)

F. G. Maier, Cypern – Insel am Kreuzweg der Geschichte (1964)

M. Markides, Annual Report of the Curator of Antiquities, Nicosia, 1914–1916

A. H. Murray - A. H. Smith - H. B. Walters, Excavations in Cyprus (1900)

J. L. Myres - M. Ohnefalsch-Richter, Catalogue of the Cyprus Museum (1899)

J. L. Myres, Handbook of the Cesnola Collection of Antiquities from Cyprus (1914)

M. Ohnefalsch-Richter, Griechische Sitten u. Gebräuche auf Cypern (1913)

E. Oberhummer, Die Insel Cypern (1903); id., RE. I a (1920) 1832 ff. s. v. Salamis

A. Palma di Cesnola, Salaminia – The History, Treasures and Antiquities of Salamis in the Island of Cyprus (1882)

L. Palma di Cesnola, Cyprus – Its Ancient Cities, Tombs and Temples (1877)

G. Perrot - Ch. Chipiez, Histoire de l'Art dans l'Antiqué III (1885)

S. Reinach, Chroniques d'Orient, Ser. I: 1883–90 (1891)

C. F. A. Schaeffer, Missions en Chypre 1932–1935 (1936); id., Stratigraphie Comparée et Chronologie de l'Asie Occidentale, IIIe et IIe Millenaires (1948); id., Ugaritica I–VI (1939–1969)

J. Stewart, Handbook to the Nicholson Museum (^{2}1948) 115 ff.

The Swedish Cyprus Expedition – Finds and Results of the Excavations in Cyprus 1927–1931, I–IV (1934–1962)

R. Tamassia, Vasi Ciprioti nelle Collezioni Veneziani: Stud. Mediterr. Arch. IX (1969) 95 ff.

J. Thimme - P. Åström - G. Lilliu - J. Wiesner, Frühe Randkulturen des Mittelmeerraumes: Kykladen – Zypern – Malta–Altsyrien (1968)

F. Unger - T. Kotschy, Die Insel Cypern (1865)

C. Watzinger, Kypros, in: Handb. d. Arch. I (1939) 824 ff.

PRE-NEOLITHIC – NEOLITHIC – CHALCOLITHIC

(cf. also above, pp. 11 ff., selected bibl.)

H.-G. Buchholz, Birth of a Culture: Archaeologia Viva No. 3 (1969) 19 ff.

H. W. Catling, Cyprus in the Neolithic and Bronze Age Periods: *CAH*. (^{2}1966) No. 43 (review: V. Karageorghis, *JHS*. 88 [1968] 215 f.; J. Mellink, *JAOS*. 88 [1968] 539 f.)

V. G. Childe, The Dawn of European Civilzation ((^{6}1957)

C. Delvoye, Remarques sur la Seconde Civilisation Néolithique du Continent Grec et des Iles Avoisinantes: BCH. 73 (1949) 29 ff.

P. Dikaios, The Excavations at Erimi 1933–35: *RDAC*. 1936, 1 ff. (also *SCE*. IV/1 A [1962] 113 ff. & Iraq 7 [1940] 69 ff. [Report on Khirokitia and Erimi]); id., Khirokitia (1953); id., Sotira (1961) & The Stone Age: *SCE*. IV/1 A (1962) 1 ff.

J. D. Evans, Excavations in the Neolithic Settlement of Knossos: *BSA*. 59 (1964) 132 ff.

J. D. Evans - C. Renfrew, Excavations at Saliagos near Antiparos: *BSA*. Suppl. V (1968)

A. Furness, The Neolithic Pottery of Knossos: *BSA*. 48 (1953) 94 ff.

M. Gimbutas, Archaeology 25 (1972), 112 ff. (Neolithic Macedonia)

E. Gjerstad, Studies on Prehistoric Cyprus (1926); id., Antiquaries Journal 6 (1926) 54 ff.

E. J. Holmberg, The Neolithic Pottery of Mainland Greece (1964)

V. Karageorghis, Philia-Drakos: *BCH*. 90 (1966) 358 ff.

E. Kunze, Orchomenos II – Die neolithische Keramik (1931)

V. Milojcic, Chronologie der Jüngeren Steinzeit in Mittel- u. Südosteuropa (1949); id., Zur Chronologie der Jüngeren Steinzeit in Griechenland: *JdI*. 65/66 (1950/51) 1 ff.; id., Die deutschen Ausgrabungen auf der Argissa-Magula in Thessalien 1 – Das präkeramische Neolithikum (1962)

V. Milojcic - H. Hauptmann, Die Funde der frühen Dimini-Zeit aus der Arapi-Magula, Thessalien (1969)

J. Mellaart, Earliest Civilizations of the Near East (1965)

G. Mylonas, The Neolithic Epoch in Greece (mod. Gk., 1928)

K. Nikolaou, The Distribution of the Settlements in Stone Age: Cyprus: Kypriakai Spoudai 31 (1967), 37 ff.

C. Renfrew, The Neolithic and Early Bronze Age Cultures of the Cyclades and their External Relations, PhD. Thesis, Cambridge (1965)

F. Schachermeyr, Zur Entstehung der ältesten Civilisation in Griechenland: La Nouvelle Clio 1/2 (1949/50) 569 ff.; id., Prähistorische Kulturen Griechenlands: RE. XXII 2 (1954) 1350 ff.; id., Die ältesten Kulturen Griechenlands (1955) & Das ägäische Neolithikum: Stud. Mediterr. Arch. VI (1964)

F. Schachermeyr - H.-G. Buchholz, Forschungsbericht über die Ausgrabungen und Neufunde zur ägäischen Frühzeit (AA. 1971, 295 ff.)

E. Stockton, Preneolithic Remains at Kyrenia, Cyprus?: RDAC. 1968, 16 ff.

Ch. Tsountas, The prehistoric citadels of Dimini and Sesklo (mod. Gk., 1908)

D. R. Theocharis, Nea Makri – Eine große neolithische Siedlung in der Nähe von Marathon: *AM*. 71 (1956) 1 ff.

Thessalika – Archaeological Review for Civilization, History and Religion of Ancient Thessaly (1958 ff.)

A. J. B. Wace - M. S. Thompson, Prehistoric Thessaly (1912)

L. Walker-Cosmopoulos, The Prehistoric Inhabitation of Corinth (1948)

T. Watkins, Ausgrabung in Philia – Auf der Suche nach den ersten Dorfgemeinschaften: *Archaeologia Viva* Nr. 3 (1969) 29 ff.

S. S. Weinberg, Aegean Chronology – Neolithic Period and Early Bronze Age: *AJA*. 51 (1947) 165 ff.; id., The Stone Age in the Aegean: *CAH*. I (²1965) Ch. 10

C. Zervos, Naissance de la Civilisation en Grèce I & II (1962/63)

ANTHROPOLOGY – PREHISTORIC FAUNA

J. L. Angel, Am. Journ. of Physical Anthropology 1 (1943) 229 ff., & 4 (1946) 69 ff.; id., *AJA*. 49 (1945) 252 ff. & The People of Lerna: *AJA*. 62 (1958) 221; id., Troja-Suppl. I (1951), & in: G. Mylonas, Aghios Kosmas (1959) 167 ff.; id., Neolithic Crania from Sotira, in: P. Dikaios, Sotira (1961) 223 ff.; id., The People of Lerna: Analysis of a Prehistoric Aegean Population (1971)

J. L. Angel, Human Skeletal Material from Franchthi Cave, in: Th. W. Jacobsen, Excavations at Porto Cheli: Hesperia 38 (1969) 380 f.

B. Axmacher - C.-H. Hjortsjö, Examen Anthropologique des Cranes Constituant le Matériel Protohistorique Exhumé à Bamboula, Chypre: Lund Univ. Årsskrift 55 (1959) No. 2

E. Breitlinger, in: W. Kraiker - K. Kübler, Kerameikos II (1939), 254

R.-P. Charles, Le Peuplement de Chypre dans l'Antiquité: *Etudes Chypriotes* II (1962); id., Anthropologie Archéologique de la Crète: *Etudes Crétoises* XVI (1965) 147 ff.

P. Ducos, Le Daim à Chypre aux Epoques Préhistoriques: RDAC. 1965, 1 ff.

S. Eberhardt, in: Festschrift G. Kiek (1965), 117 ff. (early Cycladic skeletons)

E. Fischer, in: G. Karo, Schachtgräber, 320 ff.

C. M. Fürst, Zur Anthropologie der prähistorischen Griechen in der Argolis (1930); id., Zur Kenntnis der Anthropologie der prähistorischen Bevölkerung der Insel Cypern (1933)

N. G. Gejvall, Tierreste aus Troja: Årsberättelse Lund 1937/38 & 1938/39

C.-H. Hjorstjö, To Knowledge of the Prehistoric Craniology of Cyprus: Årsberättelse Lund 1946/47

J. E. King, Mammal Bones from Khirokitia and Erimi, in: P. Dikaios, Khirokitia (1953) 431 ff.

G. Kurth, Bevölkerungsbewegungen im östlichen Mittelmeerraum: Archaeologia Viva Nr. 3 (1969) 6 ff.

G. Velde, Anthropologische Untersuchungen und Grabung in einer Höhle der jüngeren Steinzeit auf Leukas: *ZfE*. 44, 1912, 845 ff.

F. E. Zeuner - A. G. Ellis, Animal Bones, in: P. Dikaios, Sotira (1961) 235 f.

EARLY AND MIDDLE BRONZE AGE

P. Åström, The Middle Cypriote Bronze Age (1957)

L. Bernabò-Brea, Poliochni – Città Preistorica nell'Isola di Lemnos I (1964); id., *Bd'A*. 42 (1957) 193 ff.

C. W. Blegen, Korakou – A Prehistoric Settlement near Corinth (1921); id., Zygouries – A Prehistoric Settlement in the Valley of Cleonae (1928)

C. W. Blegen - A. J. B. Wace, Middle Helladic Tombs: *SymbOslo* 9 (1930) 28 ff.

K. Branigan, The Foundations of Palatial Crete – A Survey of Crete in the Early Bronze Age (1970); id., The Tombs of Mesara (A Study of Funerary Art and Ritual in Southern Crete, 2800–1300 B. C.) (1970)

H.-G. Buchholz, Der Pfeilglätter aus dem Schachtgrab von Mykene u. d. helladisáen Pfeilspitzen: *JdI*. 77 (1962) 1 ff.

W. Buttler - R. Heidenreich - W. Wrede, Vorgeschichtliches in der Stadt Samos: *AM*. 60/61 (1935/36) 112 ff.

J. L. Caskey, The Earliest Settlement at Etreusis: *Hesperia* 29 (1960) 126 ff.; id., The Early Helladic Period in the Argolid (loc. cit. 285 ff.); id., Greece, Crete and the Aegean Islands in the Early Bronze Age: *CAH*. II ²(1964) Ch. 26 & The early Bronze Age at Ayina Irini in Keos: Archaeology 23 (1970) 339 ff.

J. N. Coldstream - G. L. Huxley, Kythera: Excavations and Studies conducted by the University of Pennsylvania Museum and the British School at Athens (1972)

P. Dikaios, The Excavations at Vounous Bellapais 1931–32: Archaeologia 88 (1938) 1 ff.

W. Dörpfeld, Troja u. Ilion I & II (1902); id., Alt-Ithaka (1927)

C. Doumas, The N. P. Goulandris Collection of Early Cycladic Art (1968)

Ch. Dugas, La Céramique des Cyclades (1925)

S. Fuchs, Die griechischen Fundgruppen der frühen Bronzezeit u. ihre auswärtigen Beziehungen (1937)

H. Goldman, Excavations at Eutresis in Boiotia (1931)

E. Kunze, Orchomenos III – Die Keramik der frühen Bronzezeit (1934)

W. Lamb, Excavations at Thermi in Lesbos (1936)

F. Matz, Zur ägäischen Chronologie in der frühen Bronzezeit: *Historia* 1 (1950) 173 ff.

K. Müller, Tiryns IV – Die Urfirniskeramik (1938)

G. E. Mylonas, Excavations at Olynthos I — The Prehistoric Settlement (1929); id., Aghios Kosmas — An Early Bronze Age Settlement and Cemetery in Attica (1959)

G. A. Papabasileios, Prehistoric Tombs in Euboia (mod. Gk., 1910)

N. Sandars, The First Aegean Swords and their Ancestry: *AJA*. 65 (1961) 17 ff.

F. Schachermeyr, Welche geschichtlichen Ereignisse führten zur Entstehung der mykenischen Kultur?: *AfO*. 17 (1949) 331 ff.

R. Seager, Excavations on the Island of Mochlos (1912)

E. & J. R. Stewart, Vounous 1937/38 (1950)

J. R. Stewart, The Early Bronze Age in Cyprus: *SCE*. IV/1 A (1962) 203 ff.

F. Stubbings, Chronology of the Aegean Bronze Age: *CAH*. I ²(1962) Ch. 6

N. Valmin, Malthi – The Swedish Messenia Expedition, 1933 (1938)

A. J. B. Wace - C. W. Blegen, The Pre-Mycenaean Pottery on the Mainland: *BSA*. 22 (1916–1918) 175 ff.

P. Warren, Myrtos: an Early Bronze Age Settlement in Crete (1972); id., Minoan Stone Vases (1969)

S. S. Weinberg, The Relative Chronology of the Aegean in the Neolithic Period and Early Bronze Age, in: R. Ehrich, Relative Chronologies in Old World Archaeology (1955/²1965) 86 ff.; id., Exploring the Early Bronze Age in Cyprus: Archaeology 9 (1956) 112 ff.

St. Xanthoudides, The Vaulted Tombs of Messara (1924)

A. A. Zois, Der Kamares-Stil – Werden u. Wesen. Diss. Tübingen 1968

LATE BRONZE AGE – TRANSITION TO IRON AGE

N. Åberg, Bronzezeitliche u. früheisenzeitliche Chronologie IV – Griechenland (1933)

St. Alexiou, Katsamba – Late Minoan Tombs (mod. Gk., 1967)

P. Ålin, Das Ende der mykenischen Fundstätten auf dem griechischen Festland: Stud. Mediterr. Arch. I (1962)

P. Åström, Umfang u. Bedeutung der kyprischen Wirtschaft im 2. Jahrtausend (Extent and Importance of the Cypriot Household in the 2nd Millennium): Archaeologia Viva No. 3 (1969) 73 ff.

L. Åström, Studies in the Arts and Crafts of the Late Cypriote Bronze Age (1967)

R. D. Barnett, Phoenicia and the Ivory Trade: Archaeology 9 (1956) 87 ff.

J. Bérard, Recherches sur la Chronologie de l'Epoque Mycénienne: Mémoires de l'Acad. des Inscriptions et Belles-Lettres XV 1 (1950)

C. W. Blegen, Prosymna – The Helladic Settlement preceding the Argive Heraeum (1937); id., Troy I–IV (1950–1958)

C. W. Blegen - M. Rawson, The Palace of Nestor at Pylos in Western Messenia I (1966)

H.-G. Buchholz, Steinerne Dreifußschalen des ägäischen Kulturkreises u. ihre Beziehungen zum Osten: JdI. 78 (1963) 1 ff.

N. Calvet, Une Tombe du 11e Siècle av. J.-C. à Salamine de Chypre: Acad. des Inscr. et Belles Lettres, Comptes Rendus des Séances 1966, 348 ff.

O. Carruba, Contributo alla Storia di Cipro nel 2 Mill.: Studi Classici e Orientali 17 (1968) 5 ff.

M. A. S. Cameron, Unpublished Fresco Fragments of a Chariot Composition from Knossos: AA. 1967, 330 ff.; id., Minoan and Mycenaean Frescoes (Diss. Liverpool)

M. A. S. Cameron - M. S. F. Hood, Catalogue of Plates in Sir A. Evans' Knossos Fresco Atlas (1967)

H. W. Catling, A Bronze Greave from 13th Cent. B. C. Tomb at Enkomi: OpAth. 2 (1955) 21 ff.; id., Patterns of Settlement in Bronze Age Cyprus: OpAth. 4 (1962) 129 ff.; id., Kouklia-Evreti Tomb 8: BCH. 92 (1968) 162 ff.

E. Coche de la Ferté, Essai de Classification de la Céramique Mycénienne d'Enkomi (1951)

J.-C. Courtois, Enkomi-Alasia – Glanz u. Macht einer kyprischen Stadt (Splendour and Power of a Cypriot town): Archaeologia Viva No. 3 (1969) 93 ff.

J. F. Daniel, Two Late Cypriote III Tombs from Kourion: AJA. 41 (1947) 56 ff.

V. R. d'A. Desborough, Protogeometric Pottery (1952); id., The Last Mycenaeans and their Successors (1964)

P. Dikaios, The Bronze Statue of a Horned God from Enkomi: AA. 1962, 1 ff.; id., Enkomi – Excavations 1948–1958 I–III (1969/1970)

J. Deshayes, Argos – Les Fouilles de la Deiras (1966)

A. J. Evans, The Prehistoric Tombs of Knossos (1906); id., Shaft Graves and Bee-Hive Tombs of Mycenae (1929)

O. Frödin - A. W. Persson, Asine (1938)

A. Furtwängler - G. Löschcke, Mykenische Thongefäße (1879); id., Mykenische Vasen (1886)

A. Furumark, The Chronology of Mycenaean Pottery (1941); id., The Mycenaean Pottery – Analysis and Classification (1941); id., The Mycenaean III c Pottery and its Relation to Cypriote Fabrics: OpArch. 3 (1944) 194 ff.; id., The Settlement at Ialysos and Aegean History c. 1500–1400: OpArch. 6 (1950) 150 ff.; id., The Excavations at Sinda: OpAth. 6 (1965) 99 ff.

J. W. Graham, The Palaces of Crete (1962)

V. Hankey, Late Helladic Tombs at Khalkis: BSA. 47 (1952) 49 ff.

J. B. Hennessy, Stephania – A Middle and Late Bronze Age Cemetery in Cyprus (1965)

P. Hommel - G. Kleiner - A. Mallwitz - C. Weickert, Die Ausgrabungen beim Athena-Tempel in Milet 1957: IstMitt. 9/10 (1959/60) 1 ff.

M. S. F. Hood, Tholos Tombs of the Aegean: Antiquity 34 (1960) 166 ff.; id., Stratigraphic Excavations at Knossos 1957–1961: Kret. Chron. 15/16 (1961/62) Teil I 92 ff.

S. Iakovidis, The Athenian Acropolis during Mycenaean Times (modern Greek, 1962)

H. J. Kantor, Syro-Palestinian Ivories: JNES. 15 (1956) 153 ff.; id., Ivory Carving in the Mycenaean Period: Archaeology 13 (1960) 14 ff.

V. Karageorghis, Notes on some Myc. Survivals in Cyprus: Kadmos 1 (1962) 71 ff.; id., CVA. Cyprus I (1963) & II (1965); id., Nouveaux Documents pour l'Etude du Bronze Récent à Chypre: Etudes Chypriotes II (1965); id., An Early 11th Century Tomb from Palaepaphos: RDAC. 1967, 1 ff.; id., (Highlights of artistic creation in Cyprus): Archaeologia Viva No. 3 (1969) 131 ff.; id., Kition – Ein Handelszentrum zur Zeit Mykenes (loc. cit. 113 ff.)

G. Karo, Die Schachtgräber von Mykenai (1930)

A. D. Lacy, Greek Pottery in the Bronze Age (1967)

M. Lang, Picture Puzzles from Pylos – First Steps in the Study of Frescoes: Archaeology 13 (1960) 55 ff.; id., The Frescoes: The Palace of Nestor at Pylos II (1969)

U. Liepmann, Fragmente eines Dreifußes aus Zypern in New York u. Berlin: JdI. 83 (1968) 39 ff.

F. G. Maier, In den Nekropolen von Alt-Paphos: Archaeologia Viva Nr. 3 (1969) 116 ff.

M. B. Mackeprang, Late Mycenaean Vases: AJA. 42 (1938) 537 ff.

F. Matz, Forschungen auf Kreta 1942 (1951); id., Minoan Civilization – Maturity and Zenith: CAH. II (²1962) Ch. 4 & 12

G. H. McFadden, A Late Cypriot III Tomb from Kourion-Kaloriziki: AJA. 58 (1954) 131 ff.

R. S. Merrillees, The Cypriot Bronze Age Pottery found in Egypt: Stud. Mediterr. Arch. XVIII (1968)

V. Milojcic, Samos I – Die prähistorische Siedlung unter dem Heraion, Grabung 1953 u. 1955 (1961) (many earlier finds)

K. Müller, Tiryns III – Architektur der Burg u. des Palastes (1930)

V. Müller, Kretisch-mykenische Studien: JdI. 40 (1925), 85 ff.

G. E. Mylonas, Ancient Mycenae (1957); id., Grave Circle B of Mycenae: Stud. Mediterr. Arch. VII (1964); id., Mycenae and the Mycenaean Age (1966); id., Mycenae's Last Century of Greatness (Australian Humanities Research Council. Occasional Paper 23) (1969)

U. Naumann, Subminoische u. protogeometrische Bronzeplastik von Kreta, Diss. Hamburg 1967 (typescript; cf. Festschr. U. Jantzen [1969] 114 ff.)

L. R. Palmer, The Penultimate Palace of Knossos (1969)

L. Pernier - L. Banti, Il Palazzo Minoico di Festòs I & II (1935/1951)

A. W. Persson, The Royal Tombs at Dendra near Midea (1931); id., New Tombs at Dendra near Midea (1942)

J. du Plat Taylor, Myrtou-Pighades – A Late Bronze Age Sanctuary in Cyprus (1957)

M. R. Popham, The Last Days of the Palace at Knossos: Stud. Mediterr. Arch. V (1964); id., The Destruction of the Palace at Knossos. Pottery of the Late Minoan III A Period: Mediterr. Arch. Stud. XII (1970)

H. Reusch, Vorschlag zur Ordnung der Fragmente von Frauenfriesen aus Mykenai: AA. 1953, 26 ff. & Die zeichnerische Rekonstruktion des Frauenfrieses im böotischen Theben (1956)

G. Rodenwaldt, Tiryns II – Die Fresken des Palastes (1912); id., Der Fries des Megarons von Mykenai (1921)

B. Rutkowski, Larnaksy Egejskie (Polish, 1966)

A. E. Samuel, The Mycenaeans in History (1966)

J. Schäfer, Elfenbeinspiegelgriffe des 2. Jahrtausends: AM. 73 (1958) 73 ff.

C. F. A. Schaeffer, Enkomi-Alasia I (1952)

C. F. A. Schaeffer - J.-C. Courtois, Rapports Préliminaires sur les Fouilles d'Enkomi, in Chronique des Fouilles et Découvertes Arch. à Chypre: BCH. since 1960

E. Sjöqvist, Problems of the Late Cypriot Bronze Age (1940)

L. A. Stella, La Civiltà Micenea nei Documenti Contemporanei (1965)

F. H. Stubbings, Mycenaean Pottery from the Levant (1951); id., The Rise of Mycenaean Civilization: CAH.² II (1963) Ch. 14 & The Recession of the Mycenaean Civilization (loc. cit., Ch. 27 [1965])

C.-G. Styrenius, Submycenaean Studies (1967)

W. Taylour, The Mycenaeans (1964); id., Mycenae (1968)

N. Valmin, Malthi – The Swedish Messenia Expedition 1933 (1938)

A. J. B. Wace, A Cretan Statuette in the Fitzwilliam Museum (1927); id., Chamber Tombs at Mycenae: Archaeologia 82 (1932); id., Mycenae – An Archaeological History and Guide (1949/1964)

H. Wace, Ivories from Mycenae I – The Ivory Trio (1961)

C. Weickert, Grabungen in Milet 1938: Bericht über den VI. internat. Kongr. f. Arch., Berlin 1939 (1940) 325 ff.; id., Neue Ausgrabungen in Milet, in: Neue deutsche Ausgrabg. im Mittelmeergeb. u. im Vord. Orient (1959) 181 ff.

J. Wiesner, Grab u. Jenseits – Untersuchungen im ägäischen Raum zur Bronzezeit u. frühen Eisenzeit (1938)

CULTURAL RELATIONS – EASTERN MEDITERRANEAN

The Aegean and the Near East – Studies presented to H. Goldman (1956)

G. Bass, Cape Gelidonya – A Bronze Age Shipwreck: TrAPhSoc. N. S. 57, Part 8 (1967)

H.-G. Buchholz, Der Kupferhandel des 2. vorchristl. Jahrtausends: Festschr. Sundwall (1958) 92 ff.; id., Zur Herkunft der kretischen Doppelaxt (1959); id., Bemerkungen zu bronzezeitlichen Kulturbeziehungen im östlichen Mittelmeer: Acta Praehistorica et Archaeologica 1 (1970)

F. Cassola, La Ionia nel Mondo Miceneo (1957)

H. W. Catling - V. Karageorghis, Minoika in Cyprus: BSA. 55 (1960) 109 ff.

J. Cook, Greek Settlements in the Eastern Aegean and Asia Minor: CAH.² II (1961) Ch. 38

T. J. Dunbabin, The Greeks and their Eastern Neighbours (1957)

H. Frankfort, Studies in Early Pottery of the Near East II – Asia, Europe and the Aegean, and their Earliest Interrelations: Occasional Papers VIII (1927)

A. Furumark, The Mycenaean III c Pottery and its Relation to Cypriote Fabrics: OpArch. 3 (1944) 194 ff.

V. Hankey, Mycenaean Pottery in the Middle East – Notes on Finds since 1951: BSA. 62 (1967) 107 ff.

W. Helck, Die Beziehungen Ägyptens zu Vorderasien im 3. u. 2. Jahrtausend v. Chr. (1962)

Y. L. Holmes, The Foreign Relations of Cyprus during the Late Bronze Age. Diss. Brandeis University (1969)

J. T. Hooker, The Mycenae Siege Rhyton and the Question of Egyptian Influence: AJA. 71 (1967) 269 ff.

H. J. Kantor, The Aegean and the Orient in the 2nd Millenium B. C. (1947)

J. D. S. Pendlebury, Aegyptiaca – A Catalogue of Egyptian Objects in the Aegean Area (1930)

F. Poulsen, Der Orient u. die frühgriechische Kunst (1912)

F. Schachermeyr, Zur Entstehung der ältesten Zivilisation in Griechenland: La Nouvelle Clio 1/2 (1949/50) 567 ff.; id., Streitwagen u. Streitwagenbild im Alten Orient u. bei den mykenischen Griechen: Anthropos 46 (1951) 705 ff.; id., das Keftiu-Problem: ÖJh. 45 (1960) 44 ff.; id., Ägäis u. Orient – Die überseeischen Kulturbeziehungen von Kreta u. Mykenai mit Ägypten, der Levante u. Kleinasien unter besonderer Berücksichtigung des 2. Jahrtausends v. Chr. (1967)

W. Stevenson-Smith, Interconnections in the Ancient Near East (1965)

F. H. Stubbings, Mycenaean Pottery from the Levant (1951); id., The Expansion of the Mycenaean Civilization: CAH.² II (1964) Ch. 22 a

J. Vercoutter, L'Egypte et le Monde Egéen Préhellénique – Etude Critique des Sources Egyptiennes (1956)

A. J. B. Wace - C. W. Blegen, Pottery as Evidence for Trade and Colonization in the Aegean Bronze Age: Klio 32 (1939) 131 ff.

Ch. E. Wilbour, Travels in Egypt (1936) Pl. after p. 208

CULTURAL RELATIONS – WESTERN MEDITERRANEAN AND THE REST OF EUROPE

L. Bernabò-Brea, Sicily before the Greeks (1957); id., Alt-Sizilien (1958) & Meligunis-Lipára III (1968)

F. Biancofiore, La Civiltà Micenea nell'Italia Meridionale (1963, ²1967)

J. Boardman, Bronze Age Greece and Libya: BSA. 63 (1968) 41 ff.

H.-G. Buchholz, Keftiubarren u. Erzhandel im 2. vorchristl. Jahrtausend: PZ. 37 (1959) 1 ff.

V. G. Childe, A Bronze Dagger of Mycenaean Type from Pelynt, Cornwall: PPS. 17 (1951) 95 ff.

R. Hachmann, Bronzezeitliche Bernsteinschieber: Bayerische Vorgeschichtsblätter 22 (1957) 1 ff.

E. Sprockhoff, Nordische Bronzezeit u. frühes Griechentum: JRGZMainz 1 (1954) 28 ff.; id., Eine mykenische Bronzetasse aus Dohnsen: Germania 39 (1961) 11 ff. (doubts expressed in H.-G. Buchholz, PZ. 38 [1960] 50)

W. Taylour, Mycenaean Pottery in Italy and Adjacent Areas (1958)

N. Valmin, Das adriatische Gebiet in Vor- u. Frühbronzezeit (1938)

METALLURGY

K. Branigan, A Transitional Phase in Minoan Metallurgy, BSA. 63 (1968) 185 ff.

J. A. Charles, The first Sheffield Plate: Antiquity 42 (1968) 278 ff. (dagger from Gournia)

G. Bass, Cape Gelidonya – A Bronze Age Shipwreck: TrAPhSoc. N. S. 57, Part 8 (1967)

K. Branigan, Copper and Bronze Working in Early Bronze Age Crete: Stud. Mediterr. Arch. XIX (1968)

H.-G. Buchholz, Talanta – Neues über Metallbarren der ostmediterranen Spätbronzezeit: Schweizer Münzblätter 16 (1966) 58 ff.; id., Metallanalysen aus Zypern u. den Nachbarländern: BJbV. 7 (1967) 189 ff.

H. W. Catling, The Metal-Industry in Cyprus, Diss. Oxford (1957); id., Cypriote Bronze Work in the Mycenaean World (1964); id., Kupfer – Grundlage einer Kultur: Archaeologia Viva No. 3 (1969) 18 ff.; id., Mycenaean Bronzes: Stud. Mediterr. Arch. X (in preparation)

J. Deshayes, Les Outils de Bronze de l'Indus au Danube (1960)

R. J. Forbes, Metallurgy in Antiquity (1950); id., Bergbau – Steinbruchtätigkeit – Hüttenwesen: Arch. Hom. Ch. K (ed. by F. Matz & Buchholz, 1967)

S. Immerwahr, The Use of Tin on Mycenaean Vases: Hesperia 35 (1966) 381 ff.

St. Przeworski, Die Metallindustrie Anatoliens in der Zeit von 1500-700 v. Chr. – Rohstoffe, Technik, Produktion: Internationales Archiv f. Ethnographie – Suppl. 36 (1939)

C. Renfrew, Cycladic Metallurgy and the Aegean Early Bronze Age: AJA. 71 (1967) 1 ff.

SEALS

Note in particular the monumental project:

F. Matz, Corpus der minoischen u. mykenischen Siegel (14 volumes projected, 1964 ff.)

H. Biesantz, Kretisch-mykenische Siegelbilder – Stilgeschichtliche u. chronologische Untersuchungen (1954); id., Die minoischen Bildnisgemmen: MarbWPr. 1958, 9 ff.

H.-G. Buchholz, The Cylinder Seal, in: Cape Gelidonya – A Bronze Age Shipwreck: TrAPhSoc. N. S. 57, Part 8 (1967) 148 ff.

H. Frankfort, Cylinder Seals (1939)

A. Furumark, A Scarab from Cyprus: OpAth. 1 (1953) 47 ff.

M. Iakovidis, Ein beschrifteter Siegelzylinder aus Cypern, in: Europa – Festschr. f. E. Grumach (1967) 143 ff.; id., Perati II (1970) 322 ff.

V. E. G. Kenna, Cretan Seals – With a Catalogue of the Minoan Gems in the Ashmolean Museum (1960, review: H.-G. Buchholz, OLZ. 61 [1966] 123 ff.); id., The Seal Use of Cyprus in the Bronze Age: OpAth. 8 (1968) 23 ff.; id., Kyprische Glyptik (Cypriot gem-engraving): Archaeologia Viva No. 3 (1969), 135 ff.

F. Matz, Die frühkretischen Siegel – Eine Untersuchung über das Werden des minoischen Stiles (1928)

E. Porada, The Cylinder Seals of the Late Cypriote Bronze Age: AJA. 52 (1948) 178 ff.

M. H. Wiencke, Further Seals and Sealings from Lerna: Hesperia 38 (1969) 500 ff.

A. Xenaki-Sakellariou, Les Cachets Minoens de la Collection Giamalakis: Etudes Crétoises X (1958); id., Die mykenische Siegelglyptik: Stud. Mediterr. Arch. IX (1964)

SCRIPT AND LANGUAGE

All relevant details in: E. Grumach, Bibliographie der kretisch-mykenischen Epigraphik (1963) & Suppl. I of 1962-1965 (1967); see in particular the journals: Kadmos, Zeitschrift f. Vor- u. Frühgriechische Epigraphik (1962 ff.); Minos, Investigaciones y Materiales para el Estudio de los Textos Paleocretenses (1951 ff.); Nestor, Bibliography for Minoan and Mycenaean Writing (appears since 1957 monthly), also: Anzeiger f. d. Altertumswissenschaft 11 (1958) 193 ff. (F. Schachermeyr) & loc. cit. 16 (1963) 157 ff. (W. Merlingen).

E. L. Bennett, A Minoan Linear B Index (1953); id., The Pylos Tablets, Texts of the Inscriptions found 1939-1954 (1955)

W. C. Brice (editor), Europa – Studien zur Geschichte u. Epigraphik der frühen Aegaeis – Festschr. f. E. Grumach (1967); id., Inscriptions in the Minoan Linear Script of Class A (1961)

H.-G. Buchholz, Zur Herkunft der kyprischen Silbenschrift: Minos 3 (1955) 133 ff. & 6 (1958) 74 ff.; id., Die ägäischen Schriftsysteme u. ihre Ausstrahlung in die ostmediterranen Kulturen: Tagung der Jungius-Gesellschaft, Hamburg (1969)

S. Casson, Ancient Cyprus (1937) 72 ff. (Bronze Age script)

J. Chadwick, The Decipherment of Linear B (1958); id., The Prehistory of Greek Language: CAH.² II (1963) Ch. 49

F. Chapoutier, Les Ecritures Minoennes au Palais de Mallia (1930)

J. F. Daniel, Prolegomena to the Cypro-Minoan Script: AJA. 45 (1941) 249 ff.

P. Dikaios, The Context of the Enkomi Tablets: Kadmos 2 (1963) 39 ff.

W. Ekschmitt, Die Kontroverse um Linear B (1969)

A. J. Evans, Scripta Minoa – The Written Documents of Minoan Crete with Special Reference to the Archives of Knossos I (1909) & II – The Archives of Knossos, ed. J. L. Myres (1951)

E. Grumach, Die kretischen u. kyprischen Schriftsysteme: Hdb. Arch.² (1969) 234 ff.

A. Heubeck, Aus der Welt der frühgriechischen Lineartafeln (1966)

V. & J. Karageorghis, Quelques Observations sur l'Origine du Syllabaire Chypro-Minoen: RA. 1958, Part II 1 ff.

O. Masson, Répertoire des Inscriptions Chypro-Minoennes: Minos 5 (1957) 9 ff.; id., Les Inscriptions Chypriotes Syllabiques (1961); id., Les Ecritures Chypro-Minoennes et les autres Ecritures Chypriotes: Atti e Memorie del 1º Congr. Internaz. di Micenologia I (1967) 417 ff.; id., Kyprische Schriftsysteme vor dem Alphabet (Cypriot writing system before the alphabet): Archaeologia Viva No. 3 (1969) 149 ff.

Minoica – Festschrift zum 80. Geburtstag von J. Sundwall, ed. by E. Grumach (1958)

A. Morpurgo, Mycenaeae Graecitatis Lexicon (1963)

G. Neumann, Zum Forschungsstand beim Diskos von Phaistos: Kadmos 7 (1968) 27 ff.

L. R. Palmer, Mycenaeans and Minoans – Aegean Prehistory in the Light of Linear B Tablets (1961); id., The Interpretation of Mycenaean Greek Texts (1963)

L. Pernier, Il Disco di Festos (1909)

M. Pope, Aegean Writing and Linear A: Stud. Mediterr. Arch. VIII (1964)

G. Pugliese Carratelli, Le Scritture Cretesi-Micenee: Enciclopedia dell'Arte Antica Classica e Orientale V (1963) 88 ff.

L. A. Stella, Per la Cronologia dei Testi di Cnosso (1960)

M. Ventris - J. Chadwick, Documents in Mycenaean Greek – 300 selected Tablets from Knossos, Pylos and Mycenae with Commentary and Vocabulary (1956)

E. Vilborg, A Tentative Grammar of Myc. Greek (1960)

RELIGION

St. Alexiou, Die minoische Göttin mit erhobenen Händen: Kret. Chron. 12 (1958) 179 ff. (mod. Gk.)

H.-G. Buchholz, Zur Herkunft der kretischen Doppelaxt – Geschichte u. auswärtige Beziehungen eines minoischen Kultsymbols (1959); id., Eine Kultaxt aus der Messara: Kadmos 1 (1962) 166 ff.

A. B. Cook, Zeus – A Study in Ancient Religion I–III (1914–1940)

A. J. Evans, Mycenaean Tree and Pillar Cult: JHS. 21 (1901) 99 ff.

M. A. Gill, The Minoan Genius. Diss. Birmingham 1962 (cf. AM. 79 [1964] 1 ff.)

W. K. C. Guthrie, The Greeks and their Gods (1954); id., Early Greek Religion in the Light of the Decipherment of Linear B: BICS. 6 (1959) 35 ff.

E. Herkenrath, Mykenische Kultszenen: AJA. 41 (1937) 411 ff.

G. Karo, Die Religion des ägäischen Kreises: Bilderatlas zur Religionsgeschichte, ed. by H. Haas, Heft 7 (1925)

K. Kerenyi, Möglicher Sinn von Di-wo-nu-so-jo u. Da-da-re-jo-de: Atti e Memorie del 1º Congr. Internaz. di Mic., Rome 1967 (1968)

O. Masson, Zypern – Prähistorische Glaubensvorstellungen (Prehistoric Representations of Beliefs): Archaeologia Viva Nr. 3 (1969) 53 ff.

F. Matz, Göttererscheinung u. Kultbild im minoischen Kreta (1958); id., Minoischer Stiergott?: Kret. Chron. 15/16 (1961/62) Part I 215 ff.

M. P. Nilsson, The Minoan-Mycenaean Religion and its Survival in Greek Religion (²1950–1968); id., Geschichte der griechischen Religion I & II (1941–1950, ²1955–1961)

A. W. Persson, The Religion of Greece in Prehistoric Times (1942)

C. Picard, Les Religions Préhelléniques — Crète et Mycènes: Les Religions de l'Europe Ancienne I (1948)

V. Pöschl - H. Gärtner - W. Heyke, Bibliographie zur antiken Bildersprache (1964)

C. F. A. Schaeffer, Götter der Nord- u. Inselvölker in Cypern: AfO. 21 (1966) 59 ff.

B. Schweitzer, Rezension von ›The Minoan-Mycenaean Religion‹: Gnomon 4 (1928) & in: Zur Kunst der Antike I (1963)

E. Simon, Die Götter der Griechen (1969)

L. A. Stella, La Religione Greca nei Testi Micenei: Numen 5 (1958) 18 ff.

E. Vermeule, Götterkult: Arch. Hom. Kapitel V (in preparation)

J. Wiesner, Grab u. Jenseits – Untersuchungen im ägäischen Raum zur Bronzezeit u. frühen Eisenzeit (1938)

C. G. Yavis, Greek Altars — Origins and Typology — including the Minoan- Mycenaean Offertory Apparatus (1949)

HOMER AND THE MONUMENTS

Archaeologia Homerica – Die Denkmäler u. das frühgriech. Epos I–III, ed. by F. Matz u. H.-G. Buchholz (1967 ff.)

J. Bouzek, Homerisches Griechenland (1969)

E. Buchholz, Die homerischen Realien I–III (1871–1884)

E. Gjerstad, The Colonization of Cyprus in Greek Legend: OpArch. 3 (1944) 107 ff.

R. Hampe, Die homerische Welt im Lichte der neuen Ausgrabungen: Gymnasium 63 (1956) 1 ff.

W. Helbig, Das homerische Epos aus den Denkmälern erläutert – Archäologische Untersuchungen ²(1887)
H. L. Lorimer, Homer and the Monuments (1950)
M. P. Nilsson, Homer and Mycenae (1933)
M. Ohnefalsch-Richter, Kypros, die Bibel u. Homer (Cyprus, the Bible and Homer) (1893)
D. Page, History and the Homeric Iliad (1959)
W. Reichel, Über homerische Waffen – Archaeolog. Untersuchungen (1894/²1901)

W. Schadewaldt, Von Homers Welt u. Werk – Aufsätze u. Auslegungen zur homerischen Frage (³1959)
H. Schliemann, Ithaka, der Peleponnes u. Troja (1869/1963)
G. Starr, The Origins of Greek Civilization (1961), review: H.-G. Buchholz, Hist. Zeitschr. 196 (1963) 639 ff.
A. J. B. Wace - F. H. Stubbings, A Companion to Homer (1962), review: A. Heubeck - H.-G. Buchholz, Gnomon 36 (1964) 1 ff.
T. B. L. Webster, From Mycenae to Homer (1958)

LIST OF ABBREVIATIONS

On the whole, we have followed the abbreviations used in the Deutsches Archäologisches Institut for their archaeological bibliography (cf. *Archäologischer Anzeiger*, 1966, 589 ff. and exceptionally G. Bruns, *Zeitschriftenverzeichnis* [1964]). In the case of monographs, reports on excavations, and collective works, we generally decided on abbreviated forms of the title that will identify the full title even without this list.

Numbers in italics refer to the numbers of objects in this book which occur in the catalogue, the main text, and below the illustrations.

MONOGRAPHS — REPORTS ON EXCAVATIONS — FESTSCHRIFTEN — COLLECTED PAPERS — JOURNALS
THESES — REPORTS OF MEETINGS — SERIES

AA.	Archäologischer Anzeiger	Bd'A.	Bollettino d'Arte
AAA.	Athens Annals of Archaeology	BerRGK.	Deutsches Archäologisches Institut, Bericht der Römisch-Germanischen Kommission, Frankfurt
Åberg, Chronologie	N. Åberg, Bronzezeitliche und Früheisenzeitliche Chronologie. IV: Griechenland (1933)		
AfO.	Archiv für Orientforschung	BICS.	Bulletin of the Institute of Classical Studies, University of London
AJA.	American Journal of Archaeology		
AJPh.	American Journal of Philology	Biesantz, Siegelbilder	H. Biesantz, Kretisch-mykenische Siegelbilder, stilgeschichtliche und chronologische Untersuchungen (1954)
AM.	Mitteilungen des Deutschen Archäologischen Instituts, Athenische Abteilung		
		BJV.; BJbV.	Berliner Jahrbuch für Vor- und Frühgeschichte
AnatStud.	Anatolian Studies, Journal of the British Institute of Archaeology at Ankara	Blegen, Prosymna	C. W. Blegen, Prosymna – the Helladic Settlement Preceding the Argive Heraeum (1937)
Ant. Journ.	The Antiquaries Journal	Blegen, Troy	C. W. Blegen - J. Caskey - M. Rawson, Troy I–IV (1950–1963)
AntK.	Antike Kunst, ed. by Vereinigung der Freunde Antiker Kunst, Basel	Blegen, Zygouries	C. W. Blegen, Zygouries – a Prehistoric Settlement in the Valley of Cleonae (1928)
AnzAW.	Anzeiger für die Altertumswissenschaft		
AO.	Der Alte Orient	BMetrMus.	Bulletin of the Metropolitan Museum of Art, New York
ArchCl.	Archaeologia Classica		
Arch. Hom.	Archaeologia Homerica – Die Denkmäler und das Frühgriechische Epos, ed. by F. Matz and H.-G. Buchholz (Göttingen, 1967 ff.)	BMQ.	The British Museum Quarterly
		BMusFA.	Bulletin of the Museum of Fine Arts, Boston
		Boardman, Cret. Coll.	J. Boardman, The Cretan Collection in Oxford. The Dictaean Cave and Iron Age Crete (1961)
Arch. Rep.	cf. JHS		
ASAtene	Annuario della Scuola Archeologica di Atene	Bossert, Altanatolien	H. T. Bossert, Altanatolien. Kunst und Handwerk in Kleinasien von den Anfängen bis zum völligen Aufgehen in der griech. Kultur (1942)
BASOR.	Bulletin of the American School of Oriental Research		
BCH	Bulletin de Correspondance Hellénique	Bossert, Altkreta	H. T. Bossert, Altkreta. Kunst und Handwerk in Griechenland, Kreta

	und in der Ägäis von den Anfängen bis zur Eisenzeit. 3rd ed. (1937); cf. also H. T. Bossert, Altkreta. Kunst und Kunstgewerbe im ägäischen Kulturkreise (1921) & H. T. Bossert, 2nd ed.: Altkreta. Kunst und Handwerk in Griechenland, Kreta und auf den Kykladen während der Bronzezeit (1923)	Festschr. Gold	The Aegean and the Near East. Studies presented to Hetty Goldman on the Occasion of her 75th Birthday (1956)
		Festschr. Schefold	Gestalt und Geschichte. Festschrift Karl Schefold zu seinem 60. Geburtstag am 26. Jan. 1965: AntK., IV. Beiheft (1967)
Bossert, Altsyrien	H. T. Bossert, Altsyrien. Kunst und Handwerk in Cypern, Syrien, Palästina, Transjordanien und Arabien von den Anfängen bis zum völligen Aufgehen in der griechisch-römischen Kultur (1951)	Fimmen, Kret.-myk. Kultur; KMK.	D. Fimmen, Die kretisch-mykenische Kultur (²1924)
		Furtwängler, Kl. Schr.	A. Furtwängler, Kleine Schriften I & II, ed. J. Sieveking - L. Curtius (1912)
		Furtwängler-Löschcke, Myken. Vasen	A. Furtwängler - G. Löschcke, Mykenische Vasen, vorhellenische Thongefäße aus dem Gebiete des Mittelmeers (1886)
Boll. Paletnol. Ital.	Bollettino di Paletnologia Italiana	FuF.	Forschungen und Fortschritte
CAH.	The Cambridge Ancient History	Furumark, M P.; or: Myc. Pottery	A. Furumark, The Mycenaen Pottery, Analysis and Classification (1941)
Catling, Bronzework	H. W. Catling, Cypriot Bronzework in the Mycenaean World (1964)		
Chadwick, Linear B	J. Chadwick, The Decipherment of Linear B (1958)	Gallet de Santerre, Délos Primitive	H. Gallet de Santerre, Délos Primitive et Archaique (1958)
Class. Journ.	The Classical Journal	Glotz, Civilis. Egéenne	G. Glotz, La Civilisation Egéenne (1952)
Class. Rev.	The Classical Review		
Collignon, Cat.	M. Collignon - L. Couve, Catalogue des Vases Peints du Musée Nat. d'Athènes (1904)	Goldman, Eutresis	H. Goldman, Excavations at Eutresis in Boeotia (1931)
CRAI.	Comptes-Rendus des Séances de l'Année. Académie des Inscriptions et Belles-Lettres	Hall, Vrokastro	E. H. Hall, Excavations in Eastern Crete, Vrokastro (1914)
		Hafner, Gesch. d. griech. Kunst	G. Hafner, Geschichte der griechischen Kunst (Zürich, 1961)
CVA.	Corpus Vasorum Antiquorum	Hawes, Gournia	H. Boyd Hawes, Excavations at Gournia (1908)
Delt.	Archaiologikon Deltion (mod. Gk. with ›Chronika‹ = Chron.)	Hdb. Arch.	Handbuch der Archäologie; cf. Matz, Hdb. Arch.
Demargne, Naissance	P. Demargne, La Naissance de l'Art Grec (1964)	Hutchinson, Prehist. Crete	R. W. Hutchinson, Prehistoric Crete (1962)
Desborough, Last Myc.	V. R. d'A. Desborough, The Last Mycenaeans and their Successors, an Archaeological Survey c. 1200–c. 1000 B. C. (1964)	Hope Simpson, Atlas	R. Hope Simpson, A Gazetteer and Atlas of Mycenaen Sites: BICS. Suppl. 16 (1965)
Deshayes, Argos	J. Deshayes, Argos – les Fouilles de la Deiras (1966)	IEJ.	Israel Exploration Journal
		ILN.	Illustrated London News
Deshayes, Outils	J. Deshayes, Les Outils de Bronze de l'Indus au Danube (1960)	IstForsch.; Ist. Forsch.	Istanbuler Forschungen
		Ist. Mitt.	Istanbuler Mitteilungen
Doc. et Mon. Or. Ant.	Documenta et Monumenta Orientis Antiqui	JbZMusMainz	Jahrbuch des Römisch-Germanischen Zentralmuseums, Mainz
Dussaud, Civil. Préhell.	R. Dussaud, Les Civilisations Préhelléniques dans le Bassin de la Mer Egée (²1914)	JAOS.	Journal of the American Oriental Society
		JdI.; JdI.-Erg.-H.	Jahrbuch des Deutschen Archäologischen Instituts, and suppl.
Ephem.	Archaiologike Ephemeris (mod. Gk., Athens)	JHS.	Journal of Hellenic Studies, with ›Archaeological Reports‹ (= Arch. Rep.)
Ergon	To Ergon tis Archaiologikis Hetaireias (mod. Gk., Athens)		
EtCrét.; Et. Crét.	Etudes Crétoises (1928 ff.)	JNES.	Journal of Near Eastern Studies
Evans, PM.	A. Evans, The Palace of Minos. A Comparative Account of the Successive Stages of the Early Cretan Civilization as Illustrated by the Discoveries at Knossos I-V (1921–36/1964)	Karo, SchGr.; Schachtgr.	G. Karo, Die Schachtgräber von Mykenai (1930–33)
		Kenna, CS.	V. E. G. Kenna, Cretan Seals, with a Catalogue of the Minoan Gems in the Ashmolean Museum (1960)
Evans, PTK.; Prehist. Tombs	A. Evans, The Prehistoric Tombs of Knossos (1906)		

Kret. Chron.	Kretika Chronika (mod. Gk.)
KUML	Kuml. Årbog for Jysk Arkaeologisk Selskab
Liv. Ann.	University of Liverpool, Annals of Archaeology and Anthropology
Lorimer, HM.	H. L. Lorimer, Homer and the Monuments (1950)
MarbWPr.	Marburger Winckelmannsprogramm
Maraghiannis, Ant. Crét.	G. Maraghiannis - G. Karo, Antiquités Crétoises I–III (1908–1915)
Marinatos-Hirmer	S. Marinatos - M. Hirmer, Kreta und das mykenische Hellas (1959)
Matz, Hdb.Arch.	F. Matz, 'Die Ägäis', in: Handbuch der Archäologie II (1954)
Matz, CMS.	F. Matz, Corpus der minoischen und mykenischen Siegel (1964 ff.)
Matz, Gr. Kunst	F. Matz, Geschichte der griechischen Kunst I (1950)
Matz, Kreta-Mykene-Troja; or: KMT.	F. Matz, Kreta, Mykene, Troja – Die minoische und die homerische Welt (1956)
Matz, Siegel	F. Matz, Die frühkretischen Siegel – Eine Untersuchung über das Werden des minoischen Stiles (1928)
Matz-Buchholz, Arch. Hom.	cf. Arch. Hom.
MDOG.	Mitteilungen der Deutschen Orientgesellschaft
MGG.	Musik in Geschichte und Gegenwart
Mon. Ant.	Monumenti Antichi publicati per Cura della Accademia Nazionale dei Lincei
MonPiot	Fondation Eugène Piot, Monuments et Mémoires
Montelius, La Grèce Préclass.	O. Montelius, La Grèce Préclassique I & II (1924–28)
V. Müller, Frühe Plastik	V. Müller, Frühe Plastik in Griechenland und Vorderasien (1929)
Müller-Karpe, Hdb. d. Vorgesch.	H. Müller-Karpe, Handbuch der Vorgeschichte I & II (1966–68)
Mus. Helv.	Museum Helveticum
Mylonas, Anc. Myc.	G. E. Mylonas, Ancient Mycenae – The Capital City of Agamemnon (1957)
Mylonas, Myc. and the Myc. Age	G. E. Mylonas, Mycenae and the Mycenaean Age (1966)
Naumann, Architektur	R. Naumann, Architektur Kleinasiens von ihren Anfängen bis zum Ende der hethitischen Zeit (1955, 2nd ed. 1971)
Nilsson, MMR.	M. P. Nilsson, The Minoan-Mycenaean Religion and its Survival in Greek Religion (^{2}1950/1968)
ÖJh.	Jahreshefte des Österreichischen Archäologischen Instituts in Wien
OIP.	Oriental Institute Publications, Chicago
OLZ.	Orientalistische Literaturzeitung
OpArch.	Skrifter utgivna av Svenska Institute i Rom. Opuscula Archaeologica
OpAth.	Opuscula Atheniensia
Pendlebury, Arch. of Crete	J. D. S. Pendlebury, The Archaeology of Crete – an Introduction (1939/1963)
PEQ.	Palestine Exploration Quarterly
Perrot-Chipiez	G. Perrot - Ch. Chipiez, Histoire de l'Art dans l'Antiquité I–IX (1882–1911)
Persson, Asine	O. Frödin - A. W. Persson, Asine – Results of the Swedish Excavations 1922–1930, ed. by A. Westholm (1938)
Persson, Dendra I, II	A. W. Persson, The Royal Tombs at Dendra near Midea (1931) and New Tombs at Dendra near Midea (1942)
Phylakopi	Excavations at Phylakopi in Melos: JHS. Suppl. Paper No. 4 (1904)
Picard, Rel. Préhell.	C. Picard, Les Religions Préhelléniques – Crète et Mycènes, in: Les Religions de l'Europe Ancienne I (1948)
PM.	cf. Evans, PM.
PPS.	Proceedings of the Prehistoric Society
Prakt.	Praktika tis en Athenais Archaiologikis Hetaireias (mod. Gk.)
PZ.; Prähist. Zeitschr	Prähistorische Zeitschrift
RA.; Rev. Arch.	Revue Archéologique
REA.	Revue des Etudes Anciennes
RDAC.	Report of the Department of Antiquities, Cyprus
Reallex. Vorgesch.	Reallexikon der Vorgeschichte I–XV, ed. by M. Ebert (1924–1932)
RE.; RE.-Suppl.	Paulys Realencyclopädie der classischen Altertumswissenschaft (revised ed., 1883 ff., incl. suppl. volumes)
Reusch, Frauenfries	H. Reusch, Die zeichnerische Rekonstruktion des Frauenfrieses im böotischen Theben (1956)
Rodenwaldt, Fries	G. Rodenwaldt, Der Fries des Megarons von Mykenai (1921)
RVV.	Religionsgeschichtliche Versuche und Vorarbeiten
SB...	Sitzungsberichte der Akademie der Wissenschaften in ... (location given, e. g. SBMunich)
SCE.	The Swedish Cyprus Expedition – Finds and Results of the Excavations in Cyprus I–IV (1934–1962)
Schachermeyr, Die ältesten Kulturen	F. Schachermeyr, Die ältesten Kulturen Griechenlands (1955)
Seager, Mochlos	R. B. Seager, Explorations in the Island of Mochlos (1912)
SMEA.	Studi Micenei ed Egeo-Anatolici, in: Incunabula Graeca
Staïs, Coll. Mycén., Myc.	V. Staïs, Collection Mycénienne – Guide Illustré du Musée National d'Athènes, 2nd ed. (1909, Engl. 1926)
Stud. Mediterr. Arch.	Studies in Mediterranean Archaeology, Lund
SymbOslo	Symbolae Osloenses

TrAPhAss.	Transactions and Proceedings of the American Philological Association		from Lake Kopais to the Borders of Macedonia (1912)
TrAPhSoc.	Transactions of the American Philosophical Society	Walters, Cat. Bronzes	H. B. Walters, Catalogue of the Bronzes, Greek, Roman and Etruscan, in the Department of Greek and Roman Antiquities, British Museum (1899)
Tsountas, DS.	C. Tsountas, Hai Prohistorikai Akropoleis Diminiou kai Sesklou (mod. Gk., 1908)		
Tsountas-Manatt, Myc. Age	C. Tsountas - J. Manatt, The Mycenaean Age (1897/1903, reprint 1966)	Xénaki-Sakellariou, Cachets	A. Xénaki-Sakellariou, Les Cachets Minoens de la Collection Giamalakis (1958)
Ventris, Doc.; Documents	M. Ventris - J. Chadwick, Documents in Mycenaean Greek (1956)	Yavis, Altars	C. G. Yavis, Greek Altars. Origins and Typology. Including the Minoan-Mycenaean Offertory Apparature. An Archaeological Study in the History of Religion (1949)
Wace, ChT.	A. J. B. Wace, Chamber Tombs at Mycenae: Archaeologia 82 (1932)		
Wace, Mycenae	A. J. B. Wace, Mycenae. An Archaeological History and Guide (1949/1964)	Zervos, Crète	C. Zervos, L'Art de la Crète. Néolitique et Minoenne (1956)
Wace-Stubbings, Companion	A. J. B. Wace - F. H. Stubbings, A Companion to Homer (1962)	Zervos, Cycl.	C. Zervos, L'Art des Cyclades du Début à la Fin de l'Age de Bronze, 2500–1100 avant notre Ere (1957)
Wace-Thompson, Prehist. Thess.	A. J. B. Wace - M. S. Thompson, Prehistoric Thessaly – Being some Account of Recent Excavations and Explorations in North-Eastern Greece	Zervos, Naissance	C. Zervos, Naissance de la Civilisation en Grèce I–II (1962–1963)
		ZfE.	Zeitschrift für Ethnologie

GENERAL ABBREVIATIONS

Abh.	Abhandlung (essay)	Fasc.	Fascicle	Min.	Minoan
Abt.	Abteilung (department)	geometr.	geometrisch (geometric)	MM	Middle Minoan
Beibl.	Beiblatt (supplement)	Ges.	Gesellschaft (society)	mod. Gk.	modern Greek
Beih.	Beiheft (supplement)	Hdb.	Handbuch (handbook)	Mus.	Musée, Museo, Museum
Chron.	Chronika (mod. Gk., part of journal *Deltion*)	Inv. No.	Inventory Number	Myc.	Mycenaean
		Jahrb.	Jahrbuch, Jahrbücher (year-book[s])	NE	New Empire
Coll.	Collection			OE	Old Empire
Cret.-Myc.	Cretan-Mycenaean	Kunstgesch.	Kunstgeschichte (history of art)	progr.	programme
Cypr.	Cypriot			Rez.	Rezension (review, critique)
DAI.	Deutsches Archäologisches Institut	kypr.	kyprisch (Cypriot)		
		LH	Late Helladic	röm.	römisch (Roman)
diam.	diameter	LM	Late Minoan	SB	Sitzungsberichte (reports of meetings)
diss.	Dissertation	ME	Middle Empire		
ed.	edition, edited (number of edition indicated by superior figure)	Mel.	Meletai (mod. Gk., part of journal *Deltion*)	Staatl. Mus.	Staatliche Museen
		Metrop. Mus.	Metropolitan Museum	Suppl.	Supplement
EH	Early Helladic			s. v.	sub voce (under heading)
EM	Early Minoan	MH	Middle Helladic	Zeitschr.	Zeitschrift (journal)

Stone Age
cave dwelling, Aetolia

1a   1b

2

3

Cave dwellings and sacred caves, Crete

4

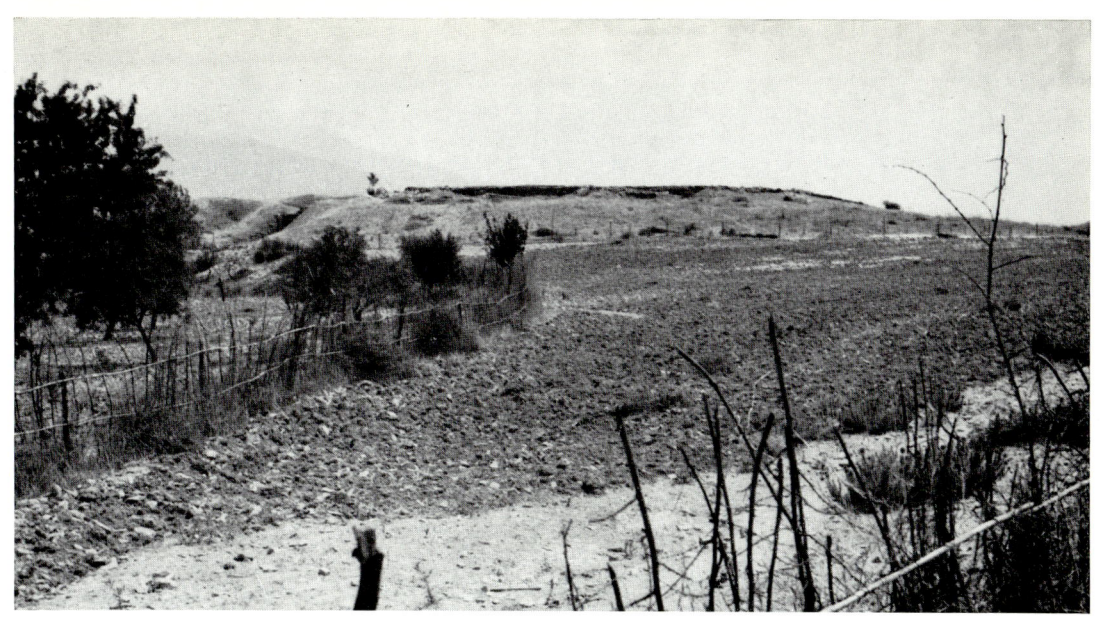

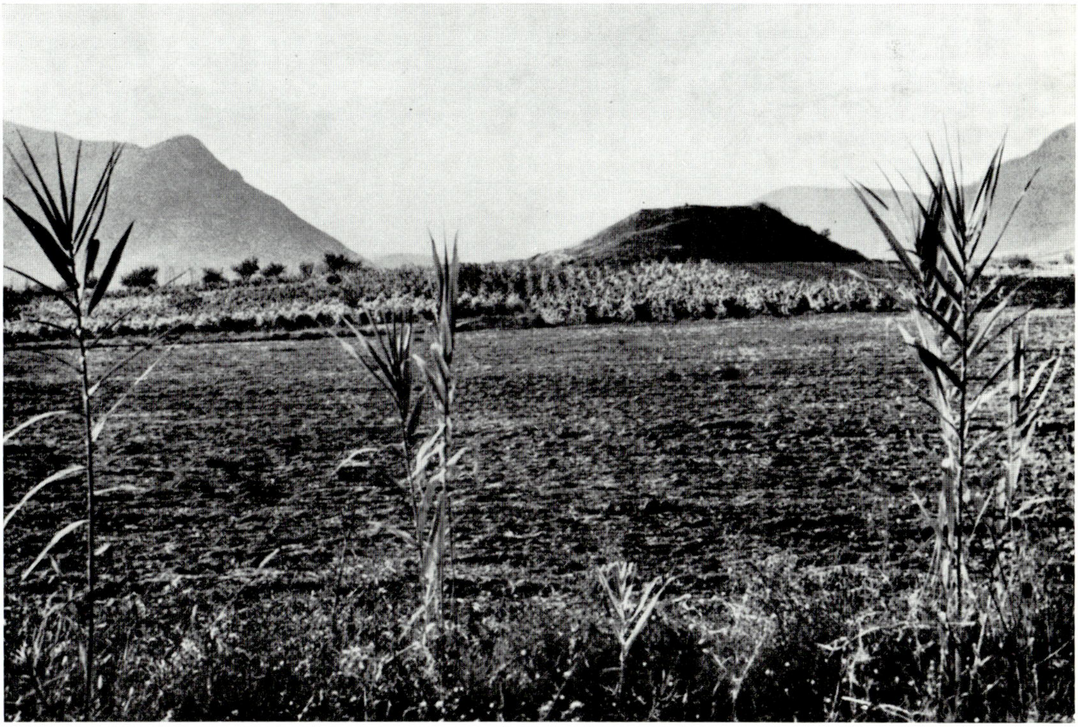

5

Neolithic hill settlements, Thessaly

Neolithic buildings, Thessaly

6,7: p. 14, Fig. 3
8–13: p. 32, Fig. 10

14

15

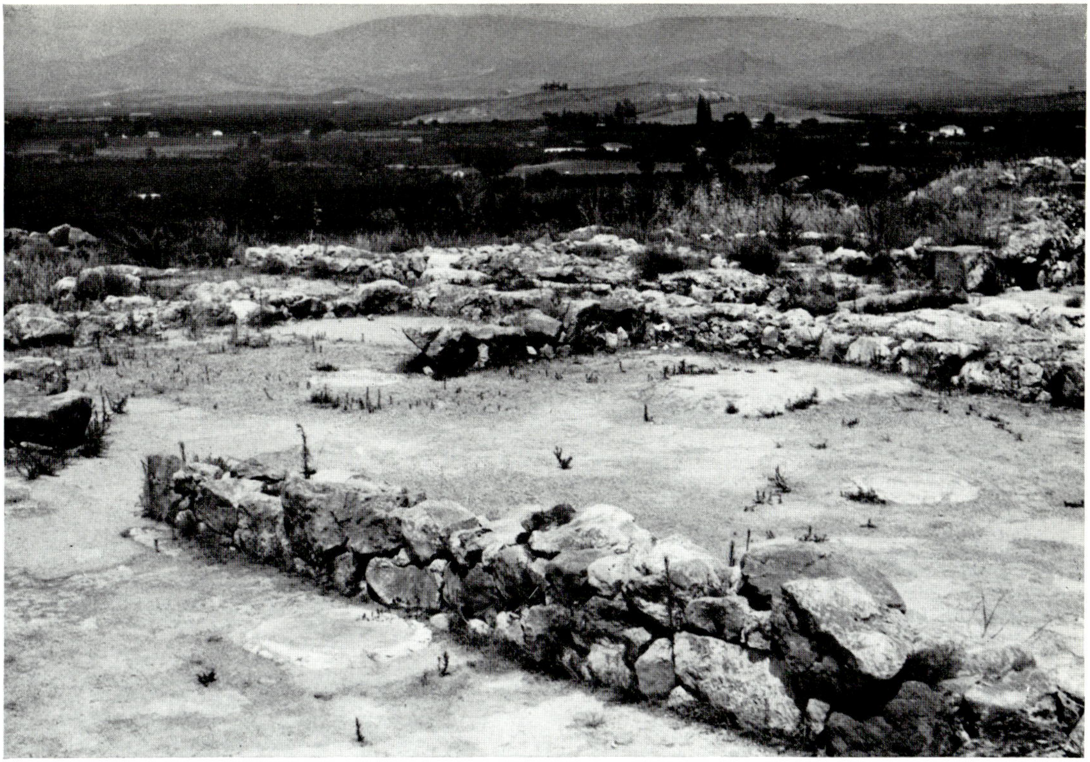

16

17

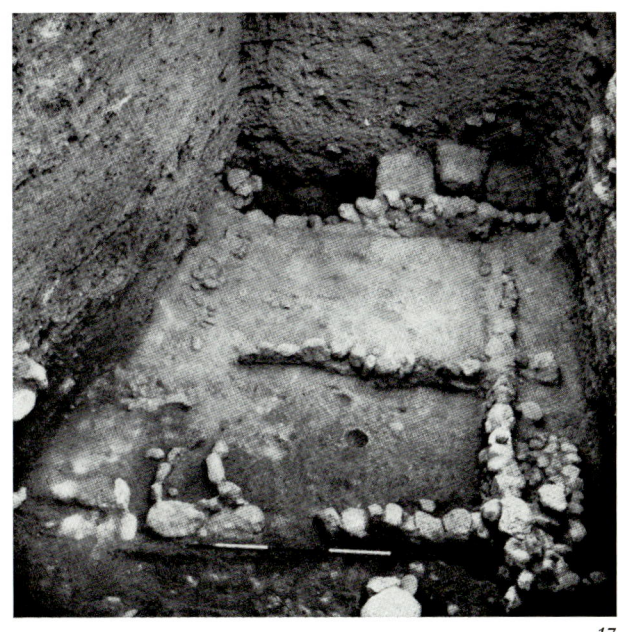

Neolithic buildings, Thessaly and Crete

18

19

20

Early Bronze Age walls; Lerna and Troy

22

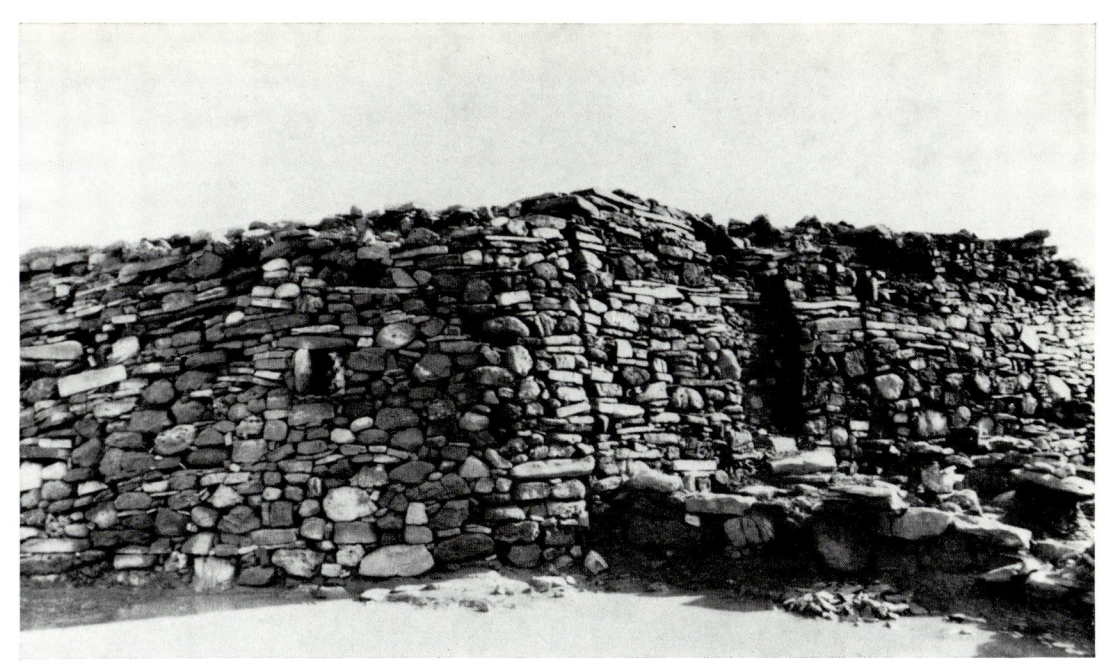

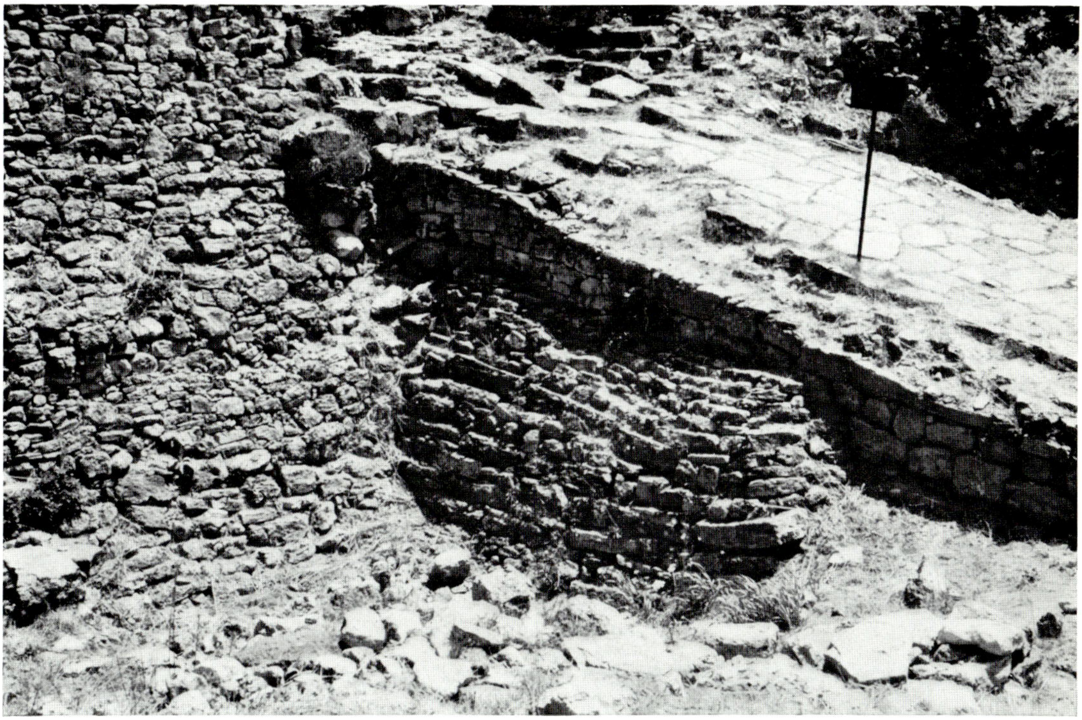

23

Early Bronze Age walls; Poliochni on Lemnos and Troy

21: p. 33, Fig. 11; *24–31:* p. 16 ff., Figs 4 and 5

32a

32b

Middle Helladic house, Olympia

196

33

34a

34b

Bronze Age buildings;
The Peloponnese and Samos

35a

35b   36

Fortification walls, Troy VI

37

38

Gate and town wall, Hagia Irini on Keos

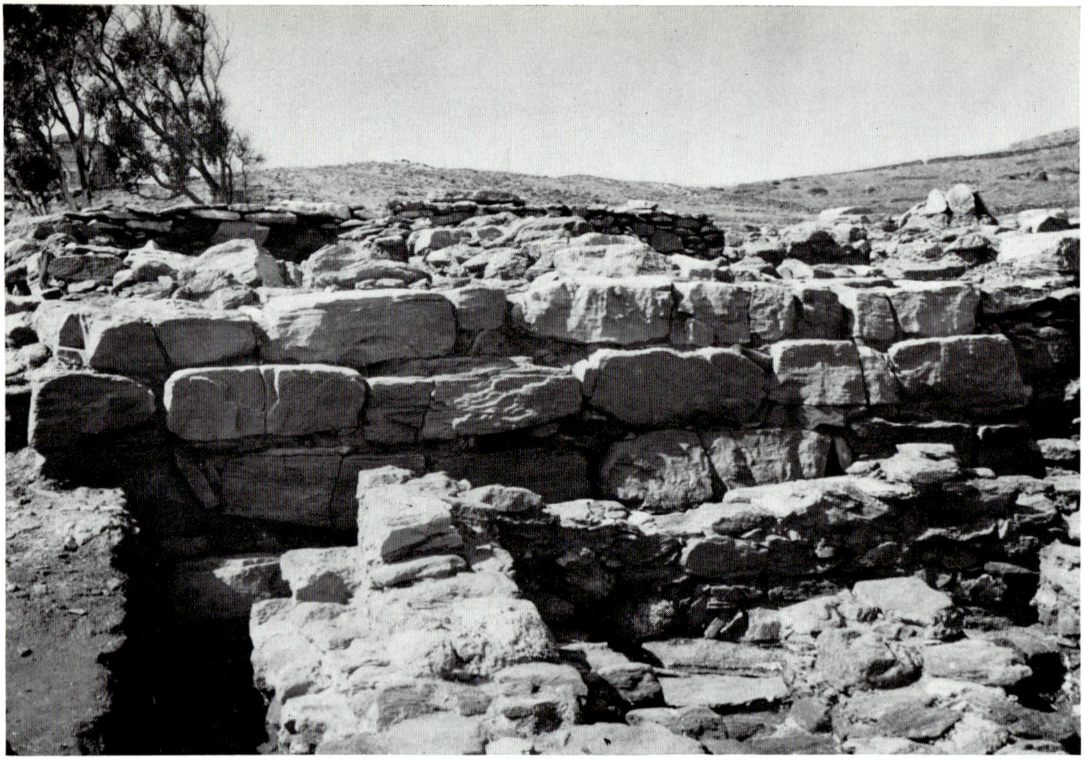

39

40

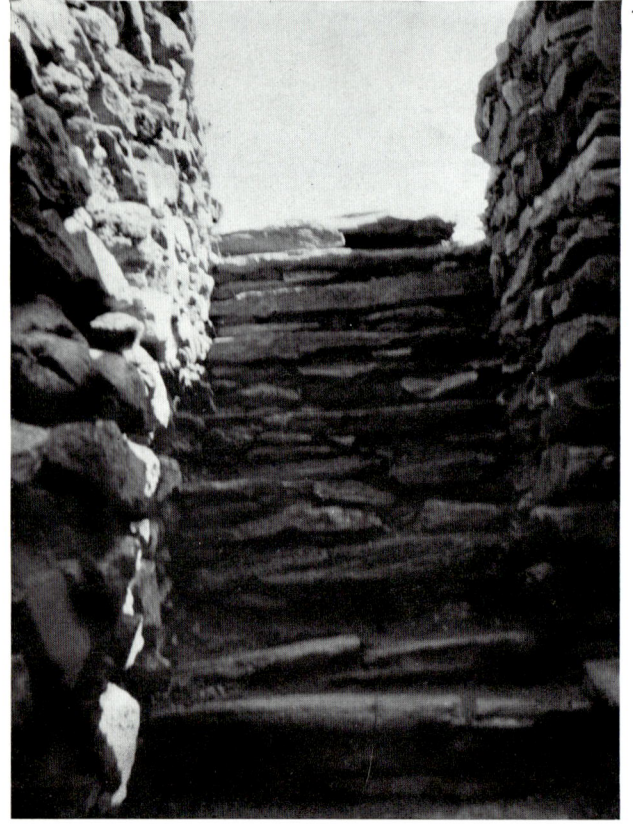

Town wall and steps,
Hagia Irini on Keos

41.42: p. 21, Fig. 6

43

44

Minoan palace; Knossos, Crete

Minoan palace; Knossos, Crete

45

46

47

48

Minoan palace; Knossos, Crete

49

50

51

pp. 204 and 205:
Details of Minoan buildings;
Knossos and Phaistos, Crete

53: p 34, Fig. 12

52

54

55

56

57

Minoan palace; Phaistos, Crete

58a

58b

Minoan palace; Phaistos, Crete

61a

60a

59

Architectural details; Phaistos, Hagia Triadha and Mallia

60b

61b

Architectural details; Hagia Triadha and Mallia

62

63

Minoan palace; Mallia, Crete

66: p. 212
67–69: p. 36, Fig. 13;
70: p. 34, Fig. 14

64

65

Minoan palace; Mallia, Crete

211

72

66

71

Minoan steps; Gournia, Mallia, Vathypetro

73

75: p. 37, Fig. 14

74

Minoan town, Gournia

76

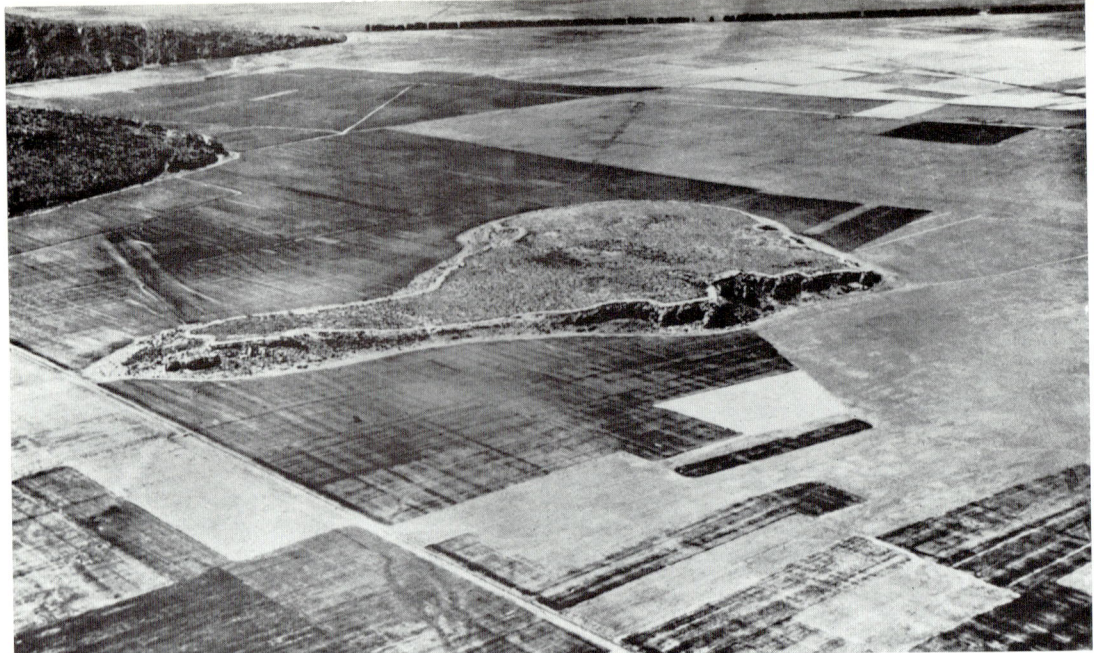

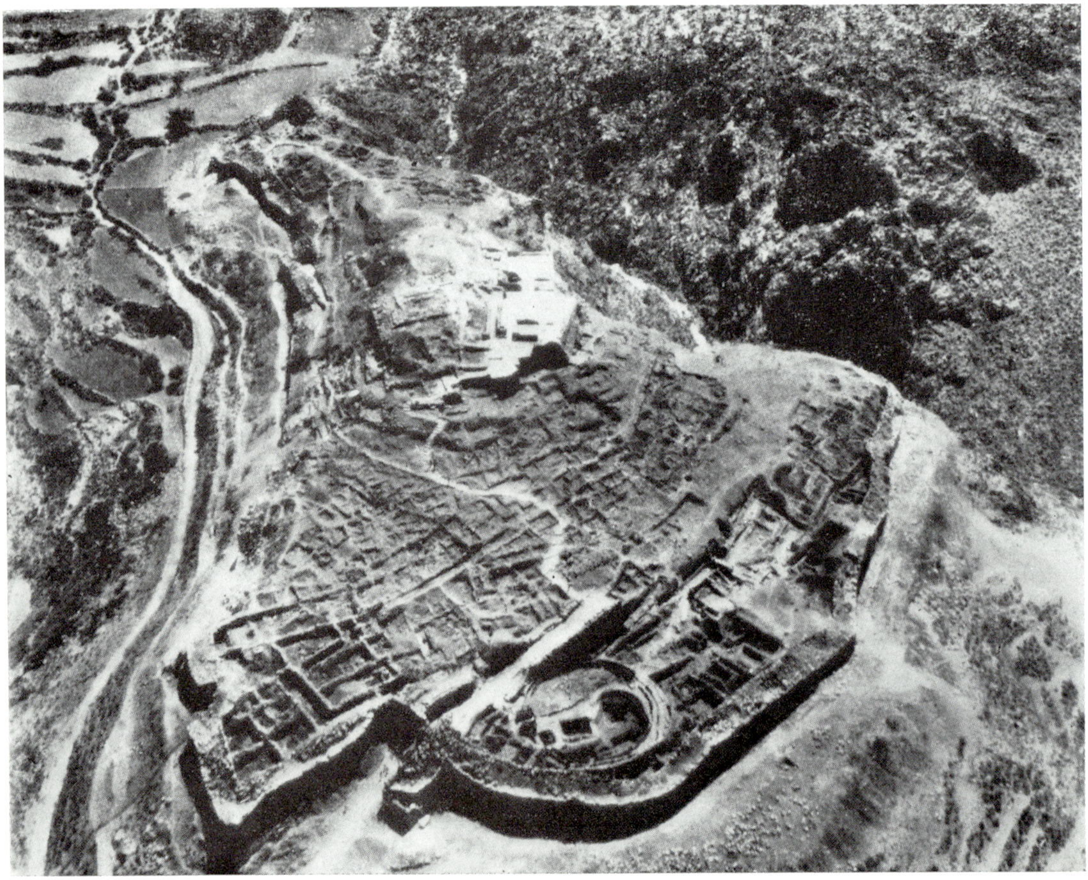

77

Aerial views of Mycenaean citadels; Gla and Mycenae

79

80 81 82

78: Colour plate 2 after p. 40 Mycenae

83

84

Mycenae

85

86

87

Mycenae 88

89

90

Mycenae; houses, steps and ramps

91a

91b

91c

Mycenae; steps
and structural details
of the Lion Gate

92

93

98

97

Mycenae, Tiryns and Kasarmi

94–96b: p. 24, Fig. 7

Tiryns

100

101

102

103a

Gates, steps and walls; Tiryns

103b

104

105

106a–108: p. 25, Fig. 8

Walls and megaron; Tiryns

p. 224:
Mycenaean acropolis, Athens
p. 225:
Mycenaean citadel, Gla in Boeotia

109

110

111

112

113

114

Gla, Boeotia

115

116

Gla, Boeotia

117

118

119

Gla, Boeotia

120.121: p. 38, Fig. 15

122

123a

123b: p. 230

So-called Palace of Nestor, Pylos

124

125

123b

So-called Palace of Nestor, Pylos

126

127

128

129.130: p. 28, Fig. 9   Sequence of courses and ashlar walls, Leukandi in Euboea

131

132

133

Early Bronze Age circular tombs, Keos and Crete

134

135

Tombs of the third and second millennia B.C., Attica and the Argolid

150

136–142: p. 41, Fig. 16;
143–149: p. 234–236
153: p. 43, Fig. 17

151

152

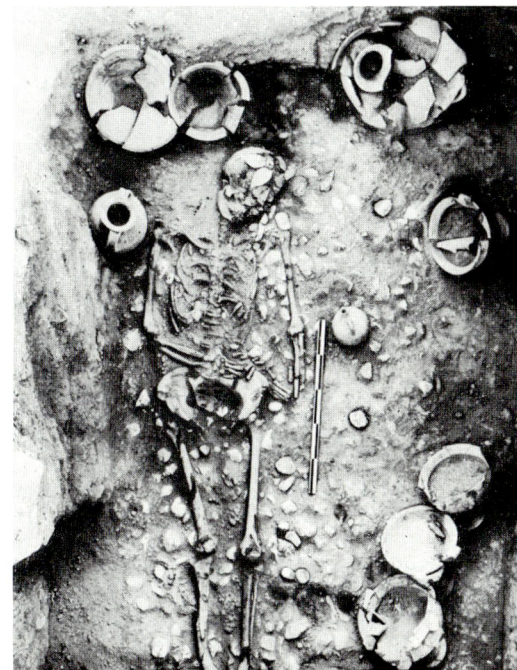

233

143

144

Knossos, 'Temple-Tomb'

145

146

Knossos, 'Temple-Tomb'

147

148

149

154

155

p. 236: Knossos, 'Temple-Tomb'

p. 237: Mycenae, Grave Circle A

156

157

158

159

Mycenae,
Grave Circle A;
Kakovatos, remains
of a tholos tomb;
Thorikos, tholos tomb

160

161

162

Tiryns and Vapheio, tholos tombs

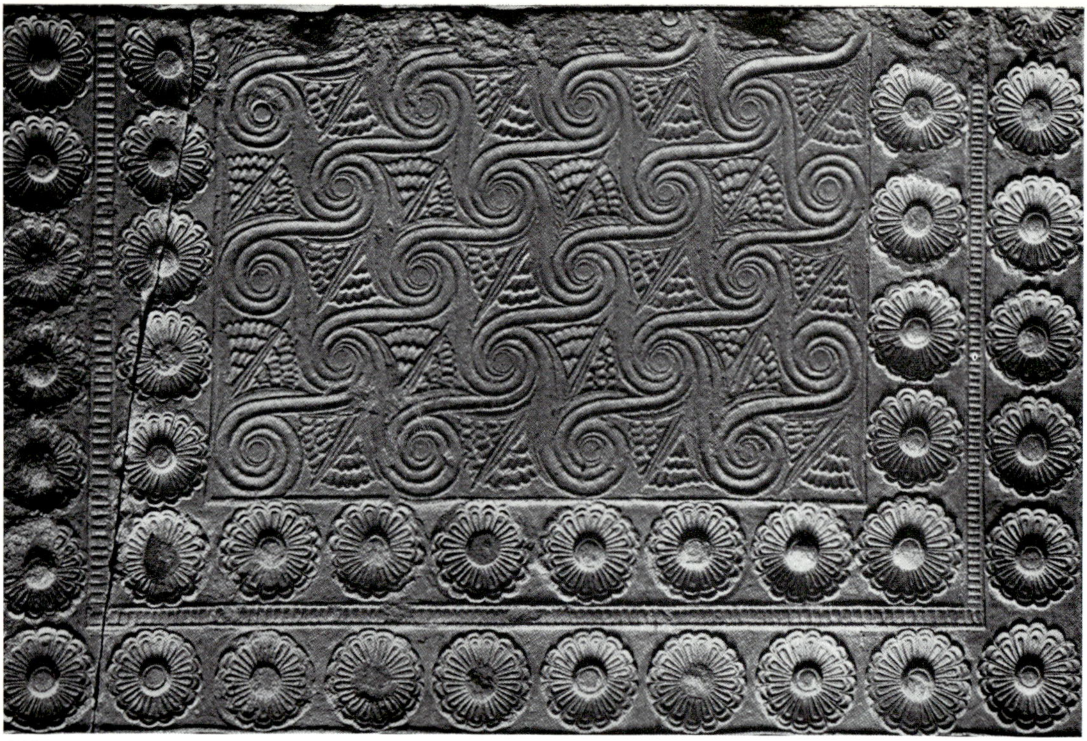

163

164

165

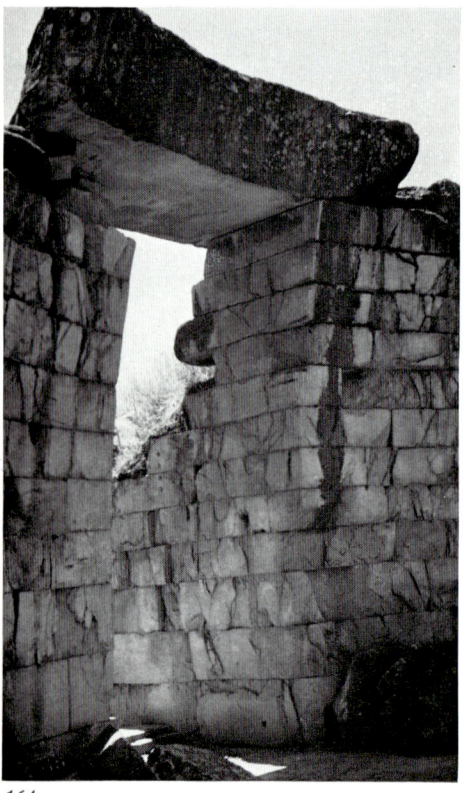

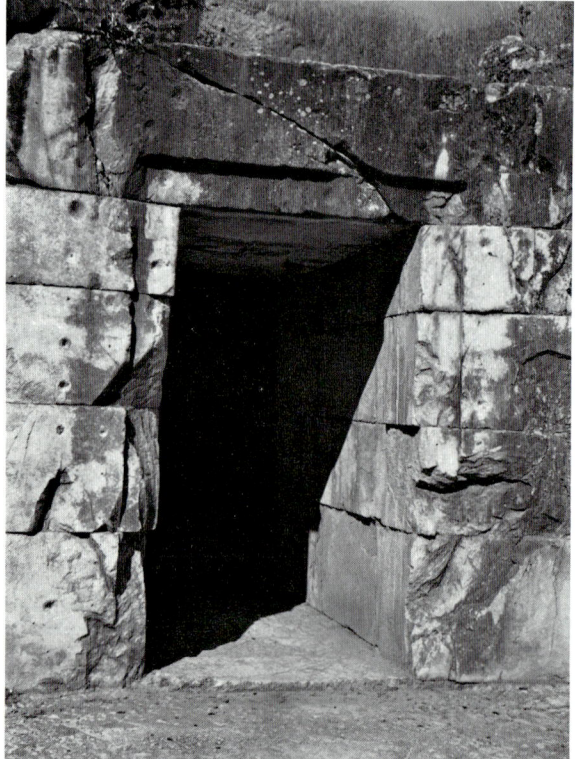

Tholos tomb, Orchomenos in Boeotia

166

167.168

169

Tholos tombs, Dendra and Mycenae

241

'Treasury of Atreus' in Mycenae

170

171

172

173

'Lion Tomb' in Mycenae

174

175

176

Mycenae, 'Tomb of Clytemnestra' *177:* Colour plate 2 after p. 40

178

179

180: p. 43, Fig. 17; *181:* p. 248

Hagios Elias in Aetolia, vaulted tombs

245

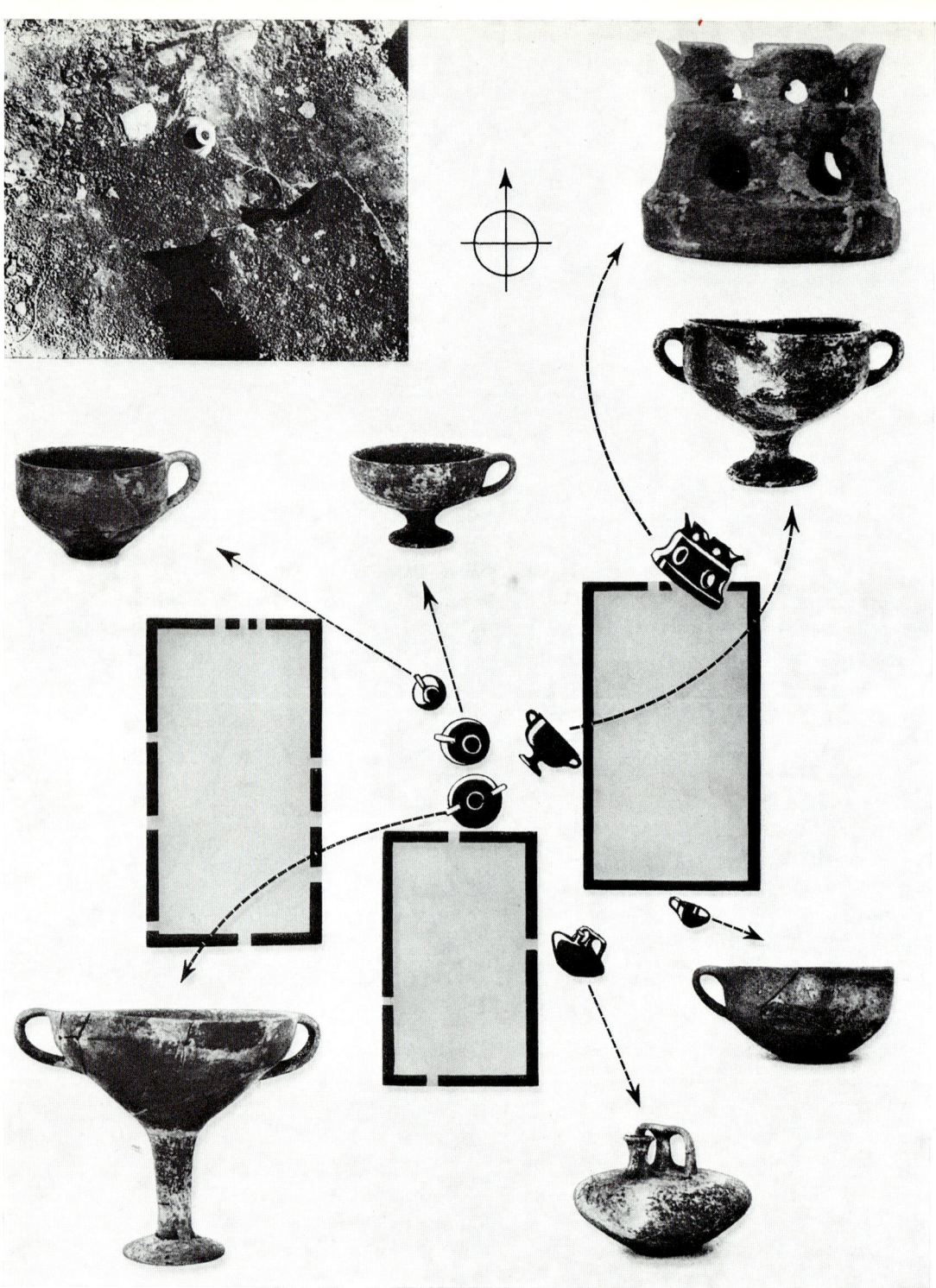

182

Tombs in Olous, eastern Crete

246

183: p. 43, Fig. 17

184

185

186

Mycenaean chamber tombs, Olympia and Tiryns

187

188

181

Pithos burial, pit grave and sacrificed horses; Mycenae, Perati and Marathon

189

190

191

Perati, Attica: necropolis of chamber tombs

193–216: p. 45, Fig. 18;
217–221.228–231:
p. 47, Fig. 19

192a–c

222 223 224 225

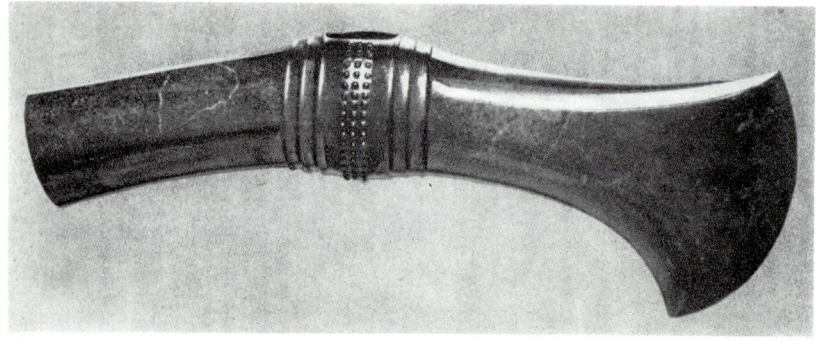

226
227

Stone implements and weapons;
Greek mainland,
Troy, Lemnos and Crete

Stone implements and weapons; Crete, Thessaly and the Argolid

251

245–289

290–308    309–336

Late Neolithic and Early Bronze Age flint and obsidian implements from Leukas

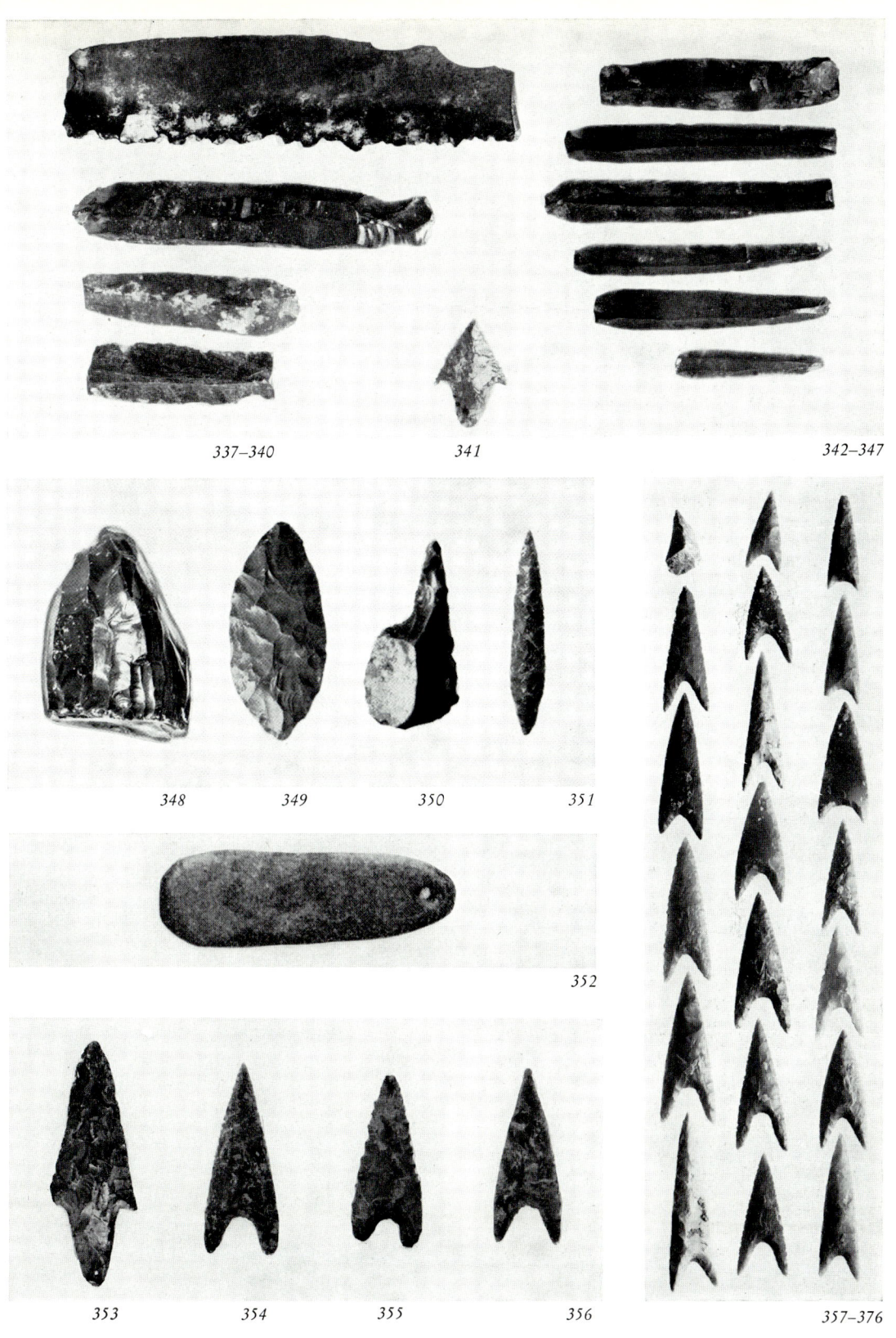

337–340   341   342–347

348   349   350   351

352

353   354   355   356   357–376

Stone and obsidian tools, arrowheads; Greek mainland, Leukas and the Cyclades

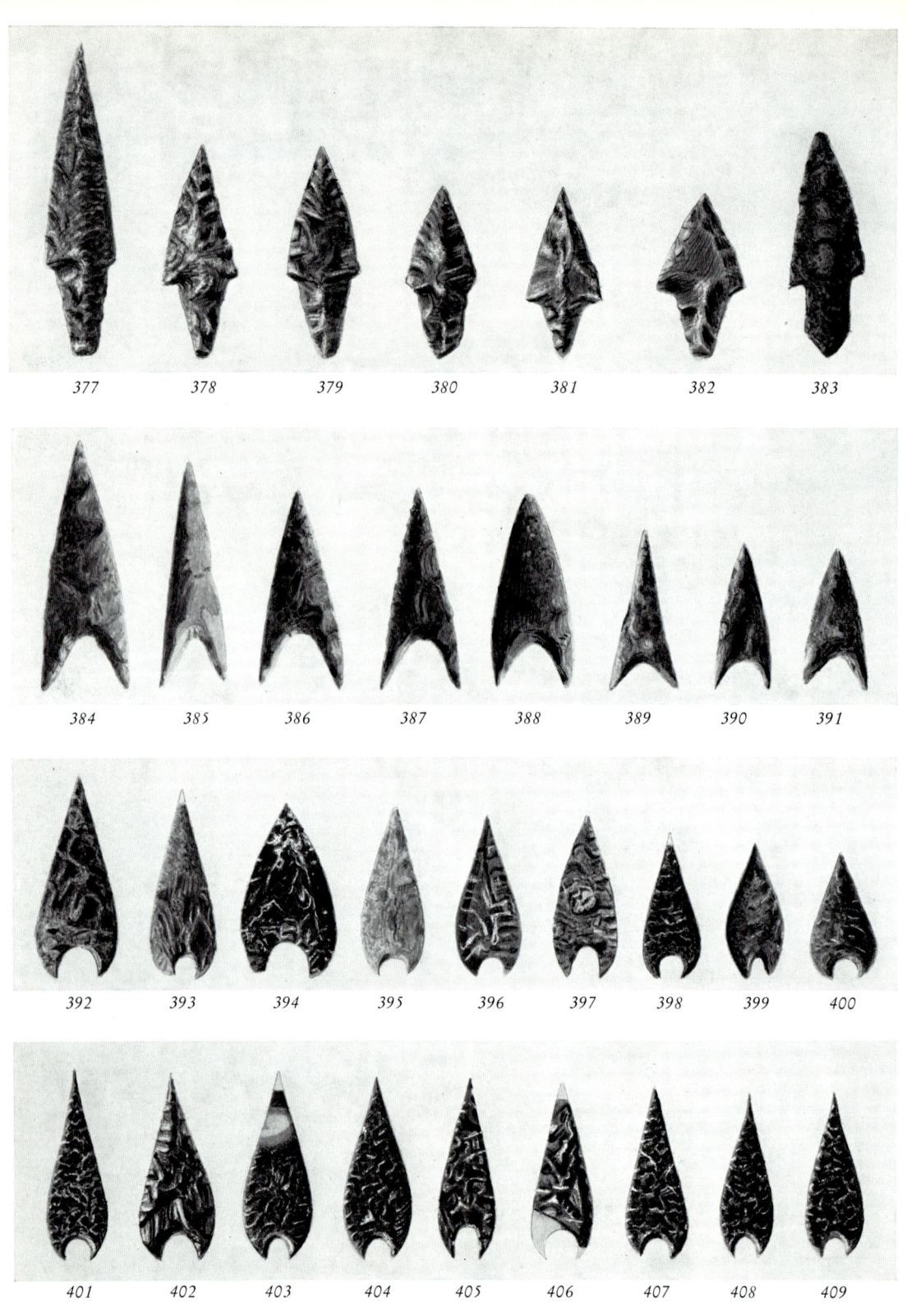

Arrowheads of flint and obsidian

410: p. 48, Fig. 20; *411.412:* p. 47, Fig. 19

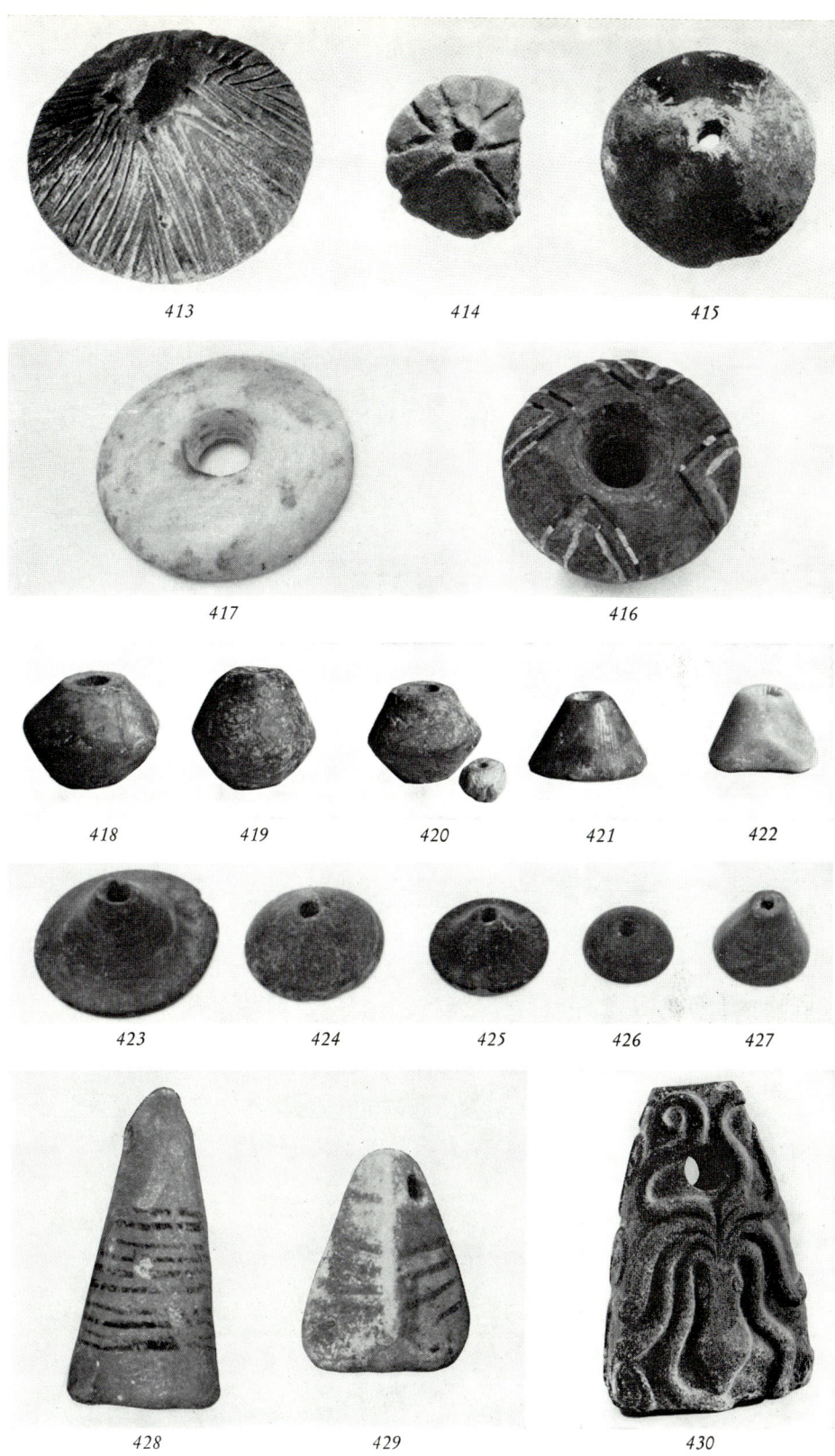

Spindle whorls, loom-weights and anchor stone (?)

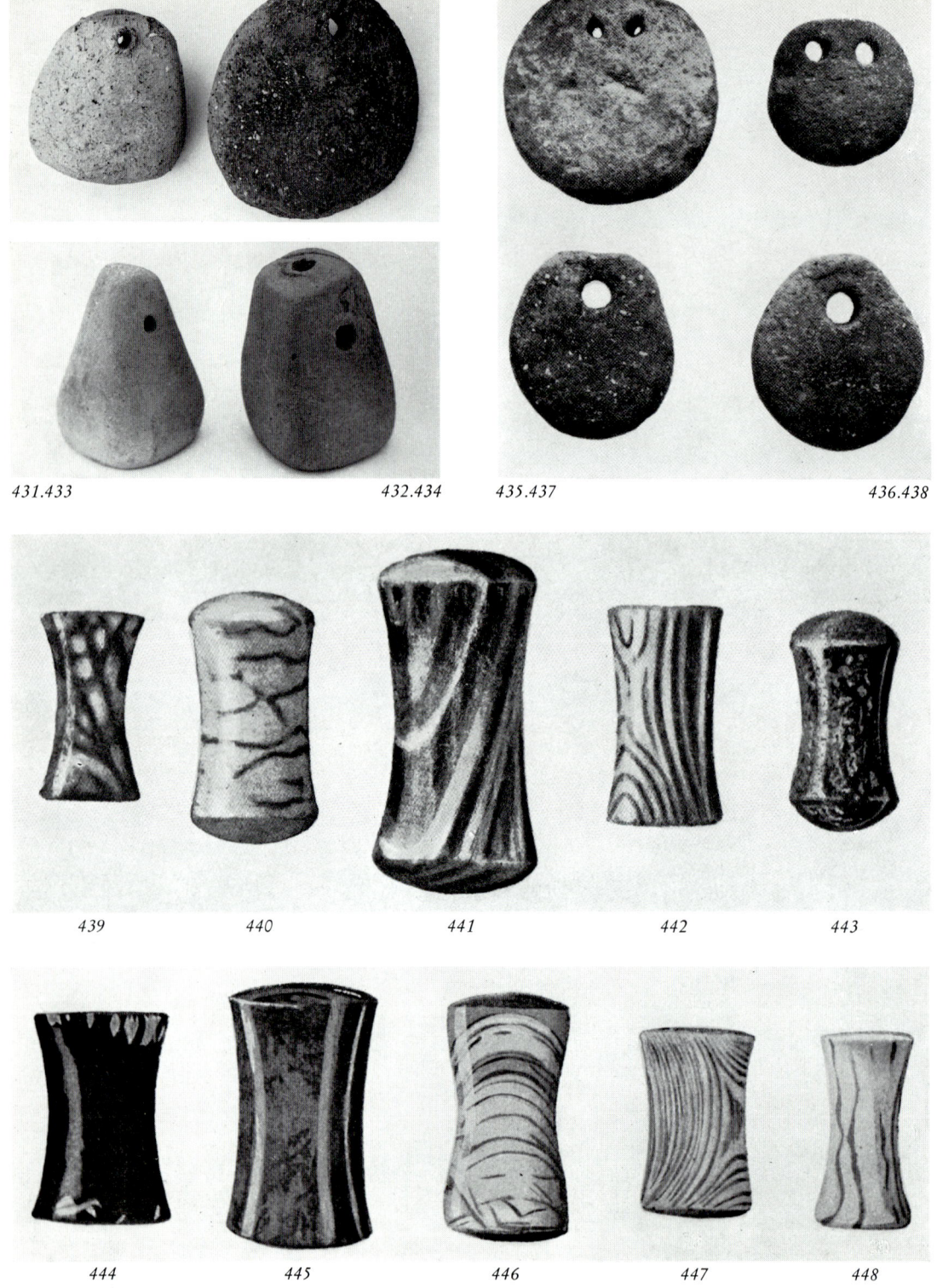

431.433   432.434   435.437   436.438

439   440   441   442   443

444   445   446   447   448

Clay loom-weights and marble pestles

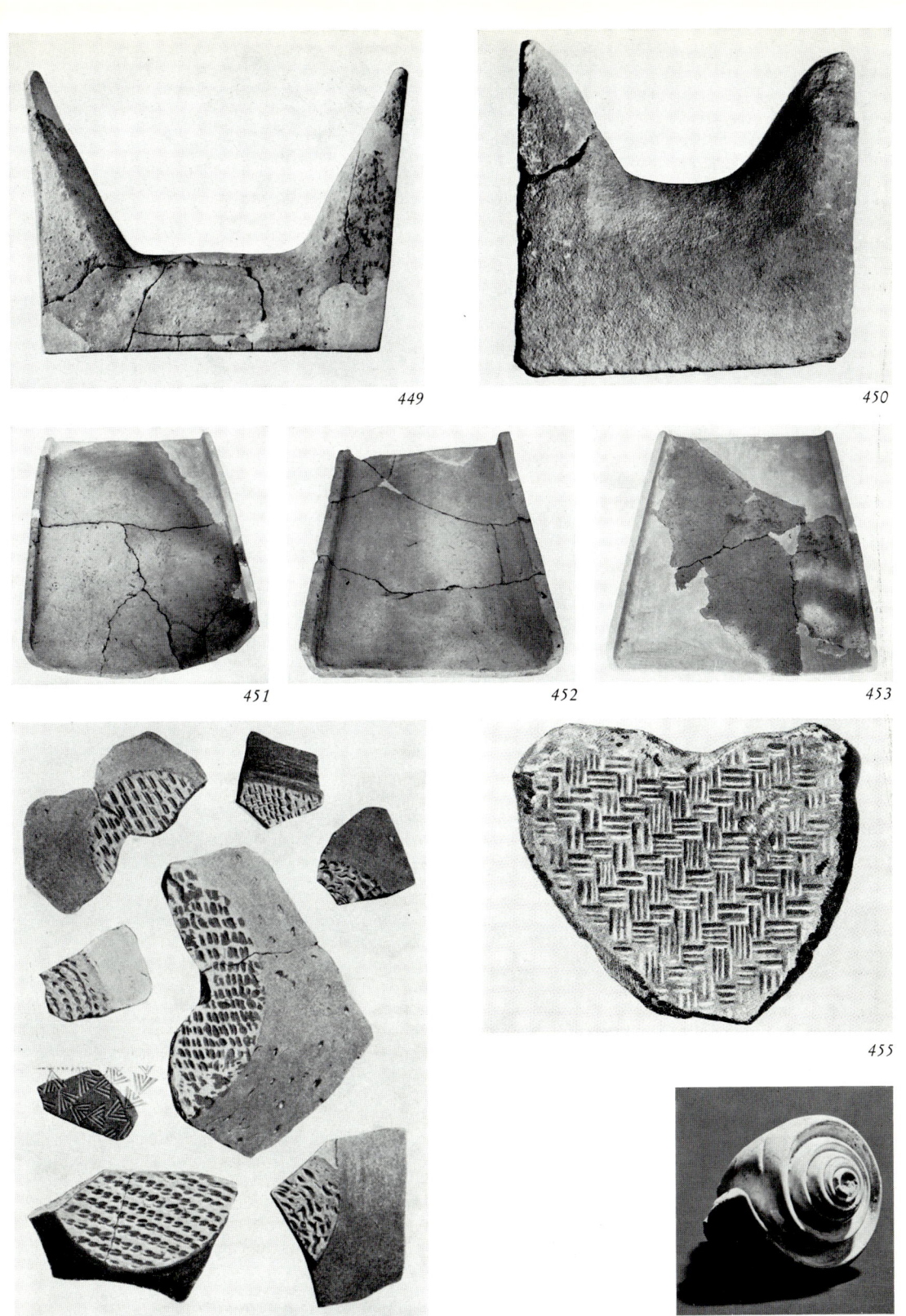

449
450
451
452
453
454a–h
455
456

Votive horns, roof tiles, mat impressions and clay spiral

458

459

460

461a

461b

Creto-
Mycenaean
moulds
and matrices

457: p. 259

Creto-Mycenaean moulds and matrices

457

462a

462b

463

464

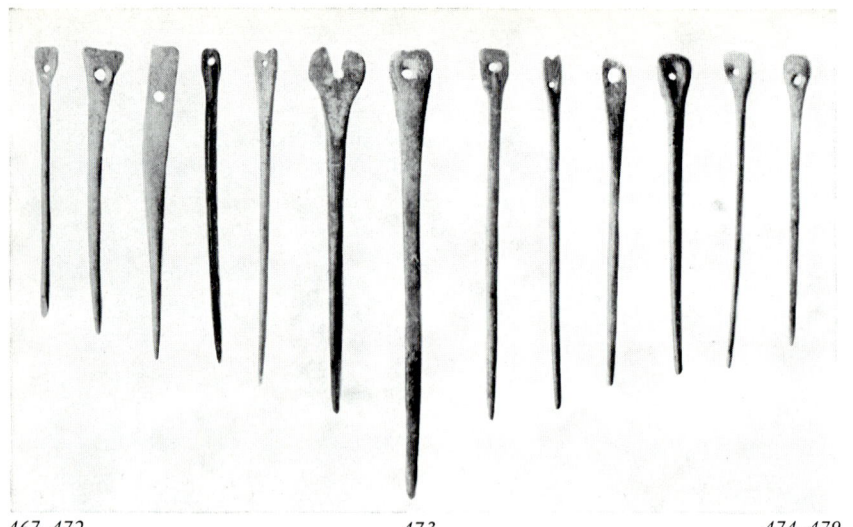
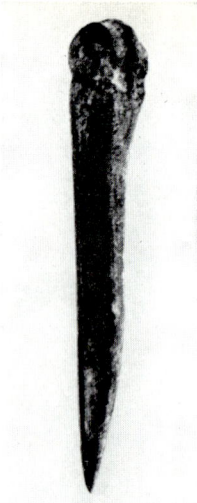

467–472　　　　　　　473　　　　　　474–479　　465

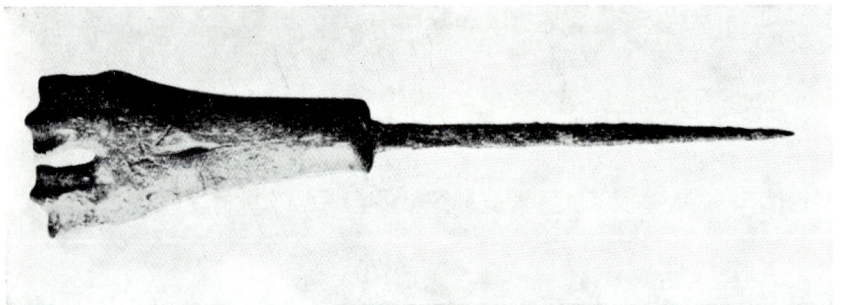
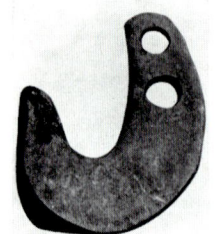

480

466

481

482–486

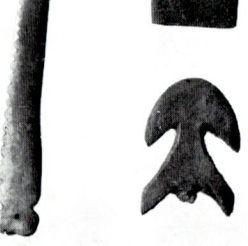

487

488–492

Bone implements;
pre-ceramic
Stone Age
and Early
Bronze Age

Bone, horn and ivory implements; Stone Age, Early and Late Bronze Age

493–498

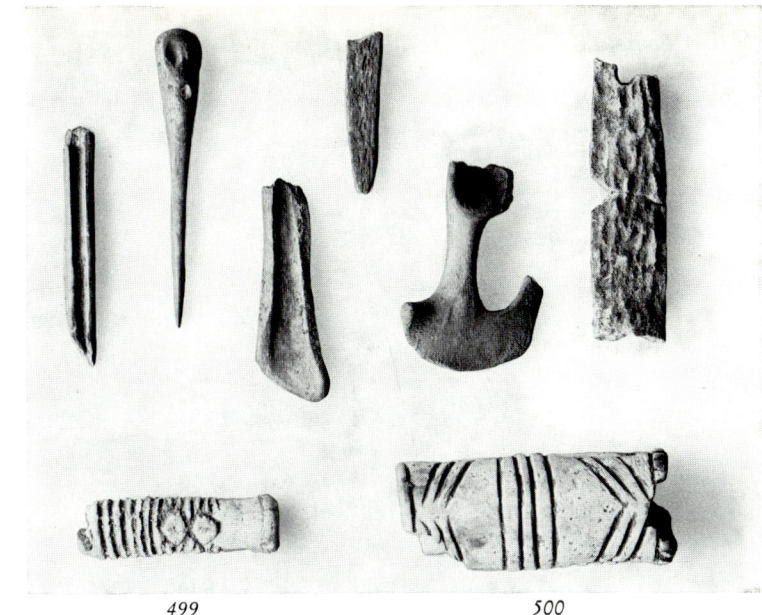

499 500

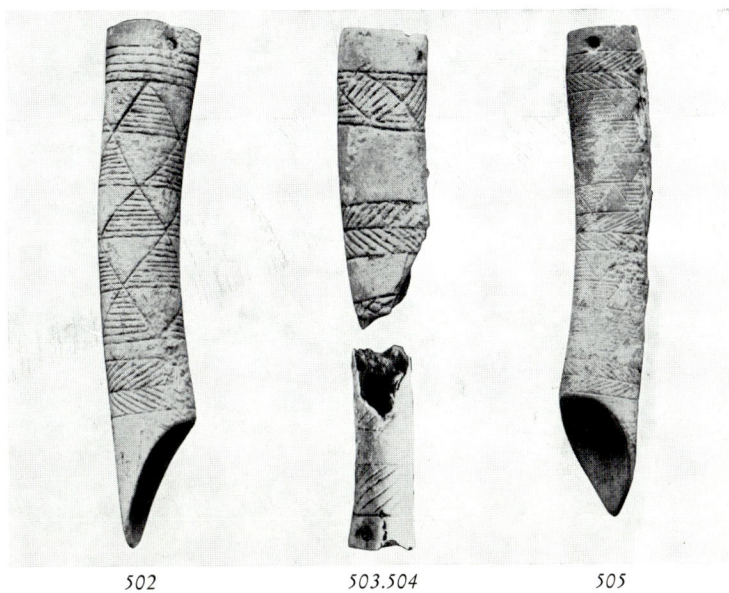

501a.b   502   503.504   505

506

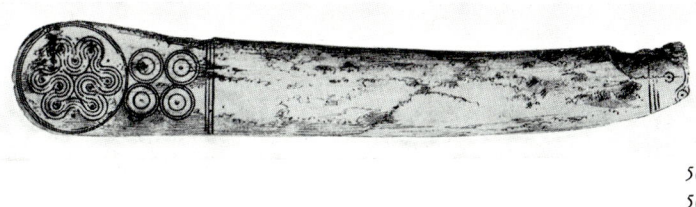

507
508

261

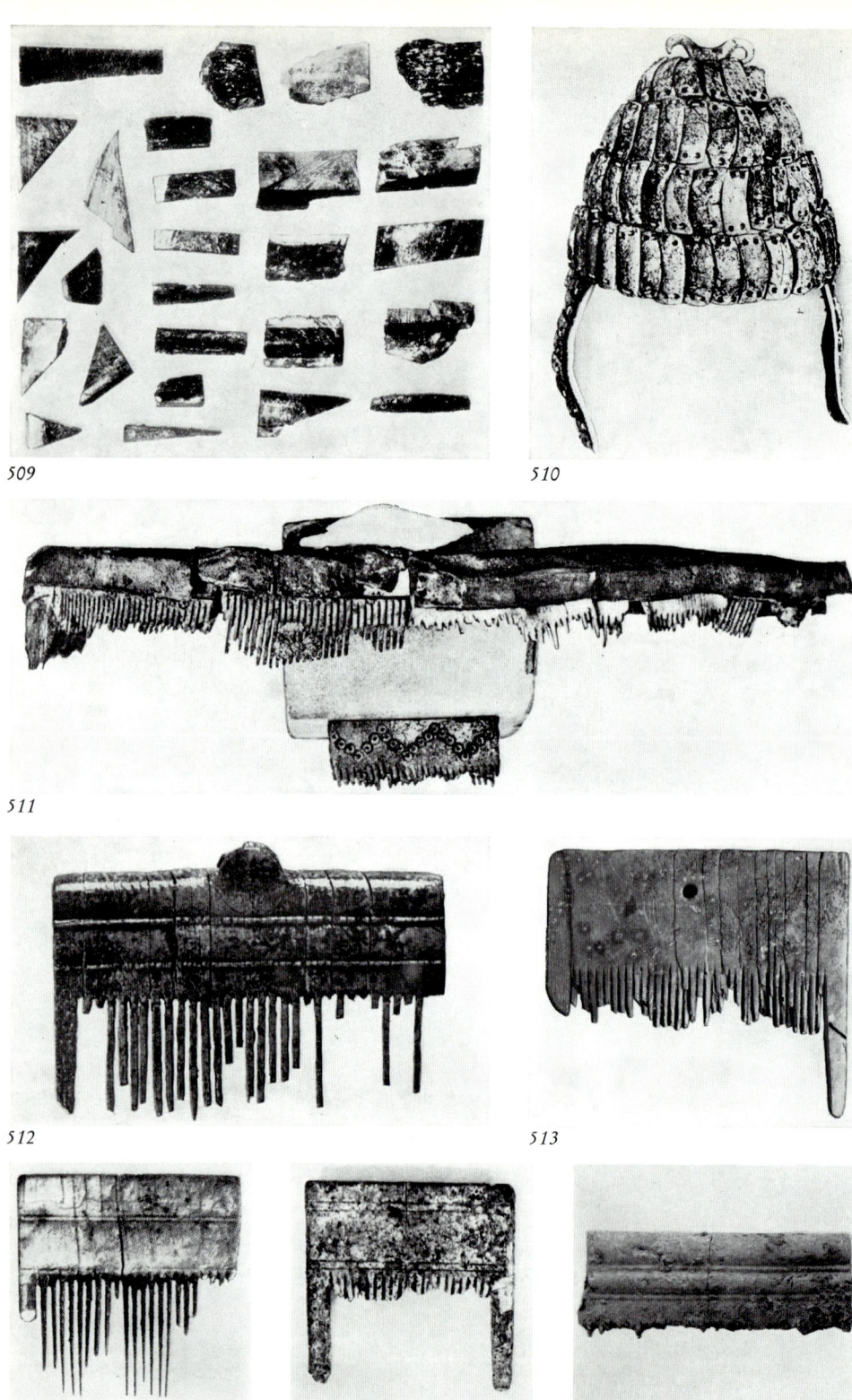

509 510

511

512 513

514 515 516

Ivory laminae, boar's tusk helmet and combs 517: p. 51, Fig. 21

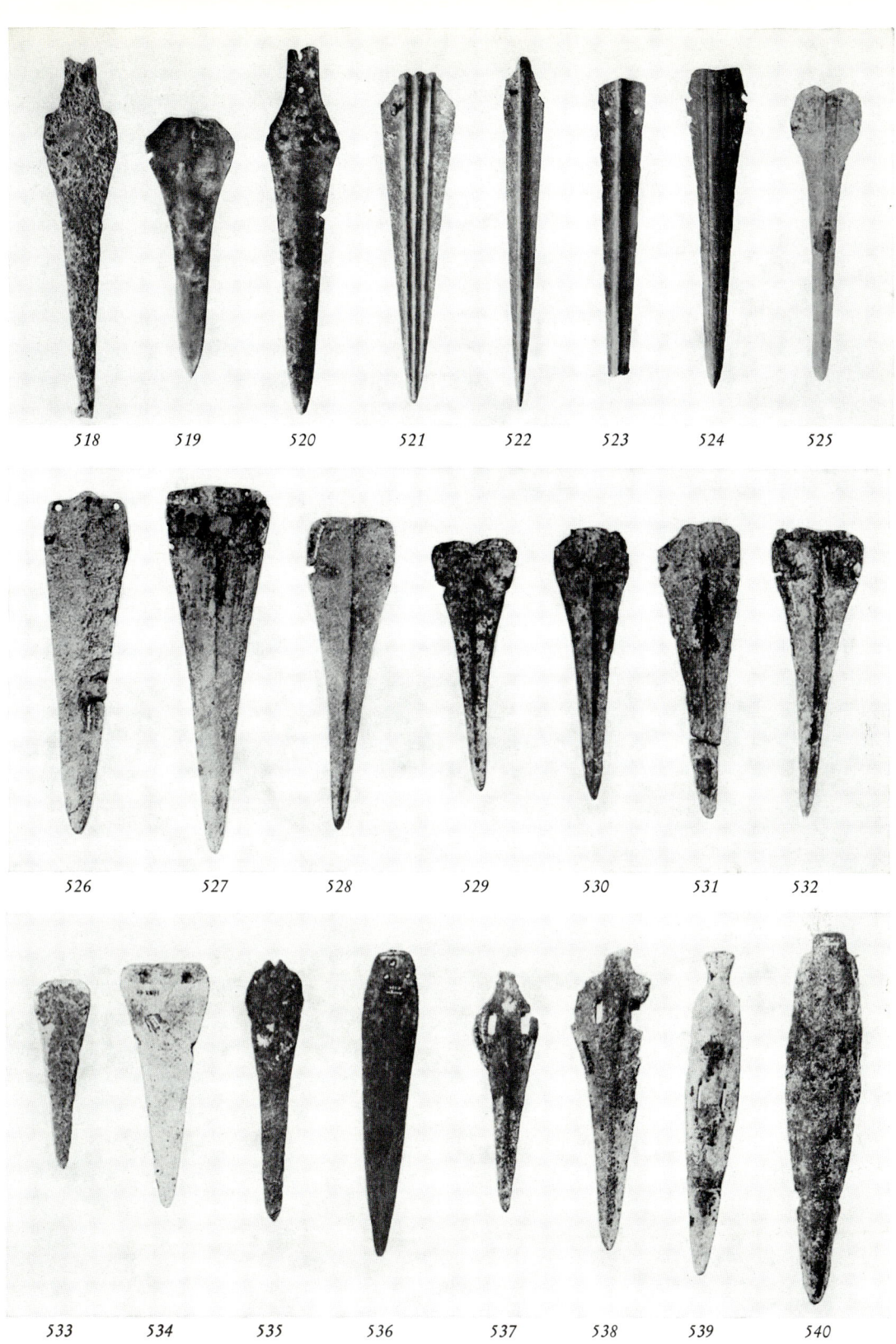

Early Bronze Age daggers

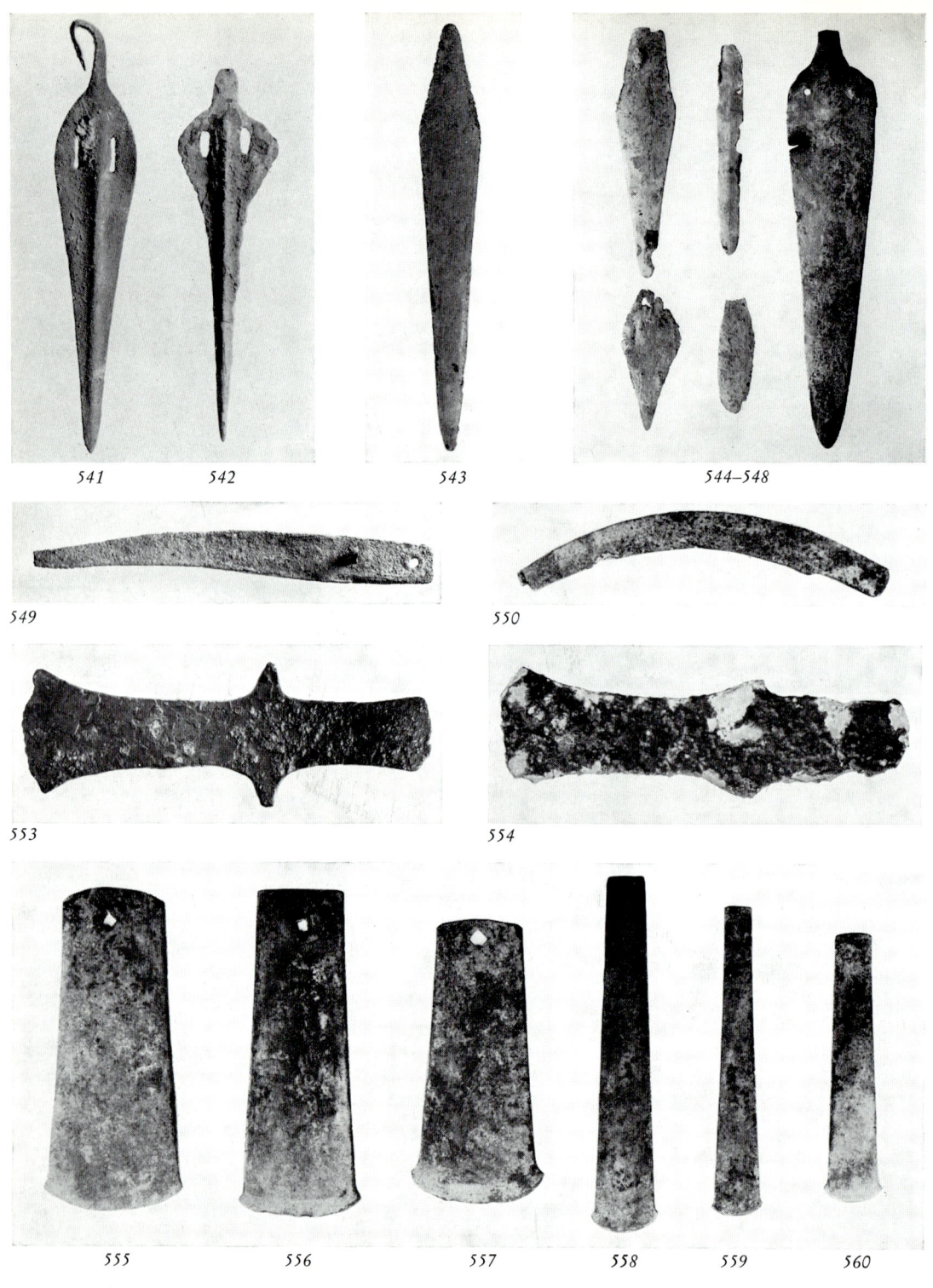

541   542   543   544–548

549   550

553   554

555   556   557   558   559   560

Daggers, knives and axes   551.552.561–563: p. 53, Fig. 22

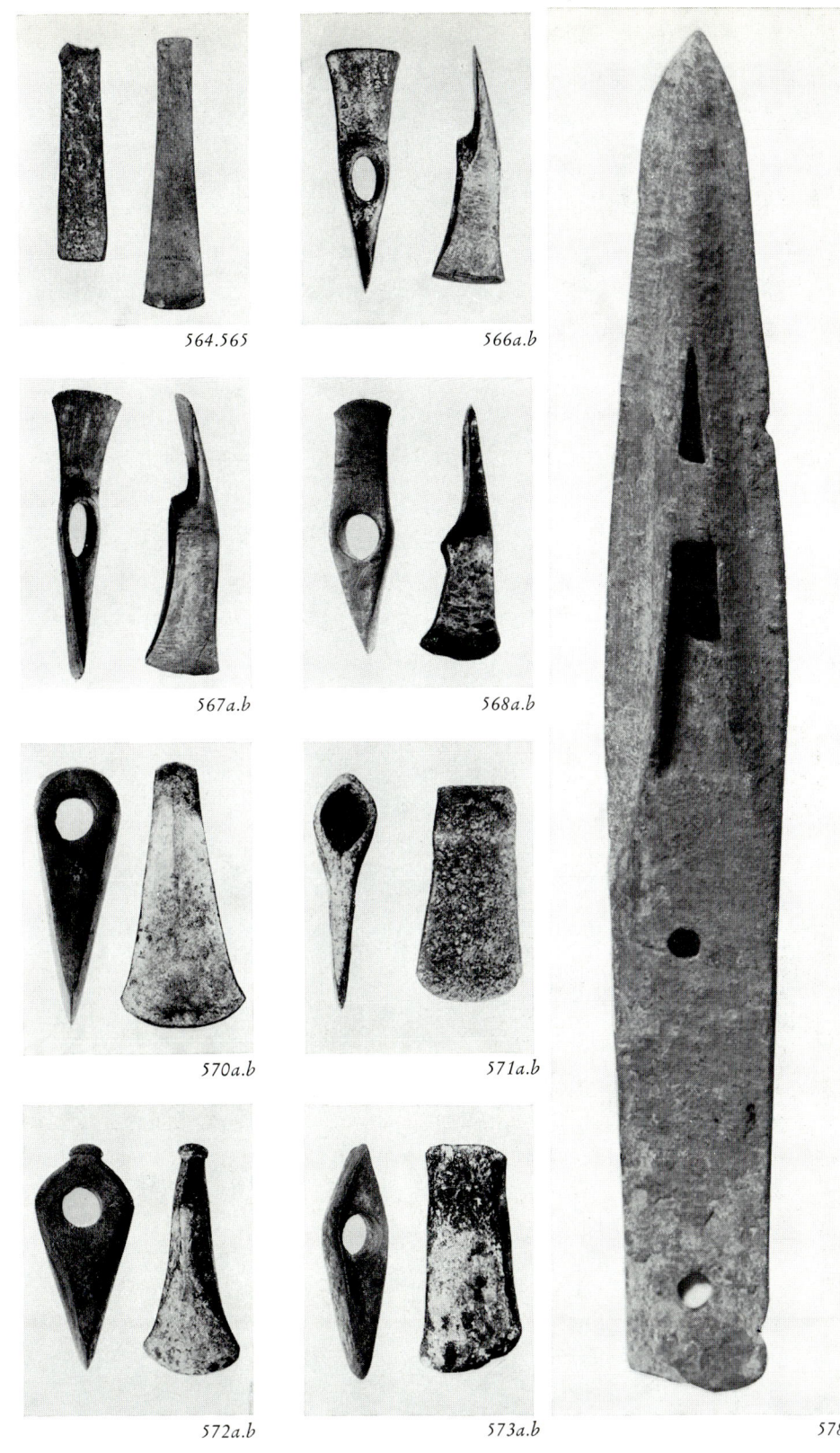

564.565
566a.b
567a.b
568a.b
570a.b
571a.b
572a.b
573a.b
578

569a.b.574a.b: p. 53, Fig. 22; 575–577: p. 266

Flat axes, picks, shaft-hole axes, and spearhead

265

575

576

577a.b

Early Bronze Age double axes   578: p. 265

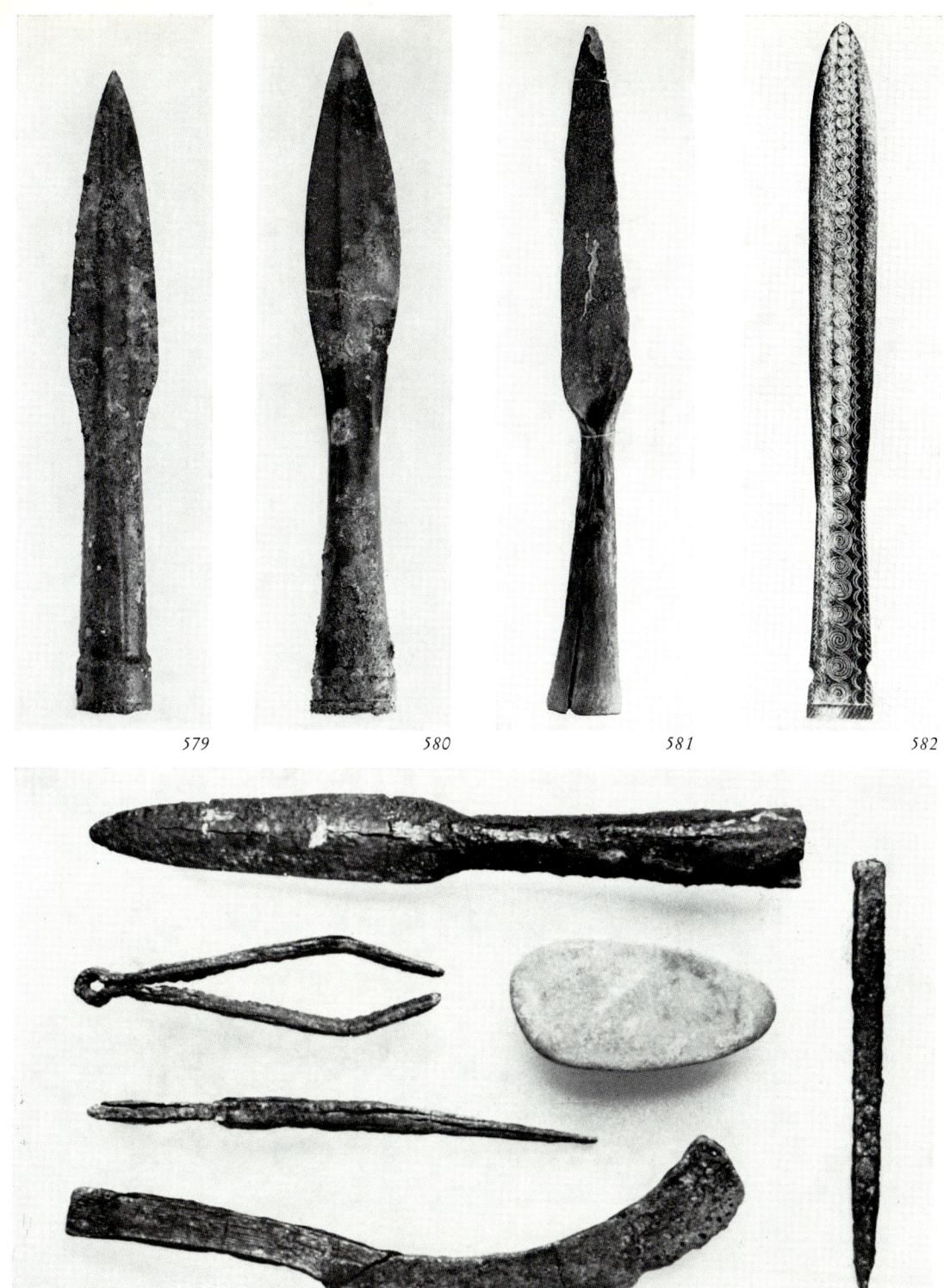

579   580   581   582

583–588

Minoan and Mycenaean spearheads, bronze implements and whetstone

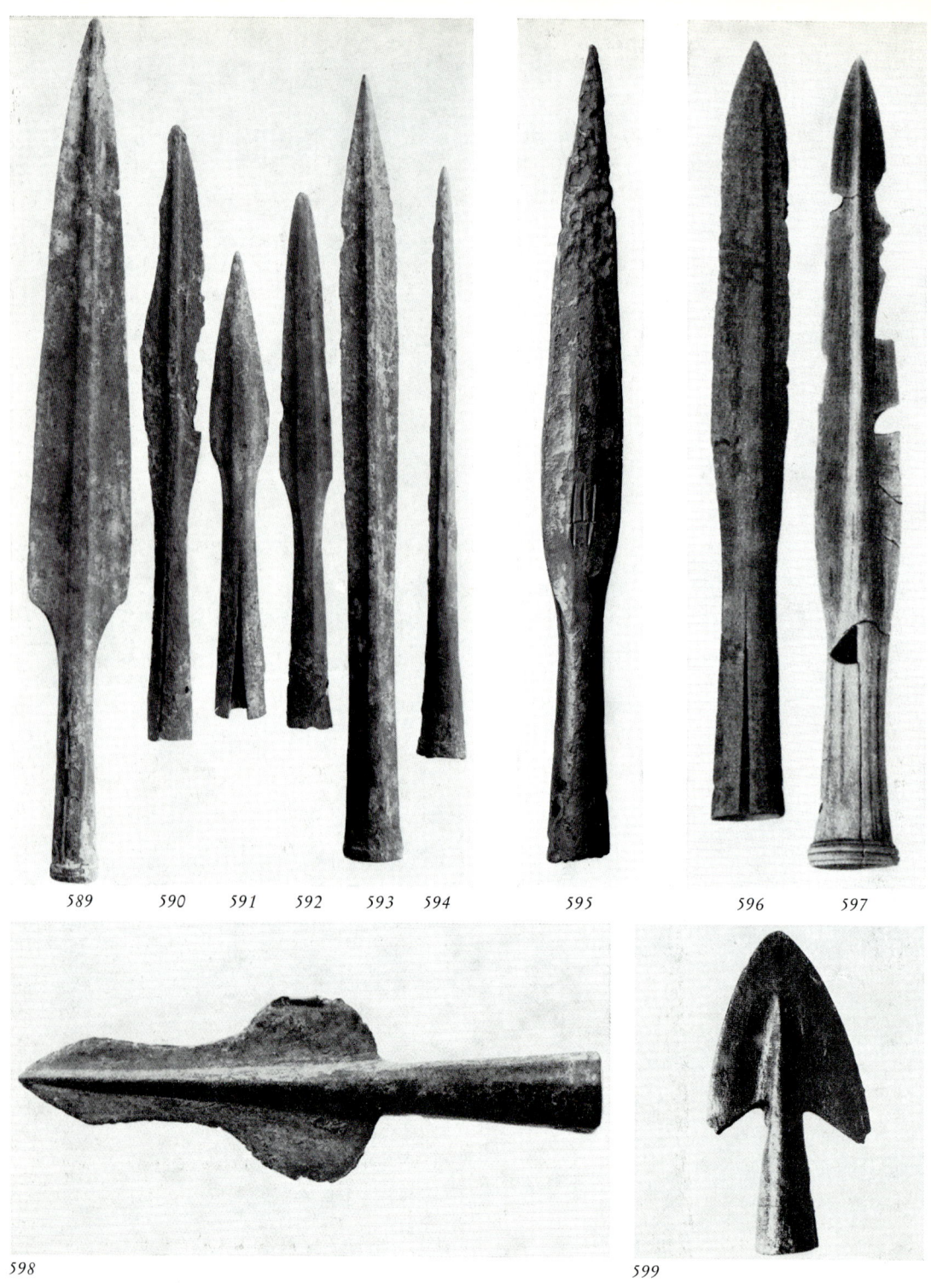

Mycenaean lanceheads, spearheads and arrowheads

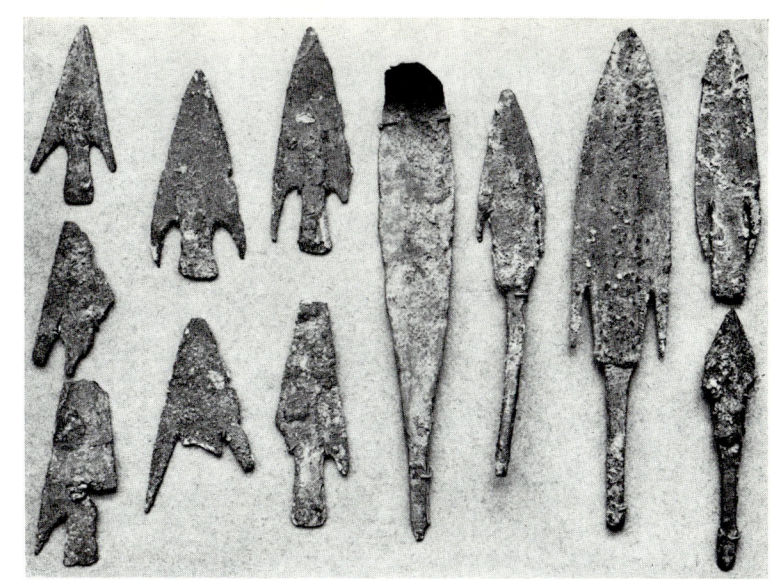

600–611

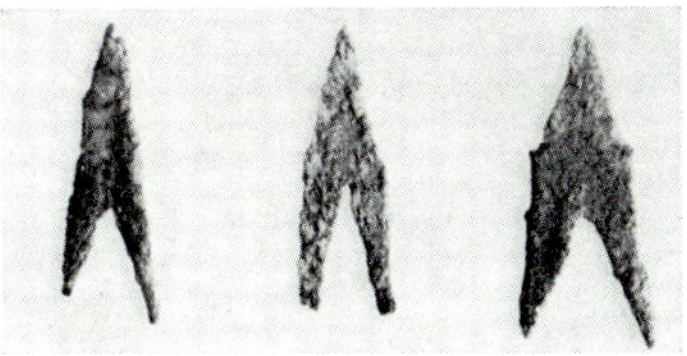

612 613 614 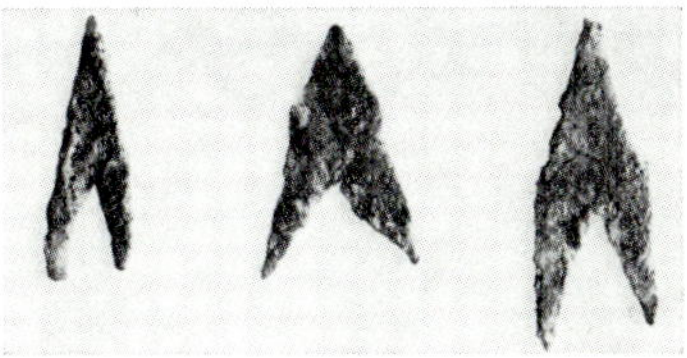   615 616 617 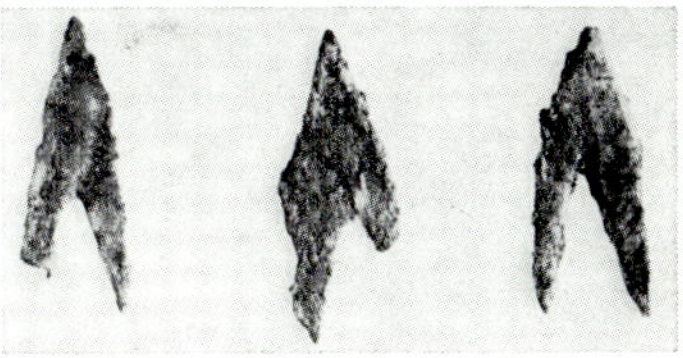   618 619 620

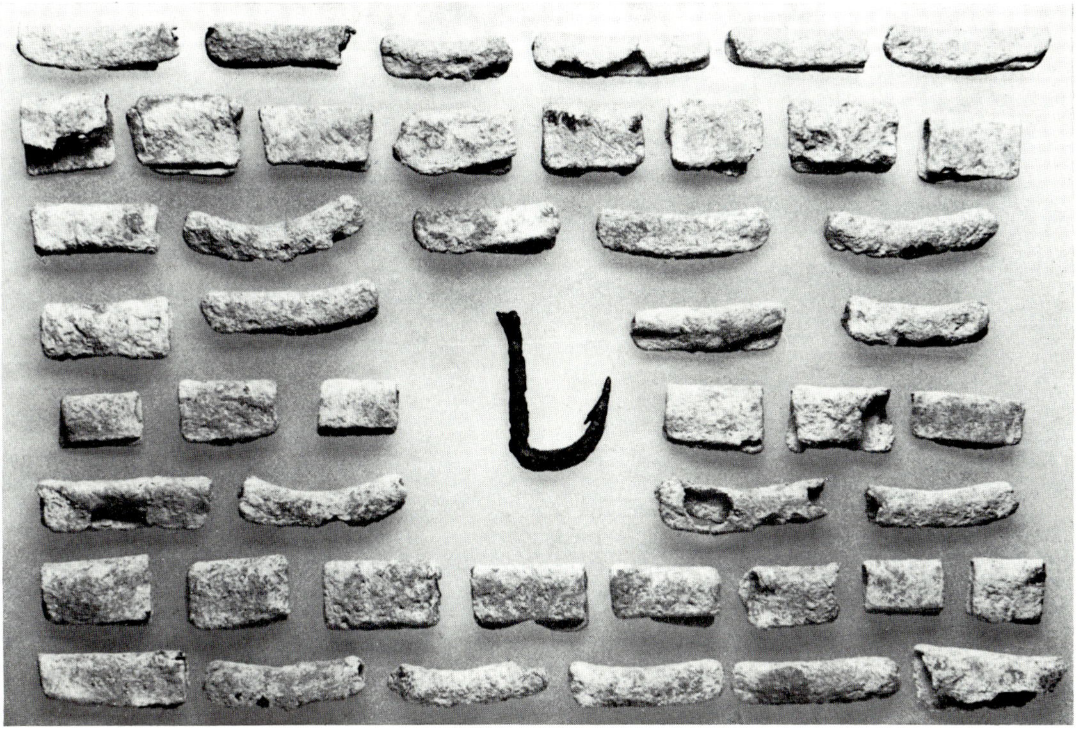

621.622

Mycenaean arrowheads. Fish-hooks and plummets from Perati, Attica

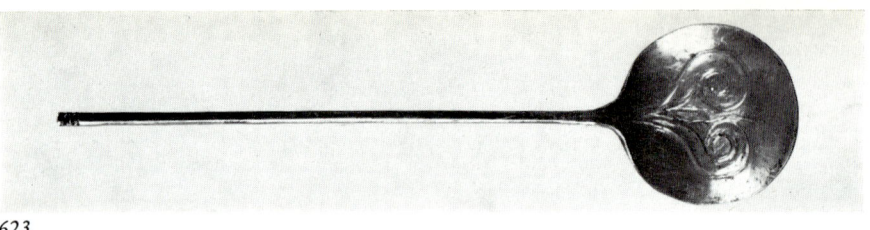

623

624

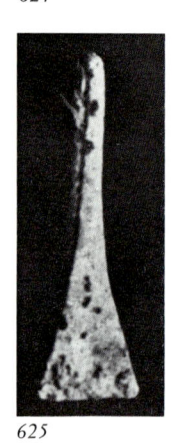

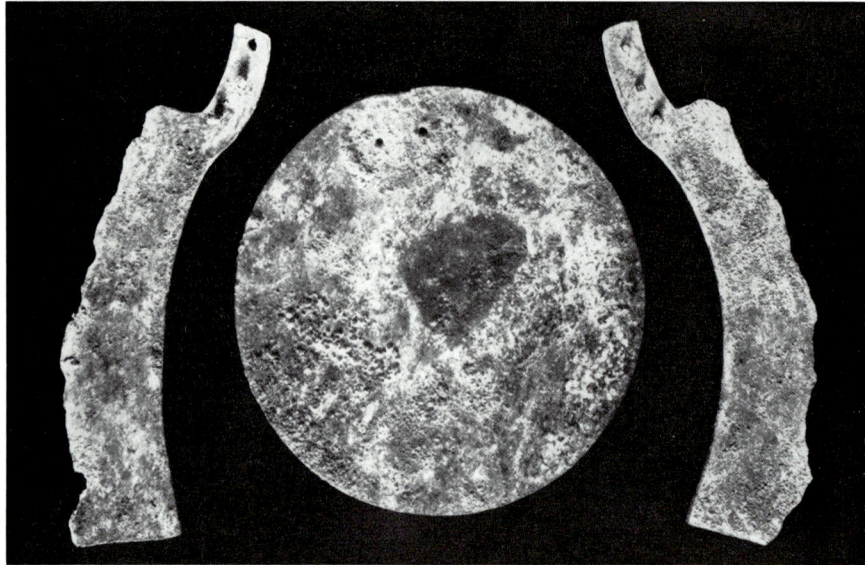

627   *626*   *628*   *625*

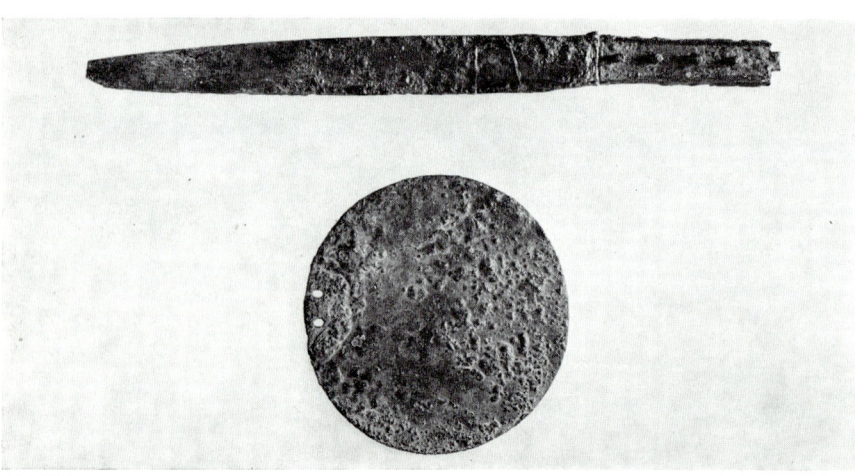

629.630

631

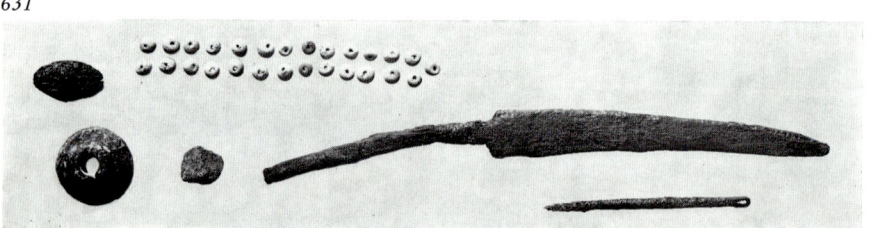

Silver spoon, bronze mirror, copper and bronze implements. Crete, Kythera and Mycenaean mainland

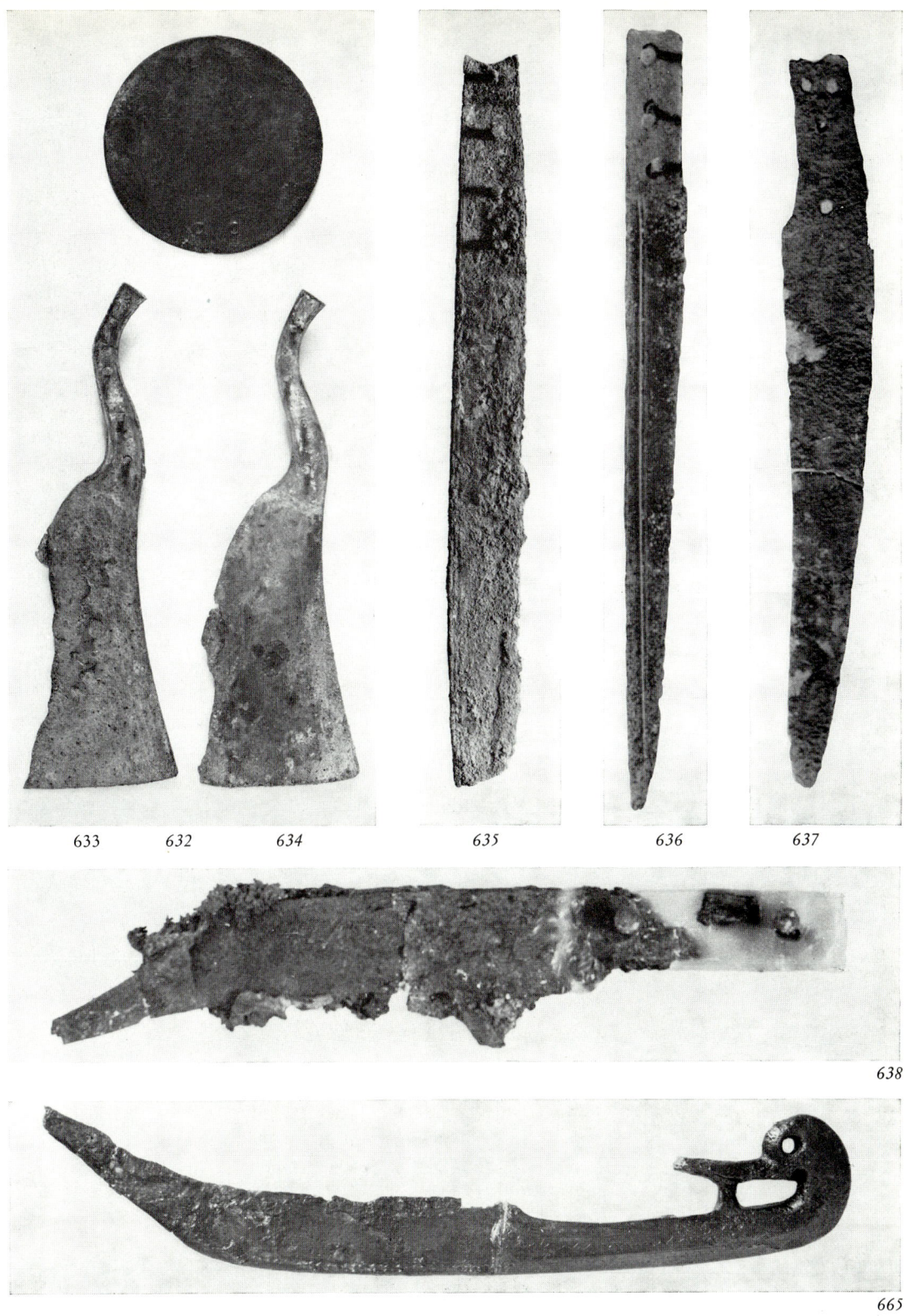

633   632   634   635   636   637

638

665

639–664: p. 55, Fig. 23   Copper, bronze and iron implements. Crete and Mycenaean mainland

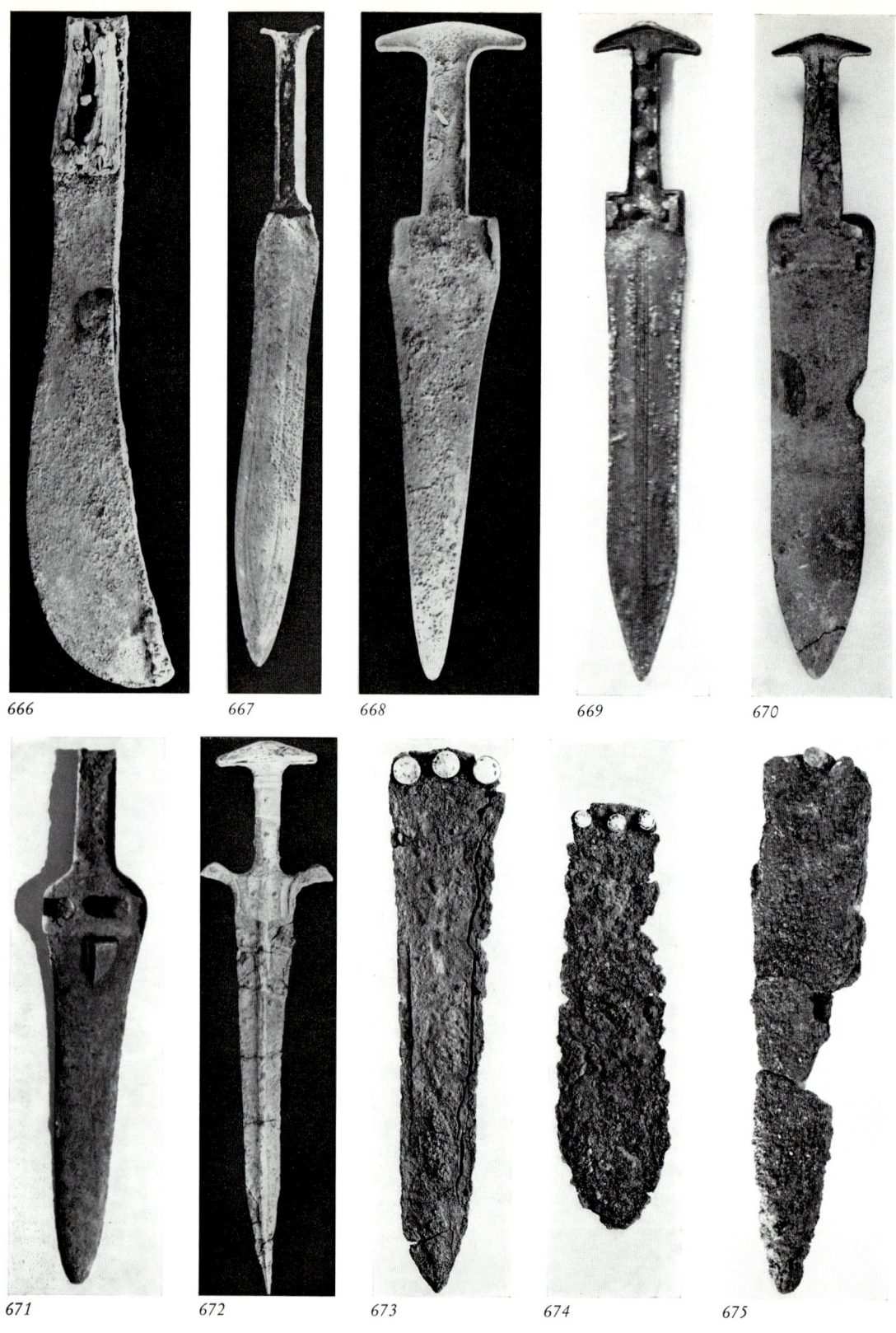

666   667   668   669   670

671   672   673   674   675

Minoan and Mycenaean daggers

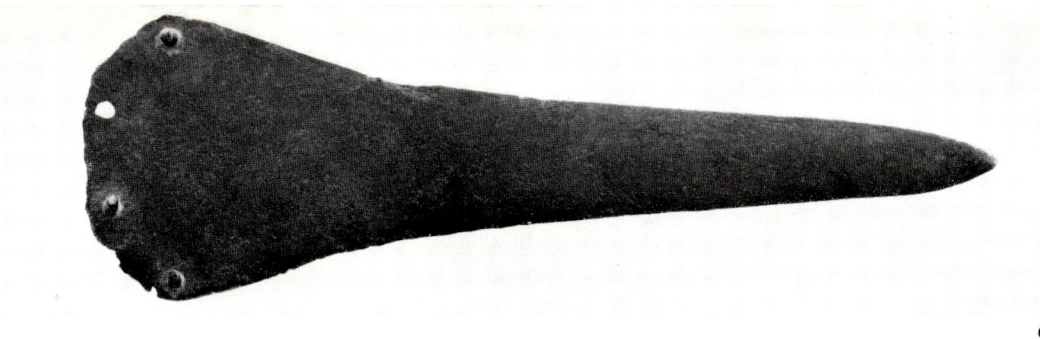

680

681

682

683

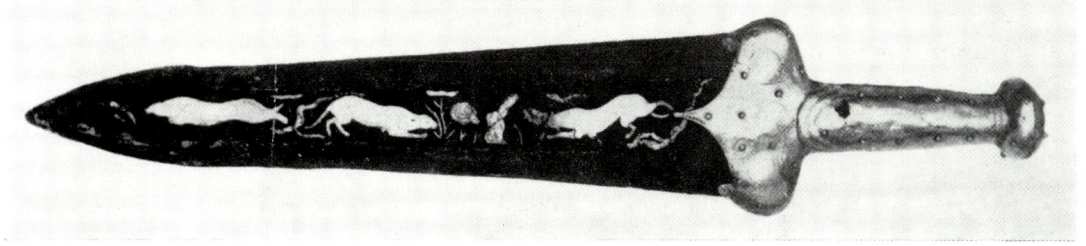

684

676–679: p. 57, Fig. 24   Mycenaean daggers

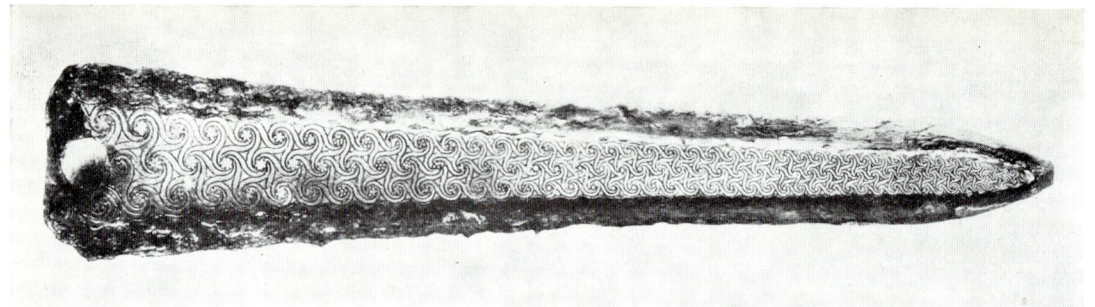

685

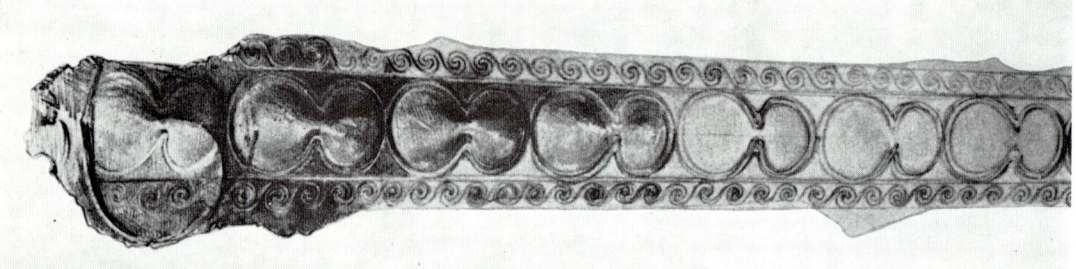

686

687

688   689   690   691

Daggers and swords

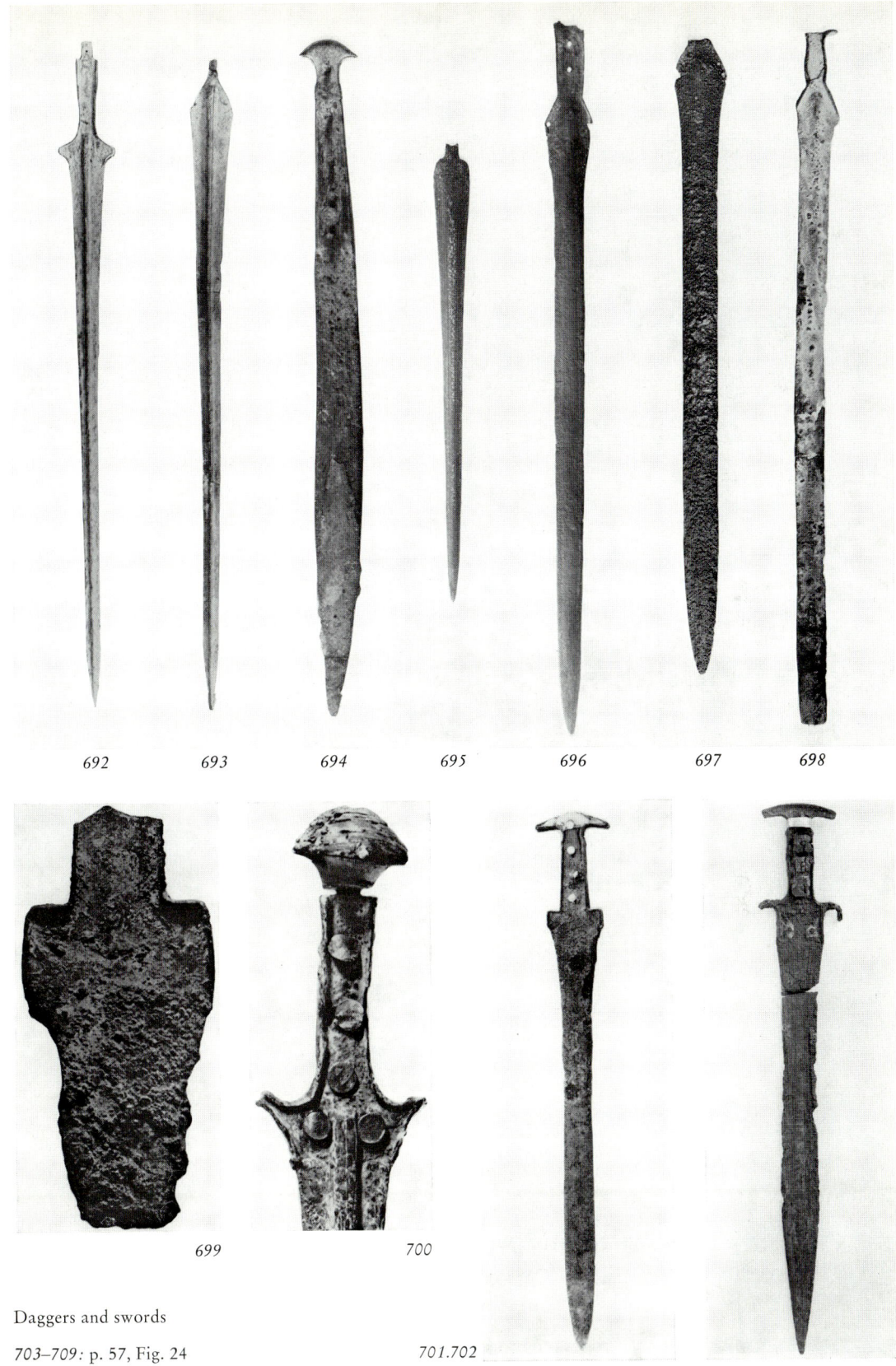

Daggers and swords

703–709: p. 57, Fig. 24

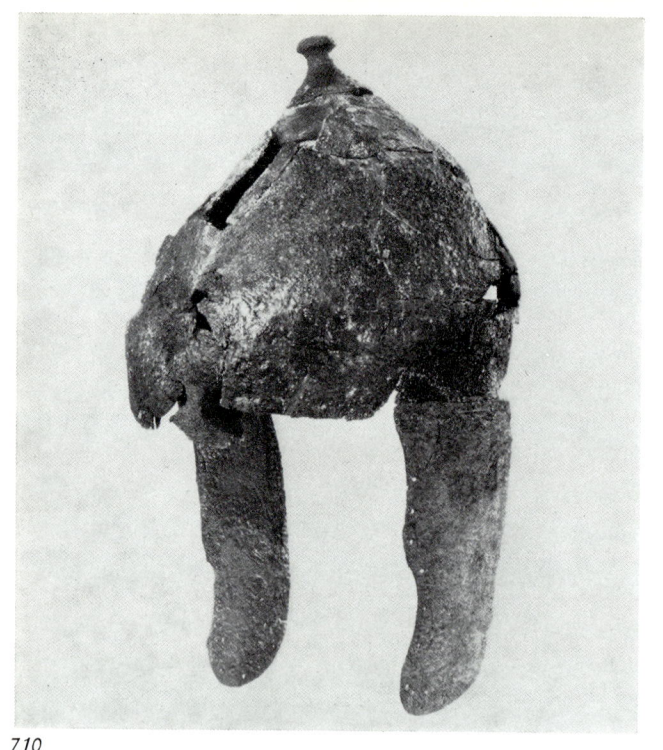

710

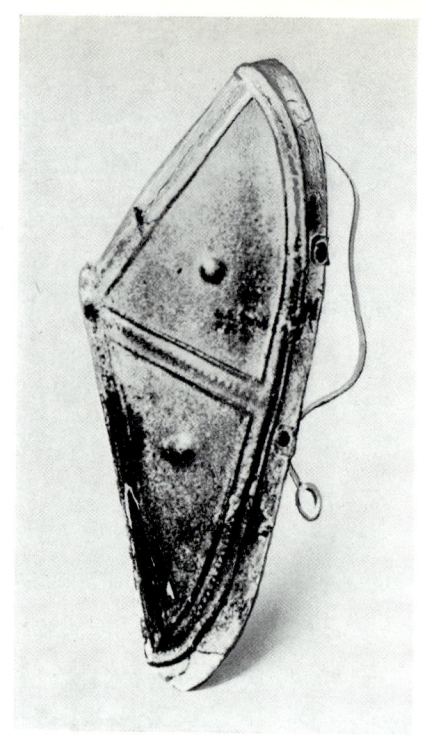

711

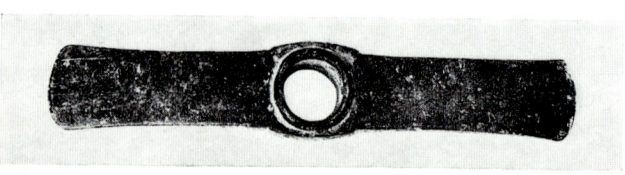

713

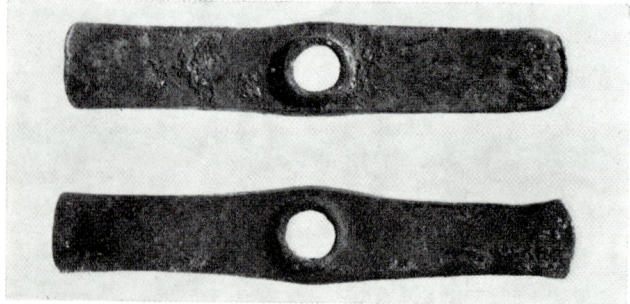

714a.715a

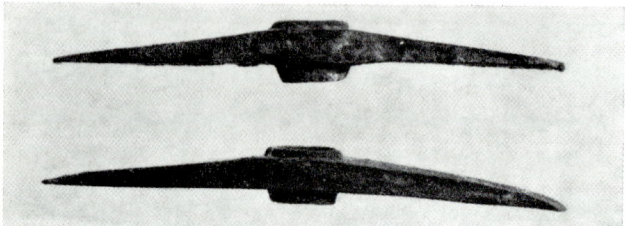

714b.715b

pp. 276 and 277:
Creto-Mycenaean defensive armour;
bronze double adzes and double axes

716.717: p. 59, Fig. 25

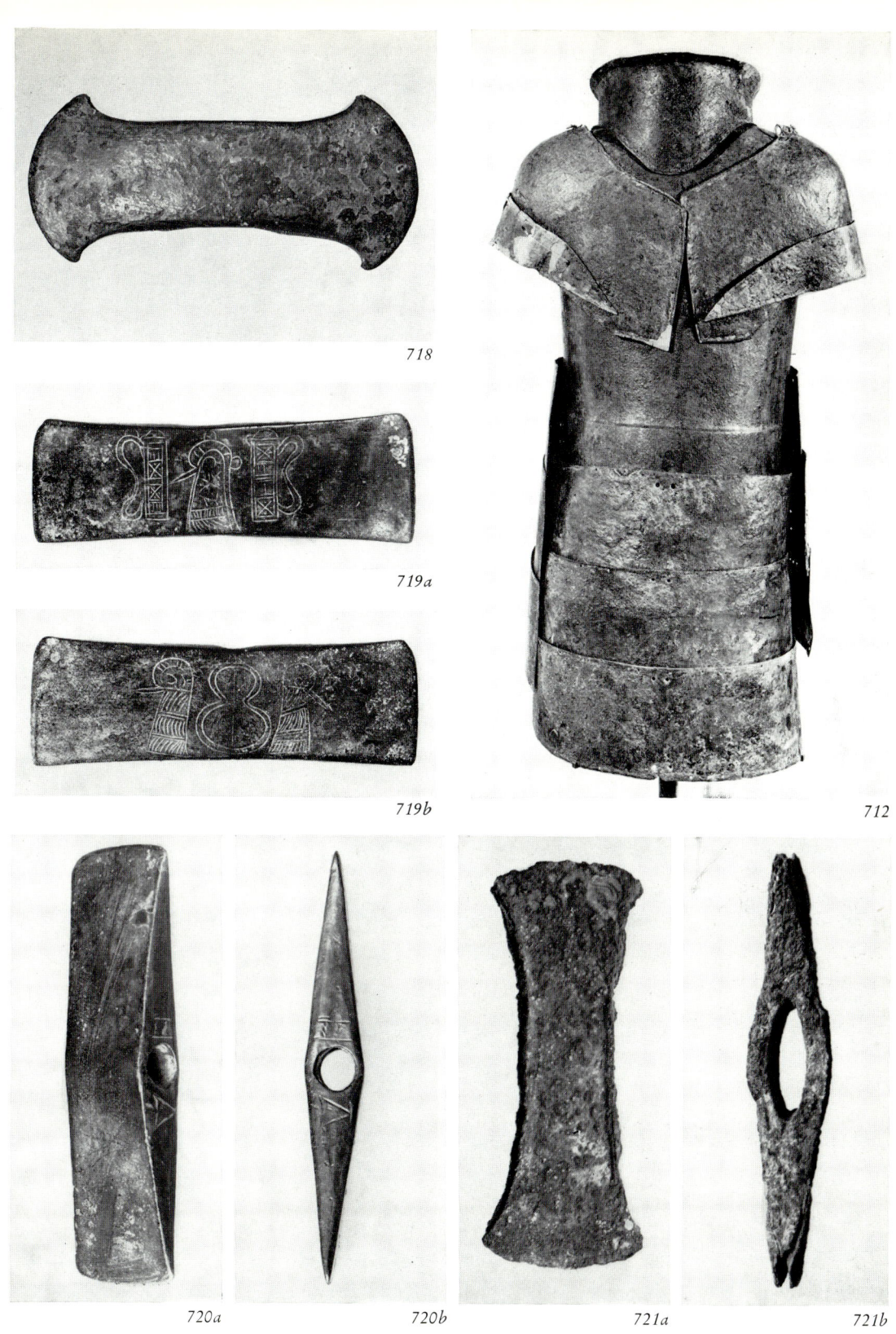

718

719a

719b

712

720a 720b 721a 721b

277

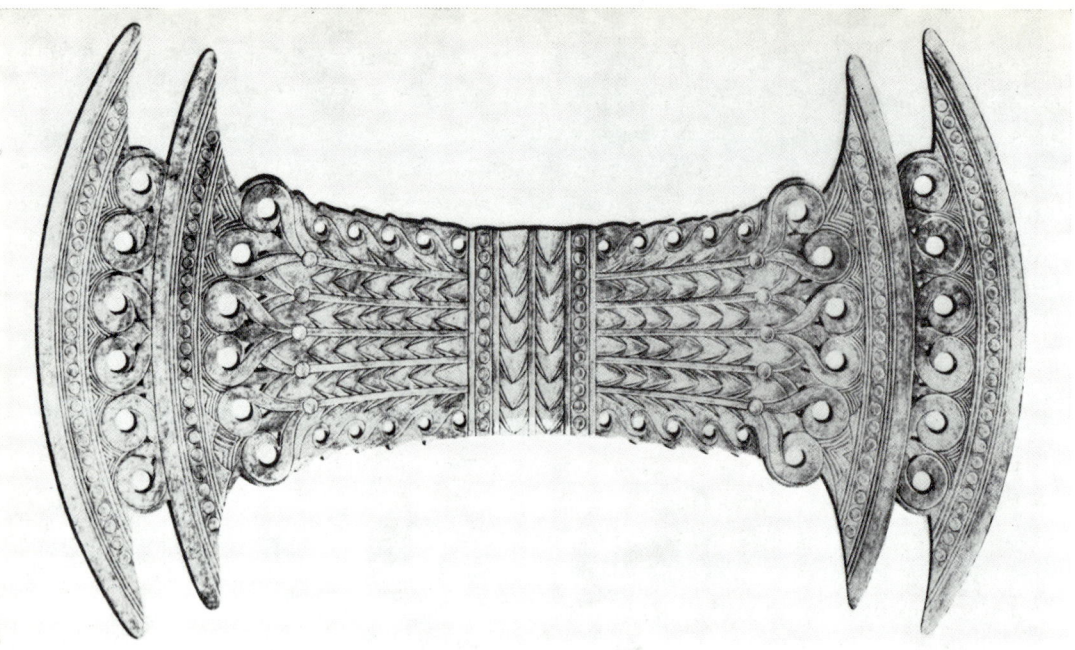

722

Bronze double axes, few of them for practical use

723–731

732–734

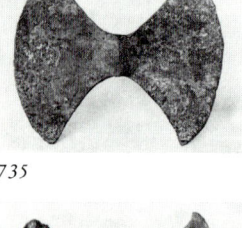

735

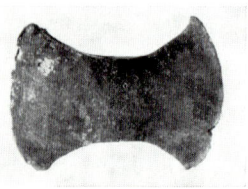

736

737

738a.b

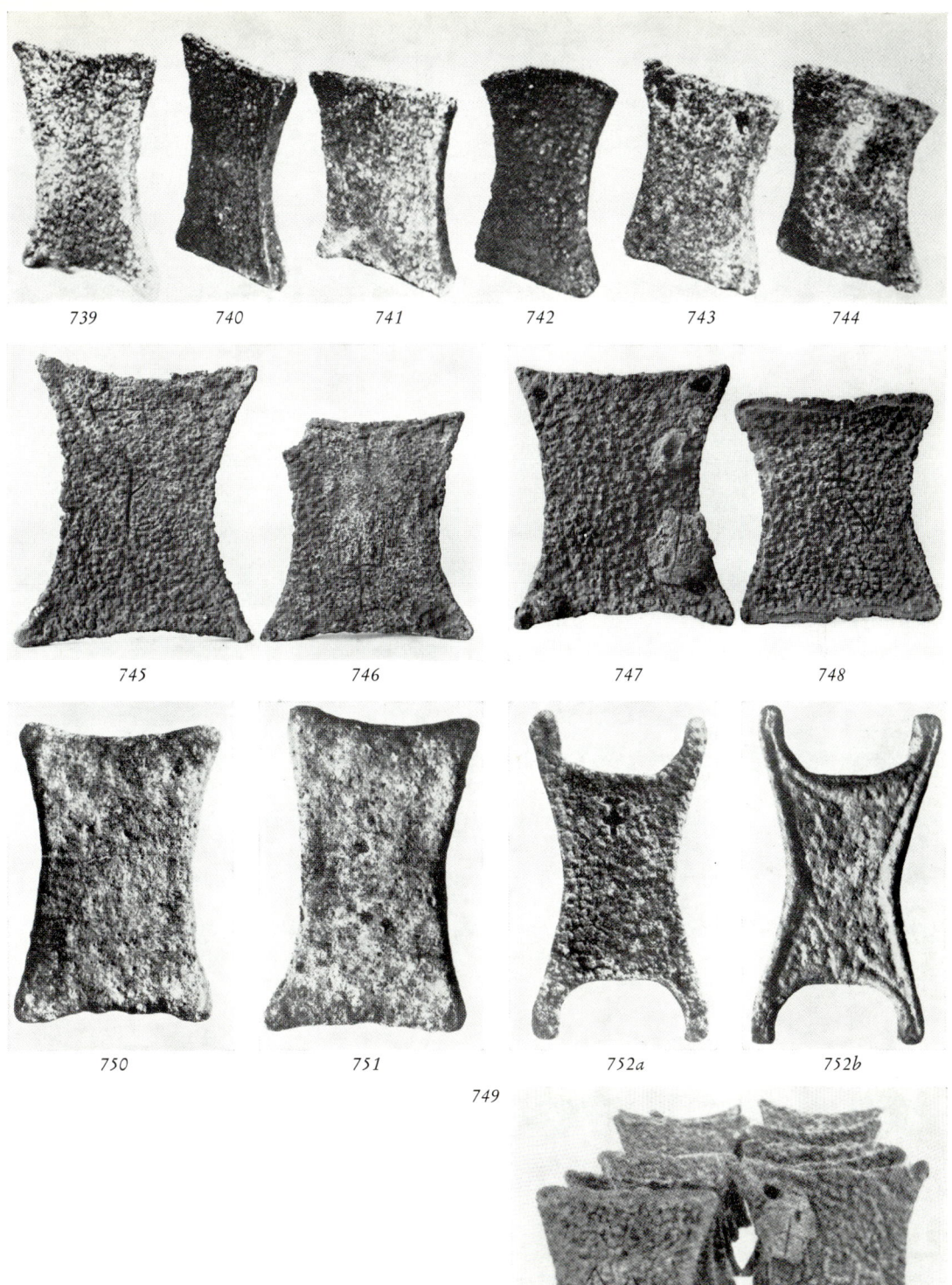

Copper ingots from Crete, Mycenae and Euboea, some with linear inscriptions; cf. distribution map p. 60, Fig. 26

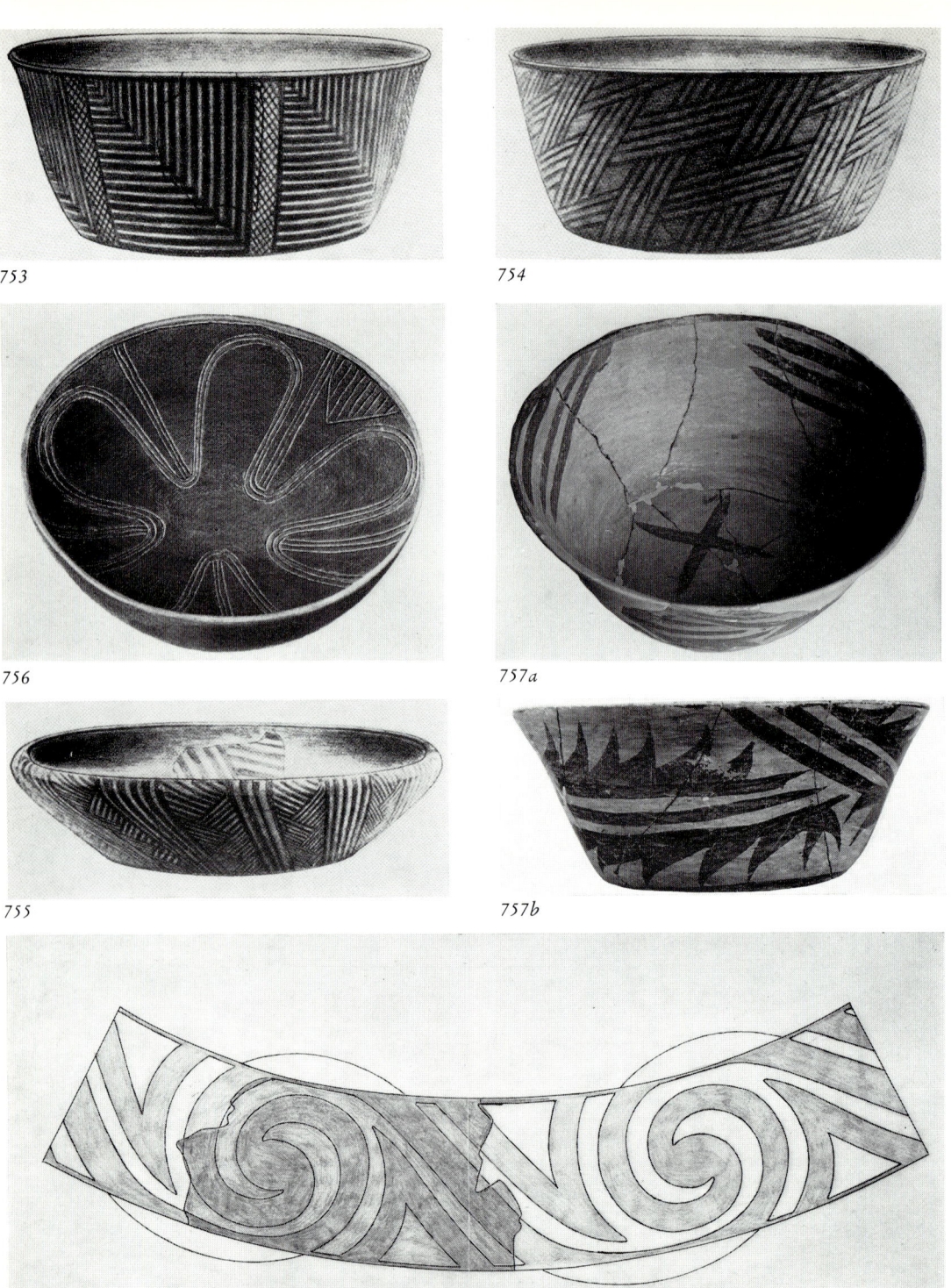

753
754
756
757a
755
757b
758

Neolithic pottery from Aegina, Leukas and Thessaly

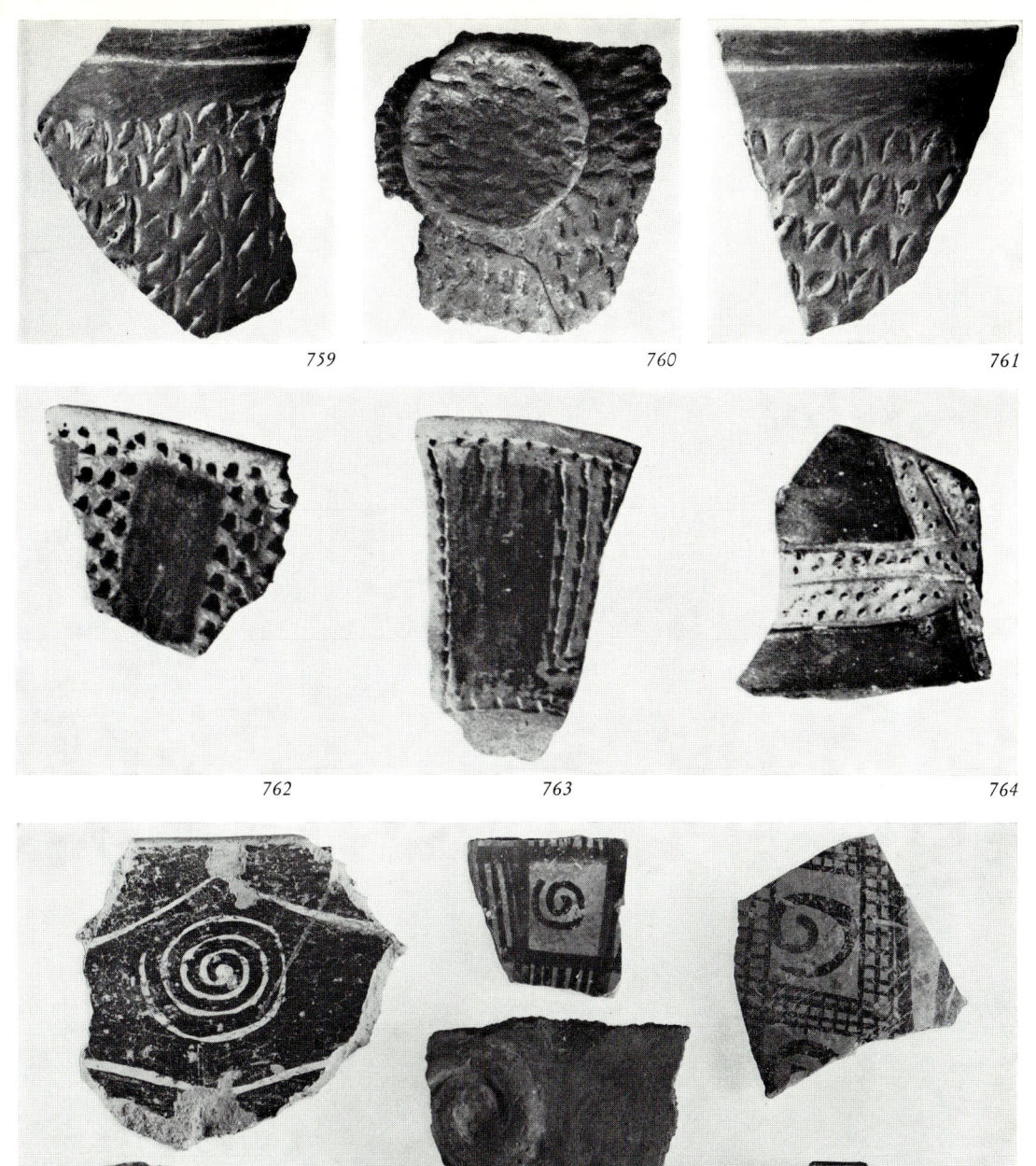

Neolithic pottery from Thessaly

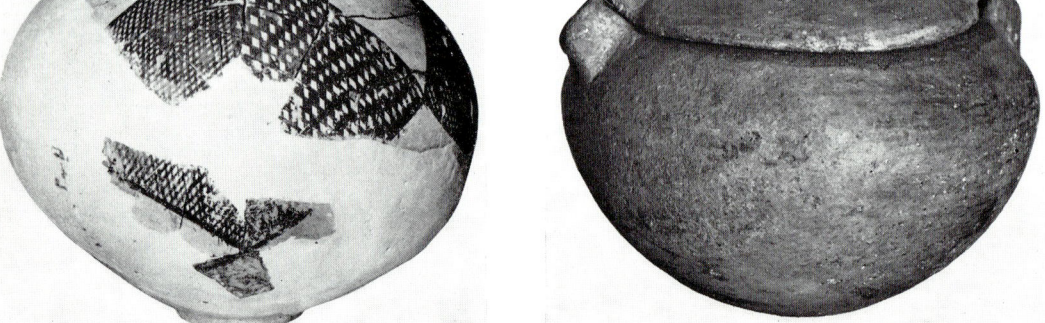

772

773

774

776

775

777

778

779

780

781

pp. 282 and 283:
Neolithic pottery
from Thessaly, Boeotia and Attica

782: Colour plate 1 after p. 8

783

784

785

786

788

787

791

pp. 284 and 285:
Neolithic and Early Bronze Age vessels
from Lemnos, Thrace, Thessaly, Boeotia,
the Poloponnese and Leukas

789

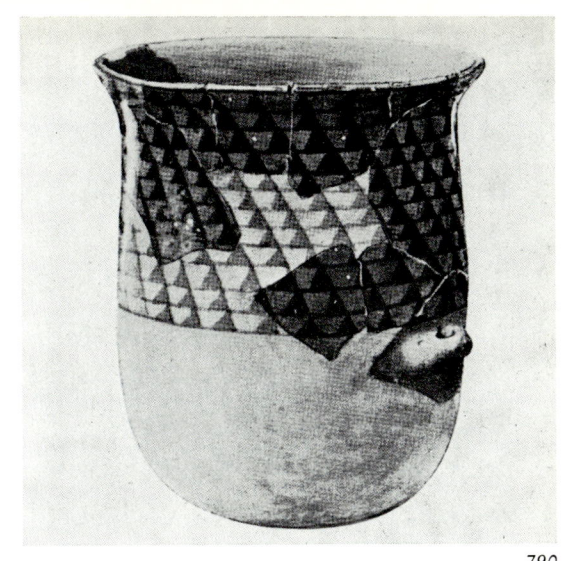
790

794

793

792a.b

795

285

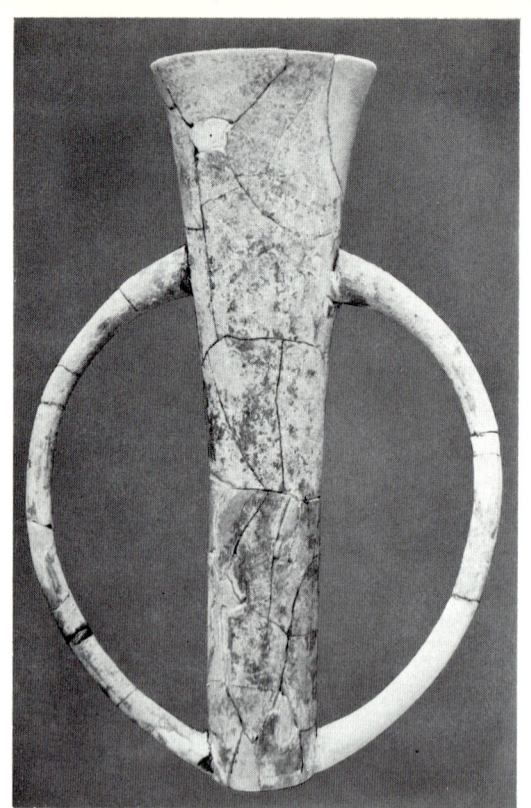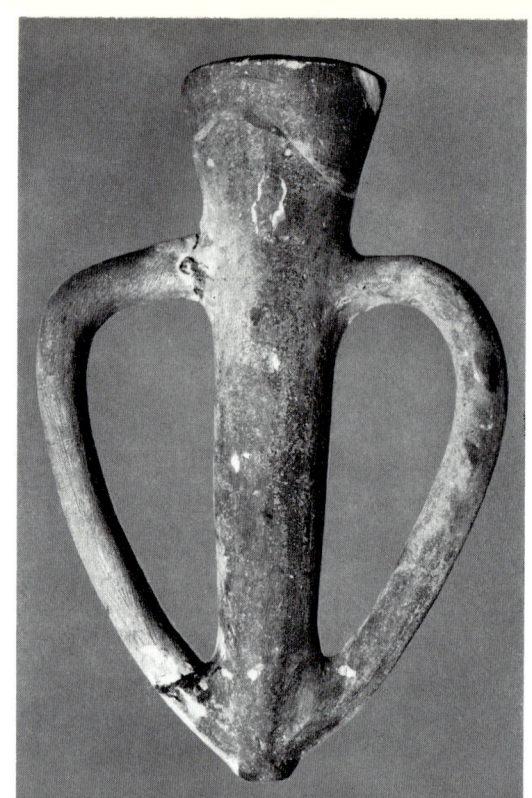

796 797

798.799

Early Bronze Age vessels from Troy, Lemnos and Boeotia

Early Bronze Age vessels from Kos, Attica and the Argolid

806 *807* *808*

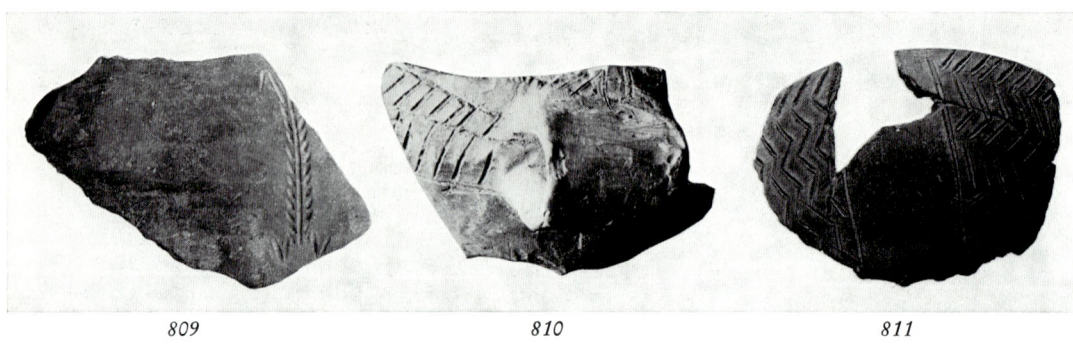

809 *810* *811*

812–815 (top row), *816–819* (bottom row)

Early Helladic pottery from Boeotia, Attica and the Argolid

820

821

Early Helladic water-jars from Orchomenos

822

823 *824*

825

826

Early Helladic pottery from Orchomenos and Leukas

827   *828*

829

Early Helladic pottery from Orchomenos

830

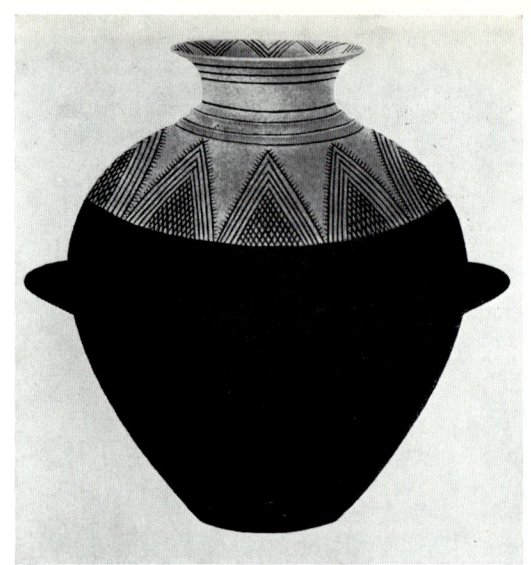
831

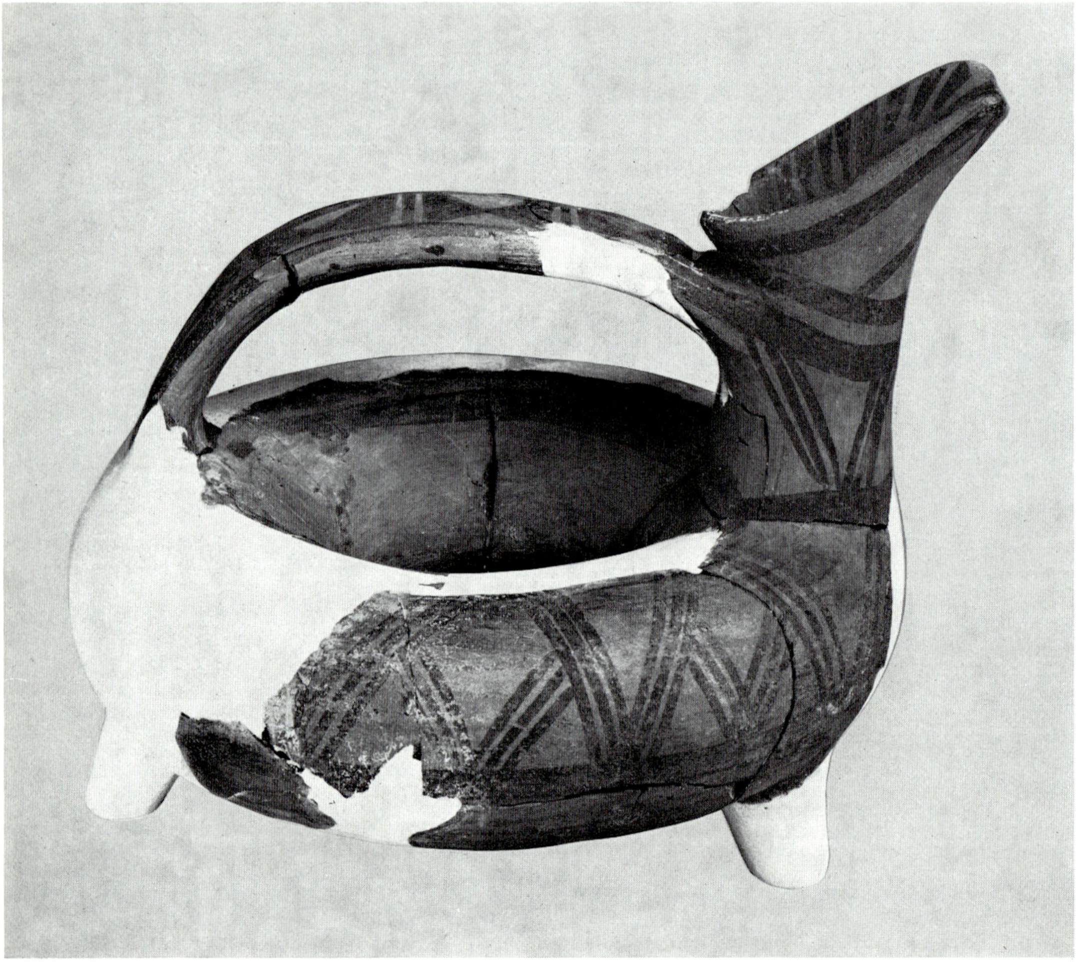

832

Early Helladic vessels from Lerna and Aegina

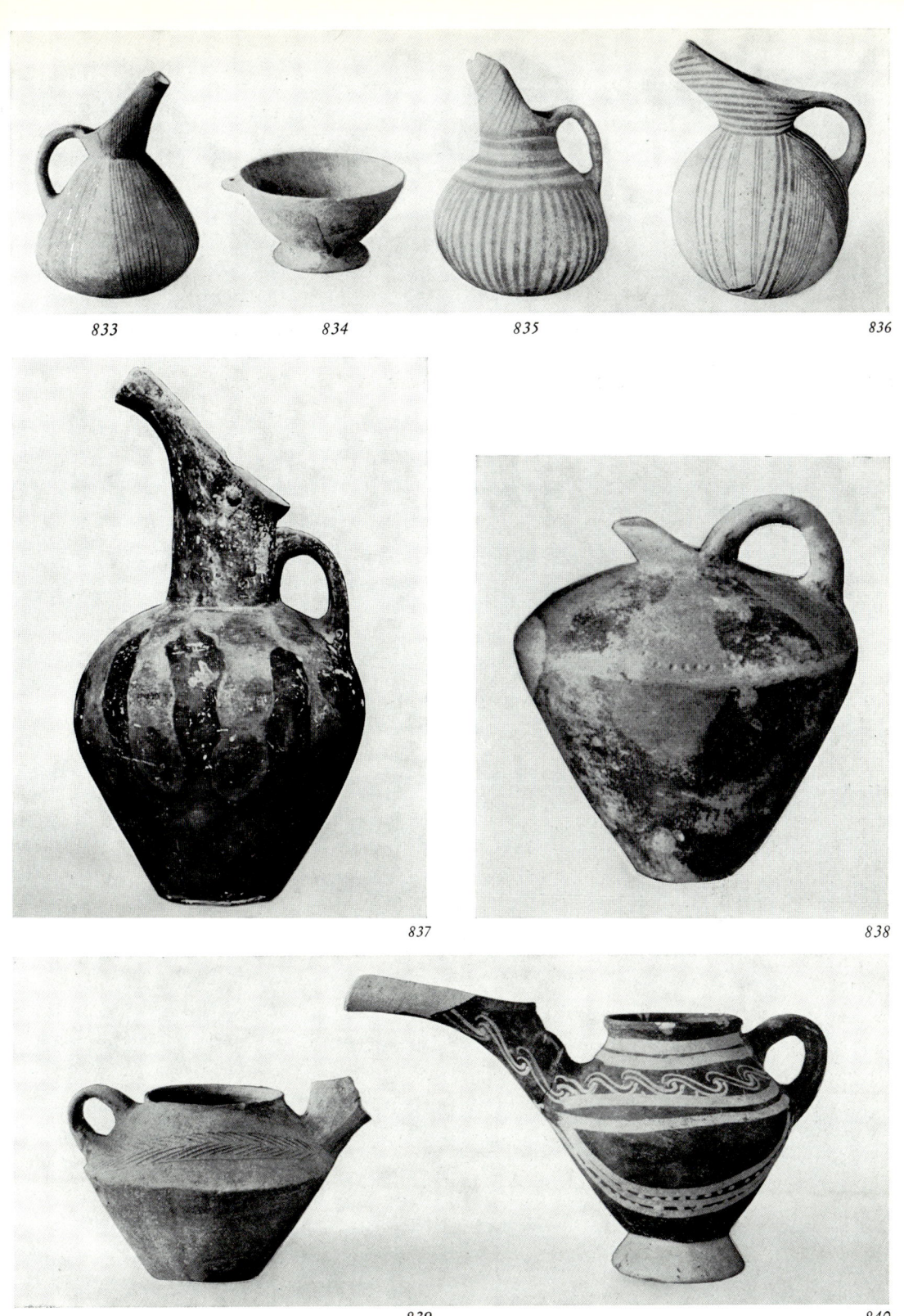

Early Minoan vessels from central and eastern Crete

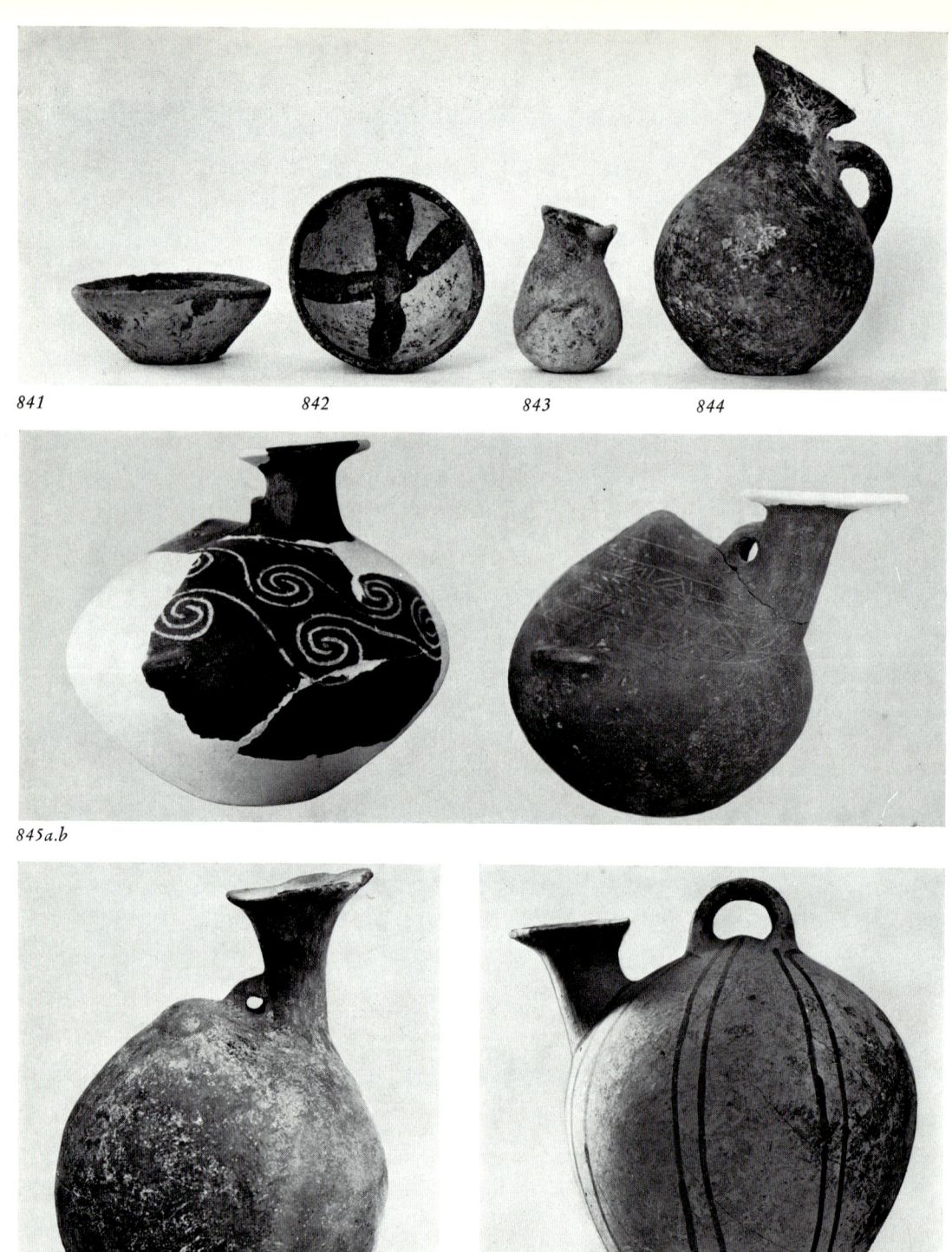

Early Bronze Age vessels from Aegina and the Cyclades

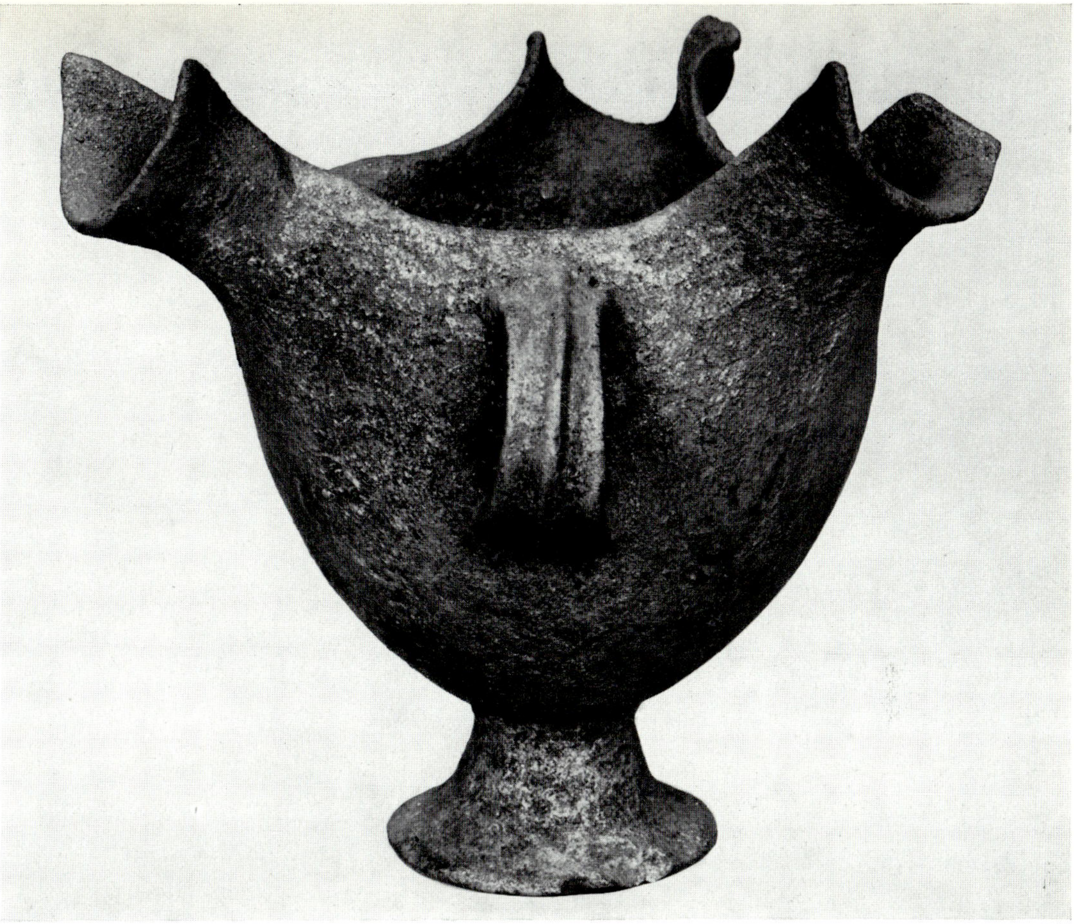

848

849

850

Early Bronze Age vessels from the Cyclades

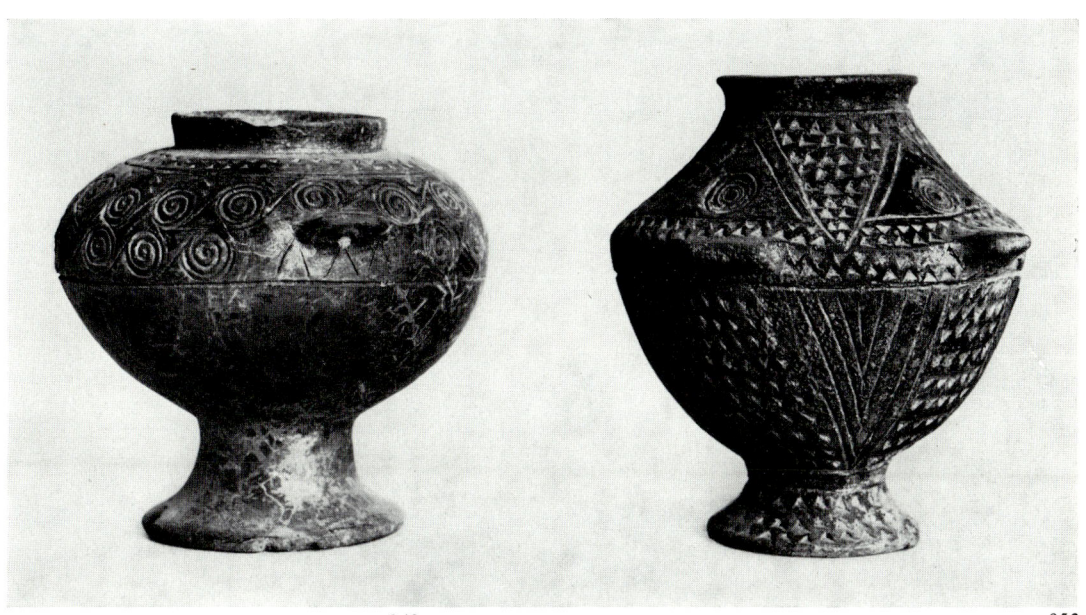

851

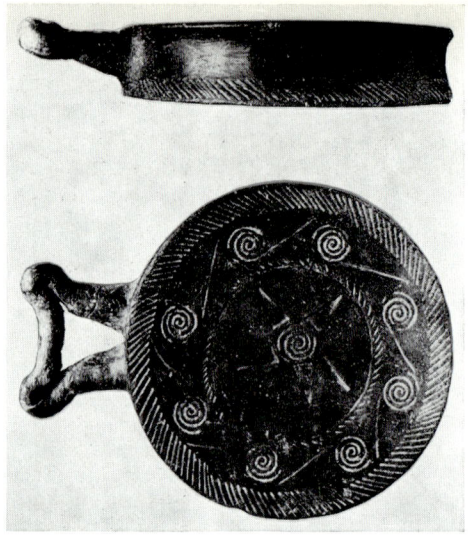

853a.b

852

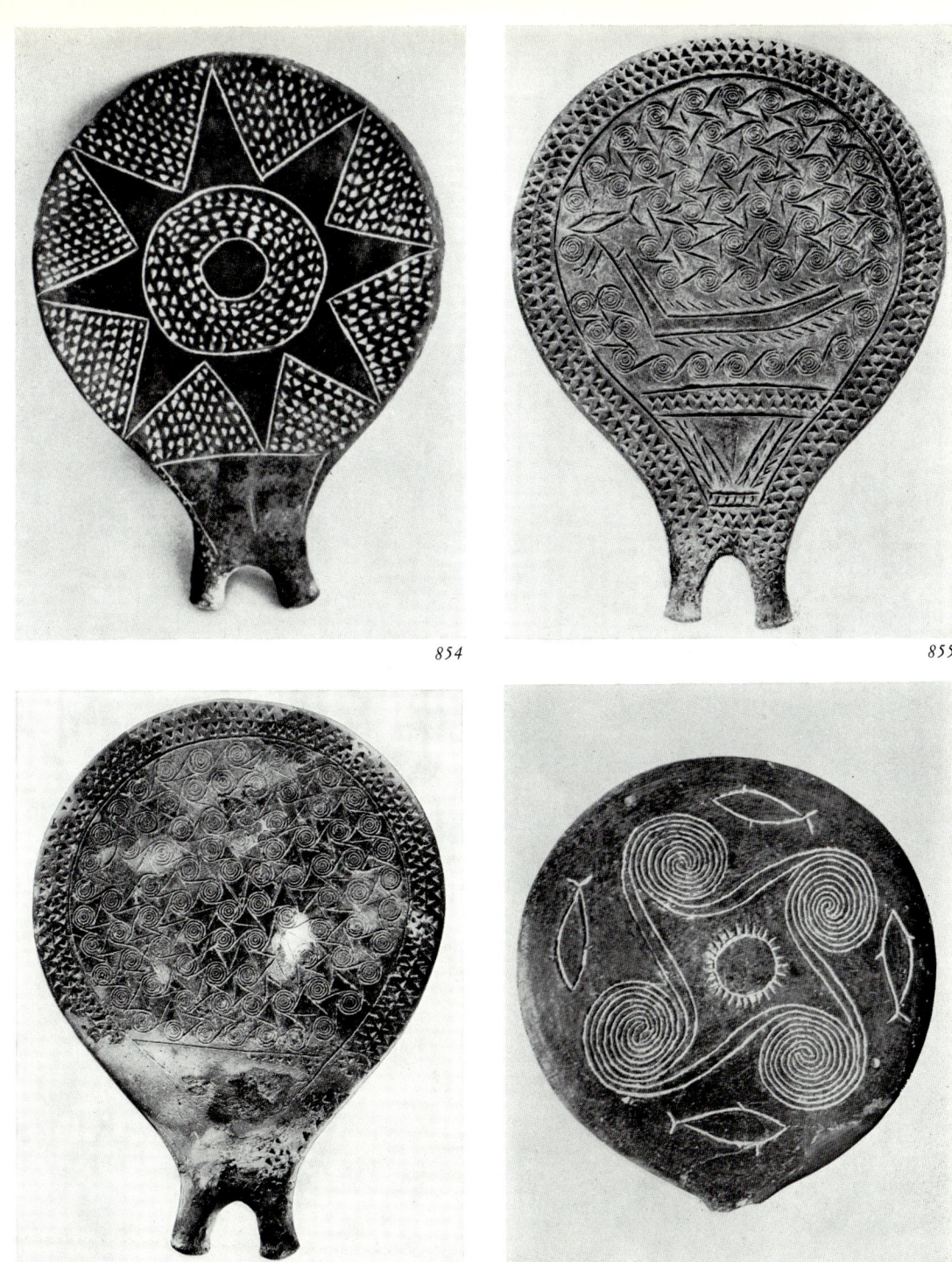

pp. 296 and 297: Pots and votive 'frying-pans' from the Early Bronze Age Cycladic culture

858
859

pp. 296 and 299:
Painted pottery of the Early
and Middle Bronze Age
from Thera, Naxos and Melos

861

863

860

862

299

864 a

864 b

865

Middle Bronze Age storage vessels; Aegina and Boeotia

866

867

870

869

868

Middle Bronze Age vessels; the Argolid, Aegina and Boeotia

871

872

873

874 875
876 877
878 879

pp. 302 and 303: Middle Helladic vessels; the Argolid and Athens

880 *881* *882* *883* *884*

Grey Minyan pottery from Orchomenos and Drachmani

885 886

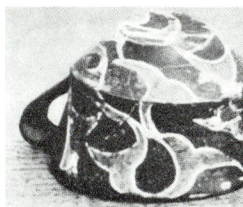 

887 888 889

891

890: Colour plate 1 after p. 8   Middle Minoan pottery; Crete

892

893

Vessels of the Cretan
Kamares Ware; Phaistos

894

895

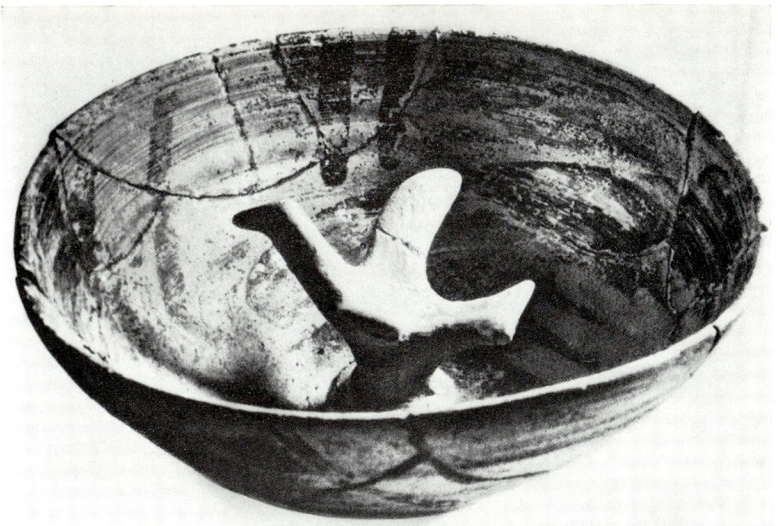

Middle Minoan vessels,
eastern and southern Crete

896

898

899

900

Middle and Late Minoan vessels

897: p. 69, Fig. 27

901

902

903 a

903 b

Late Minoan vessels (LM I); Crete and Attica

904

905

Creto-Mycenaean relief-pithoi (*906:* Stone)

906

907

908 *1146* (zu S. 354)

909

910 a.b *911*

Late Bronze Age vessels and fragments; Crete and the Peloponnese

912 a

912 b

Cretan jug
found in
Egypt

912 c

912 d

Cretan jug
found in Egypt

913

914

915

Late Minoan vessels (LM I and II); Crete

Late Bronze Age vessels; Crete, the Peloponnese and Miletus

922

923

924

925

926

927

pp. 316 and 317: Creto-Mycenaean vessels (LM/LH I and II); Crete, Aegina, Euboea and mainland

933

934

935

936 a

937 b

937 a.b

938

pp. 318 and 319:
Creto-Mycenaean vessels (LM/LH I–III);
Crete, Peloponnese, Attica and Euboea

939

940

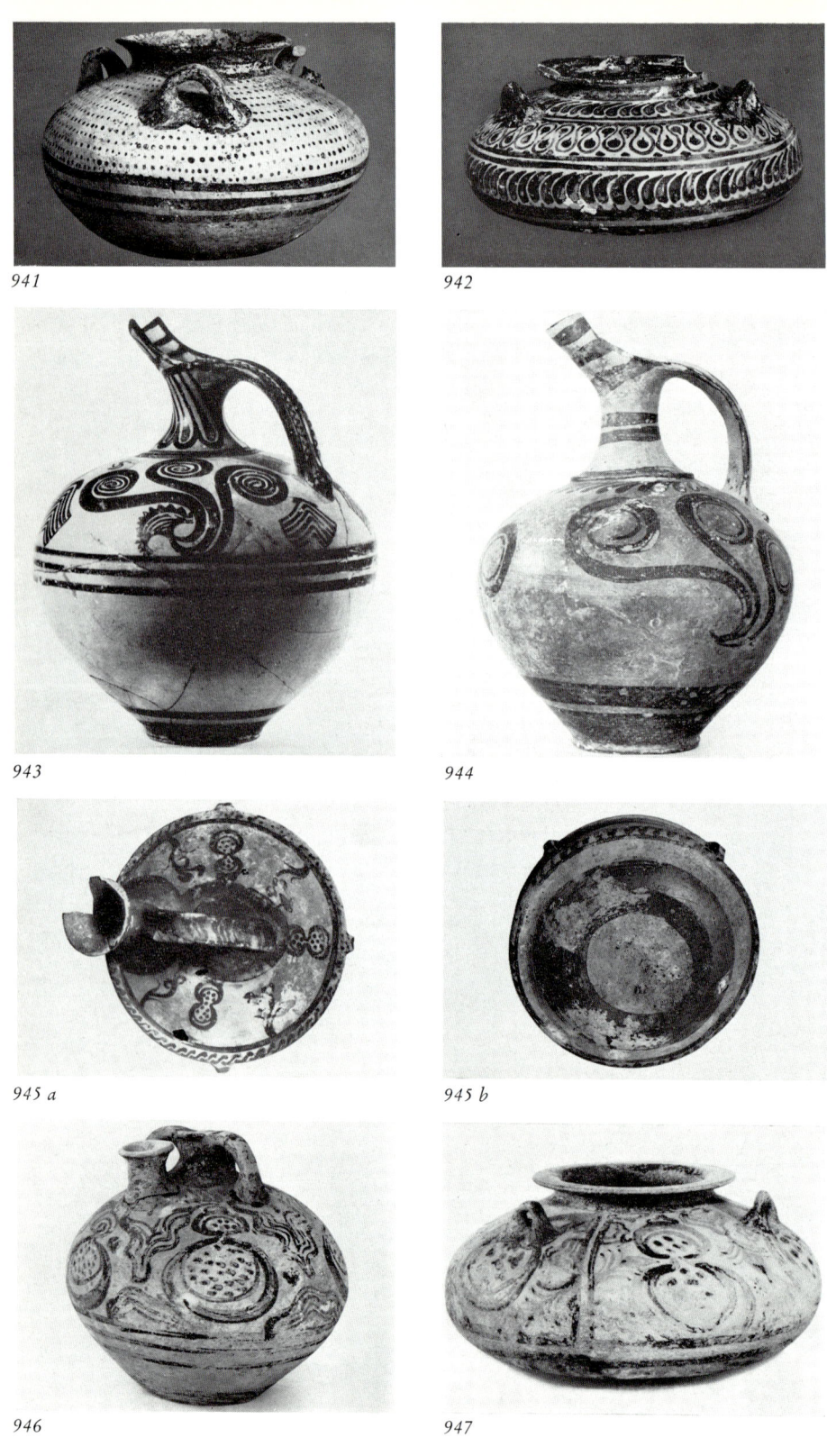

Creto-Mycenaean vessels; mainland, Euboea, Aegina, Kythera and Crete

948 949

950 a.b   951 a.b   952 a.b

953   954   955

Creto-Mycenaean vessels; Crete, Thera and Euboea

321

956 a

956 b

Mycenaean vases, imported pitcher and ivory pyxis *in situ*; chamber tomb in the Areopagus, Athens

957

958

Vases and rhyta from Rhodes, Kos, Thera and Aegina

959

960   961   962   963   964   965

Late Helladic vessels from the Argolid and unknown sites

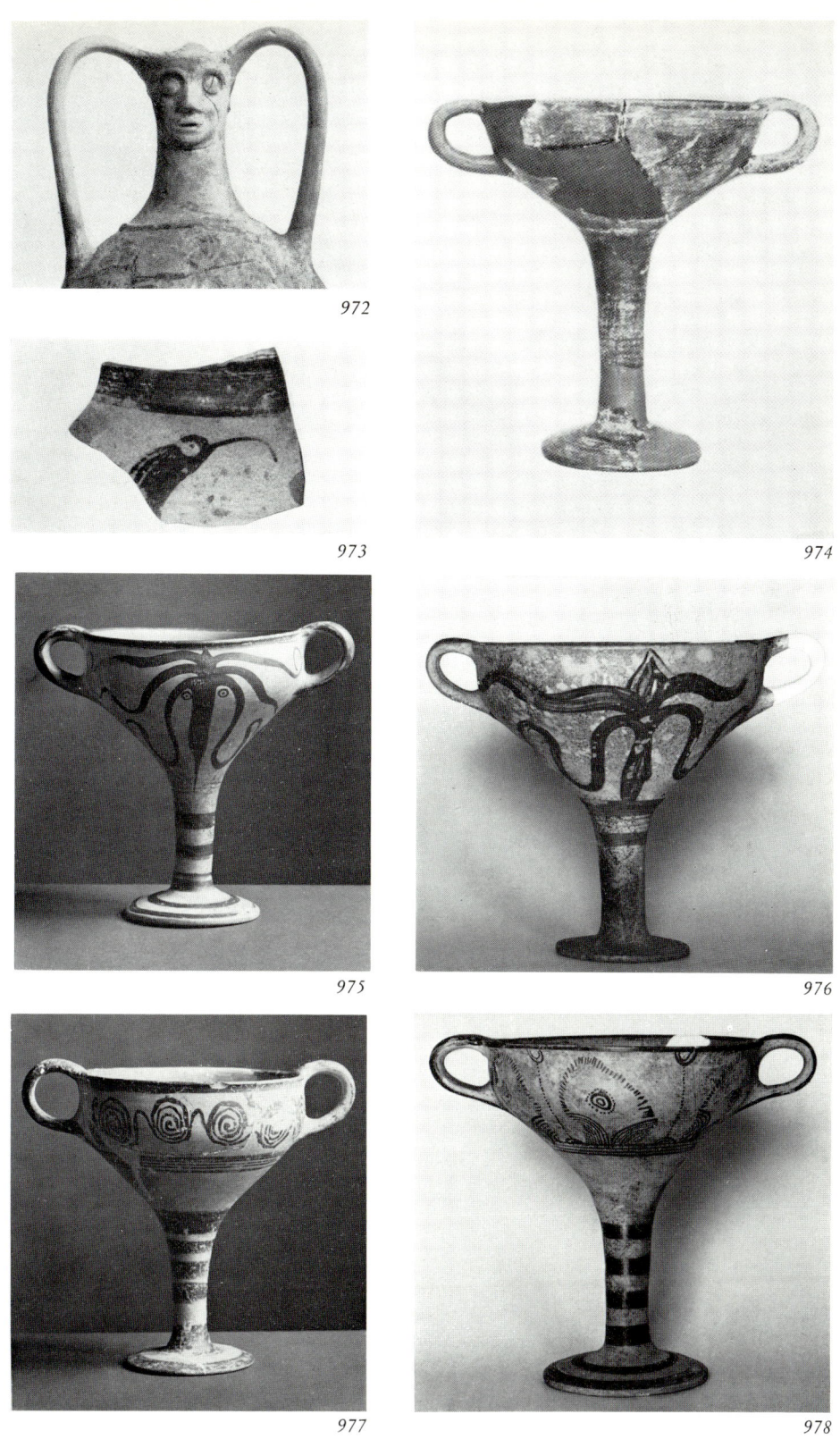

Late Helladic and Late Minoan vessels; Crete, Lesbos, Syria and unknown sites

325

979 980 981
982 983 984
985 986 987
988 989 990

Mycenaean vessels from Kythera, Elis and the Argolid

Mycenaean vases and fragments from Euboea, Attica, Keos and the Argolid

1024

1025

1026

1027

1028

1029

pp. 328 and 329: Wide-mouthed bowls and stirrup jars from the Argolid, Attica, Crete, the Cyclades and eastern Aegean

1002–1023: p. 76, Fig. 28

1030

1031

1032 a

1032 b

1033

1034

1035 1036 1037
1038 1039 1040
1041 1042

Painted vases and pictorial details from the late Aegean Bronze Age

1043

1044

Wall-paintings from Crete and Melos

1045

1046

pp. 332 and 333: Wall paintings from Hagia Triadha and Knossos

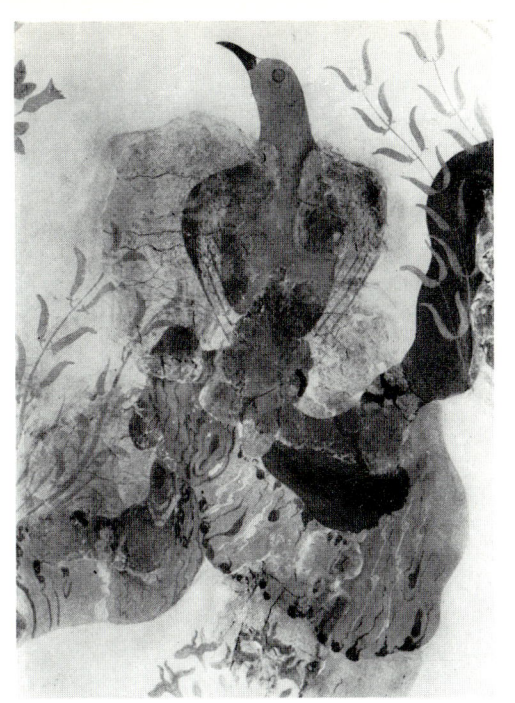

1047

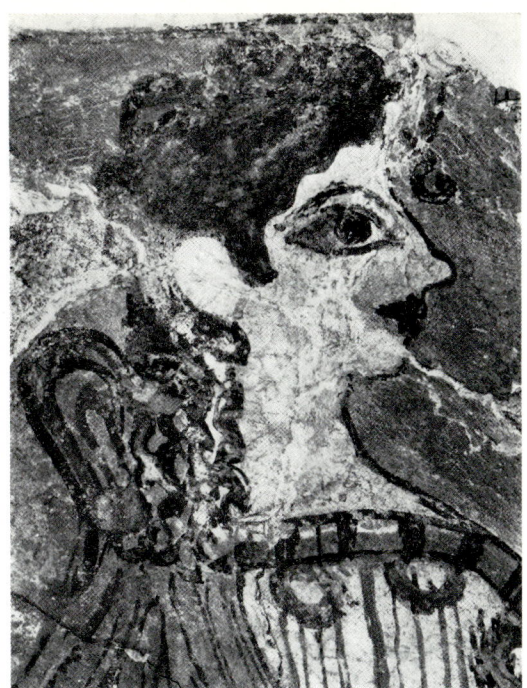

1048

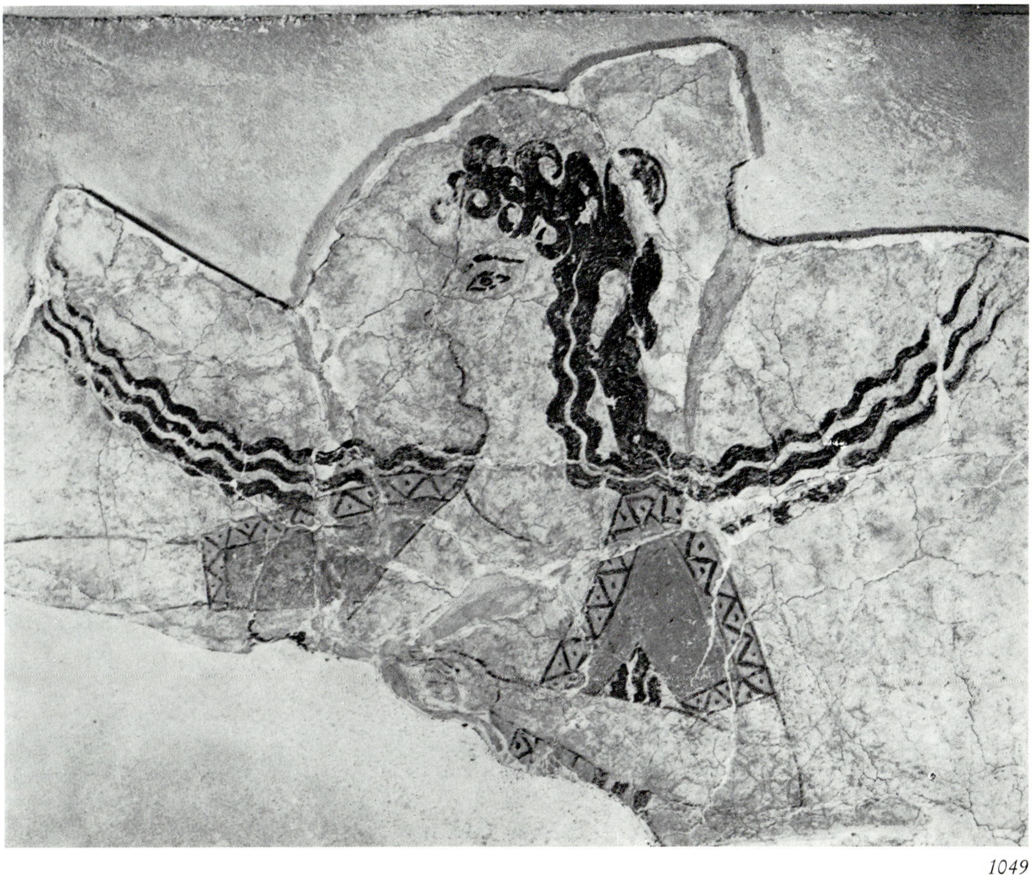

1049

1050

1051

1052

1053

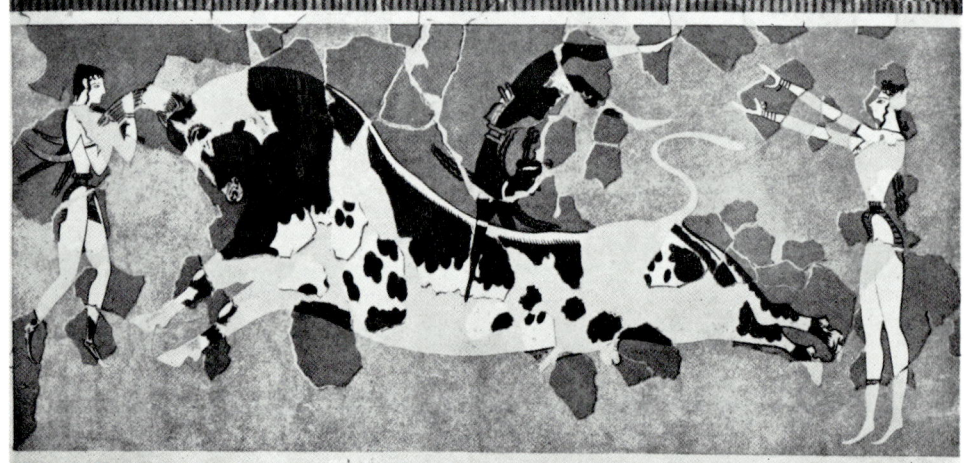
1054

334

1058

pp. 334 and 335:
Wall-paintings from
Crete and the Greek
mainland

1055–1057:
p. 79 ff., Figs 29–31

1059

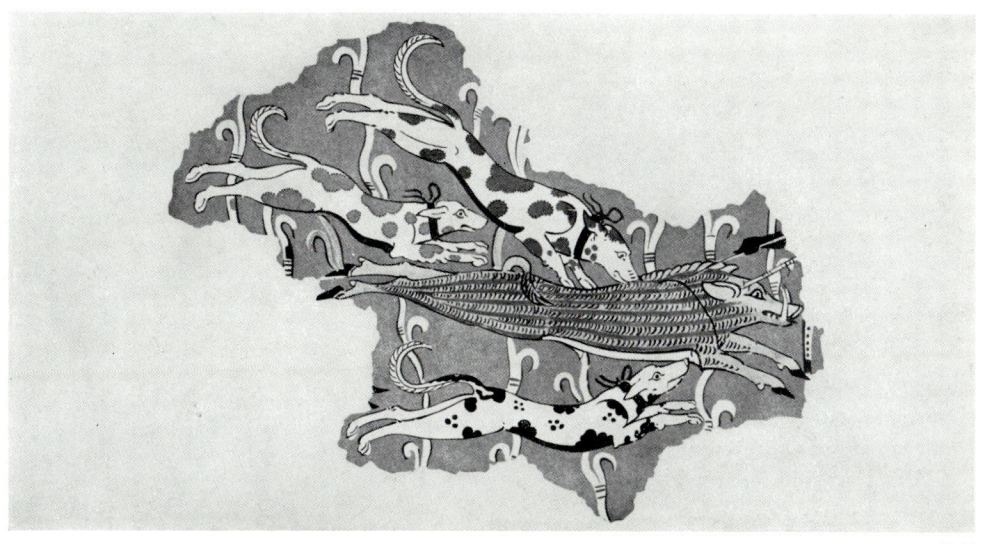

1060

335

1065 b

1066

1067

1069 a

pp. 336 and 337:
Sarcophagi from Crete
and the mainland

1068

1069 b

1061–1065 a: p. 83, Fig. 32

1069 c

Fragment of a sarcophagus from Boeotia and painted stele from Mycenae

1070

1071

1072

1073

1074

1075

Early Bronze Age objects in gold, silver and lead; Troas and the Cyclades

1076

339

1077

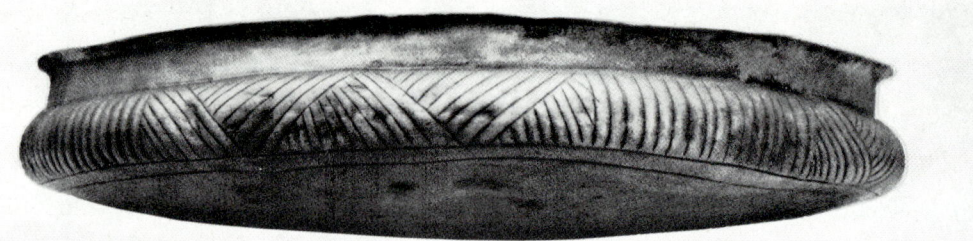

1078

1079

1080

1081

pp. 340 and 341:
Early and Middle Bronze Age vessels
in gold and silver; Euboea, the Cyclades,
the Peloponnese and eastern Crete

1082 a

1082 b

1083

1084 a

1084 d

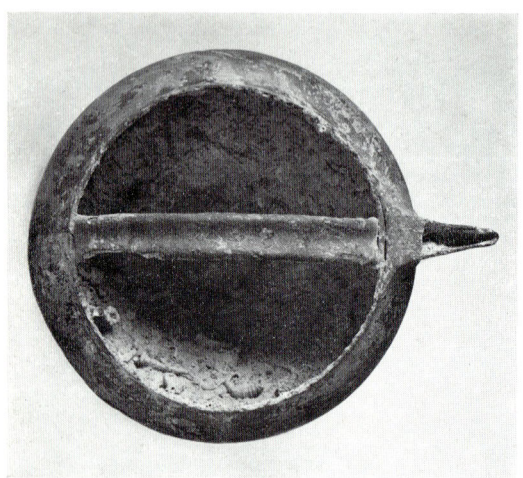

1084 b

1084 e

1084 c

1084 f

Copper cauldron from the sea off the coast of Euboea

1085

1086

1087

Mycenae,
gold vessels

1088 a

1088 b

1089

Silver jug and gold covered wooden box from Mycenae,
Grave Circle A, Shaft Grave V

1090 a

1090 b

1091 and *1092*  *1093.1094.1411*

Copper cauldron from Mycenae, Grave Circle A (cf. p. 393, *1411*)

345

Late Helladic copper hydriai from Mycenae and Dendra

1096

1095 a–o: p. 85, Fig. 33;
1100–1103: p. 87, Fig. 34

1097

1098

1099 a.b

1104 a

1104 b

1106

1105

1107

1108

1109 and 1110

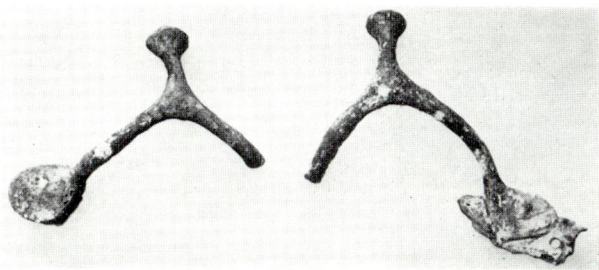

Precious metal vessels and details from vessels; wishbone handles in bronze. The Peloponnese

1111

1112

1113

1114

1115 b

1115 a

1116

Copper and bronze vessels from Dendra and Tiryns, the Argolid

1117 a

1117 b

1117 c

Gold cup from Dendra

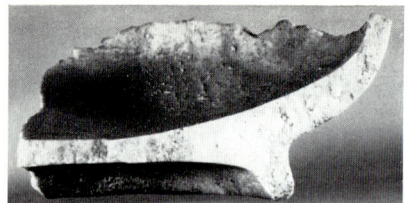

1118 a

1118 b

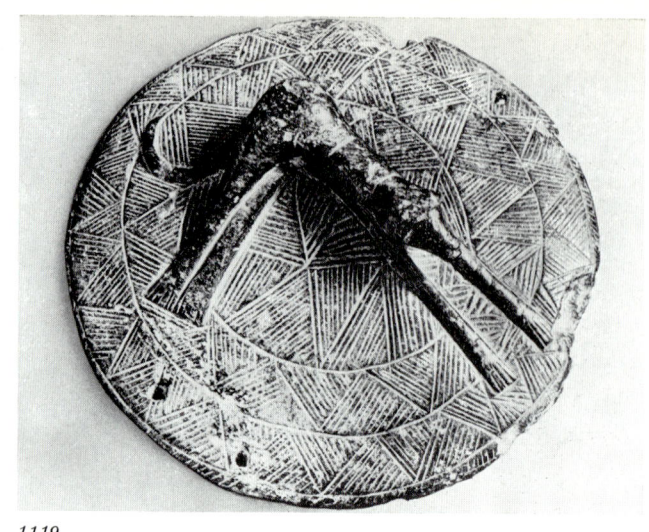

1119

1120

1121

1122 a

1122 b

pp. 350 and 351: Neolithic and Early Bronze Age stone vessels from Thessaly, the Argolid, the Cyclades and Crete

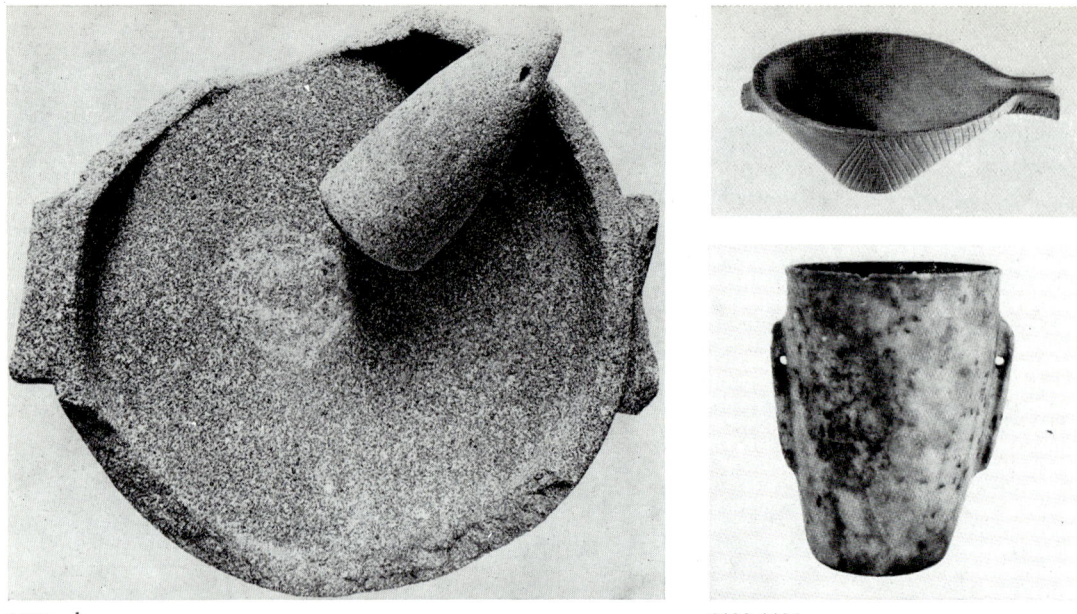

1132 a.b   *1133.1134*

1135 a–c

Early Bronze Age stone vessels from Attica, Anatolia and the Cyclades

1136

1137

1138

1139

Early Cycladic marble vessels

1140

1141 a.b

1142

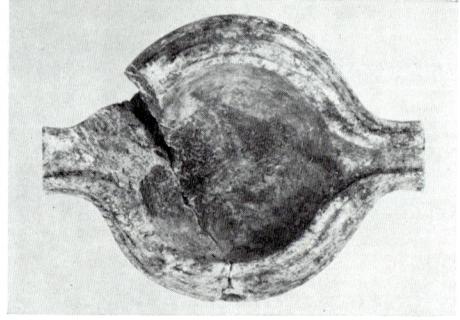

1143

1144

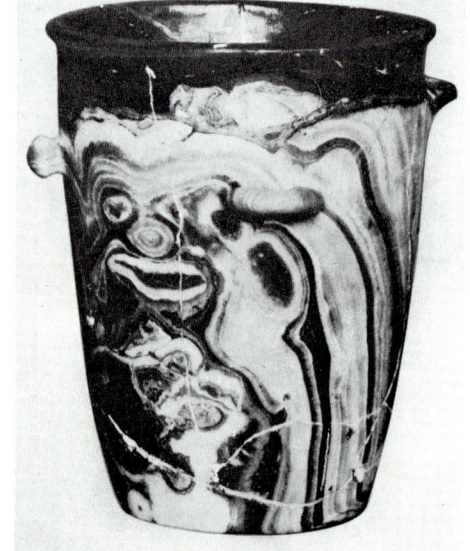

1145

Stone vessels from Crete

1146: p. 311

1147

1148

1149

1150

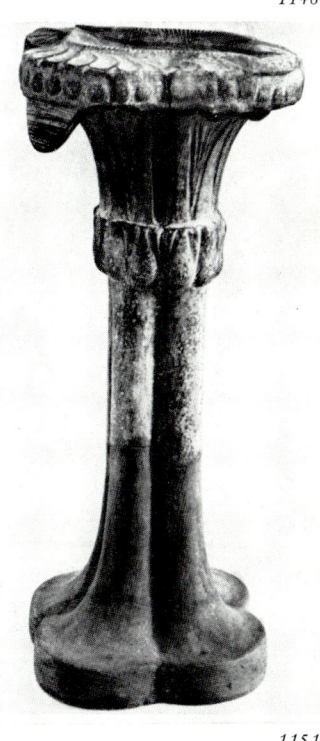
1151

Stone vessels from Crete

1153

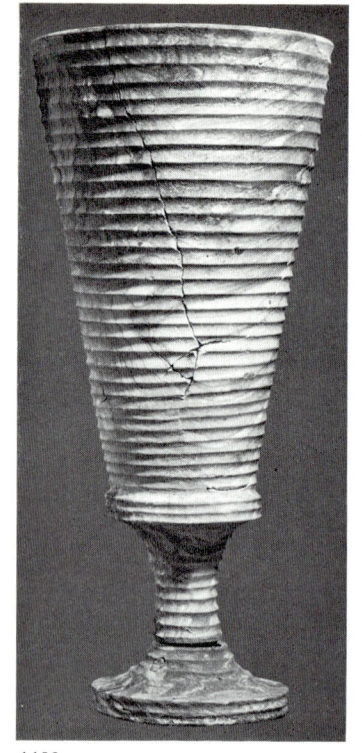

1152

1154

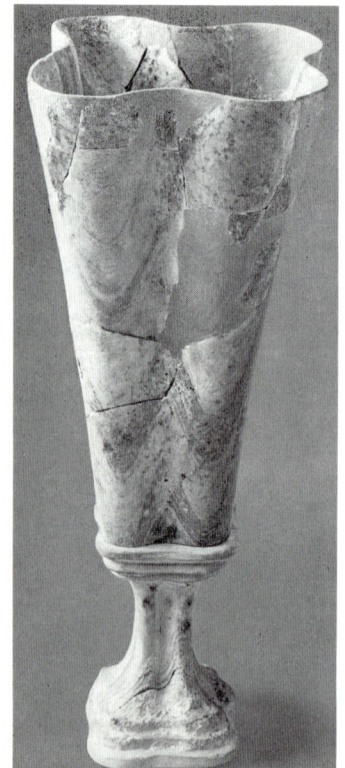

1155

1156

1157

Stone vessels from Crete, Mycenae and the Cyclades

1158   1159   1160

1162   1163

1161   1164

Stone vessels from Crete, Kythera, the Argolid and Attica

1165

1166 a

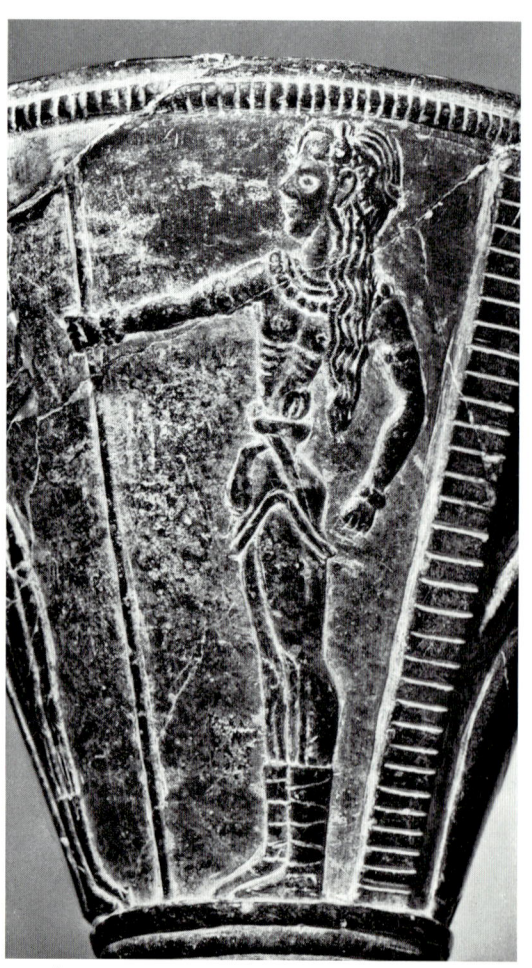

1166 b

p. 358: Stone vases with reliefs from Crete. *1167:* p. 94, Fig. 35; cf. fragment *1235*. p. 359: relief stelai from the Greek mainland and Keos

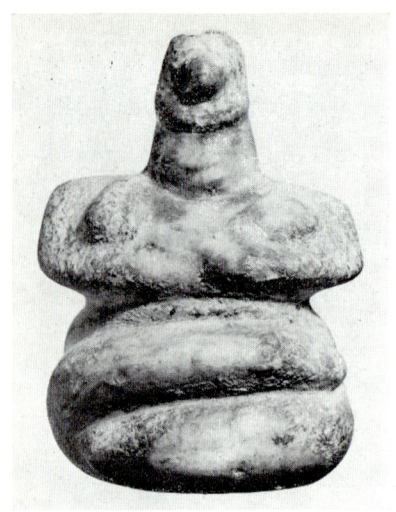

1172

1173

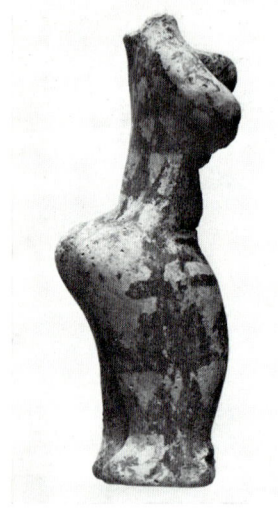

1174 a

1174 b

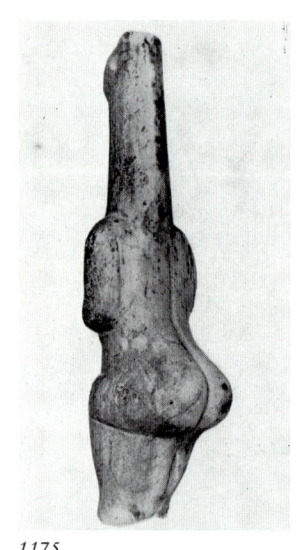

1175

1176

1177

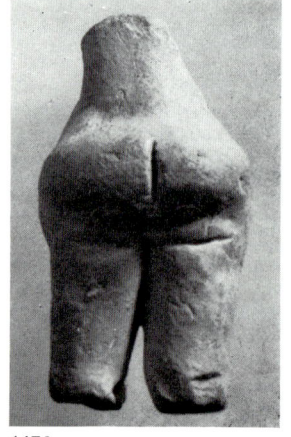

1178

1179 a

1180

1179 b

pp. 360 and 361:
Neolithic sculpture in clay, marble and limestone. Northern, central and southern Greece

1181 a

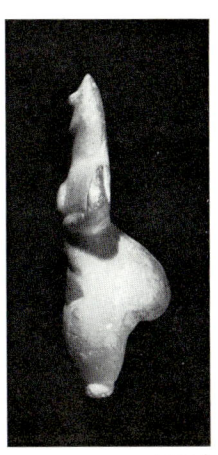

1181 b

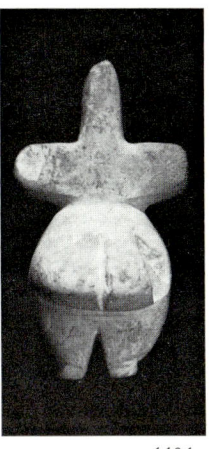

1181 c

361

1182

1183 a

1183 b

1184

1185

1186

1187 a

1187 b

1188

1189

1190

pp. 362 and 363:
Female idols and animal sculpture; Stone Age and Early Bronze Age. Crete, the Cyclades, southern and central Greece

1191 a

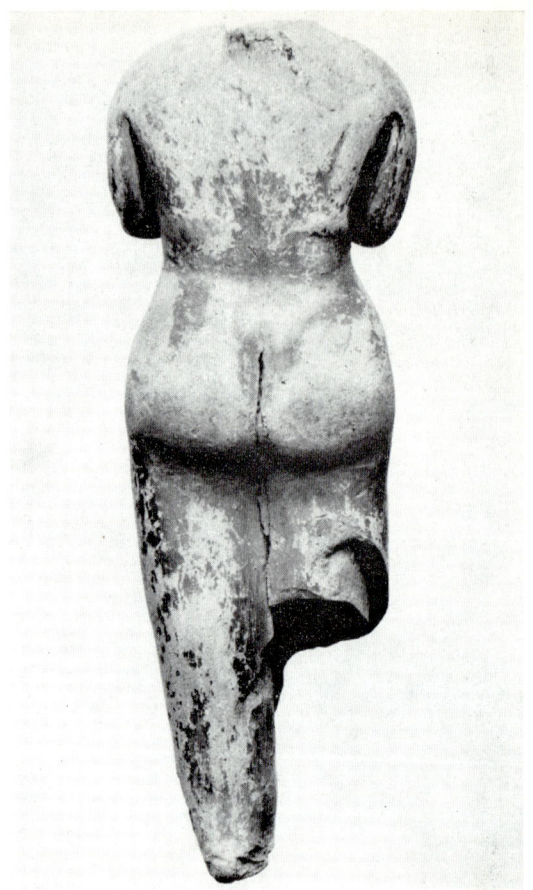

1191 b

1192 a *1192 b* *1193*

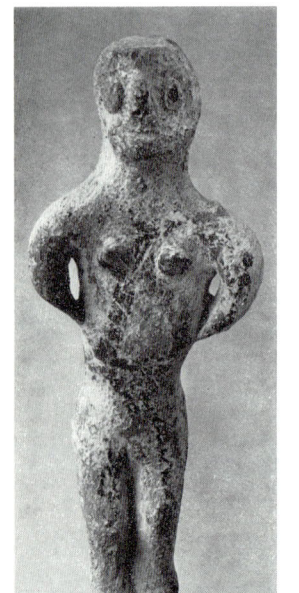

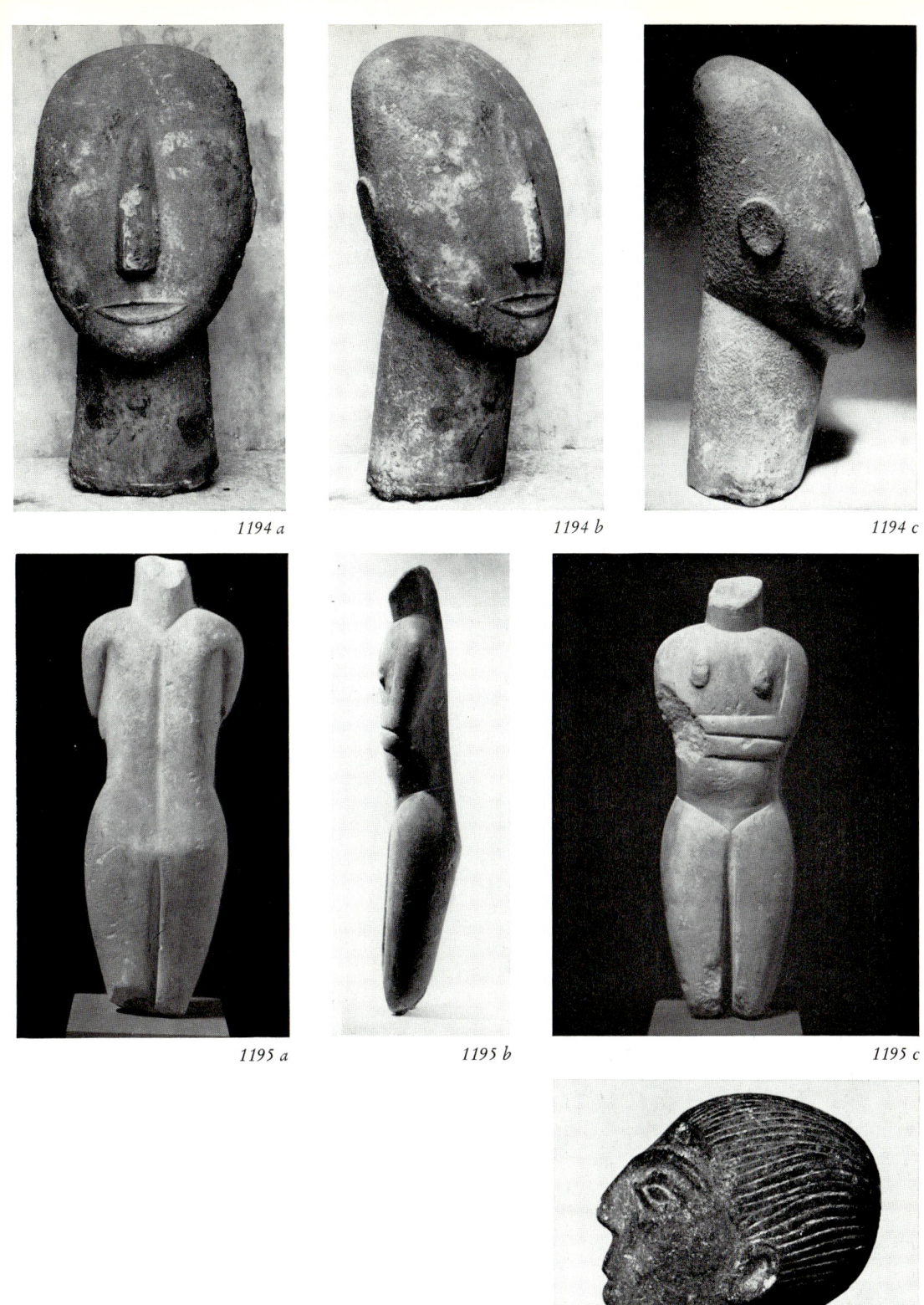

1194 a   1194 b   1194 c

1195 a   1195 b   1195 c

1196

pp. 364 and 365:
Clay statuettes and Early Cycladic marble sculpture

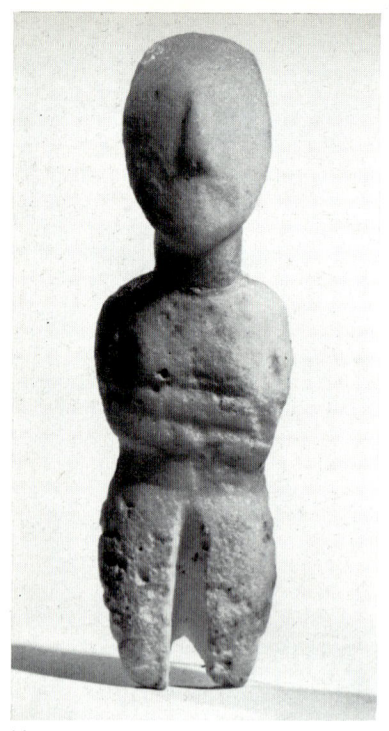
1197 a

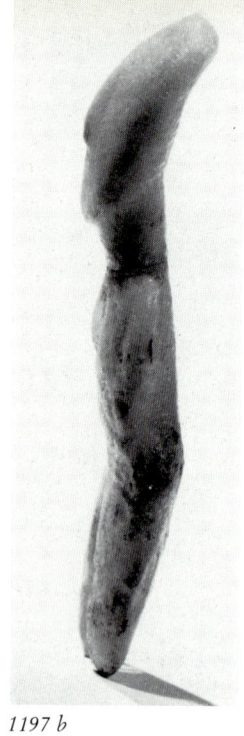
1197 b

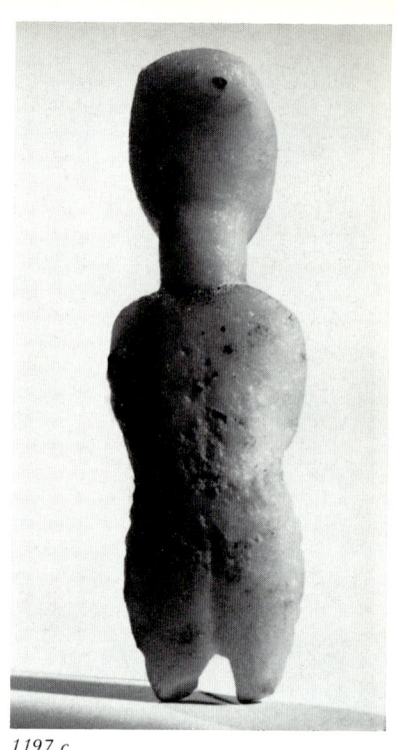
1197 c

1198

1199

1200 1201 1202 1203
1204 1205 1206 1207

pp. 366 and 367: Early Cycladic marble idols

pp. 368 and 369:
Early Cycladic
sculpture, steatite and
marble, from Crete,
Thera and Keros

1208

1209

1210

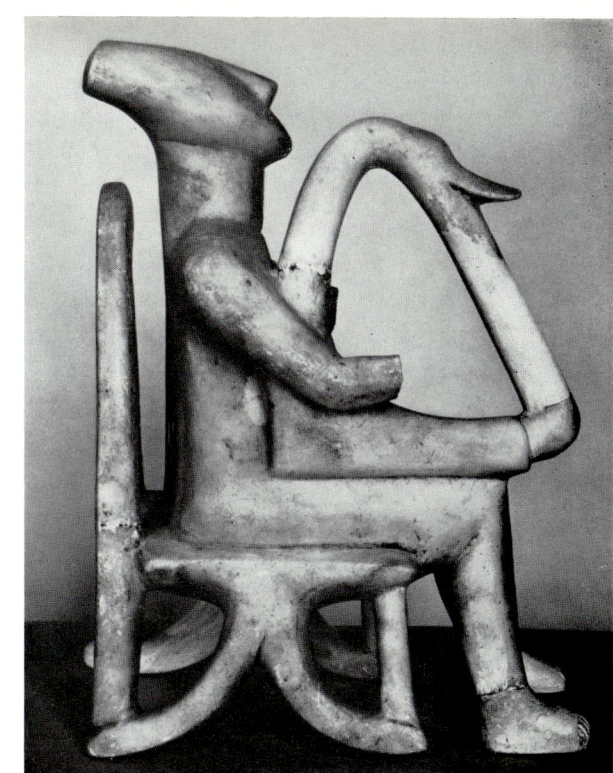

1211

1212 a

1212 b

1212 c

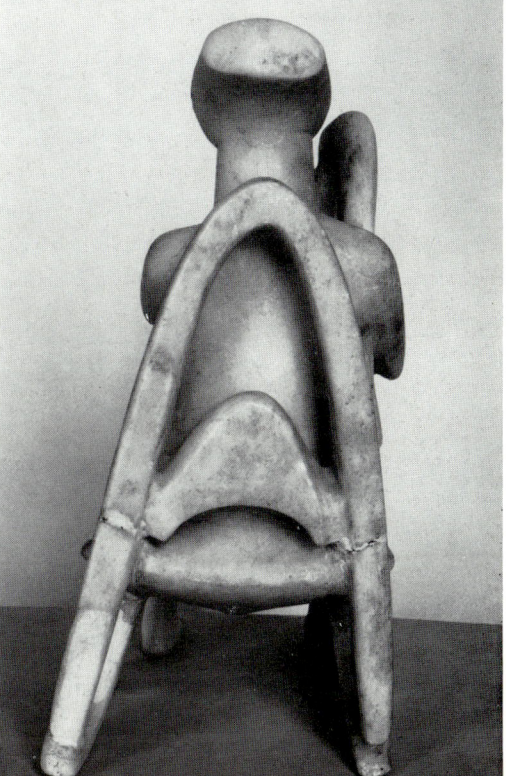

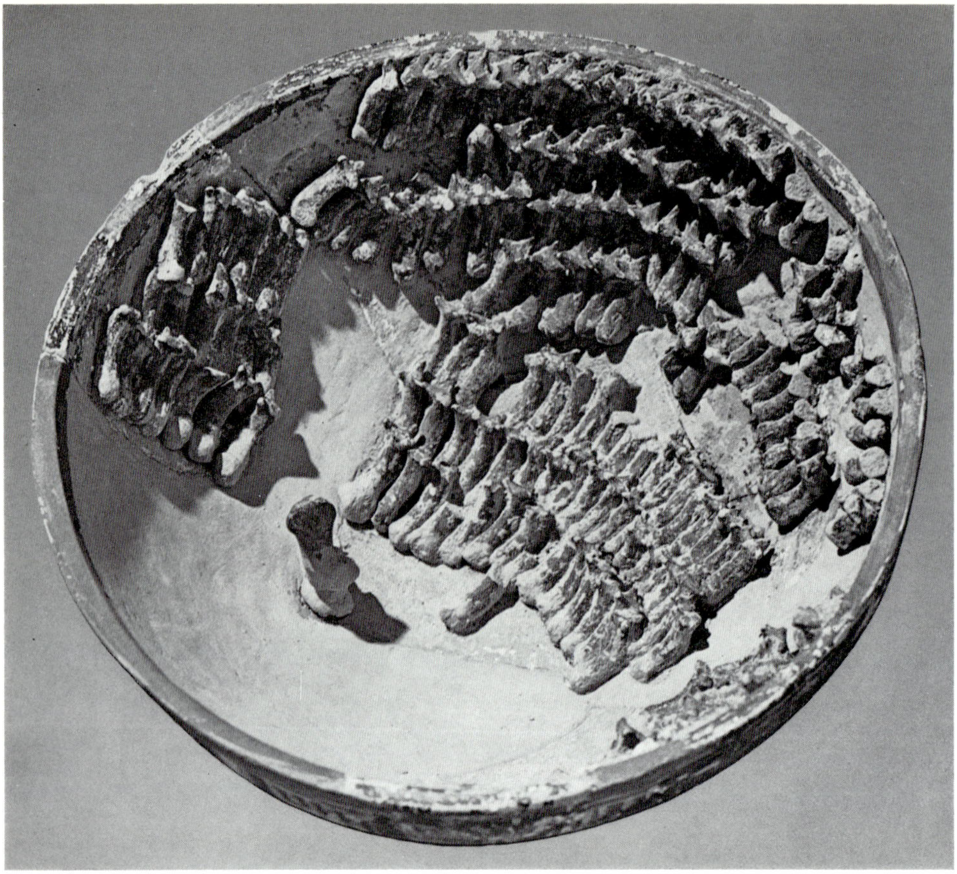

1213

1214

1215 1216 1217

pp. 370 and 371: Middle and Late Minoan clay sculpture from various Cretan sites

1218 1219 a.b

pp. 372 and 373:
Cretan clay and bronze sculpture from the mid-second millennium B.C.

1220

1221
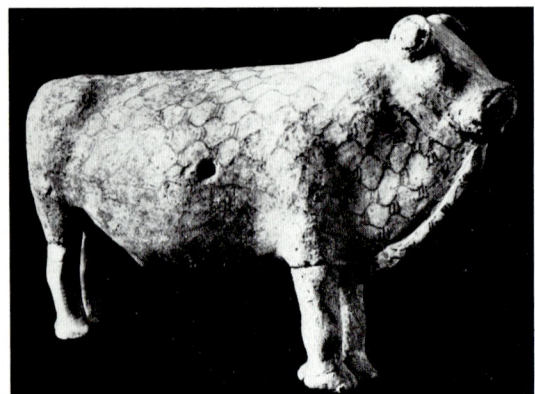

1222

1223

1224 a 1224 b
1224 c 1224 d

373

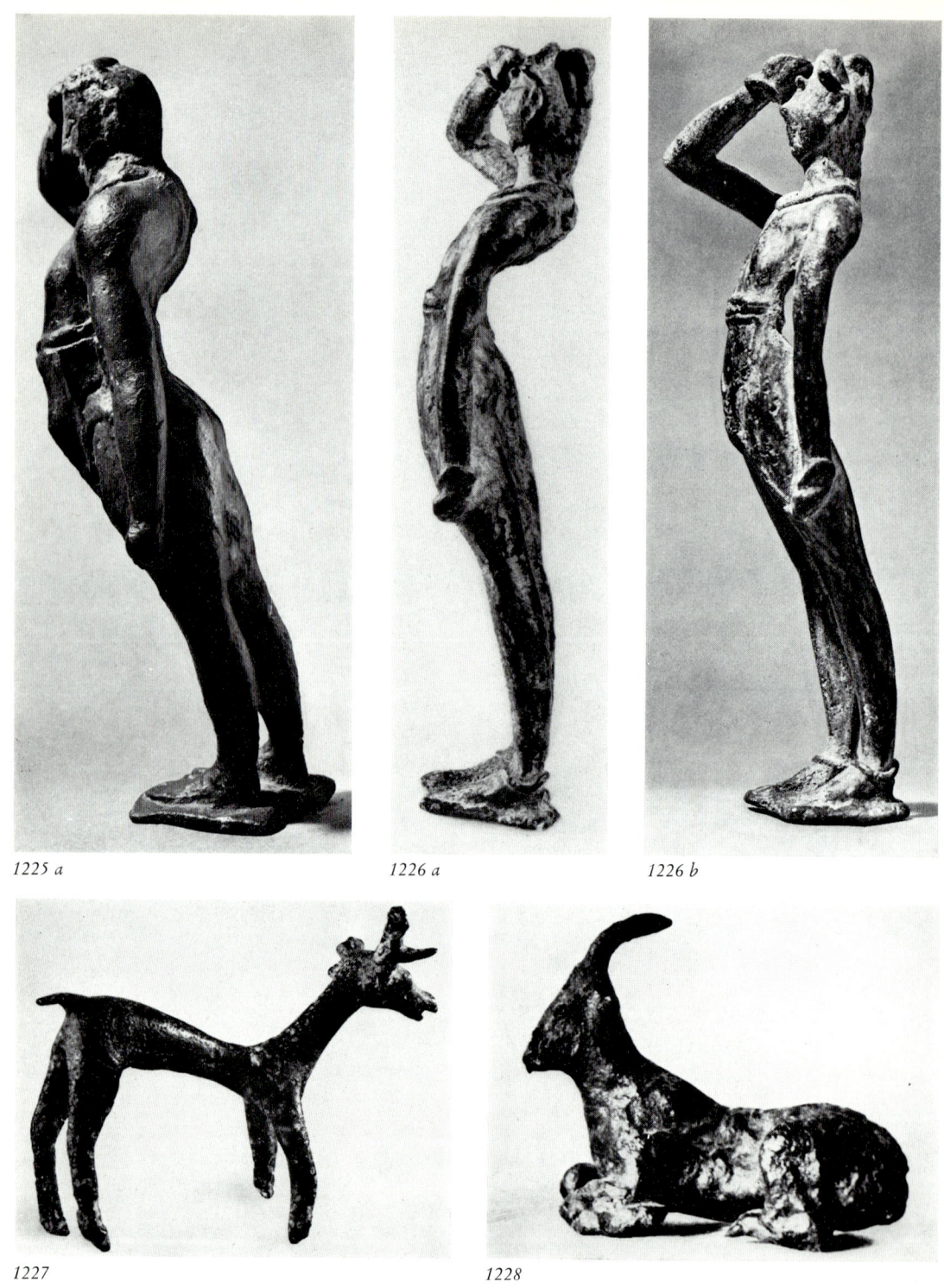

1225 a

1226 a

1226 b

1227

1228

pp. 374 and 375: Cretan bronze sculpture from the golden age of the later palaces

1229

1231

1230

1225 b

1232

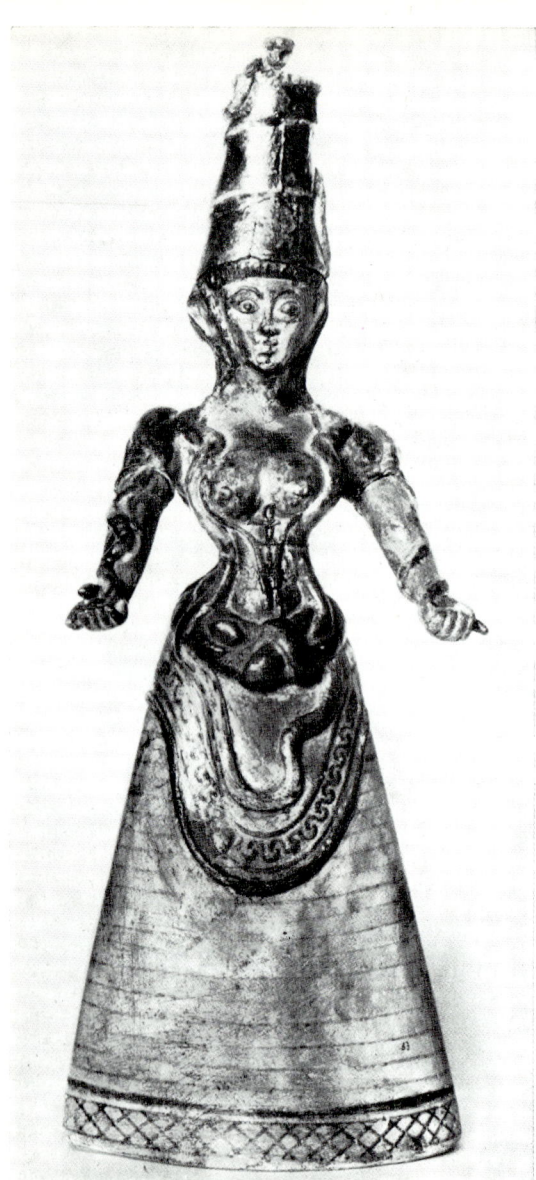

1233

1236

1234

1235

1237

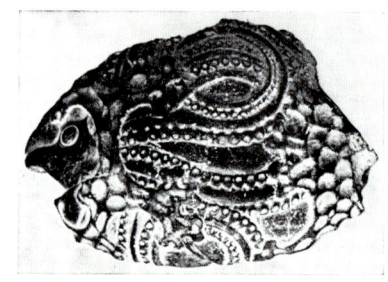

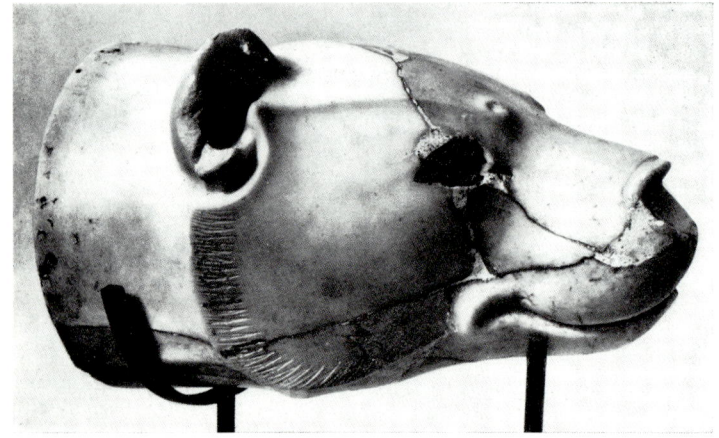

Minoan statuette of a goddess in faience and animal sculpture in stone; Crete and the Argolid

1238

1239

1240

1241

1242

Mycenaean animal-head rhyta in painted terracotta; the Argolid, Greek islands and Ras Shamra

1243

1244

1246

1245
1247 a.b

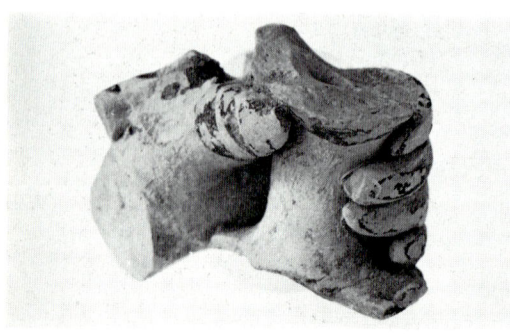

Mycenaean gold masks and fragments of clay and stucco figures; the Peloponnese

1248 a

1248 b

1248 c

1248 d

1248 e

1248 f

1249 a.b

Mycenaean terracottas from the Argolid and Attica

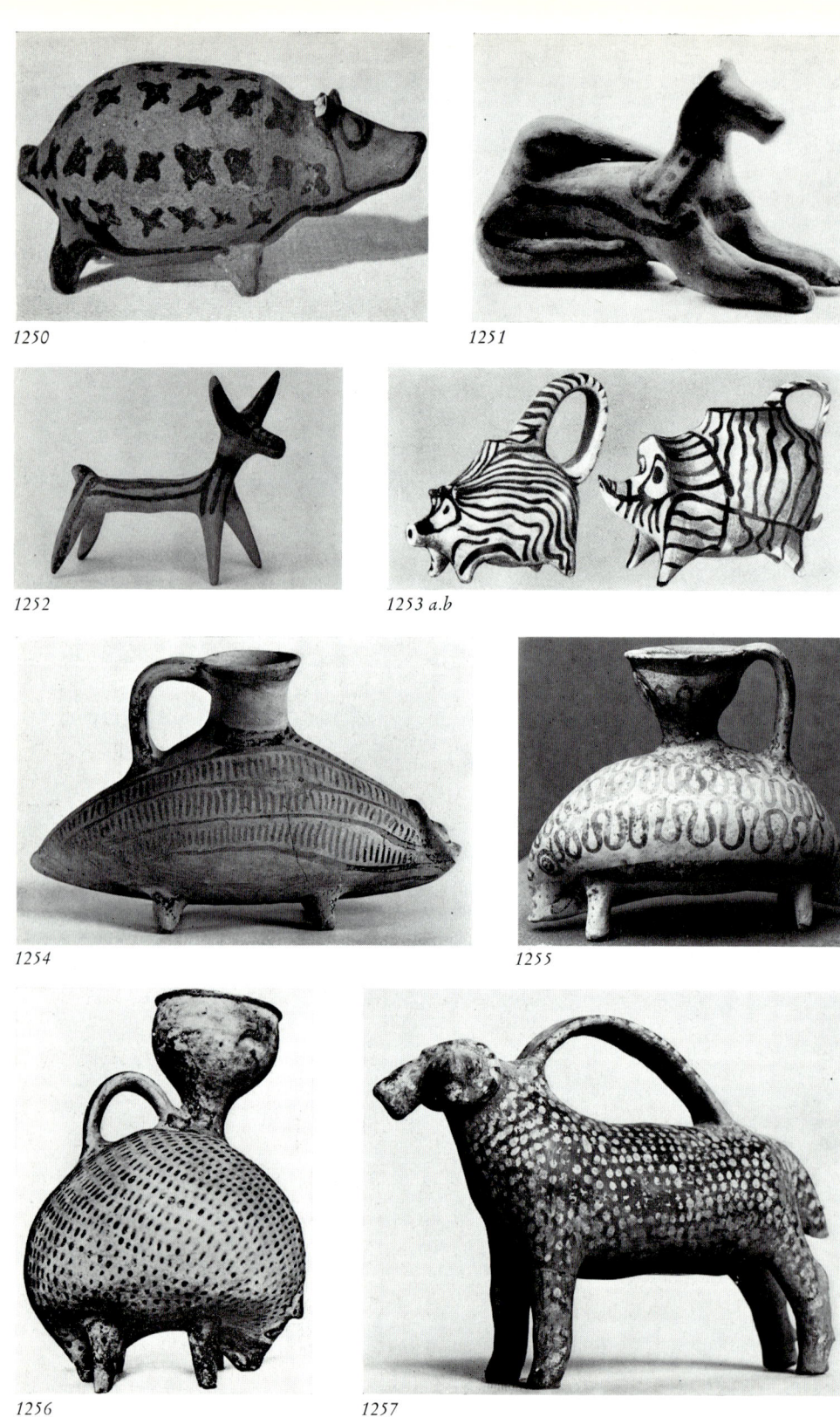

Mycenaean animal figures and vessels in the form of animals

1258 a 1259 a 1260 a 1261 a 1262 a

1258 b 1259 b 1260 b 1261 b 1262 b

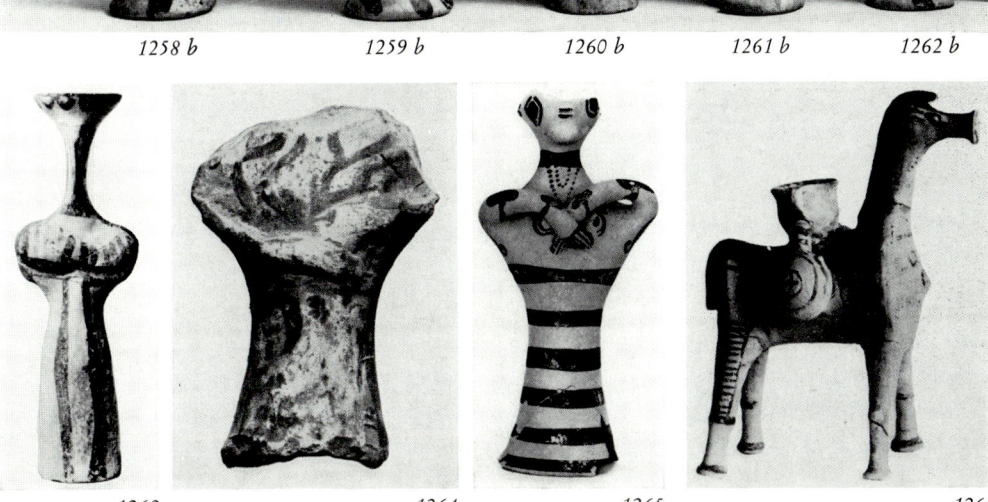

1263 1264 1265 1266

Mycenaean female idols and statuette of a horse

1267

1268

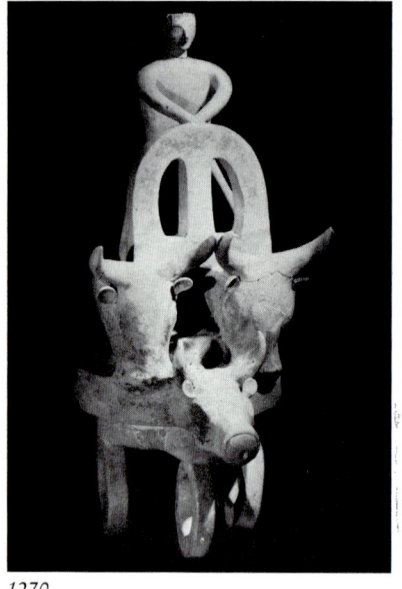

1270

1269

1271

Clay sculpture of the Late Bronze Age. Crete and Rhodes

1272

1273

1274 a.b

1275

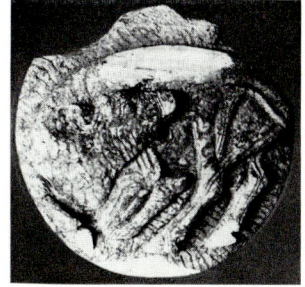

1277

1276

1278

Ivory work from mainland
in the Helladic period

1279

1281 a

1282

1280 a

1280 b

pp. 384 and 385: Ivory work from Mycenaean sites

1283

1284

1285

1286 1288 1287

1289 1290

Ivory work from Mycenaean and Near Eastern sites

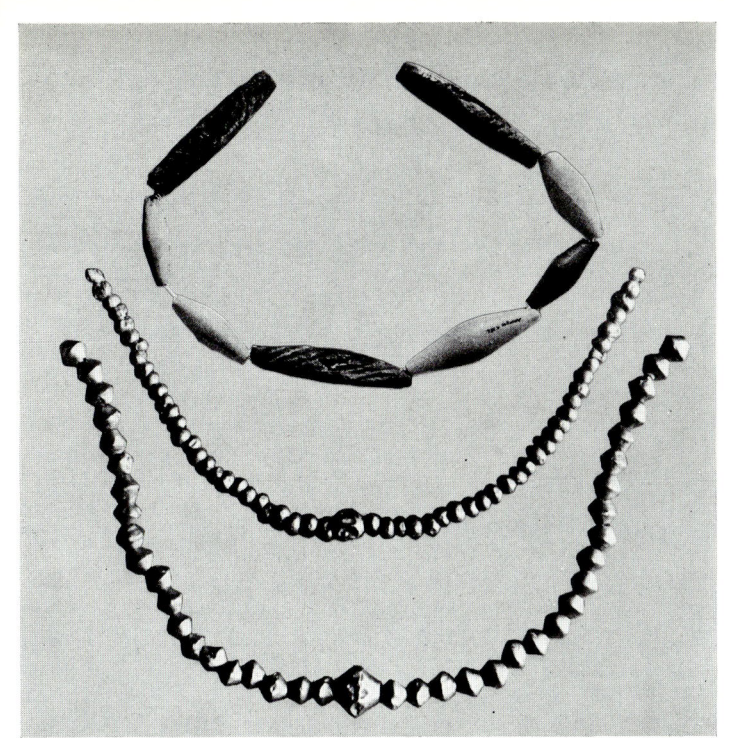

1291–1293

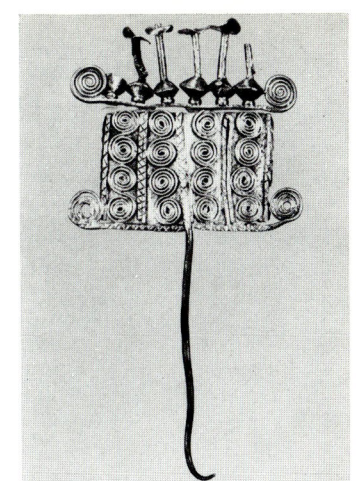

1295

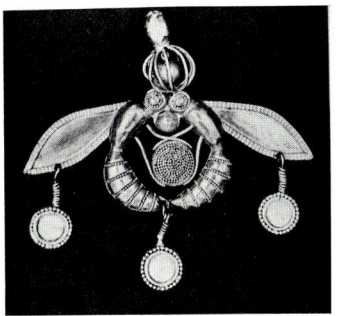

1296

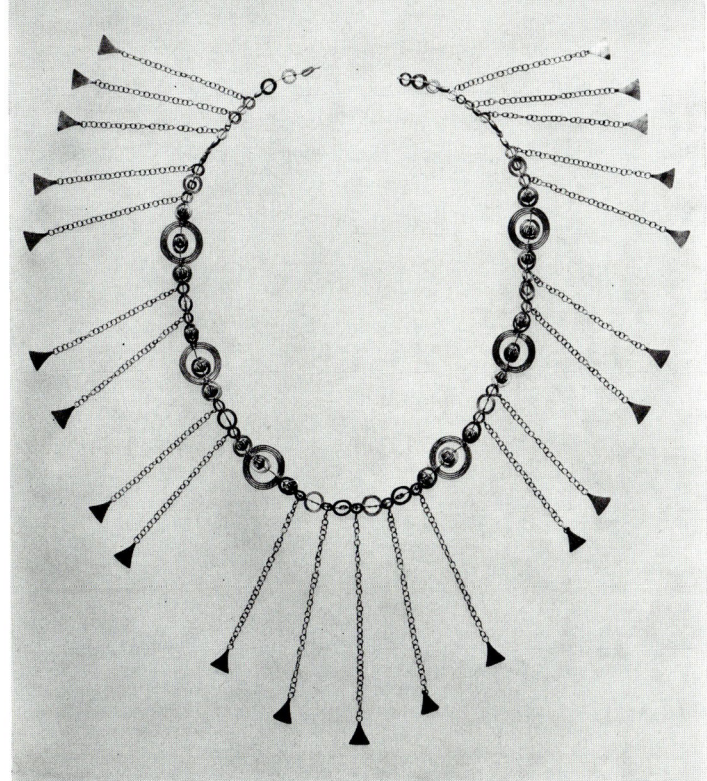

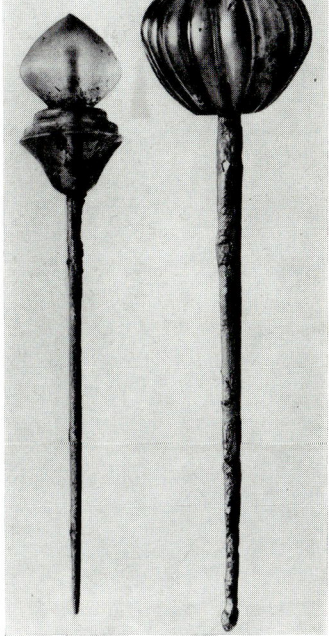

1294   1297   1298

Jewellery from Crete, the Greek islands, the mainland and Troas

1299–1302

1303

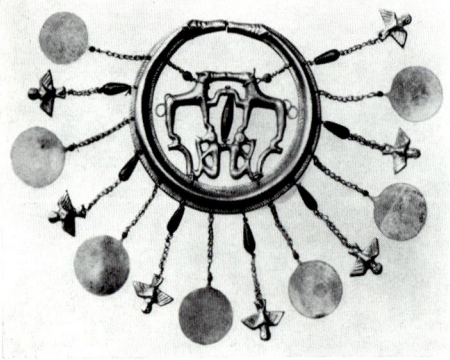

1304

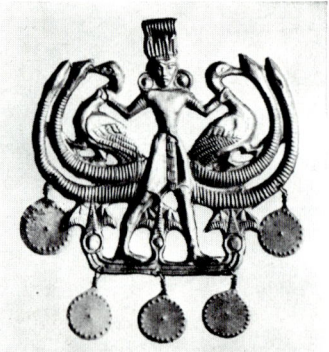

1305

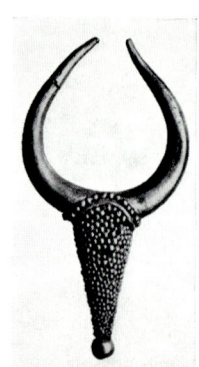

1306

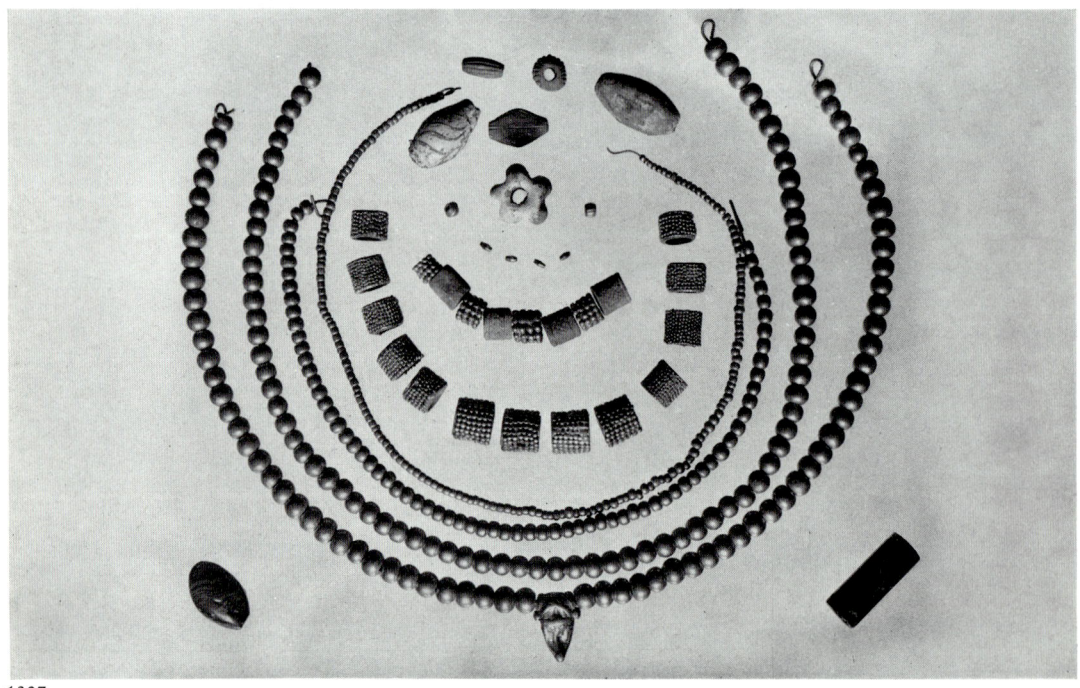

1307

Gold ornaments and pearls from Crete, Aegina, Mycenae and Tiryns

1312

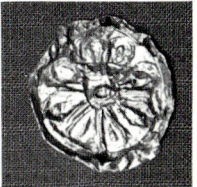

1313

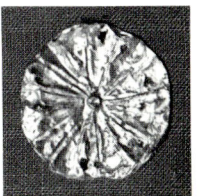

1314

1308 a–c. 1309

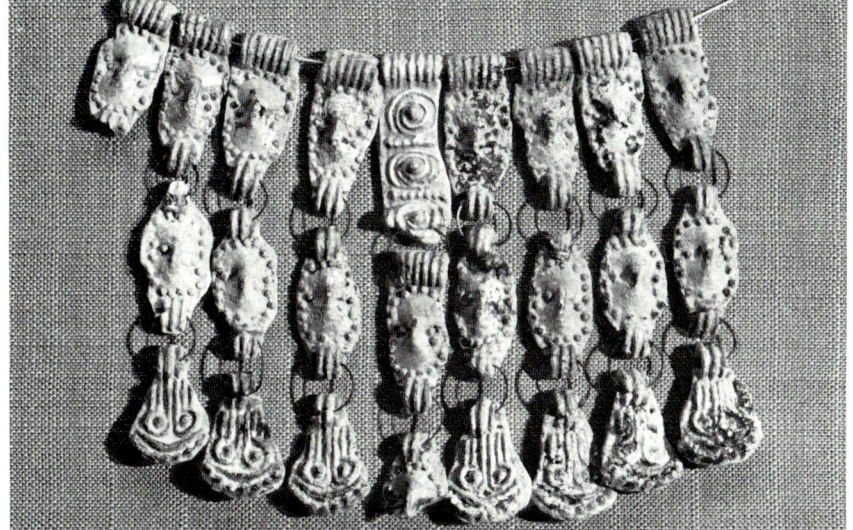

1315

1316

1310

1311

Ornaments from various sites; gold, agate, glass-paste, faience *1317–1345*: p. 109 f., Figs 36, 37

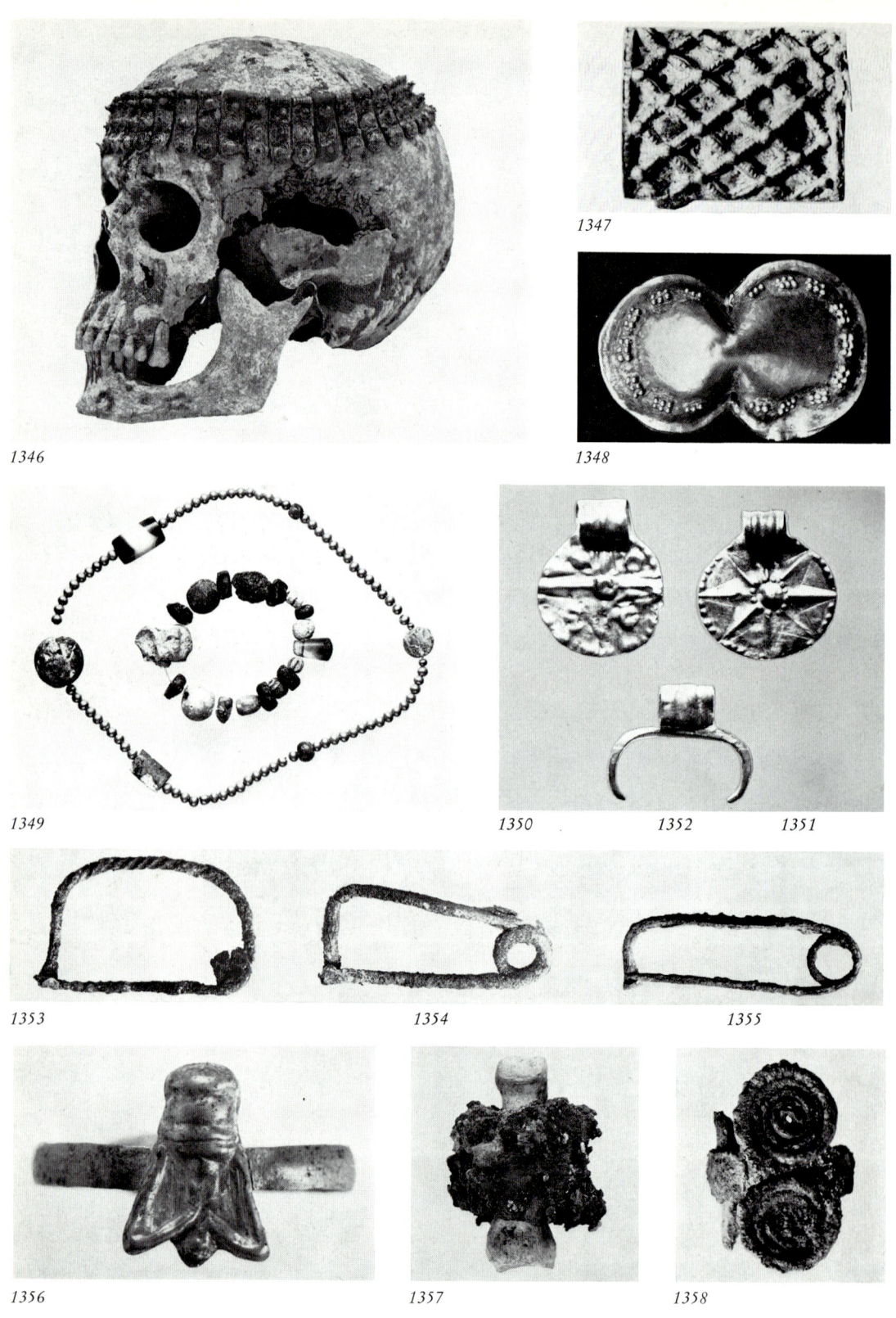

Ornaments and fibulae; from the Peloponnese, Attica and Boeotia

1359–1361   1362 a–c

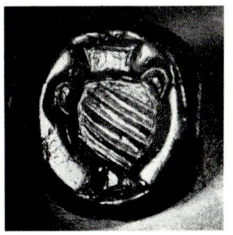
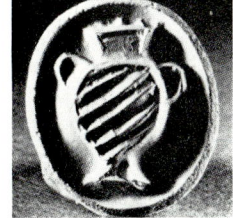

1373 a   1373 b   1374   1375

1376   1377

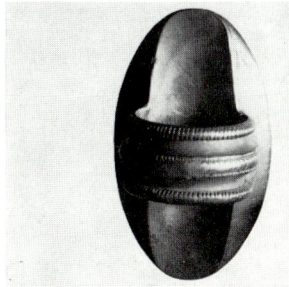

1381 a   1382   1378 a   1378 b

1379   1380

Gold rings, stamp- and cylinder-seals; Crete, the Cyclades and the mainland   1363–1372: p. 113, Fig. 38

pp. 392 and 393:
Gold rings, seals and examples of scripts

1388–1396: p. 117, Fig. 39; *1409 a–c:* p. 119, Fig. 40; *1416–1422:* p. 120 ff., Figs 41–43

1409d

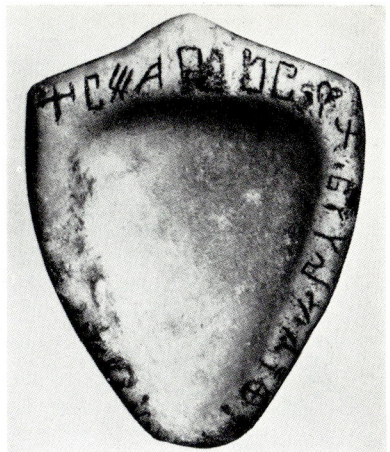

1410

1411 (s. auch S. 345)

1412

1413

1414

1415

1423

1424

Neolithic settlements in Cyprus

1436

1437

Khirokitia. Neolithic tholoi.   *1425–1435:* p. 125 ff., Figs 46–49

1438

1439

Khirokitia and Sotira. Neolithic houses

1440

1450

Sotira and Erimi. Neolithic and Chalcolithic buildings
1441–1449: p. 129 ff., Figs 50–52; *1451:* p. 132, Fig. 53; *1452:* p. 133, Fig. 54; *1453:* p. 134, Fig. 55; *1454:* p. 135, Fig. 56; *1455:* p. 136, Fig. 57

1456

1458

Enkomi and Kition. Late Bronze Age architecture

1457

1459

Enkomi and Kition. Late Bronze Age architecture

1462b

1460

Late Bronze Age fortifications

1461.1462a: p. 137, Fig. 58

1474

1473b

1463–1465a.1466–1473a: p. 141, Fig. 59; *1465b:* p. 402

Stone Age burials

1465b

1475

1477

1478

Stone Age burials

1476: p. 142, Fig. 60

1479a

1479b

1479c: p. 143, Fig. 61   Early Bronze Age chamber tomb in Philia (Vasiliko)

1480

1481

Early Bronze Age graves in Vounous

1482

1483

1484a,b: p. 133, Fig. 54   Early Bronze Age graves in Vounous

405

1485

1486

1487

1489

1488

1490

Neolithic and Chalcolithic pottery

1493

1491

1492

Chalcolithic pottery

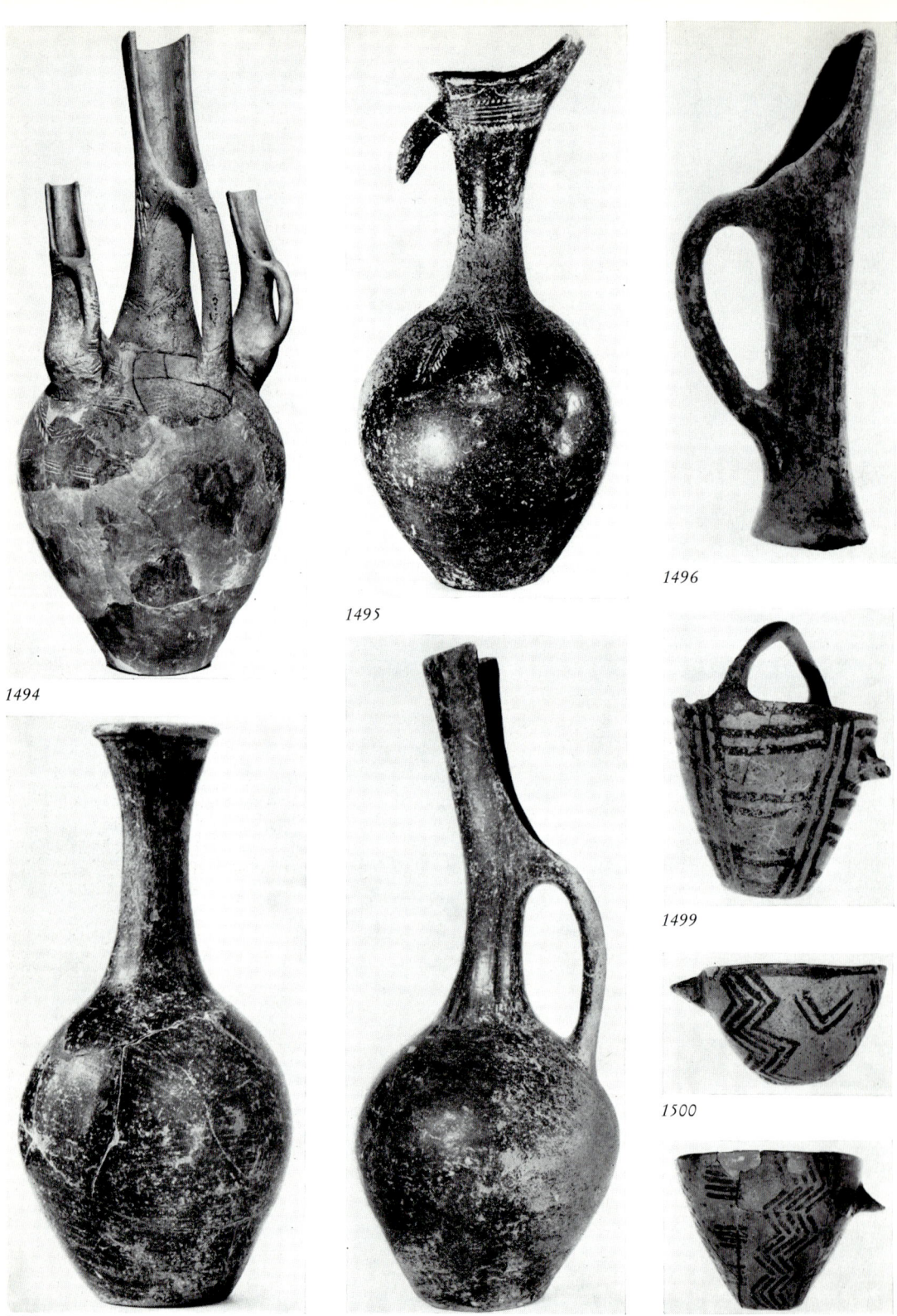

1494
1495
1496
1497
1498
1499
1500
1501

Early Bronze Age pottery

1502

1503

1504

1505

1506

Early Bronze Age red-polished pottery

1507

1508

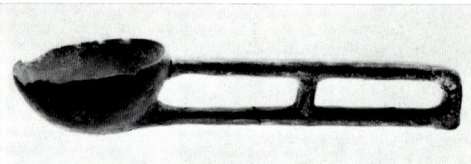

1509

1510

1511

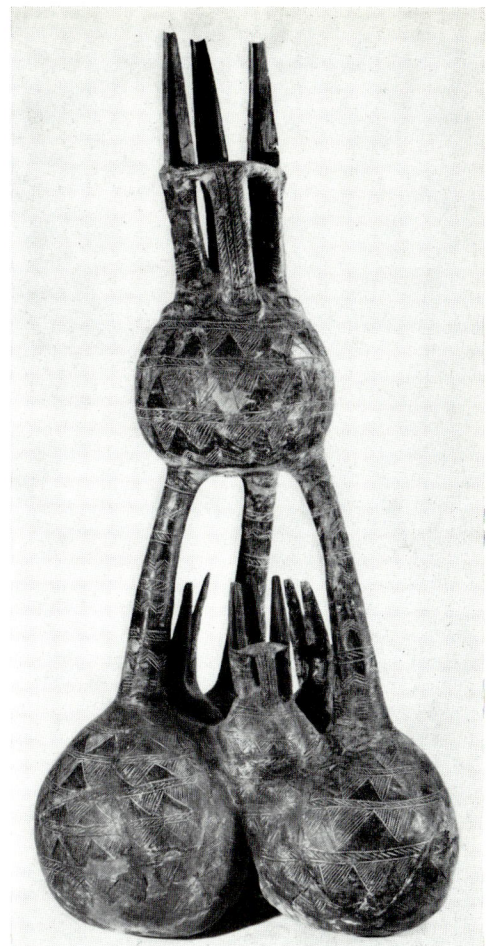

1512

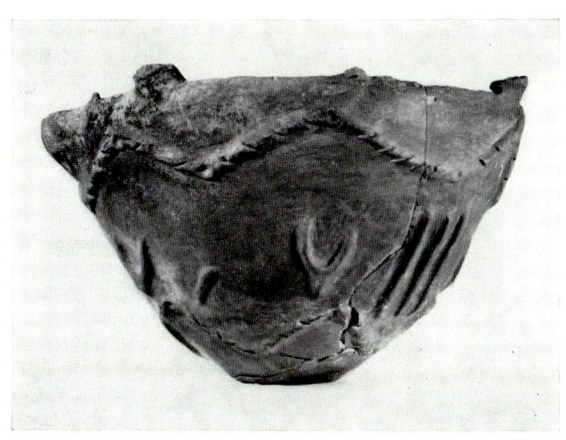

1513

1514

pp. 410 and 411: Early Bronze Age red-polished clay pottery

1515

1516

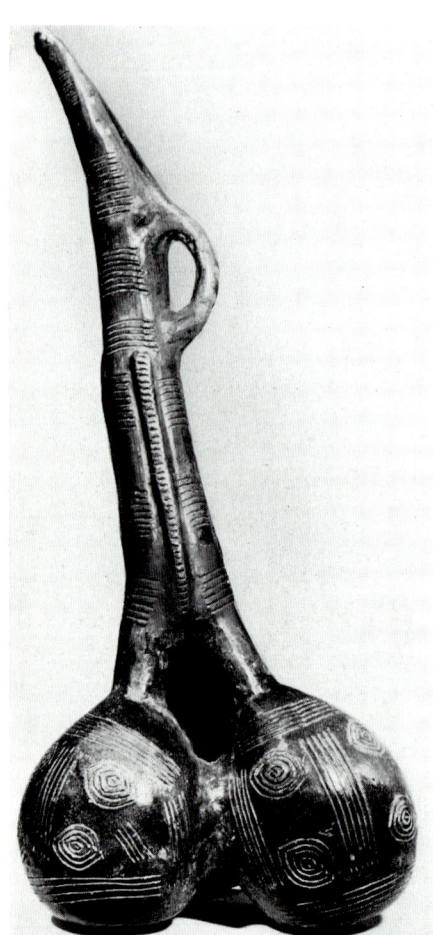

1517

1518

1519

Early Bronze Age red- and black-polished pottery

1520

1521

Early Bronze Age pyxides with lid

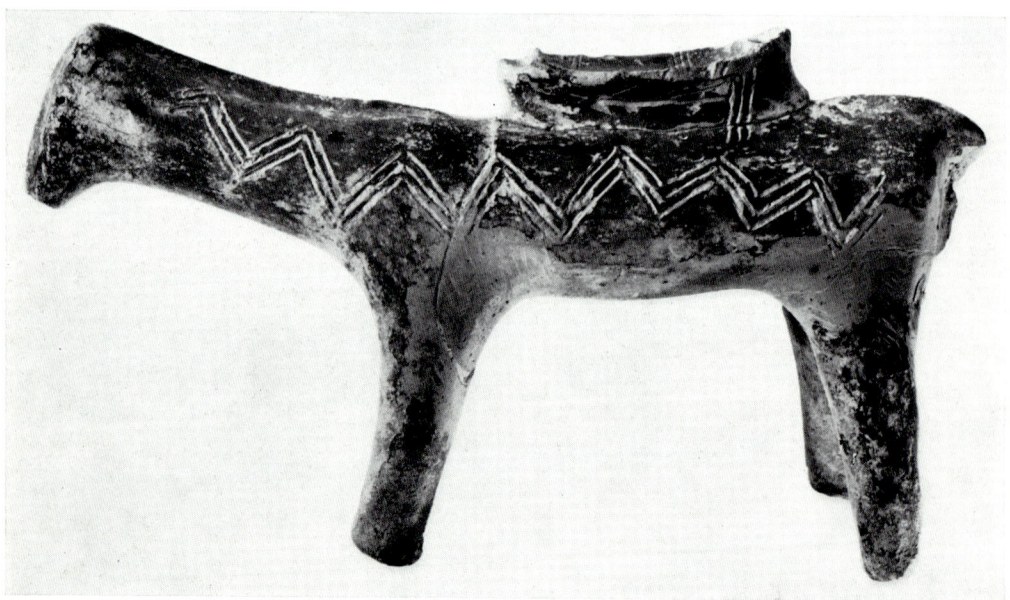

1522

1523

Votive vessel and animal figure of the Early Bronze Age

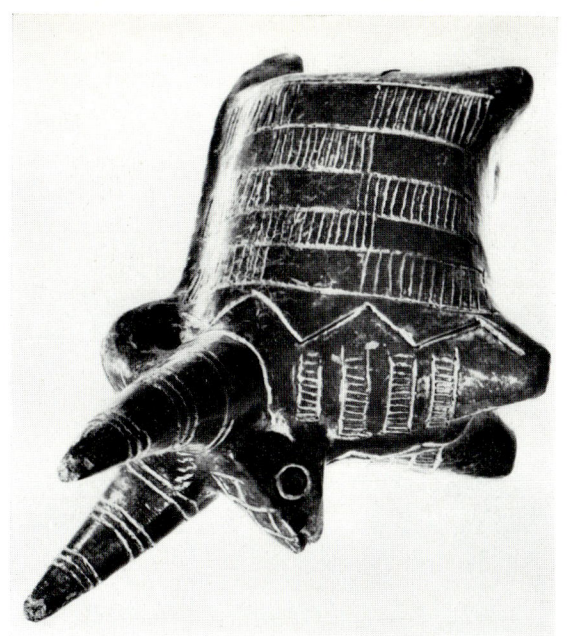

1525

1527

1524

1526

Theriomorphic Early Bronze Age vessels

1528

1529

1530

1531

1532

1533

1534

1535

1536

pp. 416 and 417
Middle Bronze Age pottery

1537

1538

1539

1540

1541

pp. 418 and 419: Middle Bronze Age pottery

1542

1543

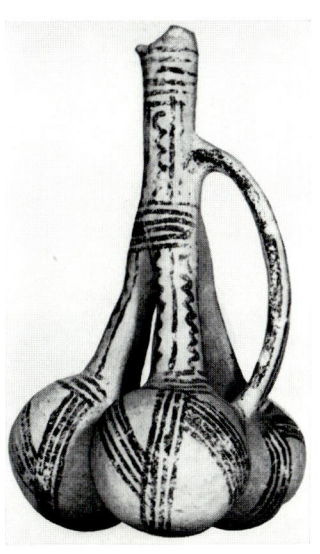
1544

1545

1546

1547

1548

1551

1549

1550 *1552*

1553

1554a

1555

1556

1557

1558

1554b: p. 422   pp. 420 and 421: Middle and Late Cypriote vessels

1559

1560

1561   1554b

Middle Bronze Age pottery and statuette

1562

1565

1563   *1564a*   *1566*

1564b: p. 424

Early and Middle Bronze Age pottery

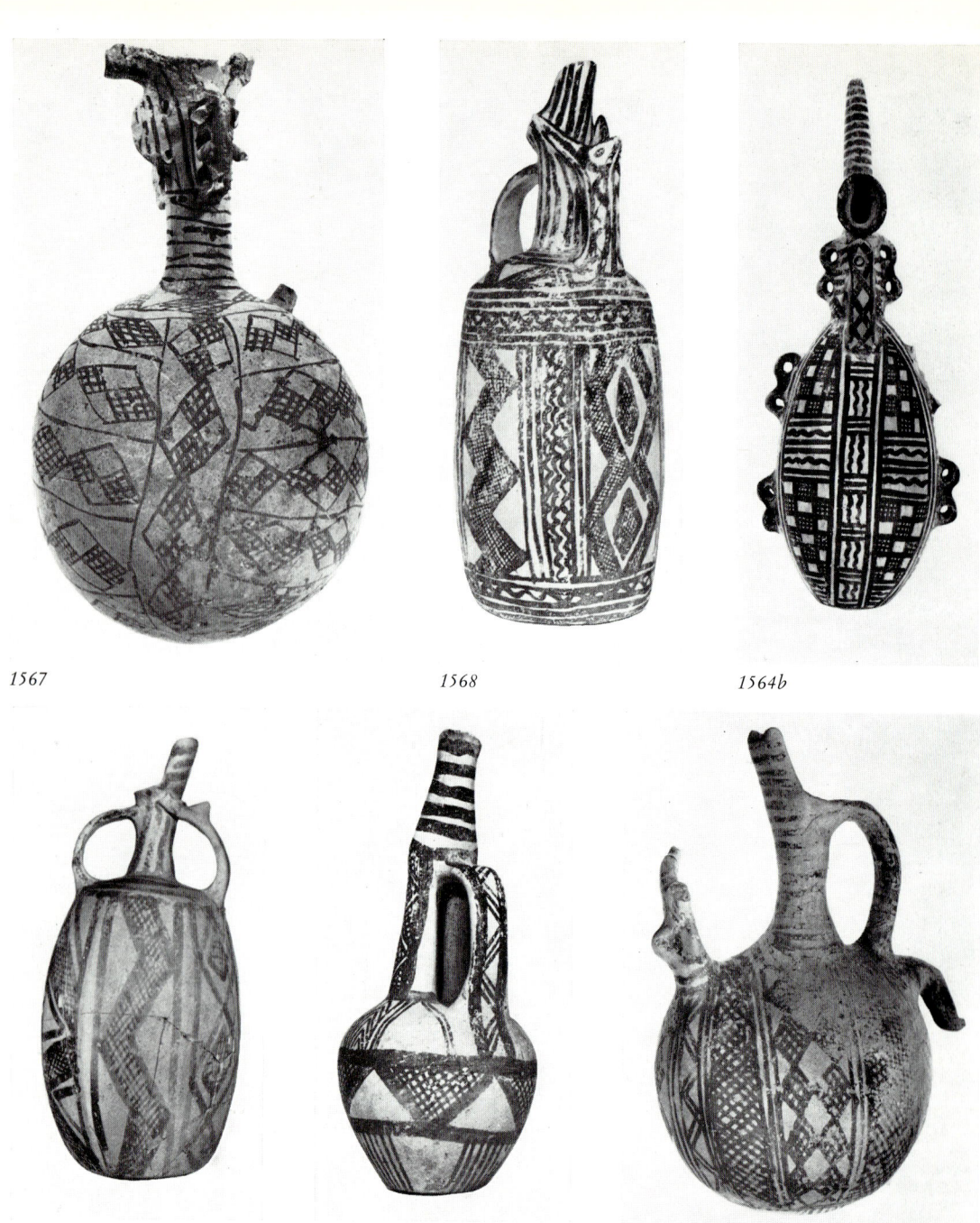

1567   1568   1564b

1569   1570   1571

Middle and Late Bronze Age Cypriote pottery

1573a   *1573b*

1572

Imported Cretan pottery, found in Cypriote graves

1574

1575

1576

pp. 426 and 427:
Bichrome vessels of the 'Late Cypriote I' period and red 'Late Cypriote II' wheelmade pottery

1577

1578

1579a 　　　*1579b* 　　　*1580*

1581　　　*1582* 　　　*1583* 　　　*1584* 　　　*1585*

1586

427

1587

1589

1590

1588

1591

Late Bronze Age Cypriote 'Base-Ring Ware'

Late Bronze Age Cypriote 'Base-Ring Ware'

1598

1599

1600

1601

1602

1603

pp. 430 and 431:
Base-Ring and Bucchero Ware from different sites in Cyprus

1604

1605

1606

1607

1608

1609

1610   *1611*

432

1612

1613

1614

1615

pp. 432 and 433: White Slip Ware

1616

1617

1618

1619

Mycenaean pottery from various sites in Cyprus, LH III a

Krater from Enkomi

Krater from Enkomi

Krater from Pyla (Verghin)

Krater from the region of Kition

Krater of unknown provenance

1625

1626

Mycenaean vases, LH III b

1627

1628

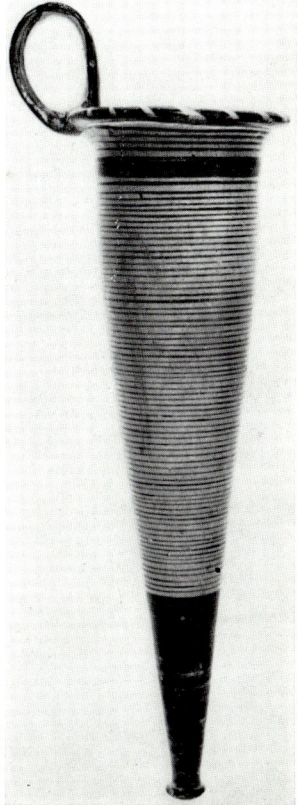

1629

Mycenaean vases, LH III b

1630

Mycenaean krater from Shemishin, LH III b

1631

1632

1633

1634

Mycenaean vessels from various sites, LH III b

Mycenaean pottery, LH III b, some imitated from local Cypriote types of vessel

1640

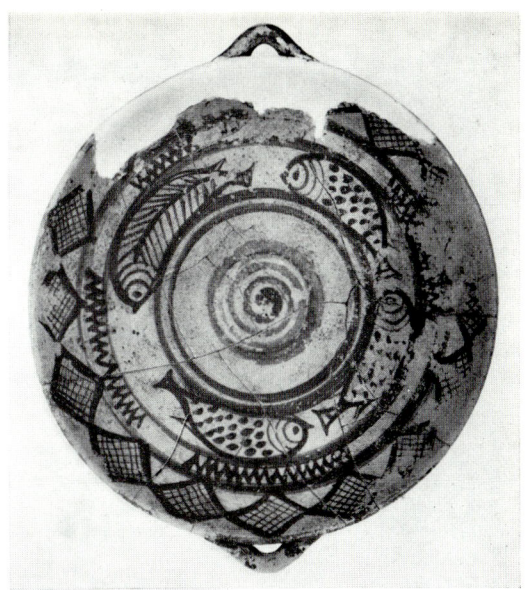
1641

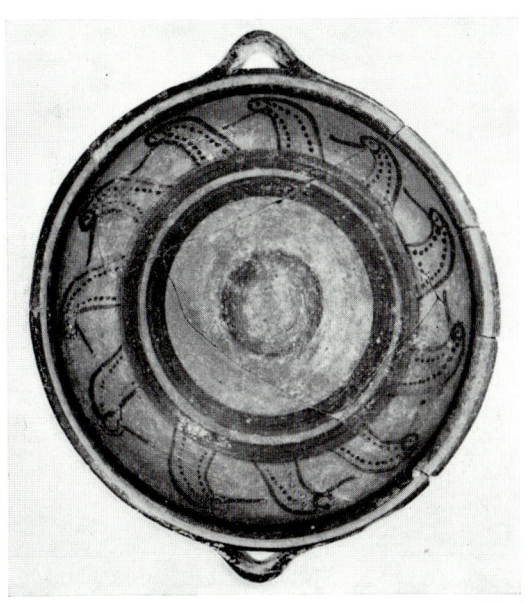
1642

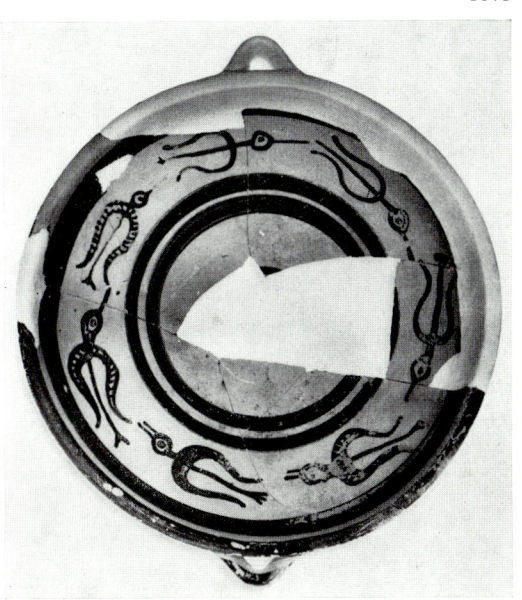
1643

Flat Mycenaean dishes, LH III b

445

1646

1647

1648

pp. 446 and 447: Mycenaean pottery, LH III b and c

1649

1650

1651a

1652

1653

pp. 448 and 449:
Askos in the form of a bird and ring kernos,
Late Cypriote III; Proto-White-Painted Ware
1651b: p. 450

1654

1655

1651b

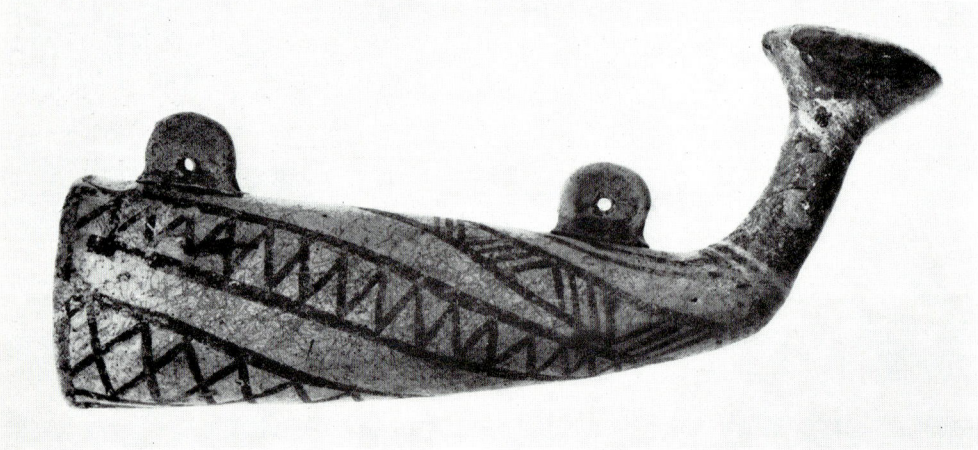

1656

Proto-White-Painted Ware

1657

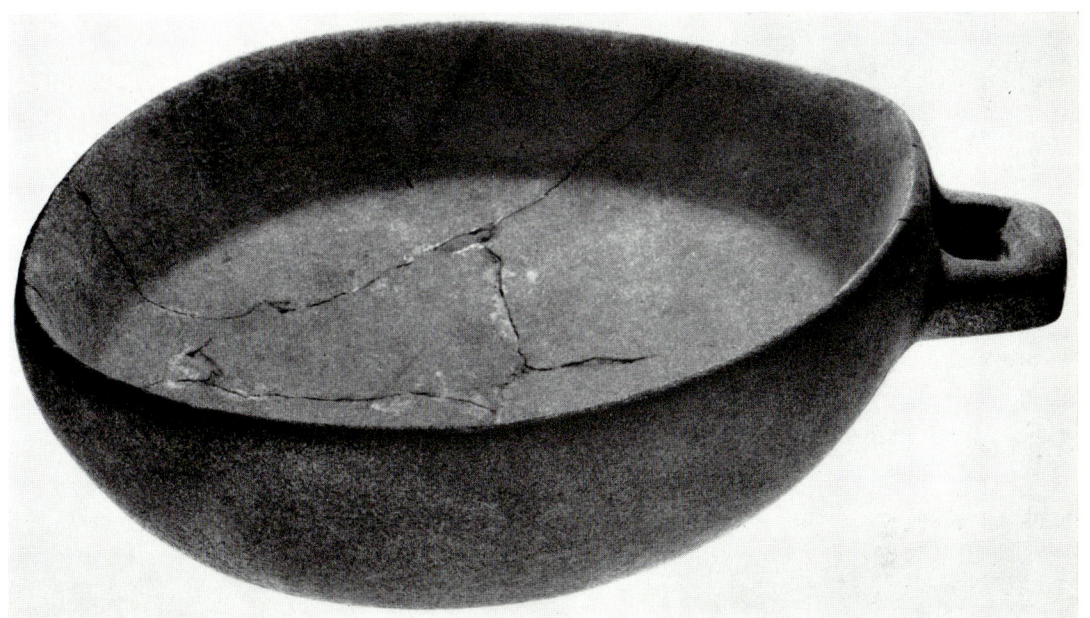

1658

1659   1660

1661   1662   1663   1664

Early Neolithic stone vessels and conical stones from Khirokitia

451

1665

1666

1667

Late Bronze Age alabaster vessels

1668a

1670

1669a

1668b

1669b

Late Bronze Age steatite vessels

453

1671a   *1671b*

Faience rhyton from Kition

1671 c.d: Colour plate 3 after p. 160

1672

1673

1674

1675

Bronze Age faience vessels from Cyprus

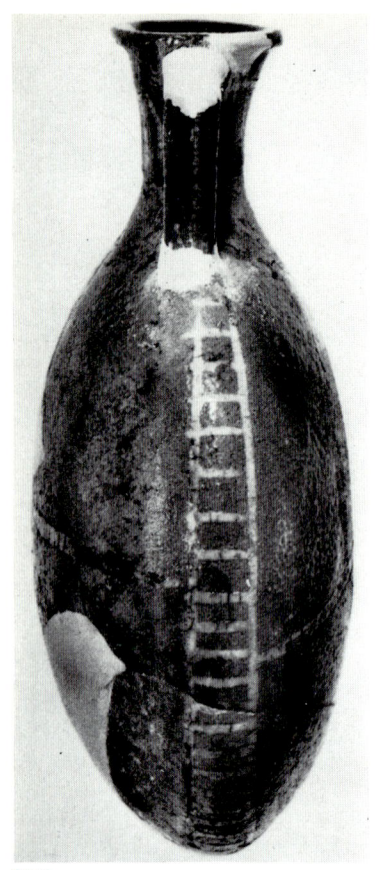

1676a 1676b

1677 1678

pp. 456 and 457: Bronze Age faience and glass-paste vessels from Cyprus

pp. 458 and 459: Bronze and silver vessels from Enkomi
1684c: Colour plate 4 after p. 168

1682
1683

1684a

1684b

1685a

1685b

pp. 460 and 461:
Four-sided bronze
cauldron stands
with wheels

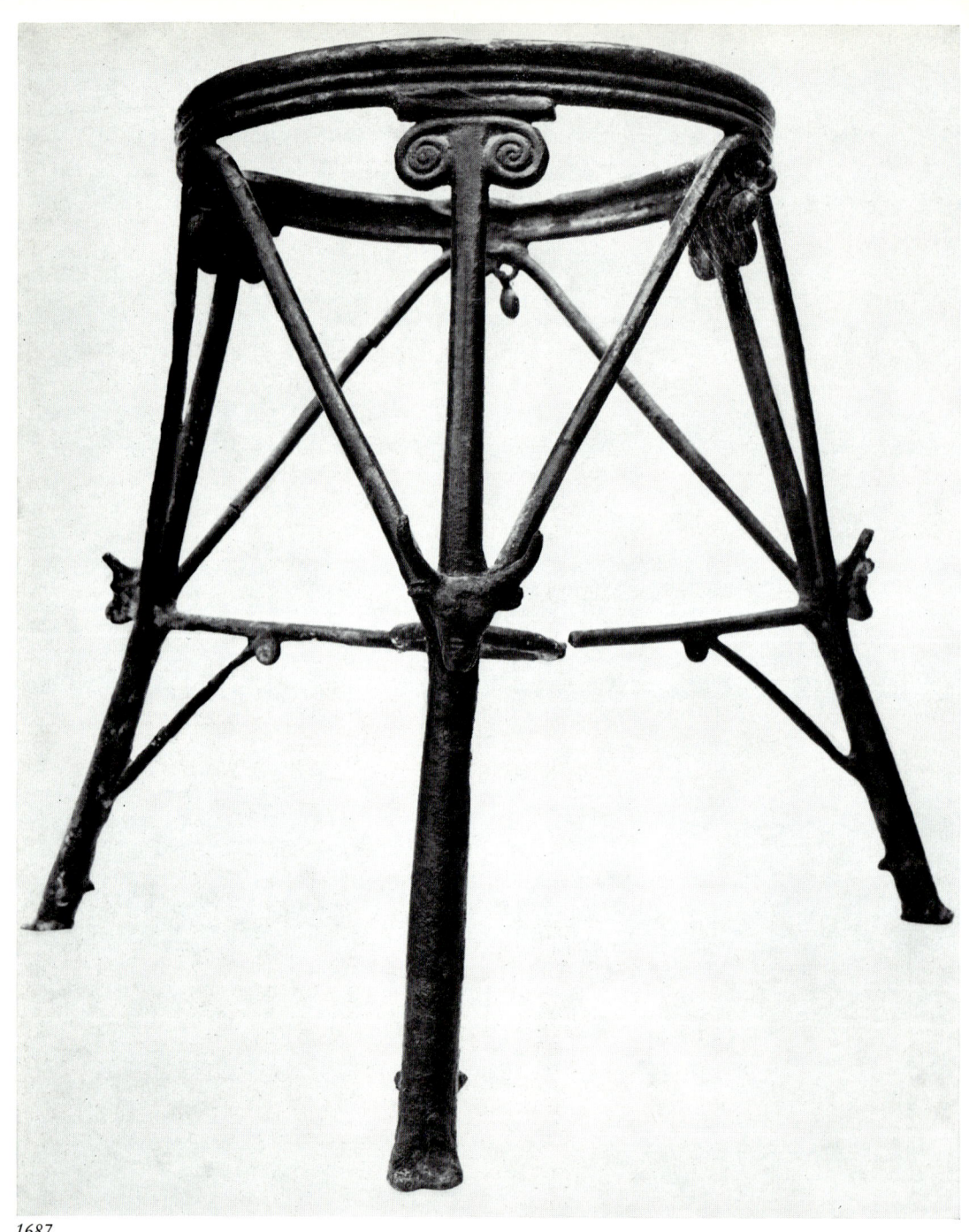

1687

pp. 462 and 463: Tripod and table with loop feet in bronze; Episkopi and Enkomi

1688a

1688b

1689

pp. 464 and 465:
Stone and clay
Neolithic free-
standing sculpture

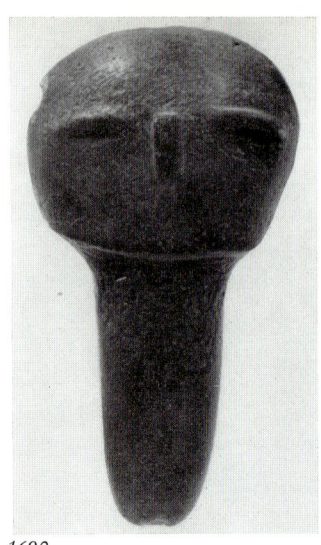

1690

1691

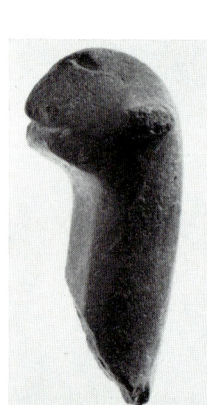

1692

1693

1694

1695

1698

1696

1697

1699

1700

1701a

1701b

1702

1703

Chalcolithic steatite idols

1704

1705

Early Bronze Age terracotta groups from Vounous

1706 1707 1708 1709

1710 1711 1712

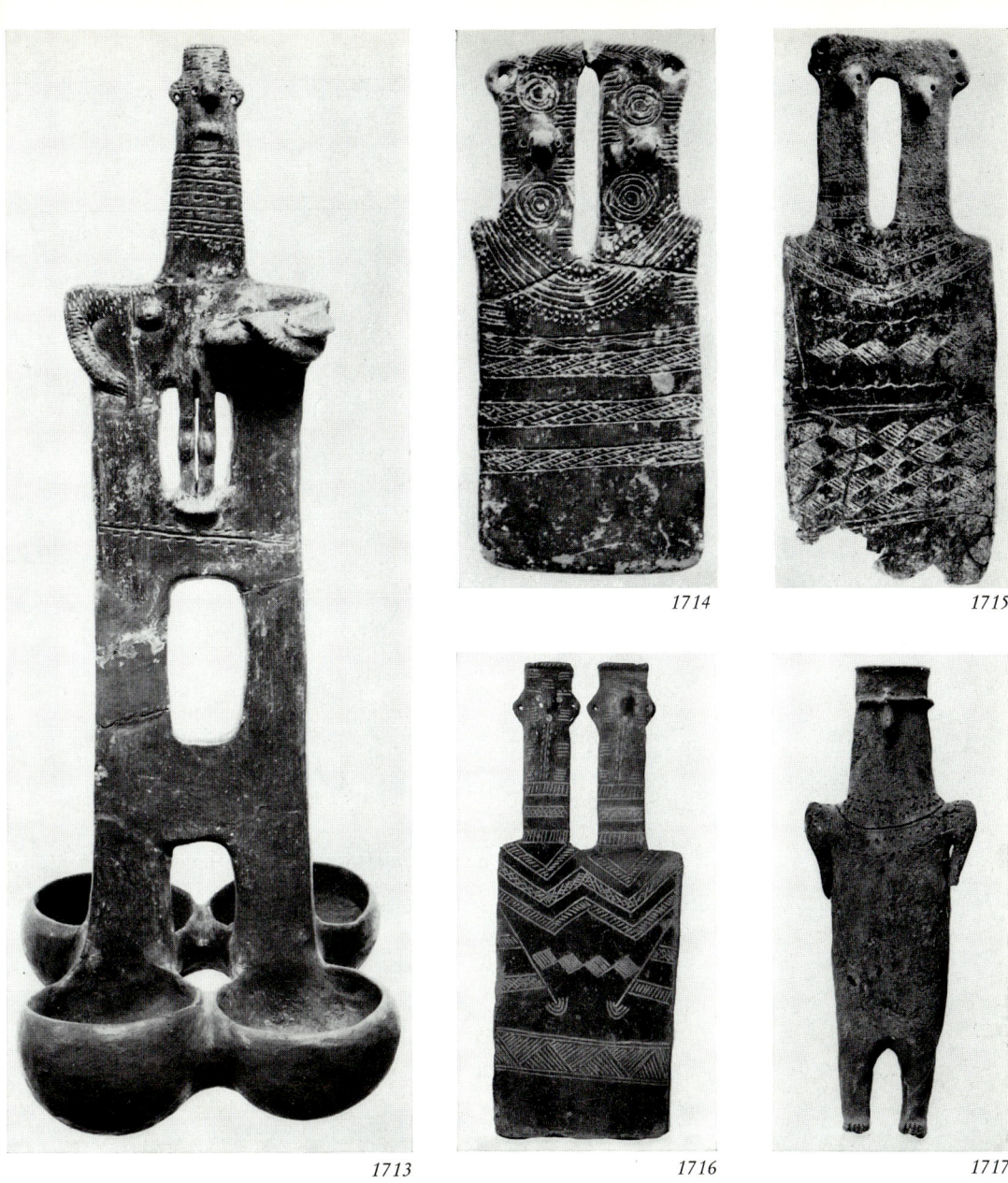

1713   1714   1715   1716   1717

pp. 468 and 469: Early Bronze Age figurative terracottas from Vounous, Lapithos and Denia. Models of daggers (*1707.1708*), dagger sheaths (*1706.1709*), brushes or combs (*1710.1711*) and spindles (*1712*); composite vessel (*1713*) and twin idols in plank shape (*1714–1716*). Middle Bronze Age idol from Akaki (*1717*).

1719

1720

1721

Late Bronze Age clay models of ships   *1718:* p. 471

1718 Middle Bronze Age clay model of a ship with crew

1722

1723

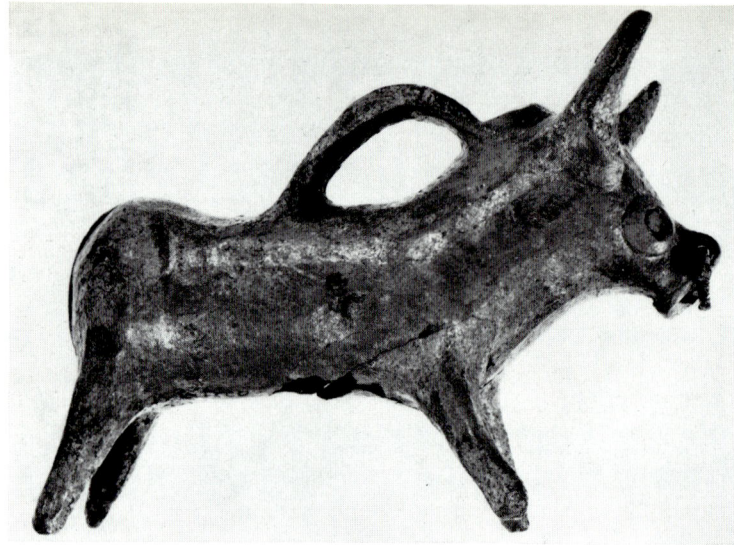

1724

1725

Late Bronze Age clay figures   *1726:* Colour plate 3 after p. 160

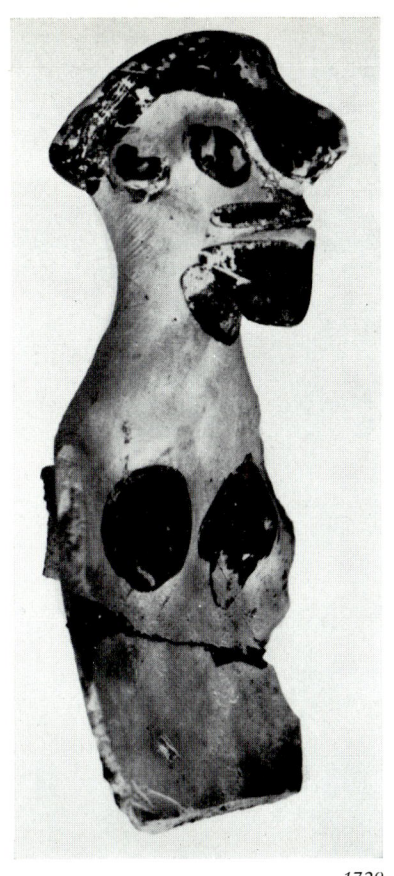

1729

1727

1730

1728

Late Bronze Age clay figures

1731
Late Bronze Age two-headed centaur from Enkomi

1732 *1733* *1734*

Late Cypriote bronze statuettes

1735a

1735b

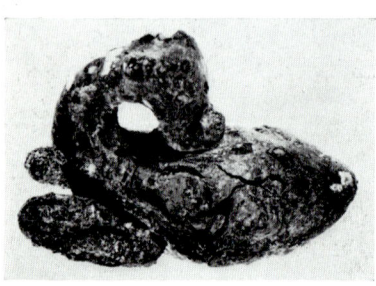

1737

pp. 746 and 477: Late Cypriote animal statuettes in bronze

1736

1738

1739

1740 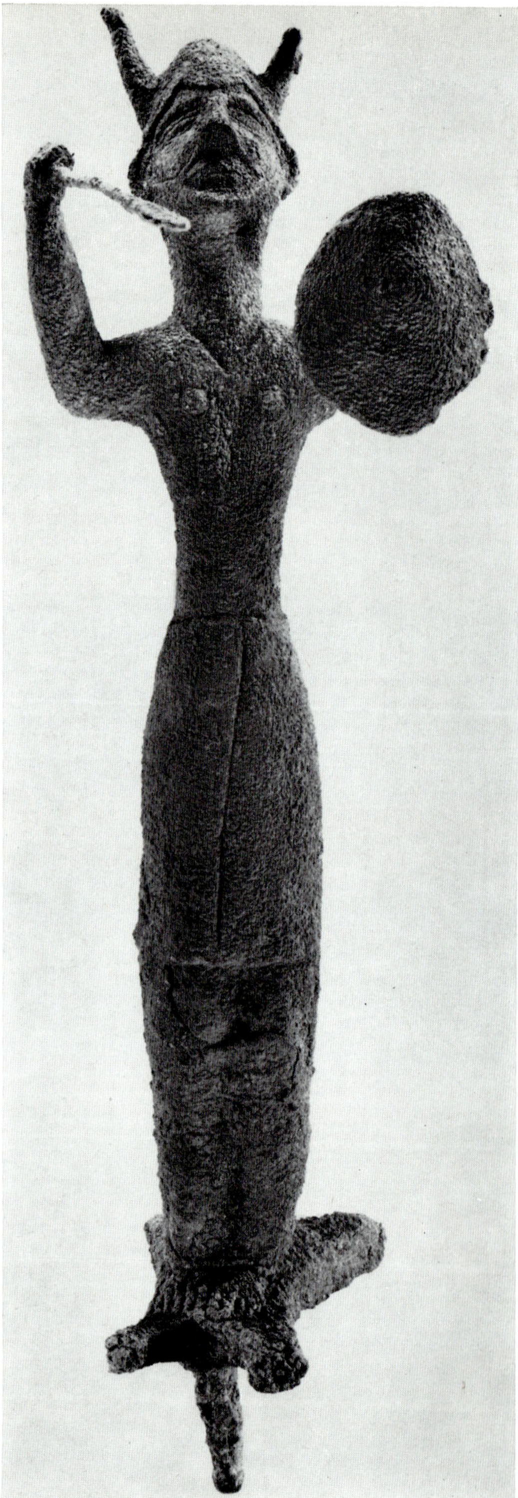 1741

Enkomi, Late Cypriote bronze figures of gods

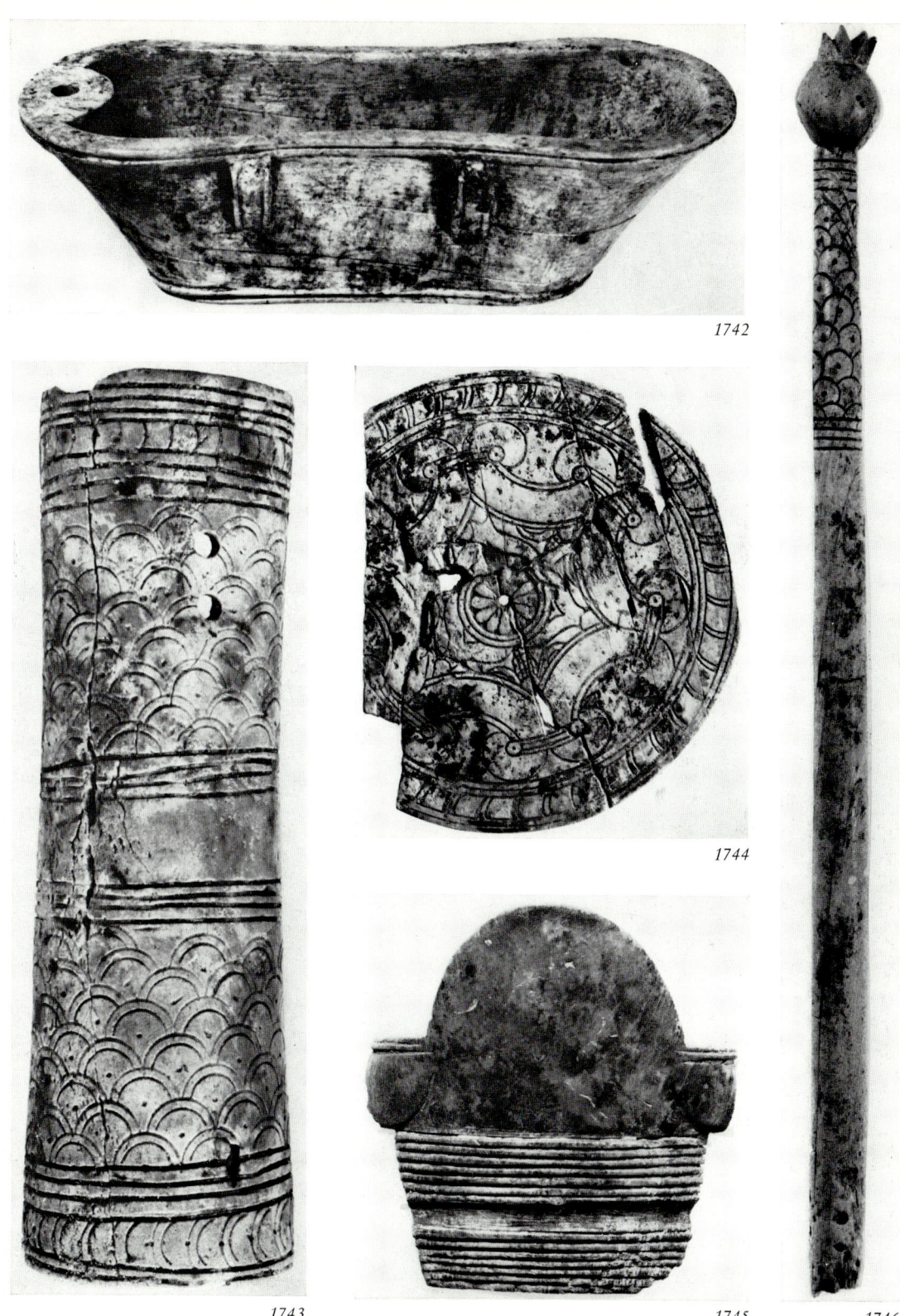

Kition, Late Cypriote ivory carvings

479

1747
Ivory mirror handle, Enkomi

1748
Ivory mirror handle,
Kouklia

1749a

1749b

Enkomi, Grave 58: ivory gaming box, Late Cypriote III. British Museum, London

482

1751

1754

1753

1750

1752

Impressions of Late Bronze Age cylinder-seals from Cyprus

1759a

1755

1756

1757

1759b

1760

Late Bronze Age seals and impressions   *1758*

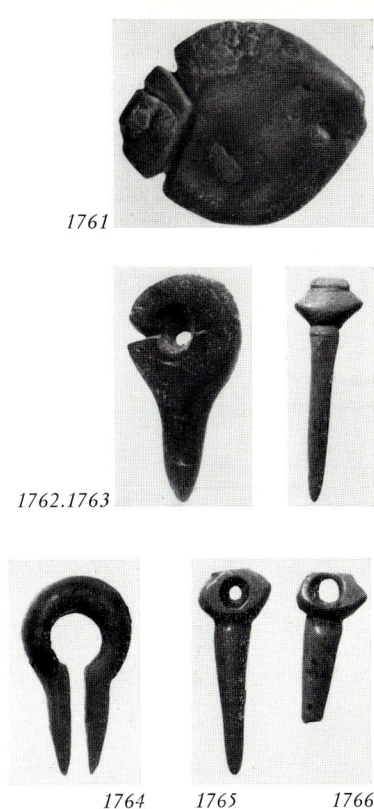

1761

1762.1763

1767   *1764*   *1765*   *1766*

Neolithic ornaments of stone and shells

1768

1769

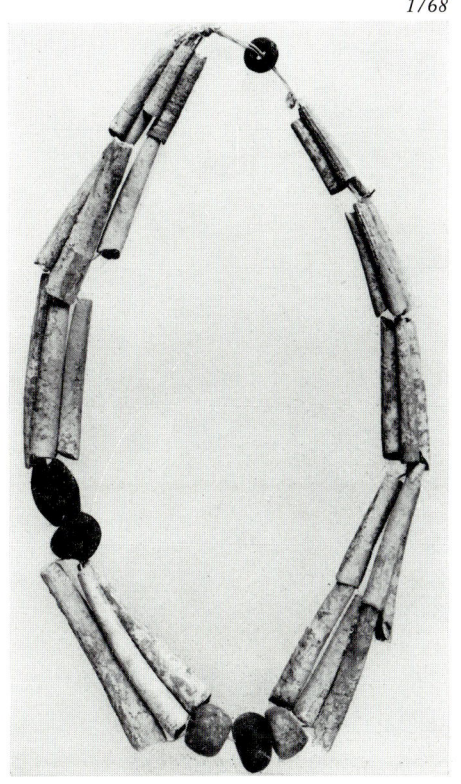

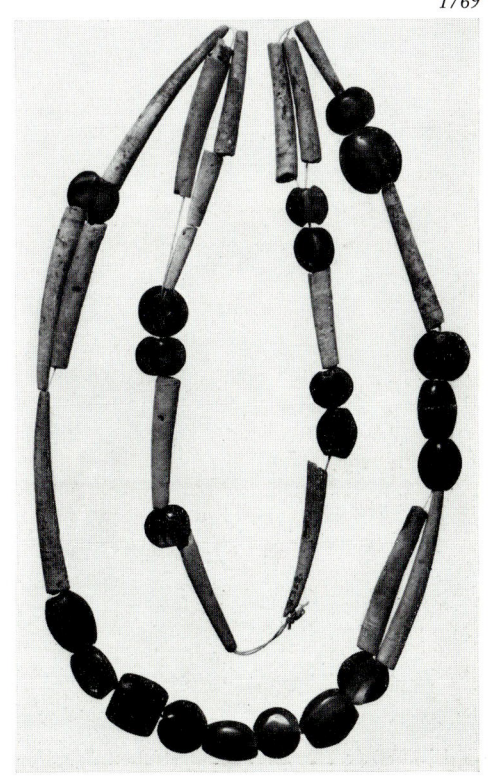

485

1770

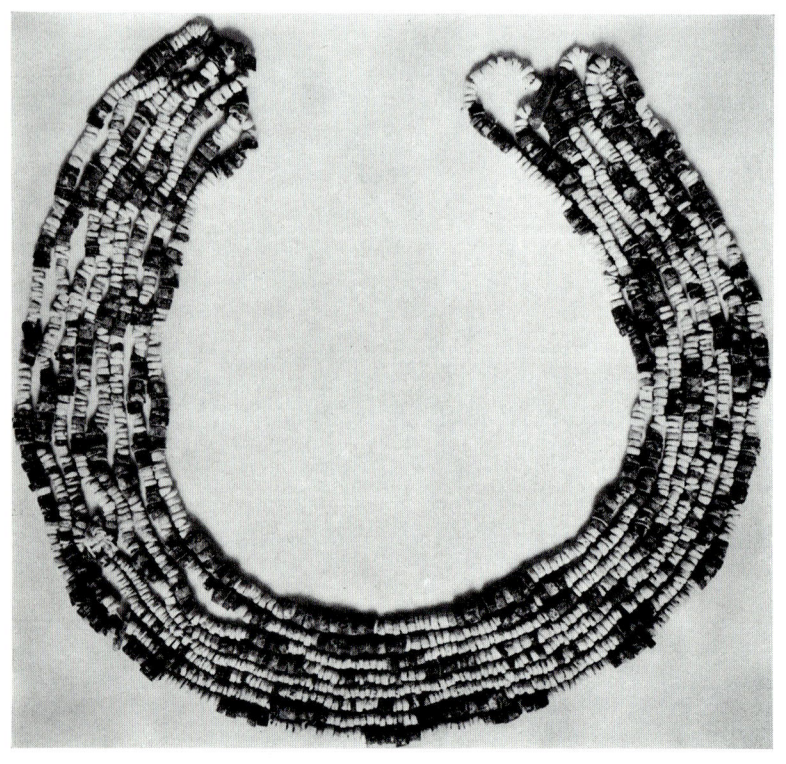

1771

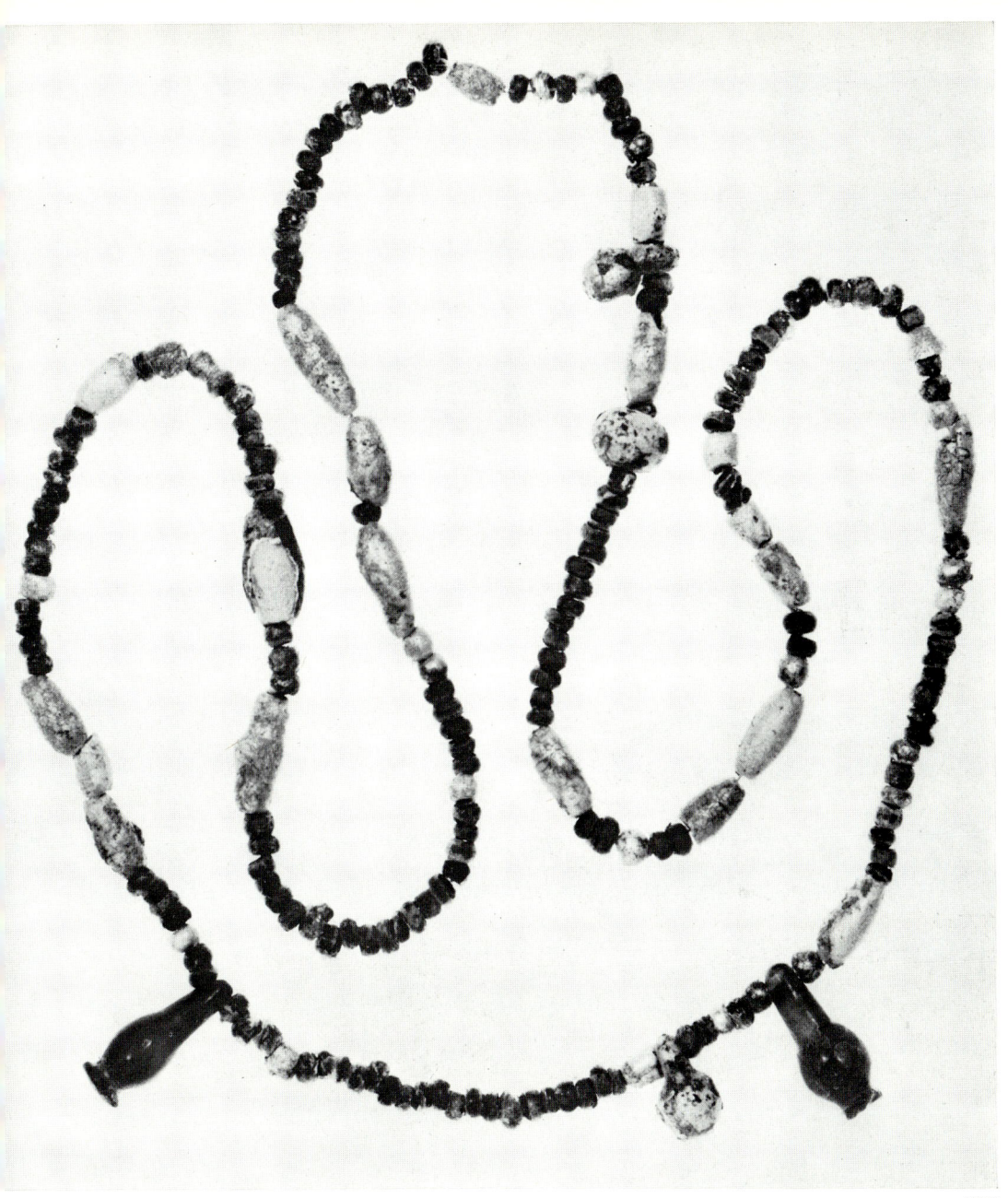

pp. 486 and 487: Early and Late Cypriote necklaces of semi-precious stones and glass-paste beads

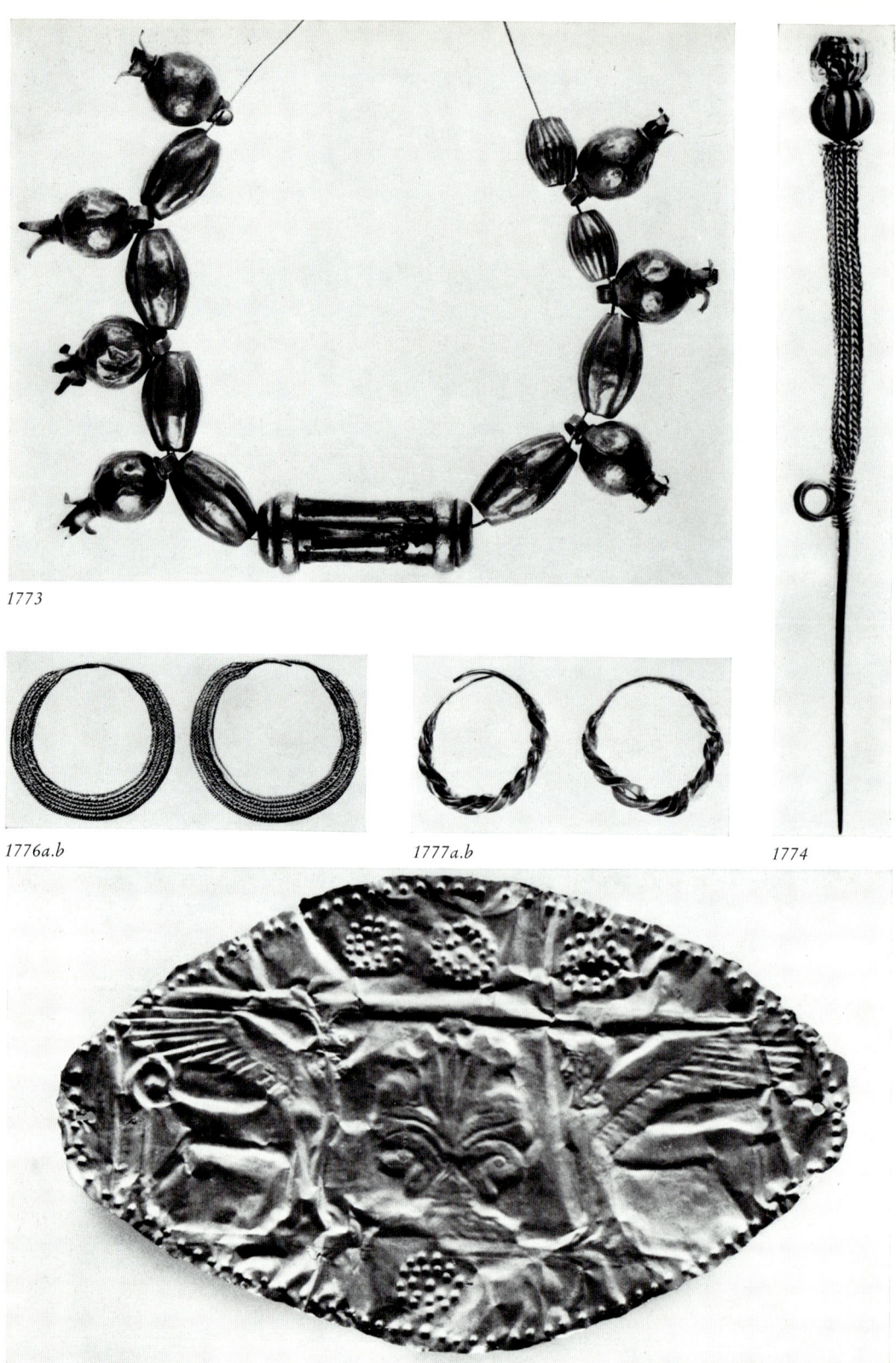

1773

1776a.b   1777a.b   1774

1775

Late Bronze Age gold ornaments

1780
1781
1782
1783
1778a.b
1779a.b

Late Bronze Age gold ornaments

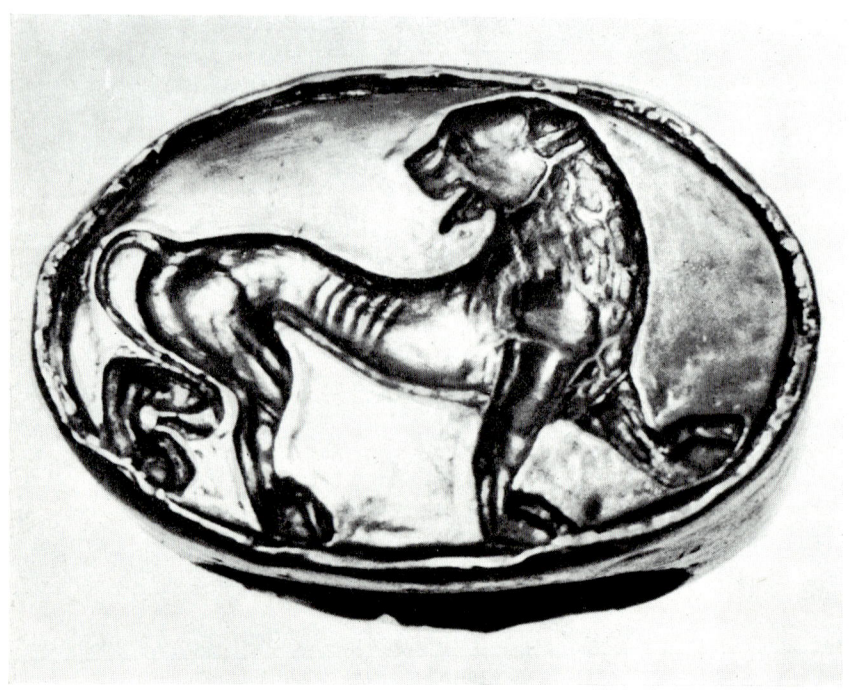

1789

1784

Late Bronze Age
gold ornaments

1785–1788: p. 491

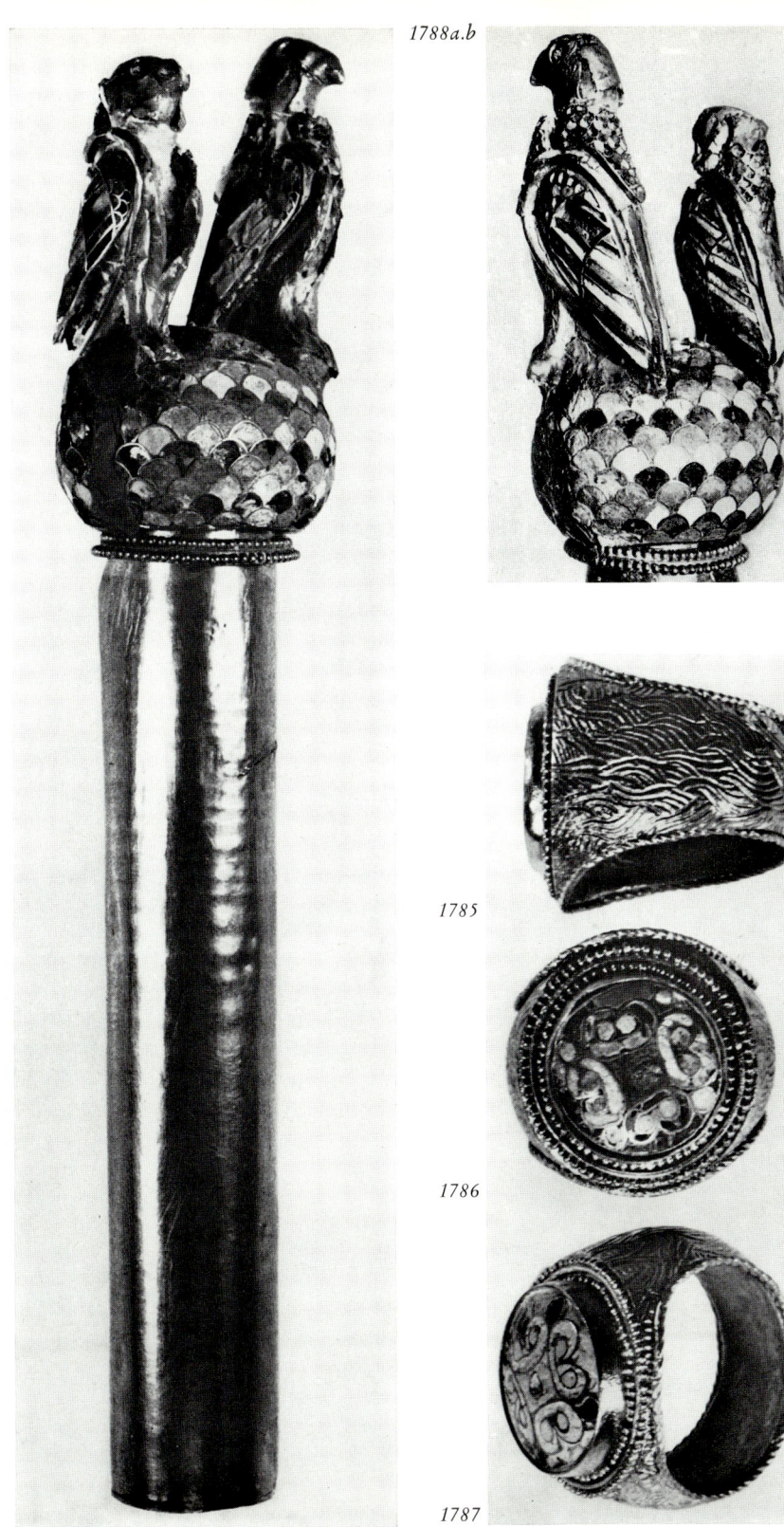

Gold sceptre and gold finger rings with enamel inlays
1788 c.d: Colour plate 4 after p. 168; *1789:* p. 490

1790

1791

1792

1793

Late Bronze Age gold ornaments from Kition and Enkomi

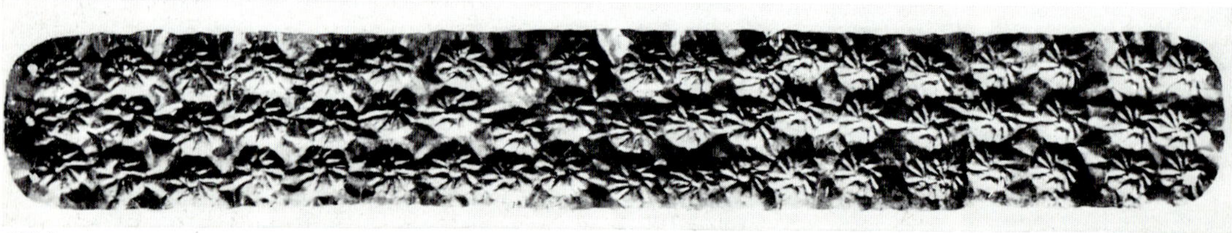

1794

1795

492

1796

1797

1798

1799

1800

1801

1802

1803

Late Bronze Age gold diadems and mouth-plates from Kition

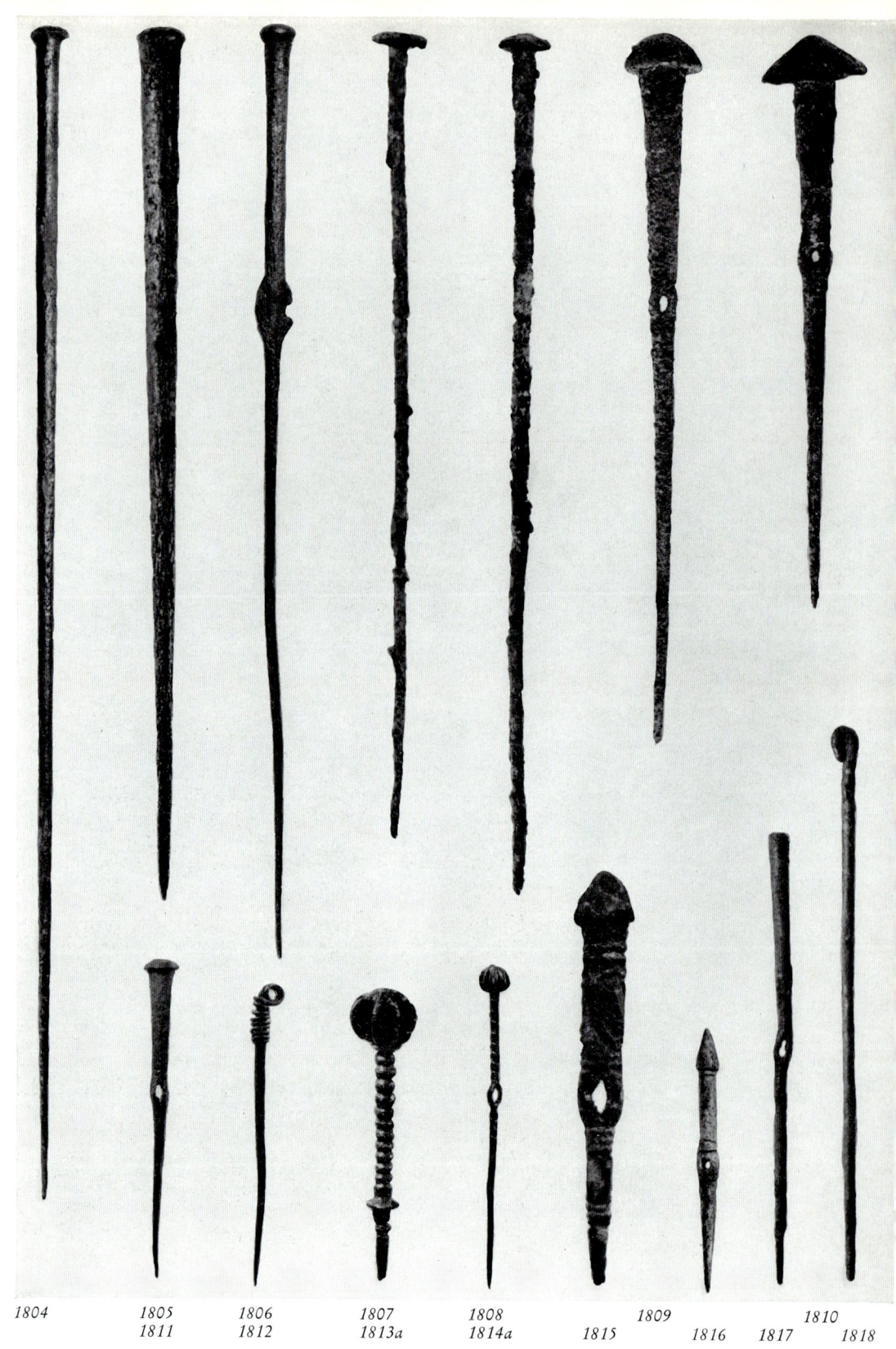

1804	1805	1806	1807	1808	1809		1810
	1811	1812	1813a	1814a	1815	1816	1817	1818

Cypriote dress pins of the second millennium B.C.

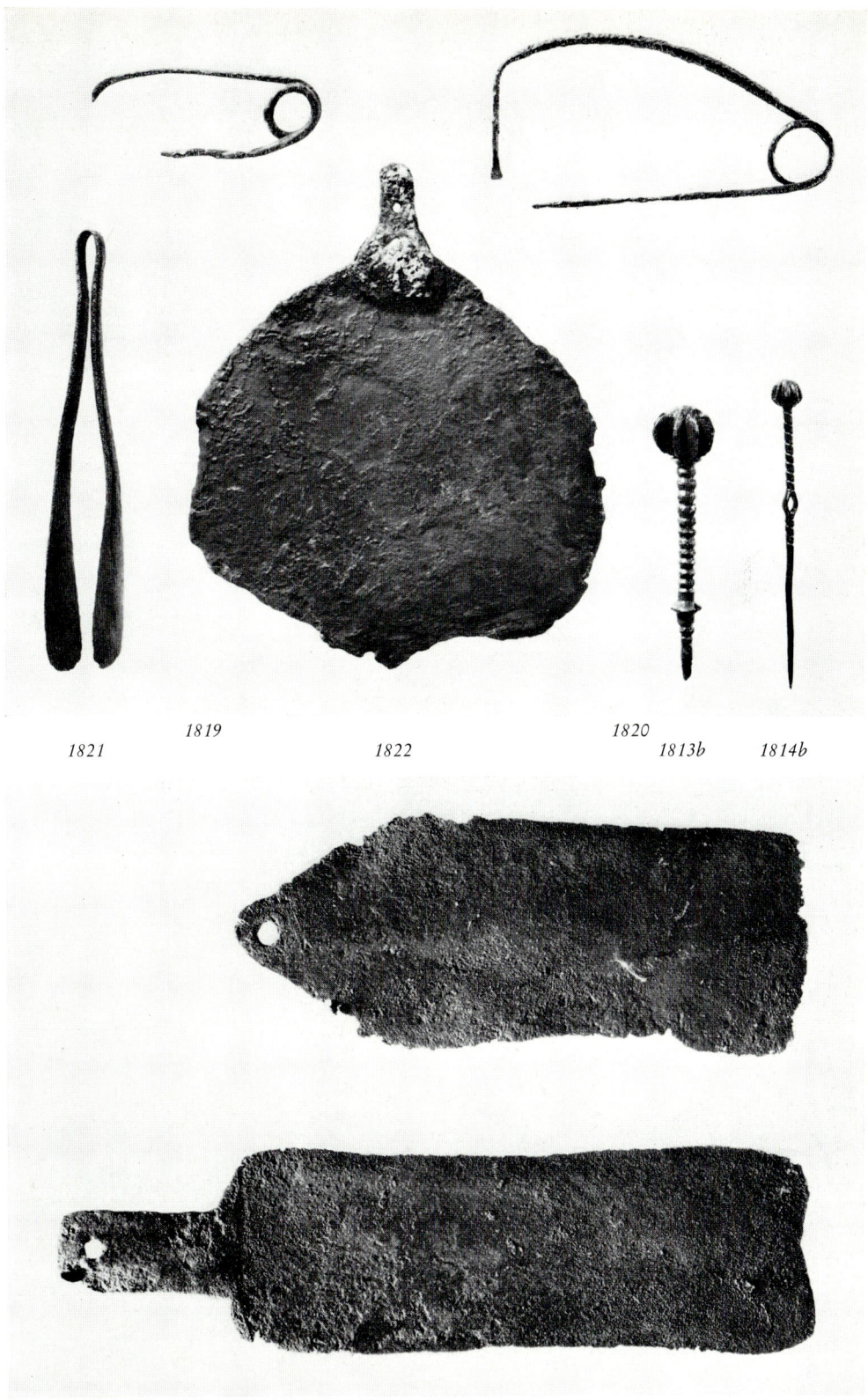

Fibulae, pins and toilet articles of the late third and the second millennium B.C.

1825a.b

1826a

1826b.c

1827a

1827b

Early and Middle Cypriote curlers in gold, silver and bronze sheet

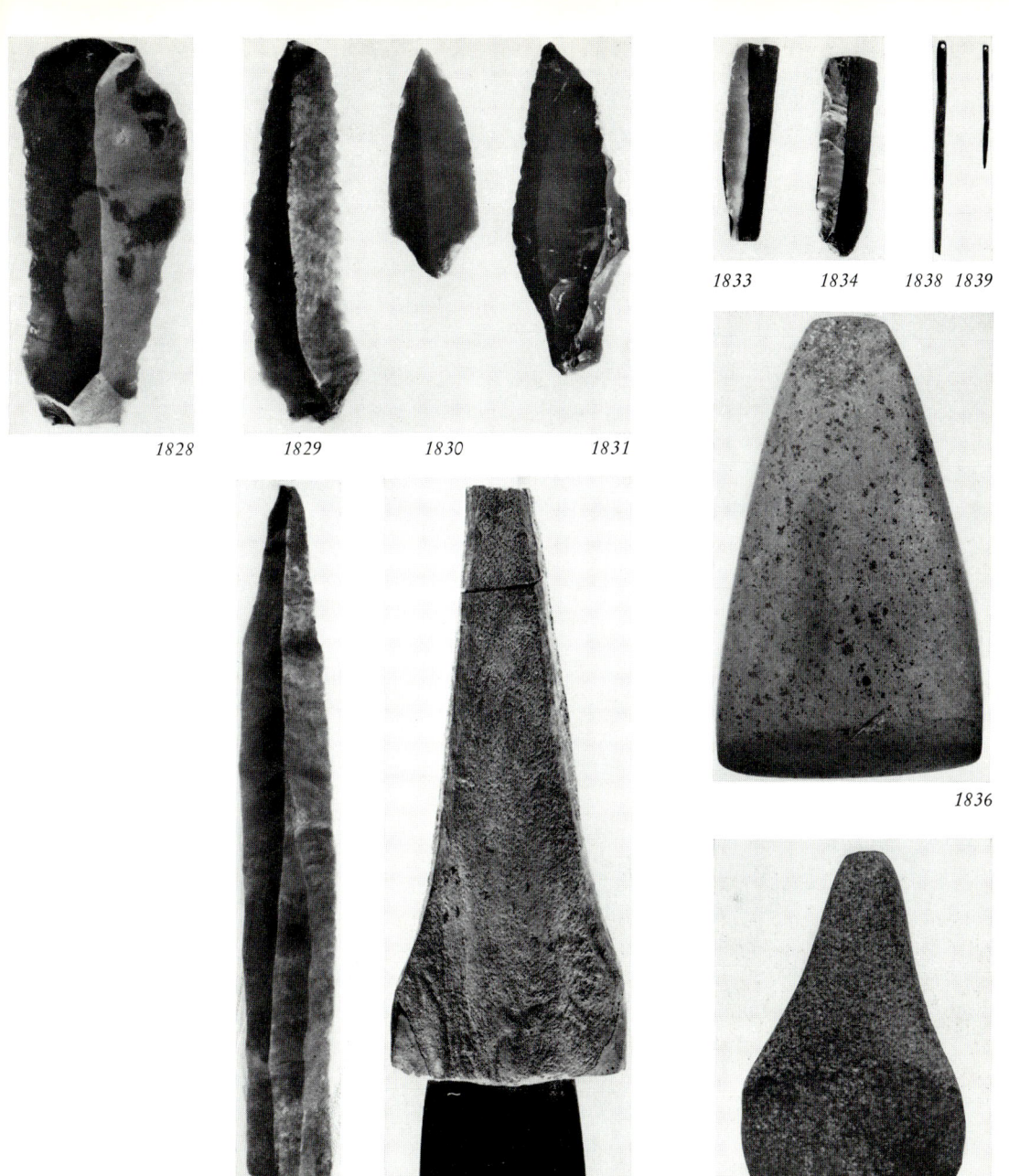

Neolithic and Chalcolithic stone and bone implements

1828 *1829* *1830* *1831* *1833* *1834* *1838* *1839*

1832 *1835* *1836* *1837*

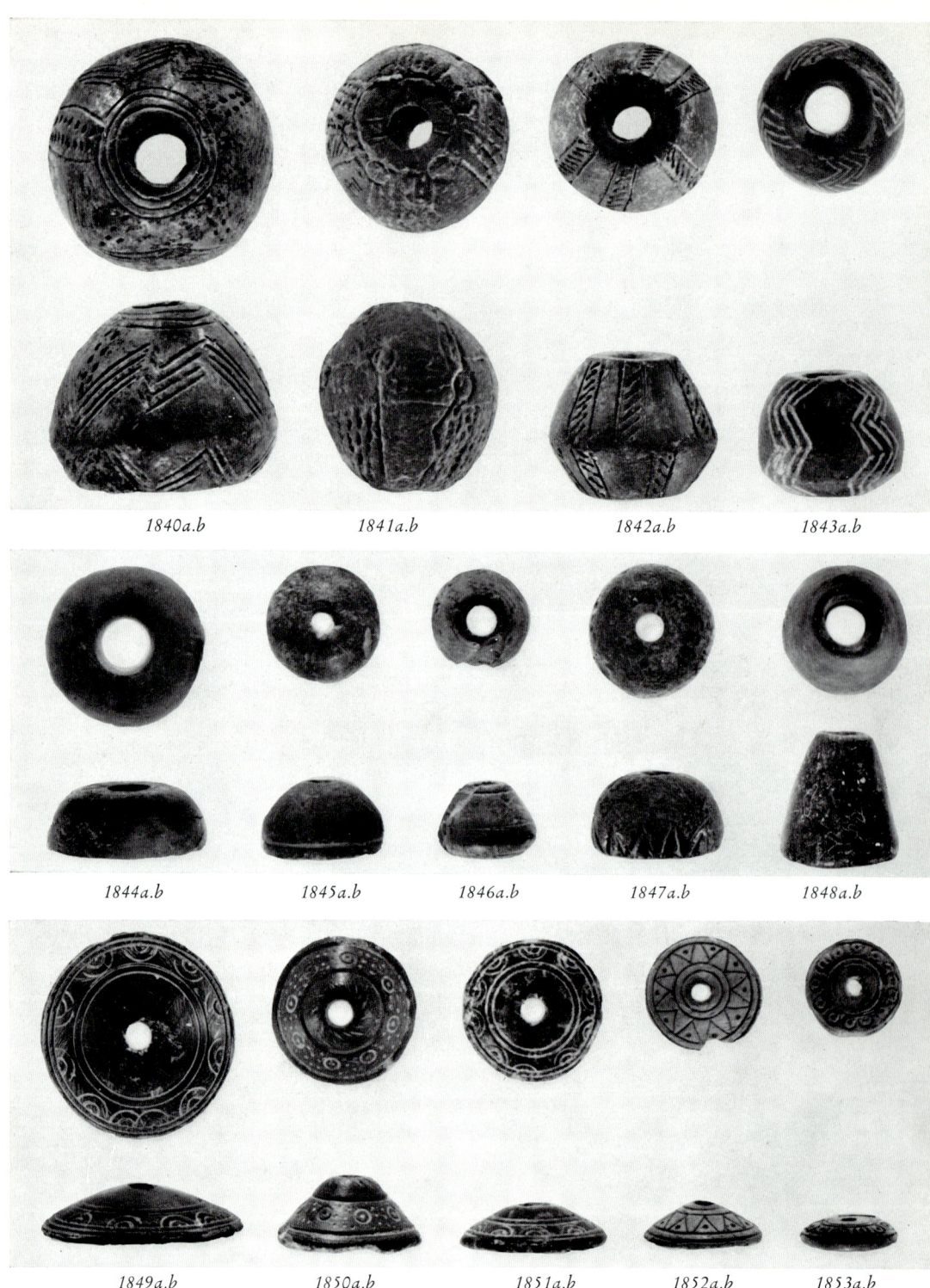

Spindle whorls in clay, ivory and steatite

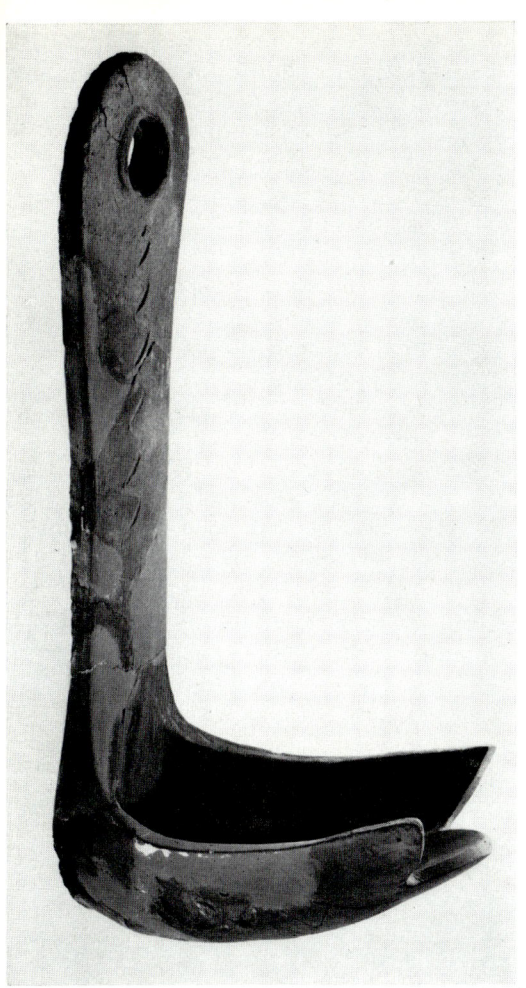

1856

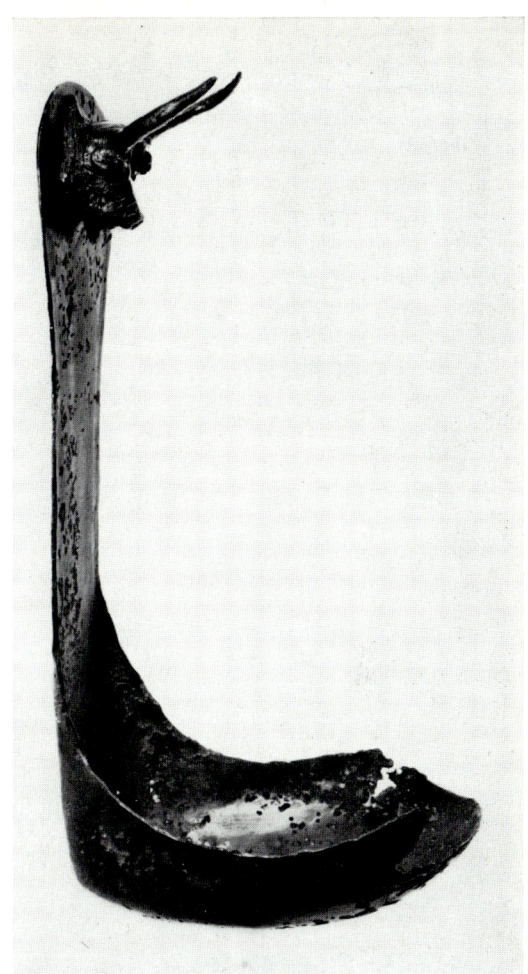

1857

1854

1855

Clay and metal lamps

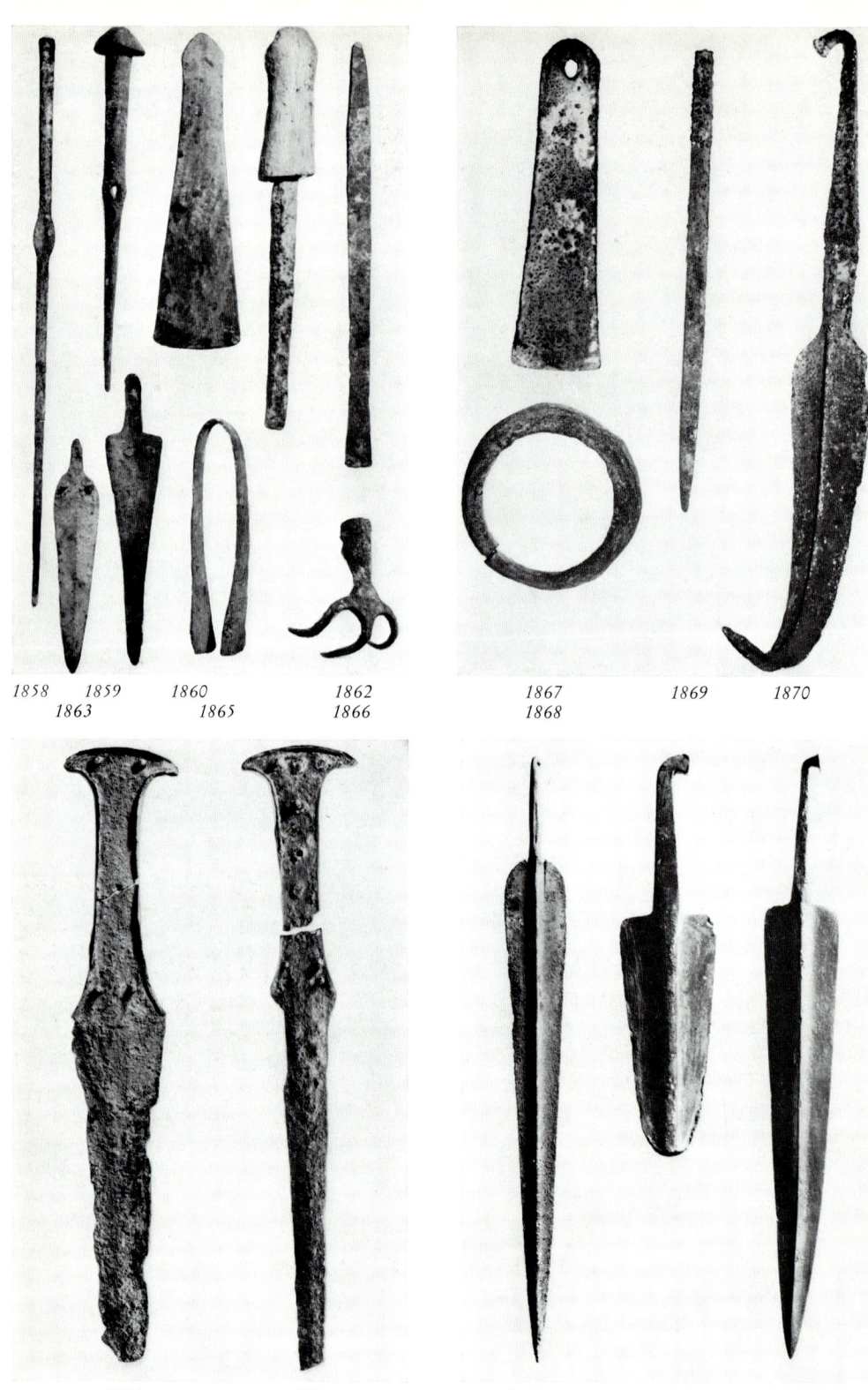

| 1858 | 1859 | 1860 | | 1862 | | 1867 | 1869 | 1870 |
| 1863 | | 1865 | | 1866 | | 1868 | | |

1874　　1875　　　　1871　1872　1873

1876

1877

1878

1879

pp. 500 and 501: Copper and bronze implements and weapons

1880

Bronze greave from Enkomi

Bronze arms and armour; except *1884:* Enkomi

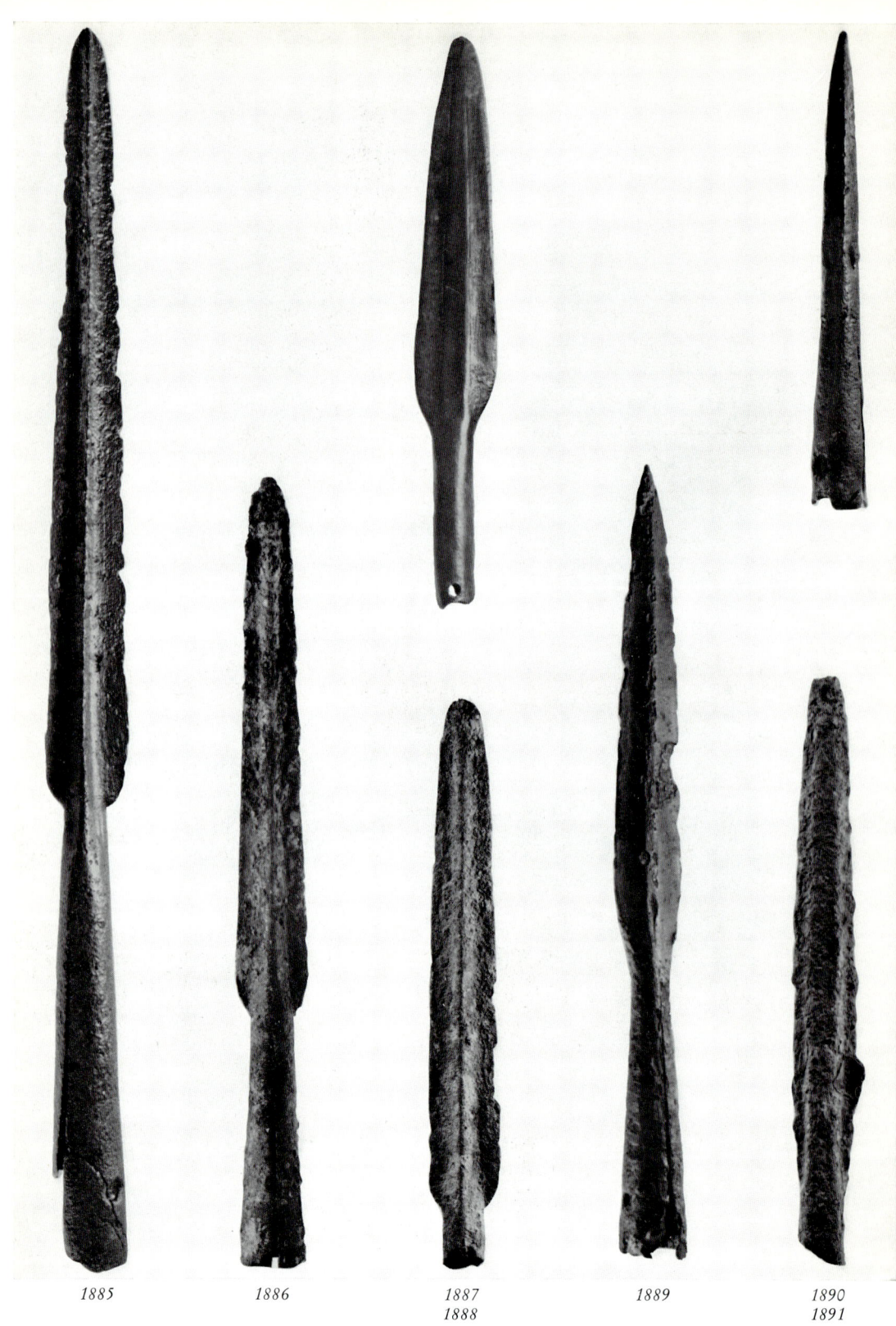

1885 1886 1887 1889 1890
             1888   1891

Bronze spearheads and lanceheads

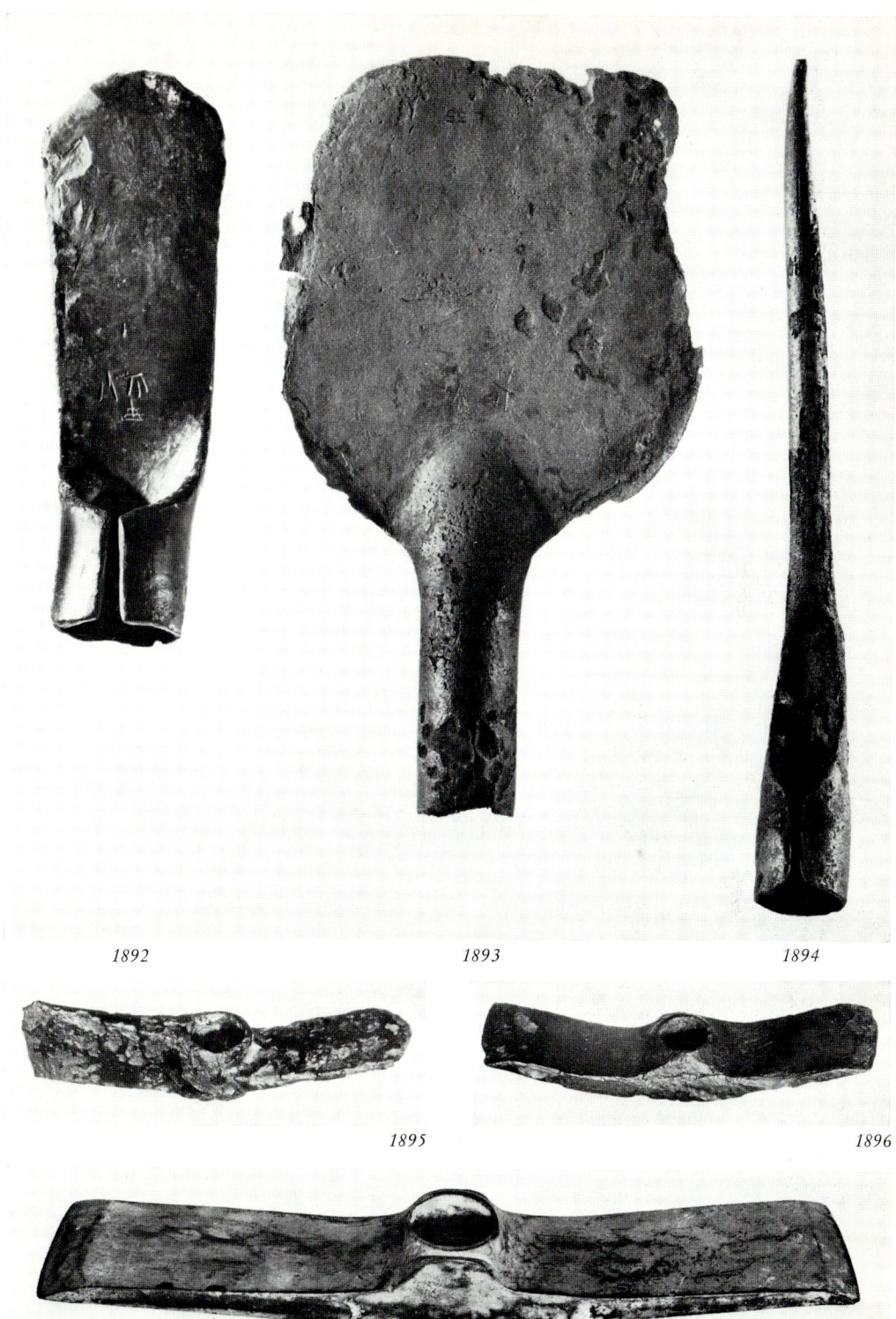

1892 1893 1894

1895 1896

1897

Bronze tools

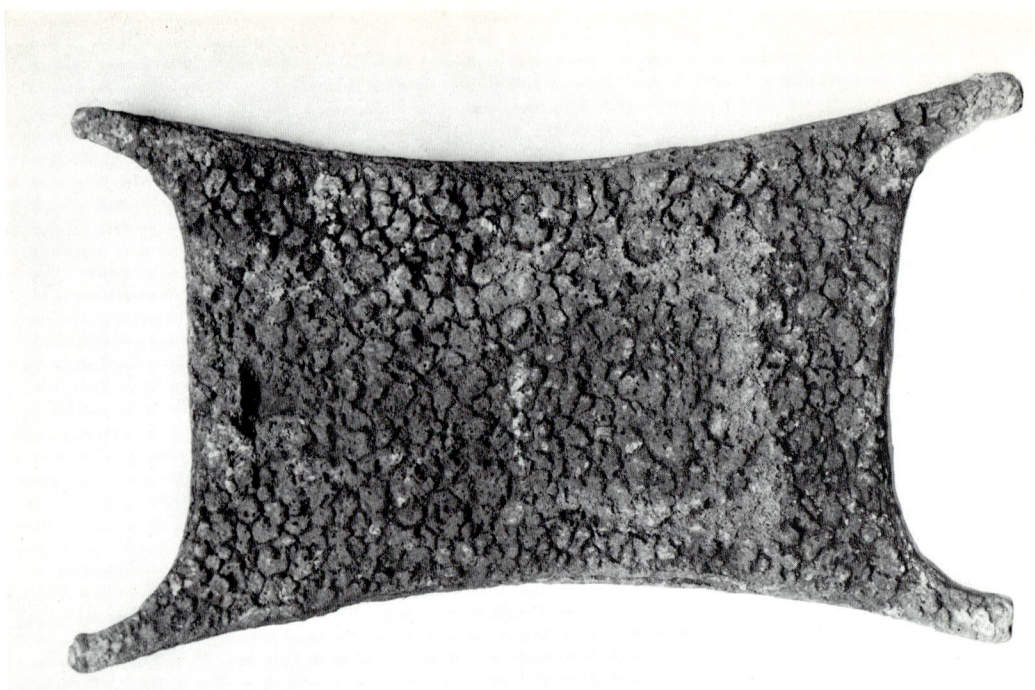

1898

1899

Cypriote copper ingots

1901

1902

1903

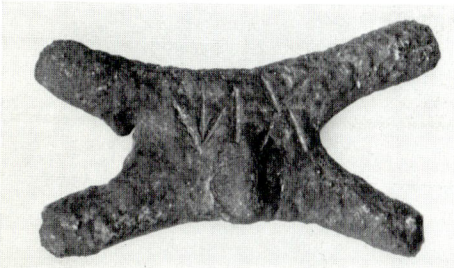

1900

1904

Cypro-Minoan syllabic scripts

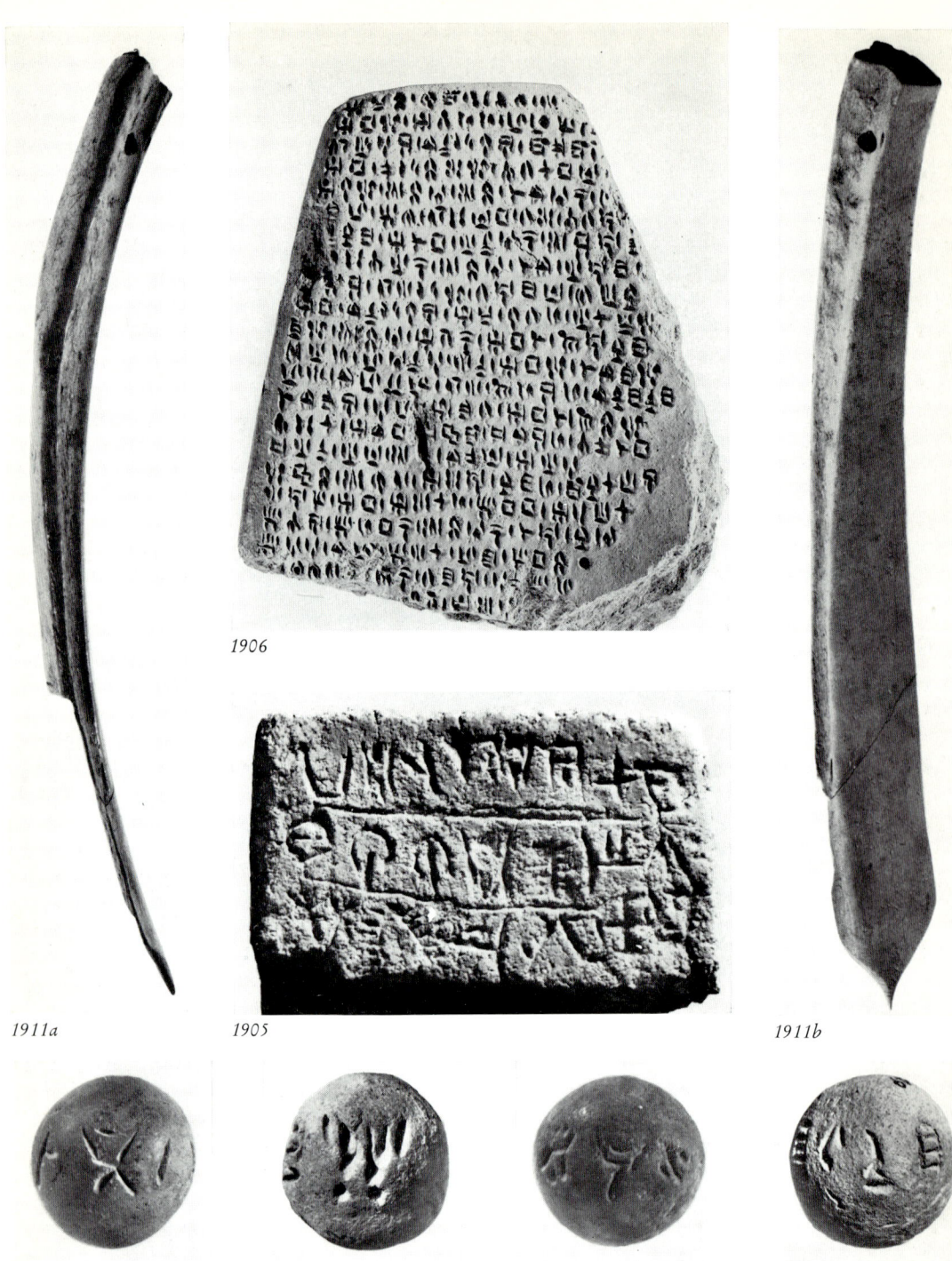

Cypro-Minoan syllabic scripts

INDEX OF SITES

INDEX OF ITEMS FROM UNKNOWN SITES

Athens, private collections, *967, 1248 a*
Basle, private collection, *917*
Bonn, *1255*
Boston, Museum of Fine Arts, *1145, 1251, 1338–45*
Budapest, Museum of Fine Arts, *1248 e*
Copenhagen, National Museum, *595*
Geneva, Musée d'Art et d'Histoire, *1402*
Giessen, private collection, *417, 423–7*
Hamburg, Museum für Kunst und Gewerbe, *227, 975, 977, 1127–30*
Herakleion, Giamalakis Collection (formerly), *231*
London, British Museum, *970*
Munich, Antikensammlungen, *966, 1256*
New York, Metropolitan Museum, *459, 1030, 1263*
New York, Pomerance Collection, *943*
Nicosia, Cyprus Museum, *1509, 1515, 1524, 1526, 1528 1530–4, 1536–41, 1543, 1544, 1549–53, 1555, 1557, 1561, 1565–7, 1570, 1576, 1583, 1584, 1587, 1588, 1590–1606, 1608, 1610–15, 1619, 1624, 1632, 1634–8, 1644, 1646, 1647, 1655, 1665, 1670, 1672–5, 1679, 1701, 1703, 1710 1718, 1720, 1723, 1725, 1729, 1730, 1777 a, b, 1805, 1807–10, 1812–15, 1817–22, 1824, 1841, 1842, 1844, 1845, 1848–53, 1857, 1860, 1863, 1864, 1871, 1873, 1876, 1878, 1879, 1884, 1885, 1887–91, 1894*
Toronto, Ontario Museum, *947*

INDEX OF SITES

Achaea, north Peloponnese, 12
Achera, Cyprus, 123; *1568, 1569, 1577, 1609, 1755–7*
Achladia, Crete, *71*
Aegina, 12, 19, 22, 31, 61, 82; *31, 753–5, 531, 832, 845 a, b, 864 a, b, 867, 868, 871, 872, 924, 941, 942, 959, 1106, 1181, 1182, 1304, 1305*
Aetolia, 12
Africa, 105
Aigion, north Peloponnese, *1310*
Aila, Naxos, *552*
Ailia, near Knossos, Crete, *39*
Akaki, Cyprus, *1717*
Akrotirak, Siphnos, 51
Alaça Hüyük, Anatolia, 26
Alalakh, Syria, 26
Alambra, Cyprus, 123, 132
Albania, *578*
Alones, see Aegina
Ambelia, Rhodes, 28
Ambelikou, north-west Cyprus, 123, 132, 138, 147; *1451*
Amnisos, Crete, 13, 79, 124; *3, 71*
Amorgos, the Cyclades, 12, 17, 51; *526–42, 550, 564, 565, 1194, 1196, 1201*
Amuq Plain, north Syria, *799*
Amyclae, Laconia, 12, 96; *1246, 1247*
Analiondas, Cyprus, *1758*
Analipsi, Peloponnese, *352*
Anatoli, near Hierapetra, Crete, *1231*
Anatolia, 9, 11, 17, 22, 26, 28, 31, 60, 84, 89, 118, 123, 132; *35, 231, 798, 799*
Andreas, see Cape Andreas, Cyprus

Angastina, Cyprus, *1547*
Angelokastrom, the Argolid, 25
Angio Vuno, Rhodes, 28
Ano Englianos, Messenia, *121–5*
Ano Zakro, see Zakro
Anoyira, Cyprus, 123
Anthedon, Boeotia, 12; *645*
Antiparos, Cyclades, 12; *348–51*
Antissa, Lesbos, 28, 124; *974*
Aphrodisias, west Anatolia, *799*
Apliki, north-west Cyprus, 166; *1856*
Apollakia, Rhodes, 28
Apollona, Rhodes, 28
Apsaktiras, Rhodes, 28
Aradippou, Cyprus, see Shemishin
Arapi magoula, Thessaly, 12, 30; *782*
Arcadia, 12, 124, 135; *789, 790*
Archanes, Crete, 13, 106; *582*
Argissa, Thessaly, 12, 95
Argive Heraion, see Prosymna
Argolid, the, 11, 13, 17, 25, 84, 95, 158; *107, 755, 927, 1252*
Argos and Heraion, 12, 25, 39, 124; *219, 596, 597, 657, 658, 660, 874, 878*
Arkades, Crete, 84; *1406*
Arkalochori, Crete, 13, 118; *705*
Arkesine, Amorgos, *540*
Arpera, Cyprus, *1529, 1681, 1902*
Asea, Arcadia, 12; *789, 790, 823, 824*
Asine, the Argolid, 12, 17, 25, 27; *554, 1115*
Asklepio, 28
Askloupis, Kos, see Kos
Aspis, the Argolid, see Argos
Asportili, Rhodes, 28
Aspripetra, Kos, 12; *646*
Athens, 12, 15, 19, 23, 51, 124, 155; *108–10, 183, 377–83, 512, 875, 879, 956, 1037, 1039, 1040, 1172, 1281*
Attica, 12, 19, 40, 89, 95, 108; *517, 777, 1031, 1175, 1311*
Avaritza, Thessaly, 95

Babes, near Olympia, 12; *680*
Balomenou magoula, Boeotia, *774, 775, 1174*
Bamboula, Cyprus, see Kourion
Berbati, the Argolid, 12, 25, 31; *451–3, 1024*
Besika-Tepe, Troas, *455*
Beyçe-Sultan, west Anatolia, 124
Beyköy, west Anatolia, 28
Blučina, Moravia, 105
Boeotia, 11, 30, 51, 82, 95; *27, 76, 111–20, 163–5, 354–6, 394, 598, 774, 775, 791, 795, 797, 810–22, 825–9, 865, 866, 869, 880, 881, 883, 1257*
Bogazköy, Anatolia, 124, 133
Bosphorus, 11
Byblos, Lebanon, 26, 124; *502*

Camirus, Rhodes, 12, 28, 124
Canaan, 23
Çandarli, Pitane, west Anatolia, 28; *1032*
Cape Andreas, Cyprus, *1424*
Cape Gelidonya, Anatolia, 124; *738; 739*

509

Çatal Hüyük, Anatolia, *466*
Cencreae, 25
Cerkessutaniye, west Anatolia, 28
Chaironeia, Boeotia, 12; *774, 775, 1174*
Chalandriani, Syros, 12, 51; *549, 849–51, 1133*
Chalkis, Euboea, 12; *662, 936, 944, 950–5, 991–3*
Chalkis, near Kalydon, *737*
Chamaizi, Crete, 18
Chania, west Crete, 13; *655*
Chaos ravine, Mycenae, 24
Charadiatika, Leukas, *575, 576*
Charadros, river, the Argolid, 25
Charvati, east Attica, *1160, 1248 b*
Chiliomodi, near Tenea, 25
Chimaria, Rhodes, 28
Chimaro, Rhodes, 28
Chios, 11, 12, 60
Chirokitia, Cyprus, see Khirokita
Choirospilia, Leukas, 12; *245–308, 493–500, 788*
Chrysolakkos, near Mallia, Crete, 36; *61, 1296*
Cilicia, *798*
Copais, Lake, Boeotia, *111*
Corcyra, 12; *695*
Corinth, 12
Corinthia, *517*
Crete, 17–19, 20, 22, 26, 29, 31, 39, 44, 51, 61, 79, 82, 89, 95–7, 108, 112, 118, 124, 133, 155; *227, 231, 621, 713, 888, 889, 917, 947, 1115, 1127–30, 1133, 1144, 1145, 1184, 1215–17, 1229, 1363, 1364, 1366, 1373, 1385, 1386, 1467, 1572, 1896*
Cyclades, the, 17, 18, 20, 30, 51, 60, 79, 89, 96; *502–5, 570–2, 852, 1078, 1121, 1135–9, 1195, 1197,* **1198, 1200,** *1202, 1204, 1206*
Cyprus, 9, 17, 19, 22, 26, 29, 31, 40, 44, 60, 61, 82, 84, 88, 89, 95, 97, 105, 108, 112, 118, 120, 123, 124; *595, 710, 711, 738, 1025, 1271, 1473*

Dardanelles, 11
Delos, 12; *1289*
Delphi, 12, 124
Dendra, the Argolid, 12, 25, 27, 82, 84; *166, 398, 401, 407, 623, 629, 630, 632–5, 659, 670, 673, 674, 694, 712,* **932,** *968, 969, 1099, 1111, 1112, 1115, 1117,* **1684**
Dereköy, Anatolia, 28
Dhenia, Cyprus, 123; *1510, 1513, 1516, 1519, 1559, 1574, 1716*
Dia, Island of, 13
Dictaean Cave, Crete, 13; *934, 935*
Dikeleia, near Larnaka, Cyprus, 82; *1754*
Dikeli (Dikili) Tash, Thrace, 12; *413–15*
Dimini, Thessaly, 12, 15, 30, 40; *4, 7, 12, 15, 16, 235–7, 783, 787*
Dipylon, see Athens
Dirmil, Anatolia, 9
Dokathismata, Amorgos, 51
Dodona, Epirus, 12; *554*
Drachmani, Phokis, *865, 882, 884*

Eflatunpinar, Anatolia, 28
Egypt, 19–23, 29, 61, 84, 89, 95, 97, 118, 123, 155, 157, 163; *851, 900, 912, 1123*
Eleona, Kos, 12; *957, 958*
Eileithyia Cave, near Amnisos, Crete, *3*
Eleona, Kos, 12; *957, 958*
Eleusis, Attica, 12; *459, 806–8*

Elis, 11, 30, 96, 124; *701*
Enkomi, east Cyprus, 22, 23, 26, 123, 134–7, 139, 158, 160, 165, 166, 172; *1356, 1455–7, 1579, 1581, 1582, 1585, 1586, 1617, 1620, 1621, 1627, 1633, 1645, 1649, 1650, 1669, 1678, 1682–4, 1688, 1726, 1731–3, 1738, 1740, 1741, 1747, 1749, 1753, 1759, 1760, 1774, 1775, 1780,* **1784, 1789, 1790,** *1854, 1880–3, 1892, 1893, 1895, 1896, 1898–901, 1903–11*
Ephesus, west Anatolia, 28
Epidauros, 25; *97*
Epiros, 11, 30; *194–9, 202–14, 223*
Episkopi, Cyprus, see Kourion
Episkopi Hierapetras, Crete, *1066*
Erimi, Cyprus, 123, 124, 125, 138, 147; *1450, 1489–92, 1828, 1836, 1839*
Eskihisar-Stratonikeia, Anatolia, 28
Etruria, 23
Euboea, 12, 17; *126–8, 502, 1078–81, 1084*
Eutresis, Boeotia, 12, 18; *394, 551, 562, 563, 569*

Fanes, Rhodes, 28
Fasilar, Anatolia, 28
Fethiye-Telmessos, south-west Anatolia, 28
Foça-Phokaia, Anatolia, 28
Franchthi Cave, near Koilada, the Argolid, 13, 179

Galaxidi, Delphi, 12; *735*
Galinoporni, Anatolia, *1542*
Gâvurkala, Anatolia, 28
Gazi, Crete, 13; *652, 1267*
Gelidonya, see Cape Gelidonya
Gezer, Palestine, *1350*
Gla, Boeotia, 12, 27, 124; *76, 111–20, 451*
Gligori Korphi, see Kamilari
Glyfada, Rhodes, 28
Gödelesin, Anatolia, 28
Gonia, near Corinth, *439*
Gordion, Anatolia, 28
Goulas, Crete, *647*
Gournia, east Crete, 13, 51; *72–4, 450, 640, 886, 914, 964, 1042, 1083*
Gouvalari, see Pylos
Gremnos magoula, Thessaly, *758, 786*
Griviglia, near Rhethymnon, Crete, 97

Hagia Irini, Cyprus, 123; *1575, 1578, 1580*
Hagia Irini, Keos, 22, 30, 79; *37–40, 131, 994, 1026, 1169*
Hagia Mavri, west Cyprus, *1689*
Hagia Paraskevi, Cyprus, *1560, 1564*
Hagia Photia, Crete, *13, 838*
Hagia Triada, south Crete, 13, 20, 22, 27, 60, 79, 82, 95, 118, 124; *60, 132, 641, 676, 718, 745–9, 885, 1043,* **1045,** *1065, 1125, 1126, 1165, 1166, 1224, 1228, 1395*
Hagios Elias, Aetolia, 82; *1, 178, 179, 224*
Hagios Elias, near Mallia, Crete, 36
Hagios Elias, near Mycenae, 78
Hagios Elias, near Tiryns, *160, 186*
Hagios Epiktetos, Cyprus, *1493*
Hagios Isidorus, Rhodes, 28
Hagios Jakovos, Cyprus, 123; *1735, 1773, 1776*
Hagios Kosmas, Attica, 12, 19, 51, 82; *134–40, 853, 925, 1132 a, b*
Hagios Mamas, near Olynthos, 12
Hagios Merkourios, Rhodes, 28

Hagios Minas, Rhodes, 28
Hagios Nikolaos, near Mallia, Crete, 36
Hagios Nikolas, Rhodes, 28
Hagios Onouphrios, south Crete, 13; *836*
Hagios Soter, Rhodes, 28
Hagios Sozomenos, Crete, 123, 133, 138
Hagios Theodoros Soleas, Alonia, *1722*
Hagios Thomas, near Palaiomyles, Cyprus, *1694*
Hala Sultan Tekké, Cyprus, 123
Haliki, Attica, *964*
Hama, Syria, *502*
Heraia, Arcadia, *1082*
Heraion, see Argos, Samos
Herakleion, Crete, 13; *1374*
Hieron, the Argolid, 25
Hirsarlik, see Troy
Horoz-Tepe, see Anatolia
Hyria Drachmani, Boeotia, 12; *1168*

Ialysos, Rhodes, 12, 27, 28, 124; *430, 710, 589–94, 600–11, 961, 1242, 1266, 1312–14*
Iasos, south-west Anatolia, 12, 28; *1134*
Idalion, Cyprus, 123; *1653*
Ilica, Anatolia, 40
Ilion, see Troy
Imbros, *223*
Inachos, river, 25
Iolkas, Thessaly, 124
Iria, Epidauria, 12; *1027*
Isopata, Crete, 13; *653, 939, 1114 a, b, 1384, 1396*
Isthmos, see Corinth
Italy, 23, 26, 61, 84
Ithaca, 12, 124
Izmir, west Turkey, 12, 28; *706*

Joannina, Epirus, *202*

Kakovatos, west Peloponnese, 12, 27, 124; *158, 393, 395, 704*
Kalavarda, Rhodes, 28
Kalavassos, Cyprus, 123, 125, 131, 138, 147; *1446–9, 1506, 1770, 1771, 1826, 1835*
Kalbaki, Epiros, *678*
Kallithea, Achaea, 12; *711*
Kalopsida, Cyprus, 123, 133, 138; *1452, 1855*
Kaloriziki, see Kourion
Kalydon, see Chalkis and Psorolithi
Kalymos, Dodecanese, 28, 60; *1032*
Kalyvia, near Phaistos, Crete, *1393*
Kamares Cave, Crete, 13
Kamilari, south Crete, 13, 22; *33, 1067, 1223*
Kaminaki, Lures, Rhodes, 28
Kaminari, Rhodes, 28
Kamini, Naxos, 29
Kampos, Laconia, 97
Kandia, the Argolid, 25
Kanli Kastelli, see Kyparissi
Kapi, Rhodes, 28
Kapros, Amorgos, *1077, 1291, 1362*
Kapsala, Amorgos, 51
Karabel, west Anatolia, 28
Karahöyük, Anatolia, 124
Karavas, Cyprus, *1830*
Kariona, Rhodes, 28
Karmi, District of Kyrenia, 123, 133, 138; *1573*
Karpass peninsula, Cyprus, 133; *1424*

Karpathos, 12, 28, 95, 124; *1239*
Karphi, Crete, 13; *643, 972, 1267, 1270*
Kasarmi, the Argolid, 12, 25; *97*
Kastello, Rhodes, 28
Kastellorizo, south-west Anatolia, 28
Kastri, Syros, 17
Kastritsa, Epirus, 12; *202–14, 679*
Katakolon, west Peloponnes, 96
Kato Zakro, see Zakro
Katsamba, north Crete, 13, 105, 120; *915, 919, 938, 1140*
Kattavia, Rhodes, 28
Katydata, Cyprus, *1727, 1840, 1874, 1875*
Kazaphani, Cyprus, 123; *1589, 1719*
Kellia, Cyprus, see Shemishin
Keos, the Cyclades, 12, 17, 22, 96, 118
Kephala, Keos, 30; *787*
Kephala, near Knossos, *458*
Kephallenia, 11, 82; *661*
Kephissos, river, 25
Kerameikos, see Athens
Keros, the Cyclades, *1211, 1212*
Khirokitia, south Cyprus, 123, 124, 138, 147; *1425–38, 1463–75, 1487, 1657–64, 1691–3, 1696–8, 1761–9, 1829, 1831, 1833, 1834, 1837*
Kition, Cyprus, 22, 123, 134, 138, 158; *1458–61, 1623, 1625, 1626, 1628, 1631, 1639–43, 1652, 1666–8, 1671, 1676, 1677, 1680, 1685, 1728, 1737, 1742–6, 1750, 1752, 1772, 1778, 1779, 1781–3, 1791–1803*
Klazomenae, west Anatolia, 28
Kleisoura, the Argolid, 25
Kleonai, Peloponnese, 25
Knossos, Crete, 13, 19, 20, 21, 27, 39, 61, 79, 84, 95, 118, 120, 124; *13, 17, 41–52, 63, 141–9, 220, 430, 458, 461, 627, 628, 642, 651, 675, 708, 714–17, 787, 901, 904, 906, 911, 926, 931, 1028, 1046–55, 1062, 1063, 1142, 1146–8, 1150, 1151, 1262, 1164, 1167, 1208, 1209, 1233, 1235–7, 1288, 1306, 1389–91, 1394, 1398, 1400, 1416–19, 1421*
Koilada, see Franchthi Cave
Kokkala, Rhodes, 28
Kokkinokremos, Cyprus, see Pyla
Kokkinopilos, Epirus, 12, 194–9
Kokkinospilia, Aetolia, 12; *178*
Kolonna Hill, Aegina, *31*
Kolophon, west Anatolia, 28
Komotini, Thrace, 12; *785*
Kontoporeia, the Argolid, 25
Kophina, Crete, *1215*
Korakou, near Corinth, 12, 25; *823, 871, 1353*
Kos, Asklepieion, 12, 28, 124; *543, 554, 646, 697, 721, 728, 802–5, 957, 958, 1353*
Kouklia west Cyprus, 26, 123, 138, 165; *1651, 1656, 1748, 1785–7*
Koumasa, south Crete, 13, 51; *523–5, 1214*
Kouphovouno, Laconia, *217, 218*
Kourion, Cyprus, 26, 138; *1504, 1687, 1788*
Koutsopodi, the Argolid, 25
Köylütolu, Anatolia, 28
Kozani, Macedonia, *192, 193*
Krini, Cyprus, 133, 138
Krokion, Thessaly, see Thebes
Ktima, west Cyprus, 123
Kufa, Rhodes, 28
Kuşadasi, west Anatolia, 28
Kydonia, 61, 84

Kyme, Euboea, 750, 751
Kymisala, Rhodes, 28
Kyparissi, Crete, *833, 835*
Kyparissia, west Peloponnese, see Peristeria
Kyra-Alonia, Cyprus, 147
Kyrenia, Cyprus, *1843*
Kythera, 12, 17, 89, 118, 124; *631, 945, 983, 984, 1161*
Kythnos, the Cyclades, 12, 51; *555–60, 568, 570, 572*
Kythrea, Cyprus, 123; *1571*

Laconia, 12, 23, 97
Lakania, Rhodes, 28
Langada, see Kos
Lapithos, north Cyprus, 26, 123, 133, 138; *1484, 1502, 1505, 1508, 1554, 1556, 1572, 1654, 1714, 1715, 1721, 1804, 1806, 1811, 1823, 1825 a, b, 1827 a, b, 1858, 1859, 1861, 1862, 1865, 1866, 1877*
Larissa, north-west Anatolia, 28
Larissa, Argos, 25; *219*
Larissa, Thessaly, 11, 12, 15; *1118, 1176*
Larnaka, see Kition
Larnakas tis Lapithou, Cyprus, *1507*
Larthos, Rhodes, 28
Lasithi district, Crete, 2, *1372*
Lebanon, see Byblos and Syria
Lebena, Crete, 51
Lechaion, Corinthia, 25
Lefka, see Leuka
Lelos, Rhodes, 28
Lemnos, 12, 51
Lerna, the Argolid, 12, 16, 17, 19, 25, 31, 40, 51; *18, 19, 25, 26, 150, 223, 823, 830, 870, 876, 877, 1191*
Lesbos, 12, 124
Leuka, Cyprus, *1847*
Leukandi, Euboea, 12, 26, 29; *126–8, 989, 999*
Leukas, 19, 39, 124; *309–36, 357–76, 384–91, 578, 756, 823, 824, 1292, 1293*
Levantine coast, 137
Lianokladi, Thessaly, 12; *779, 880*
Ligourtino, Messara, Crete, *71*
Limassol, Crete, 123; *1503, 1521*
Lindos, Rhodes, 12, 28, 124; *554*
Lipari, Acropolis, 23, 159; *1264*
Liro, Rhodes, 28
Lykia, *738*
Lythrangomi, Cyprus, *1886*
Lythrodontas, Cyprus, *1846*

Macedonia, 11, 12, 30, 45, 97
Magoulitsa, Thessaly, *760*
Mallia, Crete, 13, 20, 36, 79, 95, 108, 118, 124; *61–70, 232, 435–8, 449, 450, 457, 639, 703, 905, 1193, 1296, 1355, 1365, 1370*
Malona, Rhodes, 28
Malta, 23, 96
Maltepe, Bulgaria, 40
Malthi, Peloponnese, 12; *224, 399, 411*
Mandriko, Rhodes, 28
Maniko, Euboea, 51
Marathon, Attica, 12; *181, 780*
Margi, Cyprus, *1514*
Mari, Euphrates, 78
Maria-Tenta, Cyprus, 138
Marmara, Sea of, 11
Marmariane, Thessaly, 12; *235–7*

Maroni, Cyprus, *1618, 1629*
Maronia, Crete, *1133*
Maroniou, river, Cyprus, *1425*
Mavro Spilio, near Knossos, 27
Melathria, Laconia, 27
Melos, the Cyclades, 12, 20, 79, 89, 95, 118, 124; *1120, 1122*
Menidi, Attica, *1273*
Meniko, Cyprus, *1897*
Mersin, 124
Messara, south Crete, 13; *581*
Messena, 12, 40
Metaxata, Crete, *663*
Midea, the Argolid, 12, 25; *1158, 1159*
Milas, south-west Anatolia, 28
Miletus, south-west Anatolia, 12, 28, 124; *921, 1036*
Milia, Cyprus, *1535, 1616*
Minet-el-Beda, north Syria, *1290, 1743*
Mirabello, east Crete, *182, 1129, 1192*
Mochlos, Island of, Crete, 13, 51; *839, 1119, 1123–6, 1133, 1294, 1367, 1309*
Monastiraki, Crete, 13; *1120*
Morphou, north-west Cyprus, 123; *1545, 1546, 1548*
Mouliana, east Crete, 13, 124; *701*
Müskebi, west Anatolia, 28
Mycenae, the Argolid, 12, 22, 23, 25, 27, 40, 43, 44, 62, 79, 82, 84, 90, 95, 96, 97, 105, 118, 165; *77–96, 122, 151–7, 166–77, 180, 187, 353–6, 396, 397, 405, 406, 460, 462, 506, 507, 509–11, 513, 578, 644, 649, 650, 677, 681–3, 685, 686, 688, 709, 752, 873, 907, 927, 964, 965, 971, 989, 998, 1000, 1001, 1025, 1038, 1071, 1085–94, 1096–8, 1108, 1115, 1156, 1157, 1170, 1171, 1243–5, 2248 d, 1265, 1272, 1274–7, 1280, 1282, 1286, 1297–1303, 1379, 1383, 1387, 1388, 1399, 1411*
Myrina, *974*
Myrtou, Cyprus, 123, 138; *1736*

Nauplia, 25; *97*
Naxos, the Cyclades, 12, 27, 82, 95, 97, 118, 124; *502, 566, 567, 577, 857, 858, 999, 1076, 1137, 1207, 1238*
Nicosia, Cyprus, 123; *1734*
Nidri, see Leuka
Nirou Chani, Crete, 13; *71, 913, 940, 1149*
Niš, Yugoslavia, *574*
Nitovikla, Cyprus, 123, 133, 138; *1453*

Olous, east Crete, 13; *182, 656, 1306*
Olympia, Elis, 12, 124; *32, 184, 185, 224, 427, 823*
Olynthos, see Hagios Mamas
Omodos, west Cyprus, *1690*
Orchomenos, Boeotia, 12, 17, 18, 118, 124; *27, 163–5, 797, 810–22, 825–9, 866, 869, 880, 881, 883, 1188, 1412*
Orman magoula, near Larissa, Thessaly, *781*
Ormos Apollona, Naxos, 51
Orontes, river, Syria, see Qadesh
Otzaki Magoula, Thessaly, 12; *8, 757, 759, 761, 778*
Oxylithos Paralia, Euboea, 12; *671*

Pachyammos, Crete, 13; *1068, 1220*
Palaeoskoutella, east Cyprus, 123
Palaikastro, near Kozani, Macedonia, 12; *192, 193*
Palaikastro, east Crete, 13, 51; *234, 463, 894, 898, 920, 1041, 1149, 1213, 1371*
Palaiokastro, Kephalonia, 12; *661*
Palaiokastro-Maa, west Cyprus, 22, 123; *1462*
Palaiopyrgi, Laconia, *228*

Palaipaphos, see Kouklia
Palestine 17, 26, 159
Paliochora, Rhodes, 28
Panormos, Naxos, 51; *1187*
Pap tis Lures, 28
Paphos, *1742*
Paros, 12; *564, 565, 846, 1136, 1199, 1203*
Pediaios River, Cyprus, 137
Peloponnese, 33, 144; *223*
Pelos, Melos, 30
Pelynt, Cornwall, *699*
Pendagia, Cyprus, *1558, 1607, 1816*
Pentamodi, Malevyziou, Crete, *1061*
Perati, Attica, 12, 23, 26, 29, 39, 108, 120, 164, 172; *188–91, 508, 515, 583–8, 621, 622, 638, 665, 669, 675, 702, 985, 995, 1034, 1035, 1349–55, 1358, 1380, 1403, 1404, 1408*
Peristeria, west Peloponnese, 12, 124; *33, 451*
Perseia, see Mycenae
Petra tou Limniti, 123, 138
Petralona, 51
Phaistos, south Crete, 13, 20, 27, 34, 79, 84, 118, 124; *53–9, 65, 887, 890, 891, 892, 893, 895, 896, 933, 1028, 1219, 1230, 1232, 1401, 1409*
Phaleron, Attica, *823*
Phaneromeni, Cyprus, see Kourion
Philia, Cyprus, 123, 138, 147; *1479, 1494–1501*
Philia, Thessaly, *1359*
Phlious, the Argolid, 25
Phokis, *882*
Phrenaros, Cyprus, 138; *1832*
Phthiotic Thebes, see Thebes
Phychtia, the Argolid, 25
Phylakopi, Melos, 12, 20, 61, 124; *863, 1044, 1120, 1190, 1405*
Pilona, Rhodes, 28
Pinakiano, Kardamoutsa, Crete, *720*
Piskokephalon, east Crete, *1218*
Pitane, see Candarli, west Anatolia
Plakoto, Rhodes, 28
Platanos, south Crete, 13, 27, 51; *518–20, 624, 1368*
Poliochni, Lemnos, 12, 19, 51; *22, 28, 221, 230, 467–80, 481, 501, 543, 791, 792, 796*
Pomos, Cyprus, *1699*
Politiko, see Tamassos, Cyprus
Preveza, Epirus, *194*
Priphtiane, the Argolid, 25
Prosymna, the Argolid, 82; *402, 423, 596, 597, 687, 916, 928, 962, 965, 1109, 1110, 1116, 1234, 1248 c, 1249, 1309*
Pseira, Crete, 13; *899, 902, 929, 1126, 1128, 1221, 1222*
Psorolithi, near Kalydon, 12; *736, 737*
Psychro Cave, Crete, 13; *2, 648, 723–34*
Pyla, Cyprus, 123, 138; *1454, 1523, 1622, 1751*
Pylos, Messena, 12, 22, 38, 79, 82, 118, 121, 124; *121–5, 403, 404, 408, 409, 599, 612–20, 636, 637, 684, 1059, 1107, 1278, 1283, 1347, 1348, 1397, 1415, 1420, 1421*
Pyrasos, *1359*
Pyrgos, Attica, 12
Pyrgos, north Crete, 51

Qadesh, river Orontes, Syria, *502*
Qalaat-er-Rus, north Syria, *502*

Raphina, east Attica, *801, 823*
Ras Shamra, north Syria, 22, 26, 118, 124, 159; *502, 738, 897, 973, 1241*

Rhachmani, Thessaly, 12; *11*
Rhenia, near Olympia, *988*
Rhini, Thessaly, *10*
Rhodes, 12, 26, 28, 82, 89, 95, 96, 124, 155; *412, 423–6, 431–4, 595, 738, 1266, 1271*
Routsi, see Pylos

Salamiou-Anephani, Cyprus, *1700*
Salamis, Cyprus, 123, 137
Salamis, Island of, 23; *1037*
Saliagos, Island of, near Antiparos, 30; *348–51*
Samikon-Kleidi, Triphylia, *908, 918, 963, 980*
Samos Heraion and Tigani, 12, 17, 28, 60, 124; *34, 200, 201, 215, 216, 544–8, 798*
Samothrace, 12
Santorin, see Thera
Sardeis, Anatolia, 28
Sardinia, 23, 60, 96
Scoglio del Tonno, near Taranto, Italy, 23, 26, 61, 84; *1002–23*
Seidi Cave, Boeotia, 11
Selinos, Rhodes, 28
Seraglio, see Kos
Sesklo, Thessaly, 12, 15, 30; *6, 14, 233, 235–7, 561, 578, 757, 772, 783, 784, 787, 1173, 1177, 1178, 1180, 1359–61*
Shechem, Palestine, *1350*
Shemishin, Cyprus, *1630*
Siana, Rhodes, 28
Sicily, 60
Sinda, Cyprus, 123, 138; *1648*
Siphnos, Cyclades, 118
Sipylos (Akpinar), west Anatolia, 28
Sitiar, east Crete, 13; *463, 464, 964, 965*
Skaros Hill, see Leukas
Sklavokampos, Crete, *71*
Skopelas, 12
Skutari, Albania, *696*
Skyros, 11
Smyrna, see Izmir
Soloi, Cyprus, *1525*
Sotira, Cyprus, 123, 129, 138, 147; *1439–45, 1476–8, 1485, 1486, 1488, 1695*
Souphli magoula, Thessaly, 12, 15; *465, 466, 762–4*
Sparta, Laconia, 12, 23, 124; *1179, 1183*
Spata, east Attica, 12; *1284, 1285, 1287*
Spedos, Naxos, 51
Sphoungaras, east Crete, *838*
Staphylos, Skopelos, *689*
Stavros, Amorgos, 51
Stavros, Rhodes, 28
Stravo Kephalo, near Olympia, *981, 986, 987, 990, 1346*
Strephi, near Olympia, *909*
Synoro, Epidauria, *823*
Syria, 17, 19, 23, 60, 61, 89, 105, 108, 133, 157; *502, 638, 973, 1272*
Syros, the Cyclades, 12, 17, 30; *502–5, 798, 848, 854–6, 1186, 1205*

Tamassos-Politiko, Cyprus, 123, 164, 172; *1724*
Tanagra, Boeotia, 12
Taranto, see Scoglio del Tonno
Tarsos, 124
Teichos Dymeion, Peloponnese, 12; *514, 553*
Tekes Herakleion, Crete, *521–2*
Tell Judaida, north Syria, *553*

Tell Sukas, north Syria, 124
Telmessos, *see* Fethiye
Tenea, south of Corinth, 25
Thasos, 12
Thebes, Boeotia, 12, 27, 51, 79, 118, 124; *354–6, 392, 400, 516, 579, 580, 598, 791, 922, 923, 1058, 1143, 1308 a–c, 1315, 1316, 1356, 1357, 1357–7, 1413, 1414*
Thebes, Upper Egypt, *1100–3*
Thebes (Pthiotic), Thessaly, 12; *428, 429*
Thera (Santorin), the Cyclades, 12, 20, 79, 89, 118, 124; *841–4, 847, 859–62, 948, 960, 964, 1153, 1154, 1192, 1210*
Thermi, Lesbos, 12, 16, 18, 28, 124; *21, 24, 29*
Thespiai, Boeotia, 95
Thessaly, 11, 13, 15, 30, 40, 82, 97; *223, 235–7, 765–71, 1118, 1176*
Thorikos, Attica, 12, 124; *159*
Thrace, 11; *222, 413, 785*
Thyreatis, north Laconia, *1294*
Tigani, *see* Samos
Tiryns, the Argolid, 12, 17, 25, 29, 78, 80, 82, 85, 95, 118, 124; *98–106, 160, 161, 186, 238–44, 337–47, 481–92, 675, 697, 698, 794, 800, 809, 823, 979, 996, 997, 999, 1056, 1057, 1060, 1113, 1114, 1131, 1240, 1258–62, 1370 a–e, 1381, 1382*
Tolo, Rhodes, 28
Trauni, Rhodes, 28
Tretos, the Argolid, 25
Trianda, Rhodes, 28
Trikomo, east Cyprus, *1563*
Troas, 12; *1075, 1224, 1295*
Troulli, north Cyprus, 123, 138; *1423*
Troullos-Archanes, Crete, 118; *1410*
Troy, 12, 17, 19, 28, 84, 95, 124; *20, 23, 35, 36, 226, 416, 433, 664, 798, 799, 832, 1072–4, 1250, 1294*
Trypa, *see* Chalkis, Euboea
Tsangli, Thessaly, 12; *9, 776*
Tsani magoula, Thessaly, 12; *773*
Tylssos, Crete, 13, 29; *71, 1225, 1226*
Tzalma magoula, Thessaly, *5*

Ugarit, *see* Ras Shamra

Vagia, *see* Aegina
Vaphio, Attica, 12, 27, 124; *162, 937, 1104, 1105*
Vari, Attica, 12; *903, 1189, 1254*
Vasilia, Cyprus, 123, 138; *1867–70, 1872*
Vasiliki Anogeia, south Crete, 82
Vasiliki, east Crete, 13, 18; *30, 837, 840*
Vasiliko, *see* Philia, Cyprus
Vathy, Rhodes, 28
Vathypetro, Crete, *71*
Vergi, *see* Pyla
Vigla, Rhodes, 28
Villanova, Rhodes, 28
Vitsilia Partira, Crete, *834*
Volos, Thessaly, 12, 15, 27
Vorou Monophatziou, Crete, 13; *719, 1064*
Voula, Attica, *1248 f*
Vounous, north Cyprus, 123, 132, 138, 159; *1480–3, 1511, 1512, 1517, 1518, 1520, 1522, 1562, 1704–9, 1711–13*
Vourvatsi, Attica, *940*
Vratsi, near Tanagra, Boeotia, 82; *1069, 1070*
Vrokastro, east Crete, 13, 27, 124; *1029*
Vromousa, *see* Chalkis, Euboea
Vršac, Yugoslavia, 105

Yağri, Anatolia, 28
Yiriza, Corinthia, *439–43*

Zakro, east Crete, 13, 20, 105, 124; *75, 722, 739–44, 1155, 1163, 1227*
Zakynthos, 11, 30
Zapher Papoura, Crete, 13; *625–8, 654, 666–8, 672, 690–3, 700, 707, 1095 a–o*
Zerelia, Thessaly, 12; *229*
Zougitza Cave, near Nemea, 12
Zygouries, between Corinth and Argos, 12, 25, 51; *444–8, 454 a–h*